2005 U.S. Master™ Estate and Gift Tax Guide

CCH Editorial Staff Publication

CCH INCORPORATED
Chicago
A WoltersKluwer Company

Editorial Staff

Editor . . . . Thomas K. Lauletta, J.D.
Production . . . . Kathleen M. Higgins

2005 U.S. Master™ Estate and Gift Tax Guide was previously published by **CCH** INCORPORATED as *Federal Estate and Gift Taxes Explained.*

ISBN 0-8080-1250-9

4025 W. Peterson Ave.
Chicago, IL 60646-6085
1 800 248 3248
http://tax.cchgroup.com

Preface

The *2005 U.S. Master ™ Estate and Gift Tax Guide* is designed as a guide for tax advisors, estate representatives, and estate owners involved in federal estate and gift tax return preparation and tax payment. The explanations and filled-in forms (compiled in the Appendix for easy use) reflect major federal estate, gift, and generation-skipping transfer tax developments occurring up to the date of publication. Generally, the law applicable to decedents dying, and gifts made, in 2004 is discussed. However, changes made by the Economic Growth and Tax Relief Reconciliation Act of 2001 (P.L. 107-16) that apply to later years are highlighted throughout the *Guide*. In addition, changes made by the American Jobs Creation Act of 2004 (P.L. 108-357) have been reflected.

This book reproduces filled-in specimens of the August 2004 revision of Form 706 (United States Estate (and Generation-Skipping Transfer) Tax Return). The book also includes filled-in specimens of Form 709 (for gifts made during calendar year 2004), the federal gift tax return; Form 706-NA (Rev. January 2003), the federal estate (and generation-skipping transfer) tax return for nonresidents not U.S. citizens; Form 706-A (Rev. September 2004), the return for reporting the additional tax owing on recapture of the benefits of a special use valuation election; Form 706-QDT (Rev. January 2003), the estate tax return for qualified domestic trusts; and Form 706-D (October 2003), the form to be used by qualified heirs to report and pay the additional estate tax due under Code Sec. 2057 when certain taxable events occur with respect to qualified family-owned business interests.

In addition, the book includes filled-in specimens of the following generation-skipping transfer tax forms: Form 706-GS(D) (Rev. January 2003), Form 706-GS(D-1) (Rev. January 2003), and Form 706-GS(T) (Rev. January 2003).

The rules and principles explained in this book are accompanied by citations to the Internal Revenue Code, regulations, IRS rulings, and court decisions. These features will enable practitioners to further research the estate and gift tax law. Also included are a topical index and finding lists of forms reproduced and Code sections cited.

December 2004

Table of Contents

UNIFIED ESTATE AND GIFT TRANSFER TAX

Chapter 1

RATES AND CREDITS

¶ 10 Unified Transfer Tax Rate Schedule and Unified Credit

The basic estate and gift tax rates with respect to which the tentative tax is computed are based on a rate schedule that consists of 15 graduated rates, beginning with an 18-percent tax rate for amounts not over $10,000 and increasing to a 48-percent tax rate (for decedents dying in 2004) for amounts in excess of $2.0 million. A five-percent additional tax, which had applied to a portion of transfers in excess of $10 million, but less than $17,184,000, has been repealed with respect to decedents dying, and gifts made, after December 31, 2001 (see ¶16).

• *Impact of the 2001 Act*

The enactment of the Economic Growth and Tax Relief Reconciliation Act of 2001 (P.L. 107-16) (2001 Act) brought significant change to the transfer tax system, the most notable being the repeal of the estate and generation-skipping transfer (GST) taxes in 2010. Prior to repeal, a number of modifications are made to the maximum estate tax rate and applicable exclusion amount (see below).

Under the 2001 Act, the top marginal rate is reduced to 48 percent for decedents dying, and gifts made, in 2004, with further reductions in later years. In 2004, the effective minimum rate increases to 45 percent as a result of the operation of the applicable credit amount (¶15).

Sunset provision. In order to comply with the Congressional Budget Act of 1974, the 2001 Act provides that all provisions of, and amendments made by, the 2001 Act will not apply to estates of decedents dying, gifts made, or generation-skipping transfers after December 31, 2010. Unless Congress acts affirmatively in the interim, the Internal Revenue Code will thereafter be applied and administered as if these provisions had not been enacted.

Transfer Tax Schedule: 1984–2001

Column A *Taxable amount over*	Column B *Taxable amount not over*	Column C *Tax on amount in column A*	Column D *Rate of tax on excess over amount in column A* *Percent*
$0	$10,000	$0	18
10,000	20,000	1,800	20
20,000	40,000	3,800	22
40,000	60,000	8,200	24
60,000	80,000	13,000	26
80,000	100,000	18,200	28
100,000	150,000	23,800	30
150,000	250,000	38,800	32
250,000	500,000	70,800	34
500,000	750,000	155,800	37
750,000	1,000,000	248,300	39
1,000,000	1,250,000	345,800	41
1,250,000	1,500,000	448,300	43
1,500,000	2,000,000	555,800	45
2,000,000	2,500,000	780,800	49
2,500,000	3,000,000	1,025,800	53
3,000,000	......	1,290,800	55[1]

• ***Rate Schedule for 2002–2009***

The estate and gift tax rate schedule applicable to the estates of decedents dying and gifts made in 2002 through 2009 (the years prior to repeal of the estate tax in 2010) is as follows:

Transfer Tax Rate Schedule: 2002–2009*

(A) *Amount subject to tax more than—*	*(B)* *Amount subject to tax equal to or less than—*	*(C)* *Tax on amount in column (A)*	*(D)* *Rate of tax on excess over amount in column (A)* *Percent*
...	$10,000	...	18
$10,000	20,000	$1,800	20
20,000	40,000	3,800	22
40,000	60,000	8,200	24
60,000	80,000	13,000	26
80,000	100,000	18,200	28
100,000	150,000	23,800	30
150,000	250,000	38,800	32
250,000	500,000	70,800	34
500,000	750,000	155,800	37
750,000	1,000,000	248,300	39
1,000,000	1,250,000	345,800	41
1,250,000	1,500,000	448,300	43
1,500,000	2,000,000	555,800	45
2,000,000	2,500,000	780,800	49

[1] The U.S. Court of Appeals for the Federal Circuit has upheld a provision of the Omnibus Budget Reconciliation Act of 1993 (P.L. 103-66) that on August 10, 1993, retroactively reinstated the maximum 55-percent maximum transfer tax rate to transfers made after December 31, 1992. Prior to this change, the maximum transfer tax rate for post-December 31, 1992 transfers was 50 percent. *NationsBank of Texas, N.A.*, CA-FC, 2001-2 USTC ¶60,423, cert. denied, Oct. 7, 2002.

(A) Amount subject to tax more than—	(B) Amount subject to tax equal to or less than—	(C) Tax on amount in column (A)	(D) Rate of tax on excess over amount in column (A) Percent
2,500,000	......	1,025,800	50*

* The 2001 Act reduces the top marginal rate for years after 2002, according to the following schedule:
- 49 percent for decedents dying, and gifts made, in 2003;
- 48 percent in 2004;
- 47 percent in 2005;
- 46 percent in 2006;
- 45 percent in 2007, 2008, and 2009.

For years 2003 through 2009, the tentative tax is to be determined by using a table prescribed by the IRS, which will be the same as the rate schedule shown above except for the adjustments necessary to reflect the reductions in the maximum rate.

For the gift tax rates for gifts made after December 31, 2009, see ¶2005.

• ***Unified Credit***

The table below provides the unified credit amount for 1987-1997 and the applicable credit amount after 1997 and the applicable exemption/exclusion amount.

Year	*Applicable Credit Amount*	*Applicable Exclusion Amount*
1987-1997	$192,800	$600,000
1998	202,050	625,000
1999	211,300	650,000
2000 and 2001	220,550	675,000

As a result of changes made by the 2001 Act, different unified credit amounts apply to the estate tax and to the gift tax (see ¶15).

The estate tax unified credit (applicable credit amount) and the applicable exclusion amount for the years 2002 through 2011 appear below:

Year	*Applicable Credit Amount*	*Applicable Exclusion Amount*
2002-2003	$345,800	$1,000,000
2004-2005	555,800	1,500,000
2006-2008	780,800	2,000,000
2009	1,455,800	3,500,000
2010 (Estate Tax Repealed)	0	0
2011 (Estate Tax Reinstated)	345,800	1,000,000

The gift tax applicable credit amount for the years 2002 through 2009 will remain at $1 million.

¶ 11 Unified Rate Schedule

A single unified transfer tax applies to estate and gift taxes, effective for the estates of decedents dying, and for gifts made, after December 31, 1976.[2] The rates are progressive on the basis of cumulative lifetime transfers and those transfers occurring at death. For decedents dying or gifts made in 2004, the unified transfer tax rates range from 18 percent on cumulative transfers of $10,000 or less to a maximum rate of 48 percent, applicable to cumulative transfers over $2.0 million (see ¶10).[3]

[2] Code Sec. 2001 and Code Sec. 2502; Reg. §20.0-2 and Reg. §25.2502-1.

[3] Code Sec. 2001(c)(1). See the Appendix at ¶2600 for the current unified transfer tax rate schedule, as well as the maximum rates

¶12 Application of Unified Rate Schedule

In computing the gift tax liability for any calendar year, the unified rate schedule is applied to the transferor's cumulative lifetime taxable gifts (see Chapter 34). The term "taxable gifts" means gross gifts, minus the annual exclusion (see Chapter 36) and any allowable charitable or marital deduction (see Chapter 37). Taxable gifts for the current period are aggregated with those for all prior periods (see ¶2355) and a tentative gift tax is computed. From this amount, a second tentative tax on the gifts from prior periods only is subtracted. In both cases, the current unified rate schedule is used to compute the tentative tax.[4] The applicable credit amount (see ¶15 and ¶2376) and the credit for foreign gift taxes, if any, are subtracted to arrive at the current year's gift tax liability.

In computing the estate tax liability under the unified transfer tax system, the unified rate schedule is applied to a decedent's cumulative transfers, both during life and at death. A tentative estate tax is computed on what is sometimes referred to as the "estate tax base," which is composed of the taxable estate (the gross estate minus allowable deductions (see Chapter 6 through Chapter 24)) plus all taxable gifts made after 1976, other than gifts includible in the gross estate (see Chapter 25).[5] The gross estate tax is then calculated by subtracting the gift tax payable on the post-1976 taxable gifts (using the current unified rate schedule).[6] The applicable credit amount (see ¶15) and additional allowable credits (see Chapters 26 and 27) are then applied against the gross estate tax liability to arrive at the net estate tax due.

Special phaseout rules apply with respect to both the gift tax and the estate tax for certain large transfers made before January 1, 2002 (see ¶16 and ¶2378).

The estate tax base does not include the value of lifetime transfers that are already included in the decedent's estate, such as transfers where the decedent retained certain interests, rights, or powers in the property (see ¶30). This precludes having the same lifetime transfers taken into account more than once for transfer tax purposes. The gift tax payable on these transfers is later subtracted in determining the correct estate tax.

Special rules apply in the case of nonresidents not citizens (see ¶1635) and for certain split gifts (see ¶1426). See also ¶2350.

¶15 Unified Credit

The unified credit, now referred to as the "applicable credit amount" in Code Sec. 2010, is a one-time credit in life and at death against taxes payable on certain transfers.[7] The unified credit replaced the pre-1977 $30,000 lifetime gift tax exemption and the $60,000 estate tax exemption.[8] Although the credit must be used to offset gift taxes on lifetime transfers, regardless of the amount so used, the full credit is allowed against the tentative estate tax. The rationale for such full application is that, under Code Sec. 2001(b)(2), the estate tax payable is calculated using the cumulative transfers at life and at death and is then reduced by the amount of gift tax paid by a decedent. If a portion of the unified credit was used to avoid the payment of gift taxes, the gift tax paid reflects the amount subtracted under Code Sec. 2001(b)(2). The estate tax payable is necessarily

(Footnote Continued)

that applied to pre-1984 decedents and transfers. See also ¶2640 and ¶2650 for the separate estate tax and gift tax rates that applied to pre-1977 decedents and transfers.

[4] Code Sec. 2502(a).

[5] Code Sec. 2001(b).

[6] Code Sec. 2001(b)(2).

[7] Code Sec. 2010 and Code Sec. 2505.

[8] Code Sec. 2010 and Code Sec. 2505.

increased by the amount of the gift tax credit used. However, the credit for estate tax purposes cannot exceed the amount of the estate tax.

It should be noted that, because of the nature of the gift tax, the computation of the unified credit for gift tax purposes is different from that for estate tax purposes (see ¶2007 and ¶2376). Moreover, with the passage of the Economic Growth and Tax Relief Reconciliation Act of 2001 (P.L. 107-16) (2001 Act), the unified credit has been "de-unified": different schedules of applicable exclusion amounts apply to the estate tax and to the gift tax (see ¶10).

• *Impact of the 2001 Act*

The enactment of the 2001 Act brought significant change to the transfer tax system, the most notable being the repeal of the estate and generation-skipping transfer (GST) taxes in 2010. Prior to repeal, a number of modifications are made to the maximum estate tax rate and the estate and gift tax applicable exclusion amounts. The 2001 Act increases the *estate tax* applicable exclusion amount according to the following schedule:

- For decedents dying in 2002 and 2003: $1 million;
- For decedents dying in 2004 and 2005: $1.5 million;
- For decedents dying in 2006, 2007, and 2008: $2 million; and
- For decedents dying in 2009: $3.5 million.

The 2001 Act also increases the *gift tax* applicable exclusion amount to $1 million, beginning with gifts made in 2002. However, unlike the gradual increase in the estate tax applicable exclusion amount in the years leading up to repeal of the estate tax, the gift tax applicable exclusion amount remains at $1 million and is not indexed for inflation. For years 2002 through 2009, the amount of the gift tax unified credit is equal to (1) the applicable credit amount in effect under Code Sec. 2010(c) for such calendar year, determined as if the applicable exclusion amount were $1 million, reduced by (2) the sum of the amounts allowable as a credit under Code Sec. 2505 for all preceding calendar periods[9] (see ¶2005).

• *Computation of Credit Following Estate Tax Repeal*

The 2001 Act retains the gift tax following estate tax repeal in 2010. Gift tax liability for years after 2009 is determined by using a rate schedule created by the 2001 Act (Code Sec. 2502(a), as amended by the 2001 Act). The credit allowed against the gift tax for such years will be equal to (1) the amount of the tentative tax that would be determined under the new gift tax-only rate schedule if the amount with respect to which such tentative tax is to be computed were $1 million, reduced by (2) the sum of the amounts allowable as a credit for all preceding calendar periods[10] (see ¶2005). The gift tax rules are discussed beginning at ¶2000.

Sunset provision. In order to comply with the Congressional Budget Act of 1974, the 2001 Act provides that all provisions of, and amendments made by, the 2001 Act will not apply to estates of decedents dying, gifts made, or generation-skipping transfers after December 31, 2010. Unless Congress acts affirmatively in the interim, the Internal Revenue Code will thereafter be applied and administered as if these provisions had not been enacted.

---

[9] Code Sec. 2505(a), as amended by P.L. 107-16.

[10] Code Sec. 2505(a)(1), as amended by P.L. 107-16.

The estate tax return filing requirements have been adjusted to reflect that a return is required if the gross estate exceeds the applicable exclusion amount in effect for the calendar year of the decedent's death (¶22).

• ***Post-1997, Pre-2004 Unified Credit***

For the years 1998–2003, the unified credit was gradually increased to $345,800 and was determined by reference to the "applicable credit amount" and "the applicable exclusion amount" (formerly the exemption equivalent) ($1 million in 2002 and 2003). (See the table at ¶10.) For the years 2000 and 2001, the applicable exclusion amount was $675,000, resulting in an applicable credit amount of $220,550.

• ***Pre-1998 Unified Credit***

The unified estate and gift tax credit was $192,800 for decedents dying after 1986 and before 1998. The exemption equivalent for these years was $600,000. The unified credit for previous years appears in the Appendix at ¶2600.

The estate tax and gift tax return filing requirements reflect the exemption equivalent (see ¶22 and ¶26).

A special transitional rule applies to gifts made between September 9, 1976, and December 31, 1976.[11]

¶16 Benefits of Graduated Rates and Unified Credit Phased Out

The benefits of the graduated rates and the unified credit under the unified transfer tax system were phased out beginning with cumulative transfers above $10 million prior to 1998.[12] This was accomplished by adding five percent of the excess of any transfer over $10 million to the tentative tax computed in determining the ultimate transfer tax liability. This five-percent surtax was repealed by the Economic Growth and Tax Relief Reconciliation Act of 2001 (P.L. 107-16), effective for decedents dying, and gifts made, after December 31, 2001. (See ¶2595 regarding the "sunsetting" of this provision after December 31, 2010.)

For estates of decedents dying, and gifts made, after 1987 and before 1998, the tax was levied on amounts transferred in excess of $10 million but not exceeding $21,040,000 in order to recapture the benefit of any transfer tax rate

---

[11] Under this rule, if the $30,000 lifetime exemption was used during this period, the unified credit available for later gifts is reduced, but only to the extent of 20 percent of the exemption—up to a maximum of $6,000 (Code Sec. 2010(b) and Code Sec. 2505(b)). For example, if gifts were made during this period and the lifetime exemption was applied against a gift tax liability of $15,000, the unified credit allowable after Jan. 1, 1977, must be reduced by $3,000. Use of the $30,000 lifetime exemption on gifts made prior to September 9, 1976, does not reduce the unified credit.

In addition, with respect to lifetime gifts made in 1977, only $6,000 of the available $30,000 unified credit may be applied against gifts made after December 31, 1976, but prior to July 1, 1977. See the Appendix at ¶2600 for a year-to-year chart of the phase-in of the unified credit.

The retroactive application of this transitional rule was upheld by the U.S. Supreme Court in *A. Hemme*, SCt, 86-1 USTC ¶13,671, 476 US 1166. The estate of a decedent who had made lifetime transfers after September 8, 1976, and before January 1, 1977, and who had elected to claim the lifetime exemption of $30,000, was required to reduce its allowable unified credit by 20 percent of the claimed exemption. The Court stated that the application of the transitional rule was not unconstitutional because the amount of the credit that the estate was ultimately allotted resulted in no greater tax than that which the estate would have owed under prior law. Therefore, the application of the transitional rule to gifts made by the decedent prior to the Tax Reform Act of 1976 (P.L. 94-455) was not so arbitrary and capricious as to violate due process.

[12] Code Sec. 2001(c)(2).

below 55 percent and the unified credit. Due to mistakes in the wording of the amendment to Code Sec. 2001(c)(2) by the Taxpayer Relief Act of 1997 (P.L. 105-34), the five-percent additional tax phased out the benefits of graduated rates, but not the benefits of the unified credit (applicable credit amount), for estates of decedents dying, and gifts made, after 1997, but before 2002. Therefore, the additional tax was levied on amounts transferred in excess of $10 million, but not exceeding $17,184,000, for decedents dying after 1997. The benefit of the applicable credit amount was not recaptured.

¶ 20 Unified Rates and Credit for Nonresidents Not Citizens

Effective for the estates of decedents dying after November 10, 1988, the estate and gift tax rates applicable to U.S. citizens are also applicable to the estates of nonresident aliens.[13] With respect to the unified credit, where permitted by treaty, the estate of a nonresident alien is allowed the same unified credit as a U.S. citizen multiplied by the percentage of the total gross estate situated in the United States. In other cases, the estate of a nonresident alien is allowed a unified credit of $13,000 (which exempts the first $60,000 of the estate from estate tax) or, for residents of U.S. possessions, the greater of $13,000 or a pro rata share of $46,800 based on the percentage of property located in the United States.[14] Consistent with the repeal of the five-percent surtax applicable to U.S. citizens dying after December 31, 2001, the five-percent surtax applicable to nonresidents not citizens is also repealed with respect to such post-2001 transfers.[15]

With respect to transfers made before 2002, in order to reflect the fact that in some cases the estate of a nonresident noncitizen did not receive the same unified credit available to U.S. citizens, the additional Code Sec. 2001(c)(2) five-percent recapture rate was adjusted.[16] Accordingly, the additional five-percent rate applied to the taxable transfers of nonresident noncitizens in excess of $10 million only to the extent that it was necessary to phase out the benefit of the graduated rates and unified credit actually allowed by statute or treaty.

See ¶1615 for a list of countries that have death tax conventions in effect with the United States.

---

[13] Code Sec. 2101(a).

[14] Code Sec. 2102(c).

[15] Code Sec. 2101(b), as amended by the Job Creation and Worker Assistance Act of 2002 (P.L. 107-147).

[16] Code Sec. 2101(b).

Chapter 2
FILING REQUIREMENTS

¶ 22 Estate Tax Returns for U.S. Citizens and Residents

An estate tax return (Form 706, United States Estate (and Generation-Skipping Transfer) Tax Return) (Rev. Aug. 2004) is due within nine months after the date of a decedent's death.[1] For estates of U.S. citizens and residents dying after 1976, the filing requirements are triggered for estates that exceed the applicable exclusion amount—i.e., the amount of property sheltered from tax by the unified credit.

For decedents dying in 2004 and 2005, the applicable exclusion amount is $1.5 million (up from $1 million for decedents dying in 2002 and 2003), and the filing threshold is increased to that amount.[2] However, if lifetime gifts are made and the applicable credit amount is offset against the gift tax, this amount is reduced accordingly (see the unified credit table at ¶ 10).[3]

Filing thresholds applicable to decedents dying before 2002 are reproduced in the Appendix at ¶ 2600.

¶ 24 Estate Tax Returns for Nonresidents Not Citizens

For estates of nonresidents not citizens of the United States, the estate representative must file a return if the value of that part of the gross estate that is located in the United States exceeds $60,000 (see ¶ 1600 et seq.).[4]

¶ 26 Gift Tax Return Filing Requirements

A gift tax return (Form 709, United States Gift (and Generation-Skipping Transfer) Tax Return) (2004) is to be filed, and any gift tax is to be paid, on an annual basis. Generally, the due date for filing the annual gift tax return is April 15 following the close of the calendar year in which gifts are made (see ¶ 2052).[5] However, for a calendar year in which a donor dies, the gift tax return must be filed no later than the due date for the donor's estate tax return, including extensions.[6] These rules apply to U.S. citizens, residents, and nonresident aliens alike.

A gift tax return must be filed if the donor (1) gave gifts to any donee other than the donor's spouse that are not fully excludable from gift tax under one or a combination of the annual, educational, or medical exclusions (see ¶ 2250), (2) gave gifts to charity unless the donor transfers his or her entire interest in the

---

[1] Code Sec. 6075(a); Reg. § 20.6075-1. Extensions of time to file may be granted in certain circumstances, and an automatic six-month extension may be available for estate tax returns due after July 25, 2001 (see ¶ 66).

[2] Code Sec. 2010(c).

[3] Code Sec. 6018(a)(3).

[4] Code Sec. 6018(a)(2).

[5] Code Sec. 6075(b)(1).

[6] Code Sec. 6075(b)(3).

property transferred and no noncharitable donee receives an interest in the property, (3) gave gifts of terminable interests (other than a life estate with a general power of appointment) to his or her spouse (see ¶2318), or (4) gave gifts of any amount that are split with his or her spouse (see ¶2200).[7]

A short form gift tax return (Form 709-A, United States Short Form Gift Tax Return) (Rev. Oct. 2002) was available for filing by a husband and wife who elected split-gift treatment for pre-2003 gifts of not more than $22,000 per donee. Because Form 709-A has been declared obsolete for gifts made after December 31, 2002, Form 709 must be used to report split gifts made after this date.[8]

¶ 27 Generation-Skipping Transfer Tax Return Filing Requirements

IRS regulations detail the filing requirements for generation-skipping transfer (GST) tax returns.[9] The return requirements depend on the type of generation-skipping transfer involved. In general, in the case of a direct skip (other than from a trust), a return must be filed on or before the date on which an estate or gift tax return is required to be filed with respect to the transfer.[10] In all other cases, the due date for the return is on or before the 15th day of the fourth month after the close of the tax year of the person required to file such a return. Exceptions to these general rules are set forth in Reg. §26.2662-1 (see ¶2471).

As noted below, the type of generation-skipping transfer involved determines which return is to be used in reporting the tax.

• *Taxable Distributions*

In the case of a taxable distribution (defined at ¶2433), the transferee must report the generation-skipping transfer on Form 706-GS(D) (Generation-Skipping Transfer Tax Return For Distributions) (Rev. Jan. 2003), and the trust involved in such a transfer must file Form 706-GS(D-1) (Notification of Distribution From a Generation-Skipping Trust) (Rev. Jan. 2003) and send a copy to each distributee.[11]

• *Taxable Terminations*

The trustee in the case of a taxable termination (defined at ¶2433) is required to report the GST tax on Form 706-GS(T) (Generation-Skipping Transfer Tax Return For Terminations) (Rev. Jan. 2003).[12]

• *Direct Skips*

In specifying the form of return to be used for reporting the GST tax on direct skips (defined at ¶2433), Reg. §26.2662-1 distinguishes between *inter vivos* direct skips and direct skips occurring at death. For any direct skip that is subject to the federal gift tax and that occurs during the life of the transferor, Form 709 (United States Gift (and Generation-Skipping Transfer) Tax Return) must be filed.[13]

The GST tax that is imposed on direct skips that are subject to the estate tax and occur at the death of a decedent is reported on Form 706 (United States Estate (and Generation-Skipping Transfer) Tax Return). Schedule R-1 (Genera-

---

[7] Code Sec. 6019.
[8] Instructions for Form 709 (2004), p. 1.
[9] Reg. §26.2662-1.
[10] Code Sec. 2662(a)(2).
[11] Reg. §26.2662-1(b)(1).
[12] Reg. §26.2662-1(b)(2).
[13] Reg. §26.2662-1(b)(3)(i).

tion-Skipping Transfer Tax) of Form 706 must be filed for any direct skip from a trust if such a direct skip is subject to the estate tax.[14]

Certain *inter vivos* transfers may be subject to both gift and GST taxes. A generation-skipping transfer is subject to the gift tax if it is required to be reported on Schedule A (Computation of Taxable Gifts) of Form 709 under the rules contained in the gift tax portion of its instructions, including the split gift rules.

For a more detailed discussion of the GST tax return requirements, see Chapter 39, beginning at ¶2430.

---

[14] Reg. §26.2662-1(b)(3)(ii).

ESTATE TAX

Chapter 3

NATURE OF TAX

¶ 28 Description of Tax

The federal estate tax is an excise tax levied on the transfer of a person's property at the time of that person's death.[1] It is neither a tax on the property itself nor a tax on the privilege of an heir to receive the property.

The amount of the tax is determined by applying the relevant tax rates to the tax base or the taxable estate (see ¶12 and ¶29). With only one exception (noted below), the tax is not affected by the relationship of the beneficiaries to the decedent as is the case under inheritance tax laws in effect in many states.

A special deduction for amounts transferred to a surviving spouse reduces the size of the taxable estate of a U.S. citizen or resident if the transferred amounts meet the conditions of such deduction (see ¶1000).[2]

The estate tax is repealed with respect to decedents dying after December 31, 2009 (see ¶10).

¶ 29 Taxable Estate

The taxable estate is determined by subtracting certain deductions (see ¶780 through ¶1175) from the gross estate (see ¶150).[3] A tentative tax applies to the amount of the taxable estate and the amount of taxable gifts made after 1976, using the unified rate schedule (see ¶10). The estate tax is computed by determining the amount of the tentative tax and subtracting gift taxes paid on gifts made after 1976.[4] To the extent that the applicable credit amount was not used to offset gift taxes, the amount of estate tax is reduced.[5]

¶ 30 Gross Estate

The value of the gross estate of a decedent is the total value of the interests described in Code Sec. 2033 through Code Sec. 2044, whether real or personal, tangible or intangible, wherever situated.[6] Generally, the gross estate of a decedent is composed of the value of:

(1) all property to the extent of the decedent's interest in it at the time of the decedent's death (see ¶150);

---

[1] Code Sec. 2001(a); Reg. § 20.0-2(a).

[2] Code Sec. 2056(a).

[3] Code Sec. 2051.

[4] Code Sec. 2001(b).

[5] Code Sec. 2010.

[6] Code Sec. 2031 and Reg. § 20.2031-1, detailing certain exceptions to Code Sec. 2033 through Code Sec. 2044.

(2) any interest of the surviving spouse existing as dower or curtesy, or similar interest (see ¶175);

(3) property transferred by the decedent during life, if: (a) the transfer was made within three years before death and the transfer involved life insurance (see ¶430) or certain other property that would have been includible in the decedent's gross estate for the reasons described in (b), (c), or (d) (see ¶555); (b) the decedent had retained the income or enjoyment for life or for a period not determinable without reference to the decedent's death (see ¶570); (c) the transfer was not intended to take effect until the decedent's death and the decedent retained a reversionary interest in the property transferred (see ¶565); (d) the decedent possessed a power to change the enjoyment through a power to alter, amend, or revoke (see ¶580 and ¶585); or (e) the decedent had relinquished a right of the type referred to in (b), (c), or (d) within three years before the decedent's death (see ¶595); and

(4) certain other types of property interests, including: (a) one-half of the value of qualified joint interests (see ¶502); (b) jointly held property interests that are not qualified joint interests (the interest being based on the decedent's contribution to the purchase of joint interests) (see ¶500); (c) life insurance proceeds, if the decedent or the decedent's estate had any interest in the proceeds or held any incidents of ownership in the policy at the time of death (see ¶400); (d) property over which the decedent had a general power of appointment received from another; (e) certain annuities (see ¶700); or (f) qualified terminable interest property (see ¶773).[7]

The above summary is not all-inclusive and is subject to various qualifications. These qualifications are discussed in more detail at the paragraphs noted above.

¶ 32 Deductions

The items listed below are deductible from the amount of the gross estate in determining the taxable estate of U.S. citizens and residents:

(1) funeral expenses (see ¶785);

(2) various expenses incidental to the administration of the estate (see ¶790);

(3) losses incurred due to casualty or theft, etc., during administration (see ¶900);

(4) debts of the decedent and enforceable claims against the estate, including taxes (see ¶800);

(5) mortgages and liens (see ¶850);

(6) a marital deduction for qualifying property passing to the decedent's spouse (see ¶1000);

(7) the value of property transferred to, or for the use of, charitable, educational, religious, or public institutions, or the government (see ¶1100);

(8) the adjusted value of the decedent's qualified family-owned business interests (see ¶1150); and

(9) state death taxes paid, effective for estates of decedents dying, and generation-skipping transfers made, after December 31, 2004.[8]

---

[7] Code Sec. 2031 and Code Sec. 2033 through Code Sec. 2044.

[8] Code Sec. 2051 and Code Sec. 2053 through Code Sec. 2058.

¶ 35 Rates

The maximum transfer tax rate on cumulative lifetime and at-death transfers is 48 percent for estates of decedents dying in 2004[9] (the top marginal rate is further reduced in later years (see ¶10)). The effective minimum transfer tax rate for U.S. citizens and residents is 45 percent as a result of the operation of the unified credit applicable for 2004 and 2005 (see ¶15). However, as the applicable credit amount increases (see ¶15), the effective minimum transfer tax rate will also increase (see ¶10). In addition, with respect to transfers made before January 1, 2002, the benefits of the graduated rates are phased out, beginning with cumulative transfers exceeding $10 million (see ¶16). The tax may be further reduced by other credits (see ¶36).

¶ 36 Credits

A unified credit (applicable credit amount) is subtracted from the amount of tentative estate tax liability (see ¶15) for estates of decedents dying after 1976.[10]

In addition to the unified credit, credits are allowed in reduction of federal estate taxes for taxes paid on prior transfers to the decedent by or from a person who died within 10 years before or two years after the decedent (see ¶1300); state inheritance, estate, and succession taxes (see ¶1370: this credit is eliminated under a phaseout schedule beginning for decedents dying in 2002, and replaced by a deduction, for the estates of decedents dying after December 31, 2004); federal gift taxes paid by the decedent on pre-1977 transfers made by the decedent during his lifetime (see ¶1382); and foreign death duties paid (see ¶1401).[11] The credit allowed against the estate tax for gift tax paid on property included in a decedent's gross estate is eliminated for post-1976 gifts.

In computing the net estate tax, these credits, the sum of all gift taxes payable on gifts made after 1976, and the allowable unified credit are subtracted (see ¶1426) from the tentative tax.[12]

¶ 37 Effect of State Law

The question of whether, and the extent to which, particular property interests are owned by a decedent at death and, thus, are includible in the decedent's gross estate generally is determined on the basis of the law of the state where the decedent resided or where the property was located.[13] The federal courts will follow state law in deciding whether something is a property interest. State law, for this purpose, includes both statutes and state court decisions interpreting statutes. Therefore, it is necessary, in many cases, to refer both to the statutes and to state court decisions in determining whether a decedent owns a property interest that is includible in the gross estate.[14]

Where the type and character of property interests held and transferred by a decedent is determined with respect to state court decisions, the decisions of the highest court of a state have binding effect for federal estate tax purposes. The decision of the state's highest court can involve the actual interest to be reported on the decedent's estate tax return or it can involve the estate of another decedent under the same general factual situation. However, in a National Office Technical

---

[9] Code Sec. 2001(c)(1).

[10] Code Sec. 2010.

[11] Code Sec. 2010 through Code Sec. 2015.

[12] Code Sec. 2001(b).

[13] *J. Morgan, Exr.*, SCt, 40-1 USTC ¶9210, 309 US 78.

[14] Although state law classifies a property interest as a certain type, it is federal law that determines whether that type of interest is includible in the gross estate.

Advice Memorandum, the IRS refused to follow, for federal estate tax purposes, a decision of the Georgia Supreme Court that a decedent's power of appointment was limited by an ascertainable standard (see ¶653).[15] The lawsuit giving rise to the Georgia court's decision was a will construction proceeding filed by a bank as executor of the decedent's estate, and only the IRS, which was notified but declined to intervene, had an interest adverse to that of the estate. In the IRS's view, the decisions of a state's highest court are binding for estate tax purposes only if the underlying lawsuit was adversarial and affected the property rights of the litigants. In a separate National Office Technical Advice Memorandum, involving a Georgia decedent in a factual situation similar to that resulting in the Georgia Supreme Court's decision, the IRS also refused to accept the Georgia court's decision as controlling for estate tax purposes.[16]

Lower state court decisions are not binding for estate tax purposes, and their effect is not clear. The U.S. Supreme Court has held that, in the absence of a decision by a state's highest court, a federal court must apply what it finds the state law to be after giving "proper regard" to decisions of other courts of the state.[17] Intermediate state court decisions may be disregarded if the federal court is convinced that the highest state court would decide otherwise. A state trial court decision must also be given "proper regard" by a federal court; however, such a decision cannot have a binding effect for federal estate tax purposes.[18]

The allowance of estate tax deductions for funeral expenses, the expenses of administering a decedent's estate, claims against a decedent's estate, and mortgages on a decedent's property are all governed by the laws of the jurisdiction where the estate is being administered. Otherwise, the allowance of estate tax deductions is generally determined by the Internal Revenue Code.

¶ 38 Decedents Whose Estates Are Subject to Tax

The estate tax applies to the estate of any person who dies leaving property having a taxable situs within the United States. Its application varies in detail, however, between persons who are considered either residents or citizens of the United States and those who are considered nonresidents not citizens. The term "residence," as used with reference to any person for federal estate tax purposes, means the person's domicile, regardless of citizenship.

Generally, this publication deals with the status of estates of U.S. residents and citizens. The variations applicable to estates of decedents considered nonresidents not citizens are discussed at ¶1600 and following.

---

[15] IRS Technical Advice Memorandum 8339004 (June 14, 1983).

[16] IRS Technical Advice Memorandum 8346008 (Aug. 4, 1983).

[17] *H.J. Bosch Est.*, SCt, 67-2 USTC ¶12,472, 387 US 456, consolidated with *Second Nat'l Bank of New Haven, Ex'r (Will of F.F. Brewster)*. See also *D.L. Hastings, Pers. Rep.*, DC Md., 86-1 USTC ¶13,662.

[18] *H.J. Bosch Est.*, SCt, 67-2 USTC ¶12,472, 387 US 456, consolidated with *Second Nat'l Bank of New Haven, Ex'r (Will of F.F. Brewster)*. See also *D.L. Hastings, Pers. Rep.*, DC Md., 86-1 USTC ¶13,662.

Chapter 4
RETURNS—FORMS REQUIRED

¶ 50 Forms Required

The estate tax return, Form 706 (United States Estate (and Generation-Skipping Transfer) Tax Return) (Rev. Aug. 2004), is used to report and pay the estate tax in the case of decedents who were U.S. citizens or residents.[1] Form 706-NA (United States Estate (and Generation-Skipping Transfer) Tax Return—Estate of nonresident not a citizen of the United States) (Rev. Jan. 2003) is filed for nonresident aliens (see ¶85). Form 706-A (United States Additional Estate Tax Return) (Rev. Sept. 2004) is to be used to report the recapture of tax benefits previously enjoyed under an election to have farm or closely held business real property valued under the special use valuation provisions of Code Sec. 2032A (see ¶80).

The estate tax return must be filed within nine months after a decedent's death unless otherwise extended.[2] Payment of the tax is also due at this time unless one of the provisions for extension of time to pay tax applies (see ¶1685).[3]

If the tax cannot be finally computed within the filing period, arrangement may be made with the IRS for an extension of time for filing and payment. In order to reduce interest liability, the return may be filed with whatever necessary information is available before expiration of the filing period and with a payment of taxes based on an estimate. If the return is not filed within one year after it is due (including extensions), the right to use the alternate valuation method is lost (see ¶105).

¶ 65 Estate Tax Return

An estate tax return must be filed for the estate of every U.S. citizen or resident whose gross estate exceeds the amount of the applicable exclusion

---

[1] Discussion and examples herein are based on Form 706, as revised in August 2004, for use with respect to decedents dying in 2004.

[2] Code Sec. 6075(a); Reg. §20.6075-1 and Reg. §20.6081-1.

[3] Code Sec. 6151(a); Reg. §20.6151-1, Reg. §20.6161-1, and Reg. §20.6163-1.

amount (based on the applicable credit amount[4]) on the date of death.[5] The value of the gross estate at the date of the decedent's death is used to determine whether a return must be filed, even though the executor may elect to have the gross estate valued as of the alternate valuation date (see ¶107).[6]

The amount of the unified credit and, therefore, the applicable exclusion amount that a decedent's gross estate must exceed before a return is required depends on the date of the decedent's death (see ¶15). For decedents dying in 2004 and 2005, the decedent's representative must file a federal estate tax return only if the gross estate of the decedent exceeds the applicable exclusion amount of $1.5 million (see ¶15 for applicable exclusion amounts for 2006 and later years and ¶2600 for exclusion amounts for pre-2004 decedents). However, the applicable exclusion amount is reduced to reflect the amount of adjusted taxable gifts made by the decedent after 1976, plus the aggregate amount allowed as a specific exemption under former Code Sec. 2521 for gifts made by the decedent after September 8, 1976.[7]

An estate tax return must also be filed by the estate of a nonresident alien if the part of his or her estate situated in the United States exceeds $60,000 (after certain adjustments) at the date of death (see ¶85).

¶ 66 Time for Filing Return

Estate tax return Form 706 (United States Estate (and Generation-Skipping Transfer) Tax Return (Estate of a citizen or resident of the United States)) (Rev. Aug. 2004) or Form 706-NA (United States Estate (and Generation-Skipping Transfer) Tax Return (Estate of nonresident not a citizen of the United States)) (Rev. Jan. 2003) must be filed within nine months after the date of a decedent's death, unless a six-month extension to file the return is applied.[8] The due date is the day of the ninth calendar month after the decedent's death numerically corresponding to the date of the calendar month on which death occurred. For example, if the decedent died on February 4, 2004, the federal estate tax return must be filed on or before November 4, 2004. If there is no numerically corresponding day in the ninth month, the last day of the ninth month is the due date. Thus, if the decedent died on December 31, 2004, the due date is September 30, 2005.

Form 706-A (United States Additional Estate Tax Return) (Rev. Sept. 2004) must be filed within six months after an early disposition or cessation of qualified use of a specially valued property, that is, real property for which the special use valuation under Code Sec. 2032A is elected (see ¶80).

When the due date for the filing of an estate tax return falls on a Saturday, a Sunday, or a legal holiday, the due date for filing the return is the next succeeding day that is not a Saturday, a Sunday, or a legal holiday.[9] The term "legal holiday" means a legal holiday in the District of Columbia and, in the case of any document required to be filed or any other act required to be performed at any office of the United States outside the District of Columbia, but within an internal

---

[4] Beginning in 1998, the unified credit is determined by reference to the "applicable credit amount," and the exemption equivalent is referred to as the "applicable exclusion amount."

[5] Code Sec. 6018(a)(1) and Code Sec. 6018(a)(3).

[6] Reg. §20.6018-1.

[7] Code Sec. 6018(a)(3).

[8] Reg. §20.6081-1(b).

[9] Reg. §301.7503-1.

revenue district, the term also means a statewide legal holiday in the state where the office is located.[10]

• *Returns Mailed from Foreign Country*

The IRS will accept, as timely filed, a federal tax return, claim for refund, statement, or other document that is mailed from and officially postmarked in a foreign country on or before the last date prescribed for filing (including any extensions of time for filing). In addition, a return, refund claim, statement, or other document filed with the IRS or the Tax Court that is given to a designated international delivery service in a foreign country and recorded as described in Code Sec. 7502 before midnight on the prescribed due date will be deemed timely filed. If the last date for filing falls on a Saturday, Sunday, or legal holiday, the return or other document will be considered timely filed if it is postmarked, or given to the delivery service, on the next succeeding day that is not a Saturday, Sunday, or legal holiday. The term "legal holiday" does not include legal holidays in foreign countries unless such holidays are also legal holidays in the District of Columbia or the state where the return or other document is required to be filed.[11]

The estate tax return cannot be amended after the expiration of the extension period granted for filing. However, the estate representative may subsequently file supplemental information that may result in a finally determined tax different from the amount indicated on the return.[12]

• *Filing Extensions*

Effective for estate tax returns due after July 25, 2001, an estate will be allowed an automatic six-month extension if (1) the application (Form 4768, Application for Extension of Time to File a Return and/or Pay U.S. Estate (and Generation-Skipping Transfer Taxes)) is filed on or before the due date prescribed in Code Sec. 6075(a); (2) the application is filed with the IRS office designated in the application's instructions (excepting hand-carried documents); and (3) the application includes an estimate of the amount of estate and generation-skipping transfer tax liability for the estate.[13] A six-month extension of time for filing the return does not operate to extend the time for payment of the estate tax (but see ¶1685). Form 4768 includes a checkbox for requesting the automatic extension. A separate checkbox is provided by which an executor who is abroad may request an extension in excess of six months. The instructions state that the executor should apply for an automatic six-month extension and then apply for any additional extension and that applications for automatic and additional extensions cannot be combined on the same Form 4768.

An executor who fails to timely apply for an automatic extension is still permitted to apply for an extension by demonstrating good and sufficient cause. To support the extension for cause, the executor must attach a written statement to the Form 4768 explaining in detail why the executor was unable to request an automatic extension, why it was impossible or impractical to file the Form 706 by the due date, and why the executor should be granted an extension at the present time. Unless the executor is out of the country, an extension will not be granted for more than 6 months beyond the original due date of the estate tax return.[14]

---

[10] Reg. §301.7503-1.

[11] Rev. Rul. 2002-23, 2002-1 CB 811.

[12] Reg. §20.6081-1(c).

[13] Reg. §20.6081-1(b).

[14] Instructions for Form 4768 (Rev. Aug. 2003), p. 2.

• *Victims of Terrorist Attacks, Combat Zone Participants*

Deadlines for certain tax-related acts, such as the filing of returns and the payment of tax, may be suspended by the IRS for up to one year in response to terrorist or military attacks (see ¶1650). Additionally, a special toll-free telephone number has been created by the IRS for individuals with tax issues related to the terrorist attacks against the United States on September 11, 2001, or related to participation in a combat zone, as designated by the Department of Defense. The number (1-866-562-5227) is operated by the IRS Monday through Friday, 7:00 a.m. to 10:00 p.m., local time.[15]

¶ 67 Penalties

The willful failure to make and file the estate tax return, to pay the tax, or to keep any records or supply any information at the time or times required by law or regulation constitutes a misdemeanor.[16] These offenses are punishable by a fine of not more than $25,000 or imprisonment of not more than one year, or both, with costs of prosecution.

If the estate tax return is not filed within the prescribed time (see ¶66), the IRS will impose a penalty of five percent of the estate tax liability per month or part of a month, up to a maximum of 25 percent, until the return is filed, unless the estate representative can show that the failure to file is due to reasonable cause and not to willful neglect.[17] In addition, if the failure to file is shown to be due to fraud, the penalties range from 15 percent to a maximum of 75 percent.[18]

• *Reliance on Accountant or Attorney*

The question of whether an executor's reliance on an attorney, accountant, or other tax professional to timely file the estate tax return constitutes reasonable cause for late filing of the return has frequently been the subject of litigation. In resolving this issue, the Tax Court and several U.S. courts of appeal have utilized different approaches and arrived at conflicting results.[19] The U.S. Supreme Court, in an attempt to establish a "bright line rule" with respect to this issue, has stated that the delegation of an executor's duty to comply with unambiguous and fixed filing requirements does not relieve the executor of his or her burden to ascertain the relevant filing deadlines and to ensure that they are met.[20] Accordingly, the Court held that where an executor relies on an attorney, accountant, or tax advisor to comply with these filing requirements, the executor's reliance will not constitute reasonable cause for a late filing of the estate tax return.

The Court did recognize that where an executor relies on the erroneous advice of counsel regarding a substantive question of law (e.g., as to whether or not a tax liability exists), such reliance may constitute reasonable cause for a late filing. However, the Court chose not to define the circumstances in which this would be true. The Tax Court has explored this issue and held that a donor's reliance on the advice of her accountant regarding the necessity for filing gift tax returns was reasonable cause for her failure to file the returns. Although the

---

[15] IRS News Release IR-2001-84, Sept. 24, 2001.

[16] Code Sec. 7203.

[17] Code Sec. 6651(a)(1).

[18] Code Sec. 6651(f).

[19] *S.E. Young Est.*, 46 TCM 324, CCH Dec. 40,605(M), TC Memo. 1983-686; *M. Ferrando*, CA-9, 57-2 USTC ¶11,702, 245 F2d 582; *C.I. Lillehei Est.*, CA-3, 81-1 USTC ¶13,389, 638 F2d 65; and *A. Geraci Est.*, CA-6, 74-2 USTC ¶13,024, 502 F2d 1148, cert. denied, 420 US 992, have adopted a *per se* rule that reliance on counsel is not "reasonable cause."

[20] *R. Boyle, Exr.*, SCt, 85-1 USTC ¶13,602, 469 US 241, rev'g CA-7, 83-2 USTC ¶13,530, 710 F2d 1251.

donor's estate eventually conceded gift tax liability for stock and cash advances she had made to her son and that were never repaid, the Tax Court stated that the donor had justifiably relied on her accountant's advice that no gift tax returns were necessary because the advances were intended to be loans at the time of their making.[21] In a similar case, the Tax Court held that an executrix's reliance on her attorney's advice that no estate tax return was due because the estate was too small constituted reasonable cause that excused the executrix's failure to file.[22] The Tax Court has also held that a personal representative's reliance on the erroneous advice of her attorney that an estate was entitled to a second automatic extension of time to file the estate tax return constituted reasonable cause for the untimely filing of the return.[23]

Additionally, an estate administrator's reliance on his attorney was found by a U.S. district court in Tennessee to be reasonable cause for his failure to timely file an estate tax return. The court held that because of his age (78), poor health, and lack of experience in estate administration, the administrator was unable to deal with the "emergency situation" created by the unexpected illness of his attorney shortly before the return was due. The district court noted that the Supreme Court had expressly left open the issue of whether an executor's reliance on his attorney would be reasonable cause for delay when that reliance was due to the executor's incapacity. The court found that the administrator was incapable of exercising ordinary business care and prudence by hiring another attorney to file the return or by obtaining an extension of time in which to file and, therefore, the delay in filing was due to reasonable cause.[24]

The unusual factual circumstances in the Tennessee case limit the application of its holding. Recent decisions on this issue have uniformly held that reliance on an attorney or accountant will not excuse late filing.[25] However, another Tennessee court has held that reliance on a qualified professional's erroneous advice as to when the estate tax return was due was reasonable cause.[26]

¶ 68 Place for Filing Return

Before 2002, the estate tax return of a resident decedent was to be filed with the IRS Service Center serving the state in which the decedent was domiciled at the date of death.[27] All returns filed after 2001, other than those with a foreign, APO, or FPO address, must be filed at the IRS Service Center, Cincinnati, OH 45999. Returns with a foreign, APO, or FPO address are to be filed at the Philadelphia Service Center, Philadelphia, PA 19255. The return of a nonresident

---

[21] *S.S. Buring Est.*, 51 TCM 113, CCH Dec. 42,539(M), TC Memo. 1985-610. See also *H.J. Knott*, 55 TCM 424, CCH Dec. 44,653(M), TC Memo. 1988-120.

[22] *F.G. Paxton Est.*, 86 TC 785, CCH Dec. 43,021; *L. Chagra Est.*, 60 TCM 104, CCH Dec. 46,713(M), TC Memo. 1990-352; see also, *C.J. Autin*, 102 TC 760, CCH Dec. 41,906, regarding the gift tax.

[23] *E.E. La Meres*, 98 TC 294, CCH Dec. 48,085.

[24] *C. Brown*, DC Tenn., 86-1 USTC ¶13,656.

[25] See *L.F. Blumberg Est.*, DC Cal., 86-1 USTC ¶13,658; *G.M. Brandon Est.*, 86 TC 327, CCH Dec. 42,911, rev'd and rem'd on another issue, CA-8, 87-2 USTC ¶13,733; *R. Cox Est.*, DC Fla., 86-2 USTC ¶13,681; *S.B. Gardner Est.*, 52 TCM 202, CCH Dec. 43,285(M), TC Memo. 1986-380; and *H.E. Rothpletz Est.*, 53 TCM 1214, CCH Dec. 43,998(M), TC Memo. 1987-310; *J.K. Fleming Est.*, CA-7, 92-2 USTC ¶60,113, 974 F2d 894; *F.S. Newton Est.*, 59 TCM 469, CCH Dec. 46,546(M), TC Memo. 1990-208; *K.S. Wilbanks Est.*, 61 TCM 1779, CCH Dec. 47,153(M), TC Memo. 1991-45, aff'd, CA-11 (unpublished opinion 1-22-92); *J. Nemerov Est.*, 75 TCM 2344, CCH Dec. 52,709(M), TC Memo. 1998-186; *J.G. Maltaman Est.*, 73 TCM 2163, CCH Dec. 51,917(M), TC Memo. 1997-110.

[26] *W.F. Sharp, Jr. Est.*, DC Tenn., 97-1 USTC ¶60,268.

[27] Code Sec. 6091(b)(3).

(whether a citizen or not) must be filed with the IRS Service Center, Philadelphia, PA 19255.[28]

¶ 69 Payment of Tax

The estate tax is due and payable at the same time and place the return is due. In other words, the payment must be made with the return.[29] Thus, the estate tax is due nine months after a decedent's death, without regard to extensions of time to file (see ¶ 66).

Failure to pay the tax with the return may result in the imposition of a penalty of one-half of one percent of the estate tax liability for each month or part of a month that the tax remains unpaid, up to a maximum of 25 percent.[30] This penalty is in addition to the late-filing penalty discussed at ¶ 67. Code Sec. 6651(d) provides that in cases where a taxpayer fails to pay the tax due on notice and demand thereof by the IRS, the penalty is further increased each month. If an addition to tax applies both for failure to file a return on the due date and for failure to pay the tax on the due date, the addition for failure to file is reduced by the amount of the addition for failure to pay for any month or part of a month to which both additions apply.[31] See ¶ 1685 for details concerning extensions of time for paying the tax.

¶ 70 Persons Required to File Return

The duly qualified executor or administrator of a decedent's estate is required to file the estate tax return. If there is more than one executor or administrator qualifying, the return must be verified and signed by all.[32]

If there is no executor or administrator appointed, qualified, and acting in the United States, every person in actual or constructive possession of any property of a decedent situated in the United States is considered an "executor" for estate tax purposes and is required to make and file a return.[33]

Where two or more persons are liable for the filing of the return, it is preferable for all to join in the filing of one complete return.[34] If all of them are unable to do so, each person is required to file a return disclosing all the information each has with respect to the return (including the name of every person holding a legal or beneficial interest in the property and a full description of the property). Similarly, in the event the appointed, qualified, and acting executor or administrator is unable to make a complete return, every person holding an interest in property comprising the decedent's estate must make a return, on receipt of notice from the district director, as to the interest held by that person.[35]

The person or persons filing the estate tax return must sign, under penalty of perjury, the first declaration on page 1 of the return. If the return is prepared by an attorney or an agent for the person or persons filing the return, the attorney or agent must also sign the second declaration on page 1 under penalty of perjury.

---

[28] Announcement 2001-74, IRB 2001-28, 40.
[29] Reg. § 20.6151-1.
[30] Code Sec. 6651.
[31] Code Sec. 6651(c)(1).
[32] Reg. § 20.6018-2.
[33] Reg. § 20.6018-2.
[34] Instructions for Form 706 (Rev. Aug. 2004), p. 2.
[35] Reg. § 20.6018-2.

¶ 71 Missing Person's Return

A duty to file an estate tax return for a missing person's estate rests on any person who would be an executor or administrator of the estate in the event of the missing person's actual death. The executor or administrator must ascertain from existing facts whether the missing person is a "decedent" for purposes of filing the estate tax return.[36]

Facts establishing a missing person's death for estate tax return purposes include the following:

(1) administration of the absentee's property pursuant to adjudication by a court of competent jurisdiction;

(2) transfer to or vesting of the absentee's assets in a beneficiary pursuant to state law;

(3) taking of or receipt of the absentee's property by any person without court order or statutory authority; or

(4) circumstances indicating that the absentee's property has been disposed of as if he or she were dead.[37]

The mere appointment of a receiver for the missing person's property does not indicate that person's death for estate tax purposes in the absence of any transfer of title or assets. In any event, if the value of the missing person's estate is such as to otherwise require that an estate tax return be filed (see ¶ 22), such a return must be filed within nine months following the period of continuous and unexplained absence after which the person may be declared legally dead under applicable state law.

In a National Office Technical Advice Memorandum, the IRS has ruled that, where there is a court adjudication of death based on a presumption of death and no fixed date thereof, the date of death for federal estate tax purposes is the ending date of the state presumptive period and not the date of adjudication. In the IRS's view, any other rule would leave the determination of the date of death, for federal estate tax purposes, to the discretion of the interested party filing the petition in state court.[38]

¶ 72 Supplemental Documents

If the decedent was a U.S. resident and died testate, a certified copy of the decedent's will must be filed with the estate tax return. The executor may also file copies of any documents that the executor desires to submit in explanation of the return. Various other supplemental documents, required for the several property schedules of the return, are discussed in the following chapters.

If the decedent was a nonresident citizen, the following documents must also be filed with the return:

(1) a copy of any inventory of property and any schedule of liabilities, claims against the estate, and expenses of administration filed with the foreign court of probate jurisdiction and certified by a proper official of such court; and

---

[36] Rev. Rul. 66-286, 1966-2 CB 485, as clarified and modified by Rev. Rul. 80-347, 1980-2 CB 342, and by Rev. Rul. 82-189, 1982-2 CB 189.

[37] Rev. Rul. 66-286, 1966-2 CB 485, as clarified and modified by Rev. Rul. 80-347, 1980-2 CB 342, and by Rev. Rul. 82-189, 1982-2 CB 189.

[38] IRS Technical Advice Memorandum 8526007 (March 14, 1985).

(2) a copy of any return filed under a foreign inheritance, estate, legacy, succession, or other death tax act and certified by a proper official of the foreign tax department, if the estate is subject to such a foreign tax.[39]

Form 2848 (Power of Attorney and Declaration of Representative) must be filed in order to grant authority to an individual to represent a taxpayer before the IRS and to receive tax information (see ¶79). Form 8821 (Tax Information Authorization) is to be used to authorize any designated individual, corporation, firm, organization, or partnership to inspect and/or receive confidential information in any office of the IRS for the type of tax and years or periods listed on the form (see ¶79).

See also the material discussing the following: alternate valuation, ¶115; real estate, ¶262; stocks and bonds, ¶313; life insurance, ¶481; business interests, ¶527; miscellaneous properties, ¶535; transfers during life, ¶615; powers of appointment, ¶670; attorneys' fees, ¶792; marital deduction, ¶1075; charitable deduction, ¶1140 and ¶1141.

¶73 Execution of the Return

Form 706 (United States Estate (and Generation-Skipping Transfer) Tax Return) is used to report the estate tax. The current Form 706 is arranged in the following sequence:

- Page 1 contains questions dealing with general information pertaining to the decedent, a "Tax Computation" section (part 2), and a section for signing the return by the executor, administrator, or person in possession of the decedent's property and by the preparer of the return. The allowable unified credit is subtracted on line 11 of the "Tax Computation" section. The credits for state death taxes, federal gift taxes on pre-1977 gifts, foreign death taxes, and tax on prior transfers are claimed on Lines 13, 15, 16, and 17, respectively, of the "Tax Computation" section where applicable.

- Page 2 of Form 706 includes an "Elections by the Executor" section (part 3) in which the executor can make elections to specially value property (see ¶280 through ¶296), to use the alternate valuation date (see ¶107), and to pay tax in installments under Code Sec. 6166 or to postpone taxes under Code Sec. 6163 (see ¶1650 through ¶1685). Page 2 also contains "General Information" questions (part 4), which continue onto page 3. If question number 15 is answered in the affirmative, Schedule I (Annuities) must be completed. (Schedule I requires an executor to disclose whether a lump-sum distribution under Code Sec. 2039(f)(2) is being excluded from the gross estate.) Question number 16 requires the executor to disclose whether the decedent was the beneficiary of a trust for which the marital deduction was claimed on the estate tax return of a predeceased spouse as qualified terminable interest property (QTIP) and which is not reported as part of the decedent's gross estate. If the answer is "yes," an explanation for the failure to report such property must be attached to the return.

- Page 3 of Form 706 contains a "Recapitulation" (part 5) that has two sections. The decedent's gross estate (from Schedules A through I) is reported in the first section of the Recapitulation, and, after subtracting any qualified conservation easement exclusion (from Schedule U), the "Total gross estate" for this section is then reported on line 1 of the "Tax Computation" section (part 2) on page 1 of Form 706. The second section of the Recapitulation is used to record the deductions (from Schedules J through M and O), and the "Total allowable

---

[39] Reg. § 20.6018-4.

deductions" are then carried over and deducted on line 2 of the "Tax Computation" section on page 1.

Form 706 also includes the following schedules:

• Schedules A through I, which are used to report a decedent's gross estate.

• Schedule A-1 (Section 2032A Valuation), which is used to report information required to support the election to value certain farm and closely held business property at its special use value. Schedule A-1 includes the Notice of Election (part 2) and the Agreement to Special Valuation Under Section 2032A (part 3).

• Schedules J through M and O, which are used to report deductions.

• Schedule P (Credit for Foreign Death Taxes) and Schedule Q (Credit for Tax on Prior Transfers), which are used to report tax credits. Note that IRS Form 706-CE (Certificate of Payment of Foreign Death Tax) (Rev. May 2002) must also be filed in order to claim a credit for foreign death tax.

• Schedule R (Generation-Skipping Transfer Tax), which is used to compute the generation-skipping transfer (GST) tax payable by an estate, and Schedule R-1 (Generation-Skipping Transfer Tax—Direct Skips From a Trust—Payment Voucher), which is used for the computation of the tax payable by certain trusts that are includible in the gross estate. Only GST tax imposed as a result of a direct skip occurring at death is reported using Form 706. See Chapter 41 (¶2471 through ¶2487) for a discussion of the other forms used for reporting the GST tax.

• Schedule U (Qualified Conservation Easement Exclusion) is used to report information required to support the election to exclude a portion of the value of land that is included in the decedent's gross estate and is subject to a qualified conservation easement. The amount of the exclusion is entered on Form 706, part 5, line 11.

• A Continuation Schedule is to be used for listing additional assets from Schedules A, B, C, D, E, F, G, H, and I and additional deductions from Schedules J, K, L, M, and O if there is no more room on the particular schedule. Totals on a Continuation Schedule should be carried over to the appropriate line of the main schedule. A separate Continuation Schedule must be used for each main schedule being continued.

Money items may be shown on the return as whole-dollar amounts. The rounding off of amounts to whole-dollar figures requires the elimination of any amount less than 50 cents and an increase of any amount in the range of 50 cents to 99 cents to the next higher dollar amount.[40]

The final computation of the tax must be shown in detail. The estate tax return does not provide a detailed schedule for the purposes of this computation, however. If the executor determines that no estate tax is owed by the decedent's estate, he or she should enter a zero on line 25—"Balance due" under "Tax Computation" (Part 2) on page 1 of the return.

• ***Total Gross Estate Exceeding the Applicable Exclusion Amount***

In the case of a decedent whose total gross estate exceeds the applicable exclusion amount ($1.5 million for 2004 and 2005), the first three pages of Form

---

[40] Instructions for Form 706 (Rev. Aug. 2004), p. 2.

706 and all required supporting schedules must be filed, in accordance with the following rules:

(1) If the gross estate does not include assets reportable on Schedule A (Real Estate), Schedule B (Stocks and Bonds), Schedule C (Mortgages, Notes, and Cash), Schedule D (Insurance on the Decedent's Life), or Schedule E (Jointly Owned Property), it is not necessary to file these schedules, and a zero should be entered on the applicable line of the Recapitulation on page 3 of Form 706. However, Schedule D must be filed if it is indicated in the "General Information" portion of Form 706 (Part 4, Question 8a) that there was insurance on the decedent's life that was not included on the return as part of the gross estate.

(2) Schedule F (Other Miscellaneous Property Not Reportable Under Any Other Schedule) must be filed with every return.

(3) Schedule G (Transfers During Decedent's Life) must be filed if, as indicated in the General Information portion of Form 706 (part 4, Questions 11 and 12a), the decedent made certain types of transfers during life or if there existed at the date of death any trusts created by the decedent during his or her lifetime. Schedule H (Powers of Appointment) must be filed if it is indicated in the General Information portion of Form 706 (part 4, Question 13) that the decedent ever possessed, exercised, or released any general power of appointment.

(4) Schedule J (Funeral Expenses and Expenses Incurred in Administering Property Subject to Claims), Schedule K (Debts of the Decedent, and Mortgages and Liens), Schedule L (Net Losses During Administration and Expenses Incurred in Administering Property Not Subject to Claims), Schedule M (Bequests, etc., to Surviving Spouse), and Schedule O (Charitable, Public, and Similar Gifts and Bequests) must be filed only if a deduction is claimed for a particular item. For Schedule M, which is used to list the assets for which a marital deduction has been taken, the QTIP election is deemed to have been made if property qualifying for QTIP treatment is listed on Schedule M.

(5) Schedule P (Credit for Foreign Death Taxes) and Schedule Q (Credit for Tax on Prior Transfers) must be filed only if the particular credit is claimed.

(6) Schedule U (Qualified Conservation Easement Exclusion) must be filed if the exclusion is claimed on part 5, line 11.

¶ 74 Estate Beneficiaries

Individuals, trusts, or estates receiving benefits of $5,000 or more from the decedent's estate (other than charitable beneficiaries) are to be listed on page 2 of the Form 706 (United States Estate (and Generation-Skipping Transfer) Tax Return) estate tax return, together with their taxpayer identification numbers (Social Security numbers in the case of individuals, and employer identification numbers for trusts and other estates), relationship to the decedent, and the approximate dollar value of property received from the estate. The total of these distributions should approximate the amount of the gross estate, reduced by funeral and administration expenses, debts and mortgages, bequests to the surviving spouse, charitable bequests, and any federal and state estate and generation-skipping transfer taxes paid relating to the benefits received by the beneficiaries.

¶75 Beneficiaries Receiving Specially Valued Property

Individuals who received an interest in specially valued property (see ¶280 through ¶296) must be listed on Schedule A-1 (Section 2032A Valuation) of the estate tax return, along with their taxpayer identification numbers, relationship to the decedent, and addresses. In the case of an individual beneficiary, the identification number is the Social Security number; for trusts and estates, the employer identification number should be used.

¶78 Entering Principal and Income on Schedules

For every item of principal, any income accrued thereon at the date of the decedent's death must be separately entered on the appropriate schedule under the column headed "Value at date of death." If the alternate valuation method is elected, any includible income with respect to each item of principal must be separately entered under the column headed "Alternate value."

The information indicated by the columns headed "Alternate valuation date" and "Alternate value" should not be shown unless the executor elects the alternate valuation method. "Alternate value" information should be omitted in the space provided in the Recapitulation, part 5, Form 706 (United States Estate (and Generation-Skipping Transfer) Tax Return), if the alternate valuation method is not elected.

The items must be numbered under every schedule. The total of the items on each schedule should be shown at the bottom of the schedule, but the totals should not be carried forward from one schedule to another. The total for each schedule, however, should be entered under the Recapitulation section.

¶79 Representation by Lawyer or Agent

If the executor is to be represented by someone else before the IRS, by correspondence or otherwise, in refund claims and other matters, a power of attorney must be filed on Form 2848 (Power of Attorney and Declaration of Representative) and signed by the fiduciary.

Form 2848 authorizes a person or persons to represent an estate in a proceeding before the IRS and to receive confidential information. It also authorizes the person or persons named as a representative to perform one or more of the three following acts: (1) execute waivers (including offers of waivers) of restrictions on assessment or collection of deficiencies; (2) execute consents extending the statutory period for assessment or collection of taxes; and (3) execute closing agreements. In order to grant additional powers, such as the power to delegate authority, to substitute another representative, or to sign the return, specific language designating the additional power must be inserted. Form 8821 (Tax Information Authorization) is to be used to authorize any designated individual, corporation, firm, organization, or partnership to inspect and/or receive confidential information in any office of the IRS for the type of tax and years or periods listed on the form. It will not authorize an individual to represent a taxpayer and/or perform other acts on the taxpayer's behalf such as executing waivers, consents, or closing agreements. Form 2848 must be used for that purpose. A properly executed declaration on page 2 (part 4) of Form 706 (United States Estate (and Generation-Skipping Transfer) Tax Return) will also authorize an attorney, certified public accountant, or enrolled agent to represent the estate and receive confidential tax information, such as a copy of the closing letter.

Generally, only one power of attorney to represent the estate may be in effect in an IRS office in any one matter. Therefore, the names and addresses of all lawyers or agents to whom the executor has delegated authority to represent the estate in the matter should be included in the power of attorney. The power of attorney should be filed with the IRS District Director in whose office the estate tax return has been, or will be, filed.

Attorneys and certified public accountants are not required to be enrolled to practice before the IRS. However, they must file as evidence of recognition a written declaration stating that they are qualified and are authorized to represent the particular parties on whose behalf they are acting.[41] Attorneys are qualified if they are members in good standing of the bar of the highest court of any state, possession, territory, commonwealth, or the District of Columbia and are not currently under suspension or disbarment from practice before the IRS. Similarly, certified public accountants are qualified if they are authorized to practice as certified public accountants in any state, possession, territory, commonwealth, or the District of Columbia and are not currently under suspension or disbarment from practice before the IRS.

In both instances the declarants, of course, must be authorized to act on behalf of their clients.

Form 2848 contains a declaration to be completed, which contains the following information:

(1) A statement that the representative is authorized to represent the taxpayer as a certified public accountant, attorney, enrolled agent, enrolled actuary, unenrolled return preparer, member of the taxpayer's immediate family, officer, full-time employee, etc. An actuary enrolled by the Joint Board for the Enrollment of Actuaries may represent a taxpayer before the IRS. However, the actuary's representation is limited to certain areas of the Internal Revenue Code. See § 10.3(d)(1) of Treasury Department Circular No. 230 for a list of the Code sections involved and the areas covered by them.

(2) The jurisdiction recognizing the representative. For an attorney or certified public accountant: Enter in the "Jurisdiction" column the state, District of Columbia, possession, or commonwealth that has granted the declared professional recognition. For an enrolled agent or actuary: Enter in the "Jurisdiction" column the enrollment card number.

(3) The signature of the representative, and the date signed.

If the estate is to be represented before the IRS by an agent, the agent must be enrolled to practice in accordance with the regulations contained in the Rules on Administrative Procedure. The requirements for enrollment of agents are contained in Treasury Department Circular No. 230 (Title 31, part 10, Code of Federal Regulations), which may be obtained from the Director of Practice, U.S. Treasury Department, Washington, D.C. 20009. Unenrolled agents may represent taxpayers only under limited circumstances.[42]

Any person qualified under § 10.5(c) (relating to temporary recognition of an applicant for enrollment) or § 10.7 (relating to limited practice without enrollment in the case of a full-time employee, or a bona fide officer of a corporation,

---

[41] Statement of Procedural Rules § 601.502.

[42] Statement of Procedural Rules § 601.502.

trust, estate, association, or organized group, and certain others) of Circular No. 230 will also be recognized to practice before the IRS.[43]

¶ 80 Special Use Valuation Additional Tax—Form 706-A

Where the election to have farm or closely held business real property valued under the special use valuation provisions is made under Code Sec. 2032A, the tax benefits gained as a result are recaptured as an additional estate tax if the property is disposed of to nonfamily members or ceases to be used for farming or closely held business purposes within 10 years after the death of the decedent. Form 706-A (United States Additional Estate Tax Return) (Rev. Sept. 2004) is used to report the recapture of these tax benefits. For a discussion of the Code Sec. 2032A election, see ¶280 through ¶296.

The basic Form 706-A (Rev. Sept. 2004) computation of the additional estate tax due under Code Sec. 2032A is made on part II, lines 1–15. Lines 16–18 incorporate information relating to involuntary conversions or exchanges reported on Schedule B before arriving at the additional estate tax amount on line 19. If an individual is using Form 706-A to report an exchange or involuntary conversion, he or she should not use the same Form 706-A to report any cessations of qualified use or dispositions of specially valued property that are not exchanges or involuntary conversions.[44] A separate Form 706-A should be used for the cessations or other dispositions. However, involuntary conversions and exchanges may be reported together on the same form. A separate Form 706-A must be used for each qualified heir.

It should be noted that Form 706-A also includes a Schedule C for purposes of reporting dispositions to family members of the qualified heir.

Form 706-A must be filed with the IRS office where the decedent's estate tax return was filed. Unless an extension for filing is obtained, Form 706-A must be filed within six months after the taxable disposition or cessation of qualified use of the property.

A filled-in Form 706-A appears in the Appendix at ¶3200.

¶ 85 Nonresidents Not Citizens

An estate tax return must be filed for the estate of a nonresident not a citizen if the part of the decedent's gross estate having a situs in the United States exceeded a value of $60,000, after reduction for (1) taxable gifts made after 1976, and (2) the aggregate amount that was allowable as a specific exemption under Code Sec. 2521, as it existed prior to its repeal by the Tax Reform Act of 1976, for gifts made between September 9, 1976, and December 31, 1976.[45] Form 706-NA (United States Estate (and Generation-Skipping Transfer) Tax Return (Estate of nonresident not a citizen of the United States)) (Rev. Jan. 2003) is used for the estates of nonresidents not citizens (see ¶3260). This return must be filed and the estate tax paid (in U.S. currency at par) within nine months after a decedent's death. The estates of nonresidents who are not citizens are entitled to the same filing and payment extensions that are available to U.S. citizens and residents. Returns of nonresidents who are not citizens must be filed with the Internal Revenue Service Center, Philadelphia, PA 19255. If the decedent died testate, a certified copy of the will must be attached to the return.

---

[43] Statement of Procedural Rules § 601.502.

[44] Instructions for Form 706-A (Rev. Sept. 2004), pp. 2-3.

[45] Code Sec. 6018(a)(3).

Schedule A of Form 706-NA is used to report that portion of the nonresident alien's gross estate that is situated in the United States. See ¶1617 and ¶1620 for further details. Property reported on this schedule must be valued in U.S. dollars, and the "alternate valuation method," discussed at ¶105, can be elected. All property must be separately listed on Schedule A (page 2) and must be described in such a manner that it can be readily identified. The total value of property listed in Schedule A is reported on line 1 of Schedule B (page 2) of Form 706-NA.

Schedule E of Form 706 must be attached if, at the time of death, the decedent owned any property located in the United States in joint tenancy with the right of survivorship, as a tenant by the entirety, or with a surviving spouse as community property.

Schedule G of Form 706 must be attached to Form 706-NA if the decedent made certain lifetime transfers (described in detail in the instructions for Form 706, Schedule G) of property that was located in the United States either at the time of the transfer or at the time of the decedent's death. A Form 706 Schedule G must also be filed with Form 706-NA if the decedent created any trusts during his lifetime that were in existence at the time of transfer or at the time of the decedent's death.

Schedule H of Form 706 must be attached to Form 706-NA if the decedent, at the time of his or her death, possessed a general power of appointment over property located in the United States and/or if the decedent exercised or released such a power at any time.

If the gross estate in the United States includes any interests in property transferred to a "skip person" as defined in the Instructions to Form 706, Schedule R (Generation-Skipping Transfer Tax) and/or Schedule R-1 (Generation-Skipping Transfer Tax—Direct Skips From a Trust) must be attached.

Schedule B of Form 706-NA is used to compute the taxable estate of a nonresident alien. This schedule is filled out as follows:

(1) The decedent's gross estate located in the United States, as reported on Schedule A, is entered on line 1. The decedent's gross estate located outside the United States is then reported on line 2. The total of lines 1 and 2, or the decedent's total gross estate wherever situated, is entered on line 3.

(2) The deduction for administration expenses, claims, etc., is determined and claimed on lines 4 and 5 of Schedule B. A deduction for mortgages will be allowed only if the full value of the mortgaged property was included in the total gross estate reported on line 3.

(3) The charitable deduction is claimed on line 6. Line 6 of Schedule B indicates that Schedule O of Form 706 must be attached to support this deduction. However, the Form 706-NA instructions indicate that, if a charitable deduction is claimed under a treaty, the applicable treaty must be specified and the computation of the charitable deduction must be attached. The marital deduction that is available to the estates of decedents only under certain treaties is also claimed on line 6. Estates of decedents claiming this deduction must attach Schedule M of Form 706 and a sheet showing the computation of the amount of the deduction.

(4) The total deductions (i.e., the total of lines 5 and 6) are entered on line 7.

(5) The taxable estate is computed on line 8 by subtracting line 7 from line 1. (See ¶1625 through ¶1635 for further details concerning the allowance of deductions for the estates of nonresident aliens.)

After Schedules A and B of Form 706-NA have been completed, the "Tax Computation" section (part II) on page 1 can be completed. The taxable estate, from line 8, Schedule B, is entered on the first line of this Tax Computation section. The sum of the taxable estate (line 1) and the decedent's adjusted taxable gifts of tangible or intangible property located in the United States (line 2) is entered on line 3. The tentative tax on the total of the taxable estate and the total taxable gifts (line 3) and the tentative tax on the total taxable gifts alone (line 2) are then entered on lines 4 and 5, respectively. The amount on line 5 is then subtracted from the amount on line 4, and the resulting amount—the gross estate tax—is entered on line 6.[46]

The estate and gift tax rates applicable to the estates of U.S. citizens are also applicable to the estates of nonresident aliens.[47]

The allowable unified credit against estate taxes is entered on line 7 and any credit for state death taxes on line 9. "Other credits" (including the Canadian marital credit and the credit for federal gift taxes) are entered on line 11, the credit for tax on prior transfers on line 12 and the total of these two credits is entered on line 13. The net estate tax liability is entered on line 14 after subtracting the line 13 amount from the amount on line 10. The generation-skipping transfer tax (see instructions to Schedules R of Form 706) imposed on transfers of interests in property that is part of the gross estate in the United States is entered on line 15. The addition of lines 14 and 15 results in the amount of total transfer taxes entered on line 16. The total reductions for prior payments (line 17) and for U.S. Treasury bonds redeemed in payment of estate tax (line 18), is entered on line 19. The balance of estate tax due (computed as the amount on line 19 subtracted from the amount on line 16) is entered on line 20.

It should be noted that, where permitted by treaty, the estate of a nonresident alien is allowed the same unified credit as that of a U.S. citizen, multiplied by the proportion of the total gross estate situated in the United States. In other cases, the estate of a nonresident alien who is not a resident of a U.S. possession is allowed a unified credit of $13,000 (which exempts the first $60,000 of the estate from estate tax).[48]

---

[46] Instructions for Form 706-NA (Rev. Jan 2003), p. 4.

[47] Code Sec. 2101(b).

[48] Code Sec. 2102(c).

Chapter 5
VALUATION—DATE AND METHODS

¶ 100 Election Available

The representative of an estate has an election with respect to the time property included in the gross estate is to be valued. The representative may elect to value property as of the date of the decedent's death or as of an "alternate valuation date." The "alternate valuation date" is, generally, a date six months after the date of the decedent's death. See ¶ 107 for further details. Even property that was transferred some time before death, but that is included in the gross estate because of the retention of certain rights or for other reasons, is valued as of the date of death or as of a date six months after death.

¶ 101 Rules Applicable to Various Types of Property

Even though all property included in the gross estate is valued as of the same date—that is, the date of death or the alternate valuation date—special problems arise in valuing particular types of property. For this reason, special rules apply in valuing the various kinds of property or interests in property that might be included in the gross estate, such as: real estate; stocks and bonds; mutual funds; interests in business; notes, secured and unsecured; cash on hand or on deposit; household and personal effects; annuities, life estates, remainders, and reversions; and certain other property.

¶ 102 Request for IRS Valuation Basis

The IRS may be required to furnish a written statement explaining any determination or proposed determination of the value of an item of property in a decedent's estate. The statement must be furnished no later than 45 days after a written request by the executor or donor or 45 days after the determination or proposed determination, whichever is later.[1]

The statement must (1) explain the basis of the valuation, (2) set forth any computation, and (3) include a copy of any expert appraisal. The method used by the IRS in arriving at the valuation is not binding on the IRS.

A request for such a statement must be filed with the District Director's office that has jurisdiction over the estate tax return by the deadline for claiming a refund of the tax that is dependent on the valuation.[2]

---

[1] Code Sec. 7517.

[2] Reg. § 301.7517-1.

¶ 105 Alternate Valuation Method

The alternate valuation method for determining the value of a decedent's estate is authorized by Code Sec. 2032. The use of this method is limited to situations in which the election would reduce both the value of the decedent's gross estate and the federal estate and generation-skipping transfer tax liability of the estate.[3]

The alternate valuation date may be elected on an estate tax return that is filed no more than one year late.[4] Once elected, the use of the alternate valuation date is irrevocable.[5] Further, the alternate valuation method must be elected on the first return filed or on a subsequent return if filed by the due date of the original return.[6] Proposed amendments to the regulations would, however, provide that estates that fail to make the alternate valuation election on the last estate tax return filed before the due date, or the first return filed after the due date, would still be able to request an extension of time to make the election. The one-year filing deadline would still remain effective under the proposed amendments: No request for an extension of time to make the election will be granted if the request is submitted to the IRS more than one year after the due date of the return (including extensions of time to file that were actually granted).[7]

The alternate valuation method is not automatic. It must be expressly elected on the estate tax return by checking the box at line 1 of part 3 (Elections by the Executor) of Form 706 (United States Estate (and Generation-Skipping Transfer) Tax Return) (Rev. Aug. 2004). However, the mere failure to designate the election on the return will not necessarily preclude the use of alternate valuation. A determination of whether an election has been made must be reached by looking at all of the facts on the return.[8]

¶ 107 Applicable Alternate Valuation Dates

If the estate representative chooses the alternate valuation method, all property included in the gross estate is valued as of six months after the decedent's death, except that property sold, distributed, exchanged, or otherwise disposed of during the six months is to be valued as of the date of disposition.[9] If there is no day in the sixth month following the decedent's death that corresponds numerically to the date of death, the alternate valuation date is the last day of the sixth month.[10] The actual selling price of securities sold in arm's-length transactions during the alternate valuation period must be used in valuing such securities by a person electing the alternate valuation method.[11]

The phrase "distributed, sold, exchanged, or otherwise disposed of" includes all possible ways by which property may cease to form a part of the gross estate. Property is considered "distributed," either by the estate representative or by a trustee of property included in the gross estate, on the date on which the first of the following events occurs:

(1) entry of an order or decree of distribution (if the order or decree subsequently becomes final);

---

[3] Code Sec. 2032(c).

[4] Code Sec. 2032(d).

[5] Code Sec. 2032(d).

[6] Temp. Reg. § 301.9100-6T.

[7] Proposed amendment to Temp. Reg. § 301.9100-6T, NPRM-REG-139845-02.

[8] Rev. Rul. 61-128, 1961-2 CB 150.

[9] Code Sec. 2032(a).

[10] Rev. Rul. 74-260, 1974-1 CB 275.

[11] Rev. Rul. 68-272, 1968-1 CB 394; Rev. Rul. 70-512, 1970-2 CB 192.

(2) separation of the property from the estate or trust so that it is completely available to the distributee; or

(3) actual distribution of the property to the beneficiary or other distributee.

In order to eliminate changes in value due only to lapse of time, Code Sec. 2032 provides that any interest or estate "affected by mere lapse of time" is to be included in the gross estate under the alternate valuation method at its value as of the date of the decedent's death. Adjustments for any difference in value as of the alternate valuation date not due to mere lapse of time are allowed. Property "affected by mere lapse of time" includes patents, estates for the life of a person other than the decedent, remainders, and reversions.[12]

¶ 109 Property to Be Valued

The property to be valued as of the alternate valuation date is the property included in the gross estate on the date of the decedent's death. Property interests remain "included property" for the purpose of valuing the gross estate under the alternate valuation method even though they change in form during the alternate valuation period by being actually received or disposed of by the estate.[13] Consequently, it is necessary in every case to determine what property comprised the gross estate at the decedent's death.

The alternate valuation election applies to *all* the property included in the gross estate on the date of a decedent's death. The election cannot be applied to only a portion of such property.[14] However, the IRS has ruled that a decedent's estate could elect both to value the decedent's assets on the alternate valuation date and to value the decedent's qualifying farm property under the special use valuation provisions of Code Sec. 2032A.[15] In addition, an estate electing both the alternate valuation date and special use valuation was required to use the alternate valuation date to determine the special use value of farmland owned by the decedent. For purposes of applying the limit on the aggregate reduction in the value of qualified real property, the alternate valuation date was also to be used to compute the difference between fair market value and special use value.[16]

¶ 110 Income After Death

Rents, dividends, and interest received during the six months following the decedent's death are not includible in a decedent's gross estate by reason of the executor's election to adopt the alternate valuation method. If the right to such income has accrued at the date of death, such income is includible.

Any partial payment of the principal of interest-bearing obligations, such as notes and bonds, made between the date of death and the subsequent valuation date is includible in the gross estate at its value on the date of payment. Similarly, any advance payment of interest for a period after the subsequent valuation date made during the alternate valuation period that has the effect of reducing the value of the principal obligation as of the subsequent valuation date will be included in the gross estate at its value on the date of payment.[17] The principle applicable to interest paid in advance also applies to advance payments of rent.

---

[12] Reg. § 20.2032-1(f).

[13] Reg. § 20.2032-1(d); *N.S. Johnston Est.*, CA-5, 86-1 USTC ¶ 13,655, 779 F2d 1123, cert. denied, 6-23-86.

[14] Reg. § 20.2032-1(b)(2).

[15] Rev. Rul. 83-31, 1983-1 CB 225.

[16] Rev. Rul. 88-89, 1988-2 CB 333.

[17] Reg. § 20.2032-1(d).

Ordinary dividends out of earnings and profits declared to stockholders of record after the decedent's death are to be excluded from the alternate valuation method. However, if the effect of the declaration of dividends is that the decedent's shares of stock on the alternate valuation date do not reasonably represent the same property existing at the date of death, such dividends are includible in determining the alternate valuation to the extent paid from earnings of the corporation prior to the date of the decedent's death. For example, a stock dividend received during the alternate valuation period affects the value of the decedent's total shares so that, at the alternate valuation date, his total shares "do not reasonably represent the same property existing at the date of his death." The stock dividend is therefore includible in determining the alternate valuation of the gross estate.[18]

The IRS National Office has ruled that, under Reg. § 20.2032-1(d), post-death corporate earnings must have been declared as a dividend or otherwise distributed during the alternate valuation period for such earnings to be considered excluded property. In determining that corporate earnings were not excluded property, the IRS concluded that no distinction was to be made between the situation where the corporation was controlled by a decedent's estate, and one that was not so controlled.[19]

A mutual fund capital gains dividend declared and paid between the time of death and the alternate valuation date is not includible in the gross estate of a decedent, even though the payment reduces the value of the shares outstanding (and the asset value on the alternate valuation date), because the value of a mutual fund share is equal to a pro rata share of the fund's net assets.[20]

¶ 112 Life Insurance Policies

With respect to policies of insurance on the life of a person other than the decedent, a distinction is made, for alternate valuation purposes, as to the cause of the value increase. When the value of a policy of insurance that had been owned by the decedent on the life of another increases following the date of the decedent's death, and such increase is attributable to the payment of premiums or to interest earned, the increase is excluded from the value of the insurance as determined under the alternate valuation method.[21] However, the appreciation in the value of insurance policies caused by the *death of the insured* during the alternate valuation period after the policy owner's death is not considered property earned or accrued during that period. Therefore, the entire value of the proceeds is includible in the deceased policy owner's gross estate.[22]

¶ 115 Return Information Under Alternate Valuation Method

If the alternate valuation election is exercised, the estate tax return (Form 706, United States Estate (and Generation-Skipping Transfer) Tax Return) must set forth:

(1) an itemized description of all property included in the gross estate on the date of the decedent's death, together with the value of each item as of that date;

---

[18] Rev. Rul. 58-576, 1958-2 CB 625.

[19] IRS Technical Advice Memorandum 200343002, June 11, 2003.

[20] *R.W. Bartram*, DC Conn., 75-1 USTC ¶ 13,041. See also Rev. Rul. 76-234, 1976-1 CB 271.

[21] Rev. Rul. 55-379, 1955-1 CB 449.

[22] Rev. Rul. 63-52, 1963-1 CB 173.

(2) an itemized disclosure of all distributions, sales, exchanges, and other dispositions during the six-month period after the decedent's death, together with the dates of such dispositions; and

(3) the value of each item of property on the appropriate alternate valuation date.[23]

This information must be reflected under the appropriate columns on *each applicable* property schedule of the return.[24]

Under the column headed "Description" on the applicable schedule, a brief statement explaining the status or disposition governing the alternate valuation date must be shown for each item. For example, the statement could be one of the following: "Not disposed of within six months following death," "Distributed," "Sold," or "Bond paid on maturity." A description of each item of principal and includible income must be separately entered in the same column. The applicable date for each separate entry must be shown in the adjacent column headed "Alternate valuation date."

The amount of principal and includible income must also be shown under the heading "Alternate value." In the case of any interest or estate having a value "affected by mere lapse of time," the value shown under the heading "Alternate value" must be the adjusted value. Under the heading "Value at date of death," the amounts of the principal and includible income must again be entered separately.

Examples showing the use of Schedule A (Real Estate) and Schedule B (Stocks and Bonds) of Form 706 under the alternate valuation method appear in the Appendix at ¶2950 and ¶2960. For comparison purposes, examples illustrating the use of the same schedules for the same decedent where the alternate valuation method is not elected also appear.

¶ 120 Supplemental Documents

Statements as to distributions, sales, exchanges, and other dispositions of a decedent's property within the six-month period after the decedent's death must be supported by evidence. If a court issues an order of distribution during that period, a certified copy of the order of distribution must be submitted with the return. The Director of an IRS Service Center or the District Director may require the submission of any additional evidence deemed necessary.[25]

¶ 121 Income Tax Basis of Inherited Property

Generally, the income tax basis of property acquired from a decedent by bequest, devise, or inheritance is its fair market value on the date of the decedent's death. However, if the alternate valuation date has been elected, the basis is the fair market value of the property on the alternate valuation date.[26] If the property was sold, distributed, or disposed of within six months of death, its basis is the fair market value at the date of sale, distribution, or disposition. See ¶296 for rules on the basis of special use valuation property acquired from a decedent. (With respect to decedents dying after December 31, 2009, this stepped-up basis will no longer apply—see the heading "New Carryover Basis Rules", below.)

---

[23] Reg. §20.6018-3(c)(6).

[24] Instructions for Form 706 (Rev. Aug. 2004), p. 6.

[25] Reg. §20.6018-4(e).

[26] Code Sec. 1014, prior to amendment by P.L. 107-16, effective for decedents dying after December 31, 2009.

A special rule applies to appreciated property acquired by a decedent as a gift within one year of death if such property passes from the decedent to the original donor or to the donor's spouse.[27] The basis of such property in the hands of the original donor or his or her spouse is its basis to the decedent immediately prior to death, rather than its fair market value on the date of death. This provision is intended to prevent individuals from transferring property in anticipation of a donee's death merely to obtain a tax-free step up in basis upon receipt of the property from the donee's estate.

• *New Carryover Basis Rules*

The Economic Growth and Tax Relief Reconciliation Act of 2001 (P.L. 107-16) (2001 Act) repeals the estate tax with respect to the estates of decedents dying after December 31, 2009.[28] In connection with estate tax repeal, the "stepped-up" basis at death rules are replaced with a carryover basis regime.[29] As a result, effective for property acquired from a decedent dying after December 31, 2009, the income tax basis of property acquired from a decedent will generally be carried over from the decedent. More specifically, the recipient of the property will receive a basis equal *to the lesser of* the adjusted basis of the property in the hands of the decedent, or the fair market value of the property on the date of the decedent's death. The new basis rule replaces the stepped-up basis rules that have long applied to property received from a decedent.

As a partial replacement for the repealed basis step up, executors will be able to increase the basis of estate property by up to $1.3 million (for property passing to any designated beneficiary or beneficiaries)[30] or $3 million in the case of property passing to a surviving spouse.[31] Less generous amounts apply to nonresident alien decedents.

To effectuate the new carryover basis at death rules, executors will be required for estates of decedents dying after December 31, 2009, to file information returns with the IRS and to supply basis information to beneficiaries.[32] Failure to comply with these filing requirements will subject the executor to penalties.[33]

Sunset provision. In order to comply with the Congressional Budget Act of 1974, the 2001 Act provides that all provisions of, and amendments made by, the 2001 Act will not apply to estates of decedents dying, gifts made, or generation-skipping transfers after December 31, 2010. Unless Congress acts affirmatively in the interim, the Internal Revenue Code will thereafter be applied and administered as if these provisions had not been enacted.

---

[27] Code Sec. 1014(e), prior to amendment by P.L. 107-16, effective for decedents dying after Dec. 31, 2009.

[28] Code Sec. 2210, as added by P.L. 107-16.

[29] Code Sec. 1014(f) and Code Sec. 1022, as added by P.L. 107-16.

[30] Code Sec. 1022(b), as added by P.L. 107-16.

[31] Code Sec. 1022(c)(2), as added by P.L. 107-16.

[32] Code Sec. 6018, as added by P.L. 107-16.

[33] Code Sec. 6716, as added by P.L. 107-16.

GROSS ESTATE

Chapter 6

PROPERTY INTEREST AT TIME OF DEATH

¶ 150 What Is Included

All property owned in whole or in part by a citizen or a resident at the time of his or her death is included in the decedent's gross estate to the extent of the value of the decedent's interest in the property.[1] Foreign realty involves special rules, discussed at ¶ 251.

In the estate tax return (Form 706, United States Estate (and Generation-Skipping Transfer) Tax Return) (Rev. Aug. 2004), four schedules are concerned solely with property and interests in property that are owned by the decedent at the time of death and which pass to others either under the terms of the decedent's will or by intestacy. The four schedules are: (1) Schedule A (Real Estate); (2) Schedule B (Stocks and Bonds); (3) Schedule C (Mortgages, Notes, and Cash); and (4) Schedule F (Other Miscellaneous Property Not Reportable Under Any Other Schedule).

¶ 155 Tests for Includibility

Although the types of property reported on each of the four schedules (Schedule A (Real Estate); Schedule B (Stocks and Bonds); Schedule C (Mortgages, Notes, and Cash); and Schedule F (Other Miscellaneous Property Not Reportable Under Any Other Schedule) of Form 706 (United States Estate (and Generation-Skipping Transfer) Tax Return)) vary, the tests for determining whether particular property interests are includible in the gross estate are the same for all. Three questions arise in determining whether property should be reported in one of the above four schedules as part of the gross estate. They are:

(1) What types of property are includible in the decedent's estate?

(2) Did the decedent have an interest in such property sufficient to warrant inclusion in the decedent's gross estate of the value of the interest involved?

(3) If the decedent had an interest, did the decedent still possess it at the time of death, and to what extent?

The answers to these questions, which determine the character of property interests held and transferred by a decedent, are determined under state laws. See ¶ 37 for further details as to the application of state laws.

---

[1] Code Sec. 2033; Reg. § 20.2033-1.

Questions concerning valuation are peculiar to the specific type of property involved. They are discussed, therefore, in connection with the individual schedules dealing with the particular type of property. Similarly, the taxability of interests and transfers not governed by the general taxing statute, Code Sec. 2033, is also discussed in connection with the schedule on which such interests or transfers are reportable.

¶ 156 First Question: Type of Property

As to the first question regarding type of taxable property, there is little for the courts to decide. Usually, because the terms of Code Sec. 2033 are so general, it is conceded that all property of the decedent is taxable, unless a state law, the peculiar nature of the interest, or some other external factor suggests a means for excluding the property from the gross estate. Except where the question involves property subject to a power of appointment, it is almost a certainty that any property in which a decedent has a valuable interest at the time of death will be includible in the decedent's gross estate. Not even property set aside for the surviving spouse by state law escapes inclusion in the decedent's gross estate if it has been established that the decedent had an interest in the property.

Lump-sum Social Security death benefits payable to the decedent's surviving spouse or to any person equitably entitled to such payments are not includible in the gross estate of the decedent. Such amounts are not considered property of the decedent.[2] Uncashed Social Security benefit checks that are payable to the decedent and his or her surviving spouse are also not includible.[3] State and municipal bonds that are exempt from federal income taxation are includible in a decedent's gross estate[4] (see ¶329). An exclusion applies to Indian trust lands, royalties, and funds held by the United States as trustee under the General Allotment Act of 1887, where the decedent dies before receiving a patent in fee simple.[5] Provisions of death tax treaties with other countries also have some exclusionary effects.

¶ 157 Second Question: Sufficient Interest

The issue involved in the second question, that of the sufficiency of the decedent's interest, has almost always been a question of property law. The cases turn largely on common-law and statutory rights. Most of the cases are decided by the application of property law to the facts.

If the decedent held the property in trust for someone else, it is generally not includible. If the property is in the decedent's name for convenience, but the property belongs to another, it is not includible. Conversely, property held in the name of another for convenience, but belonging to the decedent, is includible in the decedent's gross estate.

¶ 158 Third Question: Possession at Death

The third question, regarding possession of property interest at time of death, presents most of the estate tax difficulties. This question is concerned basically with the duration of the decedent's interest and with interests that have begun to accrue or that have come into existence about the time of the decedent's death, but that have not yet come into the decedent's possession.

---

[2] Rev. Rul. 67-277, 1967-2 CB 322; Rev. Rul. 55-87, 1955-1 CB 112.

[3] Rev. Rul. 75-145, 1975-1 CB 298.

[4] Rev. Rul. 81-63, 1981-1 CB 455.

[5] Rev. Rul. 69-164, 1969-1 CB 220.

Certain general conclusions may be drawn from the decisions involving this question. If the interest came into existence prior to the decedent's death and was not defeated by death, its value at the time of death is includible in the gross estate. Thus, vested remainders are includible, but contingent remainders, defeated by the decedent's death, are not includible. Similarly, where the decedent has only a life interest under a transfer by another, nothing is left to tax at the time of the decedent's death.

If the property interest was accruing to the decedent at the time of death, and was enforceable by the decedent's estate, so much of it as had accrued at the time of death is includible in the decedent's gross estate. Therefore, accrued salary, commissions, and income are includible. But, where these items are not *required* to be paid into the decedent's estate, they are not includible, even though actually paid to the executor.

¶ 165 Community Property

Property in which a decedent had an interest at the time of death is includible in the decedent's gross estate for estate tax purposes to the extent of the value of the decedent's interest in such property. Laws in community property states, however, generally limit the extent of a person's interest in community property to one-half of the value of the property.[6]

The federal estate tax law recognizes these state limitations by purposely failing to provide a distinct, specific method of treating community property. This failure causes the application of the estate tax to be governed by state law. Consequently, only one-half of the value of each item of community property held by a decedent and the decedent's spouse may be included in the gross estate of the decedent. The IRS has ruled, in a National Office Technical Advice Memorandum, that this is true even though the decedent's estate actually received selected community assets with an aggregate date-of-death value equal to the decedent's portion of the total amount of community property.[7]

This limitation applies not only to property in which the decedent still had an interest at the time of death but also to life insurance purchased with community funds and to property which was the subject of certain lifetime transfers. However, one-half of the proceeds of life insurance policies purchased with community funds is not includible in the gross estate of the decedent if, under the facts of a particular case or the applicable state law, it can be shown that such policies were the separate property of another.[8]

¶ 170 Reciprocal Transfers

Reciprocal trusts receive special consideration. Under a reciprocal trust arrangement, each grantor (usually related to the other grantor) transfers property to a trust, at about the same time, and gives the other grantor the lifetime right to enjoy the property as beneficiary. The trust created for the beneficiary is includible in the beneficiary's gross estate when the trusts are found to be interrelated and leave the grantors in the same economic position they would have been in had they created the trusts and named themselves as beneficiaries.[9] In essence, inclusion will result when (1) the two trusts are substantially identical

---

[6] See, for example, IRS Technical Advice Memorandum 9018002 (Jan. 17, 1990).

[7] IRS Technical Advice Memorandum 8505006 (Oct. 19, 1984).

[8] *A.M. Kroloff*, CA-9, 73-2 USTC ¶12,959, 487 F2d 334; *A.G. Kern*, CA-9, 74-1 USTC ¶12,979, 491 F2d 436; *V.F. Saia Est.*, 61 TC 515, CCH Dec. 32,428 (CA-5, appeal dismissed pursuant to stipulation, 1-27-75); *E.W. Marks, Jr., Est.*, 94 TC 720, CCH Dec. 46,594.

[9] *J.P. Grace Est.*, SCt, 69-1 USTC ¶12,609, 395 US 316.

in terms, (2) the trusts were created at about the same time under some sort of arrangement, and (3) each grantor gives the other grantor approximately the same economic rights.[10]

In at least one case (*B. Bischoff Est.*[11]), the reciprocal trust doctrine has been applied, even though the trust powers exchanged did not have substantial economic value. The existence of the crossed powers in *B. Bischoff Est.* was held sufficient to cause inclusion of the corpora of two trusts in the estates of a husband and wife, each of whom had created identical trusts for the grandchildren wherein each spouse named the other as trustee. Similarly, the value of stock that a decedent transferred to his wife to hold in custody for their children under a Uniform Gifts to Minors Act was includible in his gross estate under the reciprocal trust doctrine because his wife made identical transfers of stock to him to hold in custody for the children.[12] However, in one case, the Tax Court refused to apply the doctrine to reciprocal transfers and held that the value of stock transferred by a decedent's wife to a trust that she had created with the decedent as trustee was not includible in the decedent's gross estate even though he transferred the same amount of stock to a trust that he had created with his wife as trustee. Although the decedent granted a special power of appointment to his wife over the corpus of the trust he had created, he received no such power over the trust created by his wife; however, in all other respects the terms of the trusts were identical. In the court's view, the doctrine was inapplicable because the special power of appointment held by the decedent's wife put her in an economic position different from that of the decedent.[13]

¶ 175 Dower and Curtesy

The gross estate includes the value of dower, curtesy, and all interests created by statute in lieu of dower or curtesy.[14] This is true even though the statutory interest may differ in character from dower or curtesy. Therefore, the full value of the property is required to be included, without deduction of the value of the interest of the surviving spouse, and without regard to the time when the right to such an interest arose.[15]

Arguments that dower and curtesy are not transfers by the decedent have been unsuccessful. The right of the surviving spouse to use or enjoy the property during the surviving spouse's lifetime becomes consummate by reason of the decedent's death, and this fact is sufficient support for applying a death tax.

¶ 180 Dower or Curtesy Transferred for Consideration

Transfers of property in which the decedent retains an interest, for consideration of money or money's worth, are included in the gross estate to the extent that the fair market value of the transferred property at the time of death exceeds the value of the consideration received in exchange by the decedent. The relinquishment of dower or curtesy, or a statutory estate created in lieu of dower or curtesy, is not considered the giving of consideration and may not be used in determining the reduction from the transferred property.[16] See ¶ 610 for further details.

---

[10] IRS Letter Ruling 8019041 (Feb. 12, 1980).

[11] *B. Bischoff Est.*, 69 TC 32, CCH Dec. 34,702.

[12] *Exchange Bank and Trust Co. of Florida, Exr.*, CA-FC, 82-2 USTC ¶ 13,505, 694 F2d 1261.

[13] *H. Levy Est.*, 46 TCM 910, CCH Dec. 40,323(M), TC Memo. 1983-453.

[14] Code Sec. 2034.

[15] Reg. § 20.2034-1.

[16] Code Sec. 2043(b); Reg. § 20.2043-1.

Chapter 7
REAL ESTATE

¶ 250 Real Property

The value of all real property owned by a U.S. citizen on the date of death is includible in the decedent's gross estate under Code Sec. 2033. For this purpose, it is immaterial whether the decedent was a resident or a nonresident, or whether the property came into the possession and control of the executor or administrator or passed directly to the heirs or devisees. Real property includes certain types of loans classified as real property under local law, as well as mineral rights and royalties. Real estate owned by a decedent is reported on Schedule A (Real Estate) of Form 706 (United States Estate (and Generation-Skipping Transfer) Tax Return) (Rev. Aug. 2004), unless such property is owned by a sole proprietorship. In that case, the real estate should be reported on Form 706, Schedule F (Other Miscellaneous Property Not Reportable Under Any Other Schedule) (see ¶525). Schedule A does not have to be filed with the estate tax return if the decedent did not own reportable real estate.

¶ 251 Real Property Outside the United States

The value of interests in foreign real estate, regardless of when acquired, must be included in the gross estates of property owners. In addition, the value of foreign real property acquired by a decedent after January 31, 1962, is also includible unless it was acquired by *gift, devise, inheritance, or survivorship* and the donor or prior decedent had acquired the interest in the foreign realty (or a power of appointment with respect to it) before February 1, 1962.

Capital additions or improvements to foreign real estate, to the extent they materially increase the value of the property and to the extent they are attributable to construction after January 31, 1962, must be treated in the same manner as real property acquired after that date.[1]

¶ 253 Qualified Conservation Easement Exclusion

The executor of the estate of a decedent dying after 1997 may elect to exclude from the gross estate up to 40 percent (the "applicable percentage") of the value of land that is subject to a qualified conservation easement. The amount that may be excluded from the gross estate is limited to $500,000 in 2002 or thereafter. (In prior years, the excludable amount was limited as follows: $400,000 in 2001; $300,000 in 2000; $200,000 in 1999; and $100,000 in 1998.) In addition, the exclusion applicable in any year is reduced by the amount of any charitable deduction that was taken with respect to the land under Code Sec. 2055(f).[2]

---

[1] Reg. § 20.2031-1(c).

[2] Code Sec. 2031(c).

The election is made by filing Form 706 (United States Estate (and Generation-Skipping Transfer) Tax Return), Schedule U (Qualified Conservation Easement Exclusion), and claiming the exclusion on Page 3, Part 5, line 11. Once made, the election is irrevocable.[3]

Special use valuation property. The granting of a conservation easement does not affect specially valued property under Code Sec. 2032A. Thus, the granting of such an easement is not treated as a disposition and does not trigger the additional estate tax. In addition, the existence of a qualified conservation easement does not prevent the property from subsequently qualifying for special use valuation.

Partnerships, corporations, and trusts. An interest in a partnership, corporation, or trust will qualify for the qualified conservation easement exclusion provided that at least 30 percent of the entity is owned, directly or indirectly, by the decedent, as determined under the rules applicable to the qualified family-owned business deduction under Code Sec. 2057 (see ¶1150).[4]

• ***Land Subject to a Qualified Conservation Easement***

With respect to decedents dying before January 1, 2001, land subject to a qualified conservation easement is land which, on the date of the decedent's death, is located (1) in or within 25 miles of a metropolitan area as defined by the Office of Management and Budget, (2) in or within 25 miles of a national park or wilderness area, unless the Secretary of the Treasury determines that such land is not under significant development pressure, or (3) in or within 10 miles of an Urban National Forest as designated by the Forest Service of the U.S. Department of Agriculture.

However, the Economic Growth and Tax Relief Reconciliation Act of 2001 (P.L. 107-16) (2001 Act) eliminated the aforementioned distance requirements with respect to the estates of decedents dying after December 31, 2000. For such decedents, the land needs only to be located in the United States or in a U.S. possession.[5] However, note that the provisions of the 2001 Act will expire ("sunset") after December 31, 2010, unless Congress acts in the interim to extend the 2001 Act's effectiveness.

In order to qualify for the exclusion, the land must have been owned by the decedent or a member of the decedent's family during the three-year period ending on the date of the decedent's death. Further, the land must be subject to a qualified conservation easement granted by the decedent or a member of the decedent's family. In addition, a post-mortem conservation easement may be placed on the property, provided the easement has been made no later than the date of the election.[6]

Members of the family. The Code Sec. 2032A(e)(2) definition of "member of the family" applies to the qualified conservation easement exclusion. Thus, with respect to any decedent, a member of the family is (1) an ancestor of the decedent, (2) the spouse of the decedent, (3) a lineal descendant of the decedent, of the decedent's spouse, or of a parent of the decedent, or (4) the spouse of any individual described in (3).

Debt-financed property. The exclusion does not apply to the extent that the land is debt-financed property. Thus, debt-financed property is eligible for the exclusion only to the extent of the net equity in the property. Debt-financed

---

[3] Code Sec. 2031(c)(6).

[4] Code Sec. 2031(c)(10).

[5] Code Sec. 2031(c)(8)(A)(i).

[6] Code Sec. 2031(c)(8)(A).

property means property with respect to which there is an acquisition indebtedness on the date of the decedent's death. Acquisition indebtedness includes the unpaid amount of (1) indebtedness incurred by the donor in acquiring the property, (2) indebtedness incurred before the acquisition of the property if such indebtedness would not have been incurred but for such acquisition, (3) indebtedness incurred after the acquisition of the property if such indebtedness would not have been incurred but for such acquisition and the incurrence of the indebtedness was reasonably foreseeable at the time of acquisition, and (4) the extension, renewal, or refinancing of an acquisition indebtedness.[7]

• ***Qualified Conservation Easement Defined***

A qualified conservation easement is a qualified conservation contribution, as defined in Code Sec. 170(h)(1), i.e, a contribution of a qualified real property interest to a qualified organization exclusively for conservation purposes.

A qualified real property interest means a restriction, granted in perpetuity, on the use that may be made of the real property. Conservation purposes are defined in Code Sec. 170(h)(4)(A) and include such things as the preservation of land areas for outdoor recreation or the education of the general public, the protection of natural habitat for fish, wildlife, or plants, and the preservation of open space. However, for purposes of the qualified conservation easement exclusion, the preservation of an historically important land area or an historic structure does not qualify as a conservation purpose. In addition, a *de minimis* commercial recreational activity that is consistent with the conservation purpose, such as the granting of hunting and fishing licenses, will not cause the property to fail to qualify for the exclusion.[8]

• ***Exclusion Amount***

The exclusion amount is calculated based on the value of the property after the conservation easement has been placed on the property. However, the exclusion amount does not extend to the value of any development rights retained by the decedent or the donor. Development rights are defined as any rights retained to use the land for any commercial purpose that are not subordinate to and directly supportive of the land as a farm or for farming purposes within the meaning of Code Sec. 2032A(e)(5). However, if every person in being who has an interest in the land executes an agreement to extinguish permanently some or all of any development rights retained by the donor, on or before the date the estate tax return is due, the estate tax may be reduced accordingly. If the agreement is not implemented by the earlier of the date that is two years after the decedent's death or the date of the sale of the land, an additional tax is imposed in the amount of the estate tax that would have been due on the retained development rights subject to the agreement.[9]

Impact of the 2001 Act. According to the Committee Reports accompanying the Economic Growth and Tax Relief Reconciliation Act of 2001 (P.L. 107-16) (2001 Act), the provision relating to the additional tax (discussed in the preceding paragraph) is retained after repeal of the estate tax. The provision is retained so that those persons with an interest in the land who fail to execute the agreement will remain liable for any additional tax that may be due following repeal. See ¶253 for further discussion of qualified conservation easements. (See ¶2595.)

---

[7] Code Sec. 2031(c)(4).

[8] Code Sec. 2031(c)(8)(B).

[9] Code Sec. 2031(c)(5).

Applicable percentage. If the executor makes the election, there is excluded from the gross estate the lesser of the applicable percentage of the value of the land subject to the qualified conservation easement or the exclusion limitation. The applicable percentage means 40 percent reduced, but not below zero, by two percentage points for each percentage point (or fraction thereof) by which the value of the qualified conservation easement is less than 30 percent of the value of the land.[10] For this purpose, the value of the land is determined without regard to the value of the easement and reduced by the value of any retained development rights. As a result, if the value of the easement is 10 percent or less of the value of the land before the easement, less the value of any retained development rights, the applicable percentage will be zero.

The 2001 Act provides that, effective for the estates of decedents dying after December 31, 2000, the values to be taken into account in calculating the applicable percentage are such values as of the date of the contribution of the qualified conservation easement.[11]

"Development rights" means any right to use land that is subject to a qualified conservation easement for any commercial purpose that is not subordinate to and directly supportive of the use of the land as a farm for farming purposes (within the meaning of Code Sec. 2032A(e)(5)).[12]

> *Example:* Dolores Jones died owning land subject to a qualified conservation easement. She did not retain any development rights in the property. The fair market value of the real property on the date of her death was $500,000 without the conservation easement and $400,000 with the easement. Thus, the value of the conservation easement is $100,000, or 20% of the value of real property without the easement. The applicable percentage for the estate is 20% (40% reduced by twice the difference between 30% and 20%). Therefore, the exclusion amount is $80,000 (20% of $400,000).

¶ 262 Reporting Real Property on Return

In reporting real estate that is taxable under Code Sec. 2033, the property should be described and identified in a manner that permits the IRS to locate it readily for inspection and valuation. The area of each parcel of real estate should be given. If the parcel is improved, a short statement of the character of the improvements should be included. For urban property, the following information should also be given: street and number, ward, subdivision, block, and lot. For rural property, the description should include the township, range, and any landmarks.[13]

If an item of real estate is subject to a mortgage for which the decedent's estate is liable, the full value of such property must be reflected in the relevant value column of Schedule A (Real Estate) of Form 706 (Form 706, United States Estate (and Generation-Skipping Transfer) Tax Return) (alternate or date-of-death value). In other words, if the indebtedness is enforceable against other property of the estate not subject to such mortgage, or if the decedent was personally liable for such mortgage, the full value of the property must be shown.[14] The amount of the mortgage is to be noted in the "Description" column, and it should be deducted on Schedule K (Debts of the Decedent, and Mortgages and Liens) of Form 706.

---

[10] Code Sec. 2031(c)(2).
[11] Code Sec. 2031(c)(2).
[12] Code Sec. 2031(c)(5)(D).
[13] Instructions for Schedule A, Form 706 (Rev. Aug. 2004), p. 5.
[14] Reg. § 20.2053-7.

If, however, the decedent's estate is not liable for the amount of the mortgage, only the value of the equity of redemption (or value of the property less the indebtedness) need be included in the "Value" column as part of the gross estate, and no deduction as a mortgage or lien for the indebtedness is allowable.[15] Similarly, "points" that a decedent has agreed to pay to a mortgage lender are not includible in the value of the property for estate tax purposes unless the decedent's estate is liable for payment.[16]

Real property that the decedent has contracted to purchase should be listed in Schedule A. The full value of the property and not the equity must be reflected in the value column of the schedule. The unpaid portion of the purchase price should be deducted under Schedule K. If the land is subject to a valid contract to sell entered into by the decedent, the contract, rather than the land, is reportable. It is reportable on Schedule C (Mortgages, Notes, and Cash) of Form 706.

¶ 265 Dower and Curtesy

The value of dower and curtesy (or a statutory estate created in lieu thereof) is taxable (see ¶ 175 and ¶ 180). The extent of the decedent's interest in real property may not be reduced on account of such interest or on account of homestead or other exemptions in reporting real property on the return.

¶ 270 Valuation

The value of real property, each parcel being unique in the eyes of the law, can never be determined by a set formula. Each valuation must be fixed individually in accordance with the requirements and circumstances of the particular situation.

Expert testimony is desirable in most cases, not only to apply a local or general market situation to the piece of land involved, but often to provide the primary means of establishing value for purposes of the tax. Generally, expert testimony, market activity, and local sales, rentals, and recent mortgages are important in establishing value, if the same valuation can be obtained by the use of two or more of such factors. The local tax assessment values, or only one of the above factors, will frequently not carry sufficient weight to establish valuation contrary to that set by the IRS.

The value is determined as of the date of the decedent's death unless the executor elects to use the alternate valuation date. Whatever the method of valuation employed, the method should be stated on the return. If based on an appraisal, a copy of the appraisal, together with an explanation of the basis of the appraisal, should be attached to the return.

See ¶ 280 through ¶ 296 for special use valuation of real estate of a farm or other closely held business.

¶ 275 Community Property

If community property is involved, only one-half of the value of each item of community property is to be reported on the decedent's Form 706 (United States Estate (and Generation-Skipping Transfer) Tax Return) (see ¶ 165), with an appropriate explanation. For example, the value of a decedent's one-half interest in a house and lot in Tucson, Arizona (valued at $300,000), would be reported as

---

[15] Reg. § 20.2053-7.

[16] Rev. Rul. 80-319, 1980-2 CB 252.

$150,000 on the date of death and the description would be followed by the following statement:

> One-half only of value reported because the house and lot were held in community with the surviving spouse.

Likewise, only one-half of the value of any rental income from the property would be listed.

Chapter 8
FARMS AND CLOSELY HELD BUSINESSES

¶ 280 Special Use Valuation

Real property used as a family farm or in a closely held business may be valued on the basis of its "current" use rather than on the basis of "highest and best" use.

The maximum amount by which the value of qualifying real property can be reduced under the special use valuation provision[1] is $850,000 for 2004 (indexed for inflation),[2] up from $840,000 for 2003.[3] For example, if the estate of a decedent dying in 2004 consists of qualifying real property valued at $1,250,000 on the basis of its "highest and best" use, and the property's value under the special use valuation provision is $350,000, the gross estate will be reduced by only $850,000 (although the difference in value is $900,000, the maximum reduction allowed is $850,000).

The IRS has ruled that an estate electing both the alternate valuation date and special use valuation was required to use the alternate valuation date to determine the special use value of farmland owned by the decedent at death. Additionally, in applying the applicable limit on the aggregate reduction in the value of qualified real property as a result of valuing the property for a qualified use, the difference between the fair market value and the special use value was to be determined as of the alternate valuation date.[4]

Real property may qualify for special use valuation if it is located in the United States and if it is devoted to either (1) use as a farm for farming purposes or (2) use in a closely held trade or business other than farming. In either case, there must be a trade or business use.

---

[1] Code Sec. 2032A(a); Reg. §20.2032A-8.

[2] Rev. Proc. 2003-85, IRB 2003-49, 1184.

[3] The maximum reductions based on the special use valuation provision for previous years are as follows: $820,000 for 2002; $800,000 for 2001; $770,000 for 2000; $760,000 for 1999; and $750,000 for preceding years. Code Sec. 2032A(a)(3); Rev. Proc. 2002-70, IRB 2002-46, 845; Rev. Proc. 2001-59, 2001-2 CB 623; Rev. Proc. 2001-13, 2001-1 CB 337; Rev. Proc. 99-42, 1999-2 CB 568; Rev. Proc. 98-61, 1998-2 CB 811.

[4] Rev. Rul. 88-89, 1988-2 CB 333.

¶ 281 Qualifying Conditions

In order to qualify for the special use valuation procedure, the following conditions must be satisfied:

(1) the decedent must have been a resident or a citizen of the United States and the property must be located in the United States;

(2) the property must pass to a qualified heir (see ¶282) and a requisite agreement must be filed (see ¶289);

(3) the property must be devoted to a qualified use (see ¶291) on the date of the decedent's death;

(4) the decedent or a member of the decedent's family must have owned the qualifying property and have materially participated in the operation of the farm or other business for the required period (see ¶291 and ¶292);

(5) the adjusted value of the real and personal property used in the farm or closely held business must comprise at least 50 percent of the adjusted value of the decedent's gross estate; and

(6) at least 25 percent of the adjusted value of the gross estate must be qualified real property.[5]

For purposes of the 50-percent and 25-percent tests, the special use value is not used in determining the value of property included in the gross estate. With respect to requirement (5), the value of any transfer made within three years of death (see ¶555) is includible in the decedent's gross estate for the limited purpose of determining the estate's qualification for special use valuation.[6]

The IRS has allowed an estate to combine the adjusted values of personal property used for farming, farm property, and a building used in a business other than farming in order to meet the 50-percent test for special use valuation. The personal property was used in connection with the qualifying farm property, and the real estate was otherwise eligible for special use valuation.[7]

The IRS distinguished its result from a Tax Court decision in which a decedent's estate was not entitled to elect special use valuation for farmland owned by the decedent because personal property owned and used by him in a business unrelated to farming could not be aggregated with the farmland to meet the 50-percent requirement. In the court's view, Congress enacted the special use valuation rules in order to lessen the estate tax burden that might result from valuation of real property used in the family farm or business at its highest and best use rather than at its value to the farm or business. Because the rules were designed to protect family farms and businesses, the court reasoned that personal property should be considered in meeting the percentage requirements only if it is used in the family business together with the real property that is to be specially valued.[8]

¶ 282 Qualified Heir

The term "qualified heir" (to whom special use valuation property must pass) refers to a member of the decedent's family who acquired the real property

---

[5] Code Sec. 2032A(a) and Code Sec. 2032A(b).

[6] Code Sec. 2035(d)(3). See IRS Letter Ruling 8514032 (Jan. 8, 1985); Rev. Rul. 87-122, 1987-2 CB 221.

[7] Rev. Rul. 85-168, 1985-2 CB 197.

[8] *W.H. Geiger Est.*, 80 TC 484, CCH Dec. 39,936.

from the decedent or to whom the property has passed.[9] Where there is a further disposition of any interest in the property from a qualified heir to a member of the heir's family, the family member is to be treated as a qualified heir.[10] However, the IRS has ruled that the post-1981 disposition of specially valued farm property by a qualified heir to his cousin within the recapture period resulted in imposition of the recapture tax (see ¶284). For purposes of this exception, the cousin was not considered a member of the qualified heir's family.[11]

An individual's family members are (1) the individual's ancestors, (2) the individual's spouse, (3) lineal descendants of the individual, of the individual's spouse, or of the individual's parents, and (4) the spouse of any descendant mentioned in (3).[12] In interpreting this provision, the Tax Court has held that the nephew of a decedent's predeceased spouse was not a qualified heir because he was not a lineal descendant of the decedent's parents but, rather, was a lineal descendant of the decedent's husband's parents.[13]

For purposes of the preceding discussion, a legally adopted child of an individual is treated as the individual's child by blood.

All interests in the property to be specially valued must pass to qualified heirs. Thus, if successive interests are created in the property such as, for example, a life estate followed by a remainder interest, qualified heirs must receive all interests.[14] The IRS has ruled that an estate could elect special use valuation for farm property in which a qualified heir received a life estate under the decedent's will, even though the heir also received the power to appoint the remainder interest in the property to a nonqualified heir. The election was allowed because the heir executed a qualified disclaimer (see ¶2009) of the power of appointment, thus causing the remainder interest to vest in another qualified heir.[15] However, the IRS has also disallowed special use valuation elections because not all successive interests in otherwise qualifying real property passed to qualified heirs.[16]

Two Tax Court cases have held that Reg. §20.2032A-8(a)(2) is invalid to the extent that *all* successive interests are required to go to qualified heirs.[17] In the *Davis* case, the court held that *de minimis* successive interests that do not go to qualified heirs will not prevent special use valuation for otherwise qualified property. Similarly, the *Clinard* case limited Reg. §20.2032A-8(a)(2) by holding that special use valuation is permitted where a qualified heir possesses a life estate with a special power of appointment. In other words, the fact that a qualified heir could direct that an unqualified heir receive a remainder interest would not preclude the use of special use valuation for the interest in question. Both cases recognize that where unqualified heirs are in a position to receive an interest, special use valuation will not be precluded if those interests are exceedingly remote. This principle has also been followed by the U.S. Court of Appeals for the Seventh Circuit in affirming a decision of a U.S. district court in Illinois

---

[9] Code Sec. 2032A(e)(1).

[10] Code Sec. 2032A(e)(1).

[11] Rev. Rul. 89-22, 1989-1 CB 276.

[12] Code Sec. 2032A(e)(2).

[13] *I.M. Cone Est.*, 60 TCM 137, CCH Dec. 46,722(M), TC Memo. 1990-359.

[14] Reg. §20.2032A-8(a)(2).

[15] Rev. Rul. 82-140, 1982-2 CB 208.

[16] IRS Letter Rulings 8337015 (June 7, 1983), and 8346006 (July 29, 1983).

[17] See *D. Davis IV, Est.*, 86 TC 1156, CCH Dec. 43,105, and *C.M. Clinard Est.*, 86 TC 1180, CCH Dec. 43,106.

that allowed special use valuation despite a remote possibility that the contingent remainder interest in the property could pass to nonqualified heirs.[18]

¶ 283 Valuation Methods

Two valuation methods are used for farms or closely held businesses that qualify for the special use valuation.

• *Farm Method*

If a farm qualifies for special use valuation, it may be valued on the basis of a formula of cash rentals, real estate taxes, and effective interest rates. Under the formula, the value of a farm is determined as follows:

(1) the average annual gross cash rental for comparable land used for farming purposes and located in the same region as such farm, less the average annual state and local real estate taxes for such comparable land, divided by

(2) the average annual effective interest rate for all new Farm Credit Bank loans.

Each average annual computation described in the formula is to be made on the basis of the five most recent calendar years ending before the date of the decedent's death.[19] "Net-share" rentals (i.e., crop-share rentals) may be used in the formula valuation method if cash rentals for comparable land in the same locality are not available. The amount of a net share is equal to the value of the produce received by the lessor of the comparable land on which such produce is grown minus the cash operation expenses (other than real property taxes) of growing the produce paid by the lessor.[20]

• *Multiple Factor Method for Closely Held Businesses*

If a closely held business or a farm that does not use the farm method described above qualifies for special use valuation, its valuation generally is determined by the following factors:

(1) capitalization of income;

(2) capitalization of fair rental values;

(3) assessed land values in a state that provides a differential or use value assessment law;

(4) comparable sales of other farm or closely held business land where nonagricultural use is not a significant factor in the sales price; and

(5) any other factor that fairly values the farm or closely held business value of the property.[21]

However, in applying special use valuation to farm property, the IRS has ruled that a fiduciary could not select only one of the factors enumerated in Code Sec. 2032A(e)(8) as the exclusive basis of valuation. Each factor that was relevant to the respective valuation was to be applied, although, depending on the circumstances, certain factors could be weighed more heavily than others.[22]

---

[18] *L. Smoot, Exr.*, CA-7, 90-1 USTC ¶60,002, aff'g DC Ill., 88-1 USTC ¶13,748.

[19] Code Sec. 2032A(e)(7)(A).

[20] Code Sec. 2032A(e)(7)(B).

[21] Code Sec. 2032A(e)(8).

[22] Rev. Rul. 89-30, 1989-1 CB 274.

The Tax Court has held that if an estate that has elected special use valuation has not provided all of the necessary documentation to utilize the farm method, it is deemed to have, by default, elected to use the multiple factor method.[23]

• *Change in Method*

The IRS has ruled that an estate that had made a valid special use valuation election with respect to farmland included in the decedent's gross estate could amend the election in order to substitute the farm method of valuation for the multiple factor method that was originally applied. The executor valued the decedent's farm under the multiple factor method because he was unable to obtain the information (rentals for comparable farmland) necessary for computing value under the formula method until after the return was filed. Although the special use valuation election is irrevocable, the IRS did not bar the estate from changing the method of valuation once the election was made. In addition, the IRS noted that a change from the multiple factor method is allowable even where information regarding comparable farmland was available but the executor nevertheless originally applied the multiple factor method.[24]

¶ 284 Recapture of Taxes

Tax benefits realized by an estate that elects special use valuation may be fully or partially recaptured if the qualified real property passes out of the family or ceases to be used as a farm or closely held business within a 10-year "recapture period" measured from the decedent's death (but before the death of the qualified heir).[25] Tax liability incurred as a result of such a disposition or cessation of qualified use is to be reported on Form 706-A (United States Additional Estate Tax Return) (Rev. Sept. 2004) (see the Appendix at ¶ 3200).

A second disposition of the property or cessation will not trigger a second tax on the same qualified interest.[26] Thus, where a qualified heir ceases to use the property for its qualified purpose and later sells the property within the recapture period, a recapture tax will be imposed as to the first event that triggers recapture (cessation of use), but not as to the second event (sale of the property).

The amount of the tax benefit potentially subject to recapture is the excess of the estate tax liability that would have been incurred had the special use valuation procedure not been used over the actual estate tax liability based on the special use valuation. In other words, the maximum additional or "recapture" tax is the amount that the special use valuation has saved the estate. This is called the "adjusted tax difference."[27]

The tax will be less than the maximum if the excess of the fair market value of the interest or the proceeds of an arm's-length sale over the value of the interest determined with the special use valuation is less than the "adjusted tax difference."

• *Qualified Use*

As noted above, the tax recapture provision applies if the property ceases to be used for the qualified use (see ¶ 291) under which the property qualified for the special use valuation. However, a qualified heir may begin qualified use of

---

[23] *R. Wineman*, 79 TCM 2189, CCH Dec. 53,925(M), TC Memo. 2000-193.

[24] Rev. Rul. 83-115, 1983-2 CB 155.

[25] Code Sec. 2032A(c)(1). For estates of decedents dying before 1982, the recapture period was 15 years (Code Sec. 2032A(c)(1), prior to amendment by the Economic Recovery Tax Act of 1981) (P.L. 97-34)).

[26] Code Sec. 2032A(c)(3).

[27] Code Sec. 2032A(c)(2).

the property at any time within two years of the decedent's death without triggering recapture tax; the recapture period does not begin until the qualified use begins.[28] For tax recapture purposes, a qualified use may cease even if the property continues to be used for its qualifying purpose. A cessation occurs if within the recapture period, during any eight-year period ending after the decedent's death and before the qualified heir's death, there have been periods aggregating more than three years during which there has been no "material participation" (see ¶292) by the decedent or family member in the case of property held by the decedent. In the case of property held by a qualified heir, like periods of nonparticipation by the qualified heir or a family member will result in a cessation of qualified use.[29] However, "active management" (see ¶293) will constitute material participation in the case of "eligible qualified heirs." Such heirs are the decedent's spouse or a qualified heir who is under the age of 21, a full-time student, or disabled.[30]

The decedent's surviving spouse and lineal descendants may rent special use property to a family member on a cash rental basis without triggering the recapture tax.[31] Similarly, a family trust's lease of farmland to a family farming corporation for fixed cash payments did not trigger the special use valuation recapture tax for a decedent's children, who were trust beneficiaries. They necessarily retained the financial risks of farming, as owners of the farmland and of the family farming corporation.[32] The rule allowing net cash rental to a family member was extended to lineal descendants by the Taxpayer Relief Act of 1997 (P.L. 105-34) and applies retroactively to leases executed after December 31, 1976. The Economic Growth and Tax Relief Reconciliation Act of 2001 (P.L. 107-16) (2001 Act) provides that a claim for refund or credit of any overpayment of tax resulting from the application of Code Sec. 2032A(c)(7)(E) that is otherwise barred by law will be allowed if the claim was filed before June 7, 2002.[33]

The additional tax on recaptured property is due on the day that is six months after the recapture event (premature disposition of the property or cessation of qualified use).[34] As noted at ¶288, each heir remains expressly liable for the recapture tax with respect to his or her interest in the property.

The three-year statute of limitations for assessing the recapture tax does not begin to run until the IRS is notified of the disposition or cessation.[35] In one case decided prior to the enactment of the Taxpayer Relief Act of 1997, a qualified heir's cash rental of qualified farm property to her brother constituted a cessation of qualified use resulting in liability for additional estate tax. The heir's alleged participation in the farming operations with her brother was insufficient to change the substance of the arrangement between the parties from that of a landlord-tenant relationship. However, the disclosure of the cash rental arrangement in response to a questionnaire provided by the IRS served as notification to the IRS of the cessation of qualified use and commenced the Code Sec. 2032A(f) three-year statute of limitations on assessment and collection. Accordingly, notices of deficiency that were issued more than three years after the IRS received

---

[28] Code Sec. 2032A(c)(7).

[29] Code Sec. 2032A(c)(6). See also IRS Letter Ruling 8939031 (June 30, 1989).

[30] Code Sec. 2032A(c)(7).

[31] Code Sec. 2032A(b)(5).

[32] *M. Minter*, CA-8, 94-1 USTC ¶60,160, 19 F3d 426, rev'g unpublished DC N.D. decision.

[33] Act Sec. 581, P.L. 107-16.

[34] Code Sec. 2032A(c)(4).

[35] Code Sec. 2032A(f).

notification of cessation of qualified use precluded the IRS from assessing and collecting the additional tax.[36]

• *Impact of the 2001 Act*

The Committee Reports to the 2001 Act indicate that the recapture tax imposed if property ceases to qualify for special use valuation will be retained following the repeal of the estate tax. The retention of this provision will ensure that those estates that claimed the benefit of special use valuation prior to repeal will be subject to recapture if a disqualifying event occurs after repeal. (See ¶2595.)

¶285 Pecuniary Bequests and Purchases

Normally, property qualifying for special use valuation is acquired by a qualified heir from a decedent by bequest, devise, or inheritance. However, a special use valuation election may also be allowed where property is acquired by either:

(1) a distribution of qualified property by an estate or trust in satisfaction of a pecuniary bequest; or

(2) a purchase of qualified property by a qualified heir from a decedent's estate or trust.[37]

An estate recognizes gain on such a distribution or sale only to the extent of the post-death appreciation of the property. This appreciation is equal to the difference between the property's fair market value on the date of the distribution or sale and its estate tax value as determined *without* regard to Code Sec. 2032A. In computing the gain on distribution or sale, therefore, the estate tax value will be the property's fair market value on the date of the decedent's death or the alternate valuation date.[38]

Specially valued property that is transferred to a qualified heir in satisfaction of a pecuniary bequest or that is purchased from the decedent's estate by a qualified heir is deemed to meet the holding period requirement for long-term capital gain treatment on a subsequent sale of the property to another qualified heir.[39]

¶286 Involuntary Conversions and Tax-Free Exchanges

No recapture tax (see ¶284) will be imposed where farm or closely held business property that has been specially valued is involuntarily converted. However, the proceeds from the involuntary conversion must be reinvested in real property that is used for the same qualified use as was the involuntarily converted property.[40]

No recapture tax will be imposed on an exchange of specially valued real property to the extent that the exchange qualifies as tax free under Code Sec. 1031 so long as the property received is employed in the same qualified use as was the property exchanged. Real property received in an exchange that is employed in the qualified use is known as "qualified exchange property." If both qualified exchange property and other property are received, the recapture tax is reduced by an amount bearing the same ratio to the recapture tax as the fair

[36] *M.E. Stovall*, 101 TC 140, CCH Dec. 49,183.

[37] Code Sec. 2032A(e)(9); Rev. Proc. 82-9, 1982-1 CB 413.

[38] Code Sec. 1040(a).

[39] Code Sec. 1223(12).

[40] Code Sec. 2032A(h)(1)(A).

market value of the qualified exchange property bears to the fair market value of the property that was exchanged[41] (see ¶80 and the Appendix at ¶3200).

The special use valuation provision permits the aggregation ("tacking") of ownership, qualified use, and material participation periods in the case of replacement property acquired pursuant to like-kind exchanges under Code Sec. 1031 or involuntary conversions under Code Sec. 1033.[42] This tacking is available only if the replacement property is employed in the same qualified use as was the original property, and only for that portion of the replacement property equal in value to the original property.

¶ 287 Special Lien on Qualified Property

A government lien is imposed on all qualified property for which an election to use the special use valuation procedure has been made. The lien applies to the extent of the adjusted tax difference attributable to the qualified real property. The lien arises at the time an election is filed and is to continue until the tax benefit is recaptured, until the time limit for collecting the potential liability ceases (that is, the qualified heir dies or the recapture period (see ¶284) lapses) or until it can be established to the satisfaction of the IRS that no further liability will arise. In addition, if qualified replacement property is purchased following an involuntary conversion of special use valuation property (see ¶286), the lien that was applicable to the original special use valuation property attaches to the qualified replacement property. Similarly, if specially valued property is exchanged for qualified exchange property (see ¶286), the lien attaches to the qualified exchange property.[43]

The IRS can issue a certificate of subordination of the government's lien that arose on any part of the qualified property for which the special use valuation election was made if it determines that the interests of the United States are adequately protected thereafter.[44]

¶ 288 Personal Liability for Recapture Tax

A qualified heir is personally liable for the portion of recapture tax that is imposed with respect to his or her interest in specially valued property. A qualified heir's liability is extinguished in two instances: (1) where the recapture period lapses; and (2) where the heir dies without converting or disposing of the property.[45] Additionally, a sale or other disposition by one qualified heir to another of specially valued property is not considered a recapture event and the second heir is treated as if he or she received the property from the decedent, rather than from the first heir. The second heir then becomes liable for the recapture tax and the other qualified heir (the seller) is released from further recapture tax liability.[46] Even if the second heir has paid full consideration for the property, the special estate tax lien (see ¶287) remains on the property.

• ***Discharge from Liability***

An heir may be discharged from personal liability for future potential recapture taxes imposed on the heir's interest in the qualified property by

---

[41] Code Sec. 2032A(i)(1).

[42] Code Sec. 2032A(e)(14)(A).

[43] Code Sec. 6324B; Reg. §20.6324B-1.

[44] Code Sec. 6325(d)(3).

[45] Code Sec. 2032A(c)(1).

[46] IRS Letter Ruling 8115085 (Jan. 16, 1981).

furnishing a bond for the maximum additional tax that could be imposed on the interest.[47]

The qualified heir must make written application to the IRS for determination of the maximum additional tax that could be imposed. The IRS is then required to notify the heir within one year of the date of the application of such maximum amount.[48]

¶ 289 Election and Agreement

An election to use special use valuation is to be made on Form 706 (United States Estate (and Generation-Skipping Transfer) Tax Return) (Rev. Aug. 2004) by checking the box marked "Yes" on line 2 of Part 3, the "Elections by the Executor" section on page 2 of the return (see ¶2930). Such an election may be made on a late-filed return so long as it is the first return filed.[49]

In order to make a valid election, an estate must file Schedule A-1 (Section 2032A Valuation) of Form 706 and attach all of the required statements and appraisals.[50] Schedule A-1 contains the Notice of Election and the Agreement to Special Valuation Under Section 2032A. The Notice of Election provides information such as the fair market value of the property to be specially valued, its special use valuation, and the method used in computing special use valuation.[51]

An estate may elect special use valuation for less than all of the qualified property included in the gross estate. However, property for which an election is made must have an adjusted value of at least 25 percent of the adjusted value of the gross estate.[52]

• ***Agreement***

An estate executor making the election must also complete and file with the return Schedule A-1, part 3 (Agreement to Special Valuation Under Section 2032A), signed by each person having an interest in the qualified real property for which the election is made.[53] It is immaterial whether such person is in possession of the property. In the case of a qualified heir, the agreement expresses consent to personal liability in the event of recapture of additional estate tax due to premature cessation of qualified use or disposition of the property. Signatories other than qualified heirs must express consent to collection of any such additional estate tax from the qualified property.

The IRS National Office has ruled that farmland owned by a decedent in his capacity as shareholder of a corporation could not be valued under the special use valuation provisions because the agreement filed with the election did not contain a signature that bound the corporation. The decedent had bequeathed his estate assets, including stock of the corporation, to his children. Rather than signing the agreement as representatives of the corporation, the children, who were also corporate officers, had signed it in their individual capacities.[54]

---

[47] Code Sec. 2032A(c)(5) and Code Sec. 2032A(e)(11).

[48] Code Sec. 2032A(e)(11).

[49] Code Sec. 2032A(d)(1).

[50] Form 706 (Rev. Aug. 2004).

[51] Reg. §20.2032A-8(a)(3).

[52] Reg. §20.2032A-8(a)(2). But see *M.S. Miller, Exr.*, DC Ill., 88-1 USTC ¶13,757, holding Reg. §20.2032A-8(a)(2) invalid insofar as it imposed an additional substantive requirement to the statutory rules governing qualification for special use valuation.

[53] Reg. §20.2032A-8(c). Also see *R.H. Lucas, Pers. Rep.*, CA-11, 96-2 USTC ¶60,247, barring an estate from electing under Code Sec. 2032A because the estate failed to file the recapture agreement.

[54] IRS Technical Advice Memorandum 8602007 (Sept. 7, 1985).

Similarly, the IRS ruled that a decedent's interest in farmland that was to pass to a testamentary trust created for the benefit of her two minor grandchildren was not eligible for special use valuation because the beneficiaries did not consent to be personally liable for the recapture tax. Although the recapture agreement was signed by the decedent's daughter in her capacity as trustee, she did not have the right to execute a lien in favor of the government and lacked the capacity to legally bind the two minor beneficiaries of the trust. Thus, the agreement failed to include the required signatures of qualified heirs.[55]

The Tax Court has held, however, that Reg. §20.2032A-8(c)(2) is invalid insofar as it requires that individuals having tenancy in common interests in property that is subject to a special use election sign the required recapture agreement.[56] The court noted that, although all persons having an interest in property to be specially valued must sign the recapture agreement, the surviving tenants in the instant case did not have such an interest since only the decedent's tenancy in common interests were includible in his gross estate and subject to the election.

• *Protective Election*

Where it is not certain that property meets the requirements for special use valuation, an estate may make a protective election to specially value qualified real property, contingent on the property values as finally determined meeting the requirements of Code Sec. 2032A.[57] This election is made by filing a notice of protective election with a timely estate tax return. If it is finally determined that the property qualifies for special use valuation, the estate must file an additional notice of election within 60 days of such determination. The IRS National Office has ruled that an estate could make a protective election with respect to a decedent's farmland even though, at the time the estate tax return was filed, the estate met the percentage requirements for special use valuation.[58] However, in another National Office ruling, the IRS has pointed out that neither Code Sec. 2032A nor the regulations thereunder sanction the use of a protective election as a substitute for a timely special use valuation election.[59]

• *Cure of Technically Defective Elections*

For elections made prior to August 6, 1997, if a timely special use valuation election was made and the estate tax return, as filed, evidenced substantial compliance with the requirements of the regulations relating to special use valuation, the executor of the decedent's estate had a reasonable period of time (not exceeding 90 days) in which to cure any technical defects or flaws in the form of the election that would prevent it from being valid otherwise.[60] The 90-day period commenced following the IRS's notification to the estate that a defect existed. Examples of technical defects or flaws in the election include the failure to include all required information in the notice of election and the failure to include the signatures of all persons having an interest in the qualifying property.

The Taxpayer Relief Act of 1997 (P.L. 105-34) expanded the ability of the executor to correct omissions. For elections made after August 5, 1997, the

---

[55] IRS Technical Advice Memorandum 8802005 (Sept. 29, 1987).

[56] *M.F. Pullin Est.*, 84 TC 789, CCH Dec. 42,060; *W.C. Bettenhausen Est.*, 51 TCM 488, CCH Dec. 42,887(M), TC Memo. 1986-73.

[57] Reg. §20.2032A-8(b).

[58] IRS Technical Advice Memorandum 8407005 (Nov. 8, 1983).

[59] IRS Technical Advice Memorandum 9013001 (date not given).

[60] Code Sec. 2032A(d)(3), prior to amendment by P.L. 105-34.

executor must file a timely notice of election and a recapture agreement, but need not have substantially complied with the regulations in order to be entitled to submit missing information or signatures.[61] On filing, if the election or agreement fails to include all the required information or signatures, the executor may cure the omission by providing the missing information or signatures within 90 days after receiving written notice from the IRS.

There has been much litigation with respect to whether an estate is entitled to perfect a defective special use valuation election under the substantial compliance provisions of Code Sec. 2032A(d)(3) (prior to its amendment by P.L. 105-34) and whether an executor has provided substantially all of the information required on the estate tax return for a valid special use election. The U.S. Court of Appeals for the Seventh Circuit has held that an estate was entitled to special use valuation, even though no recapture agreement was filed with the federal estate tax return. In this case, substantially all the information required for making the election was provided with the estate tax return, and the executed agreement was filed four months later.[62] However, the U.S. Court of Appeals for the Seventh Circuit later ruled that an estate's failure to submit a recapture agreement with the estate tax return could not be corrected subsequent to the due date of the return by operation of the substantial compliance doctrine, because relief under that doctrine is limited to correcting minor errors in a recapture agreement.[63]

The U.S. Court of Appeals for the Fifth Circuit has held that where an election and recapture agreement were signed by the executrix of an estate but not by any of the beneficiaries of a testamentary trust, the lack of the beneficiaries' signatures could be perfected on an amended recapture agreement filed within 90 days of the IRS's notification to the estate's representative of the defect.[64] Similarly, the U.S. Court of Appeals for the Tenth Circuit has held that an executor's failure to attach to the decedent's federal estate tax return a previously obtained appraisal of the fair market value of certain property for which a special use value election was made was not an incurable defect.[65]

In contrast, however, the U.S. Court of Appeals for the Eighth Circuit has held that a recapture agreement that failed to include the signatures of the decedent's children (who received an interest as a result of the surviving spouse's disclaimer) did not constitute substantial compliance with the requirements for special use valuation.[66] This was also found to be the case, according to the Tax Court, where the estate failed to attach any notice of election or a signed recapture agreement to a decedent's estate tax return.[67]

¶ 290 Qualified Real Property

Real property may be eligible for special use valuation if it is located in the United States and used as a farm for farming purposes or in a trade or business other than farming. Additionally, the property must satisfy the qualified use (see ¶291) and material participation (see ¶292) requirements.

---

[61] Code Sec. 2032A(d)(3), as amended by P.L. 105-34.

[62] *L. Prussner, Exrx.*, CA-7, 90-1 USTC ¶60,007.

[63] *C. Grimes Est.*, CA-7, 91-2 USTC ¶60,078.

[64] *M. McAlpine, Jr., Est.*, CA-5, 92-2 USTC ¶60,109, 968 F2d 459.

[65] *L. Doherty Est.*, CA-10, 93-1 USTC ¶60,125, 982 F2d 450.

[66] *G.L. McDonald*, CA-8, 88-2 USTC ¶13,778, cert. denied, 4-3-89.

[67] *G. Merwin Est.*, 95 TC 168, CCH Dec. 46,817.

A "farm," for purposes of the special valuation procedure, includes stock, dairy, poultry, fruit, fur-bearing animal, and truck farms, plantations, ranches, nurseries, greenhouses or other similar structures used primarily for the raising of agricultural or horticultural commodities, and orchards and woodlands.[68] The term "farming purposes" includes cultivation of the soil, raising agricultural or horticultural commodities and preparing such commodities for market, as well as the planting, cultivating, caring for, cutting down, and preparing for market of trees.[69]

Qualified property includes residences and related improvements located on the qualifying real property and occupied on a regular basis by the owner, the owner's lessee, or the owner's employees for occupational or maintenance purposes. Also considered qualified real property are roads, buildings, and other structures and improvements functionally related to the qualified use of the property.[70]

• *Qualified Woodlands*

An executor may elect special use valuation for standing timber as part of "qualified woodlands," which are identifiable areas of real property (for which business records are normally maintained) used for growing and harvesting timber.[71] A recapture tax will be imposed when the qualified heir severs or otherwise disposes of the timber during the recapture period.[72]

¶ 291 Qualified Use Requirement

Real property for which a special use valuation election is made must be devoted to a qualified farm or business use for five of the eight years prior to the decedent's death. This requirement is satisfied if either the decedent or a member of the decedent's family is utilizing the property for the qualified use.[73] The IRS National Office has interpreted the qualified use requirement to mean that the decedent or a family member must bear some of the financial risk associated with an active farm or other business.[74] In another example of this concept, the U.S. Court of Appeals for the Seventh Circuit has held that a cash lease of farm property to a nonrelative did not constitute a qualified use.[75] However, the Taxpayer Relief Act of 1997 (P.L. 105-34) provides that a qualified heir may enter into a cash lease of farm property with a member of the heir's family without triggering recapture. The provision applies retroactively to all leases entered into after December 31, 1976.

¶ 292 Determination of "Material Participation"

In order for a property to qualify for special use valuation, the decedent or a member of the decedent's family must materially participate in the farm or business operations for five of the eight years prior to the decedent's death.[76] This eight-year period is measured from the earliest of (1) the date of the decedent's death, (2) the date that the decedent became disabled, or (3) the date that the decedent retired.[77] Whether there has been "material participation" by the decedent or family members in a farm or other closely held business is

[68] Code Sec. 2032A(e)(4).

[69] Code Sec. 2032A(e)(5).

[70] Reg. § 20.2032A-3(b)(2).

[71] Code Sec. 2032A(e)(13).

[72] Code Sec. 2032A(c)(2)(E).

[73] Code Sec. 2032A(b)(1)(A)(i).

[74] IRS Technical Advice Memorandum 8201016 (Sept. 22, 1981).

[75] *T.S. Heffley, Exrx. (O. Heffley Est.)*, CA-7, 89-2 USTC ¶13,812; *M.L. Brockman, Admr. (S. Donahoe Est.)*, CA-7, 90-1 USTC ¶60,026.

[76] Code Sec. 2032A(b)(1)(C).

[77] Code Sec. 2032A(b)(4).

determined in a manner similar to that set forth in the income tax provisions relating to whether income is subject to self-employment taxes.[78] However, regulations adopted under Code Sec. 2032A[79] provide additional factors to be considered in making this determination for estate tax purposes. The standards for material participation under Code Sec. 469, governing passive activity losses, are similar to the material participation standards under Code Sec. 2032A. Consequently, the estate of a decedent who reported her losses from a ranch as passive activity losses, rather than as losses from an active trade or business, could not elect special use valuation for ranch property because the decedent had not materially participated in ranching during her lifetime.[80]

• *Employment and Management*

Although no single factor determines whether a decedent or family member has materially participated in a farm or closely held business, physical work and participation in management decisions are the principal factors to be considered. The involvement of such an individual on a full-time basis, or to any lesser extent necessary to allow the individual to manage fully the farm or business, is considered material participation. Payment of self-employment taxes on income derived from the farm or closely held business is also an indicator of material participation. Although payment of such taxes is not conclusive evidence of material participation, if no such taxes have been paid, material participation is presumed not to have occurred unless the executor demonstrates otherwise and explains why no self-employment tax was paid. In addition, all such tax determined to be due must be paid before an effective special use valuation election may be made. For this purpose, "tax determined to be due" does not include tax assessments that are barred by the statute of limitations on collection or assessment.[81]

At a minimum, an individual must regularly advise or consult with the other managing party with respect to the operation of the business and participate in making a substantial number of management decisions.[82] According to the regulations, passive collection of rents, salaries, draws, dividends, or other income does not constitute material participation, nor does the mere advancement of capital and review of crop plans or other business proposals.[83] Thus, for farmland to qualify for special use valuation when all or a portion of it is leased to nonqualified heirs, a decedent's financial stake or other involvement must be more than that of a landlord passively collecting a fixed rental from an unrelated tenant.[84]

The U.S. Court of Appeals for the Seventh Circuit has held that farmland rented pursuant to a cash lease containing a rent adjustment clause providing for a 20-percent downward adjustment of the annual rent if gross income from farm production fell below a specified amount qualified for special use valuation. The appellate court stated that the adjustment clause allocated a portion of the risk of poor yield or low crop prices to the decedent and, therefore, the income derived from the lease of the farmland was substantially based on production. However,

---

[78] Code Sec. 2032A(e)(6), referring to Code Sec. 1402(a)(1).

[79] Reg. § 20.2032A-3.

[80] IRS Technical Advice Memorandum 9428002 (Mar. 29, 1994).

[81] Reg. § 20.2032A-3(e); Rev. Rul. 83-32, 1983-1 CB 226.

[82] Reg. § 20.2032A-3(e). See also *C.E. Coon Est.*, 81 TC 602, CCH Dec. 40,478.

[83] Reg. § 20.2032A-3(a).

[84] *H.F. Sherrod Est.*, 82 TC 523, CCH Dec. 41,084, rev'd, CA-11, 85-2 USTC ¶ 13,644, 774 F2d 1057, cert. denied, 10-6-86. See *M.J. Martin et al.*, 84 TC 620, CCH Dec. 41,998, aff'd, CA-7, 86-1 USTC ¶ 13,659, 783 F2d 81.

the court noted that, as the owner of only moderately productive farmland, the decedent was subject to a higher degree of risk than would be the owner of very productive farmland because it was more likely that the rent adjustment clause would be triggered.[85]

• *Financial Risk*

Another factor considered in the determination of material participation is the extent to which an individual has assumed financial responsibility for the farm or other business. This includes the advancement of funds, and, in the case of a farm, the provision of a substantial portion of machinery, livestock, and implements used in production.

• *Residence*

For farms, hotels, or apartment buildings operated as a trade or business, an individual's maintenance of the individual's principal place of residence on the premises is a factor to be considered in determining material participation.

• *Other Considerations*

The activities of at least one family member must amount to material participation at a given time because the activities of a number of family members cannot be considered in the aggregate as material participation. Finally, if nonfamily members participate in the farm or other business, part-time activities by the decedent or family members must be pursuant to a provable oral or written arrangement providing for actual participation by the decedent or family members. For example, the hiring of a professional farm manager will not prevent satisfaction of the material participation requirement if the decedent or family member materially participates under the terms of such an arrangement.[86]

¶ 293 Active Management by Surviving Spouse

A special rule applies to liberalize the material participation requirement with respect to a surviving spouse who receives qualifying property from a decedent in whose estate the property was eligible for special use valuation (whether such valuation was actually elected). "Active management" by the surviving spouse will satisfy the material participation requirement for purposes of electing special use valuation in the surviving spouse's gross estate. The Internal Revenue Code defines active management as the making of management decisions of a business (other than daily operation decisions).[87] Combinations of activities such as inspection of crops, review of crop plans, and marketing decisions constitute active management in farming operations.[88]

The "tacking" of active management by a surviving spouse with material participation by a retired or disabled spouse is allowed in order to qualify the property for special use valuation in the spouse's estate.[89] This provision is applicable only if the spouse died within eight years of the retired or disabled spouse.[90]

---

[85] *M. Schuneman*, CA-7, 86-1 USTC ¶13,660, 783 F2d 694, rev'g DC Ill., 83-2 USTC ¶13,540, 570 FSupp. 1327.

[86] Reg. §20.2032A-3(e).

[87] Code Sec. 2032A(b)(5) and Code Sec. 2032A(e)(12).

[88] *General Explanation of the Economic Recovery Tax Act of 1981*, Staff of the Joint Committee on Taxation, p. 246.

[89] Code Sec. 2032A(b)(5).

[90] House Committee Report on the Technical Corrections Act of 1982 (P.L. 97-448).

¶ 294 Qualifying Property Passing in Trust

The rules for the special use valuation procedure apply to qualifying property that passes in trust. However, future interests in trust property will not qualify for the special use valuation. Trust property will be considered to have passed from the decedent to a qualified heir only to the extent that the qualified heir has a present interest in that trust property. Real property otherwise qualifying for special use valuation and passing to a trust may be specially valued even if the trustee has the discretionary power to fix the amounts receivable by any individual beneficiary, so long as all potential beneficiaries are qualified heirs.[91] If the decedent created successive interests in the trust property that is to be specially valued, all of those interests must be received by qualified heirs (see ¶282).

¶ 295 Community Property

Community-owned property may be valued under the special valuation rules. For purposes of determining whether community-owned real property meets the two percentage tests necessary to qualify real property for special use valuation (see ¶281), the entire value of the property must be taken into account.[92] This ensures equal treatment of community and individually owned property under the special valuation rules.

¶ 296 Basis of Special Use Valuation Property

With respect to decedents dying before January 1, 2010, the basis of specially valued property in the hands of the qualified heir is its value as determined under the special use valuation provisions.[93] In the case of a pecuniary bequest or purchase (see ¶285), the basis of the property to the qualified heir is the estate's basis in the property immediately before the distribution or sale (generally, the property's special use value) plus the amount of post-death appreciation recognized as gain by the estate.[94]

See ¶121 for a discussion of the carryover basis at death rules that will apply to decedents dying after December 31, 2009.

• ***Basis Increase on Recapture***

A qualified heir may make an irrevocable election to increase the income tax basis of special use valuation property to its fair market value on the date of the decedent's death (or on the alternate valuation date, if the estate so elected) if recapture tax is paid.[95]

---

[91] Code Sec. 2032A(g).

[92] Code Sec. 2032A(e)(10); Rev. Rul. 83-96, 1983-2 CB 156.

[93] Code Sec. 1014(a)(3), prior to amendment by P.L. 107-16.

[94] Code Sec. 1040(c).

[95] Code Sec. 1016(c).

Chapter 9
STOCKS AND BONDS

¶ 310 Inclusion of Stocks and Bonds

Stocks and bonds owned by a decedent at the date of death are includible in the decedent's gross estate under Code Sec. 2033. They are listed on Schedule B (Stocks and Bonds) of Form 706 (United States Estate (and Generation-Skipping Transfer) Tax Return) (Rev. Aug. 2004), which does not have to be filed if the decedent did not own stocks or bonds.

¶ 311 Dividends and Interest

Dividends and interest on stocks and bonds are included in the gross estate along with the securities on which they are paid. They are usually reflected separately in the same schedule used for reporting stocks and bonds.

Dividends payable to the decedent or to the decedent's estate because, on or before the date of death, the decedent was a shareholder of record must be included in the gross estate and listed on the return as separate items.[1] If dividends have merely been declared and are payable to stockholders of record on a date after the decedent's death, they are not includible in the gross estate.[2] However, they are undoubtedly reflected in the value of the stock.

On the other hand, if the stock is traded on an exchange and the stock is selling "ex-dividend" on the date of the decedent's death, the amount of the dividend must be added to the ex-dividend stock price quotation in fixing the value of the stock.[3] It should not be reported as a separate item in the return schedule. Similarly, if the stock is not traded on an exchange, the dividends must be reported when the record date for determining to whom the dividends are to be paid has passed.

Interest on bonds is includible in the bond owner's gross estate if it has accrued at the owner's date of death.[4] In the case of certain government bonds, however, interest cannot accrue between interest payment dates. With respect to these government bonds, no interest should be included for the period between the last interest payment date and the date of death.

---

[1] Reg. § 20.2033-1(b).
[2] Rev. Rul. 54-399, 1954-2 CB 279.
[3] Reg. § 20.2031-2(i).
[4] Reg. § 20.2033-1(b).

¶ 313 Reporting Stocks and Bonds on Return

A decedent's stocks and bonds are to be reported on Schedule B (Stocks and Bonds) of the estate tax return (Form 706, United States Estate (and Generation-Skipping Transfer) Tax Return). The description of the stock should indicate (1) the number of shares, (2) whether the stock is common or preferred, (3) the issue, (4) the par value, (5) the price per share, and (6) the stock CUSIP number, if available. The CUSIP number is a nine-digit number assigned to traded securities by the American Banking Association. If the stocks are listed on a stock exchange, the exact name of the corporation, and the principal exchange on which the stock is sold, should be included in the description. If the stock is not listed on an exchange, the description should include the company's principal business office.

A description of bonds should include (1) quantity, (2) denomination, (3) name of the obligor, (4) kind of bond, (5) date of maturity, (6) rate of interest payable, (7) interest due dates, and (8) the bond CUSIP number, if available. The exchange on which the bond is listed should be given. If the bond is not listed on an exchange, the principal business office of the company must be supplied.

¶ 315 Stocks and Bonds Subject to Foreign Death Duties

If an estate, inheritance, legacy, or succession tax has been paid to a foreign country on any stocks or bonds included in the gross estate, the stocks and bonds subjected to the foreign death tax should be grouped separately on Schedule B (Stocks and Bonds) of Form 706 (United States Estate (and Generation-Skipping Transfer) Tax Return) with a heading "Subjected to Foreign Death Taxes."[5]

¶ 318 Valuation

Stocks and bonds included in the gross estate are to be reported at their value on the date of death or on an alternate valuation date (generally, six months after death) if the estate representative so elects.

When the alternate valuation method is elected, the selling price of any securities sold during the six-month period will control their valuation, if the sale is an arm's-length transaction.[6] In reporting securities under the alternate valuation method, their value at the date of death, as well as that on the alternate date, should be shown on the return.

If the alternate valuation method has been elected, stock includible in the gross estate and selling "ex-dividend" must be valued at its "ex-dividend" quoted selling price as of the alternate valuation date, increased by the amount of dividends declared during the alternate valuation period and payable to stockholders of record after the alternate valuation date.[7] Although the dividends themselves are not includible in the gross estate of a decedent in such case, the value of such stock on the alternate valuation date includes the value of the right to the declared dividends.[8]

• ***Stock Held in Retirement Account***

In a case of first impression, a U.S. district court in Texas has held that the value of a decedent's retirement accounts was not discounted to reflect the income tax liability to be incurred by the beneficiaries upon distribution of the

---

[5] See Instructions for Form 706 (Rev. Aug. 2004), p. 12.

[6] Rev. Rul. 70-512, 1970-2 CB 192.

[7] Rev. Rul. 60-124, 1960-1 CB 368.

[8] *C.D. Fleming Est.*, 33 TCM 1414, CCH Dec. 32,873(M), TC Memo. 1974-307.

accounts. The estate included two employer-sponsored retirement accounts, both comprised of marketable securities. In valuing the retirement accounts, the court concluded that at the time of death the accounts were equivalent to the securities contained within them and applied the willing buyer/willing seller tests of Reg. §20.2031-1(b). According to the court, a hypothetical willing buyer of the accounts would not take the income tax liability of the beneficiaries into consideration. The court concluded that Congress had chosen to address the issue of double taxation through Code Sec. 691(c) and that permitting a valuation discount would provide the beneficiaries with "undue relief".[9]

¶ 319 Separate Appraisal of Tangible and Intangible Assets

If the value of stocks and bonds is determined by the value of the underlying assets, and these assets are both tangible and intangible ones that do not permit a separate appraisal, no general rule is applicable for valuing such assets. Each case will vary and the value of such assets must be determined on the factors present in that particular case.[10]

¶ 320 Restricted Stock

Certain shares of unregistered stock are "restricted" under federal securities law and may not be sold to the general public but may only be sold to certain types of investors and only in limited amounts. Because of these restrictions, such stock is typically discounted when valued for estate tax purposes. In determining the amount of the discount, the following factors are relevant:

(1) the earnings, net assets, and net sales of the corporation;

(2) the resale provisions found in the restriction agreements;

(3) the relative negotiating strengths of the buyer and the seller; and

(4) the market experience of freely traded securities of the same class as the restricted securities.

All relevant facts and circumstances bearing on the value of the restricted stock must be considered in arriving at the estate tax value of the stock.[11]

The IRS may contend that no discount should be allowed because the corporation could register the stock and, thus, remove the restrictions on its sale. Whether the corporation would register the stock must be resolved on the facts of each case.[12]

¶ 321 Selling Prices

The estate tax value of stocks and bonds is the fair market value per share or bond on the applicable valuation date. If there is a market for stocks or bonds on a stock exchange or in an over-the-counter market, through a broker or otherwise, the mean between the highest and lowest quoted selling prices on the valuation date is the fair market value of each share or bond.

If there were no sales on the valuation date, but there were sales on trading dates within a reasonable period both before and after the valuation date, the fair

---

[9] *L. Smith Est.*, DC Tex., 2004-1 USTC ¶60,476.

[10] Rev. Rul. 65-193, 1965-2 CB 370.

[11] Rev. Rul. 77-287, 1977-2 CB 319, amplifying Rev. Rul. 59-60, 1959-1 CB 237. See also *E.O. Sullivan Est.*, 45 TCM 1199, CCH Dec. 40,015(M), TC Memo. 1983-185, and *C. McClatchy Est.*, CA-9, 98-2 USTC ¶60,315, rev'g TC, 106 TC 206, CCH Dec. 51,277.

[12] See, e.g., *S. Brownell Est.*, 44 TCM 1550, CCH Dec. 39,459(M), TC Memo. 1982-632, and *F. Stratton Est.*, 45 TCM 432, CCH Dec. 39,597(M), TC Memo. 1982-744, both holding that a discount was allowable.

market value is determined by (1) taking the mean between the highest and lowest sales on the nearest trading date before and nearest trading date after the valuation date, (2) prorating the difference between such mean prices to the valuation date, and (3) adding or subtracting, as the case may be, the prorated portion of the difference to or from the mean price on the nearest trading date *before* the valuation date.[13]

> *Example:* Assume that sales of stock nearest the valuation date (Wednesday, June 20) occurred two trading days before (Monday, June 18) and three trading days after (Monday, June 25). Assume further that on these days the mean sale prices per share were $10 and $15, respectively. The price of $12 would be taken as representing the fair market value of a share of stock as of the valuation date:
>
> $$\frac{(3 \times 10) + (2 \times 15)}{5}$$
>
> If, instead, the mean sale prices per share on June 18 and June 25 were reversed—$15 and $10, respectively—the price of $13 would be taken as representing the fair market value.

When a decedent dies on a weekend, the stock included in the decedent's gross estate is valued at the average of the mean sale prices for Friday and Monday.[14] Where the stock begins to sell ex-dividend on the following Monday, the amount of the dividend is added to Monday's quotations to determine the mean sales price.[15]

An alternate method is provided for valuing listed bonds if the highest and lowest selling prices for such bonds are not generally available in a listing or publication on the valuation date. Generally, in such case, the fair market value of a bond at the valuation date is the mean price between the closing selling price on the valuation date and the closing selling price on the trading day before the valuation date.

Special rules are provided for cases where (1) there were no sales on the trading day before the valuation date but there were sales on a date within a reasonable period before the valuation date, (2) there were no sales within a reasonable period before the valuation date but there were sales on the valuation date, or (3) there were no sales on the valuation date but there were sales on dates within a reasonable period both before and after the valuation date.[16]

Stocks and bonds (other than Treasury bonds) that are usually traded in dollars and dollar fractions not smaller than one-eighth are to be reported in dollars and fractions smaller than eighths, for federal estate and gift tax purposes, when the mean of the high and the low quoted selling prices results in a fraction smaller than an eighth on the applicable valuation date. Treasury bonds that are normally traded in dollars and dollar fractions of thirty-seconds are to be valued and reported in dollars and fractions smaller than thirty-seconds, for estate and gift tax purposes, when the mean between the high and low selling prices results in a fraction smaller than a thirty-second.[17] Although this rule will retain its validity, it seemingly will become less important in light of several major stock exchanges (including the New York Stock Exchange and NASDAQ) replacing fractional dollars with decimal reporting of stock values.

---

[13] Reg. § 20.2031-2(b).

[14] Reg. § 20.2031-2(b).

[15] Rev. Rul. 68-610, 1968-2 CB 405.

[16] Reg. § 20.2031-2(b)(2).

[17] Rev. Rul. 68-272, 1968-1 CB 394.

In valuing listed stocks and bonds, the executor should be careful to consult accurate records to obtain values on the applicable valuation date. If stocks or bonds are listed on more than one exchange, the records of the exchange where the stocks or bonds are principally traded should be used.

If quotations of unlisted securities are obtained from brokers, copies of the letters furnishing the quotations should be attached to the estate tax return. Similarly, if evidence as to the sale of unlisted securities is obtained from officers of the issuing companies, copies of the letters furnishing the evidence should be attached to the return.[18]

¶ 322 Large Blocks of Stock

An exception to the usual procedures for valuing listed securities can sometimes be sustained if the decedent owned a large block of stock in a single company. For example, if the executor can show that the block of stock to be valued is so large in relation to the actual sales on the existing market that it could not be liquidated in a reasonable time without depressing the market, the price at which the block could be sold outside the usual market—such as through an underwriter—may be a more accurate determination of value than market quotations or a mean between the high and low on the valuation date. On the other hand, if the block of stock to be valued represents a controlling interest, either actual or effective, in a going business, the price at which other lots change hands may have little relation to its true value.[19]

The IRS has ruled that underwriters' fees incurred by an estate in selling a large block of a decedent's stock were not to be considered in determining the allowable blockage discount. The IRS noted that the estate tax value of the block of stock was the price at which it could be sold to the general public even though the estate would receive less than this price because it paid the underwriters' fees. However, because it was necessary to sell the stock in order to pay debts, expenses and taxes of the estate, the fees were a deductible administration expense.[20]

Expert testimony, together with evidence that the stock must be specially handled by one who will discount its value, is usually necessary to establish a valid "blockage" discount.

¶ 323 Lack of Sales

If stock is sold on an exchange or over the counter and there are no sales during a reasonable period beginning before and ending after the valuation date, the valuation may be based on the bid and asked prices. The fair market value is then determined by taking the mean between the bona fide bid and asked prices on the valuation date.

If there are no bid and asked prices on the valuation date, the value may be determined by (1) taking the mean between the bona fide bid and asked prices on the nearest date before and the nearest date after the valuation date, (2) prorating the difference between the mean prices to the valuation date, and (3) adding or subtracting, as the case may be, the prorated portion of the difference to or from the mean price on the nearest date before the valuation date.[21]

---

[18] See Instructions for Form 706 (Rev. Aug. 2004), p. 13.

[19] Reg. § 20.2031-2(e).

[20] Rev. Rul. 83-30, 1983-1 CB 224.

[21] Reg. § 20.2031-2(c).

¶ 324 Incomplete Prices

If actual sale prices or quoted bona fide bid and asked prices are available on a date within a reasonable period *before* the valuation date, but are not available on a date within a reasonable period *after* the valuation date, then the mean between such highest and lowest sales or bid and asked prices may be taken as the fair market value. Similarly, if prices are available within a reasonable period after, but not before, the valuation date, the mean between the highest and lowest available sales or bid and asked prices may be accepted as the value.[22]

¶ 325 Inactive and Unlisted Securities

When stock and other securities are not listed on an exchange and their value cannot be determined on the basis of sales or bid and asked prices because of the absence of sales, the value of the unlisted stock and securities is determined by taking into consideration, in addition to all other factors, the value of stock or securities of corporations engaged in the same or similar line of business that are listed on an exchange.[23] If no active market exists, consideration is also usually given (1) in the case of bonds, to the soundness of the security, the interest yield, the date of maturity, and other relevant factors, and (2) in the case of stocks, to the company's net worth, earning power, dividend-paying capacity, and other relevant factors.[24]

Complete financial and other data on which the estate bases its valuation should be submitted with the return. This information must include balance sheets (particularly the one nearest to the valuation date), and statements of the net earnings or operating results and dividends paid for each of the five years immediately preceding the valuation date.

¶ 326 Close Corporation Stock

The term "close corporation" does not appear in the regulations, which establish only general valuation rules in the absence of sales or bona fide bid and asked prices. However, a ruling by the IRS defines closely held corporations as "those corporations the shares of which are owned by a relatively limited number of stockholders." Often the entire stock issue is held by one family. The result of this situation is that little, if any, trading in the shares takes place. There is, therefore, no established market for the stock and such sales as occur at irregular intervals seldom reflect all of the elements of a representative transaction as defined by the term "fair market value."[25]

• *Valuation Factors*

The factors to be considered in determining the value of closely held stock, and of unlisted securities generally, vary with the particular facts involved. The weight to be given any one factor in any given case depends on the circumstances. Sometimes, earnings are given the greatest weight. At other times, assets of the corporation provide the best test. The existence of special conditions in the industry at the time of valuation may also have some effect.

Although no formula can be devised for the determination of the fair market value of closely held corporations or stock of corporations where market quotations are either lacking or too scarce to be recognized, all available financial data,

---

[22] Reg. § 20.2031-2(d).

[23] Code Sec. 2031(b).

[24] Reg. § 20.2031-2(f).

[25] Rev. Rul. 59-60, 1959-1 CB 237, modified by Rev. Rul. 65-193, 1965-2 CB 370, and amplified by Rev. Rul. 77-287, 1977-2 CB 319, and Rev. Rul. 83-120, 1983-2 CB 170.

as well as all relevant factors affecting the fair market value, should be considered.[26] These factors include:

(1) the nature of the business and the history of the enterprise from its inception;

(2) the economic outlook in general and the condition and outcome of the specific industry in particular;

(3) the book value of the stock and the financial condition of the business;

(4) the earning capacity of the company;

(5) the dividend-paying capacity of the company;

(6) goodwill or other intangible value of the company;

(7) sales of the stock and the size of the block to be valued;

(8) the market price of stocks of corporations engaged in the same or a similar line of business having their stocks actively traded in a free and open market, either on an exchange or over the counter; and

(9) the life insurance proceeds received by a corporate beneficiary on a policy covering the sole or controlling stockholder.

Under (9), above, the incidents of ownership in a policy of insurance on the life of a sole surviving shareholder held by the corporation will not be attributed to the insured decedent (the sole or controlling stockholder) through the decedent's stock ownership under Reg. § 20.2042-1(c) because it will be considered a nonoperating asset of the corporation in determining the stock value included in the decedent's gross estate under Reg. § 20.2031-2(f). Thus, life insurance proceeds excluded from the decedent's gross estate are considered a nonoperating asset of the corporation for purposes of valuing the stock of the decedent that is includible in his estate. However, the incidents of ownership will be attributed to the insured decedent who is the sole or controlling stockholder under Reg. § 20.2042-1(c) if such proceeds are not payable to the corporation or a third party for a valid business purpose.[27]

An additional factor to be considered is the degree of control of the business represented by the block of stock being valued.[28] Thus, if the decedent held control over the corporation, the IRS may contend that a control premium should be added to the value of the stock in determining its estate tax value. In the Tax Court's view, "a premium for control is generally expressed as the percentage by which the amount paid for a controlling block of shares exceeds the amount that would have otherwise been paid for the shares if sold as minority interests . . . ".[29] The IRS National Office has ruled that the majority voting power of shares of preferred stock in a closely held corporation owned by a decedent at death was to be considered in valuing the stock for estate tax purposes even though the voting rights expired at the owner's death.[30] With respect to the control issue, the Tax Court has held that the possibility of protracted litigation over the relative rights of different classes of stock served to limit the date-of-death value of a decedent's interest in a closely held corporation. In addition, the fact that a decedent held the largest block of shares in the company did not necessarily

[26] Rev. Rul. 77-287, 1977-2 CB 319; Rev. Rul. 59-60, 1959-1 CB 237.

[27] Reg. § 20.2031-2(f) and Reg. § 20.2042-1(c), respectively.

[28] Reg. § 20.2031-2(f).

[29] *J.E. Salsbury Est.*, 34 TCM 1441, CCH Dec. 33,503(M), TC Memo. 1975-333, at 1451.

[30] IRS Technical Advice Memorandum 8401006 (Sept. 28, 1983).

warrant a control premium where the power to unilaterally direct and change the direction of the company was not present.[31]

A determination of the value of stock in an S corporation transferred by parents to their children did not have to be reduced to reflect "tax affecting," a process whereby a discounted future cash flow of a company is adjusted downward to reflect hypothetical income tax on future corporate earnings. In upholding the Tax Court's holding, the U.S. Court of Appeals for the Sixth Circuit noted that there was a difference within the appraisal profession regarding the propriety of the "tax affecting" procedure. Further, there was no evidence that the corporation would lose its subchapter S status and be subject to taxation at the corporate level.[32]

• *Aggregation of Stock Holdings*

The IRS National Office has ruled that two blocks of stock includible in a decedent's gross estate under two different Code sections (Code Sec. 2033 and Code Sec. 2038) can be aggregated to determine the fair market value of the stock for estate tax purposes.[33] A control premium could then be applied if the aggregated stock constituted a controlling interest in a closely held corporation. Similarly, the Tax Court has held that stock held in trust over which a decedent possessed a general power of appointment was to be aggregated for valuation purposes with stock in the same company that was owned outright by the decedent.[34]

In another Technical Advice Memorandum,[35] the IRS National Office treated a decedent's voting preferred stock and voting common stock as a single controlling interest in determining the value of a decedent's gross estate under Code Sec. 2033. A control premium was applied, even though the stock passed to two different beneficiaries. However, when it came to determining the amount of the estate tax marital deduction, the block of stock that passed to the decedent's surviving spouse was valued as a separate minority interest.

A block of publicly traded stock held in a revocable trust that was includible in a decedent's gross estate under Code Sec. 2033 was not merged for valuation purposes with additional shares of the same stock in a qualified terminable interest property (QTIP) trust that was includible in her gross estate under Code Sec. 2044, the Tax Court has ruled. The IRS argued that the decedent should be considered the outright owner of a majority block of stock for purposes of valuation and that the shares should be valued at a premium rather than at a discount. In rejecting this argument, the court relied on the fact that neither Code Sec. 2044 nor the legislative history of that section indicates that the decedent should be treated as the owner of QTIP property for purposes of aggregation. The court stated that QTIP property is merely treated as passing from the surviving spouse for estate tax purposes and does not actually pass to or from the surviving spouse. Moreover, the surviving spouse could not exercise any control over the stock. Therefore, the decedent was not considered the owner of the stock in the QTIP trust for estate tax valuation purposes.[36]

---

[31] *S. Newhouse Est.*, 94 TC 193, CCH Dec. 46,411 (Nonacq.).

[32] *W. Gross, Jr.*, CA-6, 2001-2 USTC ¶60,425 (cert. den. Oct. 7, 2002), aff'g TC, 78 TCM 201, CCH Dec. 53,481(M), TC Memo. 1999-254 (gift tax decision).

[33] IRS Technical Advice Memorandum 9403002 (Sept. 17, 1993).

[34] *A. Fontana Est.*, 118 TC 318, CCH Dec. 54,693.

[35] IRS Technical Advice Memorandum 9403005 (Oct. 14, 1993).

[36] *H. Mellinger Est.*, 112 TC 26, CCH Dec. 53,218 (Acq.).

• *Effect of Buy-Sell Agreements*

Another element may also be important, however, and may limit or nullify the weight to be given to the above factors in determining the value of close corporation stock. This element is the restrictive sales agreement, primarily the mutual buy-sell type of agreement. Mutual buy-sell agreements are those whereby a corporation or individual (usually a co-stockholder) promises to buy stock, and the stockholder promises to sell, on the happening of a certain contingency, usually the stockholder's death.

The rules to determine if a buy-sell agreement will be deemed to set the estate tax value for the corporate stock to be transferred will depend on whether such agreement is between related or unrelated parties, and if related parties are involved, whether it was entered into or substantially modified after October 8, 1990.

If the parties to the agreement are not related, the regulations and case law[37] state that to establish the estate tax value of the stock to be transferred, the following four requirements must be met:

(1) the price of the stock must be fixed or determinable by a formula within the agreement;

(2) the estate must be obligated to sell the stock at the fixed price;

(3) if the decedent shareholder chooses to sell the shares during life, he or she must sell them at the price fixed by the agreement; and

(4) the agreement must represent a bona fide business arrangement, rather than a device to pass the decedent's shares to the natural objects of his or her bounty at less than full and adequate consideration.

A buy-sell agreement between family members that was created or substantially modified after October 8, 1990, will not be effective in setting the estate tax value of a closely held business unless the decedent's estate can show that the agreement:

(1) is a bona fide business arrangement;

(2) is not a device to transfer property to family members for less than full and adequate consideration; and

(3) is comparable to similar arrangements entered into by persons in arm's-length transactions.[38]

Additionally, the post-October 8, 1990, buy-sell agreement would also have to meet the requirements stated above with respect to agreements between unrelated parties.

See, also, ¶2500 for a discussion of the special valuation rules for estate freezes.

---

[37] Reg. §20.2031-2(h); *M. Caplan Est.*, 33 TCM 189, CCH Dec. 32,461(M), TC Memo. 1974-39; *O.B. Littick Est.*, 31 TC 181, CCH Dec. 23,331 (Acq.); *M.G. Seltzer Est.*, 50 TCM 1250, CCH Dec. 42,423(M), TC Memo. 1985-519.

[38] Reg. §25.2703-1(b)(1). If more than 50 percent of the value of the property subject to the buy-sell agreement is owned by persons who are not members of the transferor's family, these three requirements are deemed satisfied, thus effectively removing them with regard to buy-sell arrangements between unrelated parties.

• *Minority Discounts*

For several years, the IRS maintained that no minority discount should apply when shares in a closely held corporation were transferred from a decedent to other family members, if the corporation remained under family control after the decedent's death. Unless there was evidence of hostility among family members or other indications that the family would not cooperate in corporate matters, the IRS generally challenged the application of a minority discount in these circumstances. However, several courts disagreed with the IRS, finding it appropriate, instead, to consider *only* the decedent's shares of stock in valuing the decedent's interest in the corporation for estate tax purposes.[39] The IRS finally reversed its earlier position and announced that it would no longer disallow a minority discount solely because the transferred interest, when aggregated with interest held by other family members, was a controlling interest.[40]

Although the IRS's position is seemingly consistent with Tax Court decisions[41] that have allowed a minority discount with respect to minority family members' interests in a family corporation for purposes of both the estate tax and the gift tax, it remains uncertain how the policy announced in Rev. Rul. 93-12 will develop.

For example, the IRS, in a Technical Advice Memorandum[42] involving a donor's gift of three 30-percent blocks of stock to his three children, concluded that the "swing vote" characteristic of each 30-percent block could properly be taken into consideration for determining the fair market value of the stock for gift tax purposes. Any of the three 30-percent owners could combine with any other to control the corporation, whether the 30-percent owners were family members or outsiders. The IRS also concluded that the swing vote attribute enhanced the value of each block of stock. If the three transfers had not been made simultaneously, the second transfer of a 30-percent block would not only have possessed swing-vote value, according to the IRS, but would also have enhanced the value of the first transferee's interest. Moreover, the IRS viewed this enhancement of value as an indirect gift to the first transferee. However, the U.S. Court of Appeals for the Fifth Circuit has ruled that aggregation is not required for the valuation of fractional interests.[43]

• *Discount for Lack of Marketability*

A substantial discount may be available on the basis that the closely held stock lacks marketability, that is, that there is an absence of a ready or existing market for the sale of the securities being valued.[44] In its *Valuation Training for Appeals Officers Coursebook*, the IRS recognizes that if owners of closely held stock should try to list a block of securities on a stock exchange for sale to the public, they probably would have to make the offerings through underwriters, incurring costs for registration, distribution, and underwriters' commissions. The use of such costs to determine lack of marketability has been upheld by the courts. In

---

[39] *M. Bright Est.*, CA-5, 81-2 USTC ¶13,436, 658 F2d 999; *J.A. Propstra*, CA-9, 82-2 USTC ¶13,475, 680 F2d 1248; *W. Andrews Est.*, 79 TC 938, CCH Dec. 39,523; and *E. Lee Est.*, 69 TC 860, CCH Dec. 35,017.

[40] Rev. Rul. 93-12, 93-1 CB 202, revoking Rev. Rul. 81-253, 1981-2 CB 187, and substituting acquiescence for the nonacquiescence (1980-2 CB 2) in *E. Lee Est.*, 69 TC 860, CCH Dec. 35,017.

[41] *W. Andrews Est.*, 79 TC 938, CCH Dec. 39,523, and *E. Lee Est.*, 69 TC 860, CCH Dec. 35,017 (estate tax decisions); and *C. Ward*, 87 TC 78, CCH Dec. 43,178 (gift tax decision).

[42] IRS Technical Advice Memorandum 9436005 (May 26, 1994).

[43] *L. Bonner, Sr. Est.*, CA-5, 96-2 USTC ¶60,237, 84 F3d 196.

[44] *M. Gallo Est.*, 50 TCM 470, CCH Dec. 42,241(M), TC Memo. 1985-363.

addition, even though securities law restrictions on unregistered stock owned by a decedent terminated on his death, the date-of-death value of the stock was reduced to reflect the restrictions that existed at the time of death.[45]

• *Liquidation Discount*

A lack of marketability discount has been allowed with respect to gifts made from a father to his two sons of stock in a holding company containing built-in capital gains. Although no sale or liquidation of the stock was planned, the estate argued that as a result of the repeal of the *General Utilities* doctrine by the Tax Reform Act of 1986 (P.L. 99-514), if the holding company were liquidated, gain would be recognized and the estate should be given a discount for the potential capital gains tax. It also argued that any potential buyer would take this tax into account in fixing a purchase price. Despite the absence of plans to sell or liquidate the stock, the Tax Court allowed the discount because it found that a hypothetical willing buyer and seller would have taken the potential tax into account under the circumstances.[46] A full discount in the estate tax value of stock in a personal holding company to reflect built-in capital gains based on a liquidation of the company was allowed, rather than a lesser amount computed to estimate the capital gains liability of the company if it continued to operate as a going concern following the decedent's death. In so holding, the U.S. Court of Appeals for the Fifth Circuit[47] concluded that the Tax Court had erred in assuming that a hypothetical buyer would continue the underlying business as a going concern where the rate of return of the business was substantially lower than the rate of return that an investor would require. Allowing a reduction for the full amount of built-in capital gains based on an assumed liquidation was necessary to reflect the economic reality surrounding the decedent's stock holdings.

• *Stock Issued Pursuant to an Estate "Freeze"*

The gross estate of the owner of a closely held corporation may include preferred stock in the corporation issued pursuant to a recapitalization designed to "freeze" the value of the individual's interest in the corporation for estate tax purposes. Such a recapitalization is intended to transfer the potential appreciation of the individual's common stock to others active in operating the corporation, often younger members of the individual's family. Typically, this involves the exchange of the individual's common stock for preferred stock that has a stated par value equal to nearly all of the value of the common stock.[48] The individual also receives new common stock having only a low fair market value, and this new stock is then transferred to the younger family members.

The Revenue Act of 1987 (P.L. 100-203) added Code Sec. 2036(c), which was intended to reduce the benefits available from such an "estate freeze." Code Sec. 2036(c) was repealed retroactively by the Revenue Reconciliation Act of 1990 (P.L. 101-508) and was replaced by a series of rules intended to curb perceived valuation abuses by valuing certain interests at the time of transfer rather than by

---

[45] *C. McClatchy*, CA-9, 98-2 USTC ¶60,315, 147 F3d 1089, rev'g 106 TC 206, CCH Dec. 51,277.

[46] *A. Davis Est.*, 110 TC 530, CCH Dec. 52,764. Followed, *I. Eisenberg*, CA-2, 98-2 USTC ¶60,322, 155 F3d 50 (Acq.), rev'g and rem'g 74 TCM 1046, CCH Dec. 52,321(M), TC Memo. 1997-483; *P. Welch*, CA-6, 2000-1 USTC ¶60,372, 208 F3d 213, rev'g and rem'g 75 TCM 2252, CCH Dec. 52,689(M), TC Memo. 1998-167.

[47] *H. Jameson Est.*, CA-5, 2001-2 USTC ¶60,420, vac'g and rem'g 77 TCM 1383, CCH Dec. 53,247(M), TC Memo. 1999-43.

[48] The recapitalization is often structured as a tax-free reorganization under Code Sec. 368(a)(1)(E).

including previously transferred property in the transferor's gross estate.[49] See ¶2500 for a further description of the limitations on valuation freezes resulting from the Chapter 14 special valuation rules.

Before the Revenue Act of 1987 limited the potential benefits of estate freezes, the IRS had provided factors to be used in valuing preferred and common stock issued pursuant to an estate freeze in a ruling amplifying Rev. Rul. 59-60.[50] Generally, in valuing the preferred stock, the primary factors to be considered are the yield of the stock and the corporation's ability to pay both the stated dividend rate and the liquidation preference. The adequacy of the yield of preferred stock is to be determined by comparing its dividend rates and liquidation preferences with those of preferred stock issued by publicly traded corporations having similar assets and engaging in similar businesses. Additional factors to be considered are the voting rights of the stock, any covenants restricting its transfer, and the corporation's ability to honor any redemption privilege.

The value of the common stock issued in such a recapitalization, according to the IRS, is largely dependent on the corporation's past growth experience, the economic condition of the industry in which the corporation operates, and general economic conditions. However, under certain circumstances, voting rights of the preferred stock could increase the value of the preferred stock and reduce the value of the common stock, especially if the preferred stock has voting control of the corporation.

¶ 327 Worthless Securities

Securities reported on the estate tax return as without value, with nominal value, or obsolete should be listed last on Schedule B (Stocks and Bonds) of Form 706 (United States Estate (and Generation-Skipping Transfer) Tax Return). The address of the company, the state in which it is incorporated, and the date of incorporation should be stated. Copies of correspondence or statements used as the basis for determining that the stock is without value should be attached.

¶ 328 Mutual Fund Shares

The fair market value of shares in open-end investment companies (mutual funds) is to be set at the "bid" or public redemption price of such shares at the date of death or on the alternate valuation date if the alternate valuation method is elected.[51] In the absence of an affirmative showing of the public redemption price in effect at the time of death, the last public redemption price quoted by the company for the date of death is presumed to be the applicable public redemption price. If there is no public redemption price quoted by the company for the applicable valuation date (for example, where the valuation date is a Saturday, Sunday, or holiday), the mutual fund shares are valued by using the last public redemption price quoted by the company for the first day preceding the applicable valuation date for which there is a quotation.[52]

¶ 329 Tax-Exempt Bonds

With respect to securities of privately owned corporations, the question of taxability does not arise. If the securities were held by the decedent at the time of death (see ¶310), or if the decedent transferred them during life in a manner coming within the definitions of taxable transfers (see ¶550), the value of the

---

[49] Code Sec. 2701 through Code Sec. 2704.

[50] Rev. Rul. 83-120, 1983-2 CB 170, amplifying Rev. Rul. 59-60, 1959-1 CB 237.

[51] Reg. § 20.2031-8(b); *D.B. Cartwright*, SCt, 73-1 USTC ¶12,926, 411 US 546.

[52] Reg. § 20.2031-8(b).

securities is includible in the decedent's estate. However, where the securities involved are securities of government-created public corporations or entities, another question arises: What is the effect of provisions stating that the securities shall be exempt from tax? The courts almost invariably answer this question by stating that the federal estate tax is a tax on the transfer of property and not on the property itself—that the exemption granted the securities is an exemption from taxes on the property itself and not an exemption from excise taxes.

The various statutory provisions that exempt bonds, bills, notes, and certificates of indebtedness of the federal government or its agencies (and the interest thereon) from taxation are not applicable to estate and gift taxes. U.S. government bonds, U.S. Treasury bonds, and U.S. savings bonds are all subject to federal estate and gift taxation. Similarly, despite state statutory exemptions, state and municipal bonds are subject to estate and gift taxation. However, such bonds issued prior to March 1, 1941, and beneficially owned by a nonresident who is not a U.S. citizen and is not engaged in business in the United States at the time of death are exempt from tax because they are considered "situated outside the United States."[53]

• *Anti-* ***Haffner*** *Provision*

The Tax Reform Act of 1984 (P.L. 98-369) provided that nothing in any provision of law exempting any property from taxation will exempt the transfer of such property (or interest therein) from federal estate, gift, and generation-skipping transfer taxes.[54] This provision, in effect, reverses the decision of a U.S. district court in Illinois (later affirmed by the U.S. Court of Appeals for the Seventh Circuit) that public housing agency bonds owned by a decedent were exempt from estate taxes under a provision of the Federal Housing Act of 1937.[55] This rule, also referred to as the "anti-*Haffner* provision," is effective with respect to the estates of decedents dying, and gifts and transfers made, on or after June 19, 1984.[56]

Although the anti-*Haffner* provision was ruled unconstitutional by a U.S. district court, that decision has been reversed by the U.S. Supreme Court in *Wells Fargo Bank*.[57] The district court had held that the provision was unconstitutional because the amended legislation amounted to the imposition of a wholly new tax and the retroactive application of that tax would constitute a constitutional violation of due process and equal protection. The Supreme Court, however, held that the language of Section 5(e) of the Housing Act of 1937 exempting property from all taxation applied only to direct taxes, such as the federal income tax, but not to excise taxes, such as the federal estate tax. Because it concluded that the Housing Act did not create an estate tax exemption, the Court found it unnecessary to rule on the constitutionality of the 1984 Tax Reform Act provision.

Basing its reasoning on the principle that a tax exemption cannot be implied, the Tax Court has also refused to infer an exemption from the estate tax for public housing agency bonds. The Tax Court has concluded that because public housing agency bonds had never expressly been exempted from the federal estate tax, their value was includible in the decedent's gross estate.[58] According

---

[53] Reg. § 20.2105-1.

[54] Act Sec. 641(a), P.L. 98-369.

[55] C.C. *Haffner III, Exr.*, 84-1 USTC ¶ 13,571, 585 FSupp. 354, aff'd, CA-7, 85-1 USTC ¶ 13,611.

[56] Act Sec. 641(b)(1), P.L. 98-369.

[57] *Wells Fargo Bank et al.*, SCt, 88-1 USTC ¶ 13,759 (consolidated with *H. Rosenberg*), rev'g DC Cal., 86-2 USTC ¶ 13,703.

[58] *L.G. Egger Est.*, 89 TC 726, CCH Dec. 44,251.

to the Tax Court, the exemption contained in the Housing Act applied to direct taxes (such as the income tax) and not to the federal estate tax on transfers of property.

The 1984 Act also provides that any provision of law enacted on or after June 19, 1984, will not be construed as exempting the transfer of property from federal estate, gift, and generation-skipping transfer taxes, unless the provision refers to an appropriate rule under the Internal Revenue Code.[59] The rule denying exemption from estate and gift taxes also applies with respect to any property that was reported on an estate or gift tax return as subject to estate or gift tax.[60] Finally, with respect to a transfer of property (or interest therein) made before June 19, 1984, the Act provides that no inference is to arise that such transfer is exempt from federal estate and gift taxation.[61]

• *Reporting Requirements*

Taxpayers are required to provide the IRS with relevant information regarding the transfer of public housing bonds of a type that the district court in *Haffner* held were exempt from estate taxes. This provision is effective with respect to transfers of public housing bonds occurring after 1983 and before June 19, 1984.[62]

¶ 330 U.S. Treasury Bonds

U.S. savings bonds purchased by a decedent with the decedent's own funds are includible in the decedent's gross estate if (1) the bonds are registered in the decedent's own name, (2) the bonds are registered in the decedent's own name, but are payable to another person on the purchaser's death, or (3) the bonds are registered in the names of the decedent and another person as co-owners. Bonds purchased with the separate funds of two persons and registered in their names as co-owners are includible in the estate of the first co-owner to die, to the extent of the percentage of the purchase price that the decedent provided.[63] However, the "consideration-furnished" test does not apply to qualified joint interests (see ¶502).

Where the purchaser registers bonds in the purchaser's own name and in the name of another person as co-owners, the bonds must be surrendered to the Treasury Department and be reissued solely in the name of this other person in order to remove them from the purchaser's estate as joint property. The mere physical delivery of such jointly owned bonds to the other person, with the intent to make a gift, will not be recognized so as to remove the bonds from a purchaser's estate.[64]

In determining the value of U.S. savings bonds, a decedent's estate was not entitled to apply a discount for lack of marketability to reflect the income tax due on interest that had accrued on the bonds.[65] In so ruling, the IRS distinguished court holdings in *A. Davis Est.*[66] and *I. Eisenberg*[67] (see ¶326, under the heading "Liquidation Discount"), in which liquidation discounts on close corporation stock were allowed based on the conclusion that a hypothetical willing buyer would negotiate a discounted purchase price for the acquisition of stock because

---

[59] Act Sec. 641(a), P.L. 98-369.

[60] Act Sec. 641(b)(2), P.L. 98-369.

[61] Act Sec. 641(b)(3), P.L. 98-369.

[62] Act Sec. 642(a), P.L. 98-369.

[63] Rev. Rul. 68-269, 1968-1 CB 399.

[64] *E.G. Chandler, Exr. (M.E. Baum Will)*, SCt, 73-1 USTC ¶12,902, 410 US 257.

[65] IRS Technical Advice Memorandum 200303010 (Sept. 19, 2002).

[66] *A. Davis Est.*, 110 TC 530, CCH Dec. 52,764.

[67] *I. Eisenberg*, CA-2, 98-2 USTC ¶60,322, 155 F3d 50 (Acq.), rev'g and rem'g 74 TCM 1046, CCH Dec. 52,321(M), TC Memo. 1997-483.

the corporation owned appreciated assets with built-in capital gains. This rationale did not apply to the U.S. savings bonds, the IRS reasoned, because the U.S. government was the only buyer, and the sales price was fixed by contractual agreement at the time of original purchase.

• *Flower Bonds*

Certain issues of U.S. Treasury bonds were redeemable at their par value and accrued interest in payment of a deceased owner's federal estate taxes. All of these bonds (often known as "flower bonds") had redemption dates of November 15, 1998, or before (see ¶1665), so they are no longer viable as a tax planning device. The following discussion of flower bonds is preserved for open estates that redeemed such bonds in payment of estate tax.

If the quoted market price of such flower bonds is higher than their stated par value, they must be reported at their quoted selling price, plus accrued interest to the date of death.

If the par value is the higher value, all the Treasury bonds that actually can be applied against the tax must be included in the decedent's gross estate at their par value (and accrued interest) whether or not the estate representative elects to redeem them in payment of estate taxes. This is true even if the executor sold the bonds after the estate tax return was filed but before issuance of a notice of a deficiency against which the bonds could have been applied.[68] Those U.S. Treasury bonds in excess of a value that can be applied to the decedent's estate tax may be reported at their mean quoted market price (and accrued interest to the date of death).[69]

> ***Example:*** At the time of his death, X.L. Cant owned, in addition to other properties of substantial value, four U.S. Treasury bonds. Each bond had a redemption and par value of $100,000. All four were of an issue that could be applied, prior to maturity or call redemption date, at par value and accrued interest in payment of federal estate taxes.
>
> On the date of Cant's death, each bond had a current market quotation of $86,562. The executor of his estate, in preparing the estate tax return, determined that taxes amounting to $500,215 were payable by the estate. However, he decided to apply only two of the Treasury bonds (before maturity or call redemption date) in payment of the estate taxes owing. *All four* Treasury bonds are, nevertheless, includible in the gross estate at their par value.

¶ 331 Nonresidents Not Citizens

Except as indicated below, only property located in the United States is includible in the gross estate of a nonresident alien decedent.[70] The notable exception to this general situs rule is the stock of domestic corporations, which is includible in a decedent's gross estate, regardless of where it is located. Likewise, except as mentioned below, debt obligations (bonds, etc.) that are owned and held by a nonresident alien are considered property located within the United States if the primary obligor is a domestic corporation or other U.S. person, the United States, a state, a political subdivision of a state, or the District of Columbia.[71] For this purpose, it is immaterial whether the written evidence of the debt

---

[68] *E.G. Simmie Est.*, CA-9, 80-2 USTC ¶13,377, 632 F2d 93, and Rev. Rul. 81-228, 1981-2 CB 171.

[69] Rev. Rul. 69-489, 1969-2 CB 172.

[70] Code Sec. 2103.

[71] Code Sec. 2104.

obligation is treated as being the property itself. Currency, however, is not to be considered a debt obligation.

Short-term original issue discount obligations will not be treated as U.S. situs property for estates of decedents dying after August 5, 1997. For this purpose, a short-term obligation means an obligation payable 183 days or less from the date of the obligation's issue.[72] Additionally, debts of a domestic corporation deriving less than 20 percent of its gross income from U.S. sources for the three-year period prior to the nonresident's death are not considered as having a situs in the United States. Other debt obligations are not, according to the House Ways & Means Committee Report to the Foreign Investors Tax Act of 1966 (P.L. 89-809), to be considered property within the United States even if written evidence of the obligation that is considered as the property itself is located in the United States.[73]

The situs rules may, however, be modified by a death tax treaty with the country of domicile of the decedent (see also ¶1615).

---

[72] Code Sec. 2105(b)(4).

[73] House Ways & Means Committee Report to the Foreign Investors Tax Act of 1966 (P.L. 89-809).

Chapter 10

MORTGAGES, NOTES, CONTRACTS TO SELL LAND, AND CASH

¶ 350 Inclusion in Gross Estate

As with property interests reportable in schedules concerned with real property and stocks and bonds, the taxability of mortgages, notes, contracts to sell land, and cash is generally determined under Code Sec. 2033. These items must be valued as of the date of decedent's death unless the executor elects to have them valued as of the alternate valuation date. They are reported on Schedule C (Mortgages, Notes, and Cash) of Form 706 (United States Estate (and Generation-Skipping Transfer) Tax Return) (Rev. Aug. 2004). This schedule does not have to be filed if the decedent did not own property reportable on it.

¶ 355 Mortgages and Notes

In describing mortgages on the estate tax return (Form 706, United States Estate (and Generation-Skipping Transfer) Tax Return), the following information should be set out:

(1) face value and unpaid balance;

(2) date of mortgage;

(3) date of maturity;

(4) name of maker;

(5) property subject to mortgage; and

(6) interest dates and rate of interest.

Similar data should be shown when reporting notes.

The value of notes, whether secured or unsecured, is the amount of unpaid principal, together with accrued interest, unless the estate representative establishes a lower value or proves them worthless. If included on the return at less than face value, plus interest, the lower value must be established by satisfactory evidence. A lower value may be justified because of the interest rate or date of maturity. For example, the IRS National Office has ruled that the estate tax value of an installment note payable to a decedent was less than its face value because the note provided for payment of interest at a rate below the prevailing interest rate on the date of the decedent's death.[1] If a note is wholly or partially uncollectible because of insolvency of the debtors or any collateral for the loan is insufficient to satisfy the debt, a lower valuation is permitted.[2]

If an estate contends that the actual value of mortgages or mortgage participation certificates is less than their face value, the controlling valuation factors include (1) the valuation of real estate and any collateral covered by the mortgages, (2) arrearages in taxes and interest, (3) gross and net rentals, (4) foreclosure

---

[1] IRS Technical Advice Memorandum 8229001 (Feb. 1, 1982).

[2] Reg. § 20.2031-4.

proceedings, (5) assignment of rents, (6) prior liens or encumbrances, (7) present interest yield, (8) over-the-counter sales, and (9) bid and asked quotations. The existence of an over-the-counter market for mortgage notes and certificates and the quotations and opinions furnished by brokers and real estate appraisers will not be accepted by the IRS as conclusive evidence of their value. Where the mortgage is amply secured, the value will be the mortgage's face value plus accrued interest to date of death. Where the security is insufficient, the mortgage will be valued on the basis of the fair market value of the property less back taxes, estimated foreclosure expenses, and, where justified, the expense of rehabilitation. The estate must prove the lesser value.[3]

• *Self-Canceling Notes*

Promissory notes that by their terms are deemed canceled on the death of the payee may escape estate taxation at the payee's death, provided that the cancellation provision is part of a bargained-for exchange supported by full and adequate consideration. In so ruling, the Tax Court distinguished the situation where a decedent tries to avoid estate taxation on promissory notes held at death by canceling the indebtedness by a will provision or separate writing.[4] With regard to the income tax consequences of a cancellation of an installment obligation at death, the U.S. Court of Appeals for the Eighth Circuit agreed with the IRS[5] that the payee's estate would have to recognize, as income in respect of a decedent, deferred installment gain on the notes. Although not part of the formal holding of the case, the appellate court noted, consistent with taxing gain to the estate, that the obligor of a self-canceling installment note would have a basis in the purchased property equal to the note's face value, not just the amount of principal actually paid.[6]

¶ 360 Contracts to Sell Land

In reporting a contract to sell land on the estate tax return, it is necessary to provide the following information:

(1) name of purchaser;

(2) date of contract;

(3) description of property to be sold;

(4) sale price;

(5) initial payment;

(6) amounts of installment payments;

(7) unpaid balance of principal; and

(8) interest rate.

The listing of contracts to sell realty is a listing in lieu of the realty. If the decedent has an unpaid mortgage or other indebtedness on the property being sold under the contract and the decedent's estate is liable for it, the full value of the contract must be included as part of the gross estate. The mortgage or indebtedness is allowed as a deduction in such a case. If the decedent's estate is not liable, only the value of the redemption equity (or the value of the contract, less the mortgage or indebtedness) need be reported as part of the value in the gross estate. In no case may the deduction on account of the mortgage exceed the

---

[3] Rev. Rul. 67-276, 1967-2 CB 321.

[4] *J.A. Moss.*, 74 TC 1239, CCH Dec. 37,230 (Acq.).

[5] Rev. Rul. 86-72, 1986-1 CB 253.

[6] *J. Frane Est.*, CA-8, 93-2 USTC ¶50,386, 998 F2d 567.

liability actually contracted for. Only interest accrued to the date of the decedent's death is deductible even though the alternative valuation method is elected.[7]

¶ 365 Cash

In reporting cash on the estate tax return, cash in the decedent's possession should be listed separately from cash deposited in banks or other financial organizations.

In reporting cash deposited in financial organizations, the return should show:

(1) name and address of each organization;

(2) amount in each account;

(3) serial number or account number;

(4) nature of accounts (checking, savings, time deposit, etc.); and

(5) unpaid interest accrued from date of last interest payment to the date of death.

If statements are obtained from the financial organizations, they should be retained for inspection by the IRS.

Cash that belongs to the decedent at the time of death must be reported in full, whether in the decedent's or another's possession and whether it is on deposit in a bank. Checks outstanding at the time of death may be subtracted from the total if they are subsequently honored and charged against the decedent's account, but only if the obligation is not claimed as a deduction.[8] The amount of any check that was given under circumstances indicating a taxable lifetime transfer cannot be claimed as a deduction.

If interest on a particular savings bank account does not accrue between interest payment dates, no interest between the last interest payment date and the date of decedent's death should be included in the valuation.[9] However, if certificates of deposit can be redeemed without forfeiture of interest on the death of the owner, the interest accrued but unpaid at death is includible in the value of the certificates for estate tax purposes even if the interest would have been forfeited had the decedent redeemed the certificates prior to death.[10]

U.S. silver coins (or paper currency) that are held by a decedent at the time of death and that are worth more than their face value must be valued at their fair market value for estate tax purposes, even if the decedent had never been a coin collector.[11] If the cash consists of foreign currency or foreign bank accounts, the value should be stated in terms of the official rate of exchange.[12] Restrictions or difficulties concerning convertibility can justify a lower value.

---

[7] Reg. §20.2053-7.

[8] Reg. §20.2031-5.

[9] Rev. Rul. 55-301, 1955-1 CB 442.

[10] Rev. Rul. 79-340, 1979-2 CB 320.

[11] Rev. Rul. 78-360, 1978-2 CB 228.

[12] *A. Fry Est.*, 9 TC 503, CCH Dec. 16,030 (Acq.).

Chapter 11
LIFE INSURANCE

¶ 400 Inclusion of Life Insurance

Life insurance, for estate tax purposes, includes not only the common forms of insurance taken out by an individual on the individual's own life, but also the proceeds of certain other types of insurance policies. Proceeds of accident insurance policies, including flight insurance of the type commonly purchased at air terminals, are proceeds of life insurance for estate tax purposes.[1] Similarly included are proceeds of War Risk insurance and of National Service Life insurance. Amounts paid under group insurance and under double indemnity clauses by reason of the accidental death of an insured are also treated as the proceeds of life insurance.

The more common forms of insurance that are regarded as life insurance are ordinary life, universal life, variable life, limited payment life, endowment, term insurance, survivor life policies, split-dollar arrangements, and retired lives reserves insurance.

Insurance that a decedent may have taken out on the life of another individual is not taxed under the insurance provision of Code Sec. 2042, but, rather, under the general taxing rules of Code Sec. 2033.

The fact that a contract is called an insurance contract does not automatically entitle it to treatment as insurance for estate tax purposes if it is not, in fact, a contract of insurance. To be an insurance contract, an element of risk must be involved. The risk must be an actuarial one under which the premium cost is based on the likelihood that the insured will live for a certain period of time and under which the insurer stands to suffer a loss if the insured does not, in fact, live for the expected period.

---

[1] *M.L. Noel Est.*, SCt, 65-1 USTC ¶ 12,311, 380 US 678.

The IRS has ruled that the value of no-fault death benefits payable to the estates of a driver and a passenger who were killed in an automobile accident was includible in their gross estates as the proceeds of life insurance policies. This was so because, under applicable state law, payment of the death benefits did not preclude the decedents' estates or heirs from bringing wrongful death actions. Accordingly, because the insurer was unconditionally bound to make payment in the event of the insureds' deaths, the no-fault insurance policy had the necessary risk-shifting and risk-distributing elements necessary to be considered life insurance for purposes of Code Sec. 2042.[2]

Insurance on the decedent's life is reported on Schedule D (Insurance on the Decedent's Life) of Form 706 (United States Estate (and Generation-Skipping Transfer) Tax Return) (Rev. Aug. 2004). Schedule D does not have to be filed with the return where there is no insurance on the decedent's life. Insurance on another person's life, which is includible in the decedent's gross estate, is not reportable on Schedule D. Rather, it must be reported on Schedule F (Other Miscellaneous Property Not Reportable Under Any Other Schedule).

¶ 403 Group Insurance

Proceeds of group life insurance are treated the same as the proceeds of any other insurance. Generally, they are includible in the estate of the insured because the insured has incidents of ownership, or is regarded as having them, at the time of death.

• *Assignability*

A group-term life insurance policy, the cost of which is paid by the employer, is excludable from the estate of a deceased employee if the decedent has irrevocably assigned all interest in the policy and did not die within three years of making the assignment.[3] The assignment, in order to be valid, must not be prohibited by state law or by the terms of the policy. Most states now have specific laws permitting assignments of group life insurance policies by insured employees. However, where state law fails to affirmatively provide for assignment, but does not expressly prohibit it, it may be possible to assign the policy and to remove it from the employee's estate.[4]

The IRS will recognize assignments made by employees in those cases where the master policy permits assignments and the individual policy certificates issued to employees do not.[5] On the other hand, where the master policy did not permit assignments, an attempted assignment was held to be invalid, and the proceeds of the policy were includible in an insured-employee's gross estate.[6]

Estates of stockholder-employees of closely held corporations may face difficulty if they attempt to exclude previously assigned group life insurance from the decedent's gross estate.[7] The government has argued that a controlling stockholder had incidents of ownership over a group policy because of his right to surrender or cancel the policy while acting as a corporate officer. The U.S. Court of Claims rejected this argument in a situation involving a corporation jointly owned by two unrelated officers. However, the court indicated that this

---

[2] Rev. Rul. 83-44, 1983-1 CB 228.

[3] Code Sec. 2035.

[4] *M.J. Gorby Est.*, 53 TC 80, CCH Dec. 29,801 (Acq.); *L. Landorf, Exr.*, CtCls, 69-1 USTC ¶ 12,593, 408 F2d 461.

[5] *M.J. Gorby Est.*, 53 TC 80, CCH Dec. 29,801 (Acq.).

[6] *S.F. Bartlett Est.*, 54 TC 1590, CCH Dec. 30,278 (Acq.).

[7] *L. Landorf, Exr.*, CtCls, 69-1 USTC ¶ 12,593, 408 F2d 461.

power might exist where the decedent was the sole stockholder or, in effect, had control over minority stockholder-officers. Presently, this question remains unresolved. For corporate-owned group-term life insurance where the decedent is the sole or controlling stockholder, the power to surrender or cancel a policy held by the corporation will not be attributed to the decedent through the decedent's stock ownership to the extent the proceeds of the policy are payable to the corporation.[8] Also, the IRS has privately ruled that the sole shareholder of a closely held corporation did not possess incidents of ownership in a life insurance policy on his own life, despite his ability to terminate the policy beneficiary's employment contract, causing the distribution of insurance proceeds to a trust for the benefit of the shareholder's family.[9]

A post-1976 assignment of a group policy made by an employee within three years of death evidently will be automatically includible in the employee's estate. However, an assignment of a group-term policy within three years of death will not result in inclusion of the policy in the transferor's gross estate if the assignment was necessitated by the employer's change of insurance carrier and was made pursuant to an "anticipatory assignment" of all present and future employer-provided policies executed more than three years before the transferor's death (see ¶555).[10]

• ***Conversion Privilege***

A group-term life insurance policy can be excluded from the estate of a deceased employee even though neither the policy nor state law gives the employee the right to convert the group-term coverage to individual life insurance on termination of employment, provided the employee has irrevocably assigned all interests in such policy, and such assignment is not prohibited by state law or the policy.[11] This is true because the power to cancel the group-term policy solely by terminating employment is not considered to be an incident of insurance ownership.

In addition, the Tax Court has held, and the IRS has agreed, that a decedent's right to convert an employer-owned group policy of insurance on his life to individual insurance on termination of employment is not an incident of ownership in the policy.[12] In the view of the court and the IRS, termination of employment by an employer is not within a decedent's control, and voluntary termination would be so detrimental to an employee's economic position that a conversion privilege should not be considered an incident of ownership. Therefore, if a decedent transfers all incidents of ownership in the policy, but retains the right to convert the group coverage to an individual policy on termination of employment, the proceeds of the group policy are not includible in the decedent's gross estate.

• ***Settlement Options***

It is an open question whether the proceeds of a noncontributory group-term life insurance policy are includible in an employee's gross estate where the employee has the right to vary the time and manner in which the proceeds are payable to the beneficiaries even though, under the policy, the employee cannot

---

[8] Reg. §20.2042-1(c).

[9] IRS Letter Ruling 9421037 (Feb. 28, 1994).

[10] Rev. Rul. 80-289, 1980-2 CB 270, revoking Rev. Rul. 79-231, 1979-2 CB 323.

[11] Rev. Rul. 72-307, 1972-1 CB 307, modifying Rev. Rul. 69-54, 1969-1 CB 221.

[12] *J. Smead Est.*, 78 TC 43, CCH Dec. 38,722 (Acq.); Rev. Rul. 84-130, 1984-2 CB 194.

benefit himself or his estate.[13] The IRS maintains that the right to elect optional modes of settlement for the proceeds of life insurance on a decedent's life is an incident of ownership within the meaning of Code Sec. 2042. In addition, the IRS has announced that it will not follow the decision of the U.S. Court of Appeals for the Third Circuit in *Connelly*, which holds that the right to select such optional settlement modes is not an incident of ownership within the meaning of Code Sec. 2042 if the option merely allows the decedent to alter the time of enjoyment of the insurance proceeds.[14]

¶ 405 Death Benefits

Death benefits, payable other than under a life insurance contract, do not ordinarily qualify as proceeds of insurance. Benefits paid by employers, for example, voluntarily or otherwise, usually are lacking in some of the elements essential for qualification as insurance (see ¶420 and ¶733 for further details).

¶ 410 Insurance on the Life of Another

If a person, at the time of death, owns policies of insurance on the life of another individual, the value of such insurance is includible in the decedent's gross estate, but not as proceeds of insurance. It is included in the decedent's estate under Code Sec. 2033 as property in which the decedent had an interest at the time of death. It must be reported on Schedule F (Other Miscellaneous Property Not Reportable Under Any Other Schedule) of Form 706 (United States Estate (and Generation-Skipping Transfer) Tax Return).

The value of such insurance is the cost of replacement and not the cash surrender value. Replacement cost is the cost of buying another policy of the same value and same status on the life of the same insured. This cost can only be obtained from the insurer. If the policy has been in force for some time at the decedent's death and further premiums are to be paid, the value may be approximated by adding to the interpolated terminal reserve at the date of the decedent's death the proportionate part of the gross premium last paid before the decedent's death that covers the period extending beyond death.[15]

Conflict exists in those cases where a beneficiary-owner and the insured person die simultaneously. The IRS takes the position that the entire proceeds of a policy are to be included in the owner-beneficiary's gross estate. The courts have almost uniformly rejected this view and have held that the policy is to be valued under the interpolated terminal reserve method in accordance with Reg. §20.2031-8.[16]

If, however, a policy is sold to the insured within six months following the death of the person who owned the policy, and the estate is valued as of a date six months after the death, the amount received on the sale of the policy will govern its value for estate tax purposes. Likewise, if the policy is actually surrendered for cash during the alternate valuation period after death, the amount received should be the acceptable value. If premiums are paid by the

---

[13] See *J.H. Lumpkin, Jr., Est.*, CA-5, 73-1 USTC ¶12,909, 474 F2d 1092; *J.J. Connelly, Sr., Est.*, CA-3, 77-1 USTC ¶13,179, 551 F2d 545.

[14] Rev. Rul. 81-128, 1981-1 CB 469.

[15] Reg. §20.2031-8(a)(2).

[16] *N. Meltzer Est.*, CA-4, 71-1 USTC ¶12,754, rev'g TC, 29 TCM 265, CCH Dec. 30,004(M), TC Memo. 1970-62; *Old Kent Bank*, CA-6, 70-2 USTC ¶12,703, 430 F2d 392; *R.M. Chown Est.*, CA-9, 70-2 USTC ¶12,702, 428 F2d 1395, rev'g TC, 51 TC 140, CCH Dec. 29,202; *E.M. Wien Est.*, CA-5, 71-1 USTC ¶12,764, 441 F2d 32, rev'g TC, 51 TC 287, CCH Dec. 29,238; *E.W. Marks, Jr., Est.*, 94 TC 720, CCH Dec. 46,594.

estate preceding the sale, it is likely that the value will be the total proceeds reduced by the portion attributable to the premiums paid after death.

See also ¶112 as to appreciation in value of insurance policies during the alternate valuation period.

¶415 Life Insurance and Annuity Combination

Persons who cannot pass the physical examination on which the issuance of the usual type of life insurance contract is predicated may purchase a special type of insurance and annuity combination. The insurance portion of such a combination cannot be purchased separately. It is issued on the assumption that, if the purchaser does not live long enough to receive full benefits from the annuity portion of the combination, the amount left over from the cost of that portion will make up the difference between the price paid for the insurance portion and the total amount of the death benefit. If the person does live to receive full benefits from the annuity portion, the money paid for the insurance portion will have gathered interest for a period long enough to build up the full amount of the death benefit. The insurance company actually takes no risk.

Formerly, it was generally believed that the insurance portion of such a combination was excludable from an insured decedent's estate where the decedent had irrevocably assigned all rights in the policy to the named beneficiaries.[17] However, this tax-saving technique was apparently eliminated by a 1972 case.[18] In this case, the IRS claimed, and the Tax Court and the U.S. Court of Appeals for the Fifth Circuit agreed, that the insurance and annuity contracts were part of one transaction and, therefore, the insurance portion was includible in the decedent's estate as an annuity under Code Sec. 2039. Both courts held that the *Fidelity-Philadelphia Trust Co.* case was not controlling because it was decided before Code Sec. 2039 was enacted.

¶420 Death Benefits Under Retirement Plans

Life insurance proceeds paid under a qualified pension or profit-sharing plan are includible in the gross estate under Code Sec. 2042 (dealing with insurance), rather than Code Sec. 2039 (dealing with annuities).[19] Thus, it may be possible to have the insurance proceeds excluded from the employee's gross estate by having the employee-plan participant transfer all incidents of ownership in the policy to someone else. To be effective, this transfer would have to take place more than three years before the participant's death.

The inclusion of payments from a nonqualified employees' plan or contract depends on whether the payment is, in fact, the payment of proceeds of insurance under a policy on the life of the employee or whether the payment, in fact, represents an annuity payment.[20] (Typically, such plans provide for pension payments and for the payment of a death benefit where the employee dies before retirement.) If the payment represents insurance proceeds, the inclusion of the payment depends on whether the decedent-employee has retained "incidents of ownership" over the policy (see ¶430). If the payment is an annuity, the estate tax treatment of the payment is based on the annuity rules discussed beginning at ¶700.

---

[17] *Fidelity-Philadelphia Trust Co., Exr. (M. Haines Est.)*, SCt, 58-1 USTC ¶11,761, 356 US 274.

[18] *L. Montgomery Est.*, 56 TC 489, CCH Dec. 30,822, aff'd per curiam, CA-5, 72-1 USTC ¶12,840, cert. denied, 409 US 849; *I.T. Sussman, Exr. (J. Sussman Will)*, DC N.Y., 76-1 USTC ¶13,126.

[19] Reg. §20.2039-1(d).

[20] Reg. §20.2039-1(d).

¶ 425 Refunds in Case of Suicide

If an insured commits suicide before a policy becomes incontestable, the beneficiary will receive only a refund of premiums instead of the face amount. This refund does not constitute a payment of insurance proceeds.[21]

¶ 430 Proceeds Payable to Named Beneficiaries

Life insurance payable to named beneficiaries is subject to special rules. If the insured merely names the beneficiary, but disposes of none, or only some, of the rights that the insured normally receives under the terms of a policy, the proceeds will be includible in the decedent-insured's gross estate just like any other property. On the other hand, if the insured disposes of all rights over the policy (incidents of ownership), the entire amount of the proceeds may be kept out of the decedent's gross estate.[22]

Insurance is considered payable to a "named beneficiary" (one other than the estate) when the recipient is not required to use any of the proceeds for the benefit of the estate. Therefore, it may be paid to an executor if the executor may keep the proceeds for the executor's own benefit. It may be paid to a trustee if the trustee is not charged with a duty to apply the proceeds in payment of taxes or other estate charges. Likewise, it may be paid to a corporation, a partnership, or a profit-sharing plan.

The term "incidents of ownership" is not limited in its meaning to ownership of the policy in the technical, legal sense. The term refers to the right of the insured or the insured's estate to the economic benefits of the policy. The retention of any of the following will result in inclusion of the insurance proceeds in the gross estate:[23]

(1) the right to change beneficiaries or their shares;

(2) the right to surrender the policy for cash or to cancel it;

(3) the right to borrow against the policy reserve;

(4) the right to pledge the policy as collateral;

(5) the right to assign the policy or to revoke an assignment;

(6) the right to prevent cancellation of an insurance policy owned by an employer by purchasing the policy for its cash surrender value;[24] and

(7) a reversionary interest by which the insured or the estate of the insured may regain one or more of the above rights in the event a beneficiary should predecease the insured or if certain other contingencies should occur. (The chances that the right or rights will return to the insured must exceed five percent of the value of the policy immediately before the death of the insured.)

The possession of any of the above rights will result in inclusion of the proceeds in the insured's gross estate even if the consent of some other person is necessary for the exercise of the right. Estate tax liability depends on a general,

---

[21] *W.D. Chew, Jr., Est.*, CA-5, 45-1 USTC ¶10,181, 148 F2d 76, aff'g TC, 3 TC 940, CCH Dec. 13,953, cert. denied, 325 US 882.

[22] Code Sec. 2042; Reg. §20.2042-1(c).

[23] Code Sec. 2042; Reg. §20.2042-1(c).

[24] Rev. Rul. 79-46, 1979-1 CB 303. The Tax Court, however, has indicated that such a right is too contingent to warrant inclusion of policy proceeds in the gross estate; see, e.g., *J.C. Morrow Est.*, 19 TC 1068, CCH Dec. 19,510, and *J. Smith Est.*, 73 TC 307, CCH Dec. 36,443.

legal power to exercise ownership, without regard to actual ability to exercise it at a particular moment (as on a trans-Atlantic flight).

• *Insured Decedent as Trustee*

Powers held by a decedent as fiduciary with respect to an insurance policy on his or her life will not constitute incidents of ownership in the policy so long as (1) the powers are not exercisable for the decedent's personal benefit, (2) the decedent did not directly transfer the policy or any of the consideration for purchasing or maintaining the policy to the trust, and (3) the decedent did not retain the powers as settlor of the trust.[25] Where all of the above conditions are met, a decedent-trustee will not be deemed to have incidents of ownership in the policy even if the decedent held, at the time of death, such broad discretionary powers over the policy as the right to elect to have the proceeds made payable according to various plans, to use the loan value to pay the premiums, to borrow on the policy, to assign or pledge the policy, or to elect to receive annual dividends.[26] This IRS position is consistent with the decisions of several appellate courts.[27]

• *Transfers Within Three Years of Death*

The gross estate of a decedent who transferred all rights over an insurance policy on the decedent's life within three years of death and after 1976 includes the entire proceeds of the policy.[28] However, the proceeds are not reported on Schedule D (Insurance on the Decedent's Life) of Form 706 (United States Estate (and Generation-Skipping Transfer) Tax Return); rather, they are reported on Schedule G (Transfers During Decedent's Life).[29]

Some courts have held that, if a policy of insurance on the life of a decedent is issued within three years of death and the decedent pays the premiums, the policy proceeds are includible in the decedent's gross estate even if the decedent did not own the policy.[30] In the view of these courts, the decedent in each case effectively transferred the policy within three years of death by having it issued in the name of some other person (usually a family member) and paying the premiums. Although these cases were decided prior to the amendment of Code Sec. 2035 by the Economic Recovery Tax Act of 1981 (P.L. 97-34), the IRS National Office has adopted the reasoning of these courts and ruled that the proceeds of a policy of insurance on a decedent's life purchased within three years of the decedent's death in 1983 were includible in the decedent's gross estate even though the decedent never actually possessed any incidents of ownership in the policy.[31]

However, the U.S. Court of Appeals for the Tenth Circuit has held that the rule requiring inclusion of transfers within three years of death applies only to a gift of life insurance where the decedent retained incidents of ownership in the

[25] Rev. Rul. 84-179, 1984-2 CB 195, revoking Rev. Rul. 76-261, 1976-2 CB 276.

[26] Rev. Rul. 84-179, 1984-2 CB 195, revoking Rev. Rul. 76-261, 1976-2 CB 276.

[27] *H.R. Fruehauf Est.*, CA-6, 70-1 USTC ¶12,688, 427 F2d 80, aff'g TC, 50 TC 915, CCH Dec. 29,146; *H.R. Skifter Est.*, CA-2, 72-2 USTC ¶12,893, 468 F2d 699; and *S.A. Hunter et al.*, CA-8, 80-2 USTC ¶13,362, 624 F2d 833; but see *C.M. Rose*, CA-5, 75-1 USTC ¶13,063, 511 F2d 259; and *N.C. Terriberry*, CA-5, 75-2 USTC ¶13,088, 517 F2d 286, cert. denied, 424 US 977.

[28] Code Sec. 2035.

[29] See Instructions for Form 706 (Rev. Aug. 2004), p. 13.

[30] *D.M. Bel, Exr. (J.A. Bel Will)*, CA-5, 72-1 USTC ¶12,818, 452 F2d 683, cert. denied, 406 US 919; and *First National Bank of Oregon, Exr. (F.M. Slade Est.)*, CA-9, 74-1 USTC ¶12,966, 488 F2d 575.

[31] IRS Technical Advice Memorandum 8509005 (Nov. 28, 1984).

insurance policy under the rules of Code Sec. 2042.[32] Even though the decedent's wholly owned corporation paid the premiums on the policy, only his spouse and children, as owners and beneficiaries of the policy, held incidents of ownership. Thus, the proceeds of the life insurance policy purchased within three years of the decedent's death in 1983 were not includible in his gross estate. Other Tax Court decisions with similar fact situations have been affirmed by the U.S. Courts of Appeal for the Fifth and Sixth Circuits as well.[33] In fact, the U.S. Court of Appeals for the Fifth Circuit held that, following the amendment of Code Sec. 2035, the IRS's position was no longer substantially justified.[34]

On the other hand, the Tax Court has also held that an insurance policy on a decedent's life that was purchased by his spouse within three years of his death was includible in his gross estate in proportion to the decedent's interest in the community funds used to pay the policy premium.[35] The court stated that the payment of the policy premiums out of community property funds effected a "transfer" by the decedent of his interest in those funds, and that the ultimate effect of the transaction was similar to that which would have occurred had the decedent purchased the policy himself and then transferred all incidents of ownership to his wife.

A variation of this reasoning has been applied by some courts to require inclusion of proceeds in the gross estate where the decedent transferred funds to a trust within three years of death and the trustee purchased the policy. Two courts have held the proceeds to be includible in such a situation on the ground that the trustee acted as the decedent's agent in purchasing the policy.[36] Another court held that the proceeds would be includible in the decedent's gross estate if it could be shown that a trustee acted as her agent in purchasing a policy within three years of her death, and remanded the case to a lower court for a factual determination of the agency issue.[37] However, the Tax Court has held that even though a decedent created an irrevocable trust that purchased an insurance policy on her life within three years of her death, and she paid the policy premiums, the insurance proceeds were not includible in her gross estate because she did not possess any of the incidents of ownership in the policy.[38]

The Tax Court has held that when a wife purchased a life insurance policy on the life of her husband within three years of his death and paid for the policy out of a joint checking account, no portion of the policy proceeds was includible in the decedent's estate because no agency relationship existed between the decedent and his wife. Therefore, the decedent did not have a transferable interest in the policy that would warrant the inclusion of the insurance proceeds in his gross estate in proportion to his contributions to the joint checking account.[39] In addition, in affirming a decision of the Tax Court, the U.S. Court of

---

[32] *J. Leder Est.*, CA-10, 90-1 USTC ¶60,001, aff'g TC, 89 TC 235, CCH Dec. 44,093.

[33] *F.M. Perry, Sr., Est.*, CA-5, 91-1 USTC ¶60,064, aff'g TC, 59 TCM 65, CCH Dec. 46,442(M); *E.L. Headrick Est.*, CA-6, 90-2 USTC ¶60,049, aff'g TC, 93 TC 171, CCH Dec. 45,914.

[34] *F.M. Perry Est.*, CA-5, 91-1 USTC ¶60,073.

[35] *R.W. Hass Est.*, 51 TCM 453, CCH Dec. 42,874(M), TC Memo. 1986-63. See *M. Baratta-Lorton Est.*, 49 TCM 770, CCH Dec. 41,890(M), TC Memo. 1985-72, aff'd by CA-9, in unpublished opinion, 3-24-86.

[36] *Detroit Bank & Trust Co., Exr. (F.W. Ritter Est.)*, CA-6, 72-2 USTC ¶12,883, 467 F2d 964, cert. denied, 410 US 929; and *T. Kurihara Est.*, 82 TC 51, CCH Dec. 40,914. See also *J. Schnack*, CA-9, 88-1 USTC ¶13,768, 848 F2d 933, rev'g TC, 52 TCM 1107, CCH Dec. 43,518(M), TC Memo. 1986-570.

[37] *G.H. Hope, Exr.*, CA-5, 82-2 USTC ¶13,504, 691 F2d 786.

[38] *M.F. Richins Est.*, 61 TCM 1706, CCH Dec. 47,125(M), TC Memo. 1991-23.

[39] *L.J. Clay Est.*, 86 TC 1266, CCH Dec. 43,128. Cf. *J. Schnack*, CA-9, 88-1 USTC ¶13,768, 848 F2d 933, rev'g TC, 52 TCM

Appeals for the Sixth Circuit has held that life insurance proceeds were not includible in a decedent's gross estate where an *inter vivos* trust purchased the policy and paid the premiums pursuant to a trust agreement that permitted, but did not require, the purchase of the policy. Although the decedent contributed to the trust funds that were used to purchase the policy and pay premiums, this was not considered a sufficient nexus to establish that the decedent was indirectly paying the premiums while the trustee acted as his agent.[40]

Where the decedent-insured transfers a life insurance policy to a transferee within three years of his death and, after the assignment, the transferee pays the insurance premiums, the amount includible in the decedent's gross estate is that portion of the face value equaling the ratio of premiums paid by the decedent to the total premiums paid.[41]

¶ 435 Proceeds Payable for the Benefit of the Estate

Life insurance payable to one's estate, or to an executor or other person for the benefit of the estate, is always includible in the gross estate for estate tax purposes. It is includible even though it may have been purchased by another who retains complete control over the policy during the lifetime of the insured.[42] It is even taxable when made payable to a trustee if the trustee is required to apply the proceeds to the payment of taxes, claims, or administration expenses. If the trustee is merely *permitted* to pay such charges, however, the insurance is subject to the same rules as insurance paid to named beneficiaries.[43]

If the proceeds of an insurance policy made payable to the decedent's estate are community assets under state community property law and, as a result, one-half of the proceeds belong to the decedent's spouse, then only one-half of the proceeds are deemed to be receivable by or for the benefit of the decedent's estate.[44] Where the decedent's spouse dies before the decedent and the community property interest is not partitioned at the time of the spouse's death, the community status of the policy is retained up to the time of maturity, and a tenancy in common is created as of the spouse's date of death.[45]

Where a Louisiana decedent purchased a life insurance policy on the decedent's life during marriage, named the decedent as the policy owner, and did not transfer ownership of the policy, the policy is presumed to be community property under Louisiana law. Accordingly, one-half of the policy proceeds is includible in the decedent's gross estate under Code Sec. 2042 and Reg. § 20.2042-1(c)(5). In the event that the decedent's spouse had predeceased the decedent, one-half of the value of the policy would have been includible in the spouse's gross estate under Code Sec. 2033 and Reg. § 20.2031-8(a)(2).[46] This result is distinguishable where, under Louisiana law, a decedent used community funds to purchase a policy of insurance on the decedent's life and designated the decedent's spouse as the sole owner of the policy. In this case, no

(Footnote Continued)

1107, CCH Dec. 43,518(M), TC Memo. 1986-570.

[40] *E.L. Headrick Est.*, CA-6, 90-2 USTC ¶ 60,049, aff'g TC, 93 TC 171, CCH Dec. 45,914.

[41] *S. Friedberg Est.*, 63 TCM 3080, CCH Dec. 48,254(M), TC Memo. 1992-310.

[42] Reg. § 20.2042-1(b).

[43] *Old Colony Tr. Co., Exr. (Est. of L.E. Flye)*, 39 BTA 871, CCH Dec. 10,687 (Acq. and Nonacq.).

[44] Reg. § 20.2042-1(b).

[45] *H.R. Cavenaugh Est.*, CA-5, 95-1 USTC ¶ 60,195, aff'g in part and rev'g in part TC, 100 TC 407, CCH Dec. 49,030.

[46] *W. Burris Est.*, 82 TCM 400, CCH Dec. 54,444(M), TC Memo. 2001-210; Rev. Rul. 2003-40, IRB 2003-17, 813.

portion of the policy proceeds is includible in the decedent's gross estate at death.[47] But the U.S. Court of Appeals for the Fifth Circuit has held that the entire proceeds of community property life insurance policies on a decedent's life that were designated as payable to his estate were includible in the gross estate.[48] Although premiums were paid with community funds, under Texas law, the entire proceeds of policies made payable to a decedent's estate are includible in the gross estate if designation of the estate as beneficiary was not made in fraud of the decedent's spouse (as found by the Tax Court). The appellate court noted that the insurance proceeds were (1) payable to the decedent's estate, (2) paid to the estate, and (3) allowed to remain in the estate's possession following the surviving spouse's state court challenge regarding her community property interest and, thus, could not be characterized as not "receivable by the executor" as required under Code Sec. 2042(1).

The proceeds of an insurance policy purchased by a decedent in favor of another person or a corporation as collateral security for a loan or other accommodation are also considered to be receivable for the benefit of the estate. However, the amount of the loan outstanding at the date of the decedent's death, with interest accrued thereon to that date, will be deductible in determining the taxable estate.[49]

¶ 440 Proceeds to Pay Estate Taxes

Although attempts have frequently been made to provide an estate tax exemption for the proceeds of insurance that are used to pay estate taxes, none of the attempts in Congress have been successful. If the recipient of the proceeds is required to use them to pay taxes, the proceeds are includible in the gross estate as insurance receivable by the executor. If a person who receives the proceeds would otherwise receive them free of tax, they do not become taxable by that person's election to apply them toward payment of the estate taxes in order to prevent liquidation of other assets.

¶ 445 Marital Deduction

If an insured's spouse is named as the beneficiary under a policy of life insurance and the insured retains no incidents of ownership in the policy, the proceeds will not be included in the insured decedent's gross estate. Consequently, the Code Sec. 2056 marital deduction will not apply.

Insurance proceeds payable to the spouse or to the spouse's estate—either in a lump sum or in installments—on the condition that the spouse survive the insured by as much as six months will qualify for the marital deduction.[50] The proceeds will also qualify if they are left at interest during the life of the surviving spouse, but are to be paid to the spouse's estate or to persons the spouse may appoint following his or her death.[51]

If the insurance proceeds are to be paid to persons that the spouse may appoint, the proceeds will qualify even if provision is made for payment to contingent beneficiaries in the event the spouse fails to exercise the power. If the proceeds are to be paid in installments for at least a certain specified period of

---

[47] Rev. Rul. 94-69, 1994-2 CB 241, revoking Rev. Rul. 48, 1953-1 CB 392, and Rev. Rul. 232, 1953-2 CB 268.

[48] *W. Street Est.*, CA-5, 98-2 USTC ¶ 60,327, aff'g TC, 73 TCM 1787, CCH Dec. 51,834(M), TC Memo. 1997-32.

[49] Reg. § 20.2042-1(b).

[50] Reg. § 20.2056(b)-3.

[51] Reg. § 20.2056(b)-6.

time, or if there is to be a refund of a part of principal in the event that the spouse fails to recover a specified amount in installments, the proceeds will still qualify if any payments following the death of the surviving spouse are to be made to the spouse's estate or to persons he or she may appoint.

¶ 450 Business Insurance

Life insurance is frequently used in connection with various types of business transactions, including the funding of agreements for purchase of an insured's business interest. It may also be purchased to protect a business against loss that might occur on the death of a key employee of the business.

In these situations, the treatment of the insurance for estate tax purposes depends on the terms of the agreement, if any is involved, and on the terms of the insurance contract. In addition to affecting the treatment of the insurance for tax purposes, agreements for the purchase of a business interest can also affect the treatment of the interest itself.

Special problems arise where a closely held corporation owns insurance on the life of a stockholder-employee. The incidents of ownership held by a corporation on a corporate-owned life insurance policy covering a sole or controlling stockholder will not be attributed to the insured stockholder through his stock ownership under Code Sec. 2042 where the proceeds of such policy are received by the corporation or a third party for a valid business purpose.[52] Such proceeds are considered a nonoperating asset of the corporation in determining the stock value includible in the decedent's estate under Reg. § 20.2031-2(f). The Tax Court has ruled that the regulations do not permit the shareholder's stock to be valued by first finding the value of the stock without the insurance proceeds and then adding the proceeds.[53] Rather, the proceeds must be taken into consideration as corporate assets in determining the value of the stock.

Except for group-term life insurance, the incidents of ownership will be attributed to the insured decedent who is the sole or controlling stockholder if such proceeds are not payable to the corporation or a third party for a valid business purpose. For this purpose, a decedent is considered to be the controlling stockholder of a corporation if he owned stock possessing more than 50 percent of the total combined voting power of the corporation at the time of his death. In this regard, the IRS has ruled that life insurance proceeds were includible in a controlling shareholder's gross estate where, within three years of his death, the corporation assigned the policy for less than adequate consideration and the shareholder then disposed of his controlling interest in the corporation. Under similar circumstances, the proceeds were includible where, instead of the corporation assigning the policy, the controlling shareholder disposed of his interest in the corporation for less than adequate consideration.[54] However, in a private ruling, the IRS did not attribute incidents of ownership to the sole shareholder of a corporation who could terminate the employment contract of the beneficiary of a life insurance policy on the shareholder's life, even though the termination would cause the insurance proceeds to be distributed to a trust for the benefit of the shareholder's family.[55]

Even if the insured person is not the sole stockholder, the value of the policy may be includible if the insured retains incidents of ownership in the policy and

---

[52] Reg. § 20.2042-1(c)(6).

[53] *J.L. Huntsman Est.*, 66 TC 861, CCH Dec. 33,976 (Acq.).

[54] Rev. Rul. 90-21, 1990-1 CB 172, amplifying Rev. Rul. 82-141, 1982-2 CB 209.

[55] IRS Letter Ruling 9421037 (Feb. 28, 1994).

the policy is not used to purchase stockholdings. Inclusion resulted in such a case where an insured stockholder had rights of ownership through the policy terms, even though the premiums were paid by the corporation, the policy was assigned by the corporation as collateral for corporate loans, and the cash surrender value was reflected on the corporate books.[56] The terms of the policy should be examined to make sure that the insured has not retained ownership through them. At least one court has ruled that terms of policies could not be rebutted by external evidence that showed that the decedent-insured intended to transfer all ownership rights to a corporation.[57]

¶ 455 Insurance on Stockholder

Life insurance often is used to fund agreements for the purchase and sale of stock in a close corporation following the death of a stockholder. The life insurance proceeds are used to provide part or all of the price for which the stock is to be sold.

The insurance under such an agreement may be purchased by the corporation, by the insured, or by other stockholders. The proceeds may be payable to the corporation, to a trustee, to the insured's estate, or to a person or persons designated by the insured. The agreement may give one or both parties an option, or it may require that the insured's stock be sold by the insured's estate and purchased by the corporation or other stockholders.

If the agreement requires the purchase and sale of the stock following the death of the insured, there will be included in the insured's estate either the value of the stock that is to be sold or the proceeds of the sale of the stock. If the insured has no rights in the insurance policy that would have required inclusion of the proceeds in the insured's estate had no stock transaction been involved, only the value of the stock will be included in the insured's gross estate. Only the value of the stock is includible even if a beneficiary or beneficiaries should actually receive insurance proceeds in excess of the value of the stock. Such a situation, however, is very unlikely. Usually, the insurance proceeds are less than the amount for which the stock is to be sold.

When the agreement for the purchase and sale of the stock is a mandatory one, the agreement normally will serve to limit the amount actually to be included in the estate (but see also ¶ 326, relating to buy-sell agreements for close corporation stock). The estate tax value is limited to the amount for which the stock is actually sold. This assumes that some fair method of valuation is used to arrive at the selling price and that all elements, including goodwill, are accounted for in fixing the value. Thus, if book value is to be the basis for fixing the price, there should be no litigation concerning some other method of valuation.

In situations where the various stockholders themselves purchase the stock (known as cross-purchase arrangements), the one who dies is likely to own insurance on one or more of the other stockholders. This insurance is not treated as life insurance for tax purposes. It is treated as any ordinary estate asset. Its value is the cost of replacement rather than the cash or loan value, unless it is disposed of within six months after death and the estate is valued as of six months after death (see ¶ 410).

---

[56] *G.H. Piggot Est.*, CA-6, 65-1 USTC ¶ 12,290, 340 F2d 829, aff'g TC, 22 TCM 241, CCH Dec. 25,985(M), TC Memo. 1963-61.

[57] *H.B. Cockrill, Exr.*, DC Tenn., 69-2 USTC ¶ 12,610, 302 FSupp. 1365.

The stockholders whose lives are covered by the policies are the most likely purchasers of such insurance. Sometimes the purchase agreement requires that the insureds be given an opportunity to purchase the insurance on their own lives. The purchase opportunity is retained because they may no longer be otherwise insurable. In addition, state law may provide that the estate no longer has an insurable interest.

¶ 460 Partnership Insurance

The estate tax treatment of the proceeds of insurance and the value of the partnership interest is the same as under the stock purchase agreement. It is less likely, however, that the partnership, as opposed to the individual partners, will be the purchaser of the insurance, since premiums have to be paid out of net income after individual taxes regardless of whether the partnership or the partners purchase the insurance.

Partners who purchase life insurance on the lives of each other to fund partnership purchase agreements should make sure (1) that they are named as owner-beneficiaries of a policy on the life of an insured partner, and (2) that policy terms do not give an insured partner incidents of ownership over the policy. In such cases, the IRS has attempted to include the face amount of the policy in the insured partner's gross estate, where the face value exceeded the value of the decedent's partnership interest as agreed on. In two such cases, the IRS's attempt was unsuccessful because the Tax Court ruled that the partnership agreement controlled over the policy terms. Because the partnership agreements provided that proceeds were to be used to pay for the insured partners' interest, the court concluded that the partners could not exercise any incident of ownership that directly affected the economic benefits arising from the policies.[58]

The IRS has ruled that the proceeds of a policy of insurance on the life of a partner, which policy was owned by the partnership, were includible in the partner's gross estate because they were not payable to, or for the benefit of, the partnership.[59] The IRS concluded that the insured partner, by virtue of his one-third interest in the partnership, held an incident of ownership in the policy at death. This was so because the insured partner in his capacity as partner had the right (exercisable in conjunction with the other partners) to direct the economic benefits of the policy. However, where insurance proceeds were payable to a partnership, the Tax Court has ruled that a deceased partner's estate did not include insurance proceeds under the predecessor to Code Sec. 2042(2), despite the partner's incidents of ownership.[60] The IRS acquiesced in this result based on the fact that the value of the decedent's partnership interest reflected the payment of insurance proceeds to the partnership.

The IRS has also ruled that the proceeds of a partnership group-term insurance policy were not includible in the gross estate of an insured partner who, more than three years before his death, assigned all of the incidents of ownership in the policy to his children.[61] This was true even though the partnership retained the power to surrender or cancel the policy—a power that is an incident of policy ownership under Reg. § 20.2042-1(c)(2). Applying the rationale of regulations promulgated under Code Sec. 79 that deal with attribution of

---

[58] *B.L. Fuchs Est.*, 47 TC 199, CCH Dec. 28,186 (Acq.); *H.F. Infante Est.*, 29 TCM 903, CCH Dec. 30,250(M), TC Memo. 1970-206, CA-7, appeal dism'd, 6-2-71.

[59] Rev. Rul. 83-147, 1983-2 CB 158.

[60] *F. Knipp Est.*, 25 TC 153, CCH Dec. 21,311 (Acq.), aff'd on another issue, CA-4, 57-1 USTC ¶ 11,693, 244 F2d 436.

[61] Rev. Rul. 83-148, 1983-2 CB 157.

incidents of ownership in group-term policies held by controlled corporations, the IRS ruled that the partnership's power to surrender or cancel the policy was not to be attributed to the partner.

¶ 465 Insurance on Sole Proprietor

Insurance taken out by a sole proprietor on the proprietor's own life has the same status for estate tax purposes as insurance taken out by any individual on the individual's own life. The presence or absence of rights of ownership determines whether the proceeds are includible in the insured's estate.

The insurance may have been taken out by the employees or other persons with an insurable interest as a means of providing funds for the purchase of all or a part of the business of the sole proprietor. The status of the insurance and the interest to be sold is the same as in the case of the corporation or partnership. Either the value of the business or the proceeds of its sale will be included in the sole proprietor's gross estate. If the agreement to sell to the employees is a mandatory one, the agreement will serve to limit the amount at which the value of the interest will be fixed.

¶ 470 Key-Employee Insurance

Sometimes a corporation will purchase insurance on the life of an officer or stockholder, not to implement a purchase agreement, but to protect the corporation against the loss that it feels would result from the untimely death of the insured. This insurance is usually referred to as "key-employee insurance."

In key-employee insurance policies, the insured individuals are personally responsible for a substantial share of the company's success, so that their death may result in a loss of a certain amount of business. The insurance taken out on their lives is calculated to make up for the loss the company expects to incur. The proceeds are made payable to the corporation rather than to any individual.

A person insured under such an arrangement usually has no interest in the insurance. None of its proceeds will be included in the insured's gross estate. Its presence will, however, be felt in fixing a value for any stock that the insured may have owned in the company. The insurance is includible among corporate assets in determining the value of the insured's stock for estate tax purposes.

If, at the time of death, it does appear likely that the key employee's absence will have an adverse effect on the conduct of the business, that factor can be taken into account in fixing the value of the stock. The estate is also protected against loss resulting from the death by its right to elect to value the estate as of six months after the insured's death. Insurance of this type is sometimes purchased by partnerships or sole proprietorships, with similar results.

¶ 472 Split-Dollar Life Insurance

Split-dollar life insurance is permanent insurance acquired under an arrangement by which the company and an employee (usually a company executive) split the premium cost and the company and the executive's beneficiaries split the proceeds on an agreed basis, on the executive's death.[62] In the typical split-dollar arrangement, the executive will have the right to name the beneficiary of his or her portion of the policy (usually the term insurance component),

---

[62] See Notice 2002-8, 2002-1 CB 420, for the income tax treatment of split-dollar life insurance.

and the employer will pay the current premiums and retain the right to the cash values that accumulate under the policy.

For the employer, split-dollar plans are a cost-effective benefit aimed at retaining executives, without the administrative difficulties of a qualified plan. The executive benefits from the receipt of insurance coverage at a lower out-of-pocket cost than would otherwise be possible.

The estate tax treatment of split-dollar life insurance proceeds closely follows the general rules relating to life insurance on the life of a decedent. Such proceeds will be included in the deceased executive's gross estate if (1) the policy proceeds were paid to, of for the benefit of, his or her estate, or (2) the decedent owned incidents of ownership in the policy at his or her death. Where such proceeds are includible in the executive's gross estate, they are reportable on Form 706 (United States Estate (and Generation-Skipping Transfer) Tax Return), Schedule D (Insurance on the Decedent's Life). However, in the typical situation, the executive with an interest in a split-dollar policy will seek to avoid estate tax inclusion by a lifetime assignment of all his or her incidents of ownership in the policy to another (usually a family member). See ¶2109 for the valuation, for gift tax purposes, of an assignment of a split-dollar insurance policy.

The IRS has issued an explanation of the standards it will use in valuing current life insurance protection under what it has termed abusive split-dollar arrangements. More specifically, the IRS is targeting arrangements where a party pays inappropriately high current term insurance premiums, prepays premiums, or uses other techniques in order to understate the value of the taxable policy benefits.[63] Under such a scenario, it appears that the IRS intends to disregard policy arrangements that use two different insurance rates (one for the amount of coverage, and another one for purposes of the gift tax.)[64] Under IRS Notice 2002-59, a party participating in a split-dollar life insurance arrangement may use the premium rates in Table 2001 (see Notice 2002-8), or the insurer's lower published premium rates only for the purposes of valuing current life insurance protection and when such protection confers an economic benefit by one party on another party, disregarding the premiums actually paid by this other party. However, if one party has any right to current life insurance protection under the split-dollar arrangement, neither the premium rates in Table 2001 nor the insurer's lower published rates may be used to value such party's current life insurance protection for purposes of determining the value of any policy benefits to which another party may be entitled.

¶ 473 Survivor Life Insurance

A survivor life insurance policy (also known as a "second-to-die policy") is a single policy covering two named insureds. On the death of the first insured, no benefit is paid. The benefit is paid only on the death of the survivor. Such policies offer the practical economy of being less costly than a separate policy for each insured since there is only one death benefit.

Survivor life policies are typically used by married couples who foresee the likelihood that the surviving spouse will die with a large enough estate to face an estate tax liability. With the unlimited marital deduction, the first spouse to die usually can arrange his or her plan of disposition so that there will be no estate tax liability. However, there will be an increased estate on the death of the second spouse because of the deferral of estate tax on the assets that passed to

---

[63] Notice 2002-59, IRB 2002-36, 481.

[64] Notice 2002-8, 2002-1 CB 420.

the survivor at the death of the first spouse. The use of a survivor life policy may provide the needed liquidity for the estate of the second spouse to die.

¶ 475 Valuation

The amount to be reported if insurance proceeds are payable to or for the benefit of the estate is the amount receivable. If the proceeds are payable to a named beneficiary, the amount receivable is again the amount reportable (although not necessarily taxable). Where the proceeds are to be paid in the form of an annuity, for life or for a certain number of years, the amount to be reported is the one sum payable at death under the lump-sum option. If no lump-sum option exists, the amount to be reported is the sum used to determine the amount of the annuity.[65] As to the valuation of reversionary interests in determining taxability, see ¶530.

If the estate must sue the insurance company in order to collect policy proceeds, the amount includible with respect to the policy may be less than the face amount of the proceeds. The IRS National Office has ruled that the amount includible in a decedent's gross estate with respect to two policies of insurance on the decedent's life is the fair market value, on the date of the decedent's death, of claims resulting from lawsuits that the decedent's estate filed to obtain the proceeds payable under the policies. Neither the amount of the proceeds nor the amount received by the estate in settlement of the claims was the correct amount includible. Although Code Sec. 2042 controls the includibility of policies in the estate, it does not control the valuation of the policies which, accordingly, must be valued on the basis of all facts and circumstances existing on the date of death.[66]

¶ 477 Life Insurance Trusts

Like almost any other type of property, life insurance policies are suitable for ownership by a trust. In fact, a special type of trust optimized to hold life insurance policies—the insurance trust—is often used to accomplish tax and nontax objectives. A revocable lifetime insurance trust can provide some significant nontax advantages, such as avoidance of probate, ability to tailor distributions to the estate owner's personal wishes (rather than be tied to the insurance company's settlement options), and availability of professional management. However, to obtain the significant estate tax advantages that are available, the insurance trust must be irrevocable.

• ***Estate and Gift Tax Issues***

In order for policy proceeds received by an irrevocable insurance trust to avoid being brought back into the deceased insured's gross estate, the trustee—not the insured—must hold all incidents of ownership in the policies. Also, any insurance policies transferred into the trust must have been so transferred more than three years before the decedent's death[67] (see ¶430).

A transfer from the insured to his or her insurance trust will constitute a taxable gift. One way to avoid this potential problem would be to transfer either term policies (which would have little or no current value) or cash value policies from which nearly all of the cash value has been removed by policy loans. Another way to minimize possible gift tax liability would be for the trust to

---

[65] Reg. §20.2042-1(a)(3).

[66] IRS Technical Advice Memorandum 8308001 (Jan. 21, 1982).

[67] Code Sec. 2035.

purchase a new policy on the life of the donor from cash initially transferred to the trust. This would also avoid the "three-years-of-death rule" since the trust's purchase of the policy will not be attributed to the donor.[68]

To the extent that a transfer to the trust is a taxable gift, the trust beneficiaries, rather than the trustee, are regarded as the donees. However, in order for the transfers to the donees to be considered gifts of present, rather than future, interests (and thus qualify for gift tax annual exclusions), the donees will have to have present powers to withdraw trust property (see ¶2265).

In the typical estate planning use of an irrevocable life insurance trust, it is not contemplated—and is normally not desired—for the beneficiaries to actually exercise their yearly withdrawal powers (which are usually limited to a noncumulative right to withdraw $10,000 per year, as adjusted for inflation ($11,000 for 2002 through 2005), the amount of the gift tax annual exclusion). The fact that the beneficiaries do not choose to exercise their withdrawal power (sometimes called a "*Crummey* power"[69] after the name of the court decision that validated use of such a power) does not put the annual gift tax exclusions for transfers into the trust in jeopardy, provided that the beneficiaries have a reasonable opportunity to make such withdrawals during the calendar year in which the gift tax exclusion is claimed[70] and have not entered into an agreement with the donor that they would not exercise their powers.[71]

Unless the insured-transferor also initially transfers cash or cash-generating property into the trust to pay future policy premiums, he or she will have to make additional payments to or on behalf of the trust to keep the policies in force. These payments will also constitute taxable gifts to the beneficiaries, unless shielded by gift tax annual exclusions.

As noted above, irrevocable trusts (including insurance trusts) may contain a *Crummey* power in order to obtain gift tax annual exclusions for yearly transfers into the trust. However, there is another type of beneficiary withdrawal power—the "five by five" power—that may be used instead. This power gives trust beneficiaries a yearly noncumulative right to withdraw from the trust the greater of $5,000 or five percent of the trust principal. This power is used so as to shield the beneficiaries from being hit with gift tax if they do not exercise their yearly withdrawal rights under the trust.

Depending on the size of the principal of the insurance trust in question, a donor may be able to obtain both the full amount of the gift tax annual exclusion for yearly amounts transferred into the trust ($11,000 for 2002 through 2005) per donee, and also make sure that the beneficiaries will not be deemed to make taxable gifts by failing to exercise their withdrawal powers (the "five by five" provision). However, the donor will have to choose to forgo a portion of his or her gift tax annual exclusion, or subject the donee-beneficiaries to gift tax themselves, if the trust does not exceed $220,000.

Example (1): Ralph Law sets up an irrevocable life insurance trust for his two children, Mary and John. Each child has a noncumulative with-

---

[68] *E. Headrick Est.*, CA-6, 90-2 USTC ¶60,049; *J. Leder Est.*, CA-10, 90-1 USTC ¶60,001. In order to ensure this result, the amount of the initial trust funding should exceed the amount of the first year's policy premium, and should not be earmarked for payment of premiums (*T. Kurihara Est.*, 82 TC 51, CCH Dec. 40,914).

[69] *D.C. Crummey*, CA-9, 68-2 USTC ¶12,541, 397 F2d 82.

[70] Rev. Rul. 73-405, 1973-2 CB 321; Rev. Rul. 81-7, 1981-1 CB 474.

[71] See *M. Cristofani*, 97 TC 74, Dec. 47,491 (Acq. in result only), 1992-1 CB 1.

drawal power limited to the amount of the gift tax annual exclusion in effect in the year the withdrawal right is available (in 2004 this amount is $11,000). If in 2004 the corpus of the trust is $220,000, each child could forgo the exercise of the yearly power without incurring a gift tax liability, since the amount deemed lapsed would qualify under the "five by five" provision of the Code ($220,000 × 5% = $11,000).

However, a different result will occur if the trust corpus were only $175,000. Although Law's transfer of $11,000 to the trust would qualify for the $11,000 annual gift tax exclusion (so he would not be hit with a gift tax liability), on nonexercise of the yearly power, each of the children would be deemed to make a taxable gift of $2,250 to the trust remaindermen:

$11,000	(Annual exclusion limitation)
– 8,750	(Five by five limit: the greater of $5,000 or 5% of trust corpus: $175,000 × 5% = $8,750)
$ 2,250	Taxable gift by each beneficiary to trust remaindermen

If the insurance trust donor is faced with the problem noted in Example (1), he or she can choose between the following two broad strategies (although there are additional variations):

(1) Structure the withdrawal right, by its terms, so that it would be limited to the amount that will qualify as a five by five power. (In Example 1, such a provision would limit the beneficiaries' withdrawal rights to $8,750.) This would solve the beneficiaries' potential gift tax problem, at the cost of limiting the donor's contribution to the trust that year to $8,750. (Or, if a larger gift is made, it would be a taxable gift of a future interest by the donor.)

Or

(2) Give each of the beneficiaries a yearly withdrawal right of $11,000 under the trust. This would allow the donor to transfer up to this amount during the year without incurring a gift tax liability, but it would mean that each beneficiary, upon failure to exercise the right, would be deemed to make a taxable gift to the remaindermen equal to the amount that exceeds the five by five limit.

Which alternative is chosen will largely be determined by the facts of the individual situation, including the size of the trust subject to the power, and the respective gift tax liabilities to be faced by the donor and donees.

• *Income Tax Issues*

Although judicious use of a "five by five" beneficiary withdrawal power can avoid gift tax liability for both the trust grantor and beneficiaries, the beneficiaries may face an income tax problem if they let their withdrawal rights lapse each year. This is because, under the grantor trust provisions of the Code,[72] since the beneficiaries will retain a power in the trust after such a lapse, they will be deemed, for income tax purposes, to be the owner of the portion of the trust property attributable to such lapse.[73] Even though these powers are noncumulative, the income tax will be exacerbated with each additional year the withdrawal power lapses.

Example (2): Sally Fisher has a yearly, noncumulative "five by five" power over a trust principal of $1 million. After she allows her power to

---

[72] Code Sec. 671 through Code Sec. 677.

[73] Rev. Rul. 67-241, 1967-2 CB 225.

lapse at the end of year one, she will be deemed to be the owner of $50,000 of the trust property, or 5%.

In year two, she would be deemed the owner of the $50,000, plus an increasing portion of the trust (assuming that the value of the trust corpus does not appreciate), calculated as followed:

$50,000 × $950,000/$1,000,000 = $47,500

Thus, at the end of year two, the spouse would be the owner of $97,500 (or 9.75%) of the trust.

How severe the income tax consequences will be to the beneficiaries as a result of a yearly lapse of withdrawal powers will depend on such factors as how much income (if any) the trust is generating and the respective income tax brackets of the trust and the beneficiaries.

¶ 480 Description of Insurance on Return

All insurance on a decedent's life is reportable on Schedule D (Insurance on the Decedent's Life) of Form 706 (United States Estate (and Generation-Skipping Transfer) Tax Return). Every policy of insurance on the life of a decedent must be listed, whether or not it is included in the gross estate. The name of the insurance company and the policy number should be listed under "Description." For every policy listed, the decedent's estate should request a statement from the company that issued the policy on Form 712 (Life Insurance Statement) (see ¶ 481).

If the policy proceeds are paid in one sum, the value to be entered in the valuation column is the net proceeds received, from Form 712, line 24. However, if the policy proceeds are not paid in one sum, the value to be entered is the value of the proceeds as of the date of the decedent's death, from Form 712, line 25. If part or all of the policy proceeds are not included in the gross estate, an explanation of the reason for their exclusion must accompany the policy description.

In the case of an estate of a nonresident not a citizen, the proceeds of insurance on the nonresident's life are not taxable and need not be included in the schedule.[74]

¶ 481 Life Insurance Statement

The executor of a decedent's estate must file a Form 712 (Life Insurance Statement) with the estate tax return for every policy of life insurance on the decedent's life that is listed on the schedule and that constitutes a part of the gross estate.[75] It is also the duty of the executor to obtain the statement from the insurance company that issued the policy.

An executor should file Form 712 in order to facilitate valuation of insurance owned by the decedent on the life of another person.

¶ 485 Community Property

Special rules apply when insurance is paid for out of community funds. See ¶ 165 and ¶ 435 for a discussion of the status of community property.

---

[74] Code Sec. 2105(a).

[75] Reg. § 20.6018-4; Schedule D, Form 706 (Rev. Aug. 2004), p. 16.

Chapter 12
JOINTLY OWNED PROPERTY

¶ 500 Interest of Joint Owners

Property in which the decedent at the time of death held an interest either as a joint tenant or as a tenant by the entirety, with right of survivorship, is the subject of special treatment under the estate tax law. Such joint interests are removed from the scope of Code Sec. 2033, which provides for inclusion of property in which the decedent had an interest at death, and are taxed under the even broader concepts of Code Sec. 2040.

Ordinarily, under property law, each participant in a joint tenancy or tenancy by the entirety is regarded as owning an undivided equal share. The estate tax law follows this concept only with respect to property held jointly with right of survivorship and only if acquired by gift, devise, bequest, or inheritance.[1]

However, special rules apply to certain joint interests held by spouses, in which each spouse will be considered as owning a one-half interest in the joint property for estate tax purposes (see ¶502). Therefore, in the case of property acquired by a spouse by inheritance as a tenant by the entirety or a joint tenant with right of survivorship, one-half of the value of the property would be included in the gross estate of the first spouse to die. Similarly, in the case of three tenants of property acquired by gift as a joint tenancy, each tenant is regarded as owning one-third of the property.

For a discussion of the special rules that apply when a taxable transfer is deemed to be made with respect to jointly held property, see ¶2162.

¶ 501 Property Acquired by Purchase

The estate tax law provides a general rule in the case of property acquired by purchase and held in joint tenancy or by the entirety. The portion to be included in the deceased tenant's gross estate is based on the percentage of the decedent's contribution to the total cost. This percentage is multiplied by the fair market value of the entire property on the date of the decedent's death (or on the alternate valuation date, if so elected).[2] (Different rules apply to property acquired by married joint tenants; see ¶502.)

The value of the entire property will be included in the gross estate unless the amount contributed by the survivor is proven. In determining the amount of the survivor's contribution, any part of the contribution that was originally received from the decedent by gift cannot be included.

> *Example:* Amy Cooper and her daughter, Julie, buy a residence for $100,000 as joint tenants. Amy contributed $80,000 to the cost and Julie contributed $20,000. Amy will be regarded as having an 80% interest in the

---

[1] Reg. §20.2040-1(a)(1).

[2] Reg. §20.2040-1(a)(2).

property. If she dies first and if, on her death, the property is worth $200,000, 80%, or $160,000, will be included in her gross estate.

This provision also covers joint bank accounts and jointly held bonds, stocks, or other instruments, but has no application to property held by the decedent and any other person as tenants in common.[3]

Where property held in joint tenancy was purchased with community property funds in which the spouses had equal vested interests, one-half of the value of the jointly held property is excluded from the decedent's gross estate.[4]

A decedent's interest as a tenant in common is not reportable on Form 706 (United States Estate (and Generation-Skipping Transfer) Tax Return) (Rev. Aug. 2004), Schedule E (Jointly Owned Property), as jointly owned property. The proper schedule for reporting the property interest is dictated by the nature of the property—realty on Form 706, Schedule A (Real Estate), stocks and bonds on Form 706, Schedule B (Stocks and Bonds), etc.

In all instances where the executor or administrator seeks to exclude a part of the value of the jointly held property from the gross estate, the executor has the burden of proving a right to include the reduced value and, therefore, should be prepared to prove the extent, origin, and nature of each joint owner's interest.[5]

¶ 502 Spousal Joint Tenancies

The estate of the first spouse to die includes only one-half of the value of a "qualified joint interest" in property regardless of which spouse furnished the consideration for the property. For purposes of this provision, "qualified joint interest" is defined as any interest in property held solely by spouses as joint tenants with the right of survivorship or as tenants by the entirety.[6]

However, the U.S. Court of Appeals for the Sixth Circuit has held that a surviving spouse was entitled to a stepped-up basis for jointly held property created prior to 1977 where her husband had provided all of the consideration for the property. Because the effective date of the Economic Recovery Tax Act of 1981 (P.L. 97-34) (ERTA) (generally applicable to estates of decedents dying after December 31, 1981) did not expressly or by implication repeal the effective date of the Tax Reform Act of 1976 (P.L. 94-455), the contribution test as it existed prior to 1977 was applicable in determining the amount of jointly held property includible in the gross estate of the decedent who died after the effective date of ERTA. Accordingly, because 100 percent of the value of the jointly held property was includible in the decedent's gross estate, his surviving spouse was entitled to a stepped-up date-of-death basis for the entire property.[7] (See, also, ¶ 2107 for treatment of pre-1982 lifetime gifts of spousal joint interests.)

Effective for decedents dying after December 31, 2009, the stepped-up basis at death rules will be replaced by a modified carryover basis regime (see ¶ 121).

• *Special Rule Where Spouse Is Noncitizen*

The creation of a joint tenancy in property is generally treated as a completed gift. Before the effective date of the Technical and Miscellaneous Revenue

---

[3] Reg. § 20.2040-1(b).

[4] *J.A. Kammerdiner*, CA-9, 44-1 USTC ¶ 10,084, 140 F2d 569; Rev. Rul. 78-418, 1978-2 CB 236.

[5] Reg. § 20.2040-1(a)(2).

[6] Code Sec. 2040(b).

[7] *M.L. Gallenstein*, CA-6, 92-2 USTC ¶ 60,114, aff'g DC Ky., 91-2 USTC ¶ 60,088; *J. Patten*, CA-4, 97-2 USTC ¶ 60,279; *E.M. Baszto*, DC Fla., 98-1 USTC ¶ 60,305; and *T. Hahn*, 110 TC 140, CCH Dec. 52,606 (Acq.).

Act of 1988 (P.L. 100-647) (TAMRA), such a gift between spouses qualified for the marital deduction for estate and gift tax purposes, and only one-half of the jointly held property was included in the gross estate of the first spouse to die under the "qualified joint interest" rule described above. However, effective for gifts made to noncitizen spouses on or after July 14, 1988, TAMRA repealed the marital deduction (see ¶1000) and also provided that the entire value of jointly held property is includible in the deceased spouse's estate, reduced by the portion of the property for which consideration was received.

In determining the federal estate tax, the value of gifts includible in the gross estate is effectively reduced by the value of taxable gifts when made. Thus, for joint tenancies created on or after July 14, 1988, where the donee spouse is a noncitizen, the amount included in the gross estate of the first spouse to die is effectively reduced by the amount transferred when the tenancy was created. In the case of joint tenancies created prior to July 14, 1988, no such reduction occurred because the gift qualified for the marital deduction and was not taxable. For purposes of determining the amount of joint tenancy property includible in a decedent's gross estate, a gift made by creating a joint tenancy in property prior to July 14, 1988, is treated as consideration belonging to the surviving spouse if the transfer would have constituted a gift had the donor been a U.S. citizen. Thus, the amount of joint tenancy property included in the gross estate of the first spouse to die is reduced proportionately by the amount of the gift.[8]

¶ 510 Valuation of Jointly Owned Property

If the decedent and any person with whom the decedent held property jointly transferred that property to others during the decedent's lifetime, the transfer is reportable as a transfer made during the decedent's lifetime, rather than as jointly held property.

The principles governing valuation of jointly held property are the same as those governing other types of property. Therefore, reference should be made to the instructions preceding the various schedules for information concerning the valuation of the specific kinds of property held jointly. However, the Tax Court has ruled that fractional interest discounts and lack of marketability discounts do not apply in the valuation of joint tenancy property.[9]

¶ 515 Description on Return

Property owned at the time of death by a decedent in joint tenancy with the right of survivorship or in a tenancy by the entirety is to be reported on Schedule E (Jointly Owned Property) of Form 706 (United States Estate (and Generation-Skipping Transfer) Tax Return). If the decedent's spouse was the only other co-tenant, the tenancy constitutes a qualified joint interest (see ¶502) and is to be reported in part I of Schedule E. All other joint tenancy property must be reported in part II of Schedule E, including the names and addresses of the surviving joint owners (see ¶2990 for further details).

In reporting jointly owned property on Schedule E, a statement under the column headed "Description" must disclose whether the whole or only a part of the property is included in the gross estate. If only a part of the property is included in the gross estate, the fair market value of the whole must nevertheless be shown under "Description."

---

[8] Act Sec. 11701(l), P.L. 101-508, amending Act Sec. 7815(d)(16), P.L. 101-239.

[9] *Wayne-Chi Young Est.*, 110 TC 297, CCH Dec. 52,691.

Property in which the decedent held an interest as a tenant in common should not be listed on Schedule E. The value of the decedent's interest as a tenant in common should be returned under the schedule for real estate, or, if personal property, under such other appropriate schedule. Similarly, community property held by the decedent and spouse should be returned under appropriate other schedules. The decedent's interest in a partnership should be shown on Schedule F (Other Miscellaneous Property Not Reportable Under Any Other Schedule) of Form 706.

Chapter 13
MISCELLANEOUS PROPERTY

¶ 525 Items Termed "Miscellaneous"

The classification "Other Miscellaneous Property" on the estate tax return, Form 706 (United States Estate (and Generation-Skipping Transfer) Tax Return) (Rev. Aug. 2004), relates to property that is includible in the gross estate under Code Sec. 2033, but that does not fall within any of the preceding property-schedule classifications. It includes such items as:

(1) debts due the decedent (other than notes and mortgages included on Schedule C (Mortgages, Notes, and Cash) of Form 706);

(2) interests in business;

(3) insurance on the life of another;

(4) claims (including the value of the decedent's interest in a claim for refund of income taxes, or the amount of the refund actually received);

(5) rights;

(6) royalties;

(7) leaseholds;

(8) judgments;

(9) shares in trust funds;

(10) household goods and personal effects, including wearing apparel;

(11) farm products and growing crops;

(12) livestock;

(13) farm machinery;

(14) automobiles;

(15) reversionary or remainder interests; and

(16) Code Sec. 2044 property (property for which the marital deduction was previously allowed).

¶ 526 Reporting Property Interests

The various property interests that are described at ¶ 525 as being reportable on Form 706 (United States Estate (and Generation-Skipping Transfer) Tax Return), Schedule F (Other Miscellaneous Property Not Reportable Under Any Other Schedule), are taxable under Code Sec. 2033 as property in which the decedent had an interest at the time of death. Schedule F must be filed with Form 706.

If any of the property reportable under this category was transferred by the decedent during the decedent's life, that property should not be listed with the "miscellaneous" property. It should be reported on Schedule G (Transfers During Decedent's Life) of Form 706 for transfers during the decedent's lifetime. The method of valuing such property, however, is the same, no matter which schedule is applicable. If the transfer, by trust or otherwise, was made by a written instrument, a copy of such document should be submitted with the return.

¶ 527 Interests in Business

Business interests, other than corporate, are reported on Form 706 (United States Estate (and Generation-Skipping Transfer) Tax Return), Schedule F (Other Miscellaneous Property Not Reportable Under Any Other Schedule) as "Other Miscellaneous Property." In determining the fair market value of any business interest or intangible asset for estate tax purposes, the general approach, methods, and factors in Rev. Rul. 59-60,[1] pertaining to valuation of stock in closely held corporations, are applicable, but will not control when better evidence of value is available.

The valuation of interests in business requires great care. A fair appraisal should be made of all of the assets of the business, including goodwill. The business should be given a net value equal to the amount that a willing purchaser would pay to a willing seller in view of asset value and earning capacity. Where the decedent's interest in a partnership, for instance, is subject to an agreement to sell to survivors at a price determined by some equitable means, that price normally will determine the value. In the absence of a purchase agreement, special attention should be given to fixing an adequate figure for the value of the goodwill.

• *Documentation*

All evidence bearing on the valuation of an interest in a business should be submitted with the return. This includes copies of reports in any case in which examinations of the business have been made by accountants, engineers, or any technical experts as of or near the applicable valuation date. If the decedent owned any interest in a partnership or unincorporated business, a statement of assets and liabilities as of the valuation date and for the preceding five years, along with statements of the net earnings for the same five years, should be submitted with the return. In general, the same information should be furnished and the same methods followed as in valuing interests in close corporations.

¶ 528 Limited Interests

Annuities, interests for life or for a term of years, and remainder and reversionary interests present special valuation problems. For a commercial annuity or insurance policy on the life of a person other than the decedent that is payable under a contract with an insurance or other company regularly engaged in selling such contracts, the value is the price of a comparable contract on the applicable valuation date (see ¶760). In all other instances, the value is determined by discounting future payments.

The valuation date for such interests is the date of death regardless of whether the alternate valuation date is used. When the alternate valuation date

[1] Rev. Rul. 59-60, 1959-1 CB 237. Additional valuation information is contained in Reg. § 20.2031-3; Rev. Rul. 65-193, 1965-2 CB 370; Rev. Rul. 77-287, 1977-2 CB 319, corrected by Ann. 77-168, IRB 1977-51, 22; and Rev. Rul. 83-120, 1983-2 CB 170, which modified and amplified Rev. Rul. 59-60.

has been elected, the value at death is then adjusted for any difference in value between the date of death and the applicable valuation date that is due to causes other than the mere lapse of time.[2]

Special tables are used to determine the present value of a private annuity, an interest for life or for a term of years, and a remainder or reversionary interest (see ¶530).

¶530 Valuation of Limited Interests

The appropriate authority for determining the estate tax value of limited interests in property such as annuities, interests for life or a term of years, and remainder and reversionary interests depends on the date of the decedent's death. Limited property interests valued with respect to decedents dying after April 30, 1999, are governed by Reg. §20.2031-7.[3] In general, the fair market value of a limited interest is determined by using an actuarial factor prescribed by the Secretary of the Treasury in conjunction with the appropriate Code Sec. 7520 interest rate. The Code Sec. 7520 interest rate is computed as 120 percent of the applicable federal midterm rate (rounded to the nearest two-tenths of one percent) and is published monthly by the IRS.

For decedents dying before May 1, 1999, Reg. §20.2031-7A provides the applicable rules for valuing limited property interests, depending on whether the decedent died before 1952 (Reg. §20.2031-7A(a)), after 1951 and before 1971 (Reg. §20.2031-7A(b)), after 1970 and before December 1, 1983 (Reg. §20.2031-7A(c)), after November 30, 1983, and before May 1, 1989 (Reg. §20.2031-7A(d)), or after April 30, 1989, and before May 1, 1999 (Reg. §20.2031-7A(e)).

IRS Publication No. 1457, "Actuarial Values, Book Aleph," contains many standard actuarial factors not included in the regulations, including last-to-die factors for valuing limited property interests dependent on more than one life (Table R(2)). It also includes examples that illustrate how to compute special factors for more unusual situations. The factors set forth in Reg. §20.2031-7 and IRS Publication 1457 involving life contingencies reflect the most recent mortality data contained in the mortality component table (Table 90CM) located in Reg. §20.2031-7(d)(7). The publication is available for purchase from the Superintendent of Documents, United States Government Printing Office, Washington, D.C. 20402.

The valuation of commercial annuity contracts and insurance policies on the lives of persons other than the decedent must be determined under Reg. §20.2031-8.

See ¶2800 for a table of the applicable Code Sec. 7520 interest rates for valuation dates after 1996.

A person's age at his or her nearest birthday is to be used for computation purposes.

• *Decedents Dying After April 30, 1999*

For decedents dying after April 30, 1999, the present value of a remainder or reversionary interest postponed for a term certain is determined by multiplying the fair market value of the property by the appropriate remainder interest factor from Table B in Reg. §20.2031-7(d)(6). If the interest is postponed until after the

---

[2] Reg. §20.2032-1(f).

[3] T.D. 8886, amending Reg. §20.2031-7, was published in the *Federal Register* on June 9, 2000.

death of one individual, the appropriate remainder interest factor from Table S in Reg. §20.2031-7(d)(7) is used. The appropriate remainder interest factor is that factor that corresponds to the applicable Code Sec. 7520 interest rate and either the Table B term certain or the Table S current age of the individual who is the measuring life. The interest rate component is based on a rate that is 120 percent of the applicable federal midterm rate compounded annually for the month in which the valuation date falls. Table B and Table S, as well as other tables from the regulations that are referred to hereafter, are reproduced at ¶2700 of the Appendix.

Ordinary term-of-years and life interest. The present value of a right to receive the income of property, or to use nonincome-producing property, for a term of years or for the life of one individual is determined by multiplying the fair market value of the property by the appropriate term-of-years or life interest factor that corresponds to the applicable Code Sec. 7520 interest rate. Although the term-of-years and life interest factors are not included in Table B or Table S in Reg. §20.2031-7(d)(6) and Reg. §20.2031-7(d)(7), they may be derived mathematically. The term-of-years (income interest) factor is derived by subtracting the correlative Table B term certain remainder factor that corresponds to the applicable Code Sec. 7520 interest rate from 1.000000. Similarly, the factor for the life of one individual (life estate) is derived by subtracting the correlative Table S single life remainder factor that corresponds to the applicable Code Sec. 7520 interest rate from 1.000000. These actuarial factors for income interests and life estates are included in Table B and Table S, respectively, in IRS Publication 1457, "Actuarial Values, Book Aleph" (7-1999) (see Reg. §20.2031-7(d)(4)).

Annuities. The present value of an annuity that is payable at the end of each year for a term certain or for the life of one individual is determined by multiplying the aggregate amount payable annually by the appropriate annuity factor that corresponds to the applicable Code Sec. 7520 interest rate. These actuarial factors are included in Table B and Table S in IRS Publication 1457, "Actuarial Values, Book Aleph." Although the annuity factors are not included in Table B or Table S in Reg. §20.2031-7(d)(6) and Reg. §20.2031-7(d)(7), they may be derived mathematically. The term certain annuity factor is derived by subtracting the correlative Table B term certain remainder factor that corresponds to the applicable Code Sec. 7520 interest rate from 1.000000 and then dividing the result by the applicable Code Sec. 7520 interest rate expressed as a decimal number. Similarly, the single life annuity factor is derived by subtracting the correlative Table S single life remainder factor that corresponds to the applicable Code Sec. 7520 interest rate from 1.000000 and then dividing the result by the applicable Code Sec. 7520 interest rate expressed as a decimal number.

> ***Example:*** George Miller died in January 2004 and was entitled to receive an annuity of $24,000 a year for six years, payable at the end of each year. The Code Sec. 7520 interest rate for January 2004 is 4.2%. The Table B term certain remainder factor at 4.2% is .781257. The term certain annuity factor is 5.208167 ((1.000000 − .781257) ÷ .042). The present value of the annuity interest at the date of the decedent's death is $124,996 ($24,000 × 5.208167). (Calculations made using CCH® FinEst Calcs™.)

Certain adjustment factors must be applied to the valuations determined above if the annuity is payable at any time other than the end of each year. Table J (Reg. §20.2031-7(d)(6)) contains the adjustment factors applicable for term certain annuities if the annuity is payable at the beginning of annual, semiannual, quarterly, monthly, or weekly periods. Table K (Reg. §20.2031-7(d)(6)) contains the adjustment factors applicable if the annuity is payable at the end of semiannual, quarterly, monthly, or weekly periods. Regardless of which table applies, the product obtained by multiplying the aggregate amount payable annually by the applicable annuity factor is then multiplied by the applicable adjustment factor to obtain the present value of the annuity.

The present value of an annuity or unitrust interest that is payable for a term of years or until the prior death of an individual may be computed by following the examples set forth in Reg. § 25.2512-5(d)(2)(v).

Split-interest trusts. The fair market value of a remainder interest in a charitable remainder annuity trust (CRAT) is the net fair market value of the property placed in trust less the present value of the annuity, which can be computed by using Table S or Table B under Reg. § 20.2031-7(d).[4] The present value of an annuity interest that is payable until the earlier to occur of the lapse of a specific number of years or the death of an individual may be computed using Tables B, K, S, and 90CM, reproduced at ¶ 2700 of the Appendix. Reg. § 25.2512-5(d)(2)(v)(A) provides an example for computing the value of such an annuity interest using these tables.

The present value of a remainder interest in a pooled income fund as defined in Reg. § 1.642(c)-5 is valued pursuant to Reg. § 1.642(c)-6.

The present value of a remainder interest in a charitable remainder unitrust (CRUT) as defined in Reg. § 1.664-3 is valued pursuant to Reg. § 1.664-4 using Tables F and D or U(1) (see the Appendix at ¶ 2700). The present value of a unitrust interest that is payable until the earlier to occur of the lapse of a specific number of years or the death of an individual may be computed using Tables D, F, U(1), and 90CM pursuant to the example provided in Reg. § 25.2512-5(d)(2)(v)(B).

Exceptions to the use of standard factors. The IRS has set forth three situations under Reg. § 20.7520-3(b)(2) and (3) in which the standard actuarial factors may not be used. These include (1) transfers to high payout annuities if the annuity is expected to exhaust the fund before the last possible annuity payment is made in full, (2) transfers to split-interest trusts in which a grantor retains an income interest in a trust funded with unproductive or underproductive property, and (3) transfers with a retained life interest for which the person who is the measuring life has a terminal illness. Thus, the standard factors may not be used if the governing instrument fails to provide an income beneficiary with that degree of beneficial enjoyment of the property that the principles of the law of trusts accord to a person who is unqualifiedly designated as the income beneficiary of a trust. In addition, an individual is deemed to be terminally ill if such individual is known to have an incurable illness or other deteriorating physical condition such that there is at least a 50-percent probability that the individual will die within one year. If the individual survives for at least 18 months after the date the gift is completed, however, the presumption is made that there was no terminal illness at the time of the transfer, unless there is clear and convincing evidence to the contrary.

Transitional rules. If the date for valuing a life estate or an annuity, remainder, or reversion that is based on one or more measuring lives is after April 30, 1999, and before July 1, 1999, the present value of the interest may be determined under the tables based on either Life Table 80CNSMT under Reg. § 20.2031-7A(e)(4) or Table 90CM under Reg. § 20.2031-7(d)(7). However, the

---

[4] Reg. § 1.664-2(c).

Code Sec. 7520 interest rate will be the appropriate rate for the month in which the valuation date occurs. See Reg. § 20.2031-7(d)(3) and Reg. § 25.2512-5(d)(3).

In cases involving a charitable deduction, if the valuation date occurs after April 30, 1999, and before July 1, 1999, and an election is made under Code Sec. 7520(a) to use the Code Sec. 7520 interest rate for March 1999 or April 1999, then the tables based on the mortality experience contained in Life Table 80CNSMT must be used. If the Code Sec. 7520 interest rate for May 1999 or June 1999 is used, the tables based on either Table 80CNSMT or Table 90CM may be used. However, if the valuation date occurs after June 30, 1999, the tables based on the mortality experience contained in Table 90CM must be used, even if a prior month interest rate election under Code Sec. 7520(a) is made. See Reg. § 1.642(c)-6(e)(2), Reg. § 1.664-2(c), and Reg. § 1.664-4(e)(2).

A transitional rule is also provided if a decedent was mentally incompetent on May 1, 1999, and dies without having regained competency or dies within 90 days of the date on which the decedent first regained competency. Under the rule, the fair market value of an annuity, interest for life or a term of years, or a remainder or reversionary interest includible in the gross estate may be determined under either Reg. § 20.2031-7(d)(3) or the corresponding applicable section at the time the decedent became incompetent.

• ***Valuation Tables Prescribed by Code Sec. 7520***

Reproduced in the Appendix at ¶2700 are the tables containing actuarial factors to be used in determining the present value of certain limited interests of decedents dying after April 30, 1999, and to gifts of such interests made after that date.[5] The tables are arranged in the following order:

Table 90CM	Life Table
Table S	Single Life
Table J	Adjustment Factors
Table K	Adjustment Factors
Table B	Term Certain
Table U(1)	Single Life Unitrust
Table D	Term Certain Unitrust
Table F	Payout Factors

The following tables applicable to decedents dying, and gifts made, after April 30, 1989, and before May 1, 1999, are also reproduced. Tables S, J, K, B, D, and F, above, also apply to decedents dying, and gifts made, after April 30, 1989, and before May 1, 1999.

Table 80CNSMT	Life Table
Table S	Single Life
Table U(1)	Single Life Unitrust

• ***Software to Calculate Actuarial Factors***

CCH has several products available that help practitioners calculate the various actuarial factors contained in IRS Publications 1457 "Actuarial Values, Book Aleph" (7-1999), 1458 "Actuarial Values, Book Beth" (7-1999), and 1459 "IRS Actuarial Values, Book Gimel" (7-1999).

CCH IRS Actuarial Factors™, included on the CCH Internet Tax Research Network™, is a finding device that enables practitioners to input the applicable

[5] Reg. § 20.2031-7 and Reg. § 1.664-4; T.D. 8886, filed with the *Federal Register* on June 9, 2000. Also see IRS Publications 1457, 1458, and 1459 (available from the Superintendent of Documents, U.S. Government Printing Office, Washington, D.C. 20402).

Table (e.g., Table S, U(1), U(2)), interest rate, term of years, age, etc. that is needed and automatically calculates the factor. Users can choose factors based on Table 90CM or Table 80CNSMT. This valuable Practice Aid is included as an enhancement to the federal tax products on CCH Internet Tax Research Network™ (Federal and Financial Tabs) and CCH Solutions for Financial Planning™.

In addition to IRS Actuarial Factors, CCH® FinEst Calcs™ will calculate the remainder factors for various split-interest trusts. This software program provides for what-if scenarios and allows for the graphing of results for presentation to clients.

To subscribe to CCH Tax Research Network, or to order CCH® FinEst Calcs™ call 1-888-CCH-REPS or visit our Internet site: http://tax.cchgroup.com.

• *Decedents Dying Before May 1, 1999*

Different rules apply in the case of decedents dying before May 1, 1999.

Valuation of gross estate before January 1, 1952. In the case of a decedent dying before 1952, the present value of limited interests that are dependent upon the continuation or termination of one or more lives, or upon a term certain concurrent with one or more lives, is computed on the basis of interest at the rate of four percent a year, compounded annually, and life contingencies as to each life involved from values that are based on the Actuaries' or Combined Experience Table of Mortality, as extended.[6] This table and related factors are contained in 26 CFR Part 81 edition revised as of April 1, 1958. The present value of an interest measured by a term of years is also computed on the basis of interest at the rate of four percent a year.

Valuation of gross estate after December 31, 1951, and before January 1, 1971. In the case of a decedent dying after 1951 and before 1971, the present value of limited interests that are dependent upon the continuation or termination of one or more lives, or upon a term certain concurrent with one or more lives, is computed on the basis of interest at the rate of 3.5 percent a year, compounded annually, and life contingencies as to each life involved are taken from U.S. Life Table 38.[7] This table and related factors are contained in 26 CFR Part 20 edition revised as of April 1, 1984. The present value of an interest measured by a term of years is also computed on the basis of interest at the rate of 3.5 percent a year.

Valuation of gross estate after December 31, 1970, and before December 1, 1983. In the case of a decedent dying after 1970 and before December 1, 1983, the present value of limited interests that are dependent upon the continuation or termination of one or more lives, or upon a term certain concurrent with one or more lives, is computed on the basis of interest at the rate of six percent a year, compounded annually, and life contingencies as to each male and female life involved are taken from Table LN of former Reg. § 20.2031-10.[8] This table and related factors are contained in 26 CFR Part 20 edition revised as of April 1, 1994. The present value of an interest measured by a term of years is also computed on the basis of interest at the rate of six percent a year.

It should be noted that, with respect to interests that are dependent on the continuation or termination of one or more lives, the six-percent tables make a distinction between an interest that is based on the life of a male (Table A(1)) and one that is based on the life of a female (Table A(2)). This is true because the

---

[6] Reg. § 20.2031-7A(a).

[7] Reg. § 20.2031-7A(b).

[8] Reg. § 20.2031-7A(c).

tables use one set of actuarial assumptions for men and a different set for women. Table B is used if the interest is dependent on a term of years.

IRS Publication No. 723, "Actuarial Values I: Valuation of Last Survivor Charitable Remainders," and IRS Publication No. 723A, "Actuarial Values II: Factors at 6 Percent Involving One and Two Lives," contain many special factors involving one or two lives. Although no longer available from the Superintendent of Documents, a copy of each may be obtained from: Internal Revenue Service, CC:DOM:CORP:T:R (IRS Publication No. 723 or 723A), Room 5228, POB 7604, Ben Franklin Station, Washington, D.C. 20044.[9]

Valuation of gross estate after November 30, 1983, and before May 1, 1989. In the case of a decedent dying after November 30, 1983, and before May 1, 1989, the present value of an annuity, interest for life, or a remainder or reversionary interest that is dependent upon the continuation or termination of a single life is computed using Table A contained in Reg. §20.2031-7A(d)(6). An annuity, interest for a term of years, or a remainder or reversionary interest that is dependent upon a term certain is valued using Table B of the regulation. These tables are based on a 10-percent interest factor and are actuarially gender-neutral.

If the valuation of the interest involved is dependent upon more than one life or on a term certain that is concurrent with one or more lives, a special factor must be used. The factor is to be computed on the basis of interest at the rate of 10 percent a year, compounded annually, and life contingencies determined, as to each person involved, from the values of 1(x) that are set forth in column 2 of Table LN, contained in Reg. §20.2031-7A(d)(6). Table LN contains values of 1(x) taken from the life table for the total population appearing as Table 1 of United States Life Tables: 1969-1971, published by the Department of Health and Human Services.[10]

IRS Publication No. 723E, "Actuarial Values II: Factors at 10 Percent Involving One and Two Lives," contains special factors involving one or two lives. Although no longer available from the Superintendent of Documents, a copy of the publication may be obtained from: Internal Revenue Service, CC:DOM:CORP:T:R (IRS Publication No. 723E), Room 5228, POB 7604, Ben Franklin Station, Washington, D.C. 20044. If a special factor is required in the case of an actual decedent, the IRS will furnish the factor to the executor on request. The request must be accompanied by a statement setting forth the date of birth of each person whose life may affect the value of the interest and copies of the relevant instruments.[11]

If an annuity is payable at the end of each year for the life of an individual, its value is determined by multiplying the amount payable by the applicable factor in column 2 of Table A, taking into consideration the age of the individual whose life measures the duration of the annuity. Similarly, if the annuity is payable annually at the end of each year for a definite number of years, the amount payable is multiplied by the figure in column 2 of Table B corresponding to the number of years for which the annuity is payable.[12]

Certain adjustment factors must be applied to the valuations determined above if the annuity is payable at the end of semiannual, quarterly, monthly, or weekly periods.[13] The product of the Table A or B factors and the aggregate amount to be paid within a year is multiplied by the applicable factor below,

---

[9] Reg. §20.2031-7A(c).
[10] Reg. §20.2031-7A(d)(5).
[11] Reg. §20.2031-7A(d)(5).
[12] Reg. §20.2031-7A(d)(2).
[13] Reg. §20.2031-7A(d)(2)(ii).

depending upon when the payments are made. The factors for the various periods are as follows:

Semiannual payments	1.0244
Quarterly payments	1.0368
Monthly payments	1.0450
Weekly payments	1.0482

If an annuity for the life of an individual is payable at the beginning of annual, semiannual, quarterly, monthly or weekly periods, the general valuation procedure is slightly different. The value of that annuity is the sum of the first payment *plus* the present value of a similar annuity that would not be payable until the *end* of each payment period (determined as above).

If the first payment of an annuity for a definite number of years is payable at the beginning of the annual or other payment period, the *applicable factor* is the *product* of the factor shown in Table B multiplied by the following additional factor, as appropriate:[14]

Annual payments	1.1000
Semiannual payments	1.0744
Quarterly payments	1.0618
Monthly payments	1.0534
Weekly payments	1.0502

The estate of a decedent dying after November 30, 1983, but before August 9, 1984, can use either the 10-percent tables of Reg. §20.2031-7A(d)(6) or the six-percent tables pursuant to Reg. §20.2031-7A(c), whichever is more advantageous, to value an annuity, an interest for life or for a term of years, or a remainder or reversionary interest that is includible in the decedent's gross estate. The estate of a decedent dying on or after August 9, 1984, must use the 10-percent tables unless the estate is subject to a special rule relating to the incompetency of the decedent. Under this rule, where the valuation date is before May 1, 1989, and the decedent was subject to a mental disability on December 1, 1983, such that the disposition of his or her property could not be changed, and the decedent either dies without regaining competency or within 90 days after doing so, the decedent's estate may use either the six- or 10-percent tables.[15]

Valuation of gross estate after April 30, 1989, and before May 1, 1999. In the case of a decedent dying after April 30, 1989, and before May 1, 1999, the present value of an annuity, interest for life or a term of years, or a remainder or reversionary interest is governed by Reg. §20.2031-7A(e). Generally, the same methodologies for valuing limited property interests for decedents dying after April 30, 1999, are also applicable for decedents dying after April 30, 1989, with one major exception. The single life Table S, based on Life Table 80CNSMT, and Table 80CNSMT in Reg. §20.2031-7A(e)(4) apply. (These tables are reproduced at ¶2700 of the Appendix.) Because the Table B term certain remainder factors and the Table J and Table K annuities adjustment factors at Reg. §20.2031-7(d)(6) are not based on mortality experience, those tables also apply to decedents dying after April 30, 1989.

Although no longer available for purchase, IRS Publication No. 1457, "Actuarial Values, Alpha Volume," includes many actuarial factors and examples not contained in the regulations. Pertinent factors contained in this publication may be obtained from: CC:DOM:CORP:R (IRS Publication 1457) Room 5226, IRS, POB 7604, Ben Franklin Station, Washington, DC 20044.

---

[14] Reg. §20.2031-7A(d)(2)(iii).

[15] Reg. §20.2031-7A(d)(1).

Transitional rules. If a decedent was incompetent on May 1, 1989, such that the disposition of his or her property could not be changed, and the decedent dies either without regaining competency or within 90 days after regaining competency, the decedent's executor has an option with respect to valuation methodologies. Under such circumstances, the fair market value of an annuity, life estate, term of years, remainder and reversion included in the decedent's gross estate may be calculated under Reg. §20.2031-7A(e)(4) or under the appropriate section of the regulation that was applicable when the decedent became mentally incompetent.

¶ 534 Actuarial Factors vs. Actual Health

For estate tax purposes, the value of life and remainder interests must be determined from facts available at the time of the decedent's death. The fact that the life tenant may in fact survive the decedent by only a short period of time is not controlling. The actuarial tables in the Appendix at ¶2700 reflect the deaths of those who die prematurely as well as those who enjoy lives of greater longevity.

Nonetheless, for the estates of decedents dying, and gifts made, after December 13, 1995, IRS regulations provide that the actuarial tables may not be used to determine the present value of a limited interest if it is known at the time of the decedent's death, or at the time the gift is completed, that the individual who is a measuring life of the interest is terminally ill.[16] An individual who is known to have an incurable illness or other deteriorating physical condition is considered terminally ill if there is at least a 50-percent probability that the individual will die within one year. Under the regulations, a special actuarial factor must be computed that takes into account the projection of the actual life expectancy. However, if the individual survives for 18 months or longer after the date of the decedent's death, the individual shall be presumed to have not been terminally ill at the date of death unless the contrary is established by clear and convincing evidence. For purposes of the credit allowable to the transferee's estate for tax on a prior transfer, the value of the property shall be the value determined previously in the transferor's estate.

Prior to December 14, 1995, if it was known on the valuation date that a life tenant was afflicted with a fatal and incurable disease in its advanced stages such that death was clearly imminent, a departure from the actuarial tables could be made and the value of a life or remainder interest determined by reference to known facts based on the expert testimony of a physician.[17] Generally, cases indicate a reluctance to depart from valuations determined through the use of actuarial tables unless an incurable or fatal disease exists *and* there is evidence indicating imminent death or a life expectancy so brief as to require a departure from such tables.[18] In the majority of cases permitting departures from such tables, the life tenant's maximum actual life expectancy was one year or less.[19] These principles apply in the valuation of interests for charitable and marital deduction purposes as well. They are also applicable for purposes of computing the allowable credit for tax on prior transfers. However, the Tax Court rejected

---

[16] Reg. §20.7520-3(b)(3) and Reg. §25.7520-3(b)(3).

[17] *N.H. Jennings,* 10 TC 323, CCH Dec. 16,263 (Acq.). See *M.P. Fabric Est.,* 83 TC 932, CCH Dec. 41,667; *C. McDowell Est.,* 51 TCM 319, CCH Dec. 42,831(M), TC Memo. 1986-27.

[18] *Cont. Ill. Nat'l Bk. & Tr. Co. of Chicago,* CA-7, 74-2 USTC ¶13,034; *Mercantile-Safe Deposit & Trust Co.,* DC Md., 74-1 USTC ¶12,985, 368 FSupp. 742.

[19] *Cont. Ill. Nat'l Bk. & Tr. Co. of Chicago,* CA-7, 74-2 USTC ¶13,034.

the use of valuation tables for purposes of computing the credit in valuing a husband's usufruct interest in his wife's share of community property after their simultaneous deaths.[20]

¶ 535 Other Property Interests

The various other items reportable on Form 706 (United States Estate (and Generation-Skipping Transfer) Tax Return), Schedule F (Other Miscellaneous Property Not Reportable Under Any Other Schedule), as "Other Miscellaneous Property" are valued as indicated below.

• ***Debts Owed Decedent***

Debts owed to the decedent should be reported in the amount of the principal plus accrued interest. The executor possibly can establish a lower valuation.

• ***Leasehold Interests***

The renewal value of leases is an important factor in valuing leaseholds.

• ***Household Goods and Personal Effects***

Household goods and personal effects should be reported at the price that a willing buyer would pay a willing seller. A room-by-room itemization is desirable. All articles should be named separately. Items in the same room with individual values of not more than $100 may be grouped. A separate value should be given for each article named.[21]

The executor may furnish a sworn statement in lieu of the itemized list, however. This statement may set forth the aggregate value of the property as appraised by a competent appraiser or appraisers, or dealers in the kind of property involved (see ¶ 540).

If the estate includes articles of marked artistic or intrinsic value, such as jewelry, furs, silverware, works of art, oriental rugs, or stamp collections, and any one article is valued in excess of $3,000 or any collection of articles is valued at more than $10,000, the appraisal of an expert or experts, under oath, must be filed with the return.[22]

• ***Farm Products and Automobiles***

Farm products, growing crops (other than timber for which special use valuation is elected, see ¶ 290), livestock, farm machinery, and automobiles are valued at the price at which such items would change hands between a willing buyer and a willing seller. The fair market value is not to be determined by a forced sale price. All relevant facts and elements of value as of the applicable valuation date must be considered[23] (see ¶ 540).

Feed on hand at the date of the decedent's death, but consumed by livestock during the elected alternate valuation period is includible in the gross estate at its value on the date of disposition—the date on which it was fed to the livestock.[24] The disposition price is to be used for any farm asset that is sold or disposed of during the alternate valuation period.[25]

---

[20] *E.W. Marks Est.*, 94 TC 720, CCH Dec. 46,594. See also *A.P. Carter Est.*, CA-5, 91-1 USTC ¶ 60,054, 921 F2d 63, cert. denied.

[21] Reg. § 20.2031-6.

[22] Reg. § 20.2031-6.

[23] Reg. § 20.2031-1(b).

[24] Rev. Rul. 58-436, 1958-2 CB 366, modified by Rev. Rul. 64-289, 1964-2 CB 173 (income tax conclusions only).

[25] Rev. Rul. 68-154, 1968-1 CB 395.

• *Deferred Compensation Payments*

Many employees enter into contracts or agreements with their employers that provide for the payment of deferred compensation to the employee, usually on the employee's retirement. These contracts also usually provide for the payment of specified sums to a named beneficiary (commonly the employee's spouse) if the employee dies before retirement.

The IRS has attempted to include the commuted value of the latter payments (commonly called "death benefits") in the estates of deceased employees as property owned at death. However, most courts have held that these payments are not includible in a deceased employee's estate because the employee's interest in the employment contract is deemed to terminate at death.

The IRS has attempted to include death benefits of this type in decedents' estates under pre-1977 Code Sec. 2035 (as transfers in contemplation of death for gifts made prior to 1977) and under Code Sec. 2036 (transfers with retained life estate), Code Sec. 2037 (transfers taking effect at death), Code Sec. 2038 (revocable transfers), and Code Sec. 2039 (annuities) (see ¶733 for further details).

¶ 540 Retail Price and Auction Price

In general, the fair market value of property includible in a decedent's estate is the price at which it would change hands between a willing buyer and a willing seller, both having reasonable knowledge of relevant facts. However, if an item is generally available to the public in a particular market, the fair market value of the property is the price obtainable on the market in which it is most commonly sold to the public. If the item of property is generally obtainable by the public on the retail market, the fair market value of the item is the price at which that item or a comparable one will sell at retail in a particular geographical market.[26]

For example, the fair market value of a car (property generally obtained by the public on the retail market) is the price at which a car of the same make, model, age, and condition could be purchased by members of the public. Fair market value is *not* the price that a used-car dealer would pay for the decedent's car.

The price paid for an item in a decedent's gross estate at a public auction or in answer to a classified newspaper advertisement will also be considered its retail price.[27] There are two conditions, however. The sale must be made within a reasonable period after the applicable valuation date, and there must not be a substantial change in market conditions during that period.

---

[26] Reg. § 20.2031-1(b).

[27] Rev. Proc. 65-19, 1965-2 CB 1002.

Chapter 14
TRANSFERS DURING LIFETIME

¶ 550 Scope of Estate Tax

If the estate tax law applied only to property in which the decedent had an interest at the time of death, the application of the estate tax to any estate could easily be prevented by lifetime transactions. State laws relating to trusts and other property rights make it easy to divest oneself of title to property. At the same time, one could retain either control or beneficial ownership for life. Likewise, when persons realized that they did not have long to live, they could dispose of any remaining property by outright gift, thereby removing such property from their gross estates.

In recognition of these possibilities, Congress included within the scope of the estate tax law various types of lifetime transfers that would otherwise permit complete escape from estate taxes. In prescribing that the value of certain lifetime property transfers are includible in the gross estate, Congress provided for almost every type of lifetime gift in which the decedent did not dispose of every consequential right. These transfers normally involve transfers to trusts.

¶ 555 Transfers Within Three Years of Death

Generally, the value of outright transfers (other than transfers of life insurance) made by a decedent within three years of death is not includible in a decedent's gross estate. However, the value of property is includible in a decedent's gross estate if, within three years of death, the decedent transferred an interest in or power over the property that, if retained by the decedent, would have caused the property to be includible in the decedent's gross estate under Code Sec. 2036 (transfers with retained life estate), Code Sec. 2037 (transfers taking effect at death), Code Sec. 2038 (revocable transfers), or Code Sec. 2042 (life insurance proceeds).[1] The exercise of a general power of appointment, as defined in Code Sec. 2041 (see ¶ 650), within three years of death does not require inclusion of the property subject to the power in the decedent's gross estate under Code Sec. 2035. In addition, for decedents dying after August 5, 1997, annual exclusion gifts made from a decedent's revocable trust within three years of the decedent's death are not includible in the decedent's gross estate.[2]

---

[1] Code Sec. 2035(a).

[2] Code Sec. 2035(e).

The value of any transfer made within three years of death is includible in the decedent's gross estate for the limited purpose of determining the estate's qualification for special use valuation (see ¶280), deferral of estate taxes (see ¶1672), and stock redemptions under Code Sec. 303. Additionally, the value of such a transfer is includible in the gross estate for purposes of determining property that is subject to estate tax liens.[3] This provision is designed to preclude deathbed transfers intended to qualify the estate for such favorable treatment by reducing the amount of nonqualifying property.[4] This provision also applies to transfers to a spouse within three years of death, even though an unlimited gift tax marital deduction is available for gifts made after 1981 (see ¶1001). Note that transfers within three years of death, as well as certain transfers within 10 years of death, are also includible for purposes of the qualified family-owned business deduction (see ¶1150).

• *Gifts for Which Gift Tax Return Not Required*

The value of transfers made within three years of death that are includible in the gross estate under exceptions to the general noninclusion rule of Code Sec. 2035 is includible even if no gift tax return was required to be filed with respect to the transfer.[5] In the case of a gift to a spouse within three years of death for which no gift tax return is required because of the unlimited gift tax marital deduction, the value of the gift is includible in the decedent's gross estate for the limited purposes of determining the estate's qualification for special use valuation, deferral of estate taxes, stock redemptions under Code Sec. 303, and for purposes of determining property that is subject to estate tax liens.

• *"Gross-Up" for Gift Tax Paid on Transfers Within Three Years of Death*

Gift taxes paid on transfers made within three years of a transferor's death are includible in the decedent's gross estate.[6] The amount subject to this rule includes the tax paid by the decedent or the decedent's estate on any gift made by the decedent or his or her spouse within the three-year period ending on the date of the decedent's death. In contrast with the general rule that a period of limitations begins the day after the triggering event (here, the date of death), the triggering event is included when determining the period of limitations for Code Sec. 2035(b)[7].

> *Example:* Mel Frankerlain died on December 31, 2004, and had made a gift on December 31, 2001, for which he had paid gift tax of $5,000. Because the three-year limitation period that ends on December 31, 2004, includes December 31, 2004, this limitation period began on January 1, 2002. Thus, the $5,000 gift tax paid with respect to the December 31, 2001 transfer did not occur within three years of Frankerlain's death, and this amount is not included in his gross estate.

Within the context of computing the estate tax liability due for the amount of gift taxes "grossed up," the Tax Court has rejected an estate's argument that Code Sec. 2043(a) permitted the estate to reduce the amount of includible gift taxes by "consideration" allegedly received by the decedent for his payment of gift taxes. The court held that no reduction was allowed because (1) the plain language of Code Sec. 2035(c) (the predecessor of current Code Sec. 2035(b))

---

[3] Code Sec. 2035(c)(1)(C).

[4] *General Explanation of the Economic Recovery Tax Act of 1981*, Staff of the Joint Committee on Taxation, p. 262.

[5] Code Sec. 2035(c)(3).

[6] Code Sec. 2035(b).

[7] IRS Technical Advice Memorandum 200432016, March 10, 2004.

made no provision for the netting of consideration received, (2) the Code Sec. 2035(c) "gross-up" rule was not a "transfer" within the meaning of Code Sec. 2043(a), and (3) the decedent's obligation to pay the gift taxes arose by operation of law and not as a result of any agreement he may have made with another party.[8]

A recent court decision demonstrates that the IRS may be able to use the "step-transaction" doctrine to successfully fight a transferor's attempt to avoid the "gross-up" rule by having a spouse pay the transferor's gift tax liability. In *B. Brown*, the transferor funded, with a $3.1 million payment, an insurance trust holding a policy on his wife's life. He also transferred $1.4 million to his wife's personal checking account, from which she paid her husband's $1.4 million gift tax liability arising from the funding of the insurance trust. The court held that the transferor's death within three years of the transfer triggered application of the "gross-up" provision of Code Sec. 2035 with respect to the transferor's gross estate. In so ruling, the court disregarded the wife's payment of her husband's gift tax liability as merely a conduit to facilitate a prearranged, tax-avoidance, step transaction that did not reflect the reality of the underlying situation.[9]

The "gross-up" rule does not apply to the gift tax paid by a spouse on a gift made by the decedent within three years of death that is treated as made one-half by the spouse under the gift-splitting provisions of Code Sec. 2513.

• ***Transfer for Adequate Consideration***

Even though transferred within three years of the decedent's death, the value of property for which the decedent received a full and adequate consideration in money or money's worth is not includible in the gross estate.

¶ 565 Transfers Intended to Take Effect at Death

The estate tax law requires the inclusion in the gross estate of the value of lifetime transfers intended to take effect at death.[10]

A transfer made by the decedent and taking effect at the decedent's death is one under which possession or enjoyment of the property can be obtained only by surviving the decedent. However, such a transfer is not treated as a transfer taking effect at death unless the decedent retained a reversionary interest in the property that immediately before the decedent's death had a value in excess of five percent of the value of the transferred property.[11] In determining whether or not a reversionary interest exceeds five percent of the value of the transferred property, the value of the reversionary interest is compared with the value of the transferred property, including interests therein that are not dependent upon survivorship of the decedent. For this purpose, a reversionary interest includes a possibility that property transferred by the decedent:

(1) may return to the decedent or to the decedent's estate; or

(2) may become subject to a power of disposition by the decedent.

If the interest is in income only, a decedent does not have a reversionary interest.[12]

---

[8] *F. Armstrong, Jr. Est.*, TC, 119 TC 220, CCH Dec. 54,921.

[9] *B. Brown*, CA-9, 2003-1 USTC ¶ 60,462, cert. denied, 10/6/2003.

[10] Code Sec. 2037.

[11] Reg. § 20.2037-1(a).

[12] Reg. § 20.2037-1(c).

This reversionary interest of the decedent may be expressly written into the instrument or it may arise by way of state law.[13] In other words, it may be explicit: "To A for life, remainder to B, but if B should predecease me, then the remainder to me or my heirs." It also may be implicit: "To A for life, remainder to B if B doesn't predecease me." In the second example, the entire fee interest has not been disposed of by the decedent. There is a possibility that B will not be eligible to take after A's life estate. Since the property is not otherwise disposed of, it will revert to the decedent by operation of law.

If, in either of these cases, the reversionary interest could be valued in excess of five percent of the value of the property, the value of the property (less the value of any outstanding, preceding interests in persons other than the transferor) would be included in the decedent's gross estate. Such a valuation in excess of five percent is quite possible if only one remainderman is named. The value of such an interest is to be determined by the usual methods of valuation, including the use of mortality tables and actuarial principles (see ¶530).

A transfer intended to take effect at death will not be included in the decedent's estate if possession or enjoyment of the property could have been obtained by any beneficiary during the decedent's lifetime through the exercise of a general power of appointment that was exercisable immediately before the decedent's death.[14]

• ***Transfers Made Prior to October 8, 1949***

All transfers made prior to October 8, 1949, and intended to take effect at death, require the same estate tax consequences as those made after that date, with one exception. The reversionary interest must be expressly included in the instrument of transfer. If it arises by operation of law, the property is not included in the decedent's gross estate.[15]

¶ 570 Transfers with Possession or Enjoyment Retained

The gross estate includes the value of property or property interests transferred by a decedent, in trust or otherwise, if the decedent reserved or retained for life, or for any period not ascertainable without reference to the decedent's death, or for a period that does not in fact end before the decedent's death:

(1) the use, possession, right to the income, or other enjoyment of the transferred property; or

(2) the right, either alone or in conjunction with any other person, to designate the person or persons who will possess or enjoy the transferred property or the income therefrom.[16]

A reservation by the decedent for a period not ascertainable without reference to the decedent's death may be illustrated by the following Example.

Example: Larry Collins reserved the right to receive the income from transferred property in quarterly payments on the condition that no part of the income between the last quarterly payment and the date of his death was to be received by him or his estate.

If the decedent retained or reserved one or more of these rights or interests as to all of the property he transferred, the amount includible in the gross estate

---

[13] Reg. §20.2037-1(c); Rev. Rul. 82-24, 1982-1 CB 134.

[14] Reg. §20.2037-1(b).

[15] Reg. §20.2037-1(f).

[16] Code Sec. 2036.

is the value of the entire property transferred, less the value of any outstanding income interest that is not subject to the decedent's interest or right and that is actually being enjoyed by another person at the time of the decedent's death. If the decedent during life retained or reserved an interest or right as to only a part of the property transferred, the amount includible in the decedent's gross estate is only a corresponding portion of the entire value of the property.[17]

The use, possession, right to the income, or other enjoyment of the transferred property is considered as having been retained by or reserved to the decedent to the extent that it is to be applied toward the discharge of a legal obligation of the decedent or otherwise for the decedent's pecuniary benefit. The term "legal obligation" includes a legal obligation by the decedent during the decedent's lifetime to support a dependent.[18]

If the rights are retained for life, however, or for a period not ascertainable without reference to the decedent's death, the property will in all cases be includible unless one of the special exceptions noted below is applicable. With respect to their right to designate the person or persons who shall possess or enjoy the transferred property or income therefrom, the manner of making the transfer is immaterial. If these rights are retained, they are taxable whether made in trust or otherwise.[19] However, the Tax Court has held that the concept of a transfer with a retained life estate was not applicable to transfers that were deemed to have been made by a decedent under the Uniform Simultaneous Death Act. Thus, in a situation where a decedent and her husband died in a common accident, the proceeds of two policies of insurance on the husband's life that were payable to a trust in which the decedent had a life income interest were not includible in her gross estate, even though she owned the policies and was deemed to have survived her husband under the Uniform Simultaneous Death Act. In the court's view, the Act is intended solely to provide rules for passage of property of both decedents to their beneficiaries.[20]

If the retained use is a natural one, however, such as the use with a spouse of a home that the decedent purchased for the spouse, rather than a use that has been reserved in the instrument of transfer or by a withholding of the property from the transferee, the transfer is not taxable in the absence of an understanding or agreement, expressed or implied. Continued occupancy in a residence, where the donor and donee are husband and wife, does not itself support an inference of an agreement or understanding as to retained possession or enjoyment by the donor.[21] Where the donor and donee are persons other than husband and wife, for example, a parent and child, the IRS has ruled that the continued occupancy of the transferred realty itself implies the existence of an agreement of retained enjoyment by the donor.[22] This IRS position has been sustained by an appellate court.[23]

Where the retention of a right to income was one that did not take effect until after the death of a primary life tenant and the decedent died before the primary life tenant, the entire value of the trust, less only the value of the outstanding life estate, is includible.[24] Unrequested income amounts that were

---

[17] Reg. §20.2036-1(a).

[18] Reg. §20.2036-1(b); see *E.E. German Est.*, CtCls, 85-1 USTC ¶13,610.

[19] Reg. §20.2036-1(b)(3).

[20] *L. Goldstone Est.*, 78 TC 1143, CCH Dec. 39,138.

[21] Rev. Rul. 70-155, 1970-1 CB 189.

[22] Rev. Rul. 78-409, 1978-2 CB 234.

[23] *J.C. Guynn*, CA-4, 71-1 USTC ¶12,742, 437 F2d 1148, rev'g and rem'g DC, 70-1 USTC ¶12,661, 309 FSupp. 233. But see *Est. of S.H. Roemer*, 46 TCM 1176, CCH Dec. 40,384(M), TC Memo. 1983-509 (no implied agreement between mother and daughter).

[24] Reg. §20.2036-1(b).

irrevocably added to trust principal were includible in the gross estate of a life income beneficiary as a transfer with a retained life estate where the beneficiary had the right to income from the augmented trust principal.[25]

• *Effect of Consideration*

If the transfer was made for a consideration, the value of the consideration is deductible from the value of the property in determining the taxable value. As in the case of other transfers, the consideration is considered purely from the standpoint of monetary value. Sentimental attachments and sufficiency of consideration from a purely legal standpoint do not enter into the picture. If the value of the transferred property exceeds the value of the consideration, the difference is included in the decedent's gross estate.[26] Dispositions of life estates and remainder interests, discussed below, may not cause inclusion of the property if a seller receives the actuarial value of the interest.

• *Transfers of Stock in Closely Held Corporations*

The retention of the right to vote (either *directly or indirectly*) shares of stock in what is called "a controlled corporation," by a person who has irrevocably transferred the stock for other than full consideration after June 22, 1976, is treated as the retention of the enjoyment of the transferred shares; thus, retention of the right causes the transferred shares to be includible in such a donor's estate at death.[27] A corporation is a "controlled corporation" for purposes of this rule if, at any time after the transfer of the stock and during the three-year period ending on the date of the decedent's death, the decedent *owned* (ownership being determined by applying the "constructive ownership" rules of income tax Code Sec. 318), or *had the right* (either alone or in conjunction with any person) to vote stock possessing at least 20 percent of the total combined voting power of all classes of stock.[28] If the stock is not in a "controlled corporation," the stock is not includible in the gross estate of a decedent even if the decedent directly held the power to vote the transferred shares.

In determining whether a transferor owns at least 20 percent of the stock in a corporation, the indirect or constructive ownership rules are applied.[29] Under these rules, stock owned by the members of a transferor's family (spouse, children, grandchildren, and parents) is treated as being owned by the transferor. These rules can also apply to stock that is owned by (1) partnerships and estates, (2) trusts, and (3) corporations in which the transferor has an interest.

These rules preclude the use of a formerly popular planning device sanctioned by a 1972 U.S. Supreme Court decision that a decedent who made this type of transfer did not retain the right to enjoy the transferred stock by reason of his voting control over it, and that he did not retain the right to designate the persons who would enjoy the income from the stock (see ¶580) by reason of his ability to control corporate dividends.[30] The decedent retained the power to (1) vote the stock held by a trust, (2) veto the transfer by the trustee of any of the stock, and (3) remove the trustee and appoint another corporate trustee.

---

[25] *S. Horner, Exr.*, CtCls, 73-2 USTC ¶12,956, 485 F2d 596.

[26] Reg. §20.2043-1.

[27] Code Sec. 2036(b)(1). For an example of indirect retention of voting rights, see Rev. Rul. 80-346, 1980-2 CB 271.

[28] Code Sec. 2036(b)(2).

[29] Code Sec. 318.

[30] *M.A. Byrum, Exrx. (M.C. Byrum Will)*, SCt, 72-2 USTC ¶12,859, 408 US 125.

• ***Transfers to Family Limited Partnerships***

A transfer to a family limited partnership may also be seen by the IRS as a means of retaining control over the transferred property sufficient to cause inclusion of its value in the transferor's gross estate. Court decisions that analyze the application of Code Sec. 2036 to family limited partnership (FLP) situations usually involve a highly fact-specific investigation of the FLP agreement, the rights and discretionary powers of the decedent under it, whether the formalities of the FLP agreement actually are being followed in the FLP's operation, and the extent to which the creation of the FLP was supported by consideration.

In a recent Tax Court decision (*A. Strangi Est.*[31]), the value of property transferred by a decedent to a family limited partnership (FLP) and to the FLP's corporate general partner (the corporation) was includible in the decedent's gross estate. Two months before his death, the decedent, assisted by his attorney in fact (who was also his son-in-law), created a FLP. The decedent transferred about $10 million to the FLP (mostly in cash and securities) in exchange for a 99-percent LP interest. Concurrent with the creation of the FLP, a corporation was formed to act as the FLP's managing general partner, with the decedent purchasing a 47-percent interest in the corporation for approximately $50,000. The decedent's attorney in fact was subsequently hired to manage the day-to-day business of the corporation. The Tax Court held that the decedent had retained a right to the income from the transferred property for purposes of Code Sec. 2036(a)(1) because the documents governing the operation of the FLP and the corporation did not preclude the decedent himself, acting through his attorney in fact, from being designated as a recipient of income from those entities. Moreover, the court concluded, the decedent retained the possession or enjoyment of the transferred property because of an implied agreement among the parties that the decedent would retain the economic benefit of the transferred property. The existence of this implied agreement was supported by the transfer of the majority of the decedent's assets, the decedent's continued occupation of his residence following its transfer to the FLP, the use of entity funds to pay for the needs of the decedent and his estate, and the testamentary nature of the arrangements.

Additionally, the *Strangi* court held that the transferred property was includible in the decedent's gross estate because the decedent retained the right to designate the persons who would enjoy the transferred property.[32] The court noted that, under the FLP agreement and the corporation's shareholder agreement, the decedent could act with other shareholders to essentially revoke the FLP arrangement and thereby bring about the present enjoyment of the FLP assets. These, and other rights conferred under the FLP/corporation arrangement, were not constrained in any meaningful way by the fiduciary duties held by directors and shareholders. The Tax Court rejected the estate's argument that the creation and funding of the FLP were supported by consideration, viewing the arrangement as a mere "recycling" of value through the use of the FLP and corporate forms.

In another case, the Court of Appeals for the Third Circuit upheld a Tax Court decision holding that assets transferred by a decedent to two family limited partnerships (FLPs) were includible in the decedent's gross estate be-

---

[31] *A. Strangi Est.*, 85 TCM 1331, CCH Dec. 55,160(M), TC Memo. 2003-145, on remand from CA-5, 2002 USTC ¶60,441. See, also, *M. Harper Est.*, 83 TCM 1641, CCH Dec. 54,745(M), TC Memo. 2002-21.

[32] Code Sec. 2036(a)(2).

cause the decedent retained the enjoyment of the property during lifetime.[33] The Tax Court had concluded that the decedent's failure to retain sufficient assets to support himself for the expected duration of his life, cash distributions from the FLPs to the decedent exceeding $170,000 over two years, and the general testamentary nature of the FLP arrangements were all factors pointing to an implied agreement that the decedent would retain the benefit of the transferred property. The appellate court agreed that the decedent's relationship with the transferred assets remained the same both before and after the contribution of the assets to the FLPs.

The appellate court in *Thompson* further held that the Code Sec. 2036(a) exception for adequate and full consideration did not apply. There was no transfer for consideration because neither FLP engaged in a functioning business enterprise that provided the decedent with a substantive, non-tax benefit for transferring the assets (mainly securities) to the FLPs. Instead, the only potential benefit to the decedent for holding the assets in partnership form was the estate tax savings to be garnered from valuation discounts. The Court distinguished the result reached in *Kimbell* (discussed below), where the FLP arrangement provided the transferor with centralized management and protection from personal liability.

In another Tax Court Memorandum decision handed down six months after *Strangi*, none of the assets transferred to five family limited partnerships by a husband and wife was includible in their respective gross estates because the transfers were bona fide sales for adequate and full consideration under Code Sec. 2036(a).[34] The transfers did not constitute a mere "recycling of value", because the FLPs had economic substance and operated as joint enterprises for profit through the management of the couple's children. The transfers were motivated primarily by investment and business concerns relating to the management of the couple's assets. In addition, the couple retained assets outside of the FLPs sufficient to maintain their accustomed standard of living. Moreover, all of the partners in each of the FLPs received partnership interests proportionate to the value of the assets transferred to the FLPs and the transferred assets were properly credited to the partners' respective capital accounts.

In *D. Kimbell, Sr., Exr.*, the Court of Appeals for the Fifth Circuit reached the opposite result, holding that assets transferred to a FLP were made pursuant to a bona fide sale for adequate and full consideration.[35] In *Kimbell*, the decedent created a revocable trust, with herself and her son designated as co-trustees. Several years later, but less than three months before her death, the decedent, her son and her daughter-in-law formed a limited liability company (LLC). The decedent's revocable trust contributed $20,000 to the LLC in exchange for a 50-percent interest. The decedent's son was the sole manager of the LLC. Later that month, the revocable trust and the LLC formed the FLP under Texas law. The revocable trust contributed approximately $2.5 million in various assets (including oil and gas working and royalty interests) to the FLP in exchange for a 99-percent LP interest. The LLC received a one-percent general partner interest in exchange for its $25,000 cash contribution. The appellate court vacated the district court's grant of summary judgment[36] for the government that the forma-

---

[33] *T. Thompson Est. (B. Turner, Exrx.)*, CA-3, 2004-2 USTC ¶60,489, aff'g TC, CCH Dec. 54,890(M), 84 TCM 374, TC Memo. 2002-346.

[34] *E. Stone, III Est.*, 86 TCM 551, CCH Dec. 55,341(M), TC Memo. 2003-309.

[35] *D. Kimbell, Sr., Exr.*, CA-5, 2004-1 USTC ¶60,486.

[36] *D. Kimbell, Sr., Exr.*, DC Tex., 2003-1 USTC ¶60,455, rev'd by CA-5, 2004-1 USTC ¶60,486.

tion of the FLP was not the result of an arm's-length transaction and that the decedent's receipt of the LP interest was nothing more than a "circuitous recycling of value". Citing the Fifth Circuit's decision in *J. Wheeler*[37] as the only case on point, the court concluded that the transfer to the FLP was made for adequate and full consideration because: (1) the decedent received a partnership interest that was proportionate to the assets contributed; (2) the decedent's capital account was properly credited with the assets that she contributed; and (3) the decedent was entitled to a distribution commensurate with her capital account balance upon termination or dissolution of the FLP. The fact that the estate claimed a 49-percent discount in valuing the decedent's LP interest did not preclude a finding that the interest was adequate consideration for the transferred assets. This was so because the "willing buyer/willing seller" test could not be equated with the full consideration test under Code Sec. 2036. The court further ruled that the estate had shown that the transfer of the FLP was a bona fide sale and not a disguised gift or sham transaction. This conclusion was supported by several objective facts, including: (1) the decedent retained sufficient assets outside of the FLP for her own support and did not commingle FLP and personal assets; (2) partnership formalities were observed and the contributed assets were actually assigned to the FLP; and (3) there were credible non-tax business reasons for the formation of the FLP, including centralized management and protection from personal liability.

The law concerning the includibility of FLP assets in a transferor's gross estate under Code Sec. 2036(a) will, undoubtedly, continue to develop in future judicial decisions. However, based on the court rulings above, a taxpayer contemplating the formation of a FLP that may be vulnerable to a Code Sec. 2036 attack should consider the following:

(1) Prior to a transfer of assets to the FLP, the transferor's advisors should do a careful cash flow analysis regarding the amount of assets that will be needed to maintain the transferor's lifestyle throughout his or her expected life span.

(2) The transferor's house should probably not be placed in a FLP.

(3) Estate taxes should not be paid from FLP assets, unless these assets are includible in the gross estate.

(4) All formalities of the partnership form should be respected. The partnership should be conducted as if it were a commercial entity.

(5) Probably not all of the assets in the FLP should be financial assets: at least some of the assets should require active management.

• ***Estate Freezes***

As part of the Revenue Act of 1987 (P.L. 100-203), Code Sec. 2036(c) was enacted in an attempt to prevent perceived valuation abuses involving a strategy known as an "estate freeze." The "estate freeze" was an estate planning device whereby an older owner of a closely held business would retain an income interest in the company, usually preferred stock and certain liquidation rights, and transfer to younger members of the family an interest in the company, usually common stock, that was likely to appreciate in value. The value of the retained interests (e.g., liquidation rights) could easily be inflated, thus lowering the value of the interest transferred and reducing the amount of the taxable gift. Under the provisions of Code Sec. 2036(c), the post-transfer appreciation in value

---

[37] *J. Wheeler*, CA-5, 97-2 USTC ¶60,278.

of certain transferred property interests was includible in the transferor's gross estate.

The Revenue Reconciliation Act of 1990 (P.L. 101-508) repealed Code Sec. 2036(c) retroactive to its original effective date (December 17, 1987) and enacted the Chapter 14 special valuation rules,[38] effective for transfers after October 8, 1990 (see ¶2500). The special valuation rules take a more direct approach by providing rules for valuing the transferred interest for gift tax purposes rather than focusing on the transferor's estate.

• *Dispositions of Life Estates and Remainder Interests*

On the theory that estate tax liability for a transfer with a retained life estate arises at the time of the transfer, the U.S. Court of Appeals for the Tenth Circuit has held that the subsequent sale of the retained life interest at its fair market value reduced only the value of the taxable property.[39] There still would be included in the gross estate of the transferor the value of the property less the purchase money paid for the life estate. Accordingly, under this reasoning, to remove the transferred property from her gross estate, the transferor must have received full and adequate consideration for the interest that would otherwise be included in her gross estate.

The U.S. Court of Appeals for the Tenth Circuit later limited this theory to transfers of property solely owned by the decedent.[40] Following the decision of the U.S. Court of Appeals for the Seventh Circuit,[41] the Tenth Circuit held that the transfer with retained life estates of jointly held property for which the decedent furnished the entire consideration (and which, therefore, would have been includible in his gross estate to the extent of its entire value if held at his death) required only the inclusion in decedent's gross estate of the value of his one-half interest in the property transferred. See ¶502 for tax treatment of "qualified joint interests" created or recreated after 1976.

With respect to the issue of valuing an interest for purposes of the bona fide sale exception, the U.S. Court of Appeals for the Federal Circuit has held that where a decedent sold a remainder interest in property and retained a life interest, the payment of the actuarial value of the remainder interest did not satisfy the exception. Thus, the value of the transferred interest was includible in the decedent's gross estate (offset by the amount of consideration received, as provided under Code Sec. 2043).[42] However, both the U.S. Court of Appeals for the Third Circuit[43] and the Court of Appeals for the Ninth Circuit[44] have held that the value of the transferred remainder interest is to be the measure of whether adequate and full consideration has been received. Thus, where it is demonstrated that full price was paid for the remainder interest, no part of the

---

[38] Code Sec. 2701 through Code Sec. 2704.

[39] *C. Allen, Exr. (Allen Est.)*, CA-10, 61-2 USTC ¶12,032, 293 F2d 916, cert. denied, 368 US 944.

[40] *E. Heasty, Exr. (King Est.)*, CA-10, 67-1 USTC ¶12,442, 370 F2d 525, aff'g DC Kan., 65-1 USTC ¶12,304, 239 FSupp. 345.

[41] *H. Glaser, Jr., Admr.*, CA-7, 62-2 USTC ¶12,094, 306 F2d 57, aff'g and rev'g DC Ind., 61-2 USTC ¶12,031, 196 FSupp. 47.

[42] *G.S. Gradow*, CA-FC, 90-1 USTC ¶60,010, 897 F2d 516, aff'g ClsCt, 87-1 USTC ¶13,711, 11 ClsCt 808.

[43] *R. D'Ambrosio Est.*, CA-3, 96-2 USTC ¶60,252, rev'g and rem'g TC, 105 TC 252, CCH Dec. 50,903, cert. denied 5/19/97. See also, *J.M. Wheeler*, CA-5, 97-2 USTC ¶60,278, 116 F3d 749, which noted that selling a remainder interest for its actuarial value does not deplete a seller's estate.

[44] *C. Magnin Est.*, CA-9, 99-2 USTC ¶60,347, 184 F3d 1074, rev'g TC, 71 TCM 1856, CCH Dec. 51,127(M), TC Memo. 1996-92.

value of the transferred property will be included in the transferor's gross estate because of his or her retained income interest.

• *Trust Reimbursement of Grantor's Income Tax Liability*

Where a grantor of a trust is deemed to be its owner under the rules of Code Secs. 671–679, trust income is taxed to the grantor, rather than to the trust. The IRS has issued estate tax guidance with respect to three factual situations where a grantor trust reimbursed the grantor for tax liability assessed on trust income. In the first situation ("Scenario One"), neither applicable state law nor the trust instrument contained any provision requiring or permitting the trustee to reimburse the grantor's income tax liability. Here, because the grantor did not retain the right to have trust property used to discharge the grantor's legal obligation to pay the income tax on trust income, no portion of the trust was includible in the grantor's gross estate under Code Sec. 2036. Under Scenario Two, the trust instrument required the trustee to reimburse the grantor for income tax incurred on trust income. Here, the IRS ruled, such a retained right caused the full value of the trust's assets to be includible in the grantor's gross estate. The result would be the same if state law required the trustee to reimburse the grantor, unless the trust instrument provided otherwise. The IRS will not apply the rule announced in Scenario Two to any decedent's estate with respect to any trust that was created prior to October 4, 2004. Under Scenario Three, the trust instrument gave the trustee the discretion to reimburse the grantor. The IRS concluded that this discretionary power (whether granted by the trust instrument or by state law), did not cause estate tax inclusion of the trust's assets, even if the trustee actually did reimburse the grantor for the income tax incurred. However, the trustee's discretionary power, coupled with other facts, such as an understanding between the grantor and the trustee regarding the trustee's exercise of the discretionary power, could cause inclusion of the trust assets in the grantor's gross estate under Code Sec. 2036.[45]

• *Pre-1931 and Pre-1932 Transfers*

Special exceptions exist in the case of transfers made before March 4, 1931. The exceptions concern any of the rights described above that were retained for life or for any period that does not in fact end before the decedent's death. Similar exceptions exist with respect to transfers made before June 7, 1932, under which the rights were retained for a period not ascertainable without reference to the decedent's death. Such pre-1931 and pre-1932 transfers are not includible in the estate of a decedent unless there is some other basis for taxability, such as the retention of other rights as well.

¶ 580 Right Retained to Designate Who Shall Possess or Enjoy

The retention of income, possession, use, or enjoyment of property requires inclusion of the value of the transferred property in the gross estate under Code Sec. 2036. A transfer also will be taxed under Code Sec. 2036 if a decedent reserved or retained the right, either alone or in conjunction with any other person or persons, to designate the persons who shall possess or enjoy the property or the income therefrom. The requirements as to the period for which such designated person retains such rights are the same as if the decedent retained those rights.[46]

---

[45] Rev. Rul. 2004-64, IRB 2004-27, 7.

[46] Reg. § 20.2036-1(b).

If a grantor creates an irrevocable trust for the benefit of other persons and acts as trustee or co-trustee, and the trustees have the power to accumulate or distribute and add trust income to trust principal, the Supreme Court has held that the value of the trust property and the accumulated trust income will be included in the decedent's gross estate.[47] Each accumulation of income represents a taxable transfer. The grantor-trustee's power to deny the beneficiaries the immediate enjoyment of that income is a retention of the power to designate the persons who would enjoy the income.

The IRS has attempted to apply the rationale of this case to situations where the grantor-trustee has not directly retained the power to accumulate or distribute income but, instead, has retained only certain administrative and managerial powers over the trust. Frequently, these administrative powers are called "boiler-plate" powers. The two most common of the types of such powers causing trouble for estates are (1) the right to allocate receipts and disbursements between trust income and principal, and (2) the right to invest in "non-legal" investments. Most courts have held that the existence of these powers does not give the decedent the right to designate the persons who shall possess or enjoy the transferred property.[48] The common denominator that has led the courts to exclude these trusts has been the existence of state laws governing the duties of trustees toward income beneficiaries and remaindermen.

The IRS will include the value of irrevocable trusts in a grantor's gross estate where the trustee is given the power to accumulate or distribute income to beneficiaries and the grantor retains the right to appoint a successor trustee that includes himself.[49] The Tax Court has agreed in at least one case.[50] However, the Tax Court has refused to follow this rule in the case of a trust set up by a Texas resident who was legally incompetent at death.[51] The IRS will not include the value of the assets of such a trust in the grantor's gross estate where the grantor merely retains the right to appoint a successor corporate trustee that was not related or subordinate to the grantor after the original trustee has resigned or been removed by judicial process.[52]

The Tax Court has held that a corporate trustee's power to distribute income and principal was not attributable to the grantor simply because of the grantor's ability to remove and replace one corporate trustee with another corporate trustee, without cause. Noting that a trustee has a duty to display complete loyalty to the interests of the beneficiary, the court would not include the trust property in the grantor's estate without evidence of fraudulent collusion.[53] In another case, the U.S. Court of Appeals for the Eighth Circuit concluded that a decedent had not retained dominion and control over property that the decedent transferred to a trust by reason of his right to remove and replace trustees with successor trustees who were not related or subordinate to the decedent.[54] In view of these decisions, the IRS ruled that a grantor's reservation of an unqualified power to change corporate trustees will not result in the inclusion of the trust corpus in the grantor's gross estate.[55] The IRS has also privately ruled that an

---

[47] *C.E. O'Malley*, SCt, 66-1 USTC ¶12,388, 383 US 627.

[48] For example, see *R. Budd Est.*, 49 TC 468, CCH Dec. 28,841 (Acq.).

[49] Rev. Rul. 73-21, 1973-1 CB 405.

[50] *J.A. Alexander Est.*, 81 TC 757, CCH Dec. 40,554.

[51] *R.T. Reid Est.*, 71 TC 816, CCH Dec. 35,883.

[52] Rev. Rul. 77-182, 1977-1 CB 273, modified by Rev. Rul. 95-58, 1995-2 CB 191.

[53] *H.S. Wall Est.*, 101 TC 300, CCH Dec. 49,330.

[54] *J. Vak Est.*, CA-8, 92-2 USTC ¶60,110, rev'g and rem'g TC, 62 TCM 942, CCH Dec. 47,674(M), TC Memo. 1991-503.

[55] Rev. Rul. 95-58, 1995-2 CB 191, revoking Rev. Rul. 79-353, 1979-2 CB 325, and Rev.

income beneficiary's power to remove and replace a current trustee with a corporate trustee will not cause inclusion of the value of the trust in the beneficiary's gross estate.[56]

• *Pre-1931 and Pre-1932 Transfers*

Similarly, the same exceptions as to pre-1931 and pre-1932 transfers and the same means of escaping the tax by relinquishing rights exist (see ¶570). In addition, transfers made before June 7, 1932, are excepted if the decedent's right to govern enjoyment was reserved to the decedent in conjunction with any other person or persons. The courts, however, are not in agreement as to whether the transfer contemplated by the statute is limited to irrevocable transfers made prior to the above dates.

¶ 585 Revocable Transfers

Property transferred during lifetime is includible in the decedent's gross estate if, at the time of the decedent's death, the enjoyment of the property is subject to change through the exercise of a power to alter, amend, revoke, or terminate by the decedent alone or by the decedent in conjunction with another person. The retention of a power in conjunction with "any person" is not limited to nonbeneficiaries.

Taxation will result even though the only effect of the exercise of the decedent's power to revoke would have been to accelerate the enjoyment of principal by the beneficiaries.[57] No tax will result, however, if the power can be exercised only with the consent of all parties having an interest, vested or contingent, in the transferred property.[58]

• *Powers Resulting in Taxability*

The courts often have had to determine what is a power to alter, amend, revoke, or terminate. They have decided that the following powers result in taxability:

(1) power to revoke or terminate the trust, whether such power results in a return of corpus to the settlor or acceleration of enjoyment by the remaindermen;

(2) power to control and manage the corpus (except where such power is concerned only with mechanics or details—the designation of funds as income or principal, investment policy, the issuance of voting proxies, or other matters that do not alter the rights or interests of the beneficiaries);

(3) power to change beneficiaries or to vary the amounts distributable (except where the transfer was made prior to March 3, 1931, and the power is applicable only to income during the decedent's lifetime);

(4) power to appoint by will or to change shares by will;

(5) power to revoke that exists by virtue of state law;[59] and

(Footnote Continued)

Rul. 81-51, 1981-1 CB 458, and modifying Rev. Rul. 77-182, 1977-1 CB 273.

[56] IRS Letter Ruling 9746007 (Aug. 11, 1997).

[57] *City Bank Farmers Trust Co.*, SCt, 36-1 USTC ¶9001, 296 US 85.

[58] Reg. §20.2038-1(a)(2).

[59] *S. Swanson Est.*, FedCl, 2000-1 USTC ¶60,371, 46 FedCl 388; aff'd, CA-FC, in an unpublished opinion, 2001-1 USTC ¶60,408; *O. Casey Est.*, CA-4, 91-2 USTC ¶60,091, 948 F2d 895, rev'g TC, 58 TCM 176, CCH Dec. 46,035(M), TC Memo. 1989-511.

(6) power to invade the corpus of a trust created by another for whose benefit the decedent created a similar trust.

If the powers involved are applicable only to a part of the trust, only that part is taxable.[60]

The fact that the transferor will not benefit by exercise of the power is not important so long as the transferor can affect the interests of beneficiaries. This includes the power to distribute or accumulate trust income. Capital gains by the trust and additions to it traceable to the decedent have the same status as original corpus. Additions by a decedent to trusts created by others are governed by the decedent's right over the trusts even though the original corpus may not be taxable in his estate.

The IRS maintains that when a donor transfers property to a minor under a state Uniform Gifts to Minors Act, a Model Gifts of Securities to Minors Act, or a Uniform Transfers to Minors Act, and is acting as custodian of the custodial property at the date of death, the custodial property is includible in the custodian's gross estate.[61] This position has been uniformly sustained by the courts because a custodian has the right, under most uniform acts, to terminate the custodianship by paying over the income and principal to the minor beneficiaries at any time. If a parent transfers property and serves as custodian, the custodial property is also includible in the parent's gross estate, under Code Sec. 2036, because the parent can apply custodial funds in satisfaction of the legal obligation of support.[62] This rule has also been applied where the decedent and the decedent's spouse made reciprocal transfers to each other in custodianship for their parents.[63]

• *Powers Not Resulting in Taxability*

The courts have decided that the following do not constitute powers sufficient to cause taxability under Code Sec. 2038:

(1) power in other than the grantor to revoke the transfer or to return part of it to the grantor (but such transfers may be taxed as transfers intended to take effect at death; see ¶565);

(2) certain powers contingent on the happening of a certain event;

(3) powers as to mechanics or details only, such as powers to direct issuance of voting proxies, to help determine investment policies, and to direct investment and reinvestment of funds;

(4) power to add to corpus; and

(5) power over trusts created by others with funds not derived from the decedent and not supported by similar trusts created by others.

If the decedent-transferor was unable to relinquish a power because of the existence of a mental disability for a continuous period beginning before October 1, 1947, and ending with death after August 16, 1954, the retained power to revoke or amend will not result in tax.

---

[60] Reg. §20.2038-1.

[61] Rev. Rul. 57-366, 1957-2 CB 618, and Rev. Rul. 70-348, 1970-2 CB 193.

[62] *H. Prudowsky Est.*, 55 TC 890, CCH Dec. 30,671, aff'd per curiam, CA-7, 72-2 USTC ¶12,870, 465 F2d 62.

[63] *Exchange Bank and Trust Co. of Florida*, CA-FC, 82-2 USTC ¶13,505, aff'g ClsCt, 82-1 USTC ¶13,444, 694 F2d 1261.

• *Split-Gift Election*

Code Sec. 2038 contemplates a transfer by the decedent of the decedent's own property before death. Thus, individually owned securities transferred by the husband of a decedent to himself as custodian for his minor daughter under the Uniform Gifts to Minors Act and held by the decedent as successor custodian at the time of her death were not includible in the decedent's gross estate for estate tax purposes even though a split-gift election was made under Code Sec. 2513 and the decedent was considered a donor of half the value of the securities for gift tax purposes.[64]

¶ 590 Exercisability of Power

If the retained power comes within the scope of Code Sec. 2038, it is taxable whether exercisable by the decedent as trustee or as transferor, alone,[65] or in conjunction with trustees or outsiders. The transfer is taxable so long as any beneficiary, vested or contingent, is excluded from the group that, with the transferor, can exercise any of the powers.[66]

If the transfer was made on or before June 22, 1936, the value of an interest in property is not includible in the transferor's gross estate unless the power to alter, amend, revoke, or terminate was reserved at the time of transfer.[67] A power that is acquired by the decedent from the trustees by being appointed as a trustee some time after the transfer and not under provisions in the instrument of transfer will not result in taxability.

¶ 595 Relinquishment of Powers Within Three Years of Death

A retained power to alter, amend, revoke, or terminate a property interest that is relinquished after 1976 and within three years of the death of the holder of the power will require that the value of the property be included in the holder's gross estate.[68] However, effective for decedents dying after August 5, 1997, a transfer of property from a revocable trust within three years of the transfer of such property to the trust will not be included in the decedent's gross estate.[69] Under prior law, the U.S. Court of Appeals for the Eighth Circuit had held that irrevocable fractional interests in the corpus of a revocable trust that were assigned by a decedent to her children within three years of death were not includible in the decedent's gross estate. The fractional interests portions of the trust functioned in the same way as if the decedent had withdrawn the fractions from the initial revocable trust and transferred them to a new irrevocable trust.[70]

¶ 600 Reciprocal Transfers

Estate taxation cannot be avoided through the use of reciprocal transfers whereby two taxpayers make transfers in trust to each other of similar economic rights under substantially identical terms. Thus, two persons cannot escape the estate tax by giving the other a right that would have resulted in an estate tax if

---

[64] Rev. Rul. 74-556, 1974-2 CB 300.

[65] See *S.A. Levin Est.*, 90 TC 723, CCH Dec. 44,706, holding that the retained power need not be exercisable by the decedent in his individual capacity; the ability to exercise it as a member of the board of directors of a company in which he held the controlling interest made it taxable.

[66] Reg. § 20.2038-1(a)(2).

[67] Reg. § 20.2038-1(c).

[68] Code Sec. 2035.

[69] Code Sec. 2035(e), as amended by P.L. 105-34.

[70] *E. Kisling Est.*, CA-8, 94-2 USTC ¶ 60,176, rev'g and rem'g TC, 65 TCM 2956, CCH Dec. 49,097(M), TC Memo. 1993-262 (Acq.) (*H. McNeely*, CA-8, 94-1 USTC ¶ 60,155, followed).

the transferor had retained it for himself[71] (see ¶170). The U.S. Court of Appeals for the Sixth Circuit has held, however, that if the fiduciary powers provided to each transferee do not rise to the level of a retained economic benefit, then the value of the trusts is not included in the transferors' gross estates.[72]

¶605 Valuation Date

Property transferred by the decedent during life but included in the decedent's gross estate must be valued as of the date of the decedent's death or, if the alternate valuation date is chosen, in accordance with Code Sec. 2032 rules (see ¶105). If only a portion of the property is so transferred as to come within the terms of the statute, a corresponding proportion of the value of the property is included in the value of the gross estate. Because Code Sec. 2036 and Code Sec. 2038 overlap, the IRS will apply the Code section that results in the greatest amount being included in the gross estate.[73]

If the transferee makes additions or enhancements to the property, the enhanced value of the property at the valuation date due to such additions or enhancements is not includible in the transferor's gross estate. Because the additions were not made by the decedent, they are not deemed to be part of the transferred property. When only a portion of the value of the property is includible, the value of the whole must still be disclosed on Schedule G (Transfers During Decedent's Life) of Form 706 (United States Estate (and Generation-Skipping Transfer) Tax Return) (Rev. Aug. 2004) under the column headed "Description," together with an explanation of the proportionate inclusion.[74]

¶610 Transfers for Consideration

The value of property transferred by a decedent during life for adequate and full consideration is not includible in the decedent's gross estate. To constitute an exchange or sale for adequate and full consideration in money or money's worth, the exchange or sale must have been made in good faith. The price must have been an adequate and full equivalent and reducible to a money value. Transfers of property during lifetime made within three years of death (in the case of a decedent dying before 1982) or with rights retained (Code Sec. 2035 through Code Sec. 2038) and otherwise taxable powers of appointment (Code Sec. 2041) for less than full and adequate consideration are includible in the transferor's gross estate to the extent of the excess of the fair market value of the property (as of the valuation date) over the price or value of consideration received by the decedent.[75] The adequacy of the consideration received for a transfer is determined as of the date of the transfer and not at a later date, such as the date of the transferor's death.

For estate tax purposes (except for determining deductibility of claims against the estate (see ¶800)), the relinquishment or promised relinquishment of dower, curtesy, a statutory estate created in lieu of dower or curtesy, or other marital rights in the decedent's property or estate is not consideration in money or money's worth.[76]

---

[71] *J.P. Grace Est.*, SCt, 69-1 USTC ¶12,609, 395 US 316.

[72] *J. Green Est.*, CA-6, 95-2 USTC ¶60,216, 68 F3d 151, aff'g unreported decision.

[73] *H.B. Joy, Jr., Exr.*, CA-6, 69-1 USTC ¶12,570, 403 F2d 419, aff'g DC Mich., 67-2 USTC ¶12,482, 272 FSupp. 544.

[74] Instructions for Form 706 (Rev. Aug. 2004), p. 14.

[75] Code Sec. 2043.

[76] Code Sec. 2043(b).

A release of support rights, pursuant to a divorce decree, is consideration to the extent of the value of the rights as determined on a case-by-case basis.[77] The IRS has ruled, in a National Office Technical Advice Memorandum, that a decedent's gross estate included the value of farmland transferred by him to his children pursuant to a property settlement agreement because the decedent had retained a life estate in the property and the transfer was not made for adequate consideration. The transfer of the remainder interest in the property to the children was deemed not to have been a part of the release of the decedent's obligation to support his minor children since the divorce decree already provided for child support payments that adequately satisfied the children's need for support. Accordingly, the IRS concluded that the transfer was not made for consideration, but, rather, was based on the decedent's donative intent.[78]

Whether the consideration paid by a decedent to his father in conjunction with the father's transfer of stock into a trust naming the decedent as life beneficiary constituted a transfer with a retained life estate was decided by the U.S. Court of Appeals for the Sixth Circuit.[79] A payment made by a son in 1941 to his father in exchange for shares of stock, which were, thereafter, used to fund a trust for the benefit of the son for life and his wife and children after his death, constituted a purchase by the son of an undivided interest in approximately 11 percent of the value of the trust assets. Accordingly, the appellate court concluded that 11 percent of the value of the trust assets on the date of the son's death was includible in his gross estate as property transferred by him during his life subject to his retained life estate.

In determining, for estate tax purposes, whether the decedent received, in exchange for property transferred, property approximately equal to it in value, the transactions he made in the years just before his death are particularly subject to scrutiny. Agreements whereby the decedent has transferred property to another in return for a promise to support and care for the decedent have been found to be supported by adequate and full consideration.[80]

¶ 615 Valuation and Description on Return

Reportable lifetime transfers are, for the most part, listed on one special schedule, Schedule G (Transfers During Decedent's Life) of Form 706 (United States Estate (and Generation-Skipping Transfer) Tax Return), without regard to the kind of property transferred. Lifetime transfers of real property and certain lifetime transfers of insurance are reportable under this schedule, even though there are other schedules that are specifically concerned with the kind of property transferred. The other schedules are largely confined to property interests owned by the decedent at the time of death. Although various lifetime transfers are all reportable on Schedule G, the principles governing valuation and description of the transferred property are the same as those of the other schedules.

Copies of Form 709 (United States Gift (and Generation-Skipping Transfer) Tax Return) relating to the lifetime transfers should be attached to Schedule G of Form 706. In addition, gift taxes paid on transfers made within three years of death are to be reported on the schedule (see ¶ 555).

---

[77] Rev. Rul. 68-379, 1968-2 CB 414, Rev. Rul. 60-160, 1960-1 CB 374, and Rev. Rul. 80-82, 1980-1 CB 209; *J.H. Scholl Est.*, 88 TC 1265, CCH Dec. 43,918.

[78] IRS Technical Advice Memorandum 8526003 (no date given).

[79] *D.J. Mahoney, Jr., Exr.*, CA-6, 87-2 USTC ¶ 13,737, 831 F2d 641, rev'g DC Ohio, 86-1 USTC ¶ 13,653, cert. denied, 6-13-88.

[80] *S.A. Bergan Est.*, 1 TC 543, CCH Dec. 12,954 (Acq.).

¶ 625 Instruments Evidencing Transfers

If a transfer, by trust or otherwise, was made by a written instrument, a copy must be filed with the return. If the instrument is of public record, the copy should be certified; if not of record, the copy should be verified. The name of the transferee, date and form of the transfer, and a complete description of the property should be set forth in this schedule. Rents and other income must be included.

Chapter 15
POWERS OF APPOINTMENT

¶ 650 Powers of Appointment

The value of all property over which a decedent possessed a general power of appointment at death is includible in the decedent's gross estate.[1] The term "power of appointment" refers to a power given to the possessor by another, rather than to a power that has been created and retained by the same person. It authorizes the possessor of the power to control, with certain limitations, the ultimate disposition of the property subject to the power. The person who receives the power is usually referred to as the donee of the power.

Under some kinds of powers, the donee has almost as much authority over property as an owner of such property would have. Therefore, the creation of such a power of appointment could, in the absence of special tax treatment, afford an easy means of preventing the application of estate taxes to the estate of the donee—taxes that would be fully applicable if the property were the donee's own or had been given to the donee in fee. Code Sec. 2041 provides specifically for the taxing of property subject to powers of appointment, the provisions being based largely on how nearly the power given to the donee resembles complete ownership of the property.

Only powers defined as "general powers of appointment" result in taxability, except in certain very special cases. Basically, for tax purposes, a "general power of appointment" is one that can be exercised by the donee in favor of the donee, the donee's estate, or the creditors of the donee or the donee's estate.[2] State law is applied in determining whether the decedent has a "general power of appointment."

"Power of appointment" is defined, for estate tax purposes, to include all powers that are in substance and effect powers of appointment, regardless of the wording used in creating the power and regardless of local property law connotations. Thus, a power in a life tenant to appropriate or consume the principal of a trust may be a power of appointment.

All property over which a decedent possessed a power of appointment must be reported on Schedule H (Powers of Appointment) of Form 706 (United States Estate (and Generation-Skipping Transfer) Tax Return) (Rev. Aug. 2004). If Schedule H is filed, certified or verified copies of the instrument granting the power and of any instrument by which the power was exercised or released must be attached to the schedule. All powers of appointment must be reported even if the estate contends that property subject to a particular power is not includible in the gross estate.[3]

---

[1] Code Sec. 2041.
[2] Reg. § 20.2041-1(c).
[3] Instructions for Form 706 (Rev. Aug. 2004), p. 15.

¶ 652 General Powers of Appointment

Only powers defined as *general* powers of appointment can result in estate or gift tax liability. A "general power of appointment" is defined as "a power which is exercisable in favor of the decedent, his estate, his creditors, or the creditors of his estate."[4] However, there are exceptions, and a general power of appointment does *not* include:

(1) a power to consume, invade, or appropriate property for the benefit of the decedent, which is limited by an ascertainable standard relating to the health, education, support, or maintenance of the decedent;

(2) a power created on or before October 21, 1942, which is exercisable by the decedent only in conjunction with another person; and

(3) a power created after October 21, 1942, which is exercisable by the decedent only in conjunction with the creator of the power, or with a person having a substantial interest in the property, subject to the power, where this interest is adverse to the exercise of the power in the decedent's favor. If the power may be exercised both in favor of the decedent and of the persons whose consent the decedent must have, the power is general to the extent of the decedent's fractional interest in it.

A power of appointment created by will is, in general, considered as created on the date of the testator's death.[5] A power created by an instrument effective during the life of the creator is considered as created on the date the instrument takes effect. This is so even though at that time the power may not be exercisable, may be revocable, or the identity of the holder may not be ascertainable. If the holder of a power exercises it by creating a second power, the second power is considered as created at the time of the exercise of the first. Generally, property subject to a general power of appointment is includible in a decedent's gross estate even if at the time of death the decedent was an adjudicated incompetent, at least in the absence of a showing that the adjudication of incompetency barred exercise of the power by any person in any capacity.[6] Similarly, it has been held that property subject to a general power of appointment was includible in the decedent's gross estate even though the decedent, as a minor, was precluded by state law from exercising the power.[7]

It should be noted that the general power of appointment under Code Sec. 2041 is not necessarily equivalent to a power of appointment often given to a decedent's surviving spouse in connection with a life estate. The IRS has ruled that property that passed to a trust for the benefit of a decedent's surviving spouse did not qualify for a marital deduction, even though the spouse received a life estate in the trust corpus and a power to appoint the trust corpus to herself or her creditors, because the trustee could prevent the spouse from exercising the power. Thus, for marital deduction purposes, the power was not exercisable "alone and in all events." However, because the trustee did not have a substantial interest in the trust adverse to that of the spouse, the value of the trust corpus was includible in the spouse's gross estate as property subject to a general power of appointment.[8]

---

[4] Reg. §20.2041-1(c).

[5] Reg. §20.2041-1(e).

[6] Rev. Rul. 75-350, 1975-2 CB 366; *W.R. Boeving*, CA-8, 81-2 USTC ¶13,415; *A.L. Gilchrist Est.*, CA-5, 80-2 USTC ¶13,378, 630 F2d 340; *F. Alperstein Est.*, CA-2, 80-1 USTC ¶13,326, 613 F2d 1213, cert. denied, 446 US 918; *Pennsylvania Bank and Trust Co., Exr.*, CA-3, 79-1 USTC ¶13,299, 597 F2d 382, cert. denied, 444 US 980; and IRS Technical Advice Memorandum 9344004 (July 13, 1993).

[7] *N.E. Rosenblatt Est.*, CA-10, 80-2 USTC ¶13,374, 633 F2d 176.

[8] Rev. Rul. 82-156, 1982-2 CB 216.

¶ 653 Powers Limited by Ascertainable Standard

A power to consume, invade, or appropriate income and corpus for the donee's benefit is not a taxable general power if the power is limited by an ascertainable standard relating to the health, education, support, or maintenance of the decedent.[9] In short, the holder's duty regarding use of the power must be reasonably measurable in terms of the holder's needs for health, education, or support—or any combination of them.

The words "support" and "maintenance" are considered synonymous. Their meaning is not limited to the bare necessities of life. For example, a power of appointment will be regarded as limited by the necessary standard if it is exercisable for the holder's (1) support, (2) support in reasonable comfort, (3) maintenance in health and reasonable comfort, (4) support in the holder's accustomed manner of living, (5) education, including college and professional education, (6) health, or (7) medical, dental, hospital, and nursing expenses.

However, a power to use property for the comfort, welfare, or happiness of the holder of the power generally will not meet the required ascertainable standard for invasion. However, under Illinois law, the word "comfort" was deemed to be an ascertainable standard that refers to maintaining someone in the station of life to which the person has become accustomed.[10] In determining the existence of an ascertainable standard, it is immaterial that the trust agreement may or may not require the beneficiary first to exhaust other income.[11]

Generally, the extent of a decedent's interest is governed by state law.[12] The U.S. Court of Appeals for the Tenth Circuit has held that a decedent's power to invade the corpus of a trust for her benefit "in case of emergency or illness" was not a general power of appointment, under New Mexico law, because its exercise was limited by an ascertainable standard. Accordingly, the court held that the value of the trust corpus was not includible in the decedent's gross estate.[13] The IRS has ruled in a National Office Technical Advice Memorandum that the power of a co-trustee and life beneficiary to invade trust corpus if the trust income was not sufficient for the comfort, support, and education of the beneficiary and her children was not a general power under state law. Because the Missouri statute prohibited the trustee from exercising any power to distribute corpus to herself, regardless of whether or not the power was limited by an ascertainable standard, the power was not a general power.[14]

The U.S. Court of Appeals for the Sixth Circuit has held similarly that a decedent who was trustee and life beneficiary of a trust did not have a general power of appointment over the trust because her "right to encroach" on the corpus was limited by an ascertainable standard under Tennessee law.[15] However, the U.S. Court of Appeals for the Seventh Circuit has held that a decedent who was the trustee and one of the beneficiaries of a trust established under the terms of her predeceased husband's will held a general power of appointment over the trust corpus because she was authorized to use so much of the principal

---

[9] Reg. §20.2041-1(c)(2).

[10] *V.J. Strauss Est.*, 69 TCM 2825, CCH Dec. 50,680(M), TC Memo. 1995-248.

[11] Reg. §20.2041-1(c).

[12] But see IRS Technical Advice Memorandum 8339004 (June 14, 1983) (state supreme court decision not followed because the state court proceeding was not adversarial and, based on applicable case law and an analysis of the words used in the invasion clause, the decedent's power of appointment was general).

[13] *I.M. Sowell Est.*, CA-10, 83-1 USTC ¶13,526, 708 F2d 1564.

[14] IRS Technical Advice Memorandum 200014002 (Nov. 29, 1999).

[15] *P.W. Finlay, Exr.*, CA-6, 85-1 USTC ¶13,604, 752 F2d 246.

as she deemed appropriate for her maintenance and support. Language giving the decedent the right to use the property "for whatever purpose she desires" was found by the court to negate any ascertainable standard under Wisconsin law.[16]

¶ 655 Taxable Powers Created After October 21, 1942

A general power created after October 21, 1942, and held by the donee will result in taxability of the subject property in the donee's gross estate, if the power is held until death, whether or not the donee exercises it by will. The exercise or release of the power during the donee's lifetime will be deemed a transfer for gift tax purposes.[17]

Estate tax liability will also result if the exercise or release was effected under circumstances that would have resulted in tax under Code Sec. 2035 through Code Sec. 2038 if the property had been the decedent's own.[18]

• *Release, Lapse, and Disclaimer of Powers*

Release of a power of appointment created after October 21, 1942, will result in taxation just as completely as would an exercise of the power by will or possession at death of an unexercised power. A release of a power need not be formal or express in character. Failure to exercise a power of appointment within a specified time, so that the power lapses, is considered a release of the power.[19]

However, a lapse of the power in any calendar year during the decedent's life is considered a release for estate tax purposes only to the extent that the property over which the power existed exceeded the greater of $5,000 or five percent of the value, at the time of the lapse, of the assets out of which the exercise could have been satisfied.

> *Example:* In 2004, Jim Dorsey transferred $200,000 worth of securities in trust with provision for payment of income to his son, George, for life and the remainder to George's issue. George was also given a right to withdraw $15,000 a year from the trust fund (which neither increased nor decreased in value prior to George's death). The right is noncumulative, so that George can never withdraw more than $15,000 in any one year, even if he fails to withdraw the full amount in a preceding year.
>
> The failure to exercise his power of withdrawal in any single calendar year is considered a release to the extent that $15,000 exceeds 5% of the trust fund. Assuming that George fails to exercise his power of withdrawal for 2004, $5,000 ($15,000 – $10,000) is deemed to be a taxable transfer to the trust from George with a retained right to income. (The $5,000 stays in the trust fund of which George is life income beneficiary.) The remaining $10,000 is not considered a release because it falls within the 5% rule. The taxable proportion created by the release in 2004 at death is 1/40 ($5,000 ÷ $200,000) of the value of the trust corpus on the date of death (or alternate valuation date). If the value of the trust principal remained at $200,000 at George's death, $5,000 (1/40 × $200,000) would be included in his gross estate.

---

[16] *Independence Bank Waukesha, N.A.*, CA-7, 85-1 USTC ¶ 13,613, 761 F2d 442. See also IRS Technical Advice Memorandum 8601003 (Sept. 20, 1985) (decedent's right to invade the trust corpus for "any special need" that might arise was a general power of appointment).

[17] Code Sec. 2514(b).

[18] Code Sec. 2041(a)(2).

[19] Code Sec. 2041(b)(2).

If the failure to exercise a power, such as a right of withdrawal, occurs in more than a single year, the proportion of the property over which the power lapsed, which is to be treated as a taxable disposition, must be determined separately for each year. Thus, in the Example above, if George had failed to exercise the power of withdrawal in three separate calendar years, $15,000 would be included in his gross estate, assuming the value of the corpus subject to the power remained at $200,000. The aggregate of the taxable proportions for all years is includible in the holder's gross estate, limited only by the aggregate value of the assets out of which an exercise of the power could have been satisfied on the applicable valuation date.[20] In addition, if in the year of death, the power has not been exercised and has not lapsed, the entire amount for which the power may be exercised is includible in the decedent's gross estate.

A widow's unexercised right, during the statutory period, to take against her husband's estate does not constitute an unexercised general power of appointment within the meaning of Code Sec. 2041 because the failure to assert the inchoate right constitutes a complete and effective disclaimer or renunciation of a power of appointment by operation of law.[21]

A restriction of a trustee-beneficiary's fiduciary power by operation of state law will not be deemed to cause a lapse of a general power under Code Sec. 2514.[22]

• ***Post-1976 Disclaimers***

A post-1976 "qualified disclaimer" of a general power of appointment is not a release of the power and does not constitute a taxable gift. A "qualified disclaimer" is based on federal, rather than state, requirements[23] (see ¶2009 for details).

• ***Pre-1977 Disclaimers***

A pre-1977 disclaimer or renunciation of a general power of appointment is not considered to be a release of the power.[24] In the absence of facts to the contrary, the failure to renounce or disclaim a power within a reasonable time after learning of its existence will be presumed to constitute an acceptance of the power. A disclaimer or renunciation of a power that is unequivocal and meets the requirements of local law will not result in a taxable gift.

• ***Creation of New Power***

If a donee by will or by a lifetime transfer exercises a power of appointment (general or special) created after October 21, 1942, by creating another power, taxability will result. The property subject to the power will be included in the original donee's estate if, under local law, the power can be exercised to postpone the vesting of any estate or interest in such property, or suspend the absolute ownership or power of alienation of such property, for a period ascertainable without regard to the date of the creation of the first power.[25]

• ***Avoidance of Tax***

A donee of a power of appointment does have some measure of control over whether the property subject to a general power will be included in the donee's gross estate at death. The donee may renounce or disclaim the power when it

---

[20] Reg. § 20.2041-3(d)(5).

[21] Rev. Rul. 74-492, 1974-2 CB 298.

[22] Rev. Proc. 94-44, 1994-2 CB 683.

[23] Code Sec. 2046 and Code Sec. 2518.

[24] Reg. § 20.2041-3(d)(6).

[25] Reg. § 20.2041-3(e).

first comes to the donee's attention. If the donee follows either of these courses, the action will not create either estate or gift tax liability. The requirements for a federal "qualified disclaimer" are described at ¶2009.

A donee may escape estate tax liability by releasing or by exercising the power during life, only if the donee does not reserve rights that would cause a transfer of the donee's own property during life to be included in the gross estate. Generally, a release or exercise within three years of death will not result in inclusion of the property subject to the power in the decedent's gross estate in the case of decedents dying after 1981. When the donee seeks to keep the property out of the donee's own estate other than by a renunciation or disclaimer, the donee must consider the application of the gift tax law (see ¶2162) to his or her actions.[26]

¶665 Powers Created Before October 22, 1942

As to powers created on or before October 21, 1942, only general powers that are exercised can result in tax.[27] Under no circumstances is it necessary for the donee of the power to release it to keep it out of the estate.

If the donee does not exercise a pre-October 22, 1942 general power, and whether the donee exercises a limited or special power, no tax will result, except in one special case discussed below. Under a corresponding provision of the gift tax law (Code Sec. 2514), a complete release of a pre-October 22, 1942, general power will not result in gift tax liability or generation-skipping transfer tax consequences.[28]

If a general power of appointment created on or before October 21, 1942, is partially released so that it no longer is a general power of appointment, under certain circumstances the subsequent exercise of the power is not deemed to be the exercise of a general power of appointment. However, such partial release must have been made:

(1) before November 1, 1951; or

(2) if, on October 21, 1942, the donee of such power was under a legal disability to release the power, then within six months after the termination of such legal disability.[29]

¶670 Instruments Granting Power

If the decedent at any time possessed a power of appointment, a certified or verified copy of the instrument granting the power, together with a certified or verified copy of any instrument by which the power was exercised or released, must be filed with the return. These copies must be filed even though the executor feels that the power is not a general power of appointment or that the property is not otherwise includible in the gross estate.[30]

---

[26] Code Sec. 2514.

[27] Code Sec. 2041(a).

[28] IRS Letter Ruling 9732034 (May 15, 1997).

[29] Code Sec. 2041(a).

[30] Instructions for Form 706 (Rev. Aug. 2004), p. 15.

Chapter 16
ANNUITIES

¶ 700 General Requirements

Subject to certain limited exceptions (see ¶735, ¶737, and ¶739), all or a portion of an annuity or other payment receivable by any beneficiary by reason of surviving the decedent is includible in a decedent's gross estate.[1] The annuity or other payment is not taxable under the annuity rules unless it is payable under a contract or agreement and the following four factors exist:

(1) The contract or agreement is not a policy of insurance on the life of the decedent.

(2) The contract or agreement was entered into after March 3, 1931.

(3) The annuity or other payment is receivable by the beneficiary by reason of the beneficiary's having survived the decedent.

(4) Under the contract or agreement—

(a) an annuity or other payment was payable to the decedent, either alone or in conjunction with another, for the decedent's life or for any period not ascertainable without reference to the decedent's death or for any period that did not in fact end before the decedent's death, *or*

(b) the decedent possessed the right to receive the annuity or other payment, either alone or in conjunction with another, for the decedent's life or for any period not ascertainable without reference to the decedent's death or for any period that did not in fact end before the decedent's death.

The amount to be included in the gross estate is the value at the decedent's death of the annuity or other payment receivable by the survivor. It is immaterial whether the annuity or other payment to the survivor is payable in a lump sum or in installments. If payable in installments, it is immaterial whether the installments are in the same amount as, or in a greater or lesser amount than, the annuity or payments to the decedent.

---

[1] Code Sec. 2039(a); Reg. § 20.2039-1.

Annuities may be includible under other provisions of the Internal Revenue Code. For example, if an annuitant retained the right to have any payments due after the annuitant's death paid to the annuitant's estate or to persons whom the annuitant might subsequently designate, the amounts payable could be included as property in which the annuitant had an interest at the time of death.[2] They could also be treated as transfers in which the annuitant had reserved the power to alter, amend, or revoke.[3] The relinquishment of an annuitant's additional rights within three years of death would cause inclusion in the annuitant's gross estate.

¶ 710 "Annuity" Defined

The term "annuity" includes periodic payments for a specified period of time. The following are examples of contracts (but not necessarily the only forms of contracts) for payments that constitute annuities or other payments for the purpose of inclusion in Schedule I (Annuities) of Form 706 (United States Estate (and Generation-Skipping Transfer) Tax Return) (Rev. Aug. 2004):[4]

(1) A contract under which the decedent immediately before death was receiving or was entitled to receive, for the duration of the decedent's life, an annuity, or other stipulated payments that were to continue after the decedent's death to a designated, surviving beneficiary.

(2) A contract under which the decedent immediately before death was receiving or was entitled to receive, together with another person for their joint lives, an annuity or other stipulated payment to continue to the survivor following the death of either.

(3) A contract or agreement entered into by the decedent and the decedent's employer. Under the contract the decedent immediately before death and following retirement was receiving, or was entitled to receive, an annuity or other stipulated payment. Payments to the decedent were for the duration of the decedent's life. Thereafter, payments were to a designated beneficiary, if the beneficiary survived the decedent. (It is immaterial whether the payments after the decedent's death are fixed by the contract or subject to an option or election exercised or exercisable by the decedent.)

(4) A contract or agreement entered into by the decedent and the decedent's employer. At the decedent's death, prior to retirement or prior to the expiration of a stated period of time, an annuity or other payment was payable to a designated surviving beneficiary.

(5) A contract or agreement under which the decedent immediately before death was receiving or was entitled to receive an annuity or other payment for a stated period of time, with the annuity or other payment to continue to a designated, surviving beneficiary on the decedent's death prior to the expiration of such period.

¶ 715 Types of Payments Involved

In determining whether amounts payable under an annuity contract following the death of a primary annuitant are taxable under Code Sec. 2039, the exact method of payment following death is seldom important. It does not matter whether the payments that accrue following death are to be in the nature of:

(1) a continuing annuity to another person or persons;

---

[2] Code Sec. 2033.

[3] Code Sec. 2038.

[4] Reg. § 20.2039-1(b).

(2) a periodic payment (whether fixed in number, duration, or total amount);

(3) a lump sum based on the difference between the cost of the annuity and the total payments to the primary beneficiary; or

(4) a lump sum fixed in amount without regard to how much the primary annuitant received during the annuitant's lifetime.

The tests for includibility revolve around the rights of the primary annuitant. In addition to the annuitant's right to an annuity, the question of who paid for the annuity is important. The value of the benefits payable after the death of the primary annuitant will, however, vary with the nature of the payments.

Sometimes there are payments due that accrued to the primary annuitant before the annuitant's death. These payments generally become payable to the decedent's estate and are automatically included in the gross estate as property in which the decedent had an interest at the time of death. They are reported as miscellaneous property on Schedule F (Other Miscellaneous Property Not Reportable Under Any Other Schedule) of Form 706 (United States Estate (and Generation-Skipping Transfer) Tax Return).

¶720 Primary Annuities Purchased by Decedent as Annuitant

Proceeds of an annuity contract payable after the death of the purchaser and primary annuitant are includible in the annuitant's gross estate for estate tax purposes. They are includible whether they are paid to the estate or to a named beneficiary. It is immaterial whether they represent payments due to the primary annuitant or payments due only after the annuitant's death. An annuity purchased by a deceased primary annuitant before March 4, 1931, is excludable from a decedent's gross estate under Code Sec. 2039.

• *Partial Payments by Others*

If the primary annuitant did not pay the entire purchase price of the annuity, that part of the value of amounts payable after the primary annuitant's death that is attributable to the part of the price paid by persons other than the primary annuitant may be excluded from the primary annuitant's gross estate.[5]

• *Death Before First Payment*

Even if the primary annuitant did not receive any payments under the annuity contract because of death prior to the date when the first payment was to be made, the payments after the annuitant's death are taxable. They are taxable to the same extent as if the annuitant had lived to receive the first payment. The amount payable after the annuitant's death is includible in the gross estate in the proportion in which the annuitant provided the purchase price for the annuities.

• *Partial Payment by Employer*

The portion (if any) of the purchase price paid by an employer or former employer, under a "nonqualified" benefit plan, is deemed to have been paid by the primary annuitant if made by reason of employment.[6] This results whether the employer made the payment directly or through an employee's trust or fund forming part of a pension, annuity, retirement, bonus, or profit-sharing plan. Totally voluntary payments made by a company to its employee's widow were

---

[5] Reg. §20.2039-1(c).

[6] Reg. §20.2039-1(c).

not taxable as annuities because they were not payable to the employee during the employee's lifetime[7] (see ¶733).

See ¶735 and ¶737 for a discussion of the includibility of annuities payable under a qualified plan or trust, Keogh plan, or an individual retirement account.

¶725 Annuities Not Purchased by Decedent

The annuity provisions of Code Sec. 2039 do not apply to annuities treated as having been purchased by someone other than the primary annuitant. Nor do they apply to portions of annuities purchased by another where the decedent, as primary annuitant, did pay a part of the purchase price. Such annuities, or parts of annuities, are governed by other provisions in the estate tax law.[8]

The taxability of any after-death payments under annuities, or portions of annuities, deemed purchased by persons other than the decedent depends on the rights that the primary annuitant possesses (in addition to the right to receive an annuity for life). If the primary annuitant has no rights beyond the mere right to receive an annuity, any interest in the annuity contract or other property from which the payments stemmed ceases with the annuitant's death. Nothing remains to be taxed in the gross estate.

If any payments are to be made to the annuitant's estate after the annuitant's death, or to persons whom the annuitant names, these payments may be included in the annuitant's gross estate as property in which the annuitant had an interest at the time of death,[9] or as property over which the annuitant had a power of appointment.[10]

¶730 Service Member's Survivorship Annuities

The Tax Reform Act of 1984 (P.L. 98-369) repealed an exclusion, with respect to decedents dying after December 31, 1984, for the value of annuities receivable by a surviving spouse or certain child beneficiaries under the Retired Serviceman's Family Protection Plan or the Survivor Benefit Plan.[11] However, the repeal does not affect a decedent whose benefit was in pay status on December 31, 1984, and who, prior to July 18, 1984, made an irrevocable election to designate the form of the benefit distribution.[12]

¶733 Employees' Death Benefits

Many employers pay surviving spouses of employees sums of money that are commonly called death benefits. Such death benefits may be paid by reason of a contract with the employee or they may be paid by reason of a formal or informal company policy or plan, often on a case-by-case basis. The following comments apply to payments under "nonqualified" plans.

The inclusion of death benefits in the estates of deceased employees, as annuities, is dependent upon the terms of the particular employment contract or plan. Therefore, it is difficult to distill any general rules of law from court cases, which often seem contradictory despite the existence of common provisions in these plans or agreements. Here are a few examples of how the courts have ruled in these cases:

---

[7] *W.E. Barr Est.*, 40 TC 227, CCH Dec. 26,103 (Acq.).

[8] Reg. § 20.2039-1(a).

[9] Code Sec. 2033.

[10] Code Sec. 2041.

[11] Code Sec. 2039(c), prior to repeal by P.L. 98-369.

[12] Act Sec. 525(a), P.L. 98-369.

(1) Death benefits paid to a surviving spouse of an active employee were not includible in the employee's gross estate, as an annuity, where the employment contract provided for the payment of a salary and the death benefit, but did not provide for any retirement benefits.[13]

(2) Where the employment contract provided for annual payments for a period of 15 years starting with the employee's retirement or termination of employment and for the payment of these benefits to named beneficiaries if the employee died, the payments made to the beneficiaries were includible in the employee's gross estate where he died while employed by the company.[14] The payments were to continue so long as the decedent did not engage in certain acts that were detrimental to the operations of the company—a standard feature in many such contracts.

(3) Two courts have reached opposite conclusions concerning the inclusion of death benefits that were paid under employment contracts that provided for (a) the employment of the decedent at a fixed salary, (b) the payment of a salary to a decedent who had become disabled or ill, and (c) payments to the employees' surviving spouses after their death. (The terms of the contracts were slightly different, but both contained essentially the same standard provisions that are included in contracts of this type.) The U.S. Court of Claims (now, U.S. Court of Federal Claims) held that the "death benefit" paid to the surviving spouse was not included in the employee's gross estate because he had died before retirement.[15] A U.S. district court, on the other hand, held that the death benefit was includible in an active employee's gross estate.[16]

(4) Payments made under nonqualified employees' plans have been included in the gross estates of deceased employees where the death benefits were vested or automatically payable to the beneficiaries at the employee's death. This rule has been applied in the case of a retired employee receiving a pension[17] and in the case of an employee who was not retired.[18] If the employee has more than one type of plan, the provisions of all the plans have been examined to determine whether an annuity is payable to a beneficiary at the decedent's death.[19] The U.S. Court of Appeals for the Second Circuit has held that a survivorship annuity payable to beneficiaries only if the decedent became totally disabled during employment was too dissimilar from a true annuity and too contingent to be aggregated with other plans covering the decedent for purposes of determining whether an annuity was payable to a beneficiary at death.[20] However, a U.S. district court in Georgia construed the same plans considered by the Second Circuit and concluded that the annuity payable to a decedent's beneficiaries was includible in the decedent's gross estate because the decedent had the right during his life to receive an annuity in the event that he became totally disabled.[21]

---

[13] *F.D. Fusz Est.*, 46 TC 214, CCH Dec. 27,944 (Acq.).

[14] *E.H. Wadewitz Est.*, CA-7, 65-1 USTC ¶12,277, 339 F2d 980, aff'g TC, 39 TC 925, CCH Dec. 26,015.

[15] *C. Kramer, Exrx.*, CtCls, 69-1 USTC ¶12,585, 406 F2d 1363.

[16] *J.C. Silberman, Exr.*, DC Pa., 71-2 USTC ¶12,814, 333 FSupp. 1120.

[17] *H.C. Beal Est.*, 47 TC 269, CCH Dec. 28,204 (Acq.).

[18] *J.W. Bahen Est.*, CtCls, 62-2 USTC ¶12,091, 305 F2d 827.

[19] *J.W. Bahen Est.*, CtCls, 62-2 USTC ¶12,091, 305 F2d 827; *J. Gray, Exr.*, CA-3, 69-1 USTC ¶12,604, 410 F2d 1094.

[20] *W.V. Schelberg Est.*, CA-2, 79-2 USTC ¶13,321, 612 F2d 25. See also *G.J. Van Wye Est.*, CA-6, 82-2 USTC ¶13,485, 686 F2d 425.

[21] *J.B. Looney, Admrx.*, DC Ga., 83-2 USTC ¶13,538, 569 FSupp. 1569. Although the government prevailed in *Looney*, it moved to

(5) Death benefits that were paid to the surviving spouse of an active employee were excludable from the employee's gross estate where the benefits were paid only after a company investigation into the circumstances of the employee's family and only with the approval of the board of directors.[22]

(6) The payment of death benefit annuities to the spouses (or other dependents) of police officers and firefighters who died in the line of duty were not includible in the decedents' gross estates as annuities under Code Sec. 2039 because such payments were made under New York State and New York City Municipal codes to provide for the dependents of such decedents, rather than being made pursuant to a contract or agreement arising from the decedents' employment. Moreover, the decedents possessed no right to receive any annuity payments during life. In addition, according to the IRS, such annuities were not includible under Code Sec. 2033 because decedents possessed no property or ownership rights in these death benefits. (However, any amounts paid to a deceased police officer or firefighter that represented a return of his or her contributions to a New York City qualified pension plan were includible as property owned at death under the general tests for inclusion discussed at ¶155.)[23]

The IRS also has attempted to include death benefits under nonqualified plans or agreements as property owned at death under Code Sec. 2033 (see ¶535), as transfers with the right to govern enjoyment under Code Sec. 2036, as transfers taking effect at death under Code Sec. 2037, and as revocable transfers under Code Sec. 2038. The Tax Court and the U.S. Court of Appeals for the Second Circuit sustained the inclusion of death benefits as a transfer taking effect at death.[24] Three courts have ruled that death benefits paid pursuant to employment contracts are not includible in the gross estates of deceased employees as a revocable transfer or a transfer with the right to govern enjoyment.[25] However, the Tax Court has ruled that a post-mortem annuity payable to the surviving spouse of a decedent, the chairman of the board of directors and controlling shareholder of a closely held corporation, was includible in his gross estate as a revocable transfer.[26]

The amount includible in a deceased employee's estate is usually the present value of the payments to the beneficiary.

¶735 Annuities from Qualified Employees' Benefit Plans

Effective with respect to decedents dying after December 31, 1984, to the extent that retirement benefits payable under qualified plans fall within the annuity inclusion rules discussed at ¶700, such benefits are generally includible in a decedent's gross estate. For decedents dying before this date, a $100,000 estate tax exclusion had been available for certain retirement benefits payable

---

(Footnote Continued)

vacate the judgment of the district court when the estate appealed to CA-11, and this motion was granted on Jan. 24, 1984.

[22] *W.E. Barr Est.*, 40 TC 227, CCH Dec. 26,103 (Acq.)

[23] Rev. Rul. 2002-39, IRB 2002-27, 33.

[24] *H. Fried Est.*, CA-2, 71-2 USTC ¶12,796, 445 F2d 979, aff'g TC, 54 TC 805, CCH Dec. 30,065, cert. denied, 404 US 1016.

[25] *C. Kramer, Exrx.*, CtCls, 69-1 USTC ¶12,585, 406 F2d 1363; *L.D. Hinze*, DC Cal., 72-1 USTC ¶12,842; *J.N. Harris*, DC Cal., 72-1 USTC ¶12,845.

[26] *S.A. Levin Est.*, 90 TC 723, CCH Dec. 44,706.

under qualified plans, tax-sheltered annuities, individual retirement arrangements (¶737), and certain military retirement plans (see ¶730).[27]

• ***Exceptions for Certain Plan Participants***

Despite the general repeal of the $100,000 estate tax exclusion for plan participants dying after 1984, this $100,000 exclusion is still available if the deceased plan participant either:

(1) on December 31, 1984, was both a participant in the plan and in pay status (i.e., had received at least one benefit payment on or before December 31, 1984), and had irrevocably elected the form of the benefit before July 18, 1984; or

(2) had separated from service before January 1, 1985, and did not change the form of benefit before death.

An *unlimited exclusion* is still available if the deceased plan participant either:

(1) on December 31, 1982, was both a participant in the plan and in pay status (i.e., had received at least one benefit payment on or before December 31, 1982), and had irrevocably elected the form of the benefit before January 1, 1983; or

(2) had separated from service before January 1, 1983, and did not change the form of benefit before death.[28]

¶737 Individual Retirement Accounts

The $100,000 estate tax exclusion for individual retirement arrangements has been repealed generally with respect to decedents dying after 1984. Thus, to the extent that an IRA falls within the annuity inclusion rules discussed at ¶700, its value is generally includible in a deceased owner's gross estate. However, for decedents dying before 1985 and for certain other limited situations (see ¶735), retirement plan death benefits and annuities paid to beneficiaries of employees dying after 1976 under Keogh plans and individual retirement account plans (IRAs) are excludable from the employee's gross estate, subject to a $100,000 limitation after 1982.[29]

The IRS has ruled that the value of a decedent's IRA could not be discounted to reflect the income tax payable by IRA beneficiaries. According to the IRS, the income tax impact on the beneficiaries was analogous to the situation in which a donor transfers low-basis property by gift, where the possibility that the donee might incur income tax on a later sale of the property does not operate to decrease the value of the gift. Moreover, the IRS reasoned that the deduction permitted by Code Sec. 691(c) for income in respect of a decedent functioned as a "statutory substitute" for a valuation discount, making any additional reduction in value unwarranted.[30]

¶739 Lump-Sum Distributions

A payment from a qualified retirement plan that qualifies as an annuity (see ¶700) will generally be included in the decedent's gross estate whether or not it is received as a lump sum payment. If, however, a deceased qualified plan participant comes under one of the exceptions to the repeal of the qualified plan

[27] Code Sec. 2039(c), prior to repeal by P.L. 98-369.

[28] Instructions for Form 706 (Rev. Aug. 2004), p. 16.

[29] Code Sec. 2039(e), prior to repeal by P.L. 98-369.

[30] IRS Technical Advice Memorandum 200247001 (undated, released Nov. 22, 2002).

benefit exclusion (see ¶735), a lump-sum distribution received will qualify for the estate tax exclusion (i.e., is not treated as a lump-sum distribution) if the recipient irrevocably elects to treat the lump-sum distribution as a taxable distribution, without applying the averaging method, for income tax purposes.[31] This election is made by filing an income tax return reflecting the distribution as taxable in the year of receipt. The election is reflected on line A of Schedule I (Annuities) of Form 706 (United States Estate (and Generation-Skipping Transfer) Tax Return). If the estate tax return is filed before the income tax return, the estate tax return nevertheless may reflect the election as if it had been made.[32] If the election is made, the estate must attach a written election made by each recipient. The recipient's name, address, and identification number (usually, the Social Security number) must also be listed on this attachment.

¶745 Annuities Combined with Life Insurance

Annuities are sometimes paired with life insurance in a combination type of contract. This combination is usually effected to enable a person who might otherwise be uninsurable to enter into a contract calling specifically for the payment of "life insurance" proceeds at death. A combination annuity contract and life insurance policy on a decedent's life that matured during the decedent's lifetime is taxed as an annuity.[33] In the case of a policy that has not matured, the policy is taxed as an insurance policy if the decedent dies before the reserve value equals the death benefit. If the reserve value equals the death benefit, the policy is taxed as an annuity[34] (see ¶415).

¶750 Annuities in Which Decedent Had No Beneficial Interest

If the decedent purchased or otherwise provided for an annuity for the benefit of another person, the rules for determining taxability are different. Taxability turns on the circumstances surrounding the establishment of the annuity and on the powers, if any, retained by the decedent.

If the annuity is provided for by will, it is fully taxable. If the annuity was purchased for another individual by the decedent within three years of death, it would be includible only to the limited extent that transfers within three years of death are still includible in the gross estate of a decedent who dies after 1981[35] (see ¶555). If it was purchased more than three years before death, it cannot be included in the gross estate unless the decedent retained some control over the annuity.

Controls that would result in inclusion of an annuity in the estate include the right to change the beneficiary and the right to revoke the annuity, either by surrendering the contract for cash or by terminating it, if the interest is in a trust. The retention of controls that would require inclusion of any other types of lifetime transfers in the gross estate would similarly require the inclusion of annuities in the gross estate (see ¶570, ¶580, ¶585, and ¶590).

¶755 Special Rules for Trusts

If the decedent was an annuitant under a trust created by another person, no tax is due at the time of the decedent's death. The annuity ceases at the

---

[31] Code Sec. 2039(c) and Code Sec. 2039(f), prior to repeal by P.L. 98-369.

[32] Reg. §20.2039-4(d).

[33] Reg. §20.2039-1(d).

[34] Reg. §20.2039-1(d).

[35] Code Sec. 2035(d).

annuitant's death. However, tax consequences may result if the annuitant had certain rights in addition to the annuity or if the trust was reciprocal in nature.

The rights that can bring about inclusion of all or a portion of the fund from which the annuity stems are the same rights that would result in taxability of other interests. For example, a tax will result if the decedent is found to have a power of appointment that would require inclusion in the estate of any other property. The fact that the decedent had an annuity rather than some other type of interest does not influence the result.

If the decedent created the trust, the retention of an annuity from the trust will result in the inclusion of the value of the balance of the trust in the decedent's gross estate. Exceptions exist for certain instances if the trust was created before March 4, 1931 (see ¶570).

If a person creates an annuity interest in a trust that is to continue after the person's death, the fact that an annuity is created is of concern only if the remainder of the trust is deductible as a charitable interest or if the remainder, but not the annuity, is includible in the gross estate. In such instances, the value of the annuity must be determined before the amount of either the charitable deduction or the taxable remainder may be established (see ¶1122).

¶760 Valuation

The value of benefits under an annuity contract is determined as of the date of death of the primary annuitant. If the estate is valued under the alternate valuation method (see ¶105), the value of these benefits is little affected. Any lower value six months after the date of death is attributable to mere lapse of time.[36] The benefits paid out during the six months cannot be excluded from the evaluation.

Only that part of the value of the annuity or other payment receivable by the surviving beneficiary that the decedent's contribution to the purchase price of the contract or agreement bears to the total purchase price is actually includible in the gross estate.[37] Special annuity tables are to be used to value Civil Service temporary annuities payable to surviving children.[38]

• *Lump-Sum Payments*

If the benefits are payable in a lump sum, the amount payable is the value.

• *Installment Payments*

When the benefits are payable in installments—whether payable for a fixed period, payable in a fixed number, or payable for the life of the beneficiary—the valuation must be made on a commuted basis.

• *Insurance Company Contract*

If the payments are made under a contract issued by an insurance company, the value of a continuing annuity to the survivor is to be based on the cost of an annuity of a similar amount at the time of the decedent's death.

• *Fixed Payments*

If the payments to the survivor are fixed in duration or amount, it is likely that they will be valued as an annuity for a term certain under the tables

---

[36] *J.A. Hance Est.*, 18 TC 499, CCH Dec. 19,025 (Acq.).

[37] Reg. §20.2039-1(c).

[38] Rev. Proc. 71-7, 1971-1 CB 671.

provided pursuant to Code Sec. 7520 (IRS Publications 1457 "Actuarial Values, Book Aleph" and 1458 "Actuarial Values, Book Beth") (see ¶2700).

• *Comparable Contract Method*

If the annuity is purchased by the decedent solely for the benefit of another but is includible in the decedent's gross estate, the value will be based strictly on the cost of a comparable contract at the time of the decedent's death. If the annuity is payable from a trust or from any other source, except under a commercial annuity contract, the value is determined by applying factors obtained from tables in Publications 1457 and 1458 (see ¶2700).

• *Lottery Payments*

The value of a decedent's interests in lottery payments will be includible in the gross estate for estate tax purposes. However, the method by which the interests would be valued is subject to debate and there is now a split at the appellate court level on the question. According to a district court in California and the U.S. Court of Appeals for the Ninth Circuit, the decedent's interest would not be valued as a commercial annuity under Reg. § 20.2031-8, and departure from the private annuity Reg. § 20.2031-7 tables would be warranted if the tables produced substantially unrealistic and unreasonable results.[39] Similarly, applying the rationale of the *Shackleford* decision, the U.S. Court of Appeals for the Second Circuit reversed the Tax Court and held that, although future lottery payments constituted an annuity within the meaning of Code Sec. 7520, departure from the valuation tables provided thereunder was justified in order to account for transferability restrictions placed on the winnings under applicable state (Connecticut) law.[40]

The U.S. Court of Appeals for the Fifth Circuit specifically declined to apply the holdings in *Shackleford* and *Gribauskas* to a recent case involving the valuation of a decedent's right to receive 19 annual payments of lottery winnings. In *Cook*,[41] the Fifth Circuit held that the annuity tables of Code Sec. 7520 provided the proper method for valuing the payments because the lottery prize fell within the definition of a private annuity. The court ruled that the use of the tables did not create an unrealistic or unreasonable valuation result because a marketability discount (which the decedent's estate had claimed) was not properly applied to lottery winning. According to the court, the nonmarketability of a private annuity was an assumption underlying the annuity tables. It would be unreasonable to apply a marketability discount to the winnings, the court added, because the interest being valued was not a capital asset, but a right, independent of market forces, to receive a stated sum of money annually for a specified term. The court noted that other kinds of private annuities, such as survivor annuities payable under qualified plans and charitable remainder annuity trusts, were valued under the tables despite being nonmarketable. A dissent in *Cook* would have applied the holdings of the *Shackleford* and *Gribauskas* decisions.

¶770 Description on Return

The description of an annuity on Schedule I (Annuities) of Form 706 (United States Estate (and Generation-Skipping Transfer) Tax Return) must include the name and address of the grantor. If the annuity was payable out of a trust or

---

[39] *T. Shackleford Est.*, DC Cal., 98-2 USTC ¶60,320; 99-2 USTC ¶60,356, aff'd CA-9, 2001-2 USTC ¶60,417.

[40] *P. Gribauskas Est.*, CA-2, 2003-2 USTC ¶60,466, rev'g and rem'g TC, 116 TC 142, CCH Dec. 54,267.

[41] *G. Cook Est.*, CA-5, 2003-2 USTC ¶60,471.

other fund, the description of the annuity must identify the payment and the trust. A description of an annuity payable for a term of years must include the duration of the term and the date on which it began. If the annuity is payable for the life of a person other than the decedent, the date of birth of that person should be given.

If the annuity is under a qualified plan, the ratio of the decedent's contribution to the total purchase price of the annuity must be reported. Similarly, the ratio of the amount paid for an annuity under an individual retirement account, annuity, or bond that was not allowable as an income tax deduction under Code Sec. 219 (other than a rollover contribution) to the total amount paid for such account, annuity or bond must also be given.[42]

[42] Instructions for Form 706 (Rev. Aug. 2004), p. 17.

Chapter 17

OTHER INCLUDIBLE PROPERTY INTERESTS

¶ 773 Property Received Under Marital Deduction Rules

Property for which a marital deduction was allowed in the estate of a decedent dying after 1981 is includible in the surviving spouse's gross estate if the property is qualified terminable interest property (QTIP), as discussed at ¶ 1002.[1] The amount included in the gross estate of the surviving spouse is its fair market value on the date of death or alternate valuation date.

The main focus of litigation involving Code Sec. 2044 has been whether a particular interest is QTIP. The U.S. Court of Appeals for the Fifth Circuit, for example, has held that certain property interests the decedent received from his predeceased wife for which he elected QTIP treatment were includible in his gross estate despite the fact that neither the will nor state law expressly prohibited income accumulation. The court determined that the manifest intent of the will was not to accumulate income and, thus, the interest was QTIP.[2] In addition, the U.S. Court of Appeals for the Eleventh Circuit has held that a testamentary QTIP trust that did not entitle the surviving spouse to receive or appoint the trust income accumulating between the date of last distribution and the date of the surviving spouse's death (so-called stub income) was nonetheless QTIP. As such, the value of the interest at death was included in the surviving spouse's gross estate pursuant to Code Sec. 2044.[3]

QTIP property includible in a spouse's gross estate is considered as property passing from the spouse for estate and generation-skipping transfer tax purposes. Accordingly, such property may qualify for a marital deduction if it passes to the decedent's spouse, assuming that the spouse has remarried. Additionally, such property may qualify for a charitable deduction if it passes to a charitable organization. The basis of QTIP property acquired from a deceased spouse is its fair market value on the date of the spouse's death.[4]

If QTIP property from a prior estate is includible in a decedent's gross estate, this fact is to be indicated by answering "yes" to question 6 on page 2 of Form 706 (United States Estate (and Generation-Skipping Transfer) Tax Return) (Rev. Aug. 2004), part 4. The property is to be reported on Schedule F (Other Miscellaneous Property Not Reportable Under Any Other Schedule).[5] Question 16 on page 3 of Form 706, part 4, requires the executor to identify whether the decedent was the beneficiary of a QTIP trust for which a deduction was claimed by the predeceased spouse's estate and that is not otherwise reported on the decedent's Form 706.

---

[1] Code Sec. 2044; Reg. § 20.2044-1.

[2] *H.R. Cavenaugh Est.*, CA-5, 95-1 USTC ¶ 60,195, aff'g in part and rev'g in part TC, 100 TC 407, CCH Dec. 49,030; IRS Letter Ruling 8028765 (Sept. 18, 1980).

[3] *L.P. Shelfer Est.*, CA-11, 96-2 USTC ¶ 60,238, rev'g TC, 103 TC 10, CCH Dec. 49,967.

[4] Code Sec. 2044(c).

[5] Instructions for Form 706 (Rev. Aug. 2004), p. 11.

In construing Code Sec. 2044, the courts will apply a duty of consistency. Thus, for example, the Tax Court has held that the value of QTIP property that passed to a decedent from her predeceased husband was includible in her estate, even though the predeceased husband's estate had not made a QTIP election for the property but had claimed a marital deduction for it.[6] According to the court, the duty of consistency required inclusion in the decedent's estate because (1) the husband's estate made a factual representation in one year, (2) the IRS relied on that fact in that year, and (3) the earlier year was closed by the statute of limitations and the decedent's estate attempted to change the earlier factual representations.

• *Right of Recovery for Estate Tax*

Additional estate tax liability attributable to taxation of the QTIP in the recipient spouse's gross estate is to be borne by the person or persons receiving the property unless the recipient spouse indicates in a will or revocable trust an intent to waive any right of recovery by specifically referring to Code Sec. 2044, Code Sec. 2207A, the QTIP, or the QTIP trust.[7]

• *Unnecessary QTIP Elections*

The IRS has issued a procedure (Rev. Proc. 2001-38) under which it will treat unnecessary QTIP elections as null and void for purposes of Code Sec. 2044. A QTIP election will be deemed to be unnecessary if it is not needed to reduce the estate tax liability to zero. For example, this rule will apply where a QTIP election was made, even though the taxable estate (before the allowance of the marital deduction) was less than the applicable exclusion amount. It will also apply to a situation where QTIP elections were made for both the marital and the "credit shelter" trusts created by a decedent's estate plan where no estate tax would have been imposed regardless of whether an election was made for the credit shelter trust.[8]

A taxpayer will be required to produce sufficient evidence to establish that a particular QTIP election comes within the scope of this IRS procedure. For example, a taxpayer may produce a copy of the predeceased spouse's estate tax return to show that the election was not necessary to reduce the estate tax liability to zero. The rule is effective as of June 4, 2001, and applies to elections qualifying under the procedure, regardless of when made.

The IRS has privately ruled that the relief provisions of Rev. Proc. 2001-38 are not available where the trustee of a decedent's trust was attempting to revoke in part (rather than to totally revoke) a QTIP election that had previously been made. (A total revocation of the election would not have served the interests of the trust because it would not have reduced the decedent's estate tax liability to zero.)[9]

¶775 Excess Retirement Accumulation Tax

Prior to repeal by the Taxpayer Relief Act of 1997 (P.L. 105-34), a 15-percent additional tax was imposed on the estate of any person who died after 1986 and before January 1, 1996, with "excess qualified retirement accumulation." In general, this excise tax was an additional estate tax and was calculated indepen-

[6] *M. Letts Est.*, 109 TC 290, CCH Dec. 52,368, aff'd, CA-11, 2000-1 USTC ¶60,374, in an unpublished per curiam opinion.

[7] Code Sec. 2207A.

[8] Rev. Proc. 2001-38, 2001-1 CB 1335.

[9] IRS Letter Ruling 200219003, Feb. 5, 2002.

dently of the estate tax owed on death.[10] Thus, the credits, deductions, exclusions, or other special rules used to determine a decedent's estate tax did not affect the calculation of this excise tax. For example, the 15-percent tax could have applied, even though there was no estate tax liability. In that case, Form 706 (United States Estate (and Generation-Skipping Transfer) Tax Return) would have been filed only to report the excise tax.

The following distributions were not subject to the tax: (1) any distribution received by any person with respect to an individual as a result of the death of that individual; (2) any distribution with respect to an individual that is received by an alternate payee under a qualified domestic relations order within the meaning of Code Sec. 414(p) that is includible in the payee's income; (3) distributions attributable to investment in the contract under Code Sec. 72(f); (4) a distribution not included in gross income by reason of rollover; and (5) a distribution for health or medical benefits under Code Sec. 401(h).[11] Additionally, the following types of distributions were excluded from the determination of excess distributions pursuant to the Technical and Miscellaneous Revenue Act of 1988 (P.L. 100-647): (1) an annuity contract that is distributed to an individual and the value of which is not included in the individual's income when the contract is distributed; (2) excess deferrals as defined in Code Sec. 402(g)(2)(A)(ii); (3) excess contributions and related income as defined in Code Sec. 401(k)(8); (4) excess aggregate contributions and related income as defined in Code Sec. 401(m)(6); and (5) certain amounts withdrawn from an IRA before the due date of the return under Code Sec. 408(d)(4).

---

[10] See Temp. Reg. § 54.4981A-1T, Q&A d-9, for examples of the determination of the additional tax.

[11] Temp. Reg. § 54.4981A-1T, Q&A a-4.

DEDUCTIONS

Chapter 18

FUNERAL AND ADMINISTRATION EXPENSES

¶ 780 Deductions Allowed

A deduction from the value of the gross estate is allowed for funeral and administration expenses allowable under the laws of the jurisdiction in which the estate is being administered. The deduction is allowable even if the jurisdiction is outside the United States.[1]

Deductions are allowable both for expenses incurred in administering property subject to claims and for expenses incurred in administering property *not* subject to claims. See ¶ 805 for the allowance of deductions where the amount of deductions exceeds the value of property subject to claims. Property not subject to claims must be included in the gross estate of the decedent, and the expenses must be paid within three years after the estate tax return is filed.

In the estate tax return, funeral expenses and the expenses incurred in administering property subject to claims are reported on Schedule J (Funeral Expenses and Expenses Incurred in Administering Property Subject to Claims) of Form 706 (United States Estate (and Generation-Skipping Transfer) Tax Return) (Rev. Aug. 2004). Expenses incurred in administering property not subject to claims are deducted on Schedule L (Net Losses During Administration and Expenses Incurred in Administering Property Not Subject to Claims) of Form 706.

Amounts allowable as expenses under Code Sec. 2053 or as losses under Code Sec. 2054 for federal estate tax purposes may not again be allowed as deductions in computing the taxable income of the decedent's estate. This rule also applies to trusts or any other person who might benefit from the expense, claim, or loss item incurred. To secure a deduction for income tax purposes, a waiver of the right to claim the deductions for estate tax purposes must be filed (see ¶ 797).[2]

¶ 783 Trustees' Commissions

Trustees' commissions, if deductible, generally should be considered with expenses incurred in administering property not subject to claims. This is proper tax treatment whether the commissions are received by the executor acting as trustee or by a separate trustee.[3]

---

[1] Code Sec. 2053(a); Reg. § 20.2053-1(a)(1)(i).

[2] Code Sec. 642(g); Reg. § 20.2053-1(d).

[3] Reg. § 20.2053-3(b).

¶ 785 Funeral Expenses

Deductible funeral expenses are those amounts actually expended by the executor or administrator. Under the laws of the local jurisdiction, expenses must be payable out of the decedent's estate.[4]

Included among the expenses deductible under this classification are reasonable expenditures for a tombstone, monument, or mausoleum, or for a burial lot (whether for the decedent or the decedent's family). These expenses must be allowable under local law. Also included as a funeral expense is the cost of transportation incurred by a person who brings the decedent's body to the place of burial. Amounts paid for perpetual care of a cemetery lot or mausoleum are deductible if allowable under local law.

If a decedent dies a resident of a state in which the spouse is responsible for the payment of funeral expenses, in the absence of contrary instructions in the decedent's will, funeral expenses are not deductible.[5] The deduction must be reduced by Social Security and Veterans Administration death benefits.[6] The funeral expense deduction must be reduced by any reimbursement that is received for such expenses under a state's wrongful death statute or by the reasonable value of such a claim filed for such expenses.[7]

In community property states, the extent of deductibility depends on whether the funeral expenses are deemed to be an expense of the community estate or of the decedent's estate. If they are an expense of the community estate, only one-half the amount expended is deductible. If the expenses are allowable against the estate of the decedent, they are deductible to the extent so allowable (see ¶ 795).

¶ 790 Administration Expenses

To be deductible, administration expenses must be actually and necessarily incurred in the administration of the estate. They include those expenses incurred in (1) collection of assets, (2) payment of debt, and (3) distribution among the persons entitled to share in the estate. These expenses, in turn, include executor's commissions, attorneys' fees, and miscellaneous expenses.[8]

Administration expenses incurred for the individual benefit of the heirs, legatees, or devisees are never deductible. To be deductible, expenses must be incurred in connection with the transfer of estate property to the beneficiaries or to a trustee. Therefore, the expenses incurred in obtaining from the probate court the award of a support allowance for the widow during administration of the estate are not deductible.[9]

As to community property estates, see ¶ 795.

¶ 791 Executors' Commissions

Executors' and administrators' commissions are deductible in the amount actually paid or in an amount that, at the time the return is filed, is reasonably expected to be paid.[10] It is best that the fee be fixed by decree of the proper court. In the event that it has not been so fixed, the deduction will be allowed on the final audit of the return if:

---

[4] Reg. § 20.2053-2.

[5] Rev. Rul. 76-369, 1976-2 CB 281.

[6] Rev. Rul. 66-234, 1966-2 CB 436.

[7] Rev. Rul. 77-274, 1977-2 CB 326.

[8] Reg. § 20.2053-3(a).

[9] *W.A. Landers Est.*, 38 TC 828, CCH Dec. 25,650.

[10] Reg. § 20.2053-3(b).

(1) the District Director is reasonably satisfied that the commissions claimed actually will be paid;

(2) the amount claimed as a deduction is within the amount allowable by the laws of the jurisdiction in which the estate is being administered; and

(3) it is customary in that jurisdiction to allow such an amount in estates of similar size and character.

If the executors' commissions have not been paid at the time of the final audit of the return, the amount claimed as a deduction must be supported with an affidavit or statement signed under the penalty of perjury that the amount has been agreed on and will be paid. If the deduction is not allowed in full at the time of the final audit, the amount disallowed may be later modified on the basis of subsequent events. If the deduction is allowed in full but actual commissions are less than the amount allowed, the difference should be reported. Any resulting increase in the tax should be paid, together with interest.

If the decedent, by will, fixes the compensation payable to the estate representative, that amount is deductible. It must not exceed the compensation allowable by local law or practice, however. If the will provides that the executor should receive a bequest or devise in lieu of commissions, no deduction is available for the amount of the bequest or devise.

Although the term "executors' commissions" may be taken to include administrators' commissions, it does not include trustees' commissions, even if received by an executor or administrator as trustee. Principal commissions paid with respect to trust property included in the gross estate are deductible as expenses in connection with property not subject to claims.

As to community property estates, see ¶795.

¶792 Attorneys' Fees

Attorneys' fees are deductible, at the time the return is filed, to the extent that they have been actually paid or to the extent that it is reasonably expected that they will be paid. If, when the return is finally audited, the fees claimed have not been awarded by the proper courts and paid, they still may be allowed. It must be shown to the satisfaction of the IRS that the amount claimed will be paid and that it is reasonable for the services rendered.[11]

If the fees claimed have not been paid at the time of the final audit of the return, the amount deducted must be supported by an affidavit, or statement signed under penalties of perjury, of the executor or the attorney stating that such amount has been agreed on and will be paid. Even if part of the amount claimed is disallowed on final audit, subsequent adjustment may be made if warranted by the facts.[12] Deductible fees are those incurred for services that benefit the estate. Fees incurred by beneficiaries incident to litigation with regard to their interest are not deductible unless the litigation is essential to the proper settlement of the estate.[13]

The return, itself, can reflect only fees of which there is some knowledge at the time of preparation and filing. If there should later be litigation or other action requiring services of attorneys in finally establishing the amount of tax due, deductions on account of such fees should be claimed at the time of the contest. The IRS will not allow deductions for legal fees that are incurred in

---

[11] Reg. §20.2053-3(c).

[12] Reg. §20.2053-3(c).

[13] *P.W. Reilly Est.*, 76 TC 369, CCH Dec. 37,691 (Acq.).

litigation and that are paid after a Tax Court decision becomes final and more than three years after the filing of the estate tax return.[14] The IRS will allow a deduction and refund in such cases only where the final decision of the Tax Court allows attorneys' fees as an additional deduction. The Tax Court has held that even where the estate tax was assessed against the transferees of the estate, thereby extending the statutory period for assessing the tax one year beyond the initial three-year period, a deduction will not be allowed for legal fees paid after such three-year period.[15]

Expenses incurred in contesting the inclusion of trust property in the gross estate are deductible as expenses incurred with respect to property not subject to claims. These expenses must be paid within three years after the final date for filing the return.

As to community property estates, see ¶795.

¶793 Miscellaneous Expenses

Deductible miscellaneous administration expenses are sufficiently broad in scope to include court costs, surrogate's fees, appraisers' fees, and clerk hire. They also include the cost of storing or maintaining estate property and other expenses necessary to the preservation and distribution of the estate. Brokers' and auctioneers' fees are also deductible if the sale of the property is necessary to pay debts or administration expenses, or to effect distribution.[16]

• ***Selling Expenses***

Pursuant to IRS regulations, selling expenses (such as broker fees, survey fees, or transfer stamps) are deductible if the sale is necessary in order to pay the decedent's debts, expenses of administration or taxes, to preserve the estate, or to effect distribution.[17]

> ***Example:*** Robert Smith died on July 5, 2004. Because his estate did not have sufficient assets to pay his debts and taxes, the estate sold his residence. The selling expenses incurred in selling the residence are a deductible expense.

The Internal Revenue Code, however, allows a deduction for administration expenses that are allowable under local law.[18] The IRS has stated, and the courts have agreed,[19] that the expense must be both allowable under local law and necessary for the preservation and distribution of the decedent's estate.

• ***Interest***

Interest on loans that were incurred by estates to pay estate and inheritance taxes are deductible as an administration expense where the loans are incurred to avoid "forced" sales of estate assets and are permitted by state probate laws.[20] However, the interest is deductible only as it accrues and, therefore, no deduction may be computed based on an estimation of the interest expense.[21] Similarly,

---

[14] Rev. Rul. 78-323, 1978-2 CB 240.

[15] *D.A. Gillum*, 49 TCM 240, CCH Dec. 41,654(M), TC Memo. 1984-631.

[16] Reg. §20.2053-3(d).

[17] Reg. §20.2053-3(d)(2).

[18] Code Sec. 2053(a).

[19] *C. Swayne*, 43 TC 190, CCH Dec. 27,054; *D. Smith*, CA-2, 75-1 USTC ¶13,046, 510 F2d 479; *S. Marcus*, CA-11, 83-1 USTC ¶13,521, 704 F2d 1227; *S.L. Payne, Exr.*, DC Fla., 75-1 USTC ¶13,059; *M.F. Park*, CA-6, 73-1 USTC ¶12,913, 475 F2d 673.

[20] *J.S. Todd Est.*, 57 TC 288, CCH Dec. 31,087 (Acq.); *F.M. Hipp, Admr.*, DC S.C., 72-1 USTC ¶12,824.

[21] Rev. Rul. 84-75, 1984-1 CB 193. See IRS Technical Advice Memorandum 8450003 (Aug. 22, 1984) (timely filing of a claim for refund of estate taxes protected estate's right

interest on deferred federal estate taxes (see ¶1672) is deductible only when accrued.[22] In addition, interest on deferred state death taxes is a deductible administration expense.[23] However, interest paid with respect to recapture tax was not deductible as an administration expense because it is separately imposed on the qualified heir(s) rather than the estate.[24]

Interest on a federal estate,[25] gift,[26] or income[27] tax deficiency is a deductible administration expense to the extent the expense is allowable under local law. This is true even for interest accruing after the decedent's death.[28]

However, penalties for late filing of an estate tax return and late payment of estate taxes are not deductible on an estate tax return as administration expenses even if allowable under state law, the IRS has ruled.[29] The executor's willful failure to file the return was a breach of his fiduciary duty and, therefore, the resulting penalties were not necessary to the administration of the estate.

Interest payable on the installment payment of the estate tax is not deductible.[30]

¶794 Support of Dependents

No deduction is allowed for payments to support dependents. This does not prevent deduction of a spousal allowance in all cases. When the allowance to the surviving spouse under state law constitutes a vested right that will survive as an asset of the surviving spouse's estate in the event of remarriage or death, it will qualify for the marital deduction.

¶795 Community Property States

In community property states, the extent to which the administration expenses are deductible depends on their treatment under state law. If they are deemed to be an expense of the entire community estate under state law, only one-half of the expenses are deductible, even if the decedent directs that his estate bear all the expenses.[31] If they are regarded as expenses of the decedent alone, the entire amount may be deducted. The usual limitations on deductions generally are applicable.

¶796 Execution of Schedule

Funeral expenses and expenses incurred in administering property subject to claims are itemized on Schedule J (Funeral Expenses and Expenses Incurred in Administering Property Subject to Claims) of Form 706 (United States Estate (and Generation-Skipping Transfer) Tax Return). Funeral expenses less any amounts that were reimbursed, such as death benefits payable by the Social Security Administration and the Veterans Administration, are listed on part A. Administration expenses are to be included in the four categories under Part B.

(Footnote Continued)

to a refund based upon interest paid on a long-term loan after the expiration of the limitations period); *M. Milliken Est.*, CA-6, 97-2 USTC ¶60,287.

[22] Rev. Rul. 80-250, 1980-2 CB 278.

[23] Rev. Rul. 81-256, 1981-2 CB 183.

[24] Rev. Rul. 90-8, 1990-1 CB 173. Also see IRS Technical Advice Memorandum 8902002 (Sept. 26, 1988).

[25] Rev. Rul. 79-252, 1979-2 CB 333.

[26] *J. DeP. Webster*, 65 TC 968, CCH Dec. 33,661.

[27] *R. Maehling*, DC Ind., 67-2 USTC ¶12,486.

[28] *J. DeP. Webster*, 65 TC 968, CCH Dec. 33,661; *R. Maehling*, DC Ind., 67-2 USTC ¶12,486; *B. Turner, Exrx.*, DC Tex., 2004-1 USTC ¶60,478.

[29] Rev. Rul. 81-154, 1981-1 CB 470.

[30] Code Sec. 2053(c)(1)(D).

[31] *D.A. Stapf*, 63-2 USTC ¶12,192, 375 US 118.

The total deduction for executors' commissions should be entered at item 1, attorneys' fees should be entered at item 2, accountant fees should be entered at item 3, and miscellaneous administration expenses should be itemized under item 4 of the schedule. Schedule J must be filed only if the estate claims a deduction on item 13 of the Recapitulation (see ¶73).

An item may be entered for deduction, even though the exact amount is not known at the time the return is filed. The item must be ascertainable with reasonable certainty and be expected to be paid. No deduction may be taken on the basis of a vague or uncertain estimate. All vouchers and receipts should be retained for possible inspection by the IRS.

¶ 797 Estate Tax vs. Income Tax Deduction

The executor or administrator of an estate has the choice of claiming administration expenses and casualty losses, under Code Sec. 2053 and Code Sec. 2054, as deductions on either the decedent's estate tax return or the fiduciary income tax return, but not on both.[32] This so-called double deduction prohibition also applies to such expenses or losses that are paid or incurred by trusts or other persons, instead of the estate. In addition, the rule against double deductions applies with respect to items that would be deductible in determining the taxable amount for taxable distributions and taxable terminations under the generation-skipping transfer tax.[33]

Administration expenses that are subject to the above double deduction prohibition include executors' commissions, attorneys' fees, and other expenses that are incurred in managing, maintaining, and conserving estate assets, such as court costs, appraisal fees, custodial fees, investment counsel services, accountants' fees, etc. In addition, selling expenses may not be used to offset the sales price on a sale of property by an estate or trust in determining gain or loss on a fiduciary income tax return, if they have also been deducted as an administration expense for federal estate tax purposes.[34]

The rule against double deductions does not apply to deductions for taxes, interest, business expenses, and other items that are accrued at the date of a decedent's death, and that, therefore, are claims against his or her estate. These expenses can be claimed as an estate tax deduction and as a deduction in respect of a decedent for income tax purposes under Code Sec. 691.

The total amount of one deduction or of all deductions does not have to be treated in the same way. One deduction or portion of a deduction may be allowed for income tax purposes if the waiver is filed, while another deduction or portion is allowed for estate tax purposes. The election to treat administration expenses as income or estate tax deductions may be made on a year-to-year basis, if the required waiver is filed.[35]

If the executor decides to claim administration expenses and casualty losses as estate tax deductions, the deductions are claimed on the estate tax return. On the other hand, if the executor decides on claiming such expenses and losses as income tax deductions, the estate must file a statement, in duplicate, with the IRS indicating that the amount has not already been claimed as an estate tax deduction and that it is waiving its right to claim them as estate tax deductions.[36] A waiver of the right to the estate deduction cannot be revoked, even though it is

---

[32] Reg. § 1.642(g)-1 and Reg. § 20.2053-1(d).
[33] Code Sec. 642(g).
[34] Code Sec. 642(g).
[35] Rev. Rul. 70-361, 1970-2 CB 133.
[36] Reg. § 1.642(g)-1 and Reg. § 1.642(g)-2.

later discovered that only a portion of the deducted expenses was of any income tax benefit. Although Reg. § 1.642(g)-1 indicates that failure to file the waiver statement precludes the allowance of an income tax deduction, the Tax Court has held that items previously deducted on a federal income tax return (where no waiver was filed) can be deducted as claims against the estate so long as they were personal obligations of the decedent at death.[37] An executor's decision to claim administration expenses or casualty losses as either income tax or estate tax deductions should be based on the course of action that will produce the greatest overall tax savings, after considering the beneficiaries and the provisions of the will.

[37] *M. Love Est.*, 57 TCM 1479, CCH Dec. 45,987(M), TC Memo. 1989-470.

Chapter 19
DEBTS OF DECEDENTS

¶ 800 Claims Against the Estate

Claims against the estate that are allowable by the laws of the jurisdiction under which the estate is being administered are deductible.[1] Such claims, when founded on a promise or agreement, are deductible to the extent that they are contracted in good faith and for adequate and full consideration. To the extent that they require the making of a contribution or gift to any charitable donee, they are deductible if similar transfers by will would qualify for deduction as a charitable transfer.

The amounts that are deductible as claims against a decedent's estate are those that represent personal obligations of the decedent existing at the time of his death. Interest that has accrued to the obligations at the time of death may be added. Only interest accrued to the date of decedent's death is deductible, even though the executor elects the alternate valuation method.[2]

If the claims represent personal obligations of the decedent at the time of his death, they are deductible whether or not they are then matured. Only claims enforceable against the estate are deductible, however. Interest accruing after a decedent's death on a claim is deductible as an administration expense if payment of the debt is postponed to benefit the estate and is allowable under state law.

Generally, a claim that becomes unenforceable (and that will not be paid) because of a creditor's failure to file as required under state law is not deductible.[3] However, the U.S. Court of Appeals for the Seventh Circuit has held that an amount owed to a creditor under a compromise agreement entered into with the decedent's estate was an enforceable and, therefore, deductible, claim against the estate even though the creditor did not file a claim within the time period prescribed by state law.[4] Similarly, a U.S. district court in Illinois has allowed a deduction for late-filed claims because the enforceability of the claims at the time of death, rather than at the time of filing, was controlling.[5] However, the court denied a deduction for loans made to the decedent, the collection of which was barred by the state statute of limitations. A U.S. district court in Ohio held that a promissory note received by the executor of a decedent's estate from the decedent and payable at the decedent's death was valid and enforceable on the date of death and, therefore, was deductible even though the executor failed to

---

[1] Code Sec. 2053(a); Reg. §20.2053-1(a)(1)(iii).

[2] Reg. §20.2053-4.

[3] Rev. Rul. 60-247, 1960-2 CB 272; *F.G. Hagmann Est.*, CA-5, 74-1 USTC ¶12,996, 492 F2d 796.

[4] *B.L. Thompson*, CA-7, 84-1 USTC ¶13,568, 730 F2d 1071.

[5] *B. Greene, Exr. (A. Greene Est.)*, DC Ill., 78-1 USTC ¶13,240, 447 FSupp. 885. See also *First Interstate Bank of Arizona, Pers. Rep.*, DC Ariz., 86-1 USTC ¶13,665.

present the claim to the probate court for allowance as required under state law.[6] The Tax Court has held that the value of a decedent's obligation to pay an annuity was deductible as a claim against the estate even though the annuitant did not present a claim to the estate as required under state law.[7]

The U.S. Court of Appeals for the Tenth Circuit has held that an estate's settlement payment of a claim of tortious interference with an inheritance that was made by the decedent's descendants was not deductible as a claim against the estate. According to the court, the payment obligation did not arise out of a tort liability that was a personal obligation of the decedent that existed as the time of his death. Instead, the payment was in the nature of a nondeductible settlement of an inheritance claim.[8]

A claim that is enforceable against multiple sources of payment, but that is not asserted against the estate, is also not deductible.[9] A valid and enforceable claim that is informally presented to the executor within the period for presenting claims under state law and paid with the approval of the beneficiaries (in order to relieve the executor of personal liability) is deductible,[10] as is an informal claim that may be deemed to have been paid through the payment of a legacy to the sole beneficiary of the estate in an amount at least equal to that of the claim.[11] Life insurance proceeds paid to the decedent's former wife under a property settlement agreement incorporated in a divorce decree are deductible, even though the insurance company made such payment directly to the beneficiary and no claim was filed against the estate, where the executor would have been obligated to pay over such proceeds to the former wife if he had received such proceeds.[12]

The amount of the deduction is the value of the claim. This has led to some dispute as to whether events occurring after the decedent's death should be considered in determining the value of a claim. In the IRS view, post-death events should be considered in valuing claims against the estate.[13] However, the IRS position has been rejected in several circuit courts of appeal. The U.S. Court of Appeals for the Ninth Circuit has held that the amount of deduction allowable with respect to a lien on a parcel of real property was the amount of the claim that was due and owing on the date of the decedent's death, rather than a lower amount that was later paid in settlement of the claim.[14] Similarly, the Ninth Circuit has held that the executor of a decedent's estate properly determined, under actuarial tables, the amount of the allowable federal estate tax deduction for a claim consisting of an annuity payable to the decedent's ex-husband, even though the total value of the annuity payments actually made was far less than the annuity's actuarial value because the ex-husband died seven months after the decedent's death.[15]

A decedent's estate was permitted to claim an estate tax deduction for federal and state income tax owed at the time of the decedent's death, even though the decedent later became entitled to a refund for the tax year at issue,

---

[6] *R.C. Wilder, Exr. (C.H. Manley Est.),* DC Ohio, 83-2 USTC ¶13,546, 581 FSupp. 86.

[7] *C. McDowell Est.*, 51 TCM 319, CCH Dec. 42,831(M), TC Memo. 1986-27.

[8] *J. Lindberg*, CA-10, 99-1 USTC ¶60,334, 164 F3d 1312.

[9] *Q.P. Courtney Est.*, 62 TC 317, CCH Dec. 32,639.

[10] Rev. Rul. 75-24, 1975-1 CB 306.

[11] Rev. Rul. 60-247, 1960-2 CB 272.

[12] *W.P. Gray, Exr. (Will of W.G. Robertson),* DC Cal., 74-2 USTC ¶13,019, 391 FSupp. 693, and 78-1 USTC ¶13,244, 440 FSupp. 684.

[13] Rev. Rul. 60-247, 1960-2 CB 272.

[14] *J.A. Propstra, Pers. Rep.*, CA-9, 82-2 USTC ¶13,475.

[15] *A.E. Van Horne Est.*, CA-9, 83-2 USTC ¶13,548, 720 F2d 1114, cert. denied, May 14, 1984.

the U.S. Court of Appeals for the Tenth Circuit has held.[16] The appellate court, reversing the decision of the Tax Court,[17] held that events occurring after death are not to be considered in valuing a claim taken as an estate tax deduction under Code Sec. 2053(a)(3). The appellate court determined that it would adopt the date-of-death valuation rule of *Ithaca Trust Co.*,[18] which provides that post-mortem events are not to be considered in valuing an estate tax charitable deduction, and extend it to the estate's tax debt claim.

Also relying on *Ithaca Trust Co.*, the Court of Appeals for the Eleventh Circuit held that a deduction claimed by a decedent's estate, relating to the estate's reimbursement of gift tax liability paid by the decedent's heirs, was to be valued as of the date of death, without consideration of any post-death events.[19]

¶ 805 Claims Exceeding Assets Available for Payment

In the event that the claims against the estate exceed the value of property subject to the payment of claims, special rules apply. Deductions of such claims (together with funeral expenses, certain administration expenses, mortgages and liens) are disallowed to the extent they exceed the value of the property subject to the claims. Deductions for such amounts nevertheless will be allowed if they are actually paid before the date prescribed for filing the estate tax return.

"Property subject to claims" is the property out of which the deductible amounts would be paid under applicable law upon the settlement of the estate. The value of such property must be reduced by any administration expenses deducted against such property.[20]

The IRS takes the position that the total amount deducted as claims against the estate cannot exceed the decedent's probate estate, citing the holding in a decision of the Court of Appeals for the Third Circuit.[21] The Federal Claims Court has rejected this limitation, stating that, where local law (Ohio) subjected nonprobate trust assets, as well as probate assets, to payment of an EPA superfund liability of $750,000, the deduction as a claim against the estate was not limited to the amount of the probate assets. The Claims Court concluded that a plain reading of the statutory language of Code Sec. 2053(c)(2) did not impose the "probate estate" limitation argued by the IRS.[22]

¶ 810 Deductible Claims

The following items are among those that have been held to be deductible as claims against the estate:

(1) alimony decreed by a court but past due (if payments are to continue periodically after the decedent's death, the commuted value of such payments is also deductible[23]);

(2) commissions owed to trustee for services during decedent's lifetime;[24]

---

16 *E. McMorris Est.*, CA-10, 2001-1 USTC ¶60,396.

17 *E. McMorris Est.*, 77 TCM 1552, CCH Dec. 53,291(M), TC Memo. 1999-82.

18 *Ithaca Trust Co.*, SCt, 1 USTC ¶386, 279 US 151.

19 *E. O'Neal Est.*, CA-11, 2001-2 USTC ¶60,412, aff'g in part and vac'g and rem'g in part, DC Ala., 99-2 USTC ¶60,365.

20 Code Sec. 2053(c)(2).

21 *S. Wilson v. U.S.*, CA-3, 67-1 USTC ¶12,451, 372 F2d 232.

22 *R. Snyder Est.*, FedCl, 99-2 USTC ¶60,357.

23 Rev. Rul. 67-304, 1967-2 CB 224.

24 *F.E. Baldwin Est.*, 44 BTA 900, CCH Dec. 11,878 (Acq.).

(3) the commuted value of support payments due a decedent's wife for her release of her support and maintenance rights under a valid separation agreement;[25]

(4) amounts due on judgments against the decedent, including tort liabilities;[26]

(5) amounts due under guarantees executed by the decedent and not collectible from primary obligator; and[27]

(6) amounts due on notes.[28]

Although, as noted at (4), above, amounts paid to satisfy judgments against the decedent are deductible, the IRS has ruled that a decedent's estate could not deduct amounts paid in satisfaction of a collusive lawsuit filed against the decedent by his son.[29] In so ruling, the IRS noted that the decedent's child filed the suit pursuant to a plan to reduce federal estate taxes that was devised by a financial planner. Even though the decedent did not contest the lawsuit and a judgment was awarded to the child under a consent decree, the amounts paid in satisfaction of the claim were not deductible because the lawsuit was without merit and was merely a device to allow the transfer of property free of estate and gift taxes.

¶ 813 Medical Expenses

The medical expenses resulting from a decedent's last illness are a deductible claim against the estate. In lieu of deducting these expenses on the estate tax return, the executor may deduct these expenses on the decedent's last income tax return. However, it may be preferable for the estate to deduct these expenses on the estate tax return because the tax rate schedule for estate tax is significantly higher than the tax rate schedule for income tax. Moreover, for estate tax purposes, the medical expenses are fully deductible. The medical expenses for income tax purposes are deductible only to the extent that such expenses exceed 7.5 percent of the decedent's adjusted gross income. However, if the decision is made to deduct medical expenses on the decedent's last income tax return, a statement that such amount has not been claimed as a deduction on the estate's Form 706 (United States Estate (and Generation-Skipping Transfer) Tax Return) (Rev. Aug. 2004) and that the estate waives any right to do so in the future must be filed.[30]

In community property states, the deductibility of a decedent's medical expenses for estate tax purposes is dependent on whether such costs are treated as an expense of the community estate or of the decedent's estate.[31] If such costs are a community expense, only one-half of the costs are deductible for estate tax purposes. If such costs are allowable against the decedent's estate, they are deductible to the extent so allowed.

¶ 815 Claims Founded on Promise or Agreement

A claim against the estate based on a promise or agreement by the decedent to pay over certain property or a specified amount of money is subject to special treatment. It will be denied as a deduction except to the extent that it was

[25] Rev. Rul. 71-67, 1971-1 CB 271.

[26] *E.C. Moore, Exr.*, 21 BTA 279, CCH Dec. 6467 (Acq.).

[27] *E.L. Benz, Exr.*, CA-1, 37-2 USTC ¶9337, 90 F2d 747.

[28] *Security Tr. Co., Exr.*, 4 BTA 983, CCH Dec. 1647 (Acq.).

[29] Rev. Rul. 83-54, 1983-1 CB 229.

[30] Code Sec. 213(c); Reg. § 1.213-1(d).

[31] Rev. Rul. 78-242, 1978-1 CB 292.

contracted in good faith and for an adequate and full consideration in money or money's worth.[32]

Generally, the requirements as to consideration here are the same as those that apply in determining whether a lifetime transfer should escape inclusion in the gross estate. A special exception is provided with respect to claims made by charitable organizations. The consideration requirements are waived if the claimant is one to whom a testamentary transfer would be deductible as a charitable transfer.

• ***Claims Under a Divorce Decree***

The consideration requirement applies to claims "founded on a promise or agreement." However, claims founded on a divorce decree are not founded on an agreement and, as such, are deductible without regard to the consideration requirement so long as they meet the general requirements for deduction.[33]

The obligation to transfer property to a former spouse of the decedent is deductible as a claim against the estate if the transfer is pursuant to an agreement satisfying the conditions for the gift tax exemption under Code Sec. 2516 (see ¶2165).[34] Thus, the deduction will be available if the transfer is pursuant to a written agreement between the spouses and if divorce occurred within the three-year period beginning one year before execution of the agreement. In the event the decedent dies before the divorce, the transfer would be eligible for the marital deduction (see ¶1000).

With respect to estates of decedents dying prior to July 18, 1984, the Tax Court has held that a decedent's estate could not deduct as a claim against the estate amounts paid to the decedent's ex-wife in settlement of her right to be named beneficiary of certain life insurance policies pursuant to a separation agreement. Although the parties were divorced and the separation agreement made part of the divorce decree, the court noted that because, under applicable state law (Missouri), the divorce court had no power to award the insurance policies to the ex-wife, the amounts were paid pursuant to the separation agreement rather than pursuant to the divorce decree. Because the estate could not show that support rights relinquished by the ex-wife and the couple's children were consideration for the insurance provision in the agreement, the court denied the deduction.[35]

The U.S. Court of Appeals for the Second Circuit, in a case involving a separation agreement under a Mexican divorce decree, has indicated its disagreement with the Tax Court's position as stated above.[36] In that case, the Second Circuit held that a decedent's estate could deduct as a claim against the estate an amount paid to the decedent's ex-wife pursuant to a separation agreement because the Mexican court had incorporated the agreement (which was executed in New York) into the divorce decree, as it was empowered to do by Mexican law. However, the Second Circuit noted that the payment would have been deductible, even if it had been made pursuant to the agreement rather than to the divorce decree because the agreement was deemed made for full and adequate consideration under Code Sec. 2516, prior to amendment by the Tax Reform Act of 1984 (P.L. 98-369).[37] In the Second Circuit's view, such a holding was necessary

---

[32] Code Sec. 2053(c)(1). Also see *M. Wedum Est.*, 57 TCM 219, CCH Dec. 45,637(M), TC Memo. 1989-184.

[33] *W.E. Robinson Est.*, 63 TC 717, CCH Dec. 33,099 (Acq.), and *M.C. Watson Est.*, CA-2, 54-2 USTC ¶10,973, 216 FSupp. 941.

[34] Code Sec. 2043(b).

[35] *E. Satz Est.*, 78 TC 1172, CCH Dec. 39,151.

[36] *D.E. Natchez and P. Natchez, Exrs.*, CA-2, 83-1 USTC ¶13,519, 705 F2d 671.

[37] The decedent and his wife were divorced within two years after executing the

in view of the U.S. Supreme Court's rulings that the estate and gift tax statutes are to be construed in a similar manner.[38]

¶ 820 Taxes

As a general rule, neither inheritance nor estate taxes payable on a decedent's estate are deductible, whether payable to the state, the federal government, or to a foreign government. State and foreign death taxes with respect to decedents dying before January 1, 2005, may give rise to credits against the federal estate tax (see ¶1370). An exception is made in the case of death taxes paid on certain transfers for charitable purposes. An executor may elect to deduct such taxes on charitable transfers, rather than take the credit against the estate tax, if the decrease in the estate tax will inure solely to the benefit of the charitable transferee.[39] See, also, ¶1380 for a discussion of the state death tax deduction, which replaces the state death tax credit, effective for estates of decedents dying after December 31, 2004.

Gift taxes due and payable on all post-1976 gifts made by a decedent dying after 1976 are subtracted from the estate tax.[40]

Property taxes are deductible only if they accrued under state law prior to the decedent's death.[41]

Excise taxes incurred in selling property of a decedent are deductible as expenses of administration if the sale is necessary to (1) pay the decedent's debts, taxes, or expenses of administration, (2) preserve the estate, or (3) effect distribution.

Unpaid income taxes are deductible if they are on income properly includible in an income tax return of the decedent for a period prior to his death. If a joint income tax return was filed, the portion of the joint liability (although entirely paid by the estate) that is deductible is the amount for which the estate would be liable under local law after enforcement of any effective right of reimbursement or contribution.[42]

Interest accruing after a decedent's death on his federal and state income tax deficiencies, which are contested by an executor or administrator, is deductible as an administration expense to the extent permitted by state law.[43] For decedents dying prior to 1998, interest payable by an estate on the unpaid balance of a decedent's federal estate tax, which the estate had elected to pay in installments pursuant to Code Sec. 6166 is also deductible as an administration expense,[44] although only as the interest liability accrues.[45] However, an estate was entitled to an immediate administration expense deduction for excess Code Sec. 6166 interest that it had paid pursuant to a deficiency assessment of the IRS that was later overturned in court. On reconsideration of its prior ruling in *Succ. of B. Helis*,[46] the U.S. Court of Federal Claims has held that an estate was not entitled to an immediate administration expense deduction for excess Code Sec. 6166 interest that it had paid pursuant to an IRS deficiency assessment that was later

---

(Footnote Continued)

separation agreement, as required under Code Sec. 2516.

[38] See, e.g., C. *Harris*, SCt, 50-2 USTC ¶10,786, 340 US 106, and *Merrill v. Fahs*, SCt, 45-1 USTC ¶10,180, 324 US 308.

[39] Code Sec. 2053(d), as amended by P.L. 107-16.

[40] Code Sec. 2001.

[41] Reg. §20.2053-6.

[42] Reg. §20.2053-6.

[43] Rev. Rul. 69-402, 1969-2 CB 176.

[44] Rev. Rul. 78-125, 1978-1 CB 292, revoking Rev. Rul. 75-239, 1975-1 CB 304.

[45] Rev. Rul. 80-250, 1980-2 CB 278; *Est. of E.H. Hoover*, 49 TCM 1239, CCH Dec. 42,031(M), TC Memo. 1985-183.

[46] *Succ. of B. Helis*, FedCl, 2003-1 USTC ¶60,454, vacating, in part, the court's opinion at 2002-2 USTC ¶60,445.

judicially overturned. According to the court, the estate was not considered to have "actually and necessarily" incurred the disputed interest expense for purposes of Reg. § 20.2053-3(a) because, prior to closing, the estate was to recover the interest overpayment, along with statutory interest on that overpayment. Therefore, from an economic standpoint, the estate would be left no worse off than if its valuation figure had been accepted without litigation. Accordingly, the estate was not entitled to deduct the excess interest payments that were later refunded as part of the final judgment in the estate tax litigation.

For decedents dying after 1997, no deduction is allowable for interest payable pursuant to Code Sec. 6166.[47] Post-death interest on a decedent's gift tax liability is deductible while the gift tax liability is being contested along with the questions of whether such interest is an allowable expense under state law.[48]

¶ 825 Execution of Schedule

In claiming a deduction for claims against the estate, the claims should be itemized on Schedule K (Debts of the Decedent, and Mortgages and Liens) of Form 706 (United States Estate (and Generation-Skipping Transfer) Tax Return) (Rev. Aug. 2004). Notes unsecured by a mortgage or other lien should be listed. Any indebtedness secured by a mortgage or other lien upon property of the gross estate should be listed separately under "Mortgages and Liens." Schedule K has to be filed only if the decedent had debts that are deductible on this schedule (see ¶73). A filled-in Schedule K is reproduced in the Appendix at ¶3060.

If the amount of the debt is disputed or is the subject of litigation, only the amount that the estate representative concedes to be a valid claim is deductible. If the claim is contested, that fact must be stated on the schedule.

Full details must be included in the description of unsecured notes, including (1) the name and address of the payee, (2) the face amount of the note, (3) the unpaid balance, (4) the date and term of the note, (5) the interest rate, and (6) the date to which interest was paid prior to death. Care must be taken to state the exact nature of the claim as well as the name of the creditor. If the claim is for services rendered over a period of time, the period covered by the claim should be stated. For example: Edison Electric Illuminating Co., for electric service during April 2004, $150.

If the amount of the claim is the unpaid balance due on a contract for the purchase of any property included in the gross estate, the schedule and item number at which the property is reported must be identified. If the claim represents a joint and several liability, the facts must be fully stated and the financial responsibility of the co-obligor explained. All vouchers or original records should be preserved for inspection by the IRS.

If the executor elects to take a deduction, rather than a credit, for state and foreign death taxes on certain charitable transfers, these taxes should be listed as a debt on the "Debts of the Decedent" portion of Schedule K.[49]

¶ 830 Community Property

If debts to be listed in the return are community debts, only one-half of the amount of such community debts should be listed. An appropriate explanation should be made.

---

[47] Code Sec. 2053(c)(1)(D).

[48] *J. DeP. Webster*, 65 TC 968, CCH Dec. 33,661 (Acq.).

[49] Instructions for Form 706 (Rev. Aug. 2004), p. 18.

Chapter 20
MORTGAGES, LOSSES, AND PROPERTY NOT SUBJECT TO CLAIMS

¶ 850 Excluding Mortgages and Liens

The amounts of any mortgages and liens that are charges against the estate of the decedent or against any specific property in the estate and that date from before decedent's death are excluded from the taxable estate. If the charges are collectible against specific property only, they are excluded by including in the gross estate only the net value of the subject property. In other instances, the value of the property is first included in the gross estate in full. Then the mortgage or lien is taken as a deduction.[1]

¶ 855 Reporting Mortgage and Lien Deductions

Only obligations secured by mortgages or other liens upon property included in the gross estate at its full value (undiminished by the amount of the mortgage or lien) are to be itemized as "Mortgages and Liens" on Schedule K (Debts of the Decedent, and Mortgages and Liens) of Form 706 (United States Estate (and Generation-Skipping Transfer) Tax Return) (Rev. Aug. 2004). If the decedent's estate is liable for the amount of the indebtedness secured by such mortgage or lien, the full value of the property subject to the mortgage or lien must be included in the gross estate under the appropriate schedule. The estate is considered liable for the indebtedness if it is enforceable against other property of the estate not subject to the mortgage or lien, or if the decedent was personally liable.[2] Schedule K need only be filed if the decedent has mortgages and/or liens that are deductible on this schedule.

There are instances where the decedent's estate is not liable for the amount of a debt secured by a mortgage or lien and the amount of the debt is greater than the value of the property subject to such mortgage or lien. In these situations, it is not possible to obtain a deduction for the full amount of the debt by entering the full value of the property as a part of the gross estate and then deducting the full amount of the debt under this schedule. Where the estate is not liable, only the redemption value (or the value of the property, less the mortgage or indebtedness) is reported as part of the gross estate.

---

[1] Code Sec. 2053(a)(4); Reg. §20.2053-1(a)(1)(iv).

[2] Reg. §20.2053-7.

Generally, the amount of mortgage liability on a decedent's property is available either as a deduction from the gross estate or as a reduction in the value of the property includible in the gross estate. However, the U.S. Court of Appeals for the Eleventh Circuit disallowed a deduction for the unpaid principal balances of mortgages on two parcels of real estate that were includible in the estates of a husband and wife because the decedents were mere accommodation parties to the mortgages and notes and, thus, were not primarily liable for the indebtedness.[3]

Notes and other obligations secured by the deposit of collateral, such as stocks and bonds, should also be listed under "Mortgages and Liens" on Schedule K. Each mortgage and lien should be identified by indicating in the "Description" column the particular schedule and item number at which the property subject to the mortgage or lien is reported. The description of the obligation should show (1) the name and address of the mortgagee, payee, or obligee, (2) the date and term of the mortgage, note, or other agreement under which the indebtedness is established, (3) the face amount, (4) the unpaid balance, (5) the rate of interest, and (6) the date to which interest was paid prior to the decedent's death.

¶ 860 Limitations as to Amount

Mortgages on, or any indebtedness with respect to, property included in the gross estate are deductible only to the extent that the liability was contracted in good faith and for an adequate and full consideration in money or money's worth.[4] Only interest accrued to the date of the decedent's death is deductible, even though the estate representative elects the alternate valuation method.[5]

The IRS has ruled that a decedent's estate could claim a deduction for the full amount of a mortgage on the decedent's farmland, even though the farmland was included in the gross estate at its special use value (see ¶280 through ¶296).[6] The IRS noted that all of the property subject to the mortgage was included in the gross estate and that the estate was liable for payment of the mortgage. Generally, the amount of a mortgage for which a decedent's estate is liable is deductible from the gross estate if the full value of the property subject to the mortgage is included in the gross estate. Under the facts of the ruling, the full value of the decedent's farmland was included in the gross estate because, for estate tax purposes, the special use value of property is equivalent to its full value.

¶ 870 Community Property Subject to Mortgage or Lien

If mortgages to be listed in the return are community obligations, such status should be made clear. Only one-half of the amount should be listed as an obligation of the estate.

¶ 900 Claiming Net Losses During Administration

Casualty and theft losses that occur during settlement of the estate are deductible to the extent they are not compensated by insurance.[7] Losses with respect to an estate asset are not deductible if they occur after distribution of the asset to the beneficiary. The term "casualty losses" encompasses losses resulting

---

[3] *C.F. Theis Est.*, CA-11, 85-2 USTC ¶13,639, 770 F2d 981.

[4] Reg. §20.2053-7.

[5] Reg. §20.2053-7.

[6] Rev. Rul. 83-81, 1983-1 CB 230.

[7] Code Sec. 2054.

from fire, storm, shipwreck, and war. The loss contemplated is a loss with respect to tangible property.[8]

Depreciation in value of intangibles, even though occasioned by destruction, damage, or theft of underlying physical assets, is not deductible under Code Sec. 2054. Losses in value of intangibles can serve to reduce the taxable estate, but only if they occur within six months after death so that the intangibles may be included in the estate at their value as of a date six months after death.

Casualty and theft losses are not deductible for estate tax purposes if, at the time the return is filed, they had been claimed as an income tax deduction.[9]

¶ 910 Alternate Valuation

When the estate representative elects to value the estate as of a date six months after death, losses during this period are reflected in the value or absence of value of the damaged or lost property. Losses are shown in the values of the specific property rather than as a deductible item, except in unusual situations. The loss or theft cannot be reflected both as a deduction and in the valuation of the affected items of property.[10]

¶ 925 Reporting Net Losses

Full details of the amount and cause of loss must be reported under "Net losses during administration" on Schedule L (Net Losses During Administration and Expenses Incurred in Administering Property Not Subject to Claims) of Form 706 (United States Estate (and Generation-Skipping Transfer) Tax Return). This schedule must be filed if the estate has deductible losses. In instances where insurance payments or other compensation is received on account of loss or theft, the amount received should be stated. The property on which loss is claimed should be identified by indicating the particular schedule and item number at which the property is reported.

¶ 935 Community Property Losses

If losses have been incurred with respect to property that had been held as community property, only one-half of the amount of such losses may be listed. Such losses should be accompanied by an appropriate explanation.

¶ 950 Expenses of Property Not Subject to Claims

Expenses of administering property that is included in the decedent's gross estate, but is not subject to claims against it, are deductible under certain circumstances. Such expenses are deductible if (1) they would be allowed as deductions if the property being administered were subject to claims (see ¶ 780), and (2) they are paid before the expiration of the period of limitation for assessment (three years after the return was filed or at any time after such tax became due and before the expiration of three years after the date on which any part of such tax was paid).[11] Usually, such expenses include principal commissions paid with respect to trust property included in the gross estate and attorneys' fees incurred to contest the inclusion of trust property in the decedent's gross estate. However, they may also be incurred in connection with the collection of other assets, or the transfer or clearance of title to other property included in the decedent's gross estate but not included in the probate estate.

---

[8] Reg. § 20.2054-1.

[9] Reg. § 20.2054-1.

[10] Reg. § 20.2032-1(g).

[11] Code Sec. 2053; Reg. § 20.2053-1.

¶ 955 Reporting Expense Deductions

Amounts representing expenses incurred in administering property included in the gross estate but not subject to claims should be itemized under "Expenses incurred in administering property not subject to claims" on the lower portion of Schedule L (Net Losses During Administration and Expenses Incurred in Administering Property Not Subject to Claims) of Form 706 (United States Estate (and Generation-Skipping Transfer) Tax Return).

The names and addresses of persons to whom the expenses are payable and the exact nature of the particular expense should be stated. The property with respect to which the expense was incurred should be identified by indicating the schedule and item number at which the property is reported.

An item may be entered for deduction, even though the exact amount is not known at that time. It must be ascertainable with reasonable certainty and expected to be paid before the expiration of the period of limitation for assessment (three years after the estate tax return is filed). No deduction may be taken on the basis of a vague or uncertain estimate. All vouchers and receipts should be retained for inspection by the IRS.

Chapter 21
MARITAL DEDUCTION

¶ 1000 Transfers to Surviving Spouse

An unlimited marital deduction is available for computing the taxable estate of an individual where any part of the deceased person's estate passes or has passed to the surviving spouse. The property so passing is deductible in computing the taxable estate to the extent that it is includible in the gross estate.[1] The amount of the allowable marital deduction depends on the year of death. For estates of decedents dying after 1981, the amount of the deduction is generally unlimited. However, for estates of decedents dying after 1976 and before 1982, the deduction was limited to the greater of one-half of the adjusted gross estate or $250,000. The post-1981 rules are discussed at ¶ 1001. The pre-1982 rules are explained at ¶ 1005.

• *Requirements for Marital Deduction*

An estate tax marital deduction is available if the following general rules are met:

(1) the decedent was married at the time of his or her death (see ¶ 1015);

(2) the decedent was survived by his or her spouse (see ¶ 1030);

---

[1] Code Sec. 2056(a); Reg. § 20.2056(a)-1.

(3) the surviving spouse was a U.S. citizen, or the property interest transferred passed through a qualified domestic trust (see ¶1004);

(4) the property interest was included in the decedent's gross estate (see ¶1001);

(5) the property interest passed from the decedent to the surviving spouse (see ¶1045); and

(6) the property interest is not a nondeductible terminable interest (see ¶1020; see also, ¶1002, relating to qualified terminable interest property).

Special rules apply with respect to a claim of a marital deduction with respect to bequests to a surviving spouse who is not a U.S. citizen[2] (see ¶1004).

Property qualifying for the martial deduction is listed on Schedule M (Bequests, etc., to Surviving Spouse) of Form 706 (United States Estate (and Generation-Skipping Transfer) Tax Return) (Rev. Aug. 2004) (see ¶1065).

¶ 1001 Amount of Deduction

In general, an unlimited marital deduction is allowed the estates of decedents dying after 1981. However, estates of decedents who died after 1981, but who had executed a will or trust before 1982 containing a maximum marital deduction formula are subject to the law as in effect prior to amendment by the Economic Recovery Tax Act of 1981 (P.L. 97-34) (see ¶1005). Under prior law, the maximum estate tax marital deduction for property passing from the decedent to the surviving spouse was the greater of one-half of the decedent's gross estate or $250,000.

The marital deduction is allowed only with respect to property, the value of which is included in determining the gross estate.[3] Thus, if the surviving spouse acquired property of the decedent during the decedent's life for full consideration in money or money's worth, no deduction will be available in the decedent's estate for such transferred property.

¶ 1002 Qualified Terminable Interest Property

An estate or gift tax marital deduction is allowed for the value of qualified terminable interest property (QTIP) if the donor or decedent's executor so elects. Qualified terminable interest property is property passing from the decedent to a spouse who is entitled to all income from the property (or a portion thereof) for life, payable at least annually. This income interest is known as a "qualifying income interest." The QTIP rule is an exception to the general rule that transfers of terminable interests (such as life estates, terms for years, annuities, etc.) do not qualify for the marital deduction (see ¶1020 through ¶1029 for a detailed discussion of the terminable interest rule).[4] Under the QTIP exception, if all requirements are met, a life interest granted to a surviving spouse will not be treated as a terminable interest. The entire property subject to such an interest will be treated as passing to the spouse and, accordingly, the entire value of the transferred property will qualify for a martial deduction.[5]

The issue of whether an income interest for life fails to qualify when accumulated income for the period between the last distribution date and the date of the surviving spouse's death ("stub" income) is not distributed to the surviving spouse's estate or subject to the spouse's general power of appoint-

[2] Code Sec. 2056(d).

[3] Reg. § 20.2056(a)-2(b)(1).

[4] Code Sec. 2056(b)(1).

[5] Code Sec. 2056(b)(7).

ment has been a subject of dispute. The Tax Court held that such an interest was not a qualifying interest,[6] but this decision was reversed by the U.S. Court of Appeals for the Ninth Circuit.[7] Later, the IRS issued final regulations that agreed with the position taken by the Ninth Circuit.[8] In a case decided after issuance of the final regulations, but arising prior to their effective date, the Tax Court reasserted the position it took in *Howard*, but again was reversed, this time by the U.S. Court of Appeals for the Eleventh Circuit.[9]

With respect to the qualifying income interest requirement, the IRS has ruled that a decedent's estate could elect to treat an individual retirement account (IRA) payable to a trustee as QTIP property if the surviving spouse can compel the trustee to withdraw all of the income earned on the IRA's assets from the IRA at least annually and distribute that amount from the trust to the spouse. Under the facts of the ruling, the terms of the testamentary trust established by the deceased spouse for the benefit of the surviving spouse required the trustee to pay the surviving spouse all of the trust's income annually. The trustee was named as the beneficiary of the decedent's IRA, and the trust gave the surviving spouse the power to compel the trustee to withdraw from the IRA an amount equal to the income earned by the IRA during the year and to distribute the sum from the trust to the surviving spouse. Under these circumstances, the IRS concluded that the surviving spouse was, within the meaning of Reg. § 20.2056(b)-5, entitled to all the income for life payable at least annually. However, since the trust was a conduit for these annual payments to the surviving spouse, the decedent's executor would be required to make a valid QTIP election with respect to both the IRA and the testamentary trust.[10]

In community property states, a nonparticipant spouse may be treated as having a vested community property interest in his or her spouse's qualified plan, IRA, or simplified employee pension plan. Upon the death of a nonparticipant spouse, the nonparticipant spouse's survivorship interest in such a plan that is attributable to community property laws may be treated as QTIP.[11]

No person, including the spouse, can have the power to appoint any part of the property subject to the qualified income interest to any person other than the spouse during the spouse's life. However, creation or retention of any powers over all or a portion of the corpus is allowed, provided that all such powers are exercisable only on or after the spouse's death. Further, income interests granted for a term of years or a life interest subject to termination upon occurrence of a condition (such as remarriage) are not qualifying income interests.

• ***Specific Portion***

The marital deduction is available when the spouse is entitled to all the income from the entire interest in the property or to the income from a specific portion of the property. For example, the right to receive 60 percent (or 3/5) of the income of a trust for life or the right to receive the income for life from 60 percent of a trust would qualify for QTIP treatment if all other requirements for QTIP treatment are satisfied.[12]

---

[6] *R. Howard Est.*, 91 TC 329, CCH Dec. 45,002.

[7] *R. Howard Est.*, CA-9, 90-2 USTC ¶ 60,033.

[8] Reg. § 20.2056(b)-7(d)(4).

[9] *L. Shelfer Est.*, CA-11, 96-2 USTC ¶ 60,238, rev'g TC, 103 TC 10, CCH Dec. 49,967.

[10] Rev. Rul. 2000-2, 2000-1 CB 305.

[11] Code Sec. 2056(b)(7)(C).

[12] Reg. § 20.2056(b)-5(c), as made applicable by Reg. § 20.2056(b)-7(b)(1)(ii).

For most decedents dying after October 24, 1992, the term "specific portion" includes only amounts determined on a fractional or percentage basis, and not pecuniary amounts.

> *Example:* Alice Green's 2004 will provided for creation of a trust funded with $3 million and providing for a benefit of $70,000 per year payable to her surviving spouse for life. Assume the trust assets are producing income of 7% per year. This is not a qualifying interest on $1 million of the property despite the fact that $70,000 of income (given the 7% income level) could be translated into all of the income on $1 million of property.

Under transitional rules, a pecuniary amount can still be a specific portion under certain circumstances for decedents dying after October 24, 1992.[13]

• *Annuities*

A survivor annuity includible in a decedent's gross estate under Code Sec. 2039 where only the surviving spouse has the right to receive payments before his or her death is treated as a qualifying income interest for life.[14] There is a presumption under the Code that a QTIP election is desired. Thus, an executor who does not intend QTIP treatment must elect out of the QTIP provision.[15]

Special rules apply in the case of a decedent dying with a will or trust executed on or before October 24, 1992, that provides the surviving spouse with a lifetime annuity interest payable from the trust or other assets passing from the decedent. In such cases, the surviving spouse's annuity interest is treated as a qualifying income interest for life if the decedent was under a mental disability to change the disposition of his property on October 24, 1992, and the decedent did not regain competence before death. The annuity interest will not be treated as a qualifying income interest for life if any person other than the surviving spouse may receive, during the surviving spouse's lifetime, any distribution of the property or its income from which the annuity is payable. For purposes of the marital deduction, the deductible interest is that *specific portion* of the property that, assuming the interest rate generally applicable for the valuation of annuities under Code Sec. 2031 and Code Sec. 7520, would produce income equal to the minimum amount payable annually to the surviving spouse.[16]

A usufruct interest for life under Louisiana law constitutes a qualifying income interest for QTIP purposes.[17] The QTIP election will be available for both consumable and nonconsumable property; however, in the case of consumable property, the value of the usufruct will be includible in the surviving spouse's gross estate under Code Sec. 2044 (see ¶773) rather than under Code Sec. 2033.

• *QTIP Election*

The election to treat property as QTIP property is made on Schedule M (Bequests, etc., to Surviving Spouse) of Form 706 (United States Estate (and Generation-Skipping Transfer) Tax Return) by the estate's executor.[18] Once made, an election or failure to make an election is irrevocable.[19] A QTIP election is made on Form 706 by simply listing the qualified terminable interest property on Schedule M and deducting its value.

---

[13] Reg. §20.2056(b)-5(c)(3) and Reg. §20.2056(b)-7(e).

[14] Code Sec. 2056(b)(7)(C).

[15] Code Sec. 2056(b)(7)(C)(ii).

[16] Reg. §20.2056(b)-7(e).

[17] Code Sec. 2056(b)(7)(B)(ii).

[18] Reg. §20.2056(b)-7(b)(3).

[19] Code Sec. 2056(b)(7)(B)(v).

The election may be made for a portion of property that meets the QTIP requirements, provided that the election relates to a fractional or percentile share of the property. This fraction may be defined by means of a formula.[20]

• *Unnecessary QTIP Elections*

The IRS has issued a procedure (Rev. Proc. 2001-38) under which it will treat unnecessary QTIP elections as null and void for purposes of Code Sec. 2056. A QTIP election will be deemed to be unnecessary if is not needed to reduce the estate tax liability to zero. For example, this new rule will apply where a QTIP election was made, even though the taxable estate (before the allowance of the marital deduction) was less than the applicable exclusion amount. It will also apply to a situation where QTIP elections were made for both the marital and the "credit shelter" trusts created by a decedent's estate plan where no estate tax would have been imposed regardless of whether an election was made for the credit shelter trust.[21]

A taxpayer will be required to produce sufficient evidence to establish that a particular QTIP election comes within the scope of this IRS procedure. For example, a taxpayer may produce a copy of the predeceased spouse's estate tax return to show that the election was not necessary to reduce the estate tax liability to zero. The new rule is effective as of June 4, 2001, and applies to elections qualifying under the procedure, regardless of when made.

The IRS has privately ruled that the relief provisions of Rev. Proc. 2001-38 are not available where the trustee of a decedent's trust was attempting to revoke in part (rather than to totally revoke) a QTIP election that had previously been made with respect to the entire corpus of the decedent's marital trust. (A total revocation of the election would not have served the interests of the trust because it would not have reduced the decedent's estate tax liability to zero.)[22]

A different result was allowed, however, where a decedent's estate had *underfunded* a marital trust due to a miscalculation of the value of property passing to that trust, and had made an unnecessary QTIP election with respect to the decedent's credit shelter trust. If this error in calculating the value of the property in the marital trust had not been made, the QTIP election with respect to the marital trust would have yielded a marital deduction sufficient to reduce the estate's estate tax liability to zero. The IRS concluded that the rationale of Rev. Proc. 2001-38 would void the QTIP election for the property in the credit shelter trust. Because the estate's QTIP election for the marital trust was timely and elected in a valid manner, the marital deduction for the full value of the property actually passing to the marital trust was available, provided the estate subsequently filed a supplemental return correcting the error prior to the Code Sec. 6511 deadline for claiming a credit or refund.[23]

• *Contingent Income Interests*

Generally, an income interest will not qualify for QTIP treatment if it is contingent on the happening of some event. One exception to this rule is making the interest contingent on the election of QTIP treatment by the executor. Effective for estates whose returns are due after February 18, 1997, Reg.

---

[20] Reg. § 20.2056(b)-7(b)(2)(ii).

[21] Rev. Proc. 2001-38, 2001-1 CB 1335.

[22] IRS Letter Ruling 200219003, Feb. 5, 2002; IRS Letter Ruling 200422050, Feb. 20, 2004.

[23] IRS Letter Ruling 200323010 (Feb. 19, 2003).

§20.2056(b)-7(d)(3)(i) permits QTIP treatment to be contingent on the executor making a QTIP election. Prior to that time, the IRS successfully challenged several such contingent QTIP elections at the Tax Court,[24] only to be reversed each time.[25] The IRS finally acquiesced to this issue upon the Tax Court's abandonment of its position.[26] Certain estates of decedents whose estate tax returns were due on or before January 18, 1997, that did not make a QTIP election because the surviving spouse's interest was contingent on the executor making the election are granted an extension of time to make the election. To be eligible, the Code Sec. 6511(a) period of limitations for filing a claim for credit or refund must not have expired.[27]

• ***Protective QTIP Election***

Executors may make a protective election in certain limited circumstances. Such an election is allowed only if, at the time the estate tax return is filed, the executor of the estate reasonably believes there is a bona fide issue as to whether an asset is includible in the gross estate or as to the nature of the property the surviving spouse is entitled to receive.[28]

• ***Tax on Transfer of Interest***

Property for which a QTIP election is made will be subject to transfer taxes at the earlier of (1) the date on which the spouse disposes (by gift, sale or otherwise) of all or part of the qualifying income interest, or (2) the date of the spouse's death. If a spouse transfers the qualifying income interest during life, the entire value of the property, reduced by any amount received by the spouse upon disposition, is a taxable gift (see ¶2313).[29] Otherwise, the entire value of the property subject to the qualified income interest will be included in the spouse's gross estate at its fair market value on the date of death or on the alternate valuation date, if elected (see ¶773).[30]

The spouse or the spouse's estate may recover from the recipient of the property the gift tax paid on the remainder interest as a result of a lifetime transfer of the income interest, or the estate tax paid as a result of the inclusion of the value of the property in the spouse's gross estate, as well as any penalties or interest attributable to the additional estate or gift tax.[31]

¶1003 Split Gifts to Spouse and Charity

There is a special rule for transfers of interests in the same property to a spouse and a qualifying charitable organization. If an individual creates a qualified charitable remainder annuity trust or unitrust and the donor and his or her spouse are the only beneficiaries who are not a charitable beneficiary or an employee stock ownership plan beneficiary, the prohibition on deduction of terminable interests (see ¶1020) does not apply. The individual (or his or her estate) receives a charitable deduction for the value of the remainder interest and a marital deduction for the value of the annuity or unitrust interest, and no transfer tax is imposed.[32]

---

[24] *A. Clayton Est.*, 97 TC 327, CCH Dec. 47,612; *W. Robertson Est.*, 98 TC 678, CCH Dec. 48,310; *J. Spencer Est.*, 64 TCM 937, CCH Dec. 48,546(M), TC Memo. 1992-579.

[25] *A. Clayton Est.*, CA-5, 92-2 USTC ¶60,121, 976 F2d 1486; *W. Robertson Est.*, CA-8, 94-1 USTC ¶60,153; *J. Spencer Est.*, CA-6, 95-1 USTC ¶60,188.

[26] *W. Clack Est.*, 106 TC 131, CCH Dec. 51,193 (Acq.).

[27] Reg. §20.2056(b)-7(d)(3)(ii).

[28] Reg. §20.2056(b)-7(c).

[29] Code Sec. 2519.

[30] Code Sec. 2044.

[31] Code Sec. 2207A.

[32] Code Sec. 2056(b)(8).

If the individual transfers a qualified income interest to his or her spouse with a remainder to charity, the entire value of the property will be considered as passing to the surviving spouse, and will qualify for a marital deduction and no part of the value of the property qualifies for the charitable deduction.[33] Although, upon the spouse's death, the entire value of the property will be included in the spouse's gross estate, any property passing outright to charity may qualify for a charitable deduction.

¶ 1004 Qualified Domestic Trusts

Effective for estates of decedents dying after November 10, 1988, property passing to a surviving spouse who is not a U.S. citizen is not eligible for the estate tax marital deduction unless the property passes through a qualified domestic trust (QDOT). However, in the case of a nonresident alien whose spouse is a U.S. citizen, the marital deduction will be allowed for estate tax purposes without the need for a QDOT.

In order to be considered a QDOT, the trust instrument must provide that at least one of the trustees be a U.S. citizen or domestic corporation and that any corpus distribution be subject to the U.S. trustee's right to withhold the estate tax imposed on such distribution. For trust instruments of decedents dying after November 10, 1988, if the instrument provides that all the trustees must be either U.S. citizens or domestic corporations, then the withholding requirement is deemed satisfied regardless of whether the withholding requirement is explicitly stated in the trust instrument.[34] The trust must also meet security requirements designed to ensure collection of the estate tax imposed on the trust. The trust instrument must require that at least one of the trustees be an individual citizen of the United States or a domestic corporation.[35] In addition, if the trust assets, as of the date of the decedent's death or, if applicable, the alternate valuation date, exceed $2 million, the trust's governing instrument must require that either:

(1) during the entire term of the QDOT, at least one U.S. trustee be a bank; or

(2) the U.S. trustee furnish a bond in favor of the IRS in an amount equal to at least 65 percent of the fair market value of the trust assets; or

(3) the U.S. trustee furnish an irrevocable letter of credit issued by a U.S. branch of a foreign bank or by a foreign bank and confirmed by a U.S. bank, in an amount equal to 65 percent of the trust assets.[36]

If the fair market value of the trust assets as finally determined for federal estate tax purposes is less than $2 million, the QDOT need not meet any of the three requirements listed above if the trust instrument expressly provides that no more than 35 percent of the fair market value of the trust assets, determined annually, may be invested in real property located outside of the United States.[37]

In addition, the executor must make an irrevocable QDOT election on the estate tax return with respect to the trust. This election is made by listing the QDOT on Schedule M (Bequests, etc., to Surviving Spouse) of Form 706 (United States Estate (and Generation-Skipping Transfer) Tax Return) and taking the marital deduction therefor. However, no election may be made on a return filed more than one year after the due date of such return, including extensions.[38]

---

[33] Reg. § 20.2056(b)-9.

[34] Act Sec. 1303, Taxpayer Relief Act of 1997 (P.L. 105-34).

[35] Code Sec. 2056A(a)(1).

[36] Reg. § 20.2056A-2(d)(1)(i).

[37] Reg. § 20.2056A-2(d)(1)(ii).

[38] Code Sec. 2056A(d).

Property passing directly to the surviving spouse may qualify for the marital deduction if, before the estate tax return is filed and while the QDOT election can still be timely made, the property is transferred or irrevocably assigned to the QDOT.[39]

An estate tax is imposed on corpus distributions from the trust that are made prior to the date of the surviving spouse's death and on the value of the property remaining in a QDOT on the date of death of the surviving spouse. However, the estate tax will no longer be imposed on a QDOT after the surviving spouse becomes a U.S. citizen if (1) the spouse was a U.S. resident at the time of the decedent's death and at all times thereafter, (2) no tax was imposed on a QDOT distribution before the spouse became a U.S. citizen, or (3) the spouse elected to treat any distribution on which tax had been imposed as a taxable gift made by the spouse (thereby reducing the unified credit available to the spouse) for the purpose of determining the spouse's future estate and gift tax liability.[40] In addition, the estate tax on distributions is itself a distribution subject to the estate tax.[41] Further, a distribution of corpus from a QDOT to a surviving spouse is excluded from the estate tax if the distribution is made "on account of hardship."[42] If no property other than the property passing to the surviving spouse is transferred to the QDOT, the trust need not otherwise qualify for the marital deduction. If the trust is funded with other property passing from the decedent, however, then all of the assets in the QDOT must qualify for the marital deduction.[43]

A special rule applies if more than one QDOT exists with respect to a decedent.[44] In such cases, the amount of estate tax imposed on the trusts is determined using the highest rate of tax in effect at the time of the decedent's death, unless a U.S. citizen or domestic corporation is responsible for filing all estate tax returns for such QDOTs and meets IRS regulatory requirements.

Another special rule states that estate tax is not imposed on distributions defined as income. However, the IRS is authorized to prescribe such regulations as necessary to determine when payments under an annuity would be treated as income for purposes of the estate tax on distributions. The IRS is also empowered to prescribe regulations under which an annuity or other payment, includible in a decedent's gross estate and payable for life or a term of years, may be treated as a QDOT.[45] Such interests would include property interests that cannot be transferred to a QDOT under federal law, such as an interest in an IRA or qualified plan.[46]

Certain estate tax benefits, such as charitable and marital deductions, special use valuation, and extensions of time to pay estate tax, are allowed against the estate tax on QDOT distributions if such benefits would be allowable with respect to the estate of the surviving spouse.[47] In addition, property distributed from a QDOT during the surviving spouse's lifetime would receive a carryover basis. However, the carryover basis would be increased by an amount equal to the proportion of any QDOT estate tax paid that the net appreciation in the property bears to the distribution.[48]

---

[39] Reg. § 20.2056A-4(b)(1).

[40] Code Sec. 2056A(b)(12).

[41] Code Sec. 2056A(b)(11).

[42] Code Sec. 2056A(b)(3)(B).

[43] Reg. § 20.2056A-4(b)(1).

[44] Code Sec. 2056A(b)(2)(C).

[45] Code Sec. 2056A(e).

[46] Conference Committee Report to the Revenue Reconciliation Act of 1989 (P.L. 101-239); Reg. § 20.2056A-4(b)(7) and Reg. § 20.2056A-4(c).

[47] Reg. § 20.2056A-6(b).

[48] Reg. § 20.2056A-12.

• *Returns*

Form 706-QDT (U.S. Estate Tax Return for Qualified Domestic Trusts) (Rev. Jan. 2003) is used to report the estate tax due with respect to taxable distributions from a QDOT, the death of the noncitizen surviving spouse, the trust's ceasing to qualify as a QDOT, and hardship distributions from the trust. Form 706-QDT must be filed within nine months following the date of the surviving spouse's death or the date that the trust ceases to qualify as a QDOT. The return is due by April 15 of the year following the year in which the taxable event or hardship distribution occurs.[49] (Form 706-QDT is reproduced in the Appendix at ¶3270.)

If the estate tax for the decedent spouse's estate has not been finally determined (such as in the case where a judicial determination of the tax is pending), a tentative tax is imposed using the highest estate tax rate in effect as of the date of the decedent's death. When a final determination is made, any amount of the tentative tax that is in excess of the additional estate tax that would have been imposed had the property been included in the decedent's estate is refundable if a claim is filed not later than one year after the date of final determination. A refund of tentative tax imposed pending final resolution of estate tax liability bears interest.[50]

A trustee is personally liable for the tax, but may be discharged from such liability.[51] The tax imposed on a QDOT is treated as an estate tax with respect to the decedent spouse's estate. Therefore, it qualifies as a previously paid tax for purposes of the Code Sec. 2103 credit for tax on prior transfers, determined without regard to the date of the decedent spouse's death.[52] In addition, there is a lien against the property giving rise to such tax for 10 years after the taxable event.

¶ 1005 Pre-1982 Marital Deduction Rules

For estates of decedents dying before 1982, the maximum estate tax marital deduction for property passing from the decedent to the surviving spouse was equal to the greater of one-half of the decedent's adjusted gross estate, or $250,000.[53] Thus, estates with adjusted gross estates of less than $500,000 were provided with an additional benefit. For example, assume a spouse had died in 1981 with an adjusted gross estate of $395,000 and had passed $250,000 in property to his or her surviving spouse that qualifies for the marital deduction. This left a net estate of $145,000 subject to estate tax. However, the unified credit exemption equivalent for 1981 (see ¶2600) eliminated any estate tax liability. For the estates of decedents dying before 1977, the marital deduction was limited to 50 percent of the value of the adjusted gross estate.

• ***Transitional Rule for Pre-1982 Marital Deduction Formula Clauses***

An unlimited marital deduction is allowed for estates of decedents dying after 1981 (see ¶1001). However, many wills and trusts that were executed prior to 1982 included maximum marital deduction formula clauses under which the amount of property transferred to the surviving spouse was to be determined by reference to the maximum allowable marital deduction. Because, with respect to estates of decedents dying before 1982, the maximum estate tax deduction was the greater of $250,000 or one-half of the adjusted gross estate, many individuals

---

[49] Code Sec. 2056A(b)(5).

[50] Code Sec. 2056A(b)(2)(B).

[51] Code Sec. 2204.

[52] Reg. § 20.2056A-7.

[53] Code Sec. 2056(c), prior to its repeal by P.L. 97-34.

may not have intended any greater amount to pass to their surviving spouses as might be the case if the unlimited marital deduction were used in the computation of the marital deduction under the formula clause.

Under a transitional rule, the unlimited marital deduction is not applicable to transfers resulting from a will or trust executed before September 12, 1981, that contains a maximum marital deduction formula clause. The transitional rule applies provided that (1) the decedent died after 1981, (2) the formula clause was not amended at any time after September 12, 1981, and before the death of the decedent to refer specifically to the unlimited marital deduction, and (3) there is no state law that would construe the formula clause as referring to the unlimited marital deduction.[54]

Whether a particular will or trust contains a maximum marital deduction formula has been a frequently litigated question. The mere appearance of a marital deduction formula clause in a will or trust will not satisfy the requirements of the transitional rule. Rather, the will or trust must contain a formula *expressly* providing that the surviving spouse is to receive the maximum amount of property qualifying for the marital deduction. Any additions to the formula that might further reduce the amount received by the spouse to ensure that the unified credit or other credits of the estate are fully utilized will not be a formula clause for purposes of the transitional rule.[55]

¶ 1015 Status as Surviving Spouse

The person receiving the decedent's property for which a marital deduction is claimed must qualify as a "surviving spouse" on the date of the decedent's death. A legal separation that has not terminated the marriage at the time of death does not change the status of the surviving spouse.[56] If an interest in property passes from the decedent to a person who was the decedent's spouse, but who was not married to the decedent at the time of death, the interest is not considered as passing to the surviving spouse. If a decedent's divorce from a prior spouse is declared invalid by a state court having jurisdiction, the IRS will not allow a marital deduction for the decedent's bequest of property to a subsequent spouse.[57]

A transfer by the decedent during his lifetime to an individual to whom he was not married at the time of the transfer but to whom he was married at the time of his death and who survives him is a transfer by the decedent to his surviving spouse with respect to gifts includible in a decedent's gross estate under Code Sec. 2035.[58]

¶ 1020 Life Estate or Other Terminable Interest

Generally, no marital deduction is allowed for property interests that are terminable interests[59] (but see the exception for qualified terminable interest property, discussed at ¶ 1002). A terminable interest is an interest in property that will terminate or fail on the lapse of time or on the occurrence, or the failure

[54] Act Sec. 403(e), P.L. 97-34.

[55] *L. Neisen Est.*, CA-8, 89-1 USTC ¶ 13,790, 865 F2d 162; *F.L. Bruning Est.*, CA-10, 89-2 USTC ¶ 13,821; *S.I. Levitt Est.*, 95 TC 289, CCH Dec. 46,873; IRS Technical Advice Memorandum 9206001 (Dec. 7, 1991).

[56] *M.S. Eccles*, 19 TC 1049, CCH Dec. 19,508, aff'd on other issues by CA-4, 54-1 USTC ¶ 9129, 208 F2d 769.

[57] Rev. Rul. 67-442, 1967-2 CB 65; *W.A. Steffke Est.*, CA-7, 76-2 USTC ¶ 13,145, 538 F2d 730, cert. denied; *L.J. Goldwater Est.*, CA-2, 76-2 USTC ¶ 13,146, 539 F2d 878, cert. denied.

[58] Rev. Rul. 79-354, 1979-2 CB 334.

[59] Code Sec. 2056(b)(1).

to occur, of some event or contingency. The purpose of the rule is to require that if property is transferred to the surviving spouse, it will be includible in the surviving spouse's estate unless disposed of or dissipated during the surviving spouse's lifetime.

- ***Types of Terminable Interests***

Terminable interests include life estates, terms for years, annuities, patents and copyrights. However, a bond, note, or similar contractual obligation that would not have the effect of an annuity or a term for years, is not a terminable interest.[60] Whether or not an interest is a terminable interest is determined by state law[61] at the death of the decedent.[62]

- ***Nondeductible Terminable Interests***

A terminal interest is nondeductible if:

(1) an interest in the same property has passed (for less than adequate and full consideration in money or money's worth) from the decedent to any person other than the surviving spouse or other than the estate of the surviving spouse; and

(2) by reason of its passing, such person or his heirs or assigns may possess or enjoy any part of the property after such termination or failure of the interest passing to the surviving spouse.

It is not necessary that the contingency or event occur or fail to occur in order to make the interest terminable.[63]

Example: Tom Atwood dies leaving stocks in trust, the income to pass to his wife, Sandy, for life, with the corpus to be distributed to his son, Jason, free of the trust when he reaches maturity. If Jason predeceases Sandy, the corpus is to be turned over to Sandy, free of the trust. There is also a gift over in the event of Jason's death after the date of Sandy's death but before the date of Jason's maturity. The interest passing to Sandy on Tom's death is a nondeductible terminable interest.

An estate for the life of the surviving spouse is an interest that will terminate in all events. If conditions (1) and (2), described above, exist, it is immaterial whether the interest passing to the surviving spouse is considered a vested interest or a contingent interest. No marital deduction is allowed in any event if the life estate or terminable interest is to be acquired for the surviving spouse, pursuant to directions of the decedent, by his executor or by the trustee of a trust.[64]

If the decedent by will bequeaths a terminable interest for which a deduction is not allowed and the surviving spouse takes under the will, the marital deduction is not allowed. A deduction is denied, even though, under local law, the interest that the spouse could have taken against the will was a fee interest for which a deduction would be allowed.[65] Similarly, the marital deduction was disallowed for the interest passing to the surviving spouse as an income benefici-

---

[60] Reg. § 20.2056(b)-1(b).

[61] *H.P. Shedd Est.*, CA-9, 56-2 USTC ¶ 11,644, 237 F2d 345.

[62] *M. Kellmann, Transferee,* DC Mo., 68-1 USTC ¶ 12,518, 286 FSupp. 632.

[63] Reg. § 20.2056(b)-1.

[64] Reg. § 20.2056(b)-1(c) and (f).

[65] *E.J. Allen, Exr.*, CA-2, 66-1 USTC ¶ 12,393, cert. denied. See also IRS Letter Ruling 8236004 (May 23, 1982).

ary or annuitant under a trust in which other persons had an interest if the surviving spouse had no power over the principal.[66]

The IRS has ruled that a cash bequest that a decedent's surviving spouse elected in lieu of a life income interest in a trust pursuant to a provision in the decedent's will qualified for an estate tax marital deduction because it was not a terminable interest. However, no such deduction was allowable for an additional amount that the spouse could demand from the trustee in order to assist the spouse in purchasing a new house. In the former situation, the spouse had an absolute right to the cash bequest as of the date of the decedent's death and the election in the will was a mere procedural requirement that did not constitute an event or contingency for marital deduction purposes. The additional amount that the spouse could demand from the trustee constituted a nondeductible terminable interest because it was conditioned on the spouse's purchase of a new house.[67]

The interest of the surviving spouse is not considered a terminable interest merely because the spouse's possession or enjoyment may be affected by events not provided for by the terms of the bequest. These events are the surviving spouse's death, or loss of the property by fire, earthquake, condemnation, or nonpayment of taxes, or the fact that the property may be used up in an indefinite period of time. However, interests in patents, copyrights, and annuity contracts that will be used up in a fixed length of time are terminable interests and are not deductible if an interest of a third person in the same property will outlast the termination of the interest of the surviving spouse.[68]

Although it formerly contested the matter, the IRS now agrees that the property passing to a decedent's spouse under an "equalization clause" governing a trust created for the spouse's benefit by the decedent is not a nondeductible terminable interest.[69] Under the clause, the trustee has the power to select as the valuation date the date of death or the alternate valuation date, whichever produces the greatest tax savings, in order to determine the percentage of trust assets to be placed in the marital portion so as to equalize the estates of both spouses.

¶ 1023 Widow's Allowance—Dower Interest

An allowance to a surviving spouse for support during the period of settlement of a decedent's estate will qualify for the marital deduction if it is not classified as a terminable interest. Although a widow's (or widower's) allowance may fall within the terminable interest rule, a marital deduction can be obtained for any portion thereof that would, in any event, pass to the surviving spouse by operation of law or of the decedent's will.[70]

Whether a widow's allowance is a terminable interest is dependent upon the state statute that authorizes the support payments. If, under the authorizing state law, the widow's right to a support allowance is a vested one, her interest in the allowance will qualify for the estate tax marital deduction. If, however, the right

---

[66] *C.H. Stockdick Est.*, DC Tex., 65-2 USTC ¶12,351.

[67] Rev. Rul. 82-184, 1982-2 CB 215.

[68] Reg. §20.2056(b)-1(g).

[69] Rev. Rul. 82-23, 1982-1 CB 139; *C.W. Smith Est.*, 66 TC 415, CCH Dec. 33,862 (Acq.), aff'd per curiam, CA-7, 77-2 USTC ¶13,215, 565 F2d 455; and *V.S. Laurin Est.*, CA-6, 81-1 USTC ¶13,398, 645 F2d 8, aff'g TC, 72 TC 73, CCH Dec. 35,987 (Acq.).

[70] Rev. Rul. 82-23, 1982-1 CB 139; *C.W. Smith Est.*, 66 TC 415, CCH Dec. 33,862 (Acq.), aff'd per curiam, CA-7, 77-2 USTC ¶13,215, 565 F2d 455; and *V.S. Laurin Est.*, CA-6, 81-1 USTC ¶13,398, 645 F2d 8, aff'g TC, 72 TC 73, CCH Dec. 35,987 (Acq.).

would not survive her death or remarriage prior to the securing of an award by the court, her interest is considered a nondeductible terminable one.[71] The nature of the widow's interest in the allowance must be determined as of the date of the decedent's death.[72] The courts have ruled that widows' allowances in Illinois, Maine, Maryland, Michigan, Minnesota, Missouri, Ohio, and Oklahoma qualify for the marital deduction. (Some of these cases were decided before the *Jackson* case and may not be followed.) Widows' allowances or awards have been held to be nondeductible terminable interests in the states of California, Connecticut, Florida, Georgia, Iowa, Massachusetts, Montana, Nebraska, Oregon, Tennessee, Texas, and Wisconsin. (State laws should be consulted for possible changes that would permit a deduction.)

Dower and curtesy interests (or statutory estates in lieu thereof) may also qualify for a marital deduction, or they may not be deductible because of the terminable interest rule. The deductibility of such interests is also dependent upon state law. A deduction will be allowed if the surviving spouse has a fixed or vested right to the dower at the moment of the decedent's death and if the dower interest is an absolute interest.[73] A payment of the commuted value of a widow's dower, if requested and paid in accordance with applicable state law, also qualifies for the marital deduction if the right to it vests at the moment of the decedent-spouse's death, even though the payment is in lieu of a dower life estate in the decedent's property.[74]

Dower interests (or amounts awarded in lieu of such interests) in the states of Arkansas, Colorado, Florida, Hawaii, Illinois, Iowa, Kentucky, Montana, New York, North Carolina, South Carolina, Tennessee, and Virginia have qualified for marital deductions. If the surviving spouse does not have such a vested interest under state law, the interest will not qualify for the marital deduction. The U.S. Court of Appeals for the Fifth Circuit has held that dower interests in Alabama do not qualify for the marital deduction, but that money received in lieu of dower may qualify.[75] The Tax Court has stated, by way of dictum, that dower in New Jersey also does not qualify for the deduction.[76]

¶ 1027 Life Interest with Power of Appointment

The terminable interest rule is designed primarily to prevent the allowance of a marital deduction with respect to property that, by the terms of the transfer, is likely to escape inclusion in the gross estate of the surviving spouse. Although there is a limited elective exception to this rule for qualified terminable interest property with respect to estates of decedents dying after 1981 (see ¶ 1002), this property is includible in the surviving spouse's gross estate by specific statutory provision.[77]

When a decedent gives to his or her spouse an interest for life, together with a general power of appointment, the possibility of exclusion from the surviving spouse's gross estate is substantially removed. Therefore, such transfers (which are usually made in the form of a "marital deduction" trust), are permitted to

---

[71] Rev. Rul. 83, 1953-1 CB 395.

[72] *L.R. Jackson*, SCt, 64-1 USTC ¶ 12,221, 376 U.S. 503.

[73] Rev. Rul. 72-8, 1972-1 CB 309.

[74] Rev. Rul. 72-7, 1972-1 CB 308, modified by Rev. Rul. 83-107, 1983-2 CB 159.

[75] *F.A. Crosby, Admr.*, CA-5, 58-2 USTC ¶ 11,808, 257 F2d 515; *M.I. Hiles, Exr.*, CA-5, 63-1 USTC ¶ 12,146.

[76] *J. Nachimson Est.*, 50 TC 452, CCH Dec. 28,993.

[77] Code Sec. 2044.

qualify for the marital deduction as exceptions to the terminable interest rule, so long as they meet certain conditions.[78]

• *All of the Income Requirement*

The surviving spouse must be entitled for life to all income from the property interest and have a general power of appointment over the property. Without disqualifying the property interest from the marital deduction, a surviving spouse may be entitled to the income from a specific portion of the property interest.[79] In general, for decedents dying after October 24, 1992, a "specific portion" is a portion of a property interest determined on a fractional or percentage basis only.[80]

Prior to the enactment of Code Sec. 2056(b)(10), the U.S. Supreme Court had held that "specific portion" included a fixed dollar amount.[81] Under a transitional rule, a right to a specific amount of income will qualify for the marital deduction if the interest was created under a will or revocable trust executed before October 24, 1992, if either (1) the decedent dies within three years after October 24, 1992, or (2) on October 24, 1992, the decedent was under a mental disability to change the disposition of his or her property and did not regain competence to dispose of such property before death. The transitional rule, however, does not apply if the will or trust is amended after October 24, 1992, to increase the amount of the transfer qualifying for the marital deduction or to alter the terms by which the interest passes.[82] Under the transitional rule, a specific sum payable annually, or at more frequent intervals, out of property and its income that is not limited by the income of the property is treated as the right to receive the income from a specific portion of the property. The specific portion is the portion of the property that, assuming the interest rate generally applicable for the valuation of annuities at the time of the decedent's death, would produce income equal to such payments.

• *Annual Income Requirement*

The surviving spouse must be entitled to receive the income annually, or at more frequent intervals. Such spouse must have the power, exercisable in favor of herself or himself or of her or his estate, to appoint the property interest or specific portion from which he or she has a right to the income. Such power must be exercisable by the spouse alone and in all events. It is not necessary that the surviving spouse have the right to exercise the power during lifetime if he or she can exercise it by will and in favor of her or his estate as well as in favor of other persons. The property must not be subject to a power in any other person to appoint to anyone other than the surviving spouse any of the property for which the deduction is sought. Nor is it necessary that the property be in trust.

In determining whether a transfer meets the above requirements, state law should be consulted. For example, if the transfer does not specify the frequency of income payments, the transfer may still qualify, if, under state law, income must be distributed at least annually.

---

[78] Code Sec. 2056(b)(5).

[79] Reg. § 20.2056(b)-5.

[80] Code Sec. 2056(b)(10).

[81] *Northeastern Pennsylvania National Bank & Trust Co., Exr.*, SCt, 67-1 USTC ¶ 12,470, 387 US 213.

[82] Reg. § 20.2056(b)-5(c)(3).

• *Powers*

The IRS has issued rules that cover the power of a fiduciary to allocate income and expenses between income and principal and to provide depreciation reserves, without causing the loss or diminution of the marital deduction, where the spouse has a life estate and power of appointment.[83] A fiduciary may have these powers if state law or the governing instrument (1) prevents the fiduciary from favoring the other beneficiaries over the spouse, (2) gives the spouse enforceable rights to enjoy the trust, and (3) limits the fiduciary from making allocations, based on the composition of the assets, that would deprive the spouse of enjoyment. A fiduciary may also have discretionary powers to retain trust cash without investing it and to determine in what form distributions are to be made. These powers are permissible if the governing instrument or state law provides reasonable limitations.

A surviving spouse does not have a power of appointment exercisable by the survivor alone and in all events over that portion of a marital trust that an executor has the authority to use to pay death taxes to the federal or state government.[84] In one situation, the IRS denied a marital deduction for property that passed to a trust for the benefit of a decedent's spouse, even though the spouse received a life estate in the trust and the power to appoint the trust corpus for herself or her creditors. The spouse did not have the power to exercise the power "alone and in all events" because the trustee could prevent exercise of the power in his sole discretion if the remainder beneficiaries of the trust objected to a proposed exercise. However, because the trustee did not have a substantial interest in the trust corpus adverse to that of the spouse, the value of the trust corpus was includible in her gross estate as property subject to a general power of appointment.[85] A testamentary power of appointment over a trust was not exercisable by a surviving spouse alone and in all events where the trust agreement provided that the spouse's right to the income and principal of the trust and the testamentary general power of appointment terminated if the spouse became incompetent before either withdrawing the corpus or exercising the power of appointment.[86]

¶ 1028 Life Insurance and Annuities

The proceeds of life insurance, endowment, or annuity contracts over which a surviving spouse is given a power of appointment may qualify for a marital deduction.[87] (Also, note the treatment of certain joint and survivor annuities as discussed at ¶ 1002.) The proceeds must be payable in installments or held by the insurer subject to an agreement to pay interest. The surviving spouse alone must have the right to receive all or a specific portion of the payments to be made during his or her lifetime. If held at interest, the proceeds, following termination of the period during which interest is to be paid, may be distributed in a lump sum or in installments. The distributions of interest or installments must be made at least annually and the first payment must be made not later than 13 months after the decedent's death.

The surviving spouse must have the power to appoint the entire proceeds or the portion from which he or she is entitled to receive installments or interest distributions. The power must be in favor of that person or that person's estate,

---

[83] Rev. Rul. 69-56, 1969-1 CB 224.

[84] *M.S. Wycoff Est.*, CA-10, 74-2 USTC ¶ 13,037, 506 F2d 1144, cert. denied.

[85] Rev. Rul. 82-156, 1982-2 CB 216.

[86] *D. Walsh Est.*, 110 TC 393, CCH Dec. 52,733.

[87] Code Sec. 2056(b)(6).

regardless of whether he or she may also exercise the power in favor of others. There must be no power in any other person to appoint to any person other than the surviving spouse.

The power must also be exercisable in all events. Formal administrative restrictions on the survivor's right of withdrawal of the proceeds are considered to be for the convenience of the insurer and do not disqualify the survivor's interest from meeting the exercisable-in-all-events test.

¶ 1029 Interest of Spouse Conditioned on Survival for Limited Period

An interest passing to a surviving spouse will qualify for the marital deduction, so long as it is not terminable on other grounds, if it is conditioned upon (1) the surviving spouse's survival for six months after the death of the decedent and the spouse does not, in fact, die within this period, (2) the surviving spouse's not dying in a common disaster taking the lives of both spouses, which does not, in fact, occur, or (3) both events, and neither of them occurs.[88] The above rule does not apply to an ordinary life estate, such as a devise to the wife for her life, with remainder over to another because her death at *any* time will cause such termination or failure.

Otherwise qualifying marital bequests that are conditioned on survival to the final distribution of the decedent's estate, or to administration or settlement of the estate, are nearly always held to be terminable, even though the surviving spouse lives beyond this period. The U.S. Court of Appeals for the Second Circuit, however, has ruled that this rule had no application where state law vested real property in the surviving spouse at the date of the decedent's death.[89]

¶ 1030 Simultaneous Deaths of Joint Property Owners

For federal estate tax purposes, upon the decedent's death, any property that the decedent owned jointly with someone other than the surviving spouse is includible in the decedent's gross estate to the extent that the decedent paid for it. However, to the extent that such property passes to the surviving spouse, it qualifies for the marital deduction. If the decedent and his or her spouse are joint owners of property and it is determined that they have died simultaneously, the rule for distribution of such property may differ from general property rules, since most of the states have adopted the Uniform Simultaneous Death Act.

Section 3 of that Act provides that "Where there is no sufficient evidence that two joint tenants or tenants by the entirety have died otherwise than simultaneously the property so held shall be distributed one-half as if one had survived and one-half as if the other had survived . . .". Thus, one-half of the property will pass to one decedent's heirs and the other half will pass to the spouse's heirs.

The general tax rule that property be included in the decedent's gross estate to the extent that the decedent furnished consideration for it does not apply in the case of "qualified joint interests" owned by husbands and wives. A "qualified joint interest" created and held by a husband and wife is divided equally between the spouses for estate tax purposes. A qualified joint interest is any property owned solely by spouses in joint tenancy or tenancy by the entirety (see ¶ 502).

---

[88] Reg. § 20.2056(b)-3.

[89] *S.W. Horton Est.*, CA-2, 68-1 USTC ¶ 12,503, 388 F2d 51.

¶ 1031 Interest Passing to Unidentified Persons

A marital deduction is not allowed for property interests that may pass to unidentified persons after the death of the spouse. If it is not possible to determine the particular person or persons to whom an interest may pass from the decedent, the interest is considered as having passed to a person other than the decedent's surviving spouse. This rule is inapplicable, however, to a spouse's life interest in connection with a qualifying power of appointment.[90]

> ***Example:*** Andrew Martin, by his will, devised the family real estate and home on Elm Street to his wife, Emily, for life and then to such of his grandchildren as survive Emily, but if none survive her, then to Emily's estate. His estate elected not to treat the bequest as qualified terminable interest property. No marital deduction is allowable for either the life estate or the contingent remainder to Emily's estate. An interest in the property is considered to pass to the grandchildren. Some of them may possess or enjoy the Elm Street property upon the death of Emily. It is immaterial that the grandchildren are not in being at the time of Andrew's death.

¶ 1032 Interest in Unidentified Assets

If the interest passing to a spouse can be satisfied out of assets for which no marital deduction would be allowed, the marital deduction is affected.[91] The value of the interest passing to the spouse, for the purpose of the marital deduction, is reduced by the aggregate value of such assets.[92]

The assets out of which the interest passing to the surviving spouse may be satisfied are determined prior to payment of any general claims, but without including named property specifically bequeathed or devised.

> ***Example:*** Arthur Britton bequeathed $200,000 to his surviving spouse, Jean. The general estate includes a term-for-years interest (valued at $225,000 in determining the value of Britton's gross estate) in his country home and acreage—an interest retained by Britton after a gift of the realty to his son. If the bequest to Jean may be satisfied out of the term-for-years interest, the marital deduction with respect to the bequest of $200,000 is reduced to zero. It is immaterial whether Jean actually receives the term-for-years interest.

¶ 1033 Fiduciary's Powers to Distribute in Kind

The IRS has prescribed conditions under which the marital deduction will be allowed in cases of a pecuniary bequest in a will, or of a transfer in trust of a pecuniary amount, if the will or trust instrument either requires or permits the executor or trustee to satisfy the bequest in noncash properties selected at their values as finally determined for federal estate tax purposes.[93] The rules set out in the revenue procedure do not apply to transfers of fractional shares of the estate or to transfers of specific assets.

The marital deduction will not be allowed if the executor or trustee is required to, or has an option to, satisfy the pecuniary transfer in kind at estate tax values (and the property available for distribution includes assets that could fluctuate in value) *unless* applicable state law or the provisions of the will or trust instrument require the fiduciary to distribute to the surviving spouse either:

---

[90] Reg. § 20.2056(c)-3.
[91] Code Sec. 2056(b)(2).
[92] Reg. § 20.2056(b)-2.
[93] Rev. Proc. 64-19, 1964-1 CB (Part 1) 682.

(1) assets having an aggregate fair market value, on the dates of distribution, of not less than the amount of the pecuniary bequest or transfer in trust as finally determined for federal estate tax purposes; or

(2) assets fairly representative of appreciation or depreciation in the value of all property available for distribution in satisfaction of the pecuniary bequest or transfer.

When condition (1) or (2) is not met, the IRS will consider the property interest passing from the decedent to the surviving spouse as unascertainable at the date of death, if the property available for distribution includes assets that could fluctuate in value.

With respect to wills and trust instruments executed prior to October 1, 1964, fiduciaries and surviving spouses were given an opportunity to preserve the marital deduction otherwise lost to the estate under the above policy by executing a "side agreement."

¶ 1035 "Interest" vs. "Property"

The terms "interest" and "property," as used in connection with the marital deduction, have separate and distinct meanings. The term "property" is the more comprehensive. It includes all objects or rights that are susceptible of ownership. The term "interest" refers to the extent of ownership of property, such as a life estate in a farm. The farm is the property; the life estate is the interest. A lease is an interest, and, if the lease is transferred from the decedent at death, an interest in property is so transferred.[94]

If a decedent devises acreage to his or her spouse for life with remainder to another, both devisees have an interest in the property. If the fee is devised to a son, subject to a charge of the rents to the surviving spouse for life, both the spouse and son have an interest in the same property.

¶ 1037 Joint and Mutual Wills

Joint and mutual wills of spouses fixing disposition of their respective estates rate a note of caution: The IRS contends that joint wills so restrict the survivor's right to dispose of the property as to create a terminable interest label for the survivor's otherwise nonterminable share, even if the property had been held in joint tenancy.[95] However, the courts have made state law a key factor in generally permitting the marital deduction under the reciprocal will arrangement. Generally, the deduction will be disallowed if the terms of the wills can be enforced under state law. An agreement between the spouses can also limit disposition and create a terminable interest.[96]

¶ 1040 Valuation of Deductible Property Interest

Only the net interest received is considered in determining the value of the interest passing to the surviving spouse for purposes of the marital deduction. Any burdens on the property passing, such as mortgages, liens, and death taxes, must be subtracted from the value of the property in determining the deductible amount.[97] Similarly, the marital deduction is allowable only to the extent that

---

[94] Reg. § 20.2056(a)-2.

[95] See, e.g., IRS Technical Advice Memorandum 8105006 (Sept. 26, 1980), and IRS Technical Advice Memorandum 9023004 (Feb. 20, 1990).

[96] *A.J. Batterton, Exr.*, CA-5, 69-1 USTC ¶ 12,584, 406 F2d 247, cert. denied.

[97] Reg. § 20.2056(b)-4. See also *V.H. Chiles, Exrx.*, CA-9, 88-1 USTC ¶ 13,763.

property bequeathed to the surviving spouse exceeds in value the property such spouse is required to relinquish. This principle has major application where, in community property states, the surviving spouse elects to take under the decedent's will and allows its terms to govern the disposition of the survivor's community interest.

Where death taxes are payable out of property bequeathed to the surviving spouse or passing to him or her under state intestate laws, the computation of the marital deduction may be dependent upon the computation of such taxes. In such event, an interdependent computation is involved, which is accomplished most easily by means of computer programs designed for such computations. These interrelated computations can also be made by way of algebraic procedures (see ¶1075).

If the decedent by will leaves the residue of his or her estate to his or her surviving spouse and the surviving spouse pays, or if the estate income is used to pay, claims against the estate so as to increase the residue, such increase in the residue is acquired by purchase and not by bequest. Accordingly, the value of any such additional part of the residue passing to the surviving spouse cannot be included in the amount of the marital deduction.

The value of the marital deduction must be reduced by death taxes that the executor is authorized by will to pay out of the marital trust even though the will does not require him to pay such expenses from the marital trust and, in fact, such payments are not made from the marital trust.[98] The U.S. Supreme Court has held, however, that the payment of administration expenses that, under state law (Georgia), could be allocated to principal or income and, in fact were allocated to income, did not affect the spousal share payable from principal at death. The Court concluded that the payment of the administrative expenses did not constitute, under the rules of Reg. §20.2056(b)-4(a), a "material limitation" on the surviving spouse's right to receive the income from the trust. Therefore, the estate was not required to offset the marital deduction by the amount of expenses that could be, but were not, paid from marital deduction property.[99]

However, a different result was obtained where the administration expenses were to be paid from the *principal (corpus)*, rather than the income, from a marital trust. In *B. Brown*,[100] an estate incurred significantly larger administration expenses than it had initially claimed on the estate tax return. Upholding the decision of the lower court, the U.S. Court of Appeals for the Ninth Circuit concluded that any such increase in the estate's administration expense deduction claimed by the estate had to be offset by a corresponding decrease in the estate's marital deduction to the extent that the expenses were paid from funds otherwise earmarked for the corpus of the marital trust. Further, because the decedent's gross estate and the deductions claimed by the estate were required to be valued as of the same date, the estate was not permitted to deduct the amount of its actual administration expenses while calculating the marital deduction based on date-of-death estimated expenses.

In order to avoid the difficulty, both for taxpayers and the IRS, to determine what constitutes a "material limitation" on a surviving spouse's right to income from a marital bequest, the IRS has amended Reg. §20.2056(b)-4, effective for

---

[98] *M.S. Wycoff Est.*, CA-10, 74-2 USTC ¶13,037, 506 F2d 1144; Rev. Rul. 79-14, 1979-1 CB 309.

[99] *O. Hubert Est.*, SCt, 97-1 USTC ¶60,261.

[100] *B. Brown*, CA-9, 2003-1 USTC ¶60,462, cert. denied, 10/6/2003.

estates of decedents dying on or after December 3, 1999.[101] The amended regulation eliminates the materiality requirement. Instead, the regulations bifurcate estate expenses into estate transmission expenses and estate management expenses. Estate transmission expenses, but not estate management expenses, reduce the value of property for marital deduction purposes. Estate transmission expenses are those expenses that would not have been incurred but for the decedent's death. Estate transmission expenses include any administration expense that is not a management expense. Management expenses are expenses that would be incurred in investing, maintaining, and preserving the estate property. Pursuant to Code Sec. 2056(b)(9), the allowable amount of the marital deduction is reduced by the amount of these management expenses if they are deducted as administration expenses on the estate tax return.

Where the decedent's will does not clearly indicate what sources are to be used to pay death taxes and administration expenses, courts apply state law in determining whether marital deduction property is to be charged with these costs.[102] The Tax Court has also applied state law to determine that interest payable on federal estate tax and state inheritance tax, and on deficiencies with respect to these taxes, did not reduce the value of property passing to a surviving spouse.[103] State law provided that the interest did not have to be charged specifically to either income or principal. Thus, because a reduction of the principal by interest payments was contrary to the decedent's intent to obtain the maximum marital deduction as demonstrated by his will, the interest due was chargeable against the income of the estate.

The U.S. Court of Claims has held that the value of property passing to a marital trust under a decedent's will was to be reduced by the amount of the decedent's liability for unpaid federal gift taxes in order to determine the allowable marital deduction. This reduction was required because the property passing to the marital trust was the only source for payment of the gift tax liability available to the decedent's executors who, under applicable state law (New York), were empowered to use the property passing to the trust to pay the gift tax liability.[104]

• ***Special Use Valuation Property***

In two separate IRS Technical Advice Memoranda relating to the same estate, the IRS ruled that an estate could claim a marital deduction for the full fair market value of property distributed to a marital trust, even though a portion of this property consisted of farmland that was included in the decedent's gross estate at its special use value (see ¶280 through ¶296).[105] The IRS National Office rejected the contention of its District Office that the allowable marital deduction should be reduced by the difference between the special use value and the fair market value of the farmland. However, the IRS ruled that the marital deduction claimed by the estate was allowable because the full value of the decedent's entire interest in the farmland was includible in his gross estate. In the second ruling, the IRS clarified this statement by defining the full value of the farmland

---

[101] T.D. 8846, amending Reg. §20.2056(b)-4, filed with the *Federal Register* on Dec. 2, 1999.

[102] *G.B. Phillips*, 90 TC 797, CCH Dec. 44,717. See *J.E. Reid Est.*, 90 TC 304, CCH Dec. 44,583.

[103] *W.E. Richardson Est.*, 89 TC 1193, CCH Dec. 44,388.

[104] *W.E. Murray, Exr.*, CtCls, 82-2 USTC ¶13,488, 687 F2d 386.

[105] IRS Technical Advice Memorandum 8314001 (Sept. 22, 1982), and IRS Technical Advice Memorandum 8314005 (Dec. 14, 1982). See also IRS Technical Advice Memorandum 8509001 (Nov. 13, 1984).

to mean its special use value. Moreover, the allowance of a marital deduction based on the fair market value of the farmland did not violate the integrity of the marital deduction statute because the farmland would be includible in the spouse's gross estate at its fair market value upon her death.

However, in another Technical Advice Memorandum,[106] the IRS National Office determined that a marital bequest was overfunded when the executors used the special use value of the farm, as opposed to its fair market value when transferring property to the surviving spouse. The decedent's will directed that the spouse was to receive one-half of the adjusted gross estate but required the executor to use fair market value for transferring assets to satisfy the marital bequest. The effect of this ruling is to allow the executor to transfer less value to the surviving spouse and leave more property in the nontaxable residuary. The Tax Court has also ruled that farmland included in the decedent's gross estate at its special use value retained that value for purposes of calculating the marital deduction.[107]

¶ 1045 Passing of Interest in Property

For purposes of the marital deduction, an interest in property is considered as passing from the decedent to his or her spouse if:

(1) the interest is bequeathed or devised to the spouse by the decedent;

(2) the interest is inherited by the spouse from the decedent;

(3) the interest is the dower or curtesy interest (or statutory interest in lieu thereof) of the surviving spouse;

(4) the interest has been transferred to the spouse by the decedent at any time;

(5) the interest was, at the time of the decedent's death, held by the spouse and the decedent (or by them in conjunction with any other person) in joint ownership with right of survivorship, such joint ownership including joint tenancy, tenancy by the entirety, a joint bank account, or any other co-ownership with right of survivorship;

(6) the decedent had a power of appointment over such interest (either alone or in conjunction with another), which he exercised in favor of the spouse, or the spouse takes the interest in default upon release or nonexercise of the power; or

(7) the interest consists of proceeds of insurance on the life of the decedent, receivable by the spouse, regardless of whether the decedent had previously assigned the policy or paid the premiums by way of gift.[108]

• ***Settlement Agreements***

Property interests that a surviving spouse assigns or surrenders pursuant to a compromise agreement in settlement of a will contest are not deductible as an interest passing to the spouse.[109] Any interest received by the surviving spouse under a settlement will be regarded as having passed from the decedent to his surviving spouse if the settlement was based on an enforceable right, under state law, as properly interpreted. The U.S. Court of Appeals for the Eighth Circuit interpreted this test to mean that, where the constitutionality of a state dower

---

[106] Technical Advice Memorandum 8708001 (May 6, 1986).

[107] *H.M. Evers Est.*, 57 TCM 718, CCH Dec. 45,776(M), TC Memo. 1989-292.

[108] Code Sec. 2056(c).

[109] Reg. § 20.2056(c)-2(d)(1).

statute was uncertain at the time of settlement, the Tax Court was required to make an independent determination as to the enforceability of the surviving spouse's dower claim.[110] Consent decrees will not necessarily be accepted as a bona fide evaluation of the rights of the spouse. The key factor is whether an interest passes from the decedent to his or her surviving spouse, so that the above rules also apply in the case of an intestate decedent where there is a dispute over the statutory share of the spouse.[111]

If a surviving spouse elects to take his or her share of the decedent's estate under local law instead of taking an interest under the will, the interest the surviving spouse takes under local law is considered as passing from the decedent.[112] The failure of a surviving spouse to elect to take an interest under the local law is not considered to any extent as a purchase of the interest the surviving spouse takes under the will.

An interest transferred to a surviving spouse, pursuant to an antenuptial agreement, is property passing from a decedent to his or her surviving spouse. A marital deduction will be allowed for it if all other requirements are met.[113]

¶ 1050 Disclaimers

A "qualified disclaimer" of property, as defined at ¶ 2009, may be made by a third person so that the property may pass to the decedent's surviving spouse and qualify for the marital deduction.[114]

> *Example:* At his death, Herbert Miller's testamentary trust provided that all of the trust income be paid to Wilma, his surviving spouse, for life, with the remainder to their descendants. Wilma's interest in the trust would not qualify for the marital deduction since it is a nondeductible terminable interest (see ¶ 1020). However, the trust also authorized the trustee to distribute principal to the descendants as the trustee deemed advisable for their support and maintenance. Pursuant to powers granted by the instrument, Herbert's executor split the trust into a marital trust and a family trust, and the children disclaimed their right to principal distributions from the marital trust during Wilma's lifetime. As a result of this action, Wilma received a qualifying income interest in the marital trust, which was thereby eligible for a marital deduction under the qualified terminable interest property rules (see ¶ 1002).

If the requirements are satisfied, refusals to accept property are given effect for estate tax purposes, even if local law does not characterize such refusals as "disclaimers." For requirements of a qualified disclaimer, see ¶ 2009.

Qualified disclaimers may be made with respect to transfers that created an interest in the person disclaiming and were made after December 31, 1976.

¶ 1055 Extensions for Future Interests

A six-month extension of time is provided for payment of estate tax on reversionary or remainder interests in property that are included in the value of the gross estate.[115] The extension is granted only for the part of the tax attributable to such interests. In determining the part of the tax attributable to the

---

[110] *G.M. Brandon Est.*, CA-8, 87-2 USTC ¶ 13,733, rev'g and rem'g TC, 86 TC 327, CCH Dec. 42,911.

[111] *V. Pastor, Admr.*, DC N.Y., 75-1 USTC ¶ 13,045, 386 FSupp. 106.

[112] Reg. § 20.2056(c)-2(c).

[113] Rev. Rul. 68-271, 1968-1 CB 409.

[114] Code Sec. 2046, Code Sec. 2056, and Code Sec. 2518.

[115] Code Sec. 6163.

reversionary or remainder interests, proper effect must be given to any marital deduction allowed.

¶ 1060 Alternate Valuation Method

If the executor elects the alternate valuation method of valuing the estate (see ¶ 105), the amount of the marital deduction is governed by the value at the date of death. It is adjusted, however, for any difference in value (not due to mere lapse of time or the occurrence or nonoccurrence of a contingency) of the property as of the date six months after the date of death.[116] If the property was distributed, sold, exchanged, or otherwise disposed of during the alternate valuation period, it is to be valued as of the date of its first distribution, sale, exchange, or other disposition.

The alternate valuation election pertains only to valuation. It does not extend the time for determining the character of the interest passing to the surviving spouse.

> *Example (1):* Under Robert Babcock's will, a life estate is given to his surviving spouse, Ann, with remainder to Ann and to their son, Tom. No deduction results, even though Tom dies within the six-month period after the decedent's death.
>
> *Example (2):* Tess True's will directed the executor to sell certain described real estate and to purchase stock of X corporation with the proceeds. The executor was then to turn the stock over to True's widower. The value of the real estate at True's death was $100,000. It was sold for $120,000 by the executor prior to six months after True's death. The stock was purchased for $120,000, but had a fair market value of $80,000 at True's death.
>
> If the gross estate is valued at the date of True's death, the marital deduction is $100,000 (the value of the real estate at the time of death). That value was the value of the interest included in determining the value of the gross estate. If the value of the gross estate is determined under the alternate valuation rule the marital deduction is $120,000, the value of the real estate at the time of sale within the six-month period.

¶ 1065 Execution of Schedule

The instructions to Form 706 (United States Estate (and Generation-Skipping Transfer) Tax Return) specify items that should not be included in the marital deduction schedule, as well as the manner of listing those that may be included. Certain property interests that passed from the decedent to his or her surviving spouse are to be wholly or partially excluded from Schedule M (Bequests etc., to Surviving Spouse) of Form 706, as indicated below:

(1) When interests in the same property passed from the decedent both to his or her surviving spouse and (for less than an adequate and full consideration in money or money's worth) to some other person under such conditions that the other person may possess or enjoy any part of the property following the termination or failure of the interest therein that passed to the surviving spouse, the interest passing to the spouse must be excluded from the schedule (unless a qualified terminable interest property election is made).

> *Example (1):* Property transferred by the decedent Bill Green in the following manner is excludable from Schedule M:

---

[116] Reg. § 20.2056(b)-4.

(1) a bequest of property to his spouse for life, with remainder to his daughter; and

(2) a bequest of property to his mother for life, with remainder to his spouse, if surviving, and, if not, to his daughter and her heirs.

Under each bequest, the spouse's interest in the property may terminate or fail, and the daughter may, thereafter, possess or enjoy the property.

(2) If the decedent directs the executor or trustee to purchase for his or her surviving spouse an annuity, a life estate or estate for years in certain property, or any other property interest that may terminate or fail, the property to be used in the acquisition may not be included on the marital deduction schedule. The ownership of a bond, note, or other contractual obligation, the discharge of which would not have the effect of an annuity for life or for a term, is not considered to be a property interest that may terminate or fail.

(3) If any property passing from the decedent to his or her surviving spouse may be paid or otherwise satisfied out of a group of assets, the value of such property interest is, for the purpose of entry on the marital deduction schedule, to be reduced by the aggregate value of any assets that, if passing from the decedent to his surviving spouse, would be nondeductible terminable interests. Property interests that may be paid or otherwise satisfied out of any of a group of assets include bequests of the residue of the decedent's estate, or of a share of the residue, and cash legacies payable out of the general estate.

Example (2): Carl Banks bequeathed $100,000 to his wife. His general estate includes a term for years (value of $10,000 in determining the value of his gross estate) in an office building. This interest was retained by Banks under a deed of the building by gift to his son. The portion of the value of the specific bequest to be entered on Schedule M is $90,000.

(4) Property interests are to be excluded from the marital deduction schedule to the extent that a deduction is taken for them under other, preceding schedules (Schedule J (Funeral Expenses and Expenses Incurred in Administering Property Subject to Claims), Schedule K (Debts of the Decedent, and Mortgages and Liens), and Schedule L (Net Losses During Administration and Expenses Incurred in Administering Property Not Subject to Claims) of Form 706, inclusive). Examples of interests to be so excluded are fees or commissions and payments made in satisfaction of a claim of the surviving spouse against the estate.

(5) When a property interest passing to the surviving spouse is subject to a mortgage or other encumbrance, or when an obligation is imposed on the surviving spouse in connection with the passing of a property interest, only the net value of the interest after reduction by the amount of the mortgage or other encumbrance, or obligation, should be included on the marital deduction schedule.

¶ 1067 Listings on Schedule M

Each property interest listed on Schedule M (Bequests etc., to Surviving Spouse) of Form 706 (United States Estate (and Generation-Skipping Transfer) Tax Return) should be fully described. This includes otherwise nondeductible terminable interest property for which a qualified terminable interest property election is intended. The items should be numbered in sequence. The description must indicate the instrument (including the clause or paragraph number of the instrument, if possible) or provision of law under which each item passed to the surviving spouse. The schedule and item number of the property interest as it appears in the schedules for reporting property includible in the gross estate should also be shown where possible. The value of each item listed on the schedule should be the value determined before taking into account the effect of federal and other death taxes.

If a residuary bequest is listed on Schedule M, a copy of the computation showing how the value of such item was determined should be submitted. The computation should include a statement showing:

(1) The value of all property that is included in the decedent's gross estate but is not part of the decedent's probate estate. This includes property transferred during life but taxed under Code Sec. 2035 through Code Sec. 2038, such as lifetime transfers, jointly owned property passing to the survivor on the decedent's death, and insurance payable to specific beneficiaries.

(2) The values of all specific and general legacies or devises, with an appropriate reference in each instance to the applicable clause or paragraph of the decedent's will or codicil. (In any case where legacies are made to each member of a class—for example, $1,000 to each of the decedent's employees—only the number in each class and the aggregate value of property received by them need be furnished.)

(3) The date of birth and the gender of all persons, the duration of whose lives may affect the value of the residuary interest passing to the surviving spouse.

(4) Any other information that may appear material, such as facts relating to any claim, not arising under the will, to any part of the estate.

¶ 1068 Adjustment for Death Taxes

The total of the values listed on Schedule M (Bequests, etc., to Surviving Spouse) of Form 706 (United States Estate (and Generation-Skipping Transfer) Tax Return) must be reduced by the amount of any federal estate tax, federal generation-skipping transfer (GST) tax and state or other death and GST taxes that are payable out of, or chargeable against, the property interests (see ¶ 1075). Such amounts of taxes should be entered in the designated spaces (items (5a), (5b), and (5c)) of the schedule. Items (5b) and (5c) must be supported by an identification and computation of the amount of state or other death and GST taxes shown.[117]

¶ 1069 Supplemental Documents

If property interests passing by the decedent's will are listed on Schedule M (Bequests, etc., to Surviving Spouse) of Form 706 (United States Estate (and Generation-Skipping Transfer) Tax Return), a certified copy of the order admitting the will to probate must be submitted with the return. If, at the time the return is filed, the court of probate jurisdiction has entered any decree interpreting the will or any of its provisions affecting property interests listed on the schedule, a copy of the decree is also required. Additional evidence to support the deduction claim may be requested by the district director.

[117] Reg. § 20.2056(b)-4.

¶ 1075 Marital Deduction and Interrelated Death Taxes

The federal estate tax law contemplates that the marital deduction will be allowed only with respect to the net amount passing to the surviving spouse.[118] Any charges that reduce the amount actually passing to such spouse will reduce the deduction.

State death taxes payable out of residue, including those chargeable against the amounts passing to the surviving spouse, reduce the amount of the deduction. Because they are not deductible under the federal estate tax law, the amounts of these taxes are subject to federal estate taxes just as is any other property not passing to the surviving spouse.

Federal estate taxes payable out of the residue are also part of the taxable estate. Determination of the amount of the residue is dependent upon the marital deduction, which in turn is dependent upon the amounts of both the federal and state taxes. The computation problems may be minimized by making specific transfers to the surviving spouse and by shifting the burden of tax payment to other interests. Where it has not been feasible to prepare a will in a manner that will avoid the involved computation, special formulas must be used.

IRS Publication No. 904, "Interrelated Computations for Estate and Gift Taxes,"[119] illustrates how the allowable marital and charitable deductions may be computed in cases in which these deductions are interrelated with death taxes.

The IRS National Office will furnish taxpayers with actuarial factors and assistance in the solution of interrelated tax computation problems. Taxpayers who have difficulty with tax computations may request assistance by writing to the IRS. The request should include sufficient supporting data to enable the IRS to make the computation. For most estates, copies of the will and relevant trust instruments, a schedule of assets and deductions, and a tentative computation of state tax should accompany the request.

In the event the estate includes community property, everything passing to the surviving spouse in excess of the surviving spouse's share of such community property should be listed in this schedule, regardless of whether such excess comes from the decedent's share of the community or from his or her separate property.

Practitioners who would like to avoid the time-consuming and tedious calculations involved with using the mathematical formulae set out in Publication 904 should consider using CCH's *ProSystem fx* ® *Tax*, which contains computer programs for calculating interrelated marital and charitable deductions.

---

[118] Reg. § 20.2056(b)-4.

[119] IRS Publication No. 904, "Interrelated Computations for Estate and Gift Taxes" (Rev. May 1985). Reproduced in CCH FEDERAL ESTATE AND GIFT TAX REPORTS.

Chapter 22
CHARITABLE, PUBLIC, AND SIMILAR TRANSFERS

¶ 1100 Transfers

A charitable deduction is allowed for the value of property transferred by the decedent to or for the use of certain organizations.[1] The deduction is allowed, without limitation as to amount, for transfers of property (to the extent included in the gross estate) to or for the use of:

(1) any corporation organized and operated exclusively for (a) religious, (b) charitable, (c) scientific, (d) literary, or (e) educational purposes, including the encouragement of art and the prevention of cruelty to children or animals;

(2) the United States, or any state or political subdivision thereof or the District of Columbia, for exclusively public purposes;

(3) any veterans' organization incorporated by Act of Congress, or of its departments or local chapters or posts;

(4) a trustee or trustees, or a fraternal society, order, or association operating under the lodge system if the contributions are to be used exclusively for the purposes enumerated in (1), above; or

(5) an employee stock ownership plan if the transfer qualifies as a qualified gratuitous transfer (see ¶ 1122).

A transfer to an individual member of a religious order will not qualify as a charitable contribution, even if the member has taken a vow of poverty requiring renunciation of any inheritance in favor of the order.[2] Bequests for masses qualify only if made directly to the church and not to a priest.[3] The IRS has permitted a charitable deduction for a bequest made to a church to say masses for previously deceased members of a decedent's family. In that situation, however, the masses would have been said even if the bequest had not been made, and the bequest became part of the general funds of the church.[4] A decedent's bequest in trust for the benefit of a nonprofit cemetery association did not qualify for an estate tax charitable deduction because the trust funds were not used for an exclusively

---

[1] Code Sec. 2055; Reg. § 20.2055-1.
[2] Rev. Rul. 55-760, 1955-2 CB 607.
[3] Rev. Rul. 68-459, 1968-2 CB 411.
[4] Rev. Rul. 78-366, 1978-2 CB 241.

charitable purpose. This was true because, under the decedent's will, the bequest was to be used to maintain the decedent's cemetery plot before it was used to maintain the cemetery in general.[5]

An estate tax deduction is not allowed for a bequest to a charity if the bequest is conditioned on the approval of a third party.[6] Bequests to foreign governments and political subdivisions thereof that are used exclusively for charitable purposes are deductible.[7]

¶1101 Disqualifications

The transfer to any organization qualifying under category (1) or (3), listed at ¶1100, will not be allowed as a deduction if any part of the net earnings of the organization inures to the benefit of any private stockholder or individual. A deduction is also denied where a substantial part of the transferee's activities involves the carrying on of propaganda or some other method of influencing legislation. A deduction is denied if the transferee participates or intervenes in (including the publishing or distributing of statements) any political campaign on behalf of or in opposition to any candidate for public office.[8] In any event, the amount of the deduction cannot exceed the portion of the contributed property included in the gross estate[9] (see ¶2305).

¶1102 Form of Transfer—Disclaimers

A charitable deduction is allowable only if the transfer is made by the decedent rather than by the decedent's estate or by the beneficiaries of the estate. The transfer may be made pursuant to a will or by means of a lifetime transfer.

However, a charitable deduction is available for property that is indirectly cast into a charitable transfer by means of a "qualified disclaimer."[10] If the qualified disclaimer requirements are satisfied, refusals to accept property are given effect for estate tax charitable deduction purposes even if local law does not characterize such refusals as "disclaimers." Qualified disclaimers may be made with respect to those transfers creating an interest in the person disclaiming. For requirements of a qualified disclaimer, see ¶2009.

The complete termination of a power to consume, invade, or appropriate property for the benefit of an individual can also create a charitable deduction.[11] In order to qualify, the termination must occur before the due date of the estate tax return and before the power has been exercised.

¶1105 Qualifying Transferees

Transfers to organizations, such as the Red Cross, the Boy Scouts, the American Heart Fund, the American Cancer Society, the Salvation Army, and other well-known charitable organizations clearly qualify for the deduction. Similarly, transfers made directly to a recognized school or church organization are deductible when the transfer is to be used for educational or religious purposes.

---

[5] *First National Bank of Omaha, Exr. (Est. of G. McIninch)*, CA-8, 82-2 USTC ¶13,474, cert. denied Jan. 10, 1983; see also *Mellon Bank N.A., Exr.*, CA-3, 85-1 USTC ¶13,615, cert. denied Feb. 24, 1986.

[6] Rev. Rul. 64-129, 1964-1 CB (Part 1) 329.

[7] Rev. Rul. 74-523, 1974-2 CB 304; IRS Technical Advice Memorandum 9842004 (Jul. 7, 1998).

[8] Code Sec. 2055(a).

[9] Code Sec. 2055(d).

[10] Code Sec. 2046 and Code Sec. 2518.

[11] Reg. §20.2055-2(c).

It is advisable to consult IRS Publication No. 78 (Cumulative List of Organizations Described in Section 170(c) of the IRC of 1986) and its supplement before making charitable bequests or distributions. IRS Publication No. 78 is the official list of those organizations to which charitable contributions are deductible under Code Sec. 170 and Code Sec. 2055.[12] Failure to consult the list and contributing to a charity not listed may result in the denial of the charitable deduction. For example, a charitable deduction was denied for funds distributed to a private school that no longer had tax-exempt status.[13] According to the Tax Court, the trustees would have been aware of the revocation had they consulted IRS Publication No. 78.

Whether various types of indirect discretionary transfers are deductible is not so clear. The courts have indicated that even these transfers will qualify if the terms under which the discretionary powers may be exercised are sufficiently explicit to limit use of the funds to the purposes specified in the law. Thus, a transfer in trust can qualify, even if the trustee is given complete discretion in selecting the ultimate beneficiaries of the transferred property. In like manner, specific charitable bequests paid by a trustee of a testamentary trust can qualify for a deduction even if the trustee has complete discretion as to which assets will be used to pay the bequests.[14]

So long as it is clear that the trustee's or other third person's discretion is limited to choosing the charitable, religious, or educational organizations to receive the funds or so long as it is clear that he must expend the funds directly and only for the purposes specified in the estate tax law, the transfers may qualify. The IRS maintains that, where a trustee has the power to select the charitable beneficiaries, the deduction is available only if state law (1) upholds the validity of the charitable trust, and (2) restricts the distribution of property to an organization that qualifies for an estate tax charitable deduction.[15]

No deduction is allowed for a transfer to or for the use of certain private foundations and foreign organizations. This matter is discussed for estate and gift tax purposes at ¶2305.

¶1110 State Law Effect

State law often plays a part in determining whether a particular transfer will qualify for the charitable deduction. If the transfer is one that is void under state law, the deduction will not be allowed.[16] No deduction will be allowed even if the heirs who would otherwise receive the property take action to permit it to go to the charitable transferees, unless they make a "qualified disclaimer" (see ¶1102). On the other hand, if the transfer is merely voidable under state law and the persons who have a right to have the transfer voided fail to act, the deduction will be allowed.[17]

---

[12] IRS Publication No. 78 is available for sale from the Superintendent of Documents, U.S. Government Printing Office, Washington, D.C. 20402, and is available on the Internet at *www.irs.gov*.

[13] *S.H. Clopton*, 93 TC 275, CCH Dec. 45,978.

[14] Rev. Rul. 81-20, 1981-1 CB 471, clarified by Rev. Rul. 90-3, 1990-1 CB 174.

[15] Rev. Rul. 69-285, 1969-1 CB 222; Rev. Rul. 71-441, 1971-2 CB 335.

[16] *H.V. Watkins, Sr., Exr.*, CA-5, 43-1 USTC ¶10,042, 136 F2d 578.

[17] *M. Varick Est.*, 10 TC 318, CCH Dec. 16,258 (Acq.).

¶ 1115 Property Passing Under Power of Appointment

Property that is includible in the gross estate under Code Sec. 2041 (relating to powers of appointment, see ¶ 650) and that passes to a charitable beneficiary is considered to be a bequest by the decedent and is deductible as a charitable transfer.[18]

¶ 1120 Transfers Not Exclusively for Charitable Purposes

Special rules are provided for transfers that are not exclusively for charitable purposes.[19] An estate tax charitable deduction is allowed for the value of the charitable interest transferred to the extent that such interest is presently ascertainable and, thus, severable from the noncharitable interest. Transfers subject to a power to divert such property to noncharitable purposes are nondeductible.

Interests transferred for other than exclusively charitable purposes that are deductible include:[20]

(1) remainder interests in a charitable remainder annuity trust, a charitable remainder unitrust, or a pooled income fund (see ¶ 1122);[21]

(2) remainder interests in a personal residence (This transfer does not have to be in trust and the Tax Court has held that the transfer to charity of proceeds from the sale of a residence after the life tenant's death qualifies for the deduction.);[22]

(3) remainder interests in a farm (This transfer does not have to be in trust.);

(4) a transfer of an undivided portion, not in trust, of the decedent's entire interest for the entire term of his interest;

Example: The decedent, Tom Sanders, transfers a life estate in an office building to his wife, Lisa, for her life, retains a reversionary interest in such building, and then transfers one-half of the reversionary interest to charity while Lisa is still alive. His estate is denied a charitable deduction because an interest in the same property has already passed from Tom for private purposes and the reversionary interest is not considered the decedent's entire interest in the property.

(5) guaranteed annuity interests (An interest, whether or not in trust, involving a right to receive a guaranteed annuity, that is defined as a determinable amount paid at least annually for a specified term or for the life or lives of an individual or individuals, each of whom is living at the date of the decedent's death and can be ascertained at such date. (A charitable annuity trust is a form of a charitable lead trust; see ¶ 1123.) If not a trust, such interest must be paid by an insurance company or by an organization regularly engaged in issuing annuity contracts in order to qualify as a deductible charitable guaranteed annuity interest);

(6) unitrust income interests (An interest, whether in trust, involving the right to receive payment, not less often than annually, of a fixed percentage of the net fair market value, determined annually, of the prop-

---

[18] Code Sec. 2055(b).

[19] Code Sec. 2055(e).

[20] Reg. § 20.2055-2.

[21] Code Sec. 2055(e)(2)(A).

[22] *E.W. Blackford Est.*, 77 TC 1246, CCH Dec. 38,477. The IRS acquiesced in the result in *Blackford;* however, in the IRS's view, the remainder would be deductible only if the governing state law followed the doctrine of equitable reconversion, under which the remainderman could elect to take the property in its original form. See Rev. Rul. 83-158, 1983-2 CB 159.

erty that funds the unitrust interest. Payments under a unitrust (a form of charitable lead trust; see ¶1123) interest may be paid for a specified term or for the life or lives of an individual or individuals, each of whom must be living at the date of the decedent's death and can be ascertained at such date. If not in trust, such interest must be paid by an insurance company, or by an organization regularly engaged in issuing interests otherwise meeting the requirements of a unitrust interest, in order to qualify as a deductible charitable unitrust interest.);

(7) "conservation purpose" transfers (A deduction is also allowed for a bequest to a charitable organization exclusively for "conservation purposes" of (a) a "restriction" in perpetuity on the use of real property, e.g., easements, leases, restrictive covenants, etc., (b) remainder interests in real property, or (c) a decedent's entire interest in real property other than certain mineral rights.[23] "Conservation purposes" include the preservation of land, areas for public recreation, education, or scenic enjoyment, the preservation of historically important land or structures, or the preservation of natural environmental systems.); and

(8) artworks with retained copyrights (A charitable deduction will be allowed for the transfer of an artwork to charity even if the copyright covering the work is not so transferred.).[24]

¶ 1121 Split-Interest Transfers

Transfers involving property interests split between charitable and noncharitable beneficiaries may arise in a number of factual situations. The IRS has ruled that a decedent's estate was not entitled to an estate tax charitable deduction for the decedent's bequest of stock to charity because, under the terms of the will, the executor was to pay dividends from the stock to a noncharitable beneficiary during the period of estate administration.[25] In the IRS's view, this gave rise to a split-interest transfer because the noncharitable beneficiary's right to the dividends constituted a property right in the stock. Accordingly, the transfer was a split-interest transfer and no deduction was allowable because it was not in one of the forms required for such transfers (i.e., a charitable remainder annuity trust, charitable remainder unitrust, or pooled income fund).

Notwithstanding the position taken in the above ruling, the IRS has ruled that a decedent's bequest of the residue of his estate to charity was not a split-interest transfer, even though, pursuant to a state court order, his surviving spouse was to receive a support allowance from the residue during the period of estate administration.[26] The IRS allowed the deduction because the support allowance would be payable for only five years; the possibility that estate administration would last beyond five years was so remote as to be negligible. Because the charity was certain to receive an amount in excess of the present value of the support allowance, the IRS determined that only the charity had an interest in this amount of the residue, and, to the extent of this amount, the residuary bequest was not a split-interest transfer.

The U.S. Court of Appeals for the Eighth Circuit relied in part on this ruling in holding that a decedent's estate was entitled to an estate tax charitable deduction for a portion of the decedent's bequest to a trust having both charitable and noncharitable beneficiaries because the estate obtained a judicial modifi-

---

[23] Code Sec. 170(f)(3)(B); Reg. § 1.170A-14 and Reg. § 20.2055-2(e)(2)(iv).

[24] Code Sec. 2055(e)(4).

[25] Rev. Rul. 83-45, 1983-1 CB 233.

[26] Rev. Rul. 83-20, 1983-1 CB 231.

cation of the trust to provide for immediate distributions to the charitable remainder beneficiaries.[27] The estate executors had a motive for the reformation, arising from state fiduciary law, that was independent of tax considerations; however, the court focused on the fact that the abuses calling for application of the split-interest transfer provisions were not a concern in the case because the charitable interests passed directly to the charities under the state court order. Also relying in part on the ruling, the Eighth Circuit allowed a charitable deduction for a decedent's bequest to charity of a remainder interest in a testamentary trust that was funded with the residue of his estate because his wife elected to take against his will, under which she was entitled to a life income interest in the trust.[28] The split-interest trust requirements did not apply to bar the deduction because the wife received an interest only in that portion of the residue necessary to fund an agreement in settlement of her election, while the charity was certain to receive the rest of the residue.

• ***Charitable Split-Dollar Insurance Transactions***

In recent years, the benefits of charitable split-dollar insurance transactions have been scaled back by Congress and the IRS. Such transactions typically involve a transfer of funds by a taxpayer to a charity, with the understanding that the charity will use the funds to pay premiums on a cash value life insurance policy that benefits both the charity and the taxpayer's family. The charity or an irrevocable life insurance trust formed by the taxpayer usually purchases the insurance policy, and members of the taxpayer's family (or the taxpayer) are beneficiaries of the trust. A split-dollar agreement between the charity and the trust specifies what portion of the insurance policy premiums is to be paid by each. Generally, over the life of the split-dollar arrangement, the trust has access to a disproportionately high percentage of the cash surrender value and death benefits of the policy, compared to the percentage of premiums paid by the trust.

Code Sec. 170(f)(10) eliminates the tax benefits of charitable split-dollar arrangements. Code Sec. 170(f)(10) provides that no charitable contribution deduction will be allowed for a transfer made after February 8, 1999, to or for the use of a Code Sec. 170(c) organization, if the organization pays a premium on any personal benefit contract with respect to the transferor. A personal benefit contract includes any life insurance, annuity or endowment contract if any beneficiary under the contract is or is related to the transferor. The limitation also applies to organizations that understand or expect that any person will pay a premium on any personal benefit contract with respect to the transferor. The provision includes cross references to other Code provisions dealing with charitable contributions, including Code Sec. 2055, Code Sec. 2106(a)(2), and Code Sec. 2522.

Limited exceptions are provided for annuity contracts purchased by a charity to fund charitable gift annuities and for charitable remainder trusts that hold life insurance, annuity, or endowment contracts to pay annuity or unitrust amounts.

Reporting and excise tax requirements are also imposed. Although the reporting requirement is effective for premiums paid after February 8, 1999, the excise tax is imposed on premiums paid after December 17, 1999. Any charitable organization that pays premiums on a personal benefit contract in connection with a transfer for which a deduction is not allowed is required to pay an excise

---

[27] *W. Oetting, Exr.*, CA-8, 83-2 USTC ¶13,533, 712 F2d 358.

[28] *First National Bank of Fayetteville, Ark., Exr.*, CA-8, 84-1 USTC ¶13,558, 727 F2d 741.

tax and to report certain information related to the premium payments.[29] For purposes of this excise tax, Code Sec. 170(f)(10)(F)(ii) provides that premium payments made by any other person pursuant to an understanding or expectation described in Code Sec. 170(f)(10)(A) are treated as made by the charitable organization.

Reporting and excise tax requirements. Pursuant to IRS Notice 2000-24,[30] a charitable organization liable for excise taxes under Code Sec. 170(f)(10)(F), must file Form 4720 (Return of Certain Excise Tax on Charities and Other Persons Under Chapters 41 and 42 of the Internal Revenue Code) (2004) to report and pay the taxes due. The charitable organization must include the amount of the Code Sec. 170(f)(10)(F) tax on line 8 of part I.

Code Sec. 170(f)(10)(F)(iii) requires charitable organizations to annually report the amount of premiums paid that are subject to tax under Code Sec. 170(f)(10)(F) along with the name and taxpayer identification number of each beneficiary of a related contract. Form 8870 (Information Return for Transfers Associated with Certain Personal Benefit Contracts) (Rev. Jan. 2004) is to be used for reporting this required information.

Code Sec. 6033 requires most charitable organizations to file annual information returns. Generally, this means that a charitable organization is to file either Form 990 (Return of Organization Exempt From Income Tax) (2003), or Form 990-PF (Return of Private Foundation or Code Sec. 4947(a)(1) Nonexempt Charitable Trust Treated as a Private Foundation) (2003). Form 5227 (Split-Interest Trust Information Return) (2003) is used by a split-interest trust to report its financial activities and whether it is subject to excise taxes under Chapter 42 of the Code.

Code Sec. 170(f)(10) follows the IRS's administrative attack on charitable split-dollar arrangements in Notice 99-36, in which the IRS applied a substance-over-form approach to deny a deduction with respect to such transactions.[31] Besides denying a charitable deduction, the Notice described the IRS's intent to challenge the tax-exempt status of charities participating in split-dollar transactions.

¶ 1122 Charitable Remainder Trusts

A deductible charitable remainder interest must be in the form of an annuity trust, a unitrust, or a pooled income fund.[32]

A charitable remainder annuity trust (CRAT) is a trust from which a sum certain or a specified amount (which is not less than five percent or more than 50 percent of the initial net fair market value of all property placed in trust) is to be paid to the income beneficiary or beneficiaries. The specified amount must be paid at least annually to the income beneficiary.[33]

A charitable remainder unitrust (CRUT) is a trust that specifies that the income beneficiary or beneficiaries are to receive payments (at least annually) based on a fixed percentage (which is not less than five percent or more than 50 percent) of the net fair market value of the trust's assets as determined each year. In the alternative, a qualified charitable remainder unitrust can provide for the distribution each year of five percent of the net fair market value of its assets

---

[29] Code Sec. 170(f)(10)(F).

[30] Notice 2000-24, 2000-1 CB 952.

[31] Notice 99-36, 1999-1 CB 1284.

[32] Code Sec. 2055(e)(2)(A); *E. La Meres Est.*, 98 TC 294, CCH Dec. 48,085.

[33] Reg. § 1.664-1 and Reg. § 1.664-2, respectively.

(valued annually) or the amount of the trust income (other than capital gains), whichever is lower.[34] This payment requirement may not be discretionary with the trustee.

In addition, deficiencies in income (i.e., where the trust income was less than the stated amount payable to the income beneficiary) can be made up in later years when a CRUT's income exceeds the amount otherwise payable to the income beneficiary for that year. This is commonly referred to as a net income makeup charitable remainder unitrust (NIMCRUT). The determination of which items are trust income is to be made under state law and, therefore, cannot include such items as capital gains, which must be allocated to the trust principal. (No comparable rules are provided for CRATs.)

The Taxpayer Relief Act of 1997 (P.L. 105-34) imposed additional maximum payout and minimum charitable benefit requirements on both CRATs and CRUTs. Under the maximum payout limitation, a trust will fail to qualify as a charitable remainder trust if the annual payout exceeds 50 percent. Thus, a CRAT cannot pay out in any year an amount in excess of 50 percent of the initial fair market value of the trust's assets. A CRUT may not make an annual payout in excess of 50 percent of the fair market value of the trust's assets determined annually. The 50-percent maximum payout limitation applies to transfers in trust made after June 18, 1997.[35]

A minimum 10-percent charitable remainder value rule applies to transfers in trust made after July 28, 1997. To satisfy the rule, the value of a remainder interest in a CRAT must be at least 10 percent of the initial net fair market value of all property transferred to the trust. With respect to a CRUT, the 10-percent rule applies to each contribution of property to the trust. Under a grandfather provision, however, the 10-percent rule and the 50-percent limitation discussed above do not apply to transfers in trust under the terms of a will or other testamentary instrument executed on or before July 28, 1997, if the decedent (1) dies before January 1, 1999, without having republished the will or amended it by codicil or otherwise, or (2) was, on July 28, 1997, unable to change the disposition of the property due to a mental disability and did not regain competency before dying.[36]

Charitable remainder annuity trusts and unitrusts cannot have noncharitable remainder interests if a deduction is to be allowed. Furthermore, the remainder interest must pass to a charity on the termination of the last income interest. There may be more than one noncharitable income beneficiary, either concurrently or successively, and the income interest may be a life estate or for a term of years, but the term of years cannot be in excess of 20 years (see, however, the exception for contingency provisions in charitable remainder trusts, noted above). Under the regulations that were effective prior to July 7, 2003, no deduction was allowable if a charitable unitrust interest was preceded by a noncharitable unitrust interest; however, the Tax Court held the regulations were invalid to the extent that they prohibit a deduction in such a situation.[37] In response to this decision, Reg. §20.2055-2 and Reg. §20.2522(c)-3 have been

---

[34] Reg. §1.664-1 and Reg. §1.664-3, respectively.

[35] Code Sec. 664(d)(1)(A) and Code Sec. 664(d)(2)(A).

[36] Code Sec. 664(d)(1) and Code Sec. 664(d)(2); Act Sec. 1089(b)(6)(B) of the Taxpayer Relief Act of 1997 (P.L. 105-34).

[37] Reg. §20.2055-2(e), held partially invalid in *M.L. Boeshore Est.*, 78 TC 523, CCH Dec. 38,902, appeal dismissed CA-7, 2-10-83. The IRS has acquiesced in result only in this decision, Acquiescence Announcement, 1987-2 CB 1.

amended, effective July 7, 2003, to permit a deduction for charitable guaranteed annuity and unitrust interests that are preceded by a noncharitable annuity or unitrust interest.[38] The amendments eliminate the former requirement that a charitable interest commence no later than the start of a noncharitable interest that is in the form of a guaranteed annuity or unitrust interest. The regulations continue to require that any amounts payable for a private purpose before the expiration of the charitable interest either must be in the form of a guaranteed annuity or unitrust interest, or be payable from a separate group of assets exclusively devoted to private purposes. A trust will not qualify as a charitable remainder trust and no charitable deduction will be allowed if it is possible that federal estate and state death taxes may be payable from the trust assets.[39]

In a series of revenue procedures, the IRS has provided sample language in order to help taxpayers in drafting governing instruments for CRATs and CRUTs.[40]

• ***Life Payment to Trust for Financially Disabled Individual***

With respect to a CRUT, the IRS has allowed a limited exception to the rule that a noncharitable interest cannot exceed 20 years. That is, a CRUT will not be disqualified if unitrust amounts are paid to a separate trust for the life of an individual who is "financially disabled" for purposes of Code Sec. 6511(h)(2)(A). Under this Code section, an individual is financially disabled if the individual is unable to manage his or her financial affairs because of a medically determinable physical or mental impairment that can be expected to result in death, or which has lasted, or can be expected to last, for a continuous period of not less than 12 months. However, the IRS has indicated that a trust will qualify as a CRUT if (1) the separate trust's sole function is to receive and administer the unitrust amounts for the benefit of the financially disabled beneficiary, and (2) upon such beneficiary's death, the separate trust's remaining assets will be distributed to the beneficiary's estate or (after reimbursing the state for any Medicaid benefits provided to the beneficiary) are subject to the beneficiary's general power of appointment. In these circumstances, according to the IRS, the use of the separate trust's assets is consistent with the manner in which the beneficiary's own assets would be used. Consequently, the beneficiary is considered to have received the unitrust amounts directly from the CRUT for purposes of Code Sec. 664(d)(2)(A) and it is permissible for the CRUT's term to be for the life of the beneficiary, and not simply for a term of years. The same result applies in the case of a charitable remainder annuity trust.[41]

• ***Certain Transfers to Employee Stock Ownership Plans***

If a charitable remainder trust holds qualified employer securities transferred from a decedent dying before January 1, 1999, the securities transferred to an employee stock ownership plan in a "qualified gratuitous transfer" will

---

[38] T.D. 9068, filed with the *Federal Register* on July 3, 2003.

[39] Rev. Rul. 82-128, 1982-2 CB 71; *M. Atkinson Est.*, 115 TC 26, CCH Dec. 53,962, aff'd, CA-11, 2002-2 USTC ¶60,449, 309 F3d 1290.

[40] Rev. Proc. 90-30, 1990-1 CB 534; Rev. Proc. 90-31, 1990-1 CB 539; Rev. Rul. 92-57, 1992-2 CB 123; Rev. Proc. 2003-53, IRB 2003-31, 230; Rev. Proc. 2003-54, IRB 2003-31, 236; Rev. Proc. 2003-55, IRB 2003-31, 242; Rev. Proc. 2003-56, IRB 2003-31, 249; Rev. Proc. 2003-57, IRB 2003-31, 257; Rev. Proc. 2003-58, IRB 2003-31, 262; Rev. Proc. 2003-59, IRB 2003-31, 268; and Rev. Proc. 2003-60, IRB 2003-31, 274.

[41] Rev. Rul. 2002-20, 2002-1 CB 794, amplifying and superseding Rev. Rul. 76-270, 1976-2 CB 194.

qualify for the estate tax charitable deduction. The deduction is limited to the extent of the present value of the remainder interest in the trust.[42]

A transfer of qualified securities is treated as a qualified gratuitous transfer if (1) the securities are transferred to the trust by a decedent dying before January 1, 1999, (2) the decedent and his or her family members owned no more than 10 percent of the value of the outstanding stock at the time of the transfer to the employee stock ownership plan (ESOP), (3) the ESOP owns at least 60 percent of the value of the stock after the transfer, (4) the ESOP was in existence on August 1, 1996, (5) the employer agrees to pay an excise tax on certain prohibited distributions and allocations of the securities, and (6) no income tax deduction is allowable for the transfer. Additionally, the ESOP must meet certain antidiscrimination, administrative and distribution and allocation requirements.[43]

¶ 1123 Charitable Lead (Income) Trusts

A charitable lead trust is basically the reverse of a charitable remainder trust (see ¶ 1122). With a charitable lead trust, a charity is given an income interest for a term of years, or for the life (or lives) of designated individuals. At the end of the measuring period or the life (or lives) of the designated individuals, the property reverts to the grantor or the grantor's estate. Such an arrangement is used where a grantor has no immediate need for the income from the property to be transferred into the charitable lead trust, but still wants the property to benefit his or her chosen beneficiaries at a later date.

To sustain an estate or gift tax deduction, the payments to the charity under a charitable lead trust must be in the form of annuity or unitrust interests.[44] But there is no minimum payout requirement.

An annuity interest requires payment, at least annually, of a fixed amount for a specified term of years or the life (or lives) of named individuals.[45] Generally, the annuity interest will be a specified percentage of the value of the property transferred to the trust at the time of the transfer. The charitable lead annuity trust (CLAT) can only receive the one initial transfer of assets to it.

A unitrust interest requires payments, at least annually, of a fixed percentage of the fair market value of the trust assets as determined each year. The amount of the charitable deduction is determined by subtracting the value of the non-charitable interests from the fair market value of the property transferred to the trust.[46]

Neither the Code nor the legislative history delineates the permissible term for which a charitable guaranteed annuity interest or a unitrust interest in a lead trust must be paid. The permissible term for these interests is set forth in the regulations as either a specified term of years, or the life or lives of an individual or individuals, each of whom must be living at the date of the transfer and can be ascertained at such date.

In recent years, donors have attempted to take advantage of the existing regulations by using the life of an unrelated individual as the measuring life for the term of a charitable lead trust, to artificially inflate the charitable deduction. Sometimes referred to as "ghoul trusts," the methodology involves selection of

---

[42] Code Sec. 2055(a)(5).

[43] Code Sec. 664(g).

[44] Code Sec. 2055(e)(2)(B) and Code Sec. 2522(c)(2)(B); Reg. §20.2055-2 and Reg. §25.2522(c)-3.

[45] Rev. Rul. 85-49, 1985-1 CB 330.

[46] See, for example, IRS Letter Ruling 9737023 (June 16, 1997).

an individual who is seriously ill, but not "terminally ill," as the measuring life. Under the regulations, the annuity factor for a terminally ill person must be computed specifically to take into account that person's actual life expectancy (Reg. § 20.7520-3(b)(4), Example 1). However, because the individuals used for the measuring lives of these trusts are not terminally ill as defined by the regulations, the charitable interest is valued based on the standard actuarial tables. When the seriously ill individual dies (prematurely in comparison to what would have been expected under the actuarial tables), the amount the charity actually receives will be significantly less than the amount on which the charitable deduction was based. On the other hand, the amount transferred to the noncharitable remainder beneficiaries will be significantly greater than that subject to gift or estate tax.

This possibility is illustrated below in Example (1).

Example (1): Assume that a CLAT is established using a 40-year-old as the measuring life. One million dollars is transferred to the CLAT. The Code Sec. 7520 rate is 8% and the annuity payout rate is set at 8% of the initial value of the trust, to produce an annuity of $80,000 per year. Under these assumptions, the results are as follows:

Annuity factor: 11.3191

Present value of annuity interest: $905,528

Present value of remainder (gift) interest: $94,472

If the 40-year-old actually dies three years later, the charity would have received a total of $240,000 (3 × $80,000) in annuity payments. Assuming a 6% net return over the three-year period the remainder beneficiaries would receive approximately $936,000.

• ***Amended Regulations***

In response to these trusts, the IRS has adopted amendments to regulations[47] that limit the use of certain charitable lead trusts that use the life expectancy of a seriously ill, but not "terminally ill," person as the measuring life. Because the IRS considers such arrangements to be abusive, as well as contrary to the legislative intent of restricting a charitable deduction to specific types of split-interest transfers, the amended regulations limit the permissible term for guaranteed annuity and unitrust interests to either a specified term of years or the lives of certain individuals who are living at the date of the transfer. With respect to the latter requirement, only one or more of the following individuals may be used as measuring lives: (1) the donor; (2) the donor's spouse; and (3) a lineal ancestor (or a spouse of a lineal ancestor) of all the remainder beneficiaries. Thus, noncharitable remainder beneficiaries can include step-children and step-grandchildren of the individual who is the measuring life. Additionally, a trust will be deemed to satisfy the requirement that the measuring life be a person in the above three categories if there is a less than 15 percent probability that individuals who are not lineal descendants will receive any trust corpus. This probability must be computed, based on the current applicable Life Table contained in Reg. § 20.2031-7, as of the date of the decedent's death taking into account the interests of all primary and contingent remainder beneficiaries who

[47] T.D. 8923, filed with the *Federal Register* on Jan. 5, 2001, adopting amendments to Reg. § 20.2055-2 and Reg. § 20.2055(c)(3).

are living at that time. Example (2), below,[48] illustrates the operation of this 15-percent probability rule.

Example (2): The grantor, Jack Linko, establishes a CLAT that provides for the annuity to be paid to a charity for his life. He is age 75 on the date the CLAT is created. On Linko's death, the corpus is to pass to his only child, Julie, age 50 on the date the CLAT is created. If Julie predeceases her father, the corpus is to pass to her issue then living and if she has no living issue at that time, then to her father's heirs at law (which class could include her father's siblings, uncles, aunts, nieces, and nephews). Julie has no living children on the date the CLAT is created. Based on the current applicable Life Table contained in Reg. § 20.2031-7 (Life Table 90CM), the probability that Julie will predecease her father, and the trust will pass to individuals who are not lineal descendants of her father, is 10.462%, taking into account the interests of remainder beneficiaries living at the time the trust was created. Because the probability that the trust corpus will pass to beneficiaries who are not lineal descendants of the grantor is less than 15%, the CLAT will satisfy the requirement that all noncharitable remainder beneficiaries are lineal descendants of the grantor or the grantor's spouse.

The limitation regarding permissible measuring lives does not apply to a charitable guaranteed annuity interest or unitrust interest payable under a charitable remainder trust described in Code Sec. 664.

The regulations allow an interest payable for a specified term of years to qualify as a guaranteed annuity or unitrust interest even if the governing instrument contains a "savings clause" intended to ensure compliance with a state's rule against perpetuities. The savings clause must utilize a vesting period of 21 years after the deaths of measuring lives who are selected to maximize, rather than limit, the term of the trust.

The amended regulations apply to transfers pursuant to wills and trusts where the decedent dies on or after April 4, 2000. Exceptions would apply for a will or revocable trust executed on or before April 4, 2000, if (1) the decedent dies on or before July 5, 2001, without having republished the will or amended the trust, or (2) the decedent was under a mental disability on April 4, 2000, under a mental disability to change the disposition of the decedent's property, and either does not regain competence to dispose of such property before the date of death, or dies prior to the later of (a) 90 days after the date on which the decedent first regains competence, or (b) July 5, 2001, without having republished the will (or amended the trust) by codicil or otherwise. In addition, the charitable deduction would not be disallowed where the charitable interest is payable for the life of an individual, other than one permitted under the regulations, if the interest is reformed into a lead interest payable for a specified term of years.

Example (3): Assume an annuity interest is payable for the life of an individual who is age 40 at the time of the transfer. If the Code Sec. 7520 interest rate is 7.4%, the annuity factor from Column 1 of Table S (7.4%), contained in IRS Publication 1457, Actuarial Values, Book Aleph, for the life of an individual age 40 is 12.0587. Based on Table B (7.4%), contained in Publication 1457, the factor 12.0587 corresponds to a term of years between 31 and 32 years. Accordingly, under the proposed amendments, the annuity interest would have to be reformed into an interest payable for a term of 32 years.

---

[48] T.D. 8923.

In the case of testamentary transfers, a judicial reformation would have to be commenced prior to the later of (1) July 5, 2001, or (2) the date prescribed by Code Sec. 2055(e)(3)(C)(iii). Any judicial reformation must be completed within a reasonable time after it is commenced. A nonjudicial reformation would be permitted if effective under state law, provided it is completed by the date on which a judicial reformation must be commenced.

¶ 1124 Trust Reformation Rules

A nondeductible charitable split-interest contribution can be reformed into a deductible split-interest contribution for purposes of the income, estate, and gift tax charitable deductions.[49] No reformation occurs, however, unless a "reformable interest" is transformed into a "qualified interest" by means of a "qualified reformation."

• *Qualified Interest*

A qualified interest is an interest for which a charitable deduction is allowed under Code Sec. 2055(a).[50] If a qualified reformation occurs, the allowable charitable deduction is equal to the lesser of (1) the actuarial value of the charitable interest after the reformation, or (2) the actuarial value of the charitable interest before the reformation for which a deduction would have been allowable but for the disallowance rules of Code Sec. 2055(e)(2) (see the Appendix at ¶2700 for actuarial tables).

• *Qualified Reformation*

A qualified reformation is a reformation, amendment, construction, or other action pertaining to the governing instrument that changes a reformable interest (defined below) into a qualified interest.[51] A qualified reformation can be accomplished by any means permitted under applicable local law, provided that the change is binding on all relevant parties under applicable local law.[52]

A reformation will constitute a qualified reformation only if certain requirements are met:

(1) The difference between the actuarial value of the reformed charitable interest and the unreformed charitable interest cannot exceed five percent of the value of the interest prior to reformation. For purposes of this requirement, values are to be determined as of the date of the decedent's death.

(2) Charitable and noncharitable interests in charitable lead (income) trusts must terminate at the same time before and after reformation. The same is generally true with respect to charitable and noncharitable interests under a charitable remainder trust instrument, with the exception that a noncharitable interest for a term of years in excess of 20 years may be reduced to 20 years.

(3) The changes are made effective as of the date of the decedent's death.[53]

---

[49] Code Sec. 2055(e)(3).

[50] Code Sec. 2055(e)(3)(D).

[51] Code Sec. 2055(e)(3)(B).

[52] Senate Finance Committee Report to the Tax Reform Act of 1984 (P.L. 98-369).

[53] Code Sec. 2055(e)(3)(B).

• *Reformable Interest*

A qualified reformation cannot occur unless the interest is "reformable." In order to be considered reformable, the following requirements must be met:

(1) The interest must be of a type that would have qualified for a charitable deduction except for the charitable split-interest rules of Code Sec. 2055(e)(2).

(2) The interest of the beneficiaries, before the remainder interest vests in possession, must be expressed as either a specified dollar amount or as a fixed percentage of the fair market value of the property, taking into account the rules of Code Sec. 664(d)(3).[54]

Requirement (2) does not apply if a judicial proceeding is commenced to change the remainder interest into a qualified interest no later than 90 days after:

(1) the last day for filing the estate tax return, including extensions; or

(2) if no estate tax return is required to be filed, the last date, including extensions, for the filing of the income tax return for the first tax year the trust is required to file a return.[55]

In deciding whether an action was commenced within the required 90-day period, the actual date that the judicial proceeding was instituted governs. Thus, a judicial proceeding instituted after this deadline will not be deemed to have a retroactive effect based on probate documents filed within the 90-day period that were not in the nature of pleadings sufficient to begin an action to amend the trust.[56]

The requirement that the interests of the beneficiaries be expressed as a specified dollar amount or fixed percentage of the property's fair market value does not apply to interests passing under wills or trusts executed before 1979, or for interests for which a timely judicial reformation proceeding is instituted.[57]

Application to income and gift taxes. Rules similar to the estate tax deduction rules apply to the determination of the allowance of income and gift tax charitable deductions for split-interest contributions.

Statute of limitations on assessment. The period for assessment of any tax deficiency arising out of the application of the rules for reformation of charitable split-interest contributions will not expire before one year after the date on which the IRS is notified that the reformation has occurred.[58]

Death of noncharitable income beneficiary. If, before the due date (including extensions) for filing the estate tax return on which the charitable split-interest contribution is claimed, the reformable interest becomes a wholly charitable interest because of the death of all noncharitable income beneficiaries, or because of a termination or distribution of a trust in accordance with the terms of the trust instrument, a deduction for such interest is to be allowed as if it met the requirements of a split-interest trust on the date of the decedent's death.[59]

Remainder interest in personal residence or farm. A charitable (as well as a gift) deduction is available for the transfer of a remainder interest, not in trust, in a personal residence and farm.[60] The value of the deduction is the fair market

---

[54] Code Sec. 2055(e)(3)(C).

[55] Code Sec. 2055(e)(3)(C)(iii).

[56] *Z. Hall*, 93 TC 745, CCH Dec. 46,219.

[57] Code Sec. 2055(e)(3)(C)(iv).

[58] Code Sec. 2055(e)(3)(G).

[59] Code Sec. 2055(e)(3)(F).

[60] Reg. § 20.2055-2(e)(2).

value of the remainder interest, determined by the actuarial tables at the date of transfer, the date of death or the alternative valuation date.[61]

Contingency provisions in charitable remainder trusts. Generally, noncharitable interests in a charitable remainder trust (whether a charitable remainder annuity trust or a charitable remainder unitrust) must terminate at the end of specified lives in being or a term of years not to exceed 20 years. However, where a trust complies with the termination rule (i.e., the noncharitable interest must terminate at the end of lives in being or a term of years not exceeding 20 years), a contingency may be placed in the trust providing that the noncharitable interest is to terminate, and the charitable interest is to be accelerated, upon the happening of an event at an earlier time (e.g., the noncharitable interest may terminate on the remarriage of an individual). In such a case, the value of the charitable remainder interest is determined without regard to the contingency.[62]

• ***Effective Dates***

Code Sec. 2055(e)(3) applies to all reformations occurring after 1981.

• ***Reformation to Comply with the Minimum Charitable Benefit Rule***

A trust that fails to qualify as a charitable remainder trust by reason of the failure to satisfy the 10-percent minimum charitable benefit requirement (see ¶1122) may be reformed to increase the value of the remainder interest. Generally, the remainder interest can be increased by reducing the payout percentage and/or shortening the trust term. If not reformed, the trust may be declared void as of its inception.[63]

¶1126 Valuation of Trust Interests

An estate can claim estate tax charitable deductions for the present value of income and remainder interests in property that is bequeathed or which otherwise passes to qualifying charities. A deduction is allowed for the fair market value of a partial interest at the appropriate valuation date for transfers not exclusively for charitable purposes. The fair market value of an annuity, life estate, term for years, remainder, reversion, or unitrust interest is its present value.

For transfers not exclusively for charitable purposes (involving guaranteed annuity trusts, unitrusts, and pooled income funds—transfers (1), (5), and (6) of ¶1120 above) made by decedents dying after July 31, 1969, the rules for computing the present values of such interests for deduction purposes are as follows:

(1) The present value of a remainder interest in a charitable remainder annuity trust is determined under income tax Reg. § 1.664-2(c).

(2) The present value of a remainder interest in a charitable remainder unitrust is determined under income tax Reg. § 1.664-4 or Reg. § 1.664-4A, depending on the valuation date.

(3) The present value of a remainder interest in a pooled income fund is determined under income tax Reg. § 1.642(c)-6.

(4) The present value of a guaranteed annuity interest is determined under either estate tax Reg. § 20.2031-7 or estate tax Reg. § 20.2031-7A, depending on the date of the decedent's death (see ¶530), unless the

---

[61] Code Sec. 7520.

[62] Code Sec. 664(f).

[63] Code Sec. 2055(e)(3)(J).

annuity is issued by a company regularly engaged in the sale of annuities, in which case Reg. § 20.2031-8 should be used.

(5) The present value of a unitrust interest is determined by subtracting the present value of all interests in the transferred property other than the unitrust interest from the fair market value of the transferred property.[64]

The above regulations are applicable only where the interest is dependent upon one life.

With respect to pooled income funds in existence for less than three tax years preceding the tax year in which the transfer is made, Reg. § 1.642(c)-6(e)(3) provides the method for determining the rate of return for purposes of valuing a remainder interest in the fund.

For purposes of valuing charitable remainder interests in annuity trusts, unitrusts, and pooled income funds that are dependent upon the death of the survivor of more than one life, the IRS has issued several publications providing special factors and tables (see ¶ 530 for a discussion of these publications).

Any claim for deduction in any return (income, estate, or gift tax) for the value of a remainder interest in a trust or pooled income fund must be supported by a statement showing the computation of the present value of such interest. The IRS, on request, may furnish a factor that can be used to value such interests.

¶ 1127 Contingent Gifts

If, as of the date of a decedent's death, a transfer to a charitable organization is dependent upon performance of an act or happening of an event (whether a condition precedent or subsequent) before it takes effect (or is divested), no charitable deduction will be allowed unless the possibility that the charity may not receive the property is so remote as to be considered negligible. The requirement of an "effective transfer"[65] makes it necessary that enjoyment of the benefits of the transfer accrue in fact to the charity, so it may be immaterial that the value of the contingent interest could have been computed actuarially.

Likewise, if a bequest to charities is wholly contingent, so that no present value is determinable from known data, no deduction can be taken.[66] However, the fact that the remainder to charity is conditioned on the life tenant's dying without issue does not make the remainder contingent if the possibility of issue is extinct,[67] as, for example, where the life tenant has reached an advanced age.[68]

¶ 1128 Transfers Out of Which Death Taxes Must Be Paid

Deductions for charitable bequests are limited to the amount actually received by the charitable organization.[69] For example, where taxes are to be paid from the residuary estate and the residuary estate is left to charity, the deduction for charitable bequests must be reduced by the amount of federal estate tax payable out of the residuary estate.[70] This computation may be accomplished algebraically or by application of the principle of the converging series, which is in general use by accountants in the determination of interdependent factors.

---

[64] Reg. § 20.2055-2(f)(2)(v).

[65] Reg. § 20.2055-2(b).

[66] *A.L. Humes, Exr. (D.R. Gates Est.)*, SCt, 1 USTC ¶ 298, 276 US 487.

[67] *Provident Trust Co., Exr. (G.T. Roberts Est.)*, SCt, 4 USTC ¶ 1229, 291 US 272.

[68] *City Bank Farmers Trust Co., Exr. (T.B. Allen Est.)*, CA-2, 35-1 USTC ¶ 9079, 74 F2d 692.

[69] Code Sec. 2055(c).

[70] Reg. § 20.2055-3.

However, whether administration expenses *allocable to the income of an estate* reduce the amount of a marital or charitable deduction has been a matter of controversy among the U.S. Courts of Appeals for the Federal, Sixth and Eleventh Circuits and the Tax Court. The Federal and Sixth Circuits have held that administration expenses reduce the marital deduction regardless of whether the payment is allocated to income or to principal.[71] But the Tax Court and the Eleventh Circuit had declined to follow the reasoning of those appellate courts and had held that administration expenses allocable to the *income* of an estate do not reduce a decedent's estate's marital or charitable deduction provided that the decedent's will and applicable state law allow for the payment of administration expenses out of the estate's income.[72] Settling the split among the circuits, the U.S. Supreme Court held in *O. Hubert Est.*[73] that the executor's or trustee's discretion, under the governing instrument and local law, to pay administration expenses out of principal or income reduces the marital deduction only if such discretion constitutes a material limitation on the spouse's right to receive income. In this case, the Court found that such discretion did not constitute a material limitation.

In order to avoid the difficulty, both for taxpayers and the IRS to determine what constitutes a "material limitation" on a charity's right to income from a charitable bequest, the IRS amended Reg. §20.2055-3, effective for estates of decedents dying on or after December 3, 1999.[74] The amended regulation eliminates the materiality requirement. Instead, the regulations bifurcate estate expenses into estate transmission expenses and estate management expenses. Estate transmission expenses, but not estate management expenses, reduce the value of property for charitable deduction purposes. Estate transmission expenses are those expenses that would not have been incurred but for the decedent's death. Estate transmission expenses include any administration expense that is not a management expense. Management expenses are expenses that would be incurred in investing, maintaining, and preserving the estate property. However, the allowable amount of the charitable deduction is reduced by the amount of these management expenses if they are deducted as administration expenses on the estate tax return.

With respect to interest accruing on obligations payable from residuary principal or income, the IRS has ruled that it will not reduce the value of a residuary charitable bequest for purposes of determining the charitable deduction.[75] In light of this ruling and the results of several court decisions, the IRS revoked a prior ruling that held that the value of a decedent's bequest of his residuary estate to charity was reduced by an estimated amount of interest on deferred estate taxes because the interest was payable from the residue.[76]

---

[71] *G. Street Est.*, CA-6, 92-2 USTC ¶60,112, 974 F2d 723, rev'g in part TC, 56 TCM 774, CCH Dec. 45,201(M), TC Memo. 1988-553; *J. Burke*, CA-FC, 93-2 USTC ¶60,146, 994 F2d 1576.

[72] *O. Hubert Est.*, 95-2 USTC ¶60,209, aff'g TC, 101 TC 314, CCH Dec. 49,342, cert. granted; *F. Allen Est.*, 101 TC 351, CCH Dec. 49,346.

[73] *O. Hubert Est.*, SCt, 97-1 USTC ¶60,261.

[74] T.D. 8846, amending Reg. §20.2055-3, filed with the *Federal Register* on Dec. 2, 1999.

[75] Rev. Rul. 93-48, 1993-2 CB 270, modifying Rev. Rul. 73-98, 1973-1 CB 407.

[76] Rev. Rul. 93-48, 1993-2 CB 270, revoking Rev. Rul. 82-6, 1982-1 CB 137; *W. Richardson Est.*, 89 TC 1193, CCH Dec. 44,388; *G. Street Est.*, CA-6, 92-2 USTC ¶60,112, 974 F2d 723; *R. Whittle Est.*, CA-7, 93-1 USTC ¶60,141, 994 F2d 379.

The amount of tax actually due and paid, rather than the present (date of death) value of such tax, is the proper amount of tax to be subtracted from the charitable interest.[77]

The deduction for charitable transfers allowed for federal estate tax purposes does not always correspond with state and foreign death tax exemptions or deductions for such transfers. In instances where a transfer is deductible under federal law, but taxable under state or foreign law, the federal estate tax law authorizes a deduction for the state or foreign death taxes paid if the executor elects to take it.

In some instances, where the charitable transfer is reduced on account of state taxes and where the charitable transfer is a remainder interest, the complicated problem of interdependent taxes and deductions arises. This problem is identical in principle to the marital deduction situation at ¶1075. As in the case of the marital deduction, the problem can be avoided by providing for the payment of taxes out of other funds in the estate.

IRS Publication 904, "Interrelated Computations for Estate and Gift Taxes" (Rev. May 1985), contains examples for computing the charitable and marital deductions when these deductions are interrelated with the federal estate tax. Although no longer available from the IRS, IRS Publication 904 is reproduced in the CCH FEDERAL ESTATE AND GIFT TAX REPORTER.

Practitioners who would like to avoid the time-consuming and tedious calculations involved with using the mathematical formulae set out in Publication 904 should consider using CCH's *ProSystem fx® Tax*, which contains computer programs for calculating interrelated marital and charitable deductions.

¶1140 Execution of Schedule

Deductions authorized for charitable, public, and similar gifts and bequests should be claimed on Form 706 (United States Estate (and Generation-Skipping Transfer) Tax Return) (Rev. Aug. 2004), Schedule O (Charitable, Public, and Similar Gifts and Bequests). This schedule must be filed if the estate claims a charitable deduction on its Form 706. If the transfer was made by will, a certified copy of the order admitting the will to probate, in addition to the copy of the will, should be submitted with the return. If the transfer was made by any other written instrument, a copy of the instrument should be submitted with the return. If the instrument is of record, the copy should be certified. If not of record, the copy should be verified.[78]

If the transfer was made by will, the executor must answer questions 1a and 1b at the top of Schedule O, which deal with whether any action has been instituted to interpret or to contest the will or any provision affecting the charitable deduction and whether, according to his or her information and belief, any such action is designed or contemplated. If the executor answers "yes" to either of these questions, full details of the action or contemplated action must be submitted with the return.

If a charitable deduction is claimed for the value of a split interest in property (see ¶1121), a copy of the computation of the deduction must be attached to the return. The computation must include the dates of birth of the life tenants or annuitants whose lives may affect the value of the interest passing to

---

[77] *J.G. Buchanan, Exr. (M.L. Gillespie Est.)*, CA-3, in unpublished decision aff'g DC Pa., 74-2 USTC ¶13,008.

[78] Reg. §20.2055-1(c).

charity, and, in the case of a pooled income fund, the applicable yearly rate of return. If property passes to a charitable beneficiary as a result of a "qualified disclaimer" (see ¶1102), the executor must answer "yes" to question 2, and a copy of the written disclaimer must be attached to Schedule O.

¶ 1141 Valuation of Residuary Transfer

If a claim is made for a deduction of the value of the residue of the estate or a portion of the residue passing to charity under the decedent's will, a copy of the computation determining the value should be submitted.[79] The computation, or supporting documents, should include:

(1) a statement showing the values of all specific and general legacies or devises, indicating whether they are for charitable or noncharitable uses (Appropriate reference must be made to the applicable paragraph or section of the decedent's will or codicil. In any case where legacies are made to each member of a class, only the number in each class and the aggregate value of property received by them need be furnished.);

(2) the dates of birth of all life tenants or annuitants, the duration of whose lives may affect the value of the interest passing to charity under the decedent's will;

(3) a statement showing the value of all property that is included in the decedent's gross estate but does not pass under the will (This includes jointly owned property that passed to the survivor on decedent's death and insurance payable to specific beneficiaries.); and

(4) any other information that may appear material, such as that relating to any claim, not arising under the will, to any part of the estate. This would include a spouse's claim to dower, curtesy, or similar rights.

¶ 1142 Alternate Valuation

Even if the alternate valuation (see ¶105) is used, any charitable transfer deductible on Schedule O (Charitable, Public, and Similar Gifts and Bequests) of Form 706 (United States Estate (and Generation-Skipping Transfer) Tax Return) should be valued as of the date of the decedent's death. However, adjustment must be made for any difference in the value of the property six months after the decedent's death, or at the date of its sale or exchange within this period. No adjustment may take into account any difference in value due to mere lapse of time or to the occurrence or nonoccurrence of a contingency.[80] If a decedent gives a percentage of his or her adjusted gross estate to charity, and his or her executor elects to use the alternate valuation method, the amount of the allowable charitable deduction is determined by using the value of the decedent's adjusted gross estate as of the alternate valuation date.[81]

---

[79] Instructions for Form 706 (Rev. Aug. 2004), p. 19.

[80] Reg. §20.2032-1(g).

[81] Rev. Rul. 70-527, 1970-2 CB 193.

Chapter 23
QUALIFIED FAMILY-OWNED BUSINESS INTEREST DEDUCTION

¶ 1150 Qualified Family-Owned Business Interest Deduction

In order to alleviate the impact of the estate tax on family-owned businesses, the Taxpayer Relief Act of 1997 (P.L. 105-34) created an exclusion for a portion of qualified family-owned business interests (QFOBIs) from a decedent's gross estate. However, because it was not clear whether Code Sec. 2033A excluded property or value from the gross estate, the Internal Revenue Service Restructuring and Reform Act of 1998 (P.L. 105-206) converted the exclusion into a deduction and redesignated Code Sec. 2033A as Code Sec. 2057.[1] Effective for estates of decedents dying after December 31, 1997, and before 2004, the qualified family-owned business interest deduction, in combination with the applicable exclusion amount (unified credit), shields up to $1.3 million of qualified family-owned business interests from the estate tax.

• ***Repeal of the QFOBI Deduction***

The Economic Growth and Tax Relief Reconciliation Act of 2001 (P.L. 107-16) (2001 Act) repeals the QFOBI deduction, effective for the estates of decedents dying after December 31, 2003. The discussion in this chapter of the QFOBI deduction is retained for use with respect to open estates.

Sunset provision. In order to comply with the Congressional Budget Act of 1974, the 2001 Act provides that all provisions of, and amendments made by, the 2001 Act will not apply to estates of decedents dying, gifts made, or generation-skipping transfers, after December 31, 2010. Unless Congress acts affirmatively in the interim, the Internal Revenue Code will, thereafter, be applied and administered as if these provisions had not been enacted.

If an estate qualifies and elects to take the deduction, up to $675,000 of the adjusted value of qualified interests may be deducted from the value of a decedent's gross estate. If the maximum $675,000 deduction is elected, the applicable exclusion amount (unified credit) is limited to $625,000, regardless of the date of death. In order to coordinate the deduction with the unified credit, if less than the maximum deduction is elected, the $625,000 applicable exclusion amount is increased by the excess of $675,000 over the amount of the deduction allowed. However, the applicable exclusion amount may not be increased above the amount that would apply to the estate if no QFOBI deduction had been elected.

> ***Example (1):*** Ruth Roth dies in 2001 when the applicable exclusion amount is $675,000. Roth's estate includes $600,000 of qualified family-owned business interests and her estate qualifies for and elects a $600,000

---

[1] Code Sec. 2057.

deduction. Roth's estate will be entitled to a deduction of $600,000 and an applicable exclusion amount of $675,000. The estate is not entitled to a $700,000 applicable exclusion amount ($625,000 + ($675,000 – $600,000)) because the applicable exclusion amount cannot exceed the amount that would apply to the estate without regard to the deduction.

Example (2): Adam Brook dies in 2003 when the applicable exclusion amount (under the 2001 Act) is $1 million. Brook's estate includes $1 million of qualified family-owned business interests and his estate qualifies for and elects to take a $600,000 deduction. Brook's estate will be entitled to a Code Sec. 2057 deduction of $600,000 and an applicable exclusion amount of $700,000 ($625,000 + ($675,000 – $600,000)).

In general, to qualify for the deduction the aggregate value of the decedent's qualified family-owned business interests that are passed to qualified heirs must exceed 50 percent of the decedent's adjusted gross estate. In addition, the decedent must be a U.S. citizen or resident at the time of death, the executor must elect to make the deduction and file a recapture agreement signed by each person in being having an interest in the property, and certain other requirements must be met. The deduction is in addition to the special use valuation provisions (see ¶280) and the provisions for the installment payment of estate taxes attributable to a closely held business (see ¶1672).

¶1155 Ownership Requirement

A qualified family-owned business is any interest in a trade or business, regardless of form, with a principal place of business in the United States, the ownership of which is held at least (1) 50 percent by one family, (2) 70 percent by two families, or (3) 90 percent by three families. If held by more than one family, the decedent's family must own at least 30 percent of the trade or business.[2] A decedent is treated as engaged in a trade or business if any member of the decedent's family is engaged in the trade or business.

Members of the individual's family include (1) the individual's spouse, (2) the individual's ancestors, (3) lineal descendants of the individual, of the individual's spouse, or of the individual's parents, and (4) the spouses of any such lineal descendants.[3]

In the case of a corporation, the ownership test is met if the decedent and family members own the requisite percentage of both the total combined voting power of all classes of voting stock and the total value of all shares of all classes of stock. In the case of a partnership, the decedent and family members are required to own the requisite percentage of the capital interest in the partnership. However, the Senate Committee Report to the Taxpayer Relief Act of 1997 (P.L. 105-34) indicates that an ownership in the profits interest of a partnership is also required. Special look-through rules apply in the case of a trade or business that owns an interest in another trade or business. Whether owned directly or indirectly, each trade or business owned by the decedent and members of the family must be separately tested to determine whether the trade or business meets the requirements of a qualified family-owned business.[4]

An interest in a trade or business does not qualify if the business's or a related entity's stock or securities were publicly traded at any time within three

[2] Code Sec. 2057(e)(1).

[3] Code Sec. 2057(e)(2) and Code. Sec. 2057(i)(2).

[4] Code Sec. 2057(e)(3).

years of the decedent's death. In addition, the interest does not qualify if more than 35 percent of the adjusted ordinary gross income from the business for the year of the decedent's death was personal holding company income. The second restriction does not apply to banks and domestic building and loan associations.

The IRS has ruled that ownership of promissory notes in a family-owned company did not constitute an "interest in an entity" for purposes of the QFOBI rules. This was because the holder of a promissory note, such as the decedent, was a creditor of the entity and did not have an "interest in" the entity, as the term is used in Code Sec. 2057(e)(1)(B).[5]

¶ 1160 Valuation

The value of a trade or business qualifying as a qualified family-owned business interest (QFOBI) is reduced to the extent that the business holds certain passive assets or cash and marketable securities in excess of reasonably expected day-to-day working capital needed for the trade or business. In addition, accumulations for capital acquisitions are not considered "working capital." Further, certain other passive assets are not considered in valuing QFOBIs.

The following assets are considered passive assets and are not included in the value of a qualified family-owned business: (1) assets that produce dividends, interest, rents, royalties, annuities, and Code Sec. 543(a) personal holding company income; (2) assets that are interests in a trust, partnership, or real estate mortgage investment conduit (as described in Code Sec. 954(c)(1)(B)(ii)); (3) assets that produce no income (as described in Code Sec. 954(c)(1)(B)(iii)); (4) assets that give rise to income from commodities transactions or foreign currency gains (as described in Code Sec. 954(c)(1)(C) and Code Sec. 954(c)(1)(D)); (5) assets that produce income equivalent to interest (as described in Code Sec. 954(c)(1)(E)); and (6) assets that produce income from notional principal contracts or payments in lieu of dividends (as described in Code Sec. 954(c)(1)(F) and Code Sec. 954(c)(1)(G)). However, with respect to regular dealers in property, such property is not considered to produce passive income and, therefore, is not considered a passive asset.[6]

¶ 1165 Qualifying Estates

In order to qualify for the qualified family-owned business interest (QFOBI) deduction, the decedent must have been a U.S. citizen or resident at the time of death and the aggregate value of the decedent's qualified family-owned business interests passing to qualified heirs must exceed 50 percent of the decedent's adjusted gross estate. For this purpose, qualified heirs include any individuals who were actively employed by the trade or business for at least 10 years prior to the date of the decedent's death, as well as members of the decedent's family.

Property passing to a trust may be treated as having passed to a qualified heir if all of the beneficiaries of the trust are qualified heirs.[7] The decedent's QFOBIs passing to qualified heirs include lifetime gifts of such interests made by the decedent to members of the decedent's family to the extent that those interests are held by family members (other than the decedent's spouse) between the date of the gift and the date of the decedent's death.

---

[5] IRS Technical Advice Memorandum 2004100002, November 6, 2003.

[6] Code Sec. 2057(e)(2).

[7] Code Sec. 2057(i)(3).

• *Fifty-Percent Liquidity Test*

Generally, a 50-percent liquidity test is used to determine if this requirement is met. Under this test, the total of all transfers of QFOBIs made by the decedent to qualified heirs at the time of the decedent's death, plus certain lifetime gifts to family members, is compared to the decedent's adjusted gross estate. If the decedent held qualified family-owned business interests in more than one trade or business, all such interests are aggregated for purposes of applying the 50-percent liquidity test.

To determine whether the decedent's qualifying interests comprise more than 50 percent of the decedent's adjusted gross estate, a percentage calculation using the following numerator and denominator is used.

The numerator is determined by aggregating the value of all qualified family-owned business interests that are includible in the decedent's gross estate and that are passed from the decedent to a qualified heir, plus any lifetime transfers of such interests by the decedent to members of the decedent's family (other than the decedent's spouse), provided such interests have been continuously held by members of the family and were not otherwise includible in the decedent's gross estate. For this purpose, the qualified interests transferred to members of the family during the decedent's lifetime are valued as of the date of the transfer. This amount is then reduced by all the indebtedness of the estate, except for the following: (1) indebtedness on a qualified residence of the decedent, i.e., a residence that qualifies for the mortgage interest deduction under Code Sec. 163(h)(3); (2) indebtedness incurred to pay the educational or medical expenses of the decedent, the decedent's spouse, or the decedent's dependents; and (3) other indebtedness up to $10,000.[8]

The denominator is equal to the decedent's gross estate, reduced by any indebtedness of the estate and increased by the amount of the following transfers, to the extent not already included in the gross estate: (1) lifetime transfers of qualified business interests that were made by the decedent to members of the decedent's family (other than the decedent's spouse), provided such interests have been continuously held by members of the family, plus (2) transfers, other than *de minimis* transfers, from the decedent to the decedent's spouse that were made within 10 years of the date of the decedent's death, plus (3) any other transfers made by the decedent within three years of death, except nontaxable transfers made to members of the decedent's family.[9]

Code Sec. 303 stock redemptions. The IRS has ruled that a distribution in redemption of stock does not affect an estate's eligibility to make a QFOBI election. Under the facts of Rev. Rul. 2003-61,[10] a decedent owned shares of stock in a corporation with an adjusted value of $3 million under Code Sec. 2057(d). The value of the decedent's adjusted gross estate was $5 million under Code Sec. 2057(c). The estate executor elected to treat all of the decedent's stock as a QFOBI, claiming the maximum allowable deduction of $675,000. In order to pay the decedent's estate tax liability, the executor caused the corporation to redeem one-third of the decedent's stock in a distribution that satisfied the requirements of Code Sec. 303 (stock redemptions to pay estate taxes).

The IRS applied rules similar to the rule in Code Sec. 6166(g)(1)(B) (certain distributions do not trigger an estate's loss of the ability to pay estate taxes in

---

[8] Code Sec. 2057(d).

[9] Code Sec. 2057(b), Code Sec. 2057(c), and Code Sec. 2057(d).

[10] Rev. Rul. 2003-6 1, IRB 2003-24, 1015.

installments) to evaluate the impact of a distribution in redemption of stock with respect to a QFOBI election. Taking guidance from the installment payment provisions of Code Sec. 6166, the IRS concluded that a distribution in redemption of stock to which Code Sec. 303 applied: (1) did not affect the initial determination of whether an estate was eligible to make the QFOBI election, and (2) did not constitute a disposition that triggered an additional estate tax with respect to the QFOBI (see ¶1175, "Recapture Tax"). Accordingly, the redemption of one-third of the decedent's stock under the facts of Rev. Rul. 2003-61 did not affect the estate's QFOBI election, even though the adjusted value of the QFOBI ($2 million) following the redemption no longer exceeded 50 percent of the decedent's adjusted gross estate ($5 million).

¶1170 Participation Requirements

The decedent, or members of the decedent's family, must have owned and materially participated in the trade or business for at least five of the eight years preceding the decedent's death in order to qualify for the qualified family-owned business interest deduction.[11] In addition, a qualified heir is subject to a recapture tax if the heir, or a member of the qualified heir's family, does not materially participate in the trade or business for at least five years of any eight-year period within 10 years following the decedent's death. The definition of "material participation" provided in Code Sec. 2032A and Reg. §20.2032A-3 pertaining to special use valuation applies. The principal factors to be considered include physical work and participation in management decisions. A qualified heir will not be treated as disposing of an interest in a trade or business by reason of ceasing to be engaged in a trade or business if any member of the qualified heir's family continues in the trade or business.[12] The material participation requirement will be met with respect to a qualified heir if the heir rents qualified property to a member of the qualified heir's family on a net cash basis, and that family member materially participates in the business.[13]

¶1175 Election

For the qualified family-owned business interest (QFOBI) deduction to apply, the executor must make a Code Sec. 2057 election and file a written agreement signed by each person in being having an interest in the property consenting to the application of the additional tax.[14] The election is made by filing Schedule T (Qualified Family-Owned Business Interest Deduction) of Form 706 (United States Estate (and Generation-Skipping Transfer) Tax Return) (Rev. Aug. 2003), attaching all required statements, and deducting the value of the QFOBIs on Form 706, page 3, part 5, Recapitulation, line 22. See the Appendix at ¶3160 for an example of a filled-in Schedule T. Because the QFOBI deduction has been repealed with respect to estates of decedents dying after December 31, 2003, Form 706 (Rev. Aug. 2003) is the last revision of the estate tax return that contains Schedule T.

• *Recapture Tax*

An additional tax is imposed if any of the following recapture events occurs within 10 years of the decedent's death and before the qualified heir's death: (1) the qualified heir ceases to meet the material participation requirements; (2) the qualified heir disposes of any portion of his or her interest in the family-owned

---

[11] Code Sec. 2057(b)(1)(D).

[12] Code Sec. 2057(f)(3).

[13] Code Sec. 2057(b)(1)(D).

[14] Code Sec. 2057(h).

business, other than by a disposition to a member of the qualified heir's family or through a conservation contribution under Code Sec. 170(h); (3) the principal place of business of the trade or business ceases to be located in the United States; or (4) the qualified heir loses U.S. citizenship.

The recapture tax may be avoided if a qualified heir loses U.S. citizenship, provided the trade or business assets are placed into a qualified trust meeting the requirement similar to that for a qualified domestic trust under Code Sec. 2056A(a) or certain other security arrangements are met. The recapture period may be extended up to two years if the qualified heir does not begin to use the property for a period of up to two years after a decedent's death.

The recapture tax is a personal liability of each qualified heir to the extent of the portion of the additional tax that is imposed with respect to his or her interest in the qualified family-owned business.[15]

> ***Example:*** John, Beth, and Sue Milton inherit equal qualified family-owned business interests from their father, and the estate elects special tax treatment. Only Sue continues to materially participate in the family business. Such participation by a family member causes all three children to meet the participation requirements. However, during the fourth year following the decedent's death, Sue ceases to materially participate in the business and neither John nor Beth participates. As a result, each of the three children would be personally liable for the portion of the recapture tax attributable to his or her interest.

A qualified heir uses Form 706-D (United States Additional Estate Tax Return Under Code Sec. 2057) (Rev. Oct. 2000), to report and pay the additional estate tax. Form 706-D is due within six months after the recapture event occurs. See the Appendix at ¶3210 for an example of a filled-in Form 706-D.

• ***Impact of the 2001 Act***

The Committee Reports to the Economic Growth and Tax Relief Reconciliation Act of 2001 (P.L. 107-16) (2001 Act) indicate that the recapture tax imposed under Code Sec. 2057(f) if property ceases to qualify for the QFOBI deduction will be retained after repeal of the QFOBI deduction in 2004 and the repeal of the estate tax generally (2010). The provision is retained so that estates that claimed the benefit of the deduction before repeal will be subject to recapture if a disqualifying event occurs following repeal.

• ***Amount of Additional Estate Tax***

The additional estate tax is based on when the recapture event occurs in relation to the decedent's death. If the recapture event occurs within the first six years of material participation, 100 percent of the reduction in estate tax attributable to the heir's interest plus interest is recaptured. Thereafter, the applicable percentage is 80 percent in the seventh year, 60 percent in the eighth year, 40 percent in the ninth year, and 20 percent in the 10th year.[16]

---

[15] Code Sec. 2057(f).

[16] Code Sec. 2057(f)(2)(B).

DETERMINATION AND PAYMENT OF TAX

Chapter 24

EXECUTOR ELECTIONS, DETERMINATION OF TAXABLE ESTATE

¶ 1190 Executor Elections

Various federal estate tax elections that are available to the executor of a decedent's estate are to be made by marking the appropriate boxes on part 3 of Form 706 (United States Estate (and Generation-Skipping Transfer) Tax Return) (Rev. Aug. 2004). (See the Appendix at ¶2930 for an example of a filled-in page 2, Form 706.)

Executor elections include elections with respect to:

(1) alternate valuation;

(2) special use valuation;

(3) installment payment of tax; and

(4) deferred payment of tax attributable to certain remainder and reversionary interests.

Qualified terminable interest property (QTIP) elections are deemed to have been made by the executor if (1) QTIP property is listed on Schedule M (Bequests, etc., to Surviving Spouse) of Form 706, and (2) the value of the property is entered as a deduction on Schedule M.

¶ 1195 General Information

Part 4 of Form 706 (United States Estate (and Generation-Skipping Transfer) Tax Return) contains general information questions relating to the decedent's death certificate, the decedent's business or occupation, the decedent's marital status, the surviving spouse's name, and the identity of individuals (other than the surviving spouse), trusts, or other estates receiving benefits (and the amount of such benefits) from the decedent's estate.

Part 4 on page 3 of Form 706 also contains questions concerning assets owned by the decedent during his or her life, such as whether the decedent received any qualified terminable interest property, owned any life insurance, possessed any retained powers, held an interest in a partnership or closely held business, etc. The purpose of this section is to alert the executor and the IRS to any assets that should be reported on the estate tax return or to remind the executor of possible elections to which the estate might be entitled. (See the Appendix at ¶2930 for examples of filled-in parts 3 and 4 of Form 706.)

¶ 1200 Recapitulation

The Recapitulation, located in part 5 on page 3 of Form 706 (United States Estate (and Generation-Skipping Transfer) Tax Return), brings together in one place the information reported in the schedules. This results in the determination of the size of the gross estate and the total allowable deductions.

With regard to the gross estate, part 5 lists the value of the estate's interest in different assets, by way of the following Form 706 schedules: Schedule A (Real Estate); Schedule B (Stocks and Bonds); Schedule C (Mortgages, Notes, and Cash); Schedule D (Insurance on the Decedent's Life); Schedule E (Jointly Owned Property); Schedule F (Other Miscellaneous Property Not Reportable Under Any Other Schedule); Schedule G (Transfers During Decedent's Life); Schedule H (Powers of Appointment); and Schedule I (Annuities). The total of these assets is then entered on line 10 of part 5. The amount claimed for the qualified conservation easement exclusion on Schedule U (Qualified Conservation Easement Exclusion) is subtracted from the gross estate. The amount of the exclusion is shown on line 11 and the total gross estate less exclusion so determined is shown on line 12 of part 5 and on line 1 of part 2 (Tax Computation).

The second half of the Recapitulation lists deductions allowed the estate that are figured on the following Form 706 schedules: Schedule J (Funeral Expenses and Expenses Incurred in Administering Property Subject to Claims); Schedule K (Debts of the Decedent, and Mortgages and Liens); Schedule L (Net Losses During Administration and Expenses Incurred in Administering Property Not Subject to Claims); Schedule M (Bequests, etc., to Surviving Spouse); and Schedule O (Charitable, Public, and Similar Gifts and Bequests).

• *Limitation on Deductions from Schedules J and K*

The amounts from Schedule J and Schedule K can be limited for purposes of determining the allowable deduction. This is the case when the sum of the items listed on Schedules J and K is more than the value (at the time of the decedent's death) of the "property subject to claims," a term that the IRS interprets as synonymous with the decedent's probate estate. In such an instance, the amount deductible is limited to the value of the property that is subject to the claims. However, if the amount actually paid at the time the return is filed is more than the amount subject to the claims, the amount actually paid, rather than the amount subject to the claims, is deductible. One court has rejected the IRS position that the amount of a decedent's probate estate limits the amount that may be deducted as a claim against the estate (see ¶805).[1]

The sum of the deductions allowable from Schedules J and K and the deductions from Schedules L, M, and O is then entered on line 23 of part 5 and on line 2 of part 2.

A sample Recapitulation section of Form 706 (filled in with respect to the estate of James X. Diversey) is reproduced in the Appendix at ¶2940.

¶ 1250 Size of Taxable Estate

In the case of a U.S. resident or citizen, the computation of the taxable estate is accomplished on part 2, page 1 (Tax Computation), of Form 706 (United States Estate (and Generation-Skipping Transfer) Tax Return). Schedule B (Taxable Estate) of Form 706-NA (United States Estate (and Generation-Skipping Transfer) Tax Return, Estate of nonresident not a citizen of the United States) (Rev. Jan. 2003) is used for this purpose by the estates of nonresidents not citizens.

---

[1] *R. Snyder Est.*, FedCl, 99-2 USTC ¶60,357.

¶ 1255 Residents and Citizens

If the decedent was a resident or a citizen of the United States, the taxable estate is determined by subtracting from the total gross estate (line 1 of part 2, Form 706 (United States Estate (and Generation-Skipping Transfer) Tax Return)) the total allowable deductions (line 2). A filled-in part 2 of Form 706 appears in the Appendix at ¶2920.

¶ 1260 Nonresidents Not Citizens

As noted above, the taxable estate of a nonresident not a citizen of the United States is computed on Schedule B (Taxable Estate) of Form 706-NA (United States Estate (and Generation-Skipping Transfer) Tax Return, Estate of nonresident not a citizen of the United States) (Rev. Jan. 2003). The gross estate situated in the United States is entered on line 1, the gross estate situated outside of the United States is listed on line 2, and the sum of lines 1 and 2 is listed on line 3.[2] The value of the gross estate outside of the United States must be supported by proof (see ¶85).[3]

The total funeral expenses, administration expenses, debts of the decedent, mortgages and liens, and losses during the administration of the estate are entered on line 4. The allowable deduction for these expenses and debts is entered on line 5 and is computed by multiplying the total amounts of these expenses by the ratio of the gross estate within the United States (line 1) to the entire gross estate wherever situated (line 3).[4]

The amount of deductible charitable and marital transfers (line 6) is then added to the amount on line 5 to arrive at the total deductions shown on line 7. The total deductions are then subtracted from the gross estate within the United States (line 1) to arrive at the taxable estate shown on line 8.

Form 706-NA is used only for the estate of a nonresident not a citizen of the United States (see ¶1625). A filled-in Form 706-NA is reproduced in the Appendix at ¶3260.

---

2 Code Sec. 2103; Reg. §20.2103-1.

3 Reg. §20.6018-3(b).

4 Code Sec. 2106; Reg. §20.2106-1.

Chapter 25
CREDIT FOR TAX ON PRIOR TRANSFERS

¶ 1300 Effective Period of Credit

A credit is allowed against the estate tax for all or a part of the estate tax paid with respect to the transfer of property (including property passing as a result of the exercise or nonexercise of a power of appointment, see ¶ 650) to the present decedent by or from a person who died within 10 years before, or within two years after, the decedent.[1] The credit is computed on Schedule Q (Credit for Tax on Prior Transfers) of Form 706 (United States Estate (and Generation-Skipping Transfer) Tax Return) (Rev. Aug. 2004) after completing the Worksheet provided in the Instructions for Form 706. This schedule does not have to be filed if a credit is not claimed.

This credit can never be larger than it would have been if the present decedent had not received the property. Because the purpose of Code Sec. 2013 is to prevent diminution of an estate by successive taxes on the same property within a brief period, no credit is available for any gift tax that may have been paid with respect to the transfer of property to the present decedent. If the prior decedent (called the "transferor") predeceased the present decedent by more than two years, the credit allowable is reduced by 20 percent for each full two years by which the death of the transferor preceded the death of the decedent.[2] See ¶ 1325 for a table of the percentage allowable.

¶ 1310 General Requirements

The term "transferee" as used in Schedule Q (Credit for Tax on Prior Transfers) of Form 706 (United States Estate (and Generation-Skipping Transfer) Tax Return) for computing the credit for tax on prior transfers refers to the decedent for whose estate the return is filed.[3] It is not necessary that the property transferred be identified in or traced through the estate of the transferee. Nor is it necessary that the transferred property be in existence on the date of the transferee's death. It is sufficient for allowance of the credit that the transfer of the property was subject to federal estate tax in the estate of the transferor and that the specified period of time has not elapsed.[4] However, the credit cannot be waived, in whole or in part, and each transfer eligible for the credit must be taken into account in computing it.[5]

A credit may be allowed with respect to property received as the result of the exercise or nonexercise of a power of appointment. The credit is available if

---

[1] Code Sec. 2013; Reg. § 20.2013-1.

[2] Reg. § 20.2013-1.

[3] Instructions for Form 706 (Rev. Aug. 2004), p. 20.

[4] Reg. § 20.2013-1.

[5] Rev. Rul. 73-47, 1973-1 CB 397.

the property is included in the gross estate of the donee of the power. If the transferee was the transferor's surviving spouse, no credit is allowed with respect to property received to the extent that a marital deduction was allowed the transferor's estate in connection with such property.

¶ 1315 "Property" Defined

The term "property" includes, for purposes of the credit, any beneficial interest received by the transferee,[6] including Louisiana usufruct interests.[7] The transferee is considered to be the beneficial owner of the property over which the transferee received a general power of appointment. "Property" does not include interests to which the transferee received bare legal title only, such as that of a trustee. Nor does it include an interest in property over which the transferee received a power that is not a general power of appointment under Code Sec. 2041 (see ¶ 652).

In addition to property interests in which the transferee received complete ownership, credit may be allowed for tax on annuities, life estates, terms for years, remainder interests (whether contingent or vested), and other future interests to the extent that the transferee became the beneficial owner of the interest. The credit is not available when the decedent "purchases" the property, as by electing to take a life estate in a spouse's community property and thereby relinquishing property greater in value than the property the decedent obtained.[8]

Additionally, the U.S. Courts of Appeals for the Fourth and Fifth Circuits and the Tax Court have held that the credit is not available for a life estate where the transferor and the transferee die simultaneously in a common disaster.[9] The Tax Court also reached the same conclusion with respect to a Louisiana usufruct interest passing from a husband to a wife on their simultaneous deaths.[10]

¶ 1320 Maximum Amount of the Credit

The credit for tax on prior transfers is limited to the smaller of the following:

(1) the amount of the estate tax of the transferor's estate pertaining to the transfer; or

(2) the amount by which (a) an estate tax on the transferee's estate (after deducting the unified tax credit and the credits for state death taxes (prior to 2005), gift taxes, and foreign death taxes) determined without regard to the credit provided for in the schedule exceeds (b) an estate tax on the transferee's estate determined by excluding from the gross estate the net value of the transfer.[11]

Where credit for a particular foreign death tax may be taken under either the statute or a death duty convention and the credit actually is taken under the convention, credit for that foreign death tax may not be taken into consideration in computing estate tax (a) or estate tax (b).

---

[6] Reg. § 20.2013-5.

[7] Rev. Rul. 66-271, 1966-2 CB 430.

[8] *I.M. Sparling Est.*, CA-9, 77-1 USTC ¶ 13,194, 552 F2d 1340, rev'g and rem'g TC, 60 TC 330, CCH Dec. 31,996 (Acq.).

[9] *G.A. Lion Est.*, CA-4, 71-1 USTC ¶ 12,745, 438 F2d 56, aff'g TC, 52 TC 601, CCH Dec. 29,646, cert. denied; *A.P. Carter Est.*, CA-5, 91-1 USTC ¶ 60,054, rev'g DC La., 90-1 USTC ¶ 60,003, 929 F2d 699, cert. denied; *J. Harrison Est.*, 115 TC 161, CCH Dec. 54,015.

[10] *E.W. Marks, Jr., Est.*, 94 TC 720, CCH Dec. 46,594.

[11] Code Sec. 2013(c).

The amounts in (1) and (2) are computed on the Worksheet provided for Schedule Q (Credit for Tax on Prior Transfers) of Form 706 (United States Estate (and Generation-Skipping Transfer) Tax Return) (see ¶1345 and ¶3110).

¶1325 Percentage Reduction

If the transferor died within two years before or within two years after the transferee's death, the credit allowed for the tax on the prior transfer is 100 percent of the maximum amount allowable. If the transferor predeceased the transferee by more than two years, the credit allowed is a reduced percentage of the maximum amount allowable. The percentage allowable may be determined by using the following table:

Period of Time Exceeding	*Not Exceeding*	*Percent Allowable*
———	2 years	100
2 years	4 years	80
4 years	6 years	60
6 years	8 years	40
8 years	10 years	20
10 years	———	none

¶1330 Formula for Estimating Credit

The formula for estimating the credit is described below. For computation of the credit on the return, see ¶1345 and the Worksheet for Schedule Q (Credit for Tax on Prior Transfers) of Form 706 (United States Estate (and Generation-Skipping Transfer) Tax Return) and Schedule Q in the Appendix at ¶3110 and ¶3120, respectively.

(1) Determine the portion of the estate tax in the preceding estate for which the property transferred to the transferee was responsible. This portion is determined as follows:

$$\left[\ \text{Value of property transferred to decedent} \div \left\{ \text{Taxable estate of prior decedent} - \text{Death tax on prior estate} \right\} \right] \times \text{Estate tax on prior estate}$$

For purposes of the above formula, "Death tax" includes state, federal, and foreign taxes. "Estate tax" means the federal estate tax paid, increased by any credit allowed against such tax on account of gift taxes and any credit allowed on account of prior transfers to such prior decedent.

(2) Determine the estate tax (after deducting the unified credit and credits for state death taxes (prior to 2005), gift taxes, and foreign death taxes) on the transferee's estate first including and then excluding the value of the property. If the difference between the two taxes is less than the amount computed under (1), above, the credit cannot exceed such difference.

(3) If the property previously taxed was transferred to the transferee more than two years before his or her death, reduce the lesser of (1) or (2) by 20 percent for each full two years by which the original transfer preceded the transferee's death so that, if the prior transfer occurred more than 10 years before the death, no credit would be allowed.

¶ 1335 Valuation

The value of the property transferred for purposes of the formula noted above is the value at which the property was included in the transferor's estate.[12] The interest received must be able to be valued under recognized valuation principles in order to claim the credit.[13] This value must be reduced by (1) the amount of any lien or encumbrance thereon that was assumed by or imposed on the transferee at the time of acquisition, (2) the amount of death taxes that the transferee might have been required to pay, and (3) any marital deduction that might have been allowed on the transfer to the transferee.

In calculating the estate tax on the decedent's estate less the value of the transferred property, any charitable deduction is reduced in the proportion that the transferred property bears to the gross estate reduced by deductions allowed for expenses, debts, taxes, losses, and administration expenses under Code Sec. 2053 and Code Sec. 2054 (or Code Sec. 2106(a)(1) for estates of nonresident noncitizens).[14] Thus, the U.S. Court of Appeals for the Seventh Circuit held that in computing the credit for estate tax paid on prior transfers available to a deceased wife's estate, it was not necessary to reduce the value of the property she received from her predeceased husband by the amount of interest assessed and paid as a result of the husband's estate having elected to defer the payment of estate taxes under Code Sec. 6166.[15]

Property that, although difficult to value, is still capable of valuation will not result in loss of the credit. Thus, a trust provision requiring the termination of a transferee's life income interest in the event the transferee remarried did not result in the disallowance of the credit for the estate tax paid by the estate of the transferor-spouse. The IRS ruled that, because the possibility of termination of the life income interest on the remarriage of the transferee could be taken into account as a valuation factor in determining the value of the annuity includible in the transferee's gross estate, the credit for tax on prior transfers should be allowed.[16]

See ¶ 530 for further rules that apply when a life estate or remainder interest is part of the property transferred.

¶ 1340 Treatment of Additional Tax on Recapture of Special Use Valuation Realty

If the gross estate of the transferor included farm or other closely held business realty for which the special use valuation election was made (see ¶ 280), and if the additional estate tax is imposed on the transferor's estate within two years of his or her death because of the termination of a qualified use (see ¶ 284), the additional tax on recapture of the special use valuation benefits is treated as a federal estate tax payable with respect to the estate of the transferor.[17]

Further, the value of such property and the amount of the transferor's taxable estate are determined as if the special use valuation had not been elected.

---

[12] Code Sec. 2013(d); *S. Pollock Est.*, 77 TC 1296, CCH Dec. 38,503.

[13] Rev. Rul. 67-53, 1967-1 CB 265.

[14] Code Sec. 2013(c)(1).

[15] *R.M. Whittle Est.*, CA-7, 93-1 USTC ¶ 60,141, aff'g TC, 97 TC 362, CCH Dec. 47,623.

[16] Rev. Rul. 85-111, 1985-2 CB 196.

[17] Code Sec. 2013(f).

¶ 1345 Computation of the Credit

The credit for tax on prior transfers is computed in two steps. First, a Worksheet that is included in the Instructions for Form 706 (United States Estate (and Generation-Skipping Transfer) Tax Return) is used to determine the transferor's tax on prior transfers (part I of the Worksheet) and the transferee's tax on the prior transfers (part II of the Worksheet). Second, this information is transferred to Schedule Q (Credit for Tax on Prior Transfers) of Form 706, where the proper percentage (see ¶ 1325) is applied to the lesser of the transferor's tax or the transferee's tax on the transfers (see ¶ 1320) in order to compute the allowable credit.

Part I of the Worksheet and Schedule Q provide for computation of the credit in situations involving up to three transferors. If there are more than three transferors, more than one Worksheet and Schedule Q should be used and the totals for the appropriate lines should be combined.

Chapter 26

CREDITS FOR STATE DEATH TAXES AND FEDERAL GIFT TAXES

¶ 1370 State Death Tax Credit

A credit is allowed against the federal estate tax for any estate, inheritance, legacy, or succession taxes actually paid to any state of the United States or to the District of Columbia with respect to any property included in the decedent's gross estate.[1] This credit does not include, however, any taxes paid with respect to the estate of a person other than the decedent. The credit for state death taxes is available only to the extent that it does not exceed the estate's tax liability after reduction by the applicable credit amount.

• *Phaseout and Repeal of Credit*

The Economic Growth and Tax Relief Reconciliation Act of 2001 (P.L. 107-16) (2001 Act) gradually phases out the state death tax credit between 2002 and 2004, with the credit repealed for the estates of decedents dying after December 31, 2004. The credit is reduced by 25 percent for the estates of decedents dying in 2002, 50 percent for the estates of decedents dying in 2003 and 75 percent for the estates of decedents dying in 2004. Beginning in 2005, the state death tax credit is replaced by a deduction for state death taxes paid until the repeal of the estate tax in 2010 (see ¶1380).[2]

To illustrate the operation of the phase out, the maximum state death tax credit allowable for decedents dying in 2002 through 2004 under the 2001 Act (applicable to those adjusted taxable estates over $10,040,000) will be as follows: for 2002, $812,100 plus 12 percent of the excess over $10,040,000; for 2003, $541,400 plus eight percent of the excess over $10,040,000; and for 2004, $270,700 plus four percent of the excess over $10,040,000.

Sunset provision. In order to comply with the Congressional Budget Act of 1974, the 2001 Act provides that all provisions of, and amendments made by, the 2001 Act will not apply to estates of decedents dying, gifts made, or generation-skipping transfers, after December 31, 2010. Unless Congress acts affirmatively in the interim, the Internal Revenue Code will thereafter be applied and administered as if these provisions had not been enacted.

---

[1] Code Sec. 2011; Reg. §20.2011-1. *J.B. Owen Est.*, 104 TC 498, CCH Dec. 50,607 (estate denied credit for state inheritance taxes paid with respect to gifts made by a decedent within three years of his death in 1986, because the gifts were not includible in the decedent's gross estate under Code Sec. 2035(d)(1)).

[2] Code Sec. 2058, as added by P.L. 107-16.

• *Operation of State Death Tax Credit*

Where the credit is used, it is applied to the adjusted taxable estate. For purposes of computing the credit for death taxes, the taxable estate is reduced by $60,000 (the amount of the specific estate tax exemption allowed prior to 1977) to produce the adjusted taxable estate. The adjusted taxable estate against which the death tax credit is applied is determined before reduction for any gift tax credit allowable. A graduated rate table (see ¶2630) under which the maximum amount of credit allowable for state death taxes is determinable is prescribed. The credit is allowed only on that part of the adjusted taxable estate that exceeds $40,000. For decedents dying after December 31, 2001, and before January 1, 2005, once the amount is computed from the table, it must be reduced by the percentage applicable for the year of the decedent's death (see "Phaseout and Repeal of Credit", above).

Because the credit is allowed only as to the amount of state taxes actually paid, care must be taken in claiming the credit to supply the required information in full. This is particularly important where a deposit is made with the state as security for the payment of the state tax, and where discounts or refunds may be allowed by the state. This information includes data tending to show the actual amount of tax due the state that may be regarded as having been paid by a deposit, the amount of tax reasonably expected to be paid, and the identity of the property in respect to which the state tax has been paid or is to be paid.

An estate tax computation involving the state death tax credit is illustrated below:

Taxable estate	$1,800,000
Less: $60,000	60,000
Adjusted taxable estate (see below)	$1,740,000

In order to determine the "adjusted taxable estate," the taxable estate is reduced by $60,000. The state death tax credit is computed on the basis of the adjusted taxable estate, while the estate tax is computed on the basis of the taxable estate before credits:

Estate tax on taxable estate	$690,800
Less: Unified credit for 2004	555,800
Less: State death tax credit	21,300 *
Tax payable	$113,700

* Because the decedent died in 2004, the amount computed under the state death tax credit is reduced by 75 percent: $85,200 × (1 –.75) = $21,300.

Note that, in the above example, there are no taxable gifts to be considered. In addition, a state tax credit is available for any generation-skipping transfer taxes that are reported on an estate tax return. See ¶2457 for further details concerning this credit.

¶ 1372 Four-Year Period of Limitations

The credit for state death taxes must be claimed within four years after the filing of the federal estate tax return (Form 706, United States Estate (and Generation-Skipping Transfer) Tax Return (Rev. Aug. 2004). Exceptions apply where a petition has been filed with the Tax Court or where an extension of time for payment of tax or deficiency has been granted.[3]

[3] Code Sec. 2011(c).

An exception to the four-year period is made where the federal tax has been paid, a claim for credit or refund of federal estate taxes has been timely filed, and the claim is still pending on expiration of the four-year period. Under these circumstances a claim for credit of state death taxes paid can be made within 60 days after the final disposition of the claim for credit or refund of federal estate taxes.

Additionally, the IRS has ruled that an estate that elected to pay federal estate and state death taxes over a period longer than four years from the date of the filing of its estate tax return could claim a credit for state death taxes paid before the end of the extended time period elected for payment of the federal estate taxes.[4] According to the IRS, the estate would be permitted to recompute the total remaining estate tax liability whenever it submitted certification of payment of additional state death tax and, on payment in full of all state death and federal estate tax liabilities, a claim for a refund of any overpayment of estate tax could be made. However, in the event that an estate does not elect to extend the time for paying federal estate taxes, the IRS ruled that no extension of time within which to claim a refund based on the credit for state death taxes actually paid will be allowed, notwithstanding the fact that the state death taxes may be paid in installments over a period longer than four years.

¶ 1374 Taxes Paid to U.S. Possessions and Territories

Taxes paid to possessions of the United States do not qualify for the credit for state death taxes.[5] However, such taxes can qualify for the credit for foreign death taxes as described at ¶1401. Further, the credit is inapplicable for taxes paid to territories of the United States.[6]

¶ 1376 Charitable Transfers Taxed Under State Death Tax Law

Although most charitable, religious, educational, and public transfers are exempt from taxation at both the state and federal levels, some states provide for the taxation of property so transferred. Because such state taxes reduce the amount of the charitable deduction for purposes of the federal estate tax, the gross estate of a decedent would be increased to the extent of the state death tax, and, consequently, the federal estate tax would be increased.

To remedy this situation, effective for estates of decedents dying before January 1, 2005, a deduction is allowed for such state death taxes.[7] The deducted taxes, however, may not be included in those taxes on which a credit is determined. The credit, in such cases, may not exceed the lesser of:

(1) the amount of state death taxes paid, other than those on charitable transfers deductible under Code Sec. 2053(d);

(2) the amount of maximum credit for a taxable estate, determined after deducting the death taxes under Code Sec. 2053(d); or

(3) that proportion of the amount of credit for a taxable estate, determined without regard to the deduction for state death taxes, as the amount of the taxes less those for which a deduction is allowed bears to the total amount of state taxes paid.[8]

---

[4] Rev. Rul. 86-38, 1986-1 CB 296.

[5] Code Sec. 2011(a).

[6] Code Sec. 2011(a).

[7] Code Sec. 2053(d).

[8] Reg. § 20.2011-2.

¶ 1380 Deduction for State Death Taxes (Post-2004)

The Economic Growth and Tax Relief Reconciliation Act of 2001 (P.L. 107-16) (2001 Act) phases out the Code Sec. 2011 state death tax credit between 2002 and 2004 and repeals the credit for the estates of decedents dying after December 31, 2004 (see the discussion at ¶1370). Beginning in 2005, the credit is replaced by a deduction.[9] Accordingly, for the estates of decedents dying after December 31, 2004, the value of a decedent's taxable estate will be determined by deducting from the gross estate the amount of any estate, inheritance, legacy, or succession taxes actually paid to any state or the District of Columbia with respect to property included in the decedent's gross estate.

Sunset provision. In order to comply with the Congressional Budget Act of 1974, the 2001 Act provides that all provisions of, and amendments made by, the 2001 Act will not apply to estates of decedents dying, gifts made, or generation-skipping transfers, after December 31, 2010. Unless Congress acts affirmatively in the interim, the Internal Revenue Code will thereafter be applied and administered as if these provisions had not been enacted.

A limitations period is imposed under which a deduction is allowed only for those state death taxes paid and for which a deduction is claimed before the *later of*:

(1) four years after filing the estate tax return; or

(2) in a case where a timely petition for redetermination has been filed with the Tax Court, 60 days after the Tax Court decision becomes final; or

(3) when an extension of time has been granted for payment of estate tax or of a deficiency, the date the extension expires; or

(4) if a timely refund claim has been filed, then the *latest of the expiration of* (a) 60 days from the mailing of a notice to the taxpayer of a disallowance of the refund claim, (b) 60 days after a court decision on the merits of the claim becomes final, or (c) two years after a notice of waiver of disallowance is filed under Code Sec. 6532(a)(3).

However, a refund based on the deduction may be made if the refund claim is filed within the above-defined period. Any refunds made will be without interest.[10]

¶ 1382 Credit for Gift Taxes on Pre-1977 Gifts

A credit is allowed for gift taxes paid on pre-1977 gifts includible in the donor's gross estate under any one of the estate tax provisions that make prior gifts includible in the estate of the donor.[11] These provisions include (1) Code Sec. 2036, which requires the inclusion of transfers in which the transferor retains a life interest (see ¶570), (2) Code Sec. 2037, which requires the inclusion of certain retained reversionary interests (see ¶565), and (3) Code Sec. 2038, which requires the inclusion of revocable transfers (see ¶585).

The credit is allowable, even though the gift tax is paid after the decedent's death and the amount of the gift tax is deducted from the gross estate as a debt of the decedent.[12] The credit is allowed only when the gift tax has been paid on the transfer of nonprobate assets and double taxation would result.

---

[9] Code Sec. 2058, as added by P.L. 107-16.

[10] Code Sec. 2058(b), as added by P.L. 107-16.

[11] Code Sec. 2012; Reg. § 20.2012-1.

[12] Reg. § 20.2012-1(a).

• ***Limitation***

The credit is limited to the lesser of:

(1) the gift tax paid on the gift that is included in the gross estate; or

(2) the amount of estate tax attributable to the inclusion of the gift in the decedent's gross estate. This second limitation is computed as follows:[13]

$$\frac{\text{Gross estate tax, less credit for state death taxes and the unified credit}}{\text{The value of the gross estate, less all marital and charitable deductions allowable}} \times \text{The value of the gift (at the time of the gift or at time of death, whichever is lower)}$$

Form 4808 (Computation of Credit for Gift Tax) can be used to compute the credit for tax paid on pre-1977 gifts. The completed Form 4808 (or other attachment showing the computation of the credit), as well as copies of all Forms 709 evidencing payment of gift tax for pre-1977 gifts, should be attached to the transferor's Form 706 (United States Estate (and Generation-Skipping Transfer) Tax Return).

The computation of the two limitations on the amount of the credit appears below.

Example: Clay Calhoun transferred his residence by gift to his daughter, Reba, in 1974. When she received the gift, Reba agreed to allow her father to live in the house, then valued at $125,000, for the remainder of his life. Clay filed a gift tax return with respect to this transfer, paying gift tax of $21,150. (He had previously completely used up his $30,000 specific exemption by a one-time gift of $33,000 in cash to Reba in 1970.) At his death in 2004, Clay had a federal gross estate of $2.5 million, including the $270,000 value of the transferred residence on the date of his death that was included in his estate as a transfer under Code Sec. 2036. Administration and miscellaneous deductions on Clay's Form 706 equaled $85,000; no marital or charitable deductions were claimed. The transfer of the residence in 1974 was the last taxable gift made by Clay. Clay's state of domicile levied a death tax equal to the amount allowed for the state death tax credit on a decedent's federal estate tax return (Form 706).

First limitation:

Amount of gift tax paid on gift included in his gross estate: $21,150

Second limitation:

Gross estate tax:	$980,000
Less:	
Unified credit amount	555,800
State death tax credit	33,000
	$391,200

($391,200 ÷ $2,500,000) × $125,000 =
.15648 × $125,000 = $19,560

The credit allowable under Code Sec. 2012 is $19,560, the lower of the two amounts computed under the first and second limitations.

---

13 Instructions for Form 706 (Rev. Aug. 2004), p. 6.

¶ 1384 Gifts Made After 1976

No credit is allowed for any gift tax paid on gifts made after 1976 because the gift tax payable on post-1976 gifts (includible in the gross estate) is automatically reflected in determining the estate tax liability under the unified transfer tax structure (see ¶ 11 and ¶ 12).[14]

---

[14] Code Sec. 2012(e).

Chapter 27
CREDIT FOR FOREIGN DEATH TAXES

¶ 1400 Double Taxation

The federal estate tax applies to the entire estate, wherever situated, of any decedent who was either a domiciled resident or a citizen of the United States. Because many other countries levy death taxes on the transfer by nonresidents not citizens of property situated within their boundaries, the estates of many persons are subject to double taxation. The United States has entered into estate tax conventions with a number of foreign countries to provide relief from such double taxation (see ¶ 1420).

¶ 1401 Statutory Credit

To protect against double taxation, the law provides a foreign estate tax credit for U.S. citizens and residents.[1] The credit applies when double taxation arises from imposition by the United States of a tax on the entire estate and the imposition by a foreign country of an estate or other death tax on property situated within that country. For the purpose of this credit, U.S. possessions are classified as foreign countries.[2]

The foreign estate tax credit, in each case, is limited by apportionment. Only taxes attributable to property taxed in both countries may be allowed as a credit. In addition, the credit cannot exceed the portion of U.S. taxes attributable to the property taxed in both countries.

Although credits against the estate tax must be claimed within the later of four years after filing the estate tax return (Form 706, United States Estate (and Generation-Skipping Transfer) Tax Return) (Rev. Aug. 2004), before the date of any extension of time for paying the U.S. tax, or 60 days after a final Tax Court decision, an extended period within which to claim this credit is provided.[3] An extension is possible where payment of the estate tax attributable to a reversionary or remainder interest is postponed.

An executor is required to notify the IRS of any recovery of state or foreign death taxes for which credit has been claimed.[4] A redetermination of the federal estate tax on the basis of such recovery is authorized without regard to any statutory time limits that might otherwise apply.

¶ 1402 Reciprocity Requirement for Resident Aliens

Generally, the estates of resident aliens may take a credit for foreign inheritance and death taxes paid. However, the President may, by proclamation, limit the availability of the credit if (1) the foreign country of which the resident aliens

[1] Code Sec. 2014; Reg. § 20.2014-1.
[2] Code Sec. 2014(g).
[3] Code Sec. 2015.
[4] Code Sec. 2016.

are citizens does not give U.S. citizens a reciprocal credit, (2) that country, when asked to do so, has not acted to provide such a credit, and (3) it is in the public interest to deny the credit. If a citizen or subject of such foreign country dies during the proclamation period, the credit will be allowed only if the foreign country allows a similar credit in the case of U.S. citizens who are residents of the foreign country at the time of their deaths.[5]

¶ 1405 Procedure for Claiming Credit

In the case of a citizen or resident of the United States, a credit is allowed for any estate, inheritance, legacy, or succession taxes paid to a foreign country or its possessions or political subdivisions with respect to property situated in that country and included in the gross estate. Credit is authorized by statute or by treaty. Unless otherwise provided by the treaty, a comparison is made to determine which of the following amounts is greater:

(1) the amount of the total credit authorized by the statute for all death taxes (national and local) imposed in the particular foreign country; or

(2) the amount of the total credit authorized by the treaty for death taxes imposed in such foreign country.[6]

• *Political Subdivisions*

When a credit for taxes imposed by a foreign country and one or more of its political subdivisions is involved, a third alternative to the credit allowed under the tax treaty or by statute is available. If it proves the most beneficial of the three, both a credit for the combined foreign death taxes allowable under the tax treaty *and* a credit under Code Sec. 2014 for death taxes paid to each political subdivision of the country (but only to the extent the taxes were not directly or indirectly creditable under the treaty) may be taken by the decedent's estate.

• *Multiple Foreign Countries*

If credit for death taxes paid in more than one foreign country is allowable, a separate computation of the credit must be made with respect to each foreign country. For purposes of the credit, each possession of the United States is considered as a foreign country. The copies of Schedule P (Credit for Foreign Death Taxes) of Form 706 (United States Estate (and Generation-Skipping Transfer) Tax Return) on which the additional computations are made should be attached to the copy of Schedule P provided in the return.[7]

• *Limitations and Allowance*

The total amount of the credit allowable with respect to any property, whether subjected to tax by one or more than one foreign country, is limited to the amount of the estate tax attributable to such property. The anticipated amount of the credit may be computed on the return. The credit cannot be allowed until the foreign tax has been paid and a certificate on Form 706-CE (Certificate of Payment of Foreign Death Tax) (Rev. May 2002) evidencing payment of the tax is furnished.[8] The Instructions for Form 706-CE contain procedures that should be followed in those cases where a foreign government refuses to certify Form 706-CE.

---

[5] Code Sec. 2014(h).
[6] Reg. § 20.2014-4.
[7] Reg. § 20.2014-5.
[8] Reg. § 20.2014-5.

¶ 1410 Situs of Property

For purposes of the foreign death tax credit, a determination must be made as to whether a particular property is situated in the United States or a foreign country. This is made according to the same principles applicable in determining whether similar property of a nonresident not a citizen is situated within the United States for the purpose of the federal estate tax[9] (see ¶1620).

¶ 1415 Execution of Schedule P for Statutory Credit

Schedule P (Credit for Foreign Death Taxes) of Form 706 (United States Estate (and Generation-Skipping Transfer) Tax Return) must be completed if an estate claims a credit for foreign death taxes paid. In addition, estates must attach Form 706-CE (Certificate of Payment of Foreign Death Tax) to support any credit claimed.

At item 1 on Schedule P, the amount of the estate, inheritance, legacy, and succession taxes paid to the foreign country and its possessions or political subdivisions attributable to property that (1) is situated in that country, (2) is subject to such taxes, and (3) is included in the gross estate should be entered. The amount entered at item 1 should not include any tax paid to the foreign country with respect to property not situated in that country. Nor should it include any tax paid to the foreign country with respect to property not included in the gross estate.

If only a part of the property subject to such foreign taxes is both situated in the foreign country and included in the gross estate, it will be necessary to determine the portion of the taxes that is attributable to such part of the property. The Instructions for Schedule P indicate that an additional sheet showing the computation of the amount entered at item 1 must be attached.[10]

The value of the gross estate less the total of the deductions shown on Form 706, Part 5, lines 20 and 21, Recapitulation (the marital and charitable deductions, respectively) should be entered at item 2 on Schedule P.

The value of the property situated in the foreign country that is subject to the foreign taxes and included in the gross estate, less those portions of the deductions on Schedule M (Bequests, etc., to Surviving Spouse) and Schedule O (Charitable, Public, and Similar Gifts and Bequests) that are attributable to such property, should be entered at item 3 on Schedule P.

The amount shown at item 15, Part 2, Form 706, should be subtracted from the amount shown at item 14, Part 2, Form 706, and the result entered on Schedule P at item 4.

The amount of the federal estate tax attributable to the value of the property specified at item 3 is calculated at item 5.

The final entry on Schedule P at item 6—the smaller of item 1 or item 5—represents the credit that may be subtracted from the estate tax otherwise payable.

Schedule P must be filed if the estate claims a foreign death tax credit, and Form 706-CE must be filed for every such credit claimed.

---

[9] Reg. § 20.2014-1(a)(3).

[10] Instructions for Form 706 (Rev. Aug. 2004), p. 20.

An Example illustrating how the foreign death tax credit is computed and a filled-in Form 706, Schedule P, relating to the Example are reproduced in the Appendix at ¶3170.

¶1420 Execution of Schedule P for Credit Under Treaties

Where the provisions of a treaty apply to the estate of a citizen or resident of the United States, a credit is allowed for the payment of the foreign death tax or taxes specified in the treaty. Death tax conventions are in effect with the following countries:

Country	*Death Tax*
Australia	Commonwealth estate duty*
Austria	Austrian inheritance and gift taxes
Canada	Canadian income tax on certain income, profits, and gains realized in the year of death and on certain gains deemed realized at death
Denmark	Duties on inheritance and gifts
Finland	Finnish inheritance tax, the communal tax on inheritances, bequests and devises, and the "poors percentage"
France	Duties on gifts and successions
Germany	German inheritance and gift taxes
Greece	Greek inheritance tax
Ireland	Irish estate tax duty
Italy	Italian estate and inheritance taxes
Japan	Japanese inheritance tax, including gift tax
Netherlands	Netherlands succession and transfer duties at death
Norway	Norwegian tax on inheritances, including death gifts
South Africa	Union estate duty
Sweden	Swedish inheritance and gift taxes
Switzerland	Estate and inheritance taxes imposed by the cantons and their political subdivisions
United Kingdom	Capital transfer tax

Credit claimed under a treaty is, in general, computed on Schedule P (Credit for Foreign Death Taxes) of Form 706 (United States Estate (and Generation-Skipping Transfer) Tax Return) in the same manner that credit is computed under the statute. The following principal exceptions apply:

(1) the situs rules contained in the treaty apply in determining whether property was situated in the foreign country;

(2) credit may be allowed only for payment of the death tax or taxes specified in the treaty;

---

* The Commonwealth estate tax duty was abolished, effective for decedents dying after July 1, 1979.

(3) where specifically provided, the credit is proportionately shared for the tax applicable to property situated outside both countries, or that was deemed in some instances to be situated within both countries; and

(4) the amount entered as item 4 of Schedule P is the amount shown at line 14 in "Tax Computation" on page 1 of Form 706 less the total of the amounts shown at lines 15 and 17 on that page.

If a credit is claimed for tax on prior transfers, it will be necessary to complete Schedule Q (Credit for Tax on Prior Transfers) of Form 706 before completing Schedule P.[11]

See CCH TAX TREATIES REPORTS for specific rules concerning the application of the treaties.

---

[11] Instructions for Form 706 (Rev. Aug. 2004), p. 20.

Chapter 28
COMPUTATION OF TAX

¶ 1425 Unified Transfer Tax

The estate and gift tax rates are combined in a single rate schedule effective for the estates of decedents dying, and gifts made, after December 31, 1976, and before 2010. Lifetime gifts made after 1976 and transfers made at death are cumulated for estate tax purposes. Estate tax liability is determined by applying the unified transfer tax rate schedule to cumulated transfers and subtracting the gift taxes payable. A unified credit[1] (as determined by reference to an applicable credit amount for estates of decedents dying after 1997) is subtracted after determining the decedent's estate tax liability.

• ***Impact of the 2001 Act***

The enactment of the Economic Growth and Tax Relief Reconciliation Act of 2001 (P.L. 107-16) (2001 Act) brought significant change to the transfer tax system, the most notable being the repeal of the estate and generation-skipping transfer taxes in 2010. Prior to repeal, a number of modifications are made to the maximum estate tax rate and applicable exclusion amount (discussed at ¶1426).

Under the 2001 Act, the top marginal rate is reduced to 48 percent for decedents dying, and gifts made, in 2004, with further reductions in later years. In 2004 and 2005, the effective minimum rate is equal to 45 percent as a result of the operation of the applicable credit amount (¶1426).

Sunset provision. In order to comply with the Congressional Budget Act of 1974, the 2001 Act provides that all provisions of, and amendments made by, the 2001 Act will not apply to estates of decedents dying, gifts made, or generation-skipping transfers, after December 31, 2010. Unless Congress acts affirmatively in the interim, the Internal Revenue Code will thereafter be applied and administered as if these provisions had not been enacted.

• ***Unified Credit: 1977–1997***

The unified estate and gift tax credit and the exemption equivalent for the years 1977 through 1997 are as follows:

Year	*Amount of Credit*	*Amount of Exemption Equivalent*
1977	$30,000	$120,667
1978	34,000	134,000
1979	38,000	147,333
1980	42,500	161,563
1981	47,000	175,625
1982	62,800	225,000

[1] The unified credit replaced the estate-tax-specific exemption of $60,000, which applied to estates of decedents dying before Jan. 1, 1977.

Year	Amount of Credit	Amount of Exemption Equivalent
1983	79,300	275,000
1984	96,300	325,000
1985	121,800	400,000
1986	155,800	500,000
1987-1997	192,800	600,000

• ***Unified Credit: 1998–2009***

For the years 1998 through 2009, the unified credit is gradually increased to $1,455,800 (in 2009) and is determined by reference to the "applicable credit amount" and the "applicable exclusion amount" (formerly the exemption equivalent). The increase is phased in as follows:

Year	Applicable Credit Amount	Applicable Exclusion Amount
1998	$202,050	$625,000
1999	211,300	650,000
2000 and 2001	220,550	675,000

As a result of changes made by the 2001 Act, different unified credit amounts apply to the estate tax, and to the gift tax (see ¶15).

The estate tax unified credit (applicable credit amount) and the applicable exclusion amount for the years 2002 through 2009 appear below:

Year	Applicable Credit Amount	Applicable Exclusion Amount
2002–2003	$345,800	$1,000,000
2004–2005	555,800	1,500,000
2006–2008	780,800	2,000,000
2009	1,455,800	3,500,000
2010 (Estate Tax Repealed)	0	0
2011 (Estate Tax Reinstated)	345,800	1,000,000

The gift tax applicable credit amount for the years 2002 through 2009 will remain at $1 million.

¶ 1426 Computation of Tax

The basic steps in computing the tax on a post-1976 estate under the unified transfer tax system are as follows:

(1) Compute the decedent's taxable estate. The taxable estate of a U.S. citizen is determined by subtracting the total allowable deductions reported on the Recapitulation of Form 706 (United States Estate (and Generation-Skipping Transfer) Tax Return) (Rev. Aug. 2004) (see the Appendix at ¶2940), from the total gross estate reported on the Recapitulation.

(2) Compute the "adjusted taxable gifts"—the aggregate post-1976 lifetime taxable gifts, other than post-1976 gifts that are includible in the decedent's gross estate. (In limited situations, the IRS may revalue post-1976 gifts for purposes of computing a decedent's estate tax; see the discussion under the heading "Revaluing Lifetime Gifts," below).

(3) Add (1) and (2).

(4) Determine the tentative tax by applying the rates in the unified rate schedule (see ¶1430) to the amount obtained in (3).

(5) Subtract the total gift tax paid on gifts made after 1976 according to the rate schedule in effect in the year of the decedent's death (including the gift tax paid on transfers includible in the gross estate).

(6) Subtract the applicable credit amount to arrive at the estate tax payable.

See the example at ¶1428 for details of these basic steps, including how to compute gift tax on lifetime gifts.

The net estate tax payable is then computed by subtracting the following tax credits: (1) the credit for state death taxes (see ¶1370); (2) the credit for federal gift taxes on pre-1977 gifts that are includible in the decedent's gross estate (see ¶1382); (3) the credit for foreign death taxes (see ¶1400); and (4) the credit for prior transfer taxes (see ¶1300).

Two other types of taxes can be added to the net estate tax to arrive at the total amount of transfer taxes that is payable on a decedent's estate tax return: (1) the generation-skipping transfer tax on generation-skipping transfers made by the decedent at death; and (2) for decedents dying before 1997, the special estate tax that is payable on what are called "excess retirement accumulations." Only the net amount of the generation-skipping tax, as computed on Schedule R (Generation-Skipping Transfer Tax) of Form 706 (United States Estate (and Generation-Skipping Transfer) Tax Return), is entered in the computation part (see ¶3130 for further details).

• *Split Gifts*

If spouses have made split gifts, special rules apply for determining the amount of the adjusted taxable gifts includible in a decedent's estate and the amount of the gift tax offset that may be claimed on a decedent's estate tax return. These rules are dependent on whether the decedent was the donor or the consenting spouse. First, if the entire amount of the gift is includible in the donor spouse's gross estate, any gift tax paid by the consenting spouse on the gift can be claimed as part of the gift tax offset in determining the estate tax payable by the estate of the donor spouse.[2] Second, a gift is not included in the adjusted taxable gifts of a consenting spouse in those cases where the amount of the split gift was includible in the donor spouse's gross estate under Code Sec. 2035. Further, the gift tax paid by the consenting spouse is not included in the gift tax offset on the consenting spouse's estate tax return in computing the final estate tax to the extent that an offset had been used on the donor spouse's estate tax return.[3]

• *Revaluing Lifetime Gifts*

For lifetime gifts made after August 5, 1997, if the reporting of the gift meets the adequate disclosure requirements (discussed below), the IRS is not permitted to revalue a gift for purposes of computing an estate tax liability if the three-year statute of limitations on the gift has expired.[4] For post-1976 gifts made before January 1, 1997, the Tax Court held that the value of a decedent's gifts, as reported on his federal gift tax returns, could be revised even though the three-year statute of limitations period on the assessment of gift taxes had expired.[5] In so holding, the Tax Court concluded that, although Code Sec. 2504(c) would have prevented such a revaluation of prior taxable gifts for gift tax purposes, there

---

[2] Code Sec. 2001(d).
[3] Code Sec. 2001(e).
[4] Code Sec. 2001(f) and Code Sec. 6501(c)(9).
[5] *F. Smith Est.*, 94 TC 872, CCH Dec. 46,648 (Acq.).

was no corresponding provision in the estate tax area. Accordingly, the post-1976 lifetime gifts of the decedent could be revalued. However, the Taxpayer Relief Act of 1997 (P.L. 105-34) added Code Sec. 2001(f), effective with respect to gifts made after August 5, 1997, which prohibits the IRS from revaluing gifts made during life in computing adjusted taxable gifts for estate tax purposes if the gift tax statute of limitations has expired. As retroactively amended by the IRS Restructuring and Reform Act of 1998 (P.L. 105-206), in order for this provision to apply, the value of the gift in question must have been finally determined for purposes of the gift tax. The value of a gift is finally determined if the value is (1) reported on a gift tax return and is not challenged by the IRS prior to the expiration of the statute of limitations, (2) determined by the IRS and not challenged by the taxpayer in court, (3) determined by a court, or (4) agreed on by the taxpayer and the IRS in a settlement.

In order to gain the benefit of the provision that bars the IRS from an estate tax revaluation of a lifetime gift for which the statute of limitations period has expired on the gift, the gift must have been adequately disclosed.[6] According to the regulations, a transfer will be adequately disclosed on the return only if it is reported in a manner adequate to apprise the IRS of the nature of the gift and the basis for the value so reported. The IRS will consider this standard met if the gift tax return (or a statement attached to the return) provides the following information:

(1) a description of the transferred property and any consideration received by the transferor;

(2) the identify of, and the relationship between, the transferor and each transferee;

(3) if the property is transferred in trust, the trust's tax identification number and a brief description of the terms of the trust; in the alternative, a copy of the trust document;

(4) a detailed description of the method used to determine the fair market value of the property transferred, including any financial data utilized in determining the value of the interest, any restrictions on the transferred property, and a description of any discounts claimed in valuing the property; and

(5) a statement describing any position taken with respect to the gift tax return that is contrary to any proposed, temporary, or final IRS regulations or revenue ruling published at the time of the transfer.

The IRS has issued guidance[7] on how to adequately disclose a gift if the required information was not initially submitted with a gift tax return filed for the year the gift was made. In this situation, the donor must file an amended gift tax return for the calendar year in which the gift was made that includes all of the information required by the regulations (items (1)-(5), listed above). Effective for amended returns filed after August 21, 2000, the period of assessment will generally expire three years after the date the amended return is filed.

¶ 1428 Example of Application of Unified Transfer Tax

The following Example illustrates application of the unified transfer tax.

---

[6] Reg. § 301.6501(c)-1, as amended Dec. 2, 1999, by T.D. 8835.

[7] Rev. Proc. 2000-34, 2000-2 CB 186.

Example: Nora Brown made the following taxable gifts to her son, Carl.

1984	$300,000
1987	$200,000
1989	$600,000
1990	$700,000

In 2004, she died with a taxable estate of $1 million.

The total transfer taxes payable by Nora are calculated as follows:

1984	
1. Taxable gift	$300,000
2. Prior taxable gifts	$0
3. Total taxable gifts	$300,000
4. Tentative tax on line 3 amount	$87,800
5. Less: Tentative tax on prior gifts	$0
6. Balance	$87,800
7. Maximum unified credit	$96,300
8. Less: Unified credit used in prior periods	$0
9. Available unified credit	$96,300
10. Unified credit used to reduce tax	($87,800)
11. Gift tax payable (line 6 minus line 10)	$0
1987	
1. Taxable gift	$200,000
2. Prior taxable gifts	$300,000
3. Total taxable gifts	$500,000
4. Tentative tax on line 3	$155,800
5. Less: Tentative tax on prior taxable gifts	($87,800)
6. Balance	$68,000
7. Maximum unified credit	$192,800
8. Less: Unified credit used in prior periods	$87,800
9. Available unified credit	$105,000
10. Unified credit used to reduce tax	$68,000
11. Gift tax payable (line 6 minus line 10)	$0
1989	
1. Taxable gift	$600,000
2. Prior taxable gifts	$500,000
3. Total taxable gifts	$1,100,000
4. Tentative tax on line 3	$386,800
5. Less: Tentative tax on prior taxable gifts	($155,800)
6. Balance	$231,000
7. Maximum unified credit	$192,800
8. Less: Unified credit used in prior periods	($155,800)
9. Available unified credit	$37,000
10. Unified credit used to reduce tax	$37,000
11. Gift tax payable (line 6 minus line 10)	$194,000
1990	
1. Taxable gift	$700,000
2. Prior taxable gifts	$1,100,000
3. Total taxable gifts	$1,800,000
4. Tentative tax on line 3	$690,800
5. Less: Tentative tax on prior taxable gifts	($386,800)
6. Balance	$304,000
7. Maximum unified credit	$192,800
8. Less: Unified credit used in prior periods	$192,800
9. Available unified credit	$0
10. Unified credit used to reduce tax	$0

1990	
11. Gift tax payable	$ 304,000
Estate	
1. Amount of taxable estate	$1,000,000
2. Plus adjusted taxable gifts	$1,800,000
3. Estate tax base	$2,800,000
4. Tentative tax on base	$1,164,800
5. Less: Gift tax payable	($ 498,000)
6. Balance	$ 666,800
Less: Unified credit (applicable credit amount)	
7.	($ 555,800)
8. Less: Credit for state death taxes	($ 8,300)
9. Estate tax payable	$ 102,700

¶ 1430 Rate Schedule Table for Unified Tax

The unified rate schedule applicable to the estates of decedents dying, and gifts made, after 1983, but before 2002, is as follows:

Unified Tax Rate Schedule

Column A *Taxable amount over*	**Column B** *Taxable amount not over*	**Column C** *Tax on amount in column A*	**Column D** *Rate of tax on excess over amount in column A* *Percent*
$0	$10,000	$0	18
10,000	20,000	1,800	20
20,000	40,000	3,800	22
40,000	60,000	8,200	24
60,000	80,000	13,000	26
80,000	100,000	18,200	28
100,000	150,000	23,800	30
150,000	250,000	38,800	32
250,000	500,000	70,800	34
500,000	750,000	155,800	37
750,000	1,000,000	248,300	39
1,000,000	1,250,000	345,800	41
1,250,000	1,500,000	448,300	43
1,500,000	2,000,000	555,800	45
2,000,000	2,500,000	780,800	49
2,500,000	3,000,000	1,025,800	53
3,000,000	......	1,290,800	55

An additional five-percent tax was levied on amounts transferred in excess of $10 million, but not exceeding $17,184,000 prior to 2002.

Transfer Tax Rate Schedule: 2002–2009*

(A) *Amount subject to tax more than—*	*(B)* *Amount subject to tax equal to or less than—*	*(C)* *Tax on amount in column (A)*	*(D)* *Rate of tax on excess over amount in column (A)* *Percent*
...	$10,000	...	18
$10,000	20,000	$1,800	20
20,000	40,000	3,800	22
40,000	60,000	8,200	24
60,000	80,000	13,000	26
80,000	100,000	18,200	28
100,000	150,000	23,800	30
150,000	250,000	38,800	32
250,000	500,000	70,800	34

Transfer Tax Rate Schedule: 2002–2009*

(A) Amount subject to tax more than—	(B) Amount subject to tax equal to or less than—	(C) Tax on amount in column (A)	(D) Rate of tax on excess over amount in column (A) Percent
500,000	750,000	155,800	37
750,000	1,000,000	248,300	39
1,000,000	1,250,000	345,800	41
1,250,000	1,500,000	448,300	43
1,500,000	2,000,000	555,800	45
2,000,000	2,500,000	780,800	49
2,500,000	....	1,025,800	50

* A special tax rate table that applies for members of U.S. armed forces who died while on active duty in a combat zone, and for the victims of certain terrorist attacks, is reproduced in the Appendix at ¶2605.

• *Impact of the 2001 Act*

The Economic Growth and Tax Relief Reconciliation Act of 2001 (P.L. 107-16) (2001 Act) reduces the top marginal rate on taxable estates exceeding $2,000,000 for years after 2002, according to the following schedule:

- 49 percent for decedents dying, and gifts made, in 2003;
- 48 percent in 2004;
- 47 percent in 2005;
- 46 percent in 2006;
- 45 percent in 2007, 2008, and 2009.

For years 2003 through 2009, the tentative tax is to be determined by using a table prescribed by the IRS, which will be the same as the rate schedule shown above except for the adjustments necessary to reflect the reductions in the maximum rate.

Effective for estates of decedents dying, and gifts made, after December 31, 2001, the 2001 Act repeals the five-percent surtax.

Sunset provision. In order to comply with the Congressional Budget Act of 1974, the 2001 Act provides that all provisions of, and amendments made by, the 2001 Act will not apply to estates of decedents dying, gifts made, or generation-skipping transfers, after December 31, 2010. Unless Congress acts affirmatively in the interim, the Internal Revenue Code will thereafter be applied and administered as if these provisions had not been enacted.

• *Phaseout of Benefits*

The benefits of the graduated rates and the unified credit under the unified transfer tax system are phased out beginning with cumulative transfers rising above $10 million prior to 1998. This is accomplished by adding five percent of the excess of any transfer over $10 million to the tentative tax computed in determining the ultimate transfer tax liability. This five-percent surtax has been repealed, effective for estates of decedents dying after December 31, 2001.

• *Decedents Dying, and Gifts Made, After 1997 and Before 2002*

Due to mistakes in the wording of the amendment to Code Sec. 2001(c)(2) by the Taxpayer Relief Act of 1997 (P.L. 105-34), the five-percent additional tax phases out the benefits of the graduated rates, but not the benefits of the unified credit (applicable credit amount), for estates of decedents dying, and gifts made, after 1997. Therefore, the additional tax is levied on amounts transferred in excess of $10 million, but not exceeding $17,184,000 for decedents dying after 1997, but before 2002. The applicable credit amount is not recaptured.[8]

• ***Decedents Dying, and Gifts Made, After 1987 and Before 1998***

For estates of decedents dying, and gifts made, after 1987 and before 1998, the tax is levied on amounts transferred in excess of $10 million, but not exceeding $21,040,000, in order to recapture the benefit of any transfer tax rate below 55 percent, as well as the unified credit.

---

[8] Code Sec. 2001(c)(2).

Chapter 29

SPECIAL TAXPAYERS: MEMBERS OF ARMED FORCES, TERRORIST VICTIMS, AND ASTRONAUTS; NONRESIDENTS NOT CITIZENS

¶ 1550 Special Reduction for Members of Armed Forces, Terrorist Victims and Astronauts

Special estate tax relief is granted to the estates of certain members of the U.S. Armed Forces who died as a result of active duty service in a combat zone, and of certain qualifying decedents who were the victims of specified terrorist attacks. Who will qualify for this tax relief, and how the relief is computed, depends on whether the decedent died before September 11, 2001, or on or after this date. The rules for post-September 10, 2001, decedents are discussed below; the rules for pre-September 11, 2001, decedents are discussed at ¶1560.

Qualified decedents. Decedents who qualify for this tax-favored treatment include:

(1) Citizens or residents of the United States dying while in active service of the Armed Forces, if such decedent was killed in action while serving in a combat zone, or died as a result of wounds, disease, or injury suffered while serving in a combat zone, and while in the line of duty, by reason of a hazard to which such decedent was subjected as an incident of such service; and

(2) Decedents dying as a result of wounds or injuries incurred as a result of the terrorist attacks against the United States on April 19, 1995 (the Oklahoma City bombing), or September 11, 2001, or dying as a result of an attack involving anthrax occurring on or after September 11, 2001, and before January 1, 2002.[1]

The definition of "combat zone" is controlled by Code Sec. 112(c). That section defines the term to mean "any area which the President of the United States by Executive Order designates . . . as an area in which the Armed Forces of the United States are or have (after June 24, 1950) engaged in combat." For example, in 1991, the Arabian Peninsula (including the total land area of Iraq,

---

[1] Code Sec. 2201, as amended by the Victims of Terrorism Tax Relief Act of 2001 (P.L. 107-134); Reg. §20.2201-1.

Kuwait, Saudi Arabia, Oman, Bahrain, Qatar, the United Arab Emirates, and bodies of water adjacent to these countries)[2] was designated as a combat zone for Operation Desert Storm.[3] No authority has terminated this designation, which remains in effect. Effective September 19, 2001, Afghanistan was declared a combat zone.[4] Separately, the Department of Defense has certified that military personnel in Uzbekistan, Kyrgystan, Pakistan, Tajikistan, and Jordan are eligible for all combat-related tax benefits due to their direct support of military operations in Afghanistan.

The Federal Republic of Yugoslavia (Serbia/Montenegro), Albania, the Adriatic Sea, and the Ionian Sea north of the 39th parallel (including all of their air spaces) were designated as a combat zone, effective March 24, 1999, for personnel serving in NATO Operation Allied Force.[5] This extension is in addition to any other extensions for which the troops qualify. Combat zone tax treatment was also extended to those members of the Armed Forces serving in a qualified hazardous duty area.[6] Under P.L. 104-117, Bosnia, Croatia, Herzegovina, and Macedonia were designated qualified hazardous duty areas, effective November 21, 1995.

Under the Victims of Terrorism Relief Act of 2001, the executor of an eligible estate can elect not to have the special provisions of P.L. 107-134 apply, in which case estate tax liability will be calculated pursuant to the generally applicable rules. The Act also amended Code Sec. 7508A to give the IRS the power to suspend certain tax-related acts (such as the filing of returns and the payment of tax) for up to one year in cases of terrorist or military actions (see ¶1650 for IRS relief actions taken to date). The IRS can exercise this authority regardless of whether the President has declared the terrorist or military action to be in a disaster area. (In addition to the estate tax relief, the Act extended to the victims of these terrorist attacks the income tax relief provided by Code Sec. 692(c), which exempts federal military and civilian employees from income taxes in the year of their death (and generally the prior taxable year) if they die as a result of military or terrorist activity outside of the United States).

Computation of estate tax for qualified decedent (post-September 10, 2001). Unless the executor elects not to have Code Sec. 2201 apply, the federal estate tax of a qualified decedent is determined using a special rate schedule contained in Code Sec. 2201(c) (see ¶2605),[7] which sets the tax at 125 percent of the state death tax credit amount. As a result, Code Sec. 2201 will no longer reduce estate tax liability by the amount of the additional estate tax (see the discussion at ¶1560, below). However, while the special rate schedule applies in computing the estate tax under Code Sec. 2001(b) (for citizens and residents) or Code Sec. 2101(b) (for noncitizens nonresidents), the amount of the unified credit is determined as if Code Sec. 2201 did not apply.[8]

Example: Gerry Stack died in the terrorist attack against the United States on September 11, 2001. Stack's taxable estate is $10 million. The

---

[2] Notice 2003-21, IRB 2003-17, 817.

[3] Executive Order 12744, Jan. 21, 1991.

[4] Executive Order 13239, Dec. 12, 2001.

[5] Executive Order 13119, Apr. 13, 1999.

[6] P.L. 106-21, generally effective Mar. 24, 1999.

[7] Code Sec. 2201(a), as amended by the Victims of Terrorism Tax Relief Act of 2001 (P.L. 107-134).

[8] The IRS has published sample computations of the estate tax liability of post-September 10, 2001, qualified decedents under Code Sec. 2201 (Rev. Rul. 2002-86, IRB 2002-52, 993; modifying and superseding Rev. Rul. 78-361, 1978-2 CB 246).

executor of the estate did not elect out of the application of Code Sec. 2201. Stack's estate tax liability is computed as follows:

Taxable estate	$10,000,000
Federal estate tax (computed under Code Sec. 2201)	1,334,500
Unified credit	(220,550)
	$ 1,113,950
State death tax credit	(1,067,600)
Tax due	$ 46,350

• *Extension to Astronauts*

Congress, by enactment of the Military Family Tax Relief Act of 2003,[9] extended the estate tax relief applicable to members of the Armed Forces and terrorist victims to astronauts who die in the line of duty. This relief applies to estates of decedents dying after December 31, 2002.[10]

¶ 1560 Members of Armed Forces Dying Before September 11, 2001

The estates of members of the Armed Forces dying before September 11, 2001, that qualify for exemption are exempt from the "additional estate tax." Under the 1939 Code, the additional tax was the difference between the "tentative tax" and the "basic tax." For most estates, there is no longer an "additional tax," "tentative tax," or "basic tax." There is, instead, "the tax" and a "credit for state death taxes." The net tax is the difference between these two, less, of course, any other credits.

For purposes of the Armed Forces exemption, the "basic estate tax" is defined as 125 percent of the amount determined to be the maximum credit allowable for state death tax purposes.[11] The additional tax is the difference between the regular estate tax and the basic estate tax, for military personnel dying after 1976.[12] Prior to 1977, the same rule applied, except that the separate estate tax rates were used.

¶ 1565 Execution of Return

The estate tax return form does not provide instructions concerning the Armed Forces exemption. The exemption should be reflected at line 8 on the first page of Form 706 (United States Estate (and Generation-Skipping Transfer) Tax Return) (Rev. Aug. 2004), and lines 4–7 can be left blank. A notation of the reason for variation is necessary, such as—"Am. Vet. killed in action" (Code Sec. 2201).

The amount shown as the "Gross estate tax" would be an amount equal to 125 percent of the maximum credit for state death taxes. In all other respects, the form would be filled out in the same manner as for any other decedent. The "General Information" portion of Form 706 (part 4) should be supplemented with a statement concerning the basis for claiming the Armed Forces exemption.

Military service personnel and certain individuals who are serving in support of military personnel are generally granted extended filing and payment

[9] P.L. 108-121.

[10] Code Sec. 2201, as amended by the Military Family Tax Relief Act of 2003, P.L. 108-121.

[11] Code Sec. 2011(d), prior to repeal by P.L. 107-134, § 103(b)(1).

[12] For computation of the estate tax liability of military persons "missing in action" declared "killed in action" after 1976, but before September 11, 2001, see Rev. Rul. 78-361, 1978-2 CB 246.

deadlines with respect to their federal tax obligations. These provisions relate to military service personnel who are in a combat zone, contingency operation, or qualified hazardous duty area, are hospitalized as a result of injury received in a combat zone or contingency operation, or are missing in action.[13] See also ¶1650 for special rules applicable to the terrorist attacks against the United States and astronauts who die in the line of duty.

¶1600 Nonresidents Not Citizens: Special Rules

There are a number of special requirements in the estate tax law that apply only to estates of persons who are neither residents nor citizens of the United States. They affect the definition of property subject to tax, the exemption, return requirements and deductions. Some of the requirements stem from the estate tax provisions of the Internal Revenue Code and apply to estates of all such persons, except to the extent modified by treaty. Others are based on treaty provisions that limit their application to nonresidents not citizens who are residents of the country with which the treaty exists.

A number of these special requirements were discussed previously (see ¶85). Some are the subject of special instructions in the estate tax return form. The following material should be read in conjunction with specific requirements already covered.

¶1605 Residents of U.S. Possessions

Decedents who are citizens of the United States and residents of U.S. possessions at the time of their death are treated as "nonresidents not citizens of the United States," for estate tax purposes, if they acquired U.S. citizenship solely by reason of:

(1) being a citizen of the possession; or

(2) birth or residence within the possession.[14]

For such purposes, there is no distinction between possession citizens who were residents of the same possession at the time of their death as that under which they acquired their citizenship and possession citizens who reside in a U.S. possession other than the possession through which U.S. citizenship is acquired.[15]

• ***Repeal of Estate Tax in 2010***

The Economic Growth and Tax Relief Reconciliation Act of 2001 (P.L. 107-16) (2001 Act) repeals the estate tax with respect to the estates of decedents dying after December 31, 2009.[16]

Sunset provision. In order to comply with the Congressional Budget Act of 1974, the 2001 Act provides that all provisions of, and amendments made by, the 2001 Act will not apply to estates of decedents dying, gifts made, or generation-skipping transfers, after December 31, 2010. Unless Congress acts affirmatively in the interim, the Internal Revenue Code will thereafter be applied and administered as if these provisions had not been enacted.

---

[13] Code Sec. 7508, as amended by P.L. 108-121; Reg. §301.7508-1.

[14] Code Sec. 2209; Reg. §20.2209-1.

[15] Rev. Rul. 74-25, 1974-1 CB 284.

[16] Code Sec. 2210.

¶ 1615 Death Tax Conventions

If a death tax convention is applicable to the estate of a decedent who is a nonresident not a citizen, both the treaty and the regulations issued pursuant to the treaty should be consulted.[17]

Death duty conventions are in effect with each of the countries listed below. The provisions of a convention apply in the case of a decedent dying on or after the effective date shown.

Country	*Effective Date*
Australia*	January 7, 1954
Austria	July 1, 1983
Canada (a revised protocol, signed March 17, 1995, to Income Tax Treaty)	November 10, 1995
Denmark	November 7, 1984
Finland	December 18, 1952
France	October 1, 1980
Germany (modified by protocol signed December 14, 1998, and entered into force on December 14, 2000)	January 1, 1979
Greece (modified by protocol (affecting situs of real property) signed February 12, 1964, which went into effect October 27, 1967)	December 30, 1953
Ireland	December 20, 1951
Italy	October 26, 1956
Japan	April 1, 1955
Netherlands	February 3, 1971
Norway	December 11, 1951
South Africa	July 15, 1952
Sweden	September 5, 1984
Switzerland	September 17, 1952
United Kingdom	November 11, 1979

* Note: The Commonwealth estate tax duty for Australia was abolished, effective for the estates of decedents dying after July 1, 1979.

The U.S.-Germany estate tax treaty did not preempt a state (Maryland) statute of limitations for filing a refund claim for estate inheritance taxes, the Maryland Court of Appeals held.[18] In denying the refund claim, the appellate court concluded that because the treaty was binding on the U.S. government, but not its political subdivisions, it did not apply to state inheritance taxes and related statutes of limitations.

If, with regard to a tax treaty, a U.S. taxpayer believes that the actions of the United States, the other country party to the treaty (called the "treaty country"), or both, have resulted in taxation that is inconsistent with treaty provisions, the tax treaty will generally permit the taxpayer to request competent authority assistance. The IRS Director, International, acts as the competent authority for the United States, and is charged with administering tax treaties. Under procedures set forth by the IRS, a request for assistance may be filed at any time after an action results in taxation that is not in accordance with the provisions of the applicable treaty. The request, which must be in letter form and addressed to the Director, International, must include (among other information) a brief description of the relevant activities or other circumstances involved in the issues being raised and an explanation of the relief being sought. Special simplified proce-

[17] See CCH TAX TREATIES REPORTS.

[18] *J. Arrowsmith*, Md. Ct. App., 2001-2 USTC ¶ 60,421.

dures are available in "small cases" where the proposed adjustment does not exceed $200,000 ($1 million in the case of a partnership or corporation).[19]

¶ 1617 Gross Estate

The gross estate of a nonresident not a citizen of the United States is determined in the same manner as that of a U.S. citizen or resident. It includes not only all property beneficially owned by the decedent, but also joint estates with right of survivorship, tenancies by the entirety, community property, property transferred by the decedent during his or her lifetime, and property subject to the decedent's general power of appointment (see Chapter 6 through Chapter 17). However, the taxable estate is the part of the gross estate situated in the United States, less the authorized deductions.[20]

Only the part of the gross estate situated in the United States should be listed on the appropriate schedules (see ¶85 and ¶1620). The term "United States," when used in a geographical sense, includes only the states and the District of Columbia. Property transferred during the decedent's lifetime, and includible in the gross estate under one of the transfer provisions (Code Sec. 2035 through Code Sec. 2038), is deemed situated in the United States if it was so situated at the time of the transfer or at the time of death.

¶ 1620 Property Situated in the United States

Although the situs rules controlling the inclusion of property in estates of nonresidents not citizens may be modified under the provisions of an applicable death tax treaty with the United States, in general, only property located in the United States is includible in the gross estate of a nonresident not a U.S. citizen. Property located within the United States is reported on Schedule A (Gross Estate in the United States) of Form 706-NA (United States Estate (and Generation-Skipping Transfer) Tax Return) (Rev. Jan. 2003). Schedule E (Jointly Owned Property), Schedule G (Transfers During Decedent's Life), and Schedule H (Powers of Appointment) of Form 706 (United States Estate (and Generation-Skipping Transfer) Tax Return) must be attached to the return if the decedent transferred certain property or if the decedent possessed, exercised, or released a general power of appointment in U.S. property (see ¶85 for further details).

• ***Stocks and Bonds***

The notable exception to this general situs rule is the stock of domestic corporations. This stock is includible in the gross estate regardless of where located. Debt obligations (bonds, etc.) that are owned and held by a nonresident not a citizen are considered property located within the United States if the primary obligor is a domestic corporation or other U.S. person, the United States, a state, a political subdivision of a state, or the District of Columbia.[21]

For this purpose, it is immaterial whether the written evidence of the debt obligation is treated as being the property itself. Currency, however, is not to be considered a debt obligation.

---

[19] Rev. Proc. 2002-52, IRB 2002-31, 242, modifying and superseding Rev. Proc. 96-14, 1996-1 CB 626, Rev. Proc. 96-13, 1996-1 CB 616, Rev. Proc. 91-26, 1991-1 CB 543, Rev. Proc. 91-23, 1991-1 CB 534, amplifying Rev. Proc. 96-53, 1996-2 CB 375, and clarifying Rev. Rul. 92-75, 1992-2 CB 197.

[20] Code Sec. 2106; Reg. §20.2106-1.

[21] Code Sec. 2104.

If the obligation is a debt of a resident alien individual or domestic corporation that meets the 80-percent-foreign-business requirement, it will be treated as having a foreign situs.[22]

Effective for estates of nonresident, non-U.S. citizen decedents dying after December 31, 2004, new rules apply to a portion of stock held in a regulated investment company (RIC). (See the heading "Stock in Regulated Investment Companies", below.)

• ***Deposits with U.S. Financial Institutions and Insurers***

Funds deposited by or for a nonresident alien in a U.S. bank (including a domestic banking branch of a foreign corporation), a savings and loan, or similar association or held by a domestic insurance company under an agreement to pay interest are not includible in a decedent's gross estate if the monies are not effectively connected with the conduct of a trade or business within the United States by the decedent.[23] Deposits with a foreign branch of a domestic corporation or partnership, if such branch is engaged in the commercial banking business, are also excludable from the gross estate.[24]

A nonresident alien's U.S. bank deposits, chartered savings institution accounts, and amounts held by insurance companies will not be treated as property located within the United States for federal estate tax purposes, if the interest paid on these amounts would have been treated as nontaxable foreign-source income for federal income tax purposes. To be exempt from federal income tax as foreign-source income, the interest from these deposits must not be "effectively connected" with the conduct of a trade or business within the United States.[25]

• ***Stock in Regulated Investment Companies***

Effective for estates of nonresident, non-U.S. citizens dying after December 31, 2004, and before January 1, 2008,[26] a portion of stock in a regulated investment company (such as a mutual fund) owned by such a decedent will be treated as property without the United States.[27] Accordingly, such property will not be includible in the gross estate of such shareholder for federal estate tax purposes. The portion that is exempt from taxation is determined at the end of the quarter of the tax year of the regulated investment company (RIC) immediately preceding the decedent's date or death, or other time to be prescribed by regulation. The exempt amount is the proportion of the RIC's assets that were qualifying assets with respect to the decedent in relation to the total assets of the RIC. Qualifying assets are those assets that, if owned by the decedent, would have been:

(1) bank deposits that are exempt from income tax;

(2) portfolio debt obligations;

(3) certain original issue discount obligations;

(4) debt obligations of a U.S. corporation that are treated as giving rise to foreign source income; and

---

[22] Code Sec. 861(a)(1)(A).

[23] Code Sec. 2105(b).

[24] Code Sec. 2105(b).

[25] Code Sec. 864(c).

[26] Code Sec. 2105(d)(3), as added by the American Jobs Creation Act of 2004 (P.L. 108-357).

[27] Code Sec. 2105(d)(1), as added by the American Jobs Creation Act of 2004 (P.L. 108-357).

(5) other property not within the United States.[28]

• *Certain Other Properties*

The following special rules exist for determining whether property is situated in the United States:

(1) Real property and tangible personal property are within the United States if physically located therein.

(2) Proceeds of insurance on the life of a nonresident not a citizen of the United States are not situated in the United States.[29]

(3) Works of art are not considered situated in the United States if they were (a) imported into the United States solely for exhibition purposes, (b) loaned for such purposes to a public gallery or museum, no part of the net earnings of which inures to the benefit of any private stockholder or individual, and (c) on exhibit (or en route to or from exhibition) in such public gallery or museum at the time of the owner's death.[30]

¶ 1625 Deduction of Administration Expenses and Claims

Estates of nonresidents not citizens of the United States may deduct the following items: (1) funeral expenses; (2) administration expenses; (3) claims against the estate; (4) unpaid mortgages and other liens; and (5) losses incurred during the settlement of the estate arising from fires, storms, shipwrecks, or other casualties, or from theft, if such losses are not compensated for by insurance or otherwise.[31] However, the amount of the deduction is limited to the proportion of the nonresident noncitizen's gross estate located in the United States divided by the entire gross estate wherever it is located. This deduction is computed by completing lines 4 and 5 of Schedule B (Taxable Estate) of Form 706-NA (United States Estate (and Generation-Skipping Transfer) Tax Return).

It is immaterial whether the amounts to be deducted were incurred or expended within or without the United States. However, no deduction may be taken unless the value of the entire gross estate wherever situated is entered on line 3 of Schedule B of Form 706-NA. The entire gross estate must be valued as of the date of the decedent's death. However, if the alternate valuation is adopted under Schedule A (Gross Estate in the United States) of Form 706-NA, such alternate valuation must be applied to the entire gross estate.

• *Substantiation*

Adequate proof in support of item 2 (gross estate outside the United States) and item 4 (deductible expenses before limitation) of Schedule B must be submitted; otherwise, this deduction will be disallowed. With respect to line 2, a certified copy of the foreign death tax return should be submitted. If no such return was filed, a certified copy of the estate inventory, together with the schedule of debts and charges filed in conjunction with the estate administration proceedings or with the foreign probate court, should be submitted. Additional proof may be required in specific cases.

With respect to line 4, the exact nature and amount of each expense or claim, as well as the name of the creditor, must be fully described and, if relating to particular property, the property must be identified. Death taxes, taxes on

---

[28] Code Sec. 2105(d)(2), as added by the American Jobs Creation Act of 2004 (P.L. 108-357).

[29] Code Sec. 2105(a).

[30] Code Sec. 2105(c).

[31] Code Sec. 2106.

income received after death, and property taxes accrued after death are not deductible. Deductions for debts and mortgages are limited to that part of the debt that was contracted in good faith for money or money's worth. Mortgages are deductible only if the full value of the mortgaged property is included on line 3 (entire gross estate wherever located).[32]

¶ 1630 Charitable, Public, and Similar Gifts and Bequests

Except as provided otherwise by treaty, a charitable deduction may be taken only if the transfer was to a corporation or association organized in the United States or to trustees for use in the United States.[33] The Tax Court has ruled that a charitable deduction was denied to the extent that the bequest, made to a Canadian registered charity, was paid solely out of funds and property located outside of the United States (which meant that such funds and property were not subject to the U.S. estate tax). In so holding, the court concluded that a revised tax protocol adopted with respect to the U.S.-Canadian death tax treaty (see ¶1615) did not change this result.[34] If a charitable deduction is claimed, Schedule O (Charitable, Public, and Similar Gifts and Bequests) of Form 706 (United States Estate (and Generation-Skipping Transfer) Tax Return) must be attached. In addition, if a charitable deduction is claimed under a treaty, the applicable treaty must be specified and a computation of the deduction attached.

• ***Marital Deduction***

Effective for estates of decedents dying after November 10, 1988, the marital deduction will be allowed for estate tax purposes in the case of a nonresident alien whose spouse is a U.S. citizen or, where the spouse is not a U.S. citizen, if the property passes by way of a qualified domestic trust.[35] Executors claiming the deduction should do so on line 6 on Schedule B (Taxable Estate) of Form 706-NA (United States Estate (and Generation-Skipping Transfer) Tax Return). Additionally, Schedule M (Bequests, etc., to Surviving Spouse) of Form 706 (United States Estate (and Generation-Skipping Transfer) Tax Return), and a statement showing the computation of the deduction, should be attached. The estates of nonresident aliens dying prior to November 11, 1988, could not claim marital deductions, unless the individual was a resident of a country that had entered into a treaty with the United States permitting his or her estate to claim a marital deduction.[36]

¶ 1635 Rates and Exemption

The gift and estate tax rates applicable to U.S. citizens also apply to the estate of a nonresident alien.[37] Effective for estates of decedents dying after December 31, 2001, the five-percent surtax that had existed before passage of the Economic Growth and Tax Relief Reconciliation Act of 2001 (P.L. 107-16) also has been eliminated with respect to the estates of nonresidents not citizens.[38] Prior to this repeal, the surtax applied to the estates of nonresidents not citizens, but the amount of the surtax was adjusted to reflect the fact that, in some cases, the estate of a nonresident noncitizen does not receive the same unified credit available to U.S. citizens. Accordingly, the additional five-percent rate that was imposed on decedents who died, and on gifts made, after 1987, but before 2002, applied to

---

[32] Instructions for Form 706-NA (Rev. Jan 2003), p. 3.

[33] Code Sec. 2106(a)(2)(A).

[34] *A. Silver*, 120 TC 430, CCH Dec. 55,150.

[35] Code Sec. 2056(d).

[36] Reg. § 20.2056(a)-1.

[37] Code Sec. 2101(b).

[38] Code Sec. 2101(b), as amended by the Job Creation and Worker Assistance Act of 2002 (P.L. 107-147).

the taxable transfers of nonresident noncitizens in excess of $10 million only to the extent that it was necessary to phase out the benefit of the graduated rates actually allowed by statute or treaty.[39]

Where permitted by treaty, the estate of a nonresident alien is allowed the unified credit available to a U.S. citizen multiplied by the proportion of the total gross estate situated in the United States. In other cases, a unified credit of $13,000 is allowed. The estate of a resident of a U.S. possession is entitled to a unified credit equal to the greater of (1) $13,000, or (2) $46,800 multiplied by the proportion that the decedent's gross estate situated in the United States bears to the total gross estate of the decedent wherever situated.[40] In the case of the estate tax provisions relating to expatriation to avoid estate tax, the credit allowable is $13,000.[41] (But see, also, the discussion below with respect to individuals who have expatriated after June 3, 2004.)

The executor of an estate of a nonresident who is not a citizen of the United States must file an estate tax return on Form 706-NA if that part of the gross estate that is located in the United States exceeds $60,000, reduced by (1) the total taxable gifts made by the decedent after December 31, 1976, and (2) the aggregate amount allowed as a specific exemption under Code Sec. 2521 (as in effect before its repeal by the Tax Reform Act of 1976 (94-455)) with respect to gifts made by the decedent after September 8, 1976, and before January 1, 1977.[42]

• *Expatriate Alternative Estate Tax Regime Revised*

If a former U.S. citizen or long-term resident who is subject to the alternative tax regime of Code Sec. 877(b) dies within 10 years of relinquishment of citizenship or residency, an estate tax is imposed on the transfer of U.S.-situs property, including the decedent's pro rata share of the U.S. property held by a foreign corporation pursuant to Code Sec. 2107(b). This provision, added by the American Jobs Creation Act of 2004 (2004 Jobs Act) (P.L. 108-357), applies to individuals who expatriate after June 3, 2004. The estate tax is computed on the taxable estate, as determined by Code Sec. 2106, using the same estate tax rate schedule used for the estate of a U.S. citizen or resident.[43] A former citizen or long-term resident is subject to the alternative tax regime if the individual: (1) has average annual net income tax for the five-year period preceding the loss of U.S. citizenship in excess of $124,000; (2) has a net worth on that date of $2,000,000 or more; or (3) fails to certify compliance with all federal tax obligations for the five-year period, unless he or she is a dual citizen or minor without substantial contact with the United States.[44] However, if, pursuant to Code Sec. 877(g), as added by the 2004 Jobs Act, the former citizen or long-term resident is present in the United States for a period of 30 days or more in any calendar year that ends during the 10-year period following relinquishment of citizenship or long-term residency and dies within that same calendar year, he or she is treated as a resident of the United States for federal estate tax purposes. Thus, all property in which the former citizen or long-term resident has an interest is includible in his or her gross estate, wherever located, including foreign assets.

Comment: The estate of a former citizen or long-term resident decedent who dies within 10 years of relinquishment of citizenship or long-term

[39] Code Sec. 2101(b)(2).

[40] Code Sec. 2102(c)(2).

[41] Code Sec. 2107(c).

[42] Code Sec. 6018(a)(2) and (3); Instructions for Form 706-NA (Rev. Jan. 2003), p. 1.

[43] Code Sec. 2107(a), as amended by the American Jobs Creation Act of 2004 (P.L. 108-357).

[44] Code Sec. 877(a), as amended by the American Jobs Creation Act of 2004 (P.L. 108-357).

residency and who is subject to the alternative tax regime is still only entitled to an applicable credit amount of $13,000 (unless otherwise specified by treaty, the estate is allowed a share of the unified credit that is proportionate to the decedent's U.S. estate).[45] However, it would seem to be the correct result that if a former citizen or long-term resident is treated as a U.S. resident for estate tax purposes under the new law, then the higher applicable credit amount used for U.S. residents ($555,800 in 2004 and 2005, sheltering $1,500,000) would apply.

• ***Impact of the 2001 Act***

The Economic Growth and Tax Relief Reconciliation Act of 2001 (P.L. 107-16) (2001 Act), which repeals the estate tax in 2010, makes several changes to the estate and gift tax rates and the applicable exclusion (and, hence, credit) amount in the years preceding repeal (see ¶1425).

Sunset provision. In order to comply with the Congressional Budget Act of 1974, the 2001 Act provides that all provisions of, and amendments made by, the 2001 Act will not apply to estates of decedents dying, gifts made, or generation-skipping transfers, after December 31, 2010. Unless Congress acts affirmatively in the interim, the Internal Revenue Code will thereafter be applied and administered as if these provisions had not been enacted.

[45] Code Sec. 2102(c)(3)(A).

Chapter 30
PAYMENT OF THE TAX

¶ 1650 Date of Filing and Payment

The estate tax is due and payable at the same time the return is due. Thus, payment is due nine months after the date of death. It must be paid within the time prescribed to avoid the assessment of various penalties. Extensions of time for payment may be granted (see ¶ 66), but such extensions, although preventing the application of certain penalties, do not entirely prevent the assessment of interest. Applicable with respect to estate tax returns due after July 25, 2001, an estate will be allowed an automatic six-month extension of time to file Form 706 (United States Estate (and Generation-Skipping Transfer) Tax Return) (Rev. Aug. 2004) beyond the date prescribed by Code Sec. 6075(a) (generally nine months after death) if (1) Form 4768 (Application for Extension of Time To File a Return and/or Pay U.S. Estate (and Generation-Skipping Transfer) Taxes), is filed on or before the Code Sec. 6075 due date, (2) the application is filed with the IRS office designated in the application's instructions (excepting hand-carried documents), and (3) the application includes an estimate of the amount of estate and generation-skipping transfer tax liability for the estate.[1]

The due date for payment is the same numbered day of the ninth month after the date of death as that day of the month in which death occurred. If there is no similarly numbered day in the ninth month, the tax is deemed to be due on the last day of that month. For example, if the date of death were May 31, 2001, the due date would be February 28, 2002. If the due date falls on a Saturday, Sunday, or legal holiday, the return is due on the next day that is not a Saturday, Sunday, or legal holiday.[2]

• *Tax Relief for Victims of Hurricane Ivan*

Taxpayers affected by Hurricane Ivan will have until December 30, 2004, to file tax returns and make tax payments that would otherwise be due in the period between September 13 and December 30, 2004.[3] The Hurricane Ivan disaster areas include 12 Alabama counties, 16 Florida counties, eight Louisiana parishes, and 10 Mississippi counties. For purposes of the tax relief, affected taxpayers include individuals and business located in the disaster areas, those whose tax records are located in the disaster areas, and relief workers. The designated extension period for returns and other tax payments is September 13

---

[1] Reg. § 20.6161-1(c)(2) and Reg. § 20.6081-1(b).

[2] Code Sec. 7503.

[3] IRS News Release IR-2004-118, Sept. 22, 2004.

through December 30, 2004. Affected taxpayers will have until December 30, 2004, to file tax returns or make tax payments that have either an original or extended due date falling within the extension period. The IRS will abate interest and any late filing or late payment penalties that would otherwise apply to returns or payments subject to the extensions. In addition, affected taxpayers will have until December 30, 2004, to perform certain time-sensitive actions (see ¶2610). To qualify for relief, affected taxpayers should put "Hurricane Ivan" in red ink at the top of the return. Taxpayers located in the disaster area should contact the IRS if they receive penalties for filing returns or paying taxes late.

• *Tax Relief for Victims of Hurricane Frances*

Taxpayers affected by Hurricane Frances will have until December 30, 2004, to file tax returns and make tax payments that would otherwise be due in the period between September 3 and December 30, 2004.[4] The Hurricane Frances disaster area consists of 36 Florida counties. For purposes of tax relief, affected taxpayer include individuals and businesses located in the disaster area, those whose tax records are located in the disaster area, and relief workers. The designated extension period for returns and other tax payments is September 3 through December 30, 2004. Affected taxpayers will have until December 30, 2004, to file tax returns or make tax payments that have either an original or extended due date falling within the extension period. The IRS will abate interest and any late filing or late payment penalties that would otherwise apply to returns or payments subject to the extensions. In addition, affected taxpayers will have until December 30, 2004, to perform certain time-sensitive actions (see ¶2610). To qualify for relief, affected taxpayers should put "Hurricane Frances" in red ink at the top of the return. Taxpayers located in the disaster area should contact the IRS if they receive penalties for filing returns or paying taxes late.

• *Tax Relief for Victims of Tropical Storm Bonnie and Hurricane Charley*

The IRS has announced[5] that taxpayers in the areas struck by Tropical Storm Bonnie and Hurricane Charley will have until December 30, 2004, to filed tax returns and make tax payments that would otherwise be due in the period between August 11 and December 30, 2004. The IRS had originally set October 15, 2004, as the deadline for this relief, but extended it to December 30, 2004, because most of the disaster area in the counties struck by Tropical Storm Bonnie and Hurricane Charley were later struck by Hurricane Frances.[6] The Tropical Storm Bonnie and Hurricane Charley disaster area consists of 25 Florida counties. For purposes of tax relief, affected taxpayers include individuals and businesses located in the disaster area, those whose tax records are located in the disaster area, and relief workers. The designated extension period for returns and other tax payments is August 11 through December 30, 2004. Affected taxpayers will have until December 30, 2004, to file tax returns or make tax payments that have either an original or extended due date falling within the extension period. The IRS will abate interest and any late filing or late payment penalties that would otherwise apply to returns or payments subject to the extensions. In addition, affected taxpayers will have until December 30, 2004, to perform certain time-sensitive actions (see ¶2610). To qualify for relief, affected taxpayers should put "Bonnie/Charley" in red ink at the top of the return. Taxpayers located in

---

[4] IRS News Release IR-2004-115, Sept. 10, 2004.

[5] IRS News Release IR-2004-108, Aug. 16, 2004.

[6] IRS News Release IR-2004-115, Sept. 10, 2004.

the disaster area should contact the IRS if they receive penalties for filing returns or paying taxes late.

• *Tax Relief for California Wildfire Victims*

Residents of Southern California struck by wildfires had until December 29, 2003, to file tax returns or make tax payments that had either an original or extended due date falling within the period of October 21 through December 29, 2003.[7] The counties located in the disaster area and covered by the relief include Los Angeles, San Bernardino, San Diego, and Ventura. As a result of the extension, the IRS abated interest and any late filing or payment penalties that would have otherwise applied. The IRS also gave affected taxpayers until December 29, 2003, to complete other time-sensitive actions (see ¶2610).

IRS Web Site on Disaster Area Tax Relief

A new page on the IRS Web site provides information on the tax relief available to taxpayers in declared disaster areas, dating back to August 2004. The page includes previous releases for victims of storms, floods, and hurricanes, as well as other state-specific declarations. The releases identify the affected localities, the extension period for returns and other tax payments, and the applicable disaster designation. The Web address is: http://www.irs.gov/newsroom/article/0,,id=129002,00.html.

• *Tax Relief for Victims of Hurricane Isabel*

Taxpayers residing in the areas struck by Hurricane Isabel (the District of Columbia, and parts of Delaware, Maryland, North Carolina, and Virginia) had until November 18, 2003, to file tax returns or make tax payments that have either an original or extended due date falling within the period running from September 18 through November 18, 2003. Eligible taxpayers include individuals and businesses located in the disaster area, those whose tax records are located in the disaster area, and relief workers. As a result of the extensions to file and pay taxes, the IRS abated interest and any late filing or payment penalties that would have otherwise applied. The IRS also gave affected taxpayers until November 18, 2003, to complete other time-sensitive actions (described at ¶2610).[8]

• *Tax Relief for Victims of Power Blackout*

Tax relief was granted to taxpayers affected by the power blackout in the northeastern United States that occurred on August 14, 2003. Accordingly, the IRS considered as timely any tax returns or payments due from August 15, 2003, through August 22, 2003, if they were completed by August 22, 2003. The "affected taxpayers" eligible for relief include individuals and businesses located in the blackout areas, and those whose tax records are located in the area of the power blackout.[9]

• *Extension to Victims of Terrorist Attacks and Astronauts*

Congress, by enactment of the Victims of Terrorism Relief Act of 2001,[10] extended the estate tax exemption applicable to members of the military who die in a combat zone (see ¶1560, and the special estate tax rate schedule reproduced in the Appendix at ¶2605) to civilians who died as a result of certain terrorist attacks. Under P.L. 107-134, tax relief is extended to victims of the September 11,

---

[7] IRS News Release IR-2003-126, Oct. 28, 2003.

[8] IRS News Release IR-2003-112, Sept. 24, 2003.

[9] IRS News Release IR-2003-100, Aug. 15, 2003.

[10] P.L. 107-134.

2001 terrorist attacks,[11] as well as to the victims of the April 19, 1995 bombing of the Alfred P. Murrah Federal Building in Oklahoma City, and to individuals who died from anthrax-related attacks occurring on or after September 11, 2001, and before January 1, 2002.[12] Under this provision, the executor of an eligible estate can elect not to have the special provisions of P.L. 107-134 apply, in which case estate tax liability will be calculated pursuant to the generally applicable rules. The Act also amended Code Sec. 7508A to give the IRS the power to suspend certain tax-related acts (such as the filing of returns and the payment of tax) for up to one year in cases of terrorist or military actions. The IRS can exercise this authority regardless of whether the President has declared the terrorist or military action to be in a disaster area. (In addition to the estate tax relief, the Act extended to the victims of these terrorist attacks the income tax relief provided by Code Sec. 692(c), which exempts federal military and civilian employees from income taxes in the year of their death (and generally the prior taxable year) if they die as a result of military or terrorist activity inside or outside of the United States.)

Procedures for determining whether a terrorist or military action has occurred for purposes of Code Sec. 692(c)(2) have been issued by the IRS, effective May 10, 2004. If a determination is made that a terrorist or military action has occurred, the IRS may exercise the authority under Code Sec. 7508A to disregard a period of up to one year for determining (1) the timeliness of acts under Code Sec. 7508(a)(1), (2) the amount of any addition to tax, and (3) the amount of any credit or refund.[13]

The Military Family Tax Relief Act of 2003[14] further extended the estate tax relief available applicable to the Armed Forces and terrorist victims to astronauts who die in the line of duty. This relief applies to estates of decedents dying after December 31, 2002.[15] The Act also amended Code Sec. 7508 to give extensions of time for performing certain acts to members of the Armed Forces serving in contingency operations.[16]

Estate tax refund opportunity until January 22, 2003. The executor of the estate of a decedent who qualifies under the provisions of P.L. 107-134 (above) is to compute the decedent's estate tax liability based on a special rate table contained in Code Sec. 2201(c) (see the Appendix at ¶2605). Estate tax returns containing a computation based on this schedule must be mailed to the following address: Internal Revenue Service, E & G Department/Stop 824T, 201 W. Rivercenter Blvd., Covington, KY 41011.

Estate executors had until January 22, 2003, to file for an estate tax refund based on this special rate schedule.[17]

Victim compensation fund recoveries. The IRS has concluded that there will be no estate tax consequences if an estate or beneficiary receives a recovery from the September 11th Victim Compensation Fund.[18]

---

[11] The victims of the September 11, 2001 terrorist acts include the individuals killed in the attacks on the World Trade Center, the Pentagon, and the crash of United Airlines Flight 93 in Somerset County, Pennsylvania (IRS Publication 3920 (Feb. 2002), Tax Relief for Victims of Terrorist Attacks, p. 1).

[12] Code Sec. 692(d)(4) and Code Sec. 2201, as amended by P.L. 107-134.

[13] Rev. Proc. 2004-26, IRB 2004-19, 890.

[14] P.L. 108-121.

[15] Code Sec. 2201, as amended by the Military Family Tax Relief Act of 2003 (P.L. 108-121).

[16] Code Sec. 7508, as amended by the Military Family Tax Relief Act of 2003 (P.L. 108-121).

[17] IRS Publication 3920 (Feb. 2002), Tax Relief for Victims of Terrorist Attacks, p. 10.

[18] IRS Publication 3920 (Feb. 2002), p. 10.

Toll-free IRS answer line. The IRS has set up a special toll-free telephone number for individuals with tax questions related to the terrorist attacks against the United States on September 11, 2001, or related to participation in a combat zone, as designated by the Department of Defense. Taxpayers whose ability to meet their federal tax obligations has been affected by the events of September 11 can call the IRS at 1-866-562-5227 on Monday through Friday, 7 a.m. to 10 p.m.[19]

Tax obligations falling between September 10-24, 2001. The due date for *all* federal tax obligations falling between September 10, 2001, and September 24, 2001, was postponed until September 24, 2001, for all taxpayers who, regardless of their location, have difficulty meeting their tax obligations. This postponement covers the filing of returns and claims for refund, payment of tax, making elections, and the filing of any other tax document.[20]

Disruptions in transportation and delivery services. Taxpayers who had difficulty in meeting their federal tax obligations because of disruptions in the transportation and delivery of documents by mail or private delivery services resulting from the terrorist attack, but who did not otherwise qualify for relief under Code Sec. 7508A, had until November 15, 2001, to file returns and make payments required to be made from September 11, 2001, through October 31, 2001.[21]

Affected taxpayers in presidentially declared disaster area. In Notice 2001-61, certain affected taxpayers, including estates and trusts, were granted both a 120-day postponement and a six-month extension of time to file returns (and to pay the tax shown or required to be shown on those returns) that would have been due on or after September 11, 2001, and on or before November 30, 2001. Affected taxpayers unable to meet tax-related deadlines for acts required to be performed between September 11, 2001, and ending on November 30, 2001, were granted a 120-day postponement of time to meet the tax deadline.[22] Affected taxpayers whose previously granted extensions of time to file their 2000 individual income tax returns were to expire on or after December 1, 2001, and on or before January 31, 2002, were granted additional relief. These taxpayers were given an additional extension until February 15, 2002, to file their returns (Notice 2001-68[23]). Included among the transfer tax-related relief acts covered were filing a claim for a credit of state death taxes and a claim for foreign death taxes, electing alternate valuation on a late-filed estate tax return, making a qualified disclaimer, and making a qualified domestic trust election. A complete list of transfer tax-related acts eligible for postponement[24] is reproduced in the Appendix at ¶2610. In addition, affected taxpayers were provided a 60-day postponement for filing Tax Court petitions that otherwise would have had to be filed during the month of December 2001.

In addition to those persons described in Reg. §301.7508A-1(d)(1) as affected taxpayers, taxpayers affected by the terrorist attack included (1) victims of the crashes, including those on the planes and those on the ground, of the four commercial jets hijacked on September 11, 2001, as well as persons missing as a result of the attacks, (2) all workers assisting in the relief activities in the covered disaster areas and in Pennsylvania, regardless of whether they were affiliated with a recognized government or philanthropic organization, and (3) taxpayers

---

[19] IRS News Release, IR-2001-84, Sept. 24, 2001.

[20] Notice 2001-63, 2001-2 CB 308.

[21] Notice 2001-61, 2001-2 CB 305.

[22] Notice 2001-61, 2001-2 CB 305.

[23] Notice 2001-68, 2001-2 CB 504.

[24] Rev. Proc. 2004-13, IRB 2004-4, 335, superseding Rev. Proc. 2002-71, IRB 2002-46, 850.

whose place of employment was located within the presidentially declared disaster area. For purposes of this relief, the presidentially declared disaster areas cover Bronx, Kings, New York (boroughs of Brooklyn and Manhattan), Queens, and Richmond counties in New York and Arlington County in Virginia.[25]

In Notice 2002-40,[26] the IRS granted relief from the running of interest and the failure to pay penalties relating to payments for which Notice 2001-61 or Notice 2001-68 had extended or postponed the due dates. Notice 2002-40 applied only to income taxes and certain excise and employment taxes. In Announcement 2003-18,[27] the IRS extended the interest and failure to pay penalty relief described in Notice 2002-40 to payments associated with federal estate tax returns for which Notice 2001-61 or Notice 2001-68 had extended or postponed the due dates, for the period of the extension or postponement provided in those notices. In general, the relief will apply to any affected taxpayer filing an estate tax return: (1) for which necessary tax records were located in the covered disaster area (as defined in Notice 2001-61); (2) signed and filed by a person who resided in the covered disaster area; or (3) signed and filed by a corporate fiduciary who was administering the estate from a place of business located in the covered disaster area.

The IRS stated that it is unable to identify the taxpayers who are eligible for the relief described in Announcement 2003-18. Therefore, taxpayers who believe they are eligible for relief should either call the Estate and Gift Tax Department at (866) 699-4083 (toll-free), Monday through Friday from 7:00 a.m. to 7:00 p.m., or write to the Cincinnati Compliance Service Center, Estate and Gift Tax Department, Attn: Stop 824, 201 W. River Center Blvd., Covington, KY 41011.

¶ 1660 Place of Payment

The law requires that the tax be paid without any need for assessment or notice and demand to the internal revenue officer with whom the estate tax return is filed.[28] For U.S. citizens and residents, the location where the estate tax return must be filed depends on the state of the decedent's residence at death, and the date of the decedent's death. All estate tax returns filed after 2001, other than those with a foreign, APO, or FPO address, are to be filed with the IRS Service Center, Cincinnati, OH 45999.[29] A listing of the filing locations appears in the Appendix at ¶2850. If the decedent was a nonresident citizen, the return must be filed with the IRS Service Center, Philadelphia, Pennsylvania 19255. However, if the decedent is a nonresident alien, the estate must file Form 706-NA (United States Estate (and Generation-Skipping Transfer) Tax Return—Estate of Nonresident Not a Citizen of the United States) (Rev. Jan. 2003).

¶ 1662 Method of Filing the Return

Unless the estate tax return is hand-delivered to the IRS Service Center at which the return is to be filed, the Form 706 (United States Estate (and Generation-Skipping Transfer) Tax Return) and accompanying schedules, attachments, and payments (if any) normally should be mailed by U.S. Postal Service certified or registered mail or by one of the IRS designated private delivery services, no later than the due date for filing the return. Although the Internal Revenue Code does not require a particular mode of delivery of estate tax returns, returns sent

---

25 Notice 2001-61, 2001-2 CB 305.

26 Notice 2002-40, 2002-1 CB 1152.

27 Announcement 2003-18, IRB 2003-13, 675.

28 Code Sec. 6151; Reg. §20.6081-1(b).

29 Announcement 2001-74, 2001-2 CB 40.

via U.S. Postal Service or designated private delivery services (listed below) will be given the benefit of the rule that deems a timely mailed return to have been timely filed and payment timely received (provided that payment of tax was included with the return).[30]

The following private delivery services qualify for the timely mailing as timely filing/paying rule, effective September 5, 2002:[31]

(1) Airborne Express (Airborne): Overnight Air Express Service, Next Afternoon Service, and Second Day Service;

(2) DHL Worldwide Express (DHL): DHL "Same Day" Service and DHL USA Overnight;

(3) Federal Express (FedEx): FedEx Priority Overnight, FedEx Standard Overnight, FedEx 2 Day, FedEx International Priority, and FedEx International First; and

(4) United Parcel Service (UPS): UPS Next Day Air, UPS Next Day Air Saver, UPS 2nd Day Air, UPS 2nd Day Air A.M., UPS Worldwide Express Plus, and UPS Worldwide Express.

• ***Cover (Transmittal) Letter Accompanying the Return***

Although not required by the Internal Revenue Code, it is advisable to send an accompanying cover or transmittal letter with the return. This letter can serve the following purposes: (1) identification of the return filed and payment made (including prior payments); (2) discussion of specific issues that the estate would like to highlight; (3) communication of certain tax elections (such as request for discharge of fiduciary liability); and (4) request for the IRS to acknowledge receipt of the return.

The cover letter, addressed to the appropriate IRS Service Center, should normally contain the following information:

(1) name of decedent;

(2) decedent's Social Security number;

(3) decedent's date of death;

(4) recitation of fiduciary's capacity;

(5) statement of tax paid with return (if any due), and statement of prior payments made;

(6) statement of any issues that the estate would like to highlight;

(7) statement of elections to be made, such as a request for discharge of fiduciary liability; and

(8) request for the IRS to acknowledge receipt of return. In order for the IRS to respond as requested, the fiduciary should include a duplicate copy of the cover letter with a designated place for signature of IRS personnel, and a postage paid, self-addressed envelope.

¶ 1665 Form of Payment

The tax may be paid by check, draft, money order, credit card, or debit card. Payment by check, draft, or money order should be made out to the "United States Treasury," rather than to the "IRS."

---

[30] Code Sec. 7502.

[31] Notice 2002-62, IRB 2002-39, 574, modifying and superseding Notice 97-26, 1997-1 CB 413, and Notice 2001-62, 2001-2 CB 307.

The decedent's name, Social Security number and "Form 706" should be written on the check, draft, or money order in order to assist the IRS in posting it to the proper account. If the amount of tax paid with the return is different from the amount of the net estate tax payable as computed on the return, the executor should explain the difference in an attached statement. For example, the executor should indicate that he or she has made prior payments to the IRS in the statement.

Effective for tax payments made after December 31, 1998, the IRS is authorized to accept payment of taxes by credit or debit card. A payment by credit or debit card is deemed made when the card issuer authorizes the transaction, provided that the payment is actually received in the ordinary course of business. Although the IRS is prohibited from imposing a fee on individuals who pay their taxes by such methods, third-party service providers contracted to process the credit and debit card transactions are not prohibited from charging fees.[32]

• *Partial Payments*

If additional taxes, penalty, and interest have been assessed against a taxpayer and the taxpayer provides specific written directions as to how his or her partial payment is to be applied, the IRS will apply the payment in accordance with such directions. However, if the taxpayer does not provide such written directions, the IRS will apply the payment to periods in the order of priority that will serve the "best interest" of the IRS. The payment will be applied to satisfy the liability for successive periods, in descending order of priority, until the payment is fully absorbed. If the amount applied is less than the liability, the amount will be applied to tax, penalty, and interest, in that order. Similar rules will apply for payments made pursuant to the terms of offers in compromise and collateral agreements.[33]

• *Flower Bonds*

Treasury bonds of certain issues (known as "flower" bonds) formerly were redeemable at par (plus the accrued interest from the last preceding date to the date of redemption) on the death of the owner, at the option of the representatives of, or persons entitled to, his or her estate. They could be redeemed for the purpose of having the proceeds applied in payment of the estate taxes on the decedent's estate. These bonds are no longer useful estate tax planning tools because the last available issue of flower bonds remaining for payment of estate taxes carried a due date of November 15, 1998. Treasury obligations issued after March 3, 1971, will not be redeemable at par value in payment of estate taxes.[34]

¶ 1672 Estate Tax on Closely Held Business Interests

The estate of an individual who dies owning a closely held business interest may qualify for a special elective method of paying the estate tax attributable to the interest. Effective for estates of decedents dying after 1981, estate tax on a closely held business interest may be deferred for up to 14 years, with the estate making annual payments of interest only for the first four years and paying the balance in 10 annual installments of principal and interest. This deferral is permitted only if the value of the interest exceeds 35 percent of the decedent's adjusted gross estate.

---

[32] Reg. § 301.6311-2.

[33] Rev. Proc. 2002-26, 2002-1 CB 746, superseding Rev. Rul. 73-304, 1973-2 CB 42, Rev. Rul. 73-305, 1973-2 CB 43, and Rev. Rul. 79-284, 1979-2 CB 83.

[34] Act Sec. 4, P.L. 92-5.

- ***Installment Payments***

If more than 35 percent of the adjusted gross estate is an interest in a farm or other closely held business, an executor may elect to defer payments of tax attributable to the interest for five years (paying interest only) and, thereafter, pay the tax in equal installments over the next 10 years.[35] The maximum payment period, however, is 14 years rather than 15 years because the due date for the last payment of interest coincides with the due date for the first installment of tax. For purposes of the 35-percent rule, the adjusted gross estate consists of the gross estate less debts, expenses, claims, and losses deductible under Code Sec. 2053 or Code Sec. 2054.

For decedents dying prior to 1998, interest is payable at a special four-percent rate on the estate tax attributable to the first $1 million in value of a farm or other closely held business. For decedents dying after 1997, the four-percent rate is replaced with a two-percent rate that applies to the first $1 million of *taxable* value of a farm or closely held business. In addition, effective for estates of decedents dying after December 31, 1997, the $1 million ceiling is indexed annually for inflation.[36]

For purposes of the 35-percent rule, an "interest in a closely held business" is defined as:

(1) an interest as a proprietor in a business carried on as a proprietorship;

(2) an interest as a partner in a partnership carrying on a trade or business (a) with no more than 15 partners, or (b) where 20 percent or more of its assets help determine the decedent's gross estate; or

(3) stock in a corporation carrying on a trade or business (a) with no more than 15 stockholders, or (b) where 20 percent of its voting stock is included in determining the decedent's gross estate.[37]

But see, also, the heading "Impact of the 2001 Act", below, discussing the expansion of the permissible number of partners or shareholders to 45, effective for estates of decedents dying after December 31, 2001.

Property owned through a corporation, partnership, estate, or trust is regarded as proportionately owned by shareholders, partners, or beneficiaries. For purposes of this election, interests in two or more closely held businesses are treated as an interest in a single closely held business if 20 percent or more of the total value of each business is included in the decedent's gross estate.[38]

The election to defer and pay in installments estate tax attributable to a decedent's closely held business interest is made by attaching to a timely filed estate tax return a notice of election containing the following information:

(1) the decedent's name and taxpayer identification number as they appear on the estate tax return;

(2) the amount of tax to be paid in installments;

(3) the date selected for payment of the first installment;

(4) the number of annual installments, including the first installment, in which the tax is to be paid;

(5) the properties shown on the estate tax return that constitute the closely held business interest (identified by schedule and item number); and

---

[35] Code Sec. 6166.

[36] Code Sec. 6601(j).

[37] Code Sec. 6166(b)(1).

[38] Code Sec. 6166(c).

(6) the facts supporting the conclusion that the estate qualifies for the deferral and installment election.

If it is not certain at the time for filing the estate tax return that the estate qualifies for the election, the estate may make a protective election. A final election notice is then filed within 60 days after it is determined that the estate qualifies for the election. The final notice must contain the information noted above.[39]

• *Impact of the 2001 Act*

The Economic Growth and Tax Relief Reconciliation Act of 2001 (P.L. 107-16) (2001 Act) increases the number of allowable partners and shareholders that a closely held business cannot exceed from 15 to 45, effective for the estates of decedents dying after December 31, 2001.[40]

Sunset provision. In order to comply with the Congressional Budget Act of 1974, the 2001 Act provides that all provisions of, and amendments made by, the 2001 Act will not apply to estates of decedents dying, gifts made, or generation-skipping transfers, after December 31, 2010. Unless Congress acts affirmatively in the interim, the Internal Revenue Code will thereafter be applied and administered as if these provisions had not been enacted.

• *Holding Company Stock*

The stock of a holding company that directly or indirectly (through one or more other holding companies) owns stock in a closely held active trade or business will be considered stock in the business company for purposes of Code Sec. 6166 and, thus, may qualify for installment payment of estate taxes.[41] A "holding company" is defined as any corporation holding stock in another corporation.[42] A "business company" is any corporation carrying on a trade or business.[43] The provisions relating to the installment payment of estate taxes for holding company stock generally are effective with respect to estates of decedents dying after July 18, 1984. However, if on June 22, 1984, and at all times prior to the decedent's death, a corporation has 15 or fewer shareholders (45 or fewer, for decedents dying after December 31, 2001; see above), and the stock of the corporation is included in the decedent's gross estate, the stock of all wholly owned subsidiaries, at the executor's election, may be treated as one corporation.[44]

In order for holding company stock to qualify for the election, several requirements applicable to closely held business interests generally must be met. First, the interest that is held by the holding company must meet the general rule of Code Sec. 6166(b)(1)(C) requiring that (1) a closely held business have 15 or fewer shareholders (45 or fewer, for decedents dying after December 31, 2001; see above), or (2) the decedent own 20 percent or more of the corporation's voting stock. Second, the value of the business interest held by the holding company must exceed 35 percent of the value of the decedent's adjusted gross estate. Only the portion of the holding company stock that represents direct or indirect ownership of nonreadily tradable stock in a business company qualifies for the election.[45]

---

[39] Reg. § 20.6166-1(d).

[40] Code Sec. 6166(b)(1)(B)(ii), Code Sec. 6166(b)(1)(C)(ii), and Code Sec. 6166(b)(9)(B)(iii)(I), as amended by P.L. 107-16.

[41] Code Sec. 6166(b)(8).

[42] Code Sec. 6166(b)(8)(D)(i).

[43] Code Sec. 6166(b)(8)(D)(ii).

[44] Act Sec. 1021(d), P.L. 98-369.

[45] Code Sec. 6166(b)(8)(B).

For purposes of determining whether the decedent, through holding company stock, owned at least 20 percent of the value of the voting stock of the business company, holding company stock will be treated as voting stock to the extent that the holding company's stock owns directly (or indirectly through one or more other holding companies) voting stock in the business company.[46]

• *Impact of the 2001 Act*

The 2001 Act clarifies the application of the Code Sec. 6166 rules by providing that only the stock of holding companies, not that of operating subsidiaries, must be nonreadily tradable in order to qualify for installment payments. However, such qualifying businesses are only entitled to make installment payments over five years rather than 10 years.[47] These amendments apply to the estates of decedents dying after December 31, 2001. However, see discussion of Sunset provision, above.

• *Making the Election*

Elections with respect to holding company stock are to be made by including on the notice of election a statement that such an election is being made and the facts forming the basis for the conclusion that the estate qualifies for such an election. If such an election is made, the special interest rate and the five-year deferral of principal payments provisions are not available. If the executor fails to state the amount of tax to be paid in installments or the number of installments, the election is presumed to be for the maximum amount payable and for payment thereof in 10 equal annual installments.[48]

• *Attribution of Ownership*

For installment payment purposes, all stock and partnership interests of a decedent and his family will be considered owned by the decedent.[49] Family members whose interests will be considered held by the decedent in order to meet these requirements are brothers and sisters, spouse, grandparents (ancestors), and children and grandchildren (lineal descendants).

• *Special Attribution Election*

A special attribution-of-ownership rule applies if the executor of the estate so elects. This rule provides that all nonreadily tradable stock and all partnership capital interests of a decedent and the decedent's family will be considered owned by the decedent for purposes of determining whether 20 percent of the corporation or partnership is includible in the decedent's gross estate.[50] Family members whose interests will be considered as held by the decedent are brothers, sisters, spouse, ancestors, and lineal descendants.

If the benefits of this rule are elected, the estate is deemed to have elected to pay the tax attributable to the business interest in 10 installments beginning on the due date for payment of the decedent's estate tax; there is no deferral period. Additionally, the special interest rate applied under the regular deferral and installment election is not available.[51]

It should be noted that the stock or partnership interest attributed to a decedent under this rule is attributed only for purposes of the 20-percent require-

---

[46] Code Sec. 6166(b)(8)(C).

[47] Code Sec. 6166(b)(8)(B), as amended by P.L. 107-16.

[48] Temp. Reg. § 301.9100-6T.

[49] Code Sec. 6166(b)(2)(D).

[50] Code Sec. 6166(b).

[51] Code Sec. 6166(b)(7)(A)(iii).

ments. Thus, the value of the attributed stock or partnership interest is not included in the decedent's gross estate for purposes of the 35-percent rule.

• ***Installment Payment Denied for Passive Assets***

In the case of all corporations and partnerships, only active business assets are considered for purposes of meeting the 35-percent-of-adjusted-gross-estate test discussed above, as well as for determining the value of the business interest qualifying for the election.[52] However, this rule does not apply for purposes of the accelerated payment provisions (see below). Any asset other than an asset used in carrying on a trade or business constitutes a passive asset. This definition includes stock in another corporation unless (1) the stock is deemed to be held by the decedent by reason of the holding company rules of Code Sec. 6166(b)(8) (see above), and (2) the stock qualifies under the 35-percent-of-adjusted-gross-estate test.

An exception is provided for certain active corporations, whereby such corporations will be treated as one corporation if:

(1) a corporation owns at least 20 percent of the value of the voting stock of another corporation, or such corporation has no more than 15 shareholders; and

(2) at least 80 percent of the value of each such corporation is attributable to assets used in carrying on a trade or business.[53]

For purposes of applying the 80-percent-of-value test ((2), above) to the corporation holding stock in a second corporation, the second corporation's stock will not be considered.

• ***Impact of the 2001 Act***

Effective for the estates of decedents dying after December 31, 2001, stock in certain qualifying lending and finance businesses will be treated as stock in an active trade or business for purposes of the installment payment of estate taxes.[54] However, the five-year deferral of principal is not available to such businesses, and they are entitled to make installment payments over five years rather than over 10 years.[55]

In order to be considered a qualifying lending and finance business, the entity must have:

(1) conducted "substantial activity" with respect to the lending and finance business immediately prior to the decedent's death; or

(2) during three of the five tax years prior to the decedent's death:

(a) employed at least one full-time manager and 10 full-time non-owner employees; and

(b) earned at least $5 million in gross receipts from lending and finance activities.[56]

In addition, the term "lending and finance business" is defined as a trade or business that is engaged in:

(1) making loans;

---

[52] Code Sec. 6166(b)(9).

[53] Code Sec. 6166(b)(9)(iii).

[54] Code Sec. 6166(b)(10), as added by P.L. 107-16.

[55] Code Sec. 6166(b)(10)(A)(ii) and Code Sec. 6166(b)(10)(A)(iii), as added by P.L. 107-16.

[56] Code Sec. 6166(b)(10)(B)(i), as added by P.L. 107-16.

(2) purchasing or discounting accounts receivable, notes, or installment obligations;

(3) renting and leasing of real and tangible personal property; and

(4) rendering services or making facilities available in the ordinary course of a lending or finance business.

The term would also include the rendering of services or making facilities available in connection with activities described in items (1) through (4) that are carried on by a corporation rendering such services or making facilities available, or another corporation that is a member of an affiliated group, as defined in Code Sec. 1504 (without regard to Code Sec. 1504(b)(3)).[57] However, the definition of a qualified lending and finance business does *not* include an interest in an entity if the stock or debt of that entity was readily tradable on an established securities market or secondary market at any time during the three years preceding the decedent's death.[58] However, see discussion of Sunset provision, above.

• ***Acceleration of Unpaid Taxes***

Under certain conditions, taxes that have been deferred under Code Sec. 6166 will become due. The following rules govern this acceleration of unpaid taxes:[59]

(1) Portions of an interest representing less than 50 percent of the value of the decedent's interest in a closely held business may be disposed of and/or withdrawn before payment of the balance of the estate taxes attributable to the interest will be accelerated. For this purpose, dispositions and withdrawals are aggregated.

(2) The transfer of the decedent's interest in a closely held business on the death of the original heir, or on the death of any subsequent transferee receiving the interest as a result of the 60prior transferor's death, will not cause acceleration of taxes if each subsequent transferee is a family member (within the meaning of Code Sec. 267(c)(4))[60] of the transferor.

(3) A delinquent payment of interest or tax will accelerate the due date of the unpaid tax balance if the full amount of payment is not paid within six months of the original due date. However, the late payment will not be eligible for the special two-percent interest rate (see ¶1680), and a penalty of five percent per month of the amount of the payment will be imposed.

(4) If the estate has undistributed net income for any tax year ending on or after the due date for the first installment, the estate will pay an amount equal to any undistributed net income for any tax year in liquidation of the unpaid portion of the tax.

For purposes of acceleration of estate taxes deferred under Code Sec. 6166, all of the following will be considered as dispositions:

(1) disposition of any interest of holding company stock that was included in the decedent's gross estate;

---

[57] Code Sec. 6166(b)(10)(B)(ii), as added by P.L. 107-16.

[58] Code Sec. 6166(b)(10)(B)(iii), as added by P.L. 107-16.

[59] Code Sec. 6166(g)(1) and Code Sec. 6166(g)(2).

[60] An individual's family members include brothers and sisters (whether by whole or half blood), spouse, ancestors, and lineal descendants.

(2) withdrawal of money or property from the holding company attributable to any interest included in determining the decedent's gross estate;

(3) disposition of any interest in the stock of the business company by the holding company; or

(4) withdrawal of money or property from such business company attributable to such stock by the holding company owning such stock.[61]

A redemption of stock to pay death taxes under Code Sec. 303 is not considered a disposition of a portion of the business interest for purposes of determining whether the installment election has been terminated.[62]

The installment payments are subject to the quarterly interest rates (see ¶1680).

A federal court did not have jurisdiction to hear a refund suit commenced by an estate following the IRS's acceleration of the estate's estate tax liability in response to the estate's failure to make timely installment payments of tax required under Code Sec. 6166. So held the U.S. Court of Appeals for the Eighth Circuit, which concluded that it did not have subject matter jurisdiction over the estate's suit because the preconditions contained in Code Sec. 7422(j)(2) were not met.[63] Specifically, the estate (1) had not fully paid each installment of principal and interest due at the time the suit was filed, (2) had failed to pay the installments due during this litigation, and (3) had failed to pay the full amount of tax liability after acceleration by the IRS.

• ***Impact of the 2001 Act***

According to the Committee Reports to the 2001 Act, the current estate tax installment payment rules under Code Sec. 6166 will be retained after the repeal of the estate tax in 2010 so that estates that entered into installment arrangements before repeal will continue to make their payments past the repeal date. In addition, the provisions of Code Sec. 6166(g), which require the payment of unpaid tax on notice and demand if 50 percent or more of the value of the closely held business is disposed of, will be retained following repeal so that dispositions that occur after repeal will continue to subject the estate to the unpaid portion of the tax. (See ¶2595.)

¶ 1680 Discount, Interest, and Penalties

No provision is made for the allowance of a discount for payment of the tax in advance of the last day for payment. If the tax is not paid when due, various interest and other penalties may be assessed, depending on the extent and circumstances of the nonpayment.

• ***Interest***

Interest must be paid on any amount of tax that is unpaid when the return is due, without regard to any extension of time for payment.[64] Interest rates paid on underpayments and overpayments of estate tax are determined on a quarterly basis and are based on the federal short-term rate.[65] Interest accruing is compounded daily.[66]

---

[61] Code Sec. 6166(g)(1)(E) and Code Sec. 6166(g)(1)(F).

[62] Code Sec. 6166(g)(1)(B).

[63] *D. Hansen, Exr.*, CA-8, 2001-1 USTC ¶60,402.

[64] Code Sec. 6601 and Code Sec. 6611.

[65] Code Sec. 6621(b).

[66] Code Sec. 6622. See Rev. Proc. 95-17, 1995-1 CB 556, superseding Rev. Proc. 83-7, 1983-1 CB 583, for the uniform tables for

The interest rates for calendar quarters after 1993 are as follows:

Calendar Quarter Beginning:	*Rate on Underpayments:*	*Rate on Overpayments:*
10/1/2004	5%	5%
7/1/2004	4	4
4/1/2004	5	5
1/1/2004	4	4
10/1/2003	4	4
7/1/2003	5	5
4/1/2003	5	5
1/1/2003	5	5
10/1/2002	6	6
7/1/2002	6	6
4/1/2002	6	6
1/1/2002	6	6
10/1/2001	7	7
7/1/2001	7	7
4/1/2001	8	8
1/1/2001	9	9
10/1/2000	9	9
7/1/2000	9	9
4/1/2000	9	9
1/1/2000	8	8
10/1/99	8	8
7/1/99	8	8
4/1/99	8	8
1/1/99	7	7
10/1/98	8	7
7/1/98	8	7
4/1/98	8	7
1/1/98	9	8
10/1/97	9	8
7/1/97	9	8
4/1/97	9	8
1/1/97	9	8
10/1/96	9	8
7/1/96	9	8
4/1/96	8	7
1/1/96	9	8
10/1/95	9	8
7/1/95	9	8
4/1/95	10	9
1/1/95	9	8

An exception to these interest rates applies in the case of a farm or closely held business that qualifies for the 14-year installment payment election (see ¶1672). For decedents dying prior to 1998, a special four-percent interest rate is allowed on the estate tax attributable to the first $1 million in value for such farm or business.[67] The maximum amount that may be subject to the lower four-percent rate is the lesser of (1) $345,800 (the estate tax on $1 million), reduced by the amount of the allowable unified credit, or (2) the amount of estate tax that is attributable to the closely held business and that is payable in installments, as discussed at ¶1672. The current interest rates discussed above apply to the estate tax attributable to the value of property that exceeds $1 million.

(Footnote Continued)

computing interest using the Code Sec. 6622 daily compounding rules. The tables are effective for all interest computations made after December 31, 1994.

[67] Code Sec. 6601(j).

• *Decedents Dying After 1997*

For decedents dying after 1997, the four-percent rate is replaced with a special two-percent rate that applies to the first $1 million in *taxable* value (as indexed for inflation; $1,100,000 for 2002, $1,120,000 for 2003, and $1,140,000 for 2004) of a closely held business.[68] For 2004, the maximum amount eligible for the two-percent rate is $532,200 (a $1,088,000 tentative tax on $2,640,000 less the applicable unified amount of $555,800 for 2004). An executor of an estate of a decedent who died prior to 1998 may elect to apply the two-percent rate to the remaining installments.[69] The deferred estate tax in excess of the amount eligible for the two-percent rate is subject to a rate that is 45 percent of the federal underpayment rate.

Generally, interest is imposed on penalties, additional amounts, and additions to tax only if such penalty or addition is not paid within 21 calendar days (10 business days if the amount exceeds $100,000) after notice and demand, and then only for the period from the date of notice and demand to the date of payment. However, under an exception to the general rule, interest will be imposed on such additions to tax for failure to file for the period beginning on the due date of the return (including extensions) and ending on the date of payment of the addition to tax.[70]

Effective with respect to interest assessed on estate tax due for estates of decedents dying after July 30, 1996, the IRS has discretionary authority to abate the assessment of interest on any deficiency or payment attributable in whole or in part to any unreasonable error or delay by IRS employees in performing a ministerial or managerial act. An IRS error or delay will be taken into account under this provision only if no significant aspect of the error or delay is attributable to the taxpayer or to a person related to the taxpayer.[71] Taxpayers who seek abatement of interest should file Form 843 (Claim for Refund and Request for Abatement).

Interest paid on installment payments of the estate tax is not deductible as an administrative expense of the estate.[72]

• *Late Filing and Late Payment Penalties*

The penalty for failure to timely file a return is five percent for the first month of such failure and an additional five percent for each month or part of a month thereafter. The penalty may not exceed 25 percent and applies only when there is an underpayment of tax.[73]

An addition to tax is also imposed for failure to pay estate and gift taxes when due, unless the failure is shown to be for reasonable cause. The addition is one-half of one percent if the failure to pay exists no longer than a month, with an additional one-half of one percent per month during the continuance of the failure to pay, up to a maximum of 25 percent.[74]

If both a late-filing penalty and a late-payment penalty are imposed, the penalty for late payment is allowed as an offset against the penalty for late filing. Thus, in this situation, the maximum penalty is five percent per month, with a overall maximum cumulative penalty of 25 percent.[75]

---

[68] Code Sec. 6601(j); Rev. Proc. 2003-85, IRB 2003-49, 1184.

[69] Rev. Proc. 98-15, 1998-1 CB 374.

[70] Code Sec. 6601(e)(2).

[71] Reg. §301.6404-2, as adopted by T.D. 8789, Dec. 17, 1998.

[72] Code Sec. 2053(c)(1)(D).

[73] Code Sec. 6651(a)(1).

[74] Code Sec. 6651(a)(2).

[75] Code Sec. 6651(c)(1).

Fraud and negligence penalties will not apply in the case of a negligent or fraudulent failure to file a return. However, in the case of a fraudulent failure to file a return, the failure-to-file penalty is increased to 15 percent of the net amount of tax due for each month that the return is not filed, up to a maximum of five months, or 75 percent.[76]

• *Accuracy-Related Penalty*

Effective for returns due after December 31, 1989 (determined without regard to extensions), an accuracy-related penalty may be imposed with respect to any portion of an underpayment that is attributable, among other factors, to negligence or disregard of rules and regulations or any substantial understatement of estate or gift tax valuation on an estate or gift tax return.[77] The penalty is equal to 20 percent of the portion of the understatement. For estate and gift tax purposes, there is a substantial estate or gift tax valuation understatement if the value of any property claimed on any return is 50 percent or less of the amount determined to be the correct amount of such valuation. The accuracy-related penalty does not apply to any portion of an underpayment that is attributable to fraud.

The penalty is increased to 40 percent for gross valuation misstatements. A gross valuation misstatement occurs if the value of the property claimed on an estate or gift tax return is 25 percent or less than the amount determined to be correct.[78] No penalty will be imposed for a substantial valuation understatement unless the portion of the underpayment attributable to substantial valuation understatement exceeds $5,000.[79] Further, the accuracy-related penalty generally will not be imposed on any portion of an understatement if the taxpayer shows that there was a reasonable cause for the underpayment and that the taxpayer acted in good faith with respect to such portion.[80]

The U.S. Court of Appeals for the Ninth Circuit has held that where the IRS had assessed penalties based on what the Tax Court had concluded was an excessive valuation of estate assets, the IRS had the burden of proving the accuracy of its assessment.[81]

• *Fraud Penalty Coordinated with Accuracy-Related Penalty*

The fraud penalty is imposed at the rate of 75 percent of the portion of any underpayment that is attributable to fraud. The 20-percent accuracy-related penalty will not apply to any portion of an underpayment on which the fraud penalty is imposed.[82] The accuracy-related penalty may be applied to any portion of the underpayment that is not attributable to fraud; however, the taxpayer must establish the portion not attributable to fraud by a preponderance of the evidence.[83]

¶ 1682 Special Lien Procedure

If the election to pay taxes in up to 10 installments after a deferral period (see ¶ 1672) is made, a special lien procedure is available that relieves the executor from personal liability for the entire installment period.[84]

---

[76] Code Sec. 6651(f).

[77] Code Sec. 6662; Reg. § 1.6662-1, Reg. § 1.6662-2, Reg. § 1.6662-3, and Reg. § 1.6662-7.

[78] Code Sec. 6662(h).

[79] Code Sec. 6662(g)(2).

[80] Code Sec. 6664(c).

[81] *P. Mitchell Est.*, CA-9, 2001-1 USTC ¶ 60,403, aff'g in part, and vac'g and rem'g in part, 74 TCM 872, CCH Dec. 52,297(M), TC Memo. 1997-461.

[82] Code Sec. 6663.

[83] Code Sec. 6663(b).

[84] Code Sec. 6324A.

The executor and all parties having any interest in the property to which the lien is to attach must file a written agreement consenting to creation of the lien in favor of the government, in lieu of bond. The agreement must designate a responsible person to deal with the IRS as an agent for the beneficiaries and any other parties who consented to the lien. The IRS may not require a bond except to the extent that there is no adequate security for the unpaid principal plus interest.[85]

Upon election of the installment payment provision, a lien attaches to real property, and other property with a long useful life, in the amount of the deferred taxes plus the aggregate amount of interest on those taxes for the first four years of the deferral period.[86]

¶ 1685 Extension of Time for Payment

The executor of an estate can obtain a general extension of time for payment of the estate tax for a period not to exceed 12 months from the date fixed for payment of the estate tax if the executor is able to show that "reasonable cause" exists for granting the extension.[87] In addition, a discretionary extension of time to pay may be allowed for reasonable cause. The time for payment of estate taxes may be deferred for a period not in excess of 10 years.[88] "Reasonable cause" will exist under any of the following circumstances:

(1) the estate consists largely of a closely held business or farm and does not have sufficient funds to pay the tax on time;

(2) the estate is unable to gather sufficient liquid assets because of legal difficulties;

(3) the assets consist of annuities, royalties, contingent fees, or accounts receivable that are not collectible at the due date;

(4) litigation is required to collect assets in the decedent's estate;

(5) the estate must sell assets to pay the tax at a sacrifice price or in a depressed market;

(6) the estate does not—without borrowing at a rate of interest higher than that generally available—have sufficient funds to pay the entire tax and at the same time also provide for the surviving spouse's and children's allowances and outstanding claims against the estate;[89] or

(7) the estate's liquid assets are located in several jurisdictions and are not immediately subject to the executor's control.[90]

See also ¶1650 for special payment extensions allowed victims of the September 11, 2001, terrorist attack against the United States.

• ***Application for Extension***

The above extension must be applied for, in writing, by the executor on Form 4768 (Application for Extension of Time to File a Return and/or Pay U.S. Estate (and Generation-Skipping Transfer) Taxes). The application should be submitted to the Internal Revenue Service Center, Cincinnati, OH 45999 (if mailed via U.S. Postal Service) or to the Internal Revenue Service Center, 201 W. Rivercenter Blvd., Covington, KY 41019 (if sent via a courier service) and must state the period of extension requested, establish why it is impossible or imprac-

---

[85] Reg. §301.6324A-1.
[86] Code Sec. 6324A.
[87] Code Sec. 6161(a).
[88] Code Sec. 6161(a)(2).
[89] Reg. §20.6161-1(a)(1).
[90] Instructions for Form 4768 (Rev. Aug. 2003), p. 3.

tical for the executor to pay the full amount of the estate tax by the due date, and include a declaration that it is made under penalties of perjury.[91]

The District Director may require the executor to furnish security for payment of the amount for which an extension is granted.[92] Such an extension does not prevent the running of statutory interest at the rate (see ¶1680) beginning nine months after the decedent's death, although it may extend the time in which state death taxes must be paid in order to qualify as a credit against the estate tax.

Special provision is made for extending the time for payment of the tax where existence of a remainder or reversionary interest causes the executor to elect to postpone paying the tax on such interest until six months after termination of the preceding property interests. A discretionary extension of time to pay the estate tax attributable to a remainder or reversionary interest may be allowed for "reasonable cause" for additional periods not to exceed a total of three years.[93]

Notice of the exercise of this election to postpone payment of the tax in such instances must be filed with the District Director before the final date for paying the estate tax. Such notice should be accompanied by a certified copy of the will or other instrument creating the reversionary or remainder interest. Various other special requirements for this extension are set out in the regulations.

In the case of a deficiency, if "reasonable cause" is shown, an extension of time for payment may be granted under the regulations for a period not in excess of four years from the date otherwise fixed for the payment of the deficiency.[94] A satisfactory bond for not more than twice the deficiency may be required as a condition of such an extension, and the running of the statute of limitations for assessment and collection is suspended for the period of the extension. Interest at the current rate, as determined under Code Sec. 6621 (see ¶1680), is imposed until payment is made.

¶1690 Fiduciary Liability for Payment of Tax

An estate executor or other fiduciary charged with the responsibility of filing and paying estate tax must be careful that sufficient estate assets are retained for payment of estate taxes. If this is not done, the executor will be personally liable (that is, the executor's *personal* assets may be attached by the IRS) for any shortfall in the payment of tax that is attributable to the executor's distribution of estate assets to beneficiaries, rather than paying the estate taxes in full.[95] The U.S. Court of Appeals for the Eighth Circuit has held, however, that personal liability of executors cannot be established until an estate is found to be insolvent.[96]

¶1701 Requests for Factors, Computations, and Rulings

In the event that an actuarial factor (see ¶530), a computation, or a ruling is necessary to complete an estate or gift tax return, the estate representative, the donor, or the agent of either may request IRS assistance by writing to the Internal Revenue Service, Attn: CC:PA:LPD:DRU, P.O. Box 7604, Ben Franklin Station, Washington, D.C. 20044.[97] If a private delivery service is used, the address is: 1111 Constitution Ave., N.W., Attn: CC:PA:LPD:DRU, Room 6561, Washington, D.C. 20224.

---

[91] Reg. §20.6161-1(b). Instructions for Form 4768 (Rev. Aug. 2003), p. 3.

[92] Code Sec. 6165.

[93] Code Sec. 6163.

[94] Code Sec. 6161(b).

[95] 31 U.S.C. §192; Reg. §20.2002-1.

[96] *B. Schwartz and M.L. Raskin Est.*, CA-8, 77-2 USTC ¶13,201, 560 F2d 311.

[97] Rev. Proc. 2004-1, IRB 2004-1, 1.

The IRS is authorized to charge user fees for requests for rulings, determination and opinion letters, and similar requests. Pursuant to this authority, the IRS is presently imposing a $275 user fee for determination letters issued by District Directors with respect to estate, gift, and generation-skipping tax matters.[98]

The IRS ordinarily will not issue "comfort rulings," defined as letter rulings that involve an issue that is "clearly and adequately addressed" by statute, regulations, court decisions, revenue rulings and procedures, or other authority published in the Internal Revenue Bulletin.[99] In addition to the "comfort ruling" policy, the IRS continues to use other measures, including specific no-rule areas (see ¶1705), model documents, published ruling checklists, and automatic action revenue procedures.[100]

- *Information Necessary*

The IRS annually issues a general checklist questionnaire that must be included with all ruling requests.[101] In addition, the IRS has issued a checklist specifically related to estate, gift, and generation-skipping transfer tax issues that is effective for all ruling requests made on or after March 13, 1991.[102] The issuance of the checklist was in response to the fact that many ruling requests did not include all of the information required for the IRS to consider them.

The estate and gift tax checklist includes the following questions:

(1) Have you read and complied with the requirements and procedures of the Associate Chief Counsel (Technical), including the checklist, as set forth in the "-1" revenue procedure of the current calendar year [e.g., Rev. Proc. 2004-1, IRB 2004-1, 1]? The "-1" revenue procedure is published in the first IRB of the year.

(2) Have you read section 3 of the "-3" revenue procedure of the current calendar year, which sets forth issues on which the IRS will not rule? The "-3" revenue procedure is published in the first IRB of the year.

(3) Is the requested ruling within the no-rule area in the "-3" revenue procedure?

(4) If the request involves a will, a trust instrument, a deed of conveyance, or a contract, is a copy of the document attached?

(5) If the answer to item (4) is yes, and the document has not been executed, is a statement attached from the individual requesting the ruling that they have a present intention to execute the document?

(6) If the request involves an outright gift (as opposed to a gift in trust), is a copy of any deed of gift or other documents concerning the gift attached?

(7) If the request involves a disclaimer, is a copy of the disclaimer attached?

(8) If the request involves a disclaimer, is a complete description of the property to be disclaimed attached?

(9) If the request involves a decedent's estate tax and the estate tax return is due to be filed shortly, has a request for an extension of time to file the return been submitted to the District Director with jurisdiction over the return?

---

[98] Rev. Proc. 2004-1, IRB 2004-1, 1.

[99] Rev. Proc. 2004-1, IRB 2004-1, 1.

[100] Rev. Proc. 90-42, 1990-2 CB 420.

[101] Rev. Proc. 2004-1, IRB 2004-1, 1, Appendix A.

[102] Rev. Proc. 91-14, 1991-1 CB 482, Appendix A.

¶ 1705 Subjects for Which Rulings Will Not Be Issued

The IRS will not ordinarily issue advance rulings or determination letters with respect to the following subjects:

(1) whether the settlement of a charitable remainder trust upon the termination of the noncharitable interest is made within a reasonable period of time;

(2) the allowance deductions for amounts paid or permanently set aside for charitable purposes if there is a possibility that the corpus of a trust or estate may be invaded; and

(3) actuarial factors for valuing interest in the prospective gross estate of a living person or the prospective or hypothetical gifts of a donor.

In addition, rulings will not ordinarily be issued with respect to the following subjects:

(1) whether a pooled income fund satisfies the requirements of Code Sec. 642(c)(5) or whether certain charitable remainder trusts satisfy the requirements of Code Sec. 664;

(2) whether a transfer to a pooled income fund or charitable remainder trust qualifies for an estate or gift tax charitable deduction;

(3) whether a net income with makeup charitable remainder unitrust (NIMCRUT) qualifies as a charitable remainder trust if certain individuals can control the timing of the trust's receipt of income from a partnership or a deferred annuity contract;

(4) whether the transfer of property to a trust will be a gift of a present interest under certain circumstances;

(5) whether Code Sec. 2514(e) will be applicable if a trust beneficiary permits a power of withdrawal to lapse under certain circumstances;

(6) whether a trust will lose its grandfathered status for purposes of the generation-skipping transfer tax if the situs of the trust is changed to one outside of the United States;

(7) whether annuity interests are qualified annuity interests under Code Sec. 2702(b) if the amount of the annual annuity interest is more than 50 percent, or the remainder interest is less than 10 percent, of the initial value of the property transferred to the trust; and

(8) whether a trust with one term holder satisfies the requirements for a qualified personal residence trust.

In addition, the IRS ordinarily will not issue "comfort rulings," defined in Rev. Proc. 2004-1, IRB 2004-1, 1, as letter rulings that involve an issue that is "clearly and adequately addressed" by statute, regulations, court decisions, revenue rulings and procedures, or other authority published in the Internal Revenue Bulletin.[103]

---

[103] Rev. Proc. 2004-3, IRB 2004-1, 114.

GIFT TAX

Chapter 31

NATURE OF THE TAX

¶ 2000 Description of Gift Tax

Like the estate tax, the gift tax is an excise tax levied on transfers of property made without adequate and full consideration. Because the gift tax is a tax on the transfer of property, rather than on the property itself, its application is generally not affected by the nature of the property or by any tax exemptions accorded to such property. An exception applies with respect to nonresidents who are not citizens of the United States.

The gift tax is levied during the transferor's lifetime and is cumulative in nature. The tax is paid annually, by means of a gift tax return, Form 709 (United States Gift (and Generation-Skipping Transfer) Tax Return) (2004). The return is due on or before April 15 of the year following the calendar year in which the taxable gifts were made.

Spouses who elect to split post-December 31, 2002, gifts must, regardless of the amount of the gift, file Form 709. For split gifts not exceeding $22,000 per donee made before January 1, 2003, spouses had been able to file Form 709-A (United States Short Form Gift Tax Return) (Rev. Oct. 2002) (see ¶2200). Form 709-A has been declared obsolete for gifts made after December 31, 2002.[1]

Although the estate and generation-skipping transfer taxes are scheduled to be repealed after December 31, 2009, the gift tax will remain in effect after this date. However, several changes to the gift tax—some of which are phased in over several years—will complicate gift tax compliance and planning for several years to come:

(1) the gift tax unified credit was "de-unified" after 2001;

(2) a unified tax rate schedule will continue to apply to the estate and gift taxes for decedents dying, and gifts made, before 2010 (and will incorporate phased-in reductions to the maximum tax rate); and

(3) the maximum tax rate applicable for gifts made after December 31, 2009 (35 percent) will be considerably lower than either the current maximum unified transfer tax (48 percent for gifts made in 2004), or maximum unified transfer tax rate immediately before the repeal of the estate tax (45 percent for gifts made in 2009).

---

[1] Instructions for Form 709 (2004), p. 1.

¶ 2005 Unified Rate Schedule

In determining gift tax liability, a "tentative tax" (before the unified credit, see ¶2007) is computed under the applicable transfer tax rate schedule in Code Sec. 2001. For gifts made, and the estates of decedents dying, in 2004, the unified transfer tax rates range from an effective minimum rate (due to operation of the unified credit) of 41 percent to a maximum rate of 48 percent, applicable to cumulative transfers over $2 million. For 2003, the maximum rate was 49 percent on cumulative transfers over $2 million. For 2002, the maximum rate was 50 percent on cumulative transfers over $2.5 million. In addition, for cumulative transfers exceeding $10 million in years prior to 2002, five percent of the excess of any transfer over $10 million is added to the tentative tax computed in determining the ultimate transfer tax liability (see ¶10 for the unified transfer tax rate schedule in effect for years 1984 through 2001).

- ***Impact of the 2001 Act (2002–2009)***

The Economic Growth and Tax Relief Reconciliation Act of 2001 (P.L. 107-16) (2001 Act) repeals the estate tax in 2010. Prior to repeal, a number of modifications are made to the maximum estate and gift tax rate and applicable exclusion amount (discussed at ¶2007). Under the 2001 Act, the top marginal rate was reduced to 49 percent for gifts made, and decedents dying, in 2003, and to 48 percent for gifts made, and decedents dying, in 2004, with further reductions in later years (see ¶10 for the transfer tax rate schedule in effect for years 2002 through 2009).

- ***Impact of the 2001 Act (after 2009)***

The gift tax is retained following the repeal of the estate tax in 2010. For gifts made after December 31, 2009, the tentative tax is computed under the following rate schedule:[2]

Gift Tax Rate Schedule: After 2009

(A) Amount subject to tax more than—	*(B) Amount subject to tax equal to or less than—*	*(C) Tax on amount in column (A)*	*(D) Rate of tax on excess over amount in column (A) Percent*
...	$10,000	...	18
$10,000	20,000	$1,800	20
20,000	40,000	3,800	22
40,000	60,000	8,200	24
60,000	80,000	13,000	26
80,000	100,000	18,200	28
100,000	150,000	23,800	30
150,000	250,000	38,800	32
250,000	500,000	70,800	34
500,000	...	155,800	35

Sunset provision. In order to comply with the Congressional Budget Act of 1974, the 2001 Act provides that all provisions of, and amendments made by, the 2001 Act will not apply to estates of decedents dying, gifts made, or generation-skipping transfers, after December 31, 2010. Unless Congress acts affirmatively in the interim, the Internal Revenue Code will thereafter be applied and administered as if these provisions had not been enacted.

---

[2] Code Sec. 2502(a)(2).

The term "taxable gifts" means the gross amount of gifts less: (1) the annual exclusion per gift ($11,000 (as indexed) for gifts made in 2002 through 2004, $10,000 for gifts made after 1981 and before 2002, and $3,000 for gifts made before 1982); and (2) any charitable or marital deductions that are available for the year (or quarter).[3]

A separate unified estate and gift tax rate schedule applies to estates of, and gifts made by, nonresidents who are not citizens of the United States (see ¶2600).

For gifts made before 1977, the separate gift and estate tax rates applied, with gift taxes set at three-fourths of estate taxes. However, taxable gifts before 1977 affect the rate at which post-1976 gifts are taxed (see ¶2008).

¶ 2007 Unified Credit

The unified credit (applicable credit amount) is the amount that is subtracted from the taxpayer's gift or estate tax liability.[4] For tax years 2002 through 2009, the gift tax applicable exclusion amount remains constant at $1 million, resulting in an applicable credit of $345,800.

For years 2002 through 2009, the amount of the gift tax unified credit is equal to (1) the applicable credit amount in effect under Code Sec. 2010(c) for such calendar year, determined as if the applicable exclusion amount were $1 million, reduced by (2) the sum of the amounts allowable as a credit under Code Sec. 2505 for all preceding calendar periods.[5] However, the allowable credit for any one year may not exceed the gift tax liability for that calendar period.[6]

Prior to changes made by the 2001 Act, for years before 2004, the amount of the unified credit for gift tax (Code Sec. 2505) was equal to the unified credit for estate tax (Code Sec. 2001) (see ¶10).

• *Computation of Credit Following Estate Tax Repeal*

The 2001 Act retains the gift tax following estate tax repeal in 2010. Gift tax liability for years after 2009 is determined by using a rate schedule created by the 2001 Act. The credit allowed against the gift tax for such years will be equal to (1) the amount of the tentative tax that would be determined under the new gift tax-only rate schedule if the amount with respect to which such tentative tax is to be computed was $1 million, reduced by (2) the sum of the amounts allowable as a credit for all preceding calendar periods.[7] Because the maximum gift tax rate will be reduced to 35 percent in 2010, the $1 million gift tax credit equivalent will result in a gift tax applicable credit of $330,800.

Sunset provision. In order to comply with the Congressional Budget Act of 1974, the 2001 Act provides that all provisions of, and amendments made by, the 2001 Act will not apply to estates of decedents dying, gifts made, or generation-skipping transfers, after December 31, 2010. Unless Congress acts affirmatively in the interim, the Internal Revenue Code will thereafter be applied and administered as if these provisions had not been enacted.

• *Transitional Rule*

A special transitional rule applied to gifts during the period September 9, 1976, through December 31, 1976. To the extent that use was made of the $30,000

---

[3] Code Sec. 2503(a).

[4] Code Sec. 2505.

[5] Code Sec. 2505(a), as amended by P.L. 107-16.

[6] Code Sec. 2505(c).

[7] Code Sec. 2505(a)(1), as amended by P.L. 107-16.

lifetime exemption during this period, the allowable unified credit was reduced by an amount equal to 20 percent of the exemption. Thus, if the full $30,000 exemption was used during this period, a maximum reduction of $6,000 was made to the unified credit.

The amount of allowable credit for gifts made during the period January 1, 1977, to June 30, 1977, was limited to $6,000. However, over the full year 1977, a $30,000 credit was allowable. Thus, a donor could have used $6,000 of the credit during the first six months of 1977 and $24,000 of the credit during the second six months, for a total offset of $30,000 against gift taxes. In effect, any portion of the unified credit used against gift taxes will reduce the credit available to be used against the estate tax.

¶ 2008 Computing the Tax

The amount of gift tax payable for any calendar quarter or year, as appropriate, for gifts made after 1976 and before 2010, is determined by applying the unified rate schedule to cumulative lifetime taxable gifts and subtracting the taxes payable for prior periods.[8] Preceding periods are (1) calendar years 1932 (including only that portion of 1932 after June 6) and 1970 and all intervening calendar years, (2) the first calendar quarter of 1971 and all quarters between that quarter and the first quarter of 1982, and (3) all calendar years after 1981 and before the year for which the tax is being computed. Gifts made prior to 1977 are taken into account in the computation of post-1976 gifts (see Example, below). In computing the tax payable on post-1976 gifts, the reduction for taxes previously paid is calculated using the unified rate schedule. Then, to the extent allowable, the unified credit is used to offset the cumulative gift tax. (See ¶2378 for a discussion of the phaseout of the benefits of graduated rates and the unified credit for cumulative transfers exceeding $10 million that occurred before January 1, 2002.)

Example: In 2004, John Jones makes taxable gifts of $1,250,000. His only other taxable gifts were made prior to 1977 and amounted to $250,000. The unified transfer tax on the 2004 gifts is computed as follows:

2004 taxable gifts	$1,250,000
Pre-1977 taxable gifts	250,000
Total taxable gifts	$1,500,000
Unified transfer (tentative) tax on total gifts	$555,800
Less unified transfer (tentative) tax on pre-1977 gifts	70,800
Tentative tax on 2004 gifts	$485,000
Less applicable credit amount	345,800
Gift tax payable	$139,200

• ***Impact of the 2001 Act***

The Economic Growth and Tax Relief Reconciliation Act of 2001 (P.L. 107-16) (2001 Act) retains the gift tax following the repeal of the estate tax in 2010. After estate tax repeal, the gift tax will continue to be determined in a fashion similar to that described above. For gifts made after December 31, 2009, the gift tax imposed for each calendar year will be an amount equal to the excess of (1) a tentative tax (computed using the new rate schedule, see ¶2005) on the aggregate sum of the taxable gifts for such calendar year and for each of the preceding

[8] Code Sec. 2502 and Code Sec. 2505.

calendar periods, over (2) a tentative tax (computed using the new rate schedule) on the aggregate sum of the taxable gifts for each of the preceding calendar periods. The definition of "preceding calendar period" is not changed by the 2001 Act.[9]

Sunset provision. In order to comply with the Congressional Budget Act of 1974, the 2001 Act provides that all provisions of, and amendments made by, the 2001 Act will not apply to estates of decedents dying, gifts made, or generation-skipping transfers, after December 31, 2010. Unless Congress acts affirmatively in the interim, the Internal Revenue Code will thereafter be applied and administered as if these provisions had not been enacted.

¶ 2009 Disclaimer

If a person makes a "qualified disclaimer," as defined below, for estate, gift, or generation-skipping transfer tax purposes, the disclaimed interest in property is treated as if it had never been transferred to the person making the qualified disclaimer.[10] Rather, it is considered as passing directly from the transferor of the property to the person entitled to receive the property as a result of the disclaimer. Thus, a person who makes a qualified disclaimer is not treated as having made a gift to the person to whom the disclaimed interest passes.

A qualified disclaimer is an irrevocable and unqualified refusal to accept an interest in property that satisfies the following four conditions:

(1) the refusal must be in writing;

(2) the written refusal must be received by the transferor, his or her legal representative, or holder of legal title, no more than nine months after the later of (a) the day on which the transfer creating the interest is made, or (b) the day on which the person making the disclaimer reaches age 21;

(3) the person making the disclaimer must not have accepted the interest or any of its benefits prior to the disclaimer; and

(4) the interest must pass to a person other than the person making the disclaimer as a result of the refusal to accept the property. A surviving spouse may, under this rule, disclaim an interest in property that, as a result and without direction on his or her part, passes to a trust in which he or she has an interest. A disclaimer is not unqualified if the disclaimant receives consideration in exchange for the disclaimer. A mere expectation or unenforceable hope that something will be received in the future does not rise to the level of consideration, however. To render the disclaimer invalid, the decision to disclaim must be part of a mutually bargained-for consideration.[11]

A timely written transfer of the property by the person disclaiming the property to the person who would have received it under a disclaimer that is valid under local law is also considered a qualified disclaimer, assuming that the requirements of (2) and (3), above, have been met.[12]

A qualified disclaimer will apply for federal estate, gift, and generation-skipping transfer tax purposes (see ¶ 1050 and ¶ 2465), even if local law does not

[9] Code Sec. 2502(b).

[10] Code Sec. 2518.

[11] *L.S. Monroe*, CA-5, 97-2 USTC ¶ 60,292, rev'g in part TC, 104 TC 352, CCH Dec. 50,539.

[12] Code Sec. 2518(c)(3).

characterize such a refusal as a disclaimer. The time limits prescribed for a qualified disclaimer also will supersede the time period prescribed by local law.

• *Joint Tenancy Interests*

In general, an individual must make a qualified disclaimer of the interest to which the disclaimant succeeds on creation of a joint tenancy within nine months after the creation of the tenancy.[13] However, a qualified disclaimer of the survivorship interest must be made no later than nine months after the death of the first joint tenant to die. The timing for disclaiming the survivorship interest is not affected by the power of the disclaimant to unilaterally sever the tenancy under local law. The U.S. Court of Appeals for the Seventh Circuit has held that a surviving spouse's disclaimer of the survivorship interest in jointly held farmland within nine months of her husband's death was qualified, even though the joint tenancy was created 25 years earlier. According to the court, there was no "transfer" of the survivorship portion until the husband's death because, until that time, each tenant had the right under state law to partition the property.[14]

Similarly, the U.S. Court of Appeals for the Eighth Circuit has held that a surviving spouse's renunciation of her survivorship interest in several parcels of property that she had held in joint tenancy with her husband was timely when made within nine months of his death. On remand, the Tax Court concluded that the wife had made a qualified disclaimer and that no taxable gift resulted when the disclaimed joint interest passed to her children.[15]

With respect to a joint tenancy in real property created after July 13, 1988, between a donor and a noncitizen spouse, the surviving noncitizen spouse may disclaim any portion of the joint tenancy included in the decedent's gross estate under Code Sec. 2040.[16]

Special rules apply to disclaimers of joint tenancy interests in bank, brokerage, and investment accounts. The transfer creating the survivorship interest in a co-tenant's contributions occurs on the death of the co-tenant only if the co-tenant possessed the right to unilaterally regain sole possession of the contributions. In such case, the surviving co-tenant may make a qualified disclaimer within nine months of the deceased co-tenant's death.[17] In addition, a joint tenant may not make a qualified disclaimer of any portion of the joint interest attributable to consideration furnished by that tenant.

• *Remainder Interests*

The requirement that a disclaimer be made of an undivided interest in property prohibits an individual from disclaiming a remainder interest while retaining a life estate in the same property.[18]

A contingent remainder interest must be disclaimed within nine months after the interest becomes a completed gift for estate and gift tax purposes. In the case of a contingent remainder, a completed gift occurs when the contingent remainder interest vests.[19]

---

[13] Reg. §25.2518-2(c)(4)(i).

[14] *P.M. Kennedy*, CA-7, 86-2 USTC ¶13,699, rev'g TC, 51 TCM 232, CCH Dec. 42,804(M), TC Memo. 1986-3. Similarly, *J.O. Dancy Est.*, CA-4, 89-1 USTC ¶13,800, rev'g TC, 89 TC 550, CCH Dec. 44,184.

[15] *G.L. McDonald*, CA-8, 88-2 USTC ¶13,778, rev'g TC, 89 TC 293, CCH Dec. 44,118, cert. denied on another matter.

[16] Reg. §25.2518-2(c)(4)(ii).

[17] Reg. §25.2518-2(c)(4)(iii).

[18] Reg. §25.2518-3(b); *T. Walshire, Exr.*, CA-8, 2002-1 USTC ¶60,439.

[19] Reg. §25.2518-2(c)(5), Example 6.

Prior to the enactment of the qualified disclaimer rules in 1986, a disclaimer of property transferred to an individual was effective for federal estate and gift tax purposes only if the disclaimer was made within a reasonable time after the individual became aware of the transfer. The U.S. Supreme Court held that an attempt to disclaim a contingent interest in a trust more than 30 years after the interest was created was invalid.[20] In the Court's view, the relevant transfer occurred when the interest was created, and not when the interest became possessory on the death of the life tenant. The Supreme Court has also ruled, under the prior law, that a disclaimer must be made within a reasonable time after learning of the transfer that created the interest, regardless of when the interest vested, even if the original transfer in trust occurred prior to the enactment of the gift tax.[21]

• ***Interests Created by Will: Statutory Shares***

A disclaimer of an interest created by a decedent's will must be made within nine months of the date of the decedent's death, not within nine months after the will was admitted to probate.[22]

The IRS has concluded that a surviving spouse's disclaimer of an undivided portion of an elected statutory share constituted a qualified disclaimer where both the election and the subsequent disclaimer occurred within nine months of the decedent's death.[23] Although the exercise of the statutory election was an affirmative act that vested title to the property in the surviving spouse, it was not considered to be an acceptance of the property or its benefits that would disqualify the disclaimer under Code Sec. 2518(c). However, such a disclaimer would not be timely if it was made more than nine months after the decedent's death, even if the disclaimer was made within nine months of the statutory election to take against the will.

• ***Tax Lien Against Disclaimed Property***

The U.S. Supreme Court has held that where an individual, against whom the IRS had assessed approximately $325,000 in tax deficiencies, disclaimed rights to an inheritance from his mother, the fact that the disclaimer constituted a qualified disclaimer under federal and state law did not shield the $233,000 passing by the disclaimer from a federal tax lien.[24] In holding that the disclaimer under state law did not defeat the federal tax lien, the Court noted that once state law creates an interest in property, federal law determines whether the taxpayer's state-delineated rights qualify as property or rights under Code Sec. 6321. The Court concluded that the son exercised dominion over the property by controlling its ultimate disposition because state law gave him the right to inherit the property or to channel it to another known family member by virtue of the disclaimer. This power to channel the estate's assets was sufficient to constitute a property right or property that was subject to the government's tax liens under Code Sec. 6321. Once it has been determined that interests created under state law satisfy the federal tax lien provisions, state law cannot prevent the attachment of liens created by federal statutes in favor of the United States. Although Code Sec. 2518(a) serves to avoid the imposition of estate, gift, and generation-

---

[20] *G.F. Jewett*, SCt, 82-1 USTC ¶13,453, 455 US 305.

[21] *J.O. Irvine*, SCt, 94-1 USTC ¶60,163.

[22] *J.K. Fleming Est.*, CA-7, 92-2 USTC ¶60,113, aff'g TC, 58 TCM 1034, CCH Dec. 46,229(M), TC Memo. 1989-675.

[23] Rev. Rul. 90-45, 1990-1 CB 175.

[24] *R. Drye, Jr., et al.*, SCt, 99-2 USTC ¶60,363, aff'g CA-8, 98-2 USTC ¶50,651.

skipping transfer tax liability in situations where such liability would otherwise apply, Congress did not intend that this provision would function to block the imposition of a federal tax lien against disclaimed property interests.

¶ 2010 Transfers in Settlement of Support Obligations

An exclusion from the gift tax is provided with respect to certain transfers in settlement of support obligations.[25] The exclusion applies to transfers of property or property interests that are made under a written agreement between spouses in settlement of their marital and property rights or for the purpose of providing a reasonable allowance for the support of their children. Such transfers will be treated as having been made for full and adequate consideration, and will be exempt from gift tax under one condition—the divorce must occur within the three-year period beginning one year before the property settlement is entered into (see ¶2165).

¶ 2011 Taxable Gifts

A taxable gift may be any complete and irrevocable voluntary transfer to or for the benefit of another or others, whether in trust or otherwise, except to the extent that it is supported by full and adequate consideration in money or money's worth.[26] The gift tax is in addition to any other tax, such as federal income or generation-skipping transfer tax, paid or due on the transfer. The nature of the property transferred is not important except in the case of transfers by nonresidents who are not citizens.

The IRS has ruled that an executor or other fiduciary may waive his or her right to statutory fees and commissions without making a taxable gift.[27] In order to be effective, the waiver must evidence an intent to render a gratuitous service, and it must be executed within a reasonable time after appointment. Claiming a deduction for the fees on any tax return, however, will negate an intention to serve gratuitously.

• ***Certain Transfers in Trust***

The Economic Growth and Tax Relief Reconciliation Act of 2001 (P.L. 107-16) (2001 Act) provides that, for gifts made after December 31, 2009, a transfer in trust will be treated as a taxable gift under Code Sec. 2503 unless the trust is treated as wholly owned by the donor or the donor's spouse under the grantor trust rules contained in Code Sec. 671 through Code Sec. 679.[28] The Job Creation and Worker Assistance Act of 2002 (P.L. 107-147) provided a technical clarification that transfers in trust made after December 31, 2009, will be treated as *transfers of property by gifts*, unless the trust is wholly owned by the grantor or the grantor's spouse. This clarification is intended to allow the gift tax annual exclusion and the gift tax marital and charitable deductions to apply to transfers in trust that are taxable gifts thereunder. Transfers of property which prior to 2010 would be treated as incomplete for gift tax purposes are to be treated as transfers by gift if made after December 31, 2009.[29]

> ***Example:*** In 2010, Ed Baxter transfers property to a trust under which the income is payable to his daughter, Mary, for her life. Ed retains the

---

[25] Code Sec. 2516; Reg. §25.2516-2.

[26] Code Sec. 2512.

[27] Rev. Rul. 66-167, 1966-1 CB 20.

[28] Code Sec. 2511(c), as added by P.L. 107-16.

[29] Code Sec. 2511(c), as amended by the Job Creation and Worker Assistance Act of 2002 (P.L. 107-147).

power to determine the remainder beneficiaries and the amount each is to receive. Under Code Sec. 2511(c), as amended, the transfer is deemed a completed, taxable gift, whereas before 2010 it would not be.[30]

Sunset provision. In order to comply with the Congressional Budget Act of 1974, the 2001 Act provides that all provisions of, and amendments made by, the 2001 Act will not apply to estates of decedents dying, gifts made, or generation-skipping transfers, after December 31, 2010. Unless Congress acts affirmatively in the interim, the Internal Revenue Code will thereafter be applied and administered as if these provisions had not been enacted.

• *Grantor Trust's Reimbursement of Grantor's Tax Liability*

The IRS has recently issued gift tax guidance with respect to a grantor trust's reimbursement of the grantor's income tax liability that is attributable to the inclusion of the trust's income in the grantor's taxable income by operation of Code Sec. 671. Under the ruling, the IRS examined three different factual situations: "Scenario One", where neither applicable state law nor the trust instrument contained any provision requiring or permitting the trustee to reimburse the grantor's income tax liability; "Scenario Two", where the trust instrument required the trustee to reimburse the grantor; and "Scenario Three", where the trust instrument gave the trustee the discretion to reimburse the grantor. The IRS concluded that the grantor's payment of the income tax liability did not constitute a gift by the grantor to the trust beneficiaries in any of the scenarios discussed because the grantor, not the trust, was liable for the taxes. In addition, the IRS determined that the trust's reimbursement of the grantor, whether mandatory or discretionary under the trust instrument, was not a gift by the trust beneficiaries to the grantor.[31]

¶ 2012 Valuation

Like the estate tax, the gift tax is measured by the value of property transferred at the date of the gift.[32] With certain exceptions, the methods of determining value for gift tax purposes are the same as those for estate tax purposes (see ¶ 2100 and following).

¶ 2013 Gift-Splitting

A married donor may elect, with his or her spouse, to treat all gifts made by either (other than gifts to the other spouse) as being made one-half from each. This has the effect of doubling the annual exclusion available for each donee (thus, for 2004, $22,000 as opposed to $11,000), and allows for the possibility of utilizing both spouses' unified gift tax credit.[33] The gift-splitting right is optional and may be taken or ignored in any calendar year.[34] In order to exercise the right, the spouses must consent, on an annual basis, to treat a gift made by either as a split gift. If the consent is effective, all gifts made by either spouse to any third party must be treated in the same way. A couple may not, therefore, elect to apply the gift-splitting privilege to some gifts but not others in the same calendar year (see ¶ 2200 and following).

---

[30] Reg. § 25.2511-2(c).

[31] Rev. Proc. 2004-64, IRB 2004-27, 7.

[32] Code Sec. 2512.

[33] Code Sec. 2513.

[34] Reg. § 25.2513-1(c).

¶ 2014 Annual Exclusions

To prevent small gifts from being hampered by tax considerations, donors are allowed each year to exclude from gift tax a specified amount (known as the annual exclusion; $11,000 for 2004) for gifts made to any one donee, provided the gifts are not of future interests.[35] This exception is prompted by the belief that a gift of a future interest is more like a testamentary disposition of property than a current small gift to the donee. The future interest rule is strictly applied.

• *Inflation Adjustments*

For transfers made after 1998, the annual exclusion is indexed for inflation, although the exclusion remained at $10,000 through 2001. However, for gifts made in 2002, the annual exclusion rose to $11,000 and remained at $11,000 for 2003 and 2004.

A donor may also exclude gifts of up to $100,000 annually (indexed; $101,000 for gifts in 1999, $103,000 for gifts in 2000, $106,000 for gifts in 2001, $110,000 for gifts in 2002, $112,000 for gifts in 2003, and $114,000 for gifts in 2004) to his or her noncitizen spouse.[36]

• *Transfers to Minors*

To facilitate the making of gifts to minors, however, Congress has specified certain types of gifts that will not be treated as gifts of future interests (see ¶2270).[37]

¶ 2015 Deductions

Before applying the unified transfer tax rates, the donor may deduct the following from the value of the gifts he or she is required to report: (1) the allowable marital deduction for gifts to a spouse (see ¶2311); (2) transfers for public, charitable and religious uses (see ¶2305); and (3) any items that reduce the net value of the gift, such as partial consideration, mortgages and other charges against the specific property transferred. The tests and rules for determining the amounts of these various deductions are similar to those applied in determining the deductibility of corresponding items for estate tax purposes.

¶ 2016 Specific Exemption for Pre-1977 Gifts

In addition to the annual exclusion of $3,000 for gifts to each donee, a donor was entitled to a specific exemption of $30,000 for gifts made prior to 1977. The specific exemption was repealed, starting with gifts made in 1977, and was replaced by the unified credit (see ¶2007).

---

[35] Code Sec. 2503.

[36] Reg. §25.2503-2(f); Rev. Proc. 99-42, IRB 1999-46, 568; Rev. Proc. 2001-13, 2001-1 CB 337; Rev. Proc. 2001-59, 2001-2 CB 623; Rev. Proc. 2002-70, IRB 2002-46, 845; and Rev. Proc. 2003-85, IRB 2003-49, 1184.

[37] Code Sec. 2503(c).

Chapter 32
FORMS REQUIRED

¶ 2050 Filing by Donor

Donors are required to report gifts of present and future interests using Form 709 (United States Gift (and Generation-Skipping Transfer) Tax Return) (2004). This is the principal form that is used in the administration of the gift tax law. Spouses who elected to split pre-January 1, 2003, gifts of not more than $22,000 per year per donee could use Form 709-A (United States Short Form Gift Tax Return) (Rev. Oct. 2002). Form 709-A has been declared obsolete.[1] Other forms and documents may be necessary, depending on the circumstances (see ¶2120).

¶ 2052 Gift Tax Return Filing Requirements

Effective for gifts made after 1981, gift tax returns must be filed, and any gift tax must be paid, on an annual basis. Generally, the due date for filing the annual gift tax return will be April 15. However, for the calendar year in which the donor dies, the gift tax return will be due on the earlier of the due date (with extensions) for filing the donor's estate tax return, or the "normal" due date with respect to the gifts (April 15 following the calendar year in which the gifts were made).[2]

See ¶1650 for special tax provisions for victims of terrorist attacks against the United States.

• *Gifts in Excess of the Annual Exclusion*

Transfers of present interests in the amount of $11,000 ($10,000 for years before 2002) or less to any donee are exempt from the gift tax and do not require a gift tax return, unless gift-splitting is elected (see ¶2013). Donors making gifts that exceed $11,000 to a single donee are required to file an annual gift tax return in the year of such gifts. A return must be filed with respect to transfers in excess of $11,000 to a charitable organization if the gift is only partially deductible. However, a donor who makes a gift to charity in excess of the annual gift tax exclusion is not required to file a gift tax return if the *entire* value of the donated property qualifies for a gift tax charitable deduction.[3] A gift tax return must be filed for gifts of future interests, regardless of the amount of the gift.

A contributor making a contribution after August 5, 1997, to a qualified tuition program (QTP) that exceeds the annual exclusion limit may elect to have the contribution treated as if it were made ratably over five years.[4] A gift tax return must be filed with respect to any contribution in excess of the annual gift tax exclusion limit.

---

[1] Instructions for Form 709 (2004), p. 1.
[2] Code Sec. 6075(b).
[3] Code Sec. 6019(a)(3).
[4] Code Sec. 529(c)(2)(B).

Example: In September 2004, Heinrich Neble contributes $55,000 to a QTP, the designated beneficiary of which is his daughter, Gretchen. At Heinrich's election, the program treats the $55,000 as being paid ratably over a five-year period at $11,000 per year. Heinrich must make the election for the five-year averaging on his gift tax return.

• *Other Rules*

Married individuals who elect to split gifts (see ¶2013) must file a gift tax return, regardless of the amount of the gift.[5]

Only individuals are required to file returns. Where gifts are made by trusts, estates, partnerships, or corporations, the trust beneficiaries, the partners, or the stockholders become the donors and may incur a gift tax liability.[6]

The death of the donor before filing a gift tax return imposes the duty to file the return on the donor's executor or administrator. If a donor becomes legally incompetent before filing a gift tax return, the donor's guardian or conservator must file the return.[7]

Loans of qualified works of art (any archaeological, historic, or creative tangible personal property) to a public charity or a private operating foundation are not treated as transfers subject to federal gift tax.

¶ 2056 Place for Filing Returns

Except for donors who do not reside in the United States (see below) all gift tax returns filed after 2001 are to be filed with the IRS Service Center, Cincinnati, OH 45999.[8] Prior to 2002, donors generally filed their gift tax returns with the IRS Service Center where their federal income tax returns were filed. See ¶2850 for a list of filing locations.

With respect to gift tax returns for calendar year 2004, if a donor did not have a legal residence or a principal place of business in the United States, the gift tax return is to be filed with the IRS Service Center in Philadelphia, Pennsylvania 19255.[9]

¶ 2057 Description of Property

All property that is required to be listed on the return must be described in such a manner that it may be readily identified.[10] Thus, for example, pertinent information with respect to real estate would include a legal description, along with the street number, name and area (if the property is located in a city), and a short statement of any improvements made to the property.

¶ 2058 Supplemental Documents

A donor must provide information to support the value attributable to the gifts being made. For stock of closely held corporations or inactive stock, balance sheets of the corporation should be attached (particularly the most recent one), as should statements of net earning or operating results and dividends paid for each of the five preceding years. For every policy of life insurance listed on the return, the donor must obtain a statement by the insurance company that issued it on Form 712 (Life Insurance Statement) (Rev. May 2000). This form must then be filed with the return. If a gift was made by means of a trust, a certified or

---

[5] Instructions for Form 709 (2004), p. 1.

[6] Reg. §25.6019-1(e).

[7] Reg. §25.6019-1(g).

[8] Announcement 2001-74, 2001-2 CB 40.

[9] Instructions for Form 709 (2004), p. 4.

[10] Reg. §25.6019-4.

verified copy of the trust instrument must be submitted and the trust's identifying number must be entered on Schedule A (Computation of Taxable Gifts) of Form 709 (United States Gift (and Generation-Skipping Transfer) Tax Return). Other special documents may also be required to substantiate the value shown for the property listed on the return[11] (see ¶2120).

¶ 2065 Signatures and Declarations

In addition to the taxpayer's signature and declaration, a second declaration must be executed by the firm or person that prepared the return. Declarations that the return is true, correct, and complete, under penalties of perjury, are made at the bottom of page 1 of Form 709 (United States Gift (and Generation-Skipping Transfer) Tax Return).

¶ 2080 Penalties

Interest and penalties similar to those applicable to the estate tax apply to the failure to file a gift tax return and pay the tax when due (see ¶1680). Accordingly, there are penalties for late filing of the gift tax return,[12] and the late payment of any tax due.[13] There are also accuracy-related penalties that may apply to that portion of any underpayment attributable to negligence or disregard of rules and regulations.[14] Penalties may also be applicable where there is a substantial understatement of the value of any property shown on a gift tax return.[15] A fraud penalty may be imposed on any portion of any underpayment that is attributable to fraud. Interest must be paid on any amount of tax that is unpaid when the return is due even if the time for filing the return has been extended.

In addition to the civil penalties noted above, criminal penalties may apply.

The willful failure to pay any tax, make any return, or to keep any records or supply any information that is required under the gift tax laws or regulations constitutes a misdemeanor and may subject the donor to additional penalties.

Any person who willfully attempts in any manner to evade or defeat any gift tax is guilty of a felony. On conviction, such person may be fined not more than $100,000, or imprisoned for not more than five years, or both, and may be required to pay the costs of prosecution. Other penalties may also apply.[16]

Any person who willfully aids or assists in the preparation or presentation of a false or fraudulent notice or return, or procures, counsels, or advises the preparation or presentation of such notice or return (whether such falsity or fraud is with or without the knowledge or consent of the person required to make the notice or return) is guilty of a felony.

---

[11] Reg. §25.6019-3 and Reg. §25.6019-4.
[12] Code Sec. 6651(a)(1).
[13] Code Sec. 6651(a)(2).
[14] Code Sec. 6662.
[15] Code Sec. 6662(g); Reg. §1.6662-7.
[16] Code Sec. 7201.

Chapter 33
VALUATION

¶ 2100 Gift Date Controls

Like the estate tax, the gift tax is levied on the value of the property transferred by gift. There are, however, no alternate valuation dates. The value is determined as of the date of the gift.

¶ 2105 Method of Valuation

Generally, the method of determining value for gift tax purposes is the same as that employed for estate tax purposes. Consequently, the paragraphs cited below, which explain the methods of valuation for estate tax purposes, are pertinent:

Real estate (¶270)	Household and personal effects (¶535)
Stocks and bonds (¶318)	Other property (¶535)
Mortgages and notes (¶355)	Cash (¶365)
Interests in business (¶527)	

Annuities, life estates, remainders, and reversions (¶530)

Certain types of property interests, however, must be specifically valued for gift tax purposes. Other types of property are frequently subject to problems in valuation for gift tax purposes and, thus, are discussed specifically from a gift tax standpoint. These include transfers conditioned on survivorship, tenancies by the entirety, and life insurance and annuity contracts. In addition, Code Sec. 2701 through Code Sec. 2704 provide special valuation rules with respect to gifts involving certain intrafamily transfers of corporate, partnership, and trust interests (see ¶2500 and following).

The IRS will not issue advance rulings or determination letters with respect to actuarial factors for valuing prospective or hypothetical gifts of a donor.[1]

¶ 2106 Transfers Conditioned on Survivorship

Occasionally, a donor makes a gift of property in trust and retains no power over the trust corpus, but may, under certain contingencies, regain the corpus by surviving the various beneficiaries. An amount less than the entire value of the property transferred is taxable. The value of the gift is reduced by the present value of the donor's right to regain the corpus in the event all of the contingen-

[1] Rev. Proc. 2004-4, IRB 2004-1, 114.

cies should occur, or fail to occur, as the case may be.[2] The value of such rights is determined in accordance with the applicable actuarial tables reproduced in the Appendix at ¶2700 (see ¶530).

¶ 2107 Joint Tenancies Between Spouses

For estate tax purposes, a spouse's interest in any property owned in joint tenancy with right of survivorship is a qualified joint interest (see ¶502). Due to the unlimited gift tax marital deduction available for gifts made after 1981 (see ¶2311), the creation of a joint tenancy between spouses after 1981 is not a taxable gift.

• *Pre-1982 Tenancies in Real Property*

For tenancies created before 1982, a donor spouse may or may not have elected to treat the creation of a tenancy by the entirety in real property between the spouses as a gift. If the donor spouse elected not to treat the creation as a gift, the transaction was treated as a gift only in the event the tenancy was terminated other than by the death of one of the tenants. If the tenancy was terminated by death, its value was involved only in determining estate tax liability.[3] The above election applied only to real property and not to personal property. This election created, for joint interests created after 1976 and before 1982, a "qualified joint interest" for estate tax purposes, and such property was treated as belonging one-half to each spouse for estate tax purposes.

If the donor spouse elected not to treat the creation of a tenancy by the entirety as a gift, and the property was subsequently sold during the lives of both spouses, or if the tenancy was otherwise terminated during their joint lives, a gift was deemed to occur at the time of termination, as long as this event occurred before 1982. The termination resulted in a gift to the extent that the proportion of the total consideration furnished by the donor spouse multiplied by the value of the proceeds of termination exceeded the value of that part of the proceeds of termination received by him or her. However, the IRS has ruled that, due to the repeal of the rules governing the creation of joint tenancies in real property by spouses, a post-1981 termination of a tenancy by the entirety created before 1982 did not result in a gift to the spouse who had not contributed any of the consideration for the property, where the spouse who had purchased the property had not elected to treat the creation of the tenancy as a gift.[4] (See, also, ¶502 for decedent's treatment of pre-1977 spousal joint interests.)

• *Pre-1982 Tenancies in Personal Property*

In the case of personal property, creation of the joint interest before 1982 had to be a complete gift for gift tax purposes in order to be a "qualified joint interest." Joint bank accounts did not qualify because either co-owner could withdraw the entire amount. Therefore, the gift was incomplete.

The creation of a joint tenancy in personal property constituted a gift to the extent that a spouse's contribution exceeded his or her retained interest in the property.[5] Thus, in determining the amount of a gift where a joint tenancy in personal property was created after 1976 and before 1982, the retained interest of each spouse was considered to be one-half of the value of the personal property.

---

[2] Reg. §25.2511-1(e).

[3] Code Sec. 2515, prior to repeal by P.L. 97-34.

[4] Rev. Rul. 83-178, 1983-2 CB 171.

[5] Code Sec. 2515A(a), prior to repeal by P.L. 97-34.

¶ 2108 Joint Tenancies Between Nonspouses

The creation by one person of a joint tenancy between that person and another in certain property that the first person owned, or for which he or she provided the entire consideration, normally constitutes a gift of one-half of the value of the transferred property.[6] In instances where each party provides part of the property or consideration, the gift is equal to one-half of the value of the difference between the contributions (see ¶ 2162).

¶ 2109 Life Insurance Contracts

The value of a gift of life insurance is deemed to be equal to the cost of replacing the policy on the date of the gift. This cost may be obtained from the insurer.[7]

Sometimes, however, valuation through the sale value of a comparable contract is not readily ascertainable when the gift is of a policy that has been in force for some time and on which further premium payments are to be made. In these instances, the value may be approximated. The approximation is made by adding to the interpolated terminal reserve at the date of the gift the proportionate part of the last premium paid before the gift that covers the period extending beyond that date.

In cases where, because of the peculiar nature of the contract, approximation by this method is not close enough to the full value, some other method must be used. In no instance, however, may either the cash surrender or the loan value be used. The value should never be based on the face value of the policy except, perhaps, in the case of certain endowment policies.

Split-dollar policies. Where a donor makes a lifetime gift of a split-dollar life insurance policy (see ¶ 472), the value of the gift is the interpolated terminable reserve value (a figure obtainable from the insurance company that issued the policy), plus the proportionate part of the gross premium paid before the date of the gift, reduced by the amount of any funds provided by the employer.[8]

The IRS has issued an explanation of the standards it will use in valuing current life insurance protection under what it has termed abusive split-dollar arrangements. More specifically, the IRS is targeting arrangements where a party pays inappropriately high current term insurance premiums, prepays premiums, or uses other techniques in order to understate the value of the taxable policy benefits.[9] Under such a scenario, it appears that the IRS intends to disregard policy arrangements that use two different insurance rates (one for the amount of coverage, and another one for purposes of the gift tax).[10] Under IRS Notice 2002-59, a party participating in a split-dollar life insurance arrangement may use the premium rates in Table 2001 (see Notice 2002-8), or the insurer's lower published premium rates only for the purposes of valuing current life insurance protection and when such protection confers an economic benefit by one party on another party, disregarding the premiums actually paid by this other party. However, if one party has any right to current life insurance protection under the split-dollar arrangement, neither the premium rates in Table 2001 nor the insurer's lower published rates may be used to value such party's current life insurance protection for purposes of determining the value of any policy benefits to which another party may be entitled.

---

[6] Reg. § 25.2511-1(h)(5).

[7] Reg. § 25.2511-1(h)(8) and Reg. § 25.2512-6(a).

[8] Rev. Rul. 81-198, 1981-2 CB 188.

[9] Notice 2002-59, IRB 2002-36, 481.

[10] Notice 2002-8, 2002-1 CB 398.

Amendments to the regulations under Code Sec. 61 and Code Sec. 7872 govern the income and gift taxation of split-dollar life insurance arrangements.

The regulations provide two mutually exclusive methods for taxing split-dollar life insurance arrangements: an "economic benefit" regime,[11] (generally applicable to endorsement arrangements), and a "loan" regime,[12] (generally applicable to collateral assignments). Under a split-dollar endorsement arrangement, one party owns the policy and endorses an interest in it to another. The first party pays the premiums, but the second party makes reimbursements for his or her share of the costs. With a collateral assignment arrangement, a donee (such as a life insurance trust) owns a life insurance policy, and pays all the premiums. The donor makes advances—which in effect are no-interest loans—to the trust in the amount of the yearly increases in the cash value. At the termination of the policy or the death of the donor, the donor is entitled to the policy's cash value.

The regulations generally provide substantially different tax consequences to the parties depending on which person owns the policy. In most cases, the person named as the policy owner is treated as the owner of the contract. However, a donor is treated as the owner of a contract under a split-dollar arrangement entered into between a donor and a donee (such as a life insurance trust) if the only economic benefit available to the donee is the value of the current life insurance protection. (This is known as a "non-equity" split-dollar arrangement.)

Under the regulations, if an irrevocable insurance trust is the owner of the life insurance contract underlying the split-dollar arrangement and there is a reasonable expectation that the donor (or the donor's estate) will recover an amount equal to the premium payments, the donor's premium payments will be treated as loans made to the trust. In such a case, the value of the gift would be the amount of the premium payment less the present value of the donor's right to receive repayment. A different set of rules apply under the regulations if the donor is treated as the owner of the contract and the donor is entitled to recover premium payments from the contract proceeds.

The regulations are effective for split-dollar arrangements entered into after September 17, 2003. In addition, the regulations apply to any split-dollar life insurance arrangement entered into on or before September 17, 2003, if the arrangement is materially modified after September 17, 2003.[13]

Notwithstanding who is treated as the owner of the life insurance contract for purposes of the regulations, the gift tax consequences of a transfer of an interest in the contract to a third party continue to be determined by established gift tax principles.

¶ 2110 Annuity Contracts

The value of a gift of an annuity for the primary benefit of a donee is the cost of the contract, if the annuity is purchased at the time of the gift.[14] If the annuity benefits are not to commence until the death of the donor, who is the primary annuitant, and if the donor has actually made a taxable gift of such secondary benefits, the value of the gift is the difference between the value of the donor's interest at the time of the gift and the value of the entire contract or trust in which the interest is created.

---

[11] Reg. §1.61-22, amended by T.D. 9092.

[12] Reg. §1.7872-15, amended by T.D. 9092.

[13] Reg. §1.61-22, amended by T.D. 9092.

[14] Reg. §25.2512-6(a).

If the gift is of an interest in an annuity contract that has been in force for some time, the value must be based on the cost of an annuity contract purchased at the time of the gift with the same provision for payment in the future.

Annuities not involving any formal contract with an insurance company are valued in the same manner as for estate tax purposes (see ¶530).

¶ 2112 Stock Options

The IRS has provided a safe-harbor methodology for the estate or gift tax valuation of certain stock options.[15] This revenue procedure applies only to the transfer tax valuation of nonpublicly traded compensatory stock options (that is, stock options that are granted in connection with the performance of services, including stock options that are subject to the provisions of Code Sec. 421), on stock that, as of the valuation date, is publicly traded on an established securities market. The options to which this revenue procedure applies are referred to as "compensatory stock options."

The procedure allows for use of an option pricing model that takes into account specific factors that are similar to those established by the Financial Accounting Standards Board in "Accounting for Stock-Based Compensation," Statement of Financial Accounting Standards No. 123 (Financial Accounting Standards Board 1995) (SFAS 123). Under SFAS 123, the fair value of a stock option granted by a public entity is estimated using an option pricing model (for example, the Black-Scholes model or a binomial model) that takes into account as of the option grant date (1) the exercise price of the option, (2) the expected life of the option, (3) the current price of the underlying stock, (4) the expected volatility of the underlying stock, (5) the expected dividends on the underlying stock, and (6) the risk-free interest rate for the expected term of the option.

¶ 2115 Transfers for Consideration

The gift tax not only applies to transfers without consideration, but it also applies to sales and exchanges for less than adequate and full consideration in money or money's worth.[16] In the case of a transfer of property for less than adequate and full consideration in money or money's worth, the amount by which the value of the property exceeds the value of the consideration is a gift. Consideration that is not reducible to a money value, such as love and affection or a promise of marriage, is disregarded.

A bona fide sale, exchange, or other transfer of property in the ordinary course of business and free from any donative intent is considered to have been made for adequate and full consideration in money or money's worth.

The initial step in the creation of a family limited partnership (FLP) transaction typically includes a transfer of property to the newly created FLP, in exchange for partnership interests in the FLP. The IRS may challenge the setup of the FLP by assessing gift tax on the transfers on a determination that the FLP interests received did not constitute full and adequate consideration for the property transferred to the FLP (see ¶2545).

¶ 2116 Transfers in Settlement of Marital Rights

If a husband and wife enter into a written agreement concerning their marital and property rights, transfers made pursuant to such an agreement may,

[15] Rev. Proc. 98-34, 1998-1 CB 983.

[16] Code Sec. 2512(b).

under certain circumstances, be deemed to have been made for full and adequate consideration in money or money's worth. Transfers made on or before July 18, 1984, qualify under this rule if the parties obtained a final decree of divorce from each other within two years after entering into the settlement agreement.[17] For transfers occurring after July 18, 1984, the exemption will apply if divorce occurs within the three-year period beginning one year before the property settlement is entered into.[18] Thus, the divorce may precede the settlement agreement by as much as one year under this rule.

It is not necessary that the agreement be approved by the divorce decree. It is necessary, however, that the transfers made be in settlement of the transferee spouse's marital or property rights, or that the transfers be made to provide a reasonable allowance for the support of minor children of the marriage.

¶ 2117 Payment of Gift Tax by Donee

Although a donor is primarily liable for the gift tax, many donors transfer property with the understanding that the donee will pay the tax or that the tax will be paid from the transferred property. Gifts of this type are commonly called "net gifts." The gift tax paid by the donee may be deducted from the value of the transferred property, to compute the donor's gift tax, where it is expressly shown or implied that the payment of the tax by the donee or from the property itself is a condition of the transfer.[19] However, the value of the gift is not reduced by the amount of the donor's available unified credit that is applied to the tentative gift tax liability.[20] Any state gift tax paid by the donee pursuant to such a condition may also be deducted from the value of the gift for federal gift tax purposes to the extent that the donor would have been liable for payment of the state gift tax.[21] Special formulas must be used to compute the donor's gift tax liability, and the donor's, rather than the donee's, unified credit must be applied.[22]

The U.S. Supreme Court has held that, to the extent that the gift tax paid by the donee in a net gift situation exceeds the donor's basis in the transferred property, the donor recognizes gain on the transaction for income tax purposes.[23] Prior to that decision, several courts had ruled that the transfer of property subject to the donee's paying any gift taxes did not result in any gain being realized by the donor.[24]

An agreement between a decedent and his children, whereby the children assumed the liability for any additional gift tax in the event that the value of stock transferred to the decedent's heirs exceeded the value reported on the decedent's gift tax return, had no effect for gift tax valuation purposes, a U.S. District Court in Virginia has held.[25] The potential gift tax liability assumed by the children was entirely speculative at the time of the transfers and was not subject to any reasonable calculable estimation. Similarly, the Tax Court has rejected some donors' argument that the value of gifted property interests should be reduced to account for the donees' contingent obligation to pay additional

---

[17] Code Sec. 2516, prior to amendment by P.L. 98-369.

[18] Code Sec. 2516, as amended by P.L. 98-369.

[19] Rev. Rul. 75-72, 1975-1 CB 310.

[20] Rev. Rul. 81-223, 1981-2 CB 189.

[21] Rev. Rul. 80-111, 1980-1 CB 208

[22] IRS Letter Ruling 8035004 (Nov. 16, 1979).

[23] *V.P. Diedrich*, SCt, 82-1 USTC ¶9419, 457 US 191.

[24] See, for example, *R.H. Turner*, CA-6, 69-1 USTC ¶9416, 410 F2d 752 (Nonacq.).

[25] *F. Armstrong, Jr. Trust*, CA-4, 2002-1 USTC ¶60,427, aff'g DC Va., 2001-1 USTC ¶60,392.

estate tax that would be due under Code Sec. 2035 if either of the donors died within three years of making the gift.[26]

The IRS ruled, in a Technical Advice Memorandum,[27] that a net gift occurred where a surviving spouse made a nonqualified disclaimer of her interest in a qualified terminable interest property trust. Upon making the disclaimer, a taxable gift to the trust remaindermen occurred pursuant to Code Sec. 2519. Moreover, because the trust was includible in the surviving spouse's estate under Code Sec. 2044 (see ¶773), Code Sec. 2207A(b) statutorily shifted the burden for paying the gift tax to the remaindermen. Nonetheless, the surviving spouse remained liable for the gift tax. Thus, a net gift occurred on payment of the gift tax by the remaindermen.

¶ 2120 Supplemental Documents Required

Any documents required for an adequate explanation of the value or the basis of valuation of each gift should be filed with the return. Otherwise, full information as to the basis of valuation used should be set out in Schedule A (Computation of Taxable Gifts) of Form 709 (United States Gift (and Generation-Skipping Transfer) Tax Return).

• ***Closely Held Stock***

Stock of a closely held corporation and stock not listed on an exchange or actively traded should be valued in accordance with estate tax principles (see ¶326). Various supplemental documents are required to be filed in connection with valuation of such stock. The donor must submit (1) balance sheets of the corporation, particularly the most recent one, (2) profit and loss statements for each of the five years preceding the date of the gift, and (3) statements of dividends paid during the same five-year period.

• ***Life Insurance***

For every life insurance policy listed on the return, the donor must file Form 712 (Life Insurance Statement) (Rev. May 2000) with the return.

• ***Real Estate***

A copy of the appraisal, if available, should be submitted with the return where the gift consists of real estate.

• ***Transfers in Trust***

If the gift was made by means of a trust, a certified or verified copy of the trust instrument must be submitted and the trust's identifying number must be entered on Schedule A of Form 709.

• ***Valuation Discounts***

If the value of any gift reflects a discount for lack of marketability, minority interest, fractional interest in real estate, blockage, market absorption, or any other reason, an explanation of the discount must be attached to Schedule A of Form 709.[28]

---

[26] *C. McCord, Jr.*, 120 TC 358, CCH Dec. 55,149 (Reviewed by the Court).

[27] IRS Technical Advice Memorandum 9736001 (May 21, 1997). See also IRS Technical Advice Memorandum 200116006 (Dec. 14, 2000) and IRS Technical Advice Memorandum 200122036 (Mar. 1, 2001).

[28] Instructions for Form 709 (2004), p. 5.

The U.S. Court of Appeals for the Eighth Circuit[29] and the Tax Court[30] have held that in determining the fair market value of closely held stock for gift tax purposes, a donor was entitled to discount the net asset value of the stock to reflect the built-in capital gains the corporation would incur if it were to liquidate, distribute, or sell appreciated corporate assets. After the 1986 legislative abrogation of the *General Utilities* doctrine,[31] which allowed a corporation to liquidate and distribute appreciated or depreciated property to shareholders without recognizing built-in gain or loss, a hypothetical willing buyer would take some account of the tax consequences of contingent built-in gains on the sale of an appreciated asset owned by the corporation in valuing the corporate stock. The adjustment for potential capital gains tax liabilities was appropriate, even if no liquidation or sale of the corporation or its assets was planned at the time of the gift of the stock.

¶ 2125 IRS Statement Explaining Gift Valuation

Upon written request by a donor, the IRS is required to furnish a written statement explaining any determination or proposed determination of the value of gift property.[32] The IRS valuation statement must be furnished within 45 days after the request or the date of determination or proposed determination of value. The method and computation used in arriving at the valuation is not binding on the IRS. A request for such a statement must be filed no later than the deadline for filing a claim for refund of the tax with regard to which the valuation was made.[33]

A taxpayer may also request a statement of value for art objects from the IRS.[34] The taxpayer may rely on the valuation of the art objects when filing an income, estate or gift tax return. Statements of value will be given for art objects that have been appraised at $50,000 or more. The IRS will issue a statement of value for items appraised at less than $50,000 if at least one item of the items submitted is appraised at $50,000 or more.

---

[29] *I. Eisenberg*, CA-2, 98-2 USTC ¶60,322, Acq., IRB 1999-4, 4, vac'g and rem'g 74 TCM 1046, CCH Dec. 52,321(M), TC Memo. 1997-483.

[30] *A. Davis Est.*, 110 TC 530, CCH Dec. 52,764.

[31] P.L. 99-515, Act Secs. 631–633.

[32] Code Sec. 7517.

[33] Reg. § 301.7517-1(a).

[34] Rev. Proc. 96-15, 1996-1 CB 627, as modified by Announcement 2001-22, 2001-1 CB 895.

Chapter 34
TAXABLE GIFTS

¶ 2150 Imposition of Tax

The gift tax is an excise tax that is imposed on lifetime transfers of property for less than full and adequate consideration in money or money's worth.[1]

The tax applies "whether the transfer is in trust or otherwise, whether the gift is direct or indirect, and whether the property is real or personal, tangible or intangible; but, in the case of a nonresident not a citizen of the United States, shall apply to a transfer only if the property is situated within the United States."[2]

Gifts by U.S. citizens who are residents of U.S. possessions and who acquired their U.S. citizenship completely independent of their connections with the possessions are treated in the same manner as gifts made by resident citizens of the United States.[3] Gifts made by other citizen-residents of U.S. possessions are treated as gifts made by nonresidents not citizens of the United States.

¶ 2155 Elements of a Gift

By property law definition, a gift is a voluntary *inter vivos* transfer (in any form or manner) of property (of any kind or nature) by one person to another without consideration or compensation therefor. It is a gratuity that requires the fulfillment of three essential elements: (1) intent on the part of the donor to make a gift; (2) delivery by the donor of the subject matter of the gift; and (3) acceptance of the gift by the donee.

The presence of these elements in connection with any given transaction is determined in light of property law requirements rather than by the application of gift tax requirements. If a transfer is a gift within the meaning of property law, it is a gift for gift tax purposes as well, unless it is specifically excluded.

The property law definition of a gift is somewhat extended for gift tax purposes. Even transfers which, under contract law, constitute transfers in fulfillment of a contractual obligation rather than gifts may be treated as gifts, at least

---

[1] Code Sec. 2501; Reg. § 25.2512-8.

[2] Code Sec. 2511(a).

[3] Reg. § 25.2501-1(c).

in part, for gift tax purposes. They are deemed to be gifts to the extent that the value of the property transferred exceeds the value of the consideration received. The value used in determining the adequacy of the consideration is monetary value. Exceptions are made, however, for arm's-length business transactions and certain settlements in connection with divorces.

Although Congress dispensed with the requirement of donative intent, the courts have required that the transfer be donative in nature. In fact, except for the matter of inadequacy of consideration, the courts have generally required the property law elements of a gift to be present before a transfer may be taxed as a gift.[4] Thus, if there has been no delivery, there is no taxable gift.[5] This is so, even though the taxpayer may have announced an intention to make a gift. Similarly, if the taxpayer is incompetent and, therefore, incapable of understanding the nature of the transaction or of possessing the intention to make a gift, a transfer by him does not constitute a taxable gift. Nor is there a taxable gift of corpus until the donor relinquishes dominion and control.

¶ 2160 Specific Types of Transfers

Most types of transfers clearly fall into gift or nongift categories. In addition to direct deliveries of specific property to a donee, gifts (in the absence of consideration) include:[6]

(1) the irrevocable transfer of property pursuant to a declaration of trust;

(2) the forgiveness of a debt;

(3) the assignment of a judgment;

(4) the assignment of benefits under an insurance contract or the transfer of ownership of a policy of insurance;

(5) the payment of insurance premiums on policies owned by others and in which the donor has no interest as a beneficiary; and

(6) the purchase of an annuity contract for the benefit of another, where no control over such annuity is retained by the donor. This may extend also to secondary rights in an annuity contract under which the donor is primary beneficiary.

• *Gifts to Political Organizations*

Transfers of money or other property to a qualified political organization are not subject to the gift tax.[7] A "qualified political organization" is a party, committee, association, fund, or other organization (whether or not incorporated) that is organized and operated primarily for the purpose of directly or indirectly accepting contributions or making expenditures, or both, in order to influence or to attempt to influence the selection, nomination, election, or appointment of any individual to any public office or to any office in a political organization.[8]

• *Disclaimers*

A person who is a beneficiary, heir, or next-of-kin may refuse to accept ownership of property that would otherwise pass to him or her without being

---

[4] See, e.g., *W.H. Wemyss*, SCt, 45-1 USTC ¶10,179, 324 US 303.

[5] Reg. §25.2511-2.

[6] Reg. §25.2511-1(a).

[7] Code Sec. 2501(a)(5).

[8] Code Sec. 527(e).

subject to the gift tax. However, the refusal to accept the property must be made in the form of a "qualified disclaimer" (see ¶2009).[9]

• *Interspousal Transfers*

The payment of income taxes due on a joint income tax return by one spouse is not a taxable gift. The same rule applies to the payment of gift taxes in the case of a husband and wife who have elected the gift-splitting provisions of Code Sec. 2513 (see ¶2200).

• *Transfers Subject to Adjustment*

The IRS and the courts have disregarded adjustment clauses included in instruments of transfer that were designed to prevent the imposition of gift tax on an IRS determination that gift taxes were due.

The U.S. Court of Appeals for the Fourth Circuit has held that a trust provision nullifying a transfer that would otherwise be subject to gift tax was void as against public policy.[10] A settlor provided in a trust instrument that if any portion of the transfer in trust were subject to gift tax as determined by "final judgment or order of a competent federal court of last resort" then the property subject to the tax was not to be included in the transfer and remained the property of the settlor. The court stated that the gift tax may not be avoided in such a manner and that the condition subsequent was contrary to public policy.

Similarly, the IRS has ruled that the value of a gift of real estate was to be determined without regard to an adjustment clause in the transfer deed that provided for a recharacterization of the transfer depending on the IRS's valuation of the transferred property.[11] The IRS disregarded both an adjustment clause reconveying to the donor a fractional share of real property sufficient to reduce its value to the amount of the gift tax exclusion and one providing that the donee would transfer to the donor consideration equal to the excess of the property's value over the amount of the annual gift tax exclusion.

The IRS noted that such provisions operated to defeat what would otherwise be a gift and, thus, interfered with its enforcement of the gift tax regulations. In both cases, the IRS reasoned that the purpose of the adjustment clause was not to preserve or implement the original, bona fide intent of the parties, but, rather, to recharacterize the nature of the transaction in the event of a future adjustment to the donor's gift tax return by the IRS. Therefore, the value of the gifts was determined without regard to the adjustment clauses.

¶2161 Below-Market Interest Loans

The U.S. Supreme Court has held that an interest-free demand loan between family members constitutes a taxable gift because such loans represent the transfer of a property right consisting of the use of money.[12] The Court did not, however, address the question of how to value the gift, nor did it determine the income tax consequences, if any, arising from such a transfer. In 1985, Congress established a set of rules under which both income and gift tax liability may be imposed on loans that are either interest free or payable at a rate lower than the

---

[9] Code Sec. 2518.

[10] *F.W. Procter*, CA-4, 44-1 USTC ¶10,110, 142 F2d 824, reh'g denied, CA-4, 44-1 USTC ¶10,123, 142 F2d 828, cert. denied, 323 US 756.

[11] Rev. Rul. 86-41, 1986-1 CB 300.

[12] *E.C. Dickman*, SCt, 84-1 USTC ¶13,560, 465 US 330.

applicable federal interest rate established by statute.[13] This type of loan is known as a below-market interest loan.

Any transfer of money that provides the transferor with a right to repayment either on demand or over a period of time may be subject to the rules of Code Sec. 7872. A demand loan is considered to be a below-market interest loan and, thus, is subject to Code Sec. 7872 rules if the interest payable on it is at a rate less than the applicable federal interest rate. A term loan is considered to be below market if the amount loaned exceeds the present value of all payments due under the loan. Although Code Sec. 7872 enumerates five types of demand or term loans that come within its purview, the discussion here will be limited to the rules applicable to gift loans, i.e., those in which the lender's forgoing of interest is in the nature of a gift to the borrower.[14]

Generally, interest-free and below-market interest loans are recharacterized as arm's-length transactions in which the lender is deemed to have made the loan to the borrower at a statutory interest rate and the borrower is deemed to have paid the interest to the lender. These transactions can have both income and gift tax consequences. Thus, in the gift loan situation, the deemed interest is includible in the lender's income, may be deductible by the borrower if it would constitute home mortgage interest and the borrower itemizes nonbusiness deductions, and may be characterized as a gift to the borrower.

• ***Applicable Federal Rates***

To determine whether a loan is a below-market interest loan subject to the rules of Code Sec. 7872, it is first necessary to compare the interest rate stated in the loan with a rate published by the IRS called "the applicable federal rate." The applicable federal rate is as follows:[15]

Term of loan	*Applicable federal interest rate*
Three years or less	Federal short-term rate
More than three but no more than nine years .	Federal mid-term rate
More than nine years	Federal long-term rate

Because a demand loan is treated as a series of one-day term loans, the applicable federal rate is the federal short-term rate in effect for the period during which the forgone interest on the loan is being computed.[16]

Through 1985, the IRS determined the applicable federal rates for six-month periods, beginning on January 1 and July 1. Beginning with January 1985, the IRS, acting under its regulatory authority, began issuing alternative applicable federal rates on a monthly basis. The 1985 Imputed Interest Simplification Act (P.L. 99-121) made the monthly rates the sole factors to be used in imputing interest. The rates are based on the average market yields on outstanding marketable obligations of the United States during the one-month period ending on the 14th day of the preceding month. The applicable federal rate is the lower of the rates for the current or two preceding months.[17]

Once it has been determined that a loan is subject to the below-market interest loan rules, the amount of forgone interest that is treated as a gift must be computed by using the applicable federal rate. In some cases, a simplified rate, called the blended annual rate, applies. This rate is published annually, along

---

[13] Code Sec. 7872.

[14] Code Sec. 7872(f)(3).

[15] Code Sec. 1274(d).

[16] Code Sec. 7872(f)(2)(B).

[17] Reg. § 1.1274-4.

with the applicable federal short-term, mid-term and long-term rates for the month of July, and applies in the case of a below-market demand loan of a fixed principal amount that remains outstanding for the entire calendar year. The blended annual rate established for 2004 is 1.98 percent.[18] Forgone interest on a below-market demand loan of a fixed principal amount that remains outstanding for the entire year of 2004, therefore, is equal to the excess of 1.98 percent of the principal amount over any interest payable on the loan that was properly allocable to 2004.

> ***Example:*** Harriet Sheldon makes a demand loan in the amount of $1 million to her son, Nick, on January 1, 2004. The interest rate on the loan is 1%. The amount of forgone interest on the loan, as of December 31, 2004, is $9,800 (the excess of $19,800 (1.98% of $1 million) over $10,000 (1% of $1 million, the amount of interest payable on December 31, 2004)).

• ***Below-Market Gift Loans***

A gift loan is any below-market loan in which the lender's forgoing of interest is in the nature of a gift. Generally, any below-market interest loan that is not made in the ordinary course of business (i.e., in a bona fide, arm's-length transaction that is free from donative intent) is considered made for less than full and adequate consideration and is treated as a gift loan. Although most of these loans are made between related parties, the Conference Committee Report to the Tax Reform Act of 1984 (P.L. 98-369) clearly states that a below-market interest loan between unrelated parties may be considered a gift loan for purposes of Code Sec. 7872.

A below-market gift loan may generate both income tax and gift tax liability. One set of rules governs the gift taxation of such loans, and another set covers the income tax consequences arising from such transactions. However, there are certain statutory provisions that limit or prevent the imposition of the gift and income tax on these loans, and these exceptions are noted below.

• ***Gift Tax Liability***

The extent of a lender's federal gift tax liability on a below-market interest gift loan is dependent on whether the loan is a demand or a term loan. If a demand loan is involved, the lender is deemed to have made a gift to the borrower on the last day of each year the loan is outstanding.[19] Thus, there may be annual gift tax consequences if the demand loan continues beyond one calendar year. The amount of the gift is calculated on December 31, and is equal to the amount of interest forgone during the year.

With respect to any tax period, forgone interest is defined as an amount equal to the excess of (1) the amount of interest that would have been payable on the loan for the tax period if interest had accrued at the applicable federal rate and was payable annually on the last day of each calendar year, over (2) any interest payable on the loan properly allocable to that period.[20]

In the case of a term loan, the lender is deemed to have made a cash gift to the borrower on the date the loan was made. The amount of cash deemed transferred is equal to the excess of the amount loaned over the present value of all payments that are required to be made under the terms of the loan.[21] The present value of the payments is computed as of the date of the loan by using a

---

[18] Rev. Rul. 2004-66, IRB 2004-27, 4.

[19] Code Sec. 7872(a)(2).

[20] Code Sec. 7872(e)(2).

[21] Code Sec. 7872(b).

discount rate equal to the applicable federal rate in effect on that date, compounded semiannually. Therefore, in this situation, there will be only one taxable gift, because the amount is determined as of the date of the loan.

• *Income Tax Liability*

For federal income tax purposes, the lender in a below-market gift loan (whether term or demand) is deemed to have transferred any interest forgone to the borrower, and the borrower is then deemed to have retransferred an identical amount as interest to the lender. The transfer and retransfer of any forgone interest attributable to periods during any calendar year are deemed to have taken place on the last day of such calendar year.[22]

• *De Minimis Exception*

In the case of a gift loan between individuals, no interest will be imputed to either the borrower or the lender for any day on which the aggregate outstanding amount of loans between such individuals does not exceed $10,000.[23] However, if the loan balance exceeds $10,000 on any given date, the rules of Code Sec. 7872 will apply to the entire amount of the loan, and not just the amount in excess of $10,000. This *de minimis* exception does not apply where the loan proceeds may be directly attributed to the purchase or carrying of income-producing assets. For purposes of this exception, as well as all other provisions of Code Sec. 7872, a husband and wife are treated as one person.[24]

• *Special Rules for Gift Loans*

If the balance of all outstanding gift loans between individuals exceeds $10,000 but is not more than $100,000, the interest imputed as paid by the borrower will be limited to the borrower's net investment income for the year, provided that the loan's interest arrangement does not have tax avoidance as one of its principal purposes.[25] In determining the borrower's net investment income for purposes of this rule, the borrower is deemed to have no investment income for any year in which his net investment income is $1,000 or less. If the borrower has two or more outstanding gift loans, he must allocate his net investment income among such loans in proportion to the respective amounts that would be treated as retransferred to the lender without regard to the net investment income limitation.

For purposes of this exception, net investment income has the same meaning as that given under Code Sec. 163(d). Thus, the borrower must take into account all investment income from any source after offsetting for investment expenses (except interest) that are attributable to such income. Investment income includes gross income from interest, dividends, rents and royalties, net short-term capital gains from investment property, and amounts recaptured as ordinary income from the sale of investment property. The above rules apply to term loans made, renegotiated, extended, or revised after June 6, 1984, and demand loans outstanding after June 6, 1984.

¶ 2162 Transfers Subject to Special Rules

Special rules apply with respect to certain types of transfers, including the following:[26]

---

[22] Code Sec. 7872(a).
[23] Code Sec. 7872(c)(2).
[24] Code Sec. 7872(f)(7).
[25] Code Sec. 7872(d).
[26] Reg. § 25.2511-1(h).

(1) When a donor, with his or her own funds, creates a joint bank account in his or her name and in another's name and grants the other person the right to make withdrawals, each withdrawal by the other person constitutes a gift at the time it is made.

(2) When a joint tenancy with rights of survivorship is created in property, other than a joint bank account, the transaction constitutes a gift if the contributions of the joint tenants are unequal. The amount of the gift is a fractional share or shares of the amount by which the contribution of one joint tenant exceeds the contributions of each of the others. If there are to be two joint tenants, one-half of the excess is treated as a gift. If there are three joint tenants, two-thirds of the excess, or one-third of the excess of each, will be the subject of a gift.

(3) When community funds are used to purchase insurance on the life of one spouse and a third person is revocably named as beneficiary, the death of the insured spouse results in a taxable gift by the surviving spouse of one-half of the proceeds of such insurance.

¶ 2163 Powers of Appointment

Transferred property need not belong to the person deemed to be the donor in order for a taxable gift to occur. If the property was transferred by some other person and the taxpayer was given a general power of appointment over the property, a taxable gift occurs if the taxpayer exercises the power (in favor of anyone other than him- or herself) during his or her lifetime. Further, if the general power was created after October 21, 1942, the mere release of the power will constitute a taxable gift.[27]

The meaning of the term "general power of appointment" is the same for gift tax purposes and estate tax purposes. The rules for determining the date of creation of a power are also the same (see ¶ 652).

¶ 2164 Real Estate Jointly Held by Husband and Wife

The creation between husband and wife of a tenancy by the entirety or joint tenancy with right of survivorship in real property is not a taxable gift if the tenancy is created after 1981. However, in the case of a tenancy created before 1982, the donor spouse could have elected to treat the creation of the tenancy as a gift by filing a timely gift tax return for the period during which the tenancy was created.[28] Also see ¶ 502 for special rules involving the transfer tax treatment of joint tenancies created prior to 1977.

¶ 2165 Transfers Incident to Divorce or Separation

Transfers of property or property interests under a written agreement between spouses settling their marital and property rights are considered to be made for adequate and full consideration and are exempt from the gift tax provided divorce occurs within the three-year period beginning one year before the property settlement is entered into.[29] Thus, the divorce may precede the settlement agreement by as much as one year. The condition applies regardless of whether the divorce decree approves the written settlement agreement of the spouses.

---

[27] Code Sec. 2514.

[28] Code Sec. 2515, prior to repeal by P.L. 97-34.

[29] Code Sec. 2516.

Transfers made under the settlement agreement to provide reasonable allowance for the support of minor children of the marriage will also be exempt from gift tax.

¶ 2166 Life Insurance

Gratuitous transfers of life insurance are generally subject to the same rules as other gifts. An insured who relinquishes rights under an insurance policy in favor of another for less than full and adequate consideration makes a gift. If, however, the insured relinquishes only some rights, there is no gift unless the rights that are retained give the insured no control over the policy or the proceeds thereof.

> *Example:* Betty Williams gratuitously transfers a policy of insurance on her life to her daughter, Barbara. In transferring ownership of the policy, Betty relinquishes all of her rights except the right to change the beneficiary under certain circumstances. There is no gift for gift tax purposes.

The mere naming of a person as a beneficiary under a policy of insurance on one's life does not, by itself, constitute a gift for gift tax purposes. An irrevocable naming of the beneficiary does not constitute a gift if the insured reserves the right to surrender the policy for cash or to borrow against its cash surrender value. On the other hand, one may make a gift for gift tax purposes without disposing of every "incident of ownership" in the policy, with the result that the proceeds will be included in the insured's gross estate (see ¶ 430).

A gift of life insurance is complete when the insured disposes of all control over the policy or its reserves.[30] If the insured retains a possibility of reverter, the gift may be complete, even though the value of the possibility exceeds five percent of the value of the policy, which would require the inclusion of the proceeds in the insured's gross estate for estate tax purposes. The value of that possibility of reverter, however, may be excludable from the value of the gift for gift tax purposes.

The payment of premiums on policies of life insurance owned by another constitutes a gift whether the policy is on the life of the donor or on the life of some other person. The value of the gift is the amount of the premiums paid in the calendar year, less any dividends received by the donor as a partial return of premiums. If the premiums are paid on policies under which the donor owns rights, the premiums will not constitute gifts.

Life insurance policies may be given in trust either before or after they are paid for, or at any intermediate stage. If the trust is irrevocable, and if no strings are attached to the transfer of insurance to the trust, there is a gift of the value of the insurance at the time of the transfer. Likewise, any premium payments by the donor after the insurance has been transferred to the trust constitute gifts. If the trustee pays the premiums out of income from other assets held in trust or reinvests some of the other assets in the insurance by selling them to pay the premiums, the payment of premiums does not amount to a gift.

See ¶ 2109 for a discussion of split-dollar life insurance arrangements.

¶ 2167 Annuities

A transferor who irrevocably creates an annuity for the benefit of another makes a gift to the extent that the transfer is not supported by full and adequate

[30] Reg. § 25.2511-1(h)(8).

consideration in money or money's worth.[31] Therefore, the gratuitous purchase of an annuity contract for another constitutes a gift if the purchaser retains no rights in the contract. Similarly, the creation of an annuity in a trust or other property constitutes a taxable gift. A taxable gift is also made when a person establishes an annuity for his or her own benefit and irrevocably names another to receive certain benefits that may be payable after the annuitant's death.

• *Qualified Employee's Annuity Plans*

Effective for transfers made after October 22, 1986, there is no longer a blanket gift tax exclusion where an employee designates a survivor beneficiary in a qualified employee benefit plan.[32] For transfers made before October 23, 1986, an employee was allowed to designate a survivor beneficiary under a qualified pension plan, stock bonus plan, profit-sharing plan, or individual retirement account or annuity without incurring a gift tax as to any portion of the benefits attributable to contributions regarded as being made by the employer. However, this gift tax exclusion did not apply to the extent that designated benefits were attributable to contributions made by the employee.

• *Waiver of Survivor Benefits*

The waiver of a joint and survivor benefit or a qualified pre-retirement survivor benefit or the right to such a benefit by a nonparticipant spouse prior to the death of the participant does not result in the imposition of the gift tax.[33]

¶ 2168 U.S. Savings Bonds

The IRS has issued comprehensive rules for determining whether purchases of U.S. savings bonds are taxable transfers.[34] Bonds that are purchased with an individual's own funds and registered in the purchaser's name, but that are payable to another person on the purchaser's death, are not taxable gifts. A taxable gift is made when the purchaser has the bonds registered in another person's name. Bonds that are purchased with an individual's own funds and registered in the names of the purchaser and another person as co-owners are not taxable gifts at the date of purchase. A taxable gift will result if the other co-owner cashes them. A person who purchases bonds and names two other persons as co-owners makes a gift of one-half of the purchase price to each of the co-owners.

¶ 2170 Donor's Dominion and Control

Before the gift tax may be imposed on any transaction, the gift must be complete. If the intention to make a gift is expressed at one time, but the delivery of the property and acceptance of the gift take place at a later date, the later date governs. It is only at that time that the gift is completed. A promise to make a gift is not a gift. Even the execution of a trust instrument in itself will not constitute a gift. The property subject to such a trust must be transferred without retention of powers by the donor.[35]

A transfer in trust is not complete for gift tax purposes if the trustee is given such broad powers to invade income and corpus for the grantor's benefit that there is no assurance, at the time of the transfer, that anything of value will be paid to any other beneficiary. Such a transfer will not result in a taxable gift even

---

[31] See, for example, Rev. Rul. 69-74, 1969-1 CB 43.

[32] Code Sec. 2517, repealed by P.L. 99-514.

[33] Code Sec. 2503(f).

[34] Rev. Rul. 68-269, 1968-1 CB 399.

[35] Reg. § 25.2511-2.

though the value of the trust property is large in amount. Similarly, if creditors of the grantor can reach the trust assets under applicable state law, the transfer in trust is not a taxable gift.[36]

¶ 2171 Cessation of Dominion and Control

A gift is incomplete unless the donor has parted with dominion and control and, thus, is without power to change the disposition of the transferred property—whether for the donor's benefit or for the benefit of another. A gift is incomplete in every instance where a donor reserves the power to reassume the beneficial title to the property. It is also incomplete when a donor reserves the power to name new beneficiaries or to change the interests of the various beneficiaries.[37] The U.S. Court of Appeals for the Tenth Circuit has held that the question of whether a transfer is a completed gift for purposes of the federal gift tax is strictly a matter of federal law.[38]

A gift will not be incomplete merely because the donor reserves the power to change the manner or time of enjoyment thereof. Also, it will not be incomplete as to an intermediate vested interest, such as a life estate or an estate for years, merely because it will return to the donor at a later date.

A donor is considered to retain a power if the donor may exercise that power in conjunction with any person not having a substantial adverse interest in the disposition of the transferred property or the income therefrom. A trustee who has no other interest in the trust is not a person having an adverse interest in the disposition of the trust property or its income.

The relinquishment or termination of a power to change the disposition of the transferred property, occurring otherwise than by the death of the donor, is regarded as the event that completes the gift and causes the tax to apply. However, if a donor retains the power to change the amount of the beneficiaries' interests or to designate the beneficiary of the trust corpus, any income that is transferred to the beneficiaries before the donor designates a recipient of the corpus is not a part of the property disposed of by the designation. The income received by the beneficiaries is a taxable gift at the time the gift is completed.[39]

¶ 2175 Transfers by Nonresidents Not Citizens

Except for the estates of nonresidents not citizens who are subject to the expatriate alternative gift tax regime (discussed below), a blanket exemption from federal gift taxation is provided for all gifts by nonresidents who are not U.S. citizens of intangible property having a situs within the United States, e.g., stocks and bonds.[40]

Transfers by U.S. citizens who are residents of a U.S. possession but who acquired their U.S. citizenship solely by reason of being a citizen of the possession or by reason of birth or residence within the possession will be treated as transfers made by nonresidents who are not citizens of the United States.

---

[36] *M.M. Outwin*, 76 TC 153, CCH Dec. 37,645 (Acq.).

[37] Reg. § 25.2511-2.

[38] *Wells Fargo Bank, N.A.*, CA-10, 2003-1 USTC ¶ 60,456, rev'g *First Security Bank*, DC N.M., 2001-1 USTC ¶ 60,406.

[39] Reg. § 25.2511-2(f).

[40] Code Sec. 2501(a)(2).

• ***Alternative Gift Tax Regime for Expatriates***

Gratuitous transfers of tangible or intangible property situated in the United States by a former citizen or long-term resident who is subject to the alternative tax regime of Code Sec. 877(b), and made during the 10-year period following relinquishment of citizenship or long-term residency, are subject to federal gift tax. This provision is effective for individuals who expatriate after June 3, 2004.[41] However, if pursuant to Code Sec. 877(g), as added by the American Jobs Creation Act of 2004 (P.L. 108-357), such a former citizen or long-term resident is present in the United States for a period of 30 days or more in any calendar year that ends during the 10-year period following relinquishment of citizenship or long-term residency, he or she is treated as a resident of the United States for federal gift tax purposes. Thus, all gratuitous transfers, regardless of where the property is situated, made by such former citizen or long-term resident in the calendar year are subject to the federal gift tax.

• ***Transfer of Stock in Certain Closely Held Foreign Corporations***

Gratuitous transfers of stock in certain closely held foreign corporations, regardless of where the stock is located, by a former citizen or long-term resident who is subject to the alternative tax regime of Code Sec. 877(b), are subject to the federal gift tax, if made during the 10-year period following relinquishment of citizenship to long-term residency. This provision is effective for individuals who expatriate after June 3, 2004.[42] A foreign corporation that is subject to this gift tax rule is one in which the former citizen or long-term resident: (1) owns 10 percent or more of the total combined voting power of all classes of stock, and (2) directly or indirectly owns over 50 percent of the total combined voting power of all classes of stock or total value of stock.[43] The value of the stock for gift tax purposes is the U.S.-asset value of the stock at the time of the transfer. The U.S. asset value is equal to the proportionate share of the fair market value, at the time of the transfer, of the foreign stock transferred which the fair market value of any assets owned by the foreign corporation that are situated in the United States bears to the total fair market value of all assets owned by such foreign corporation.[44]

> ***Example:*** Marco Ferraro, owner of 75 percent of the voting block in Black Inc., a Spanish closely held corporation, transfers his interest to his two children on October 15, 2004. Ferraro, who relinquished his U.S. citizenship five years before the transfer, recently spent 45 days in the United States visiting relatives and friends. At the time of transfer, Black Inc. owned $2 million in assets, $500,000 of which were situated in the United States. On October 15, 2004, the fair market value of the transferred stock was $1.5 million. For purposes of determining Ferraro's gift tax liability on the transfer, the value of the stock is computed by first determining the fraction or percentage that the fair market value of the U.S.-situated assets bears to the fair market value of all assets owned by Black Inc. ($500,000/$2,000,000, which is 25 percent). This 25 percent amount is then applied to the fair market value of the transferred stock to determine the U.S.-asset value of the stock ($1,500,000 × 25% = $375,000).

---

[41] Code Sec. 2501(a), as amended by the American Jobs Creation Act of 2004 (P.L. 108-357).

[42] Code Sec. 2501(a)(5)(A), as added by the American Jobs Creation Act of 2004 (P.L. 108-357).

[43] Code Sec. 2501(a)(5)(B), as added by the American Jobs Creation Act of 2004 (P.L. 108-357).

[44] Code Sec. 2501(a)(5)(C), as added by the American Jobs Creation Act of 2004 (P.L. 108-357).

¶ 2180 Manner of Reporting Gifts on Return

Gifts that are subject only to the gift tax are reported in part 1 of Schedule A (Computation of Taxable Gifts) of Form 709 (United States Gift (and Generation-Skipping Transfer) Tax Return) (2004). These gifts include charitable, public, and similar gifts. Gifts that are direct skips and are subject to both the gift tax and the generation-skipping transfer tax are reported in chronological order on part 2 of Schedule A. Indirect skips from a trust that are currently subject to gift tax and may later be subject to generation-skipping transfer tax are reported on part 3 of Schedule A. Gifts to political organizations and for medical and educational purposes are exempt from the gift tax and, thus, do not have to be reported.

If the total annual gifts of present interests to any donee are more than $11,000 ($10,000 for calendar years before 2002), the donor must enter all such gifts that are made during that year to or on behalf of that donee, including those gifts that will be excluded under the annual exclusion. If the total is $11,000 or less, the donor need not enter on Schedule A any gifts (except gifts of future interests made to that donee). Gifts of future interests made during a calendar year must be reported on Schedule A regardless of their value.[45]

Where one transfer results in gifts to two individuals (such as a life estate to one person with the remainder to another person), the gift to each individual must be listed separately. Gifts made by a donor to his or her spouse should be reflected on Schedule A only if they are gifts of terminable interests. All terminable interests that pass to the spouse should be reported regardless of whether they qualify for the gift tax marital deduction (see ¶ 2313).

An annual Form 709 need not be filed if the donor's gifts consisted solely of:

(1) transfers of present interests not in excess of the annual gift tax exclusion (see ¶ 2250);[46]

(2) transfers to political organizations;

(3) qualified transfers for educational or medical expenses (see ¶ 2250); or

(4) transfers to the donor's spouse that qualify for the unlimited marital deduction (see ¶ 2311).[47]

¶ 2181 Description of Property on Return

The property comprising the gifts listed in Schedule A (Computation of Taxable Gifts) of Form 709 (United States Gift (and Generation-Skipping Transfer) Tax Return) (reproduced in the Appendix at ¶ 2950) should be described in enough detail to be easily identified. For interests in property based on the duration of a person's life, the date of birth of that person should be included in the description.[48]

• *Real Estate*

A legal description should be given for each parcel of real estate. If the property is located within a city, the name of the street, the street number, and the area of the city should be given. A short statement of any improvements to the realty should also be furnished.

---

[45] Reg. § 25.6019-1.

[46] Instructions for Form 709 (2004), p. 2.

[47] Instructions for Form 709 (2004), p. 3.

[48] Instructions for Form 709 (2004), p. 8.

• ***Bonds***

A description of bonds transferred should include (1) the number of bonds transferred, (2) the principal amount, (3) the name of the obligor, (4) the maturity date, (5) the rate of interest, (6) the date or dates when interest is payable, (7) the series number, if there is more than one issue, (8) the exchange on which the bond is listed, and (9) the CUSIP (Committee on Uniform Security Identification Procedure) number, if available (see ¶313). If the bond is not listed on an exchange, the address of the principal business office of the corporation should be given.

• ***Stocks***

A description of a gift of stock should include (1) the number of shares transferred, (2) a designation of the shares as common or preferred stock, (3) if a listed security, the principal exchange on which it is sold, and (4) the CUSIP number, if available (see ¶313). If the stock is not listed on an exchange, the description should give the location of the corporation's principal business office, the state in which the corporation was incorporated, and the date of incorporation. If the gift is of preferred stock, the description should contain the issue, the par value of the stock, the quotation at which returned, and the exact name of the corporation.

• ***Insurance Policies***

A description of life insurance policies should include the name of the insurer and the policy number.

Chapter 35
GIFT-SPLITTING

¶ 2200 Practical Effect

A gift made by a husband or wife to a third person may be treated as made one-half by each, if both spouses consent.[1] This right is an optional one that is effective only for the calendar year, or quarter for certain prior periods, for which the election is made. If the consent is effective, all gifts by the husband and wife to third persons during that calendar year or quarter must receive the same treatment. By signifying their consent, the donor and his or her spouse become jointly and severally liable for the entire gift tax for that calendar year or quarter. See ¶2205 for guidelines concerning the manner of reporting these gifts on Schedule A (Computation of Taxable Gifts) of Form 709 (United States Gift (and Generation-Skipping Transfer) Tax Return) (2004).

A short form gift tax return (Form 709-A, United States Short Form Gift Tax Return) (Rev. Oct. 2002) was available for filing by a husband and wife who elected split-gift treatment for pre-2003 gifts of not more than $22,000 per donee. Because Form 709-A has been declared obsolete for gifts made after December 31, 2002, Form 709 must be used to report split gifts made after this date.[2]

Although the Code does not limit gift-splitting treatment to separately owned property, such treatment has no significance except in the case of separate property. The purpose of gift-splitting, in fact, is to equalize the effect of the gift tax as between community and separate property.

> *Example (1):* On March 5, 2004, Tony Sheaffer made a gift to his son, Roger, of bonds worth $30,000, representing his separate property. Tony and his spouse signed the required consent form. The gift is treated as one of $15,000 by Tony and one of $15,000 by his spouse.

> *Example (2):* On February 6, 2004, Patricia Rey made a gift to her grandson, Louis, of stock worth $22,000, representing community property. Whether the consent was filed, the gift is one of $11,000 by Patricia and one of $11,000 by her spouse (see ¶2220).

The gift-splitting benefit is not available unless the donor is married at the time of the gift and does not become married to a different person before the close of the calendar year. In addition, each spouse must be a citizen or resident of the United States at the time of the gift. Finally, to qualify for the gift-splitting privilege, the spouse making the gift must not give the other spouse a general power of appointment over the property transferred.

If the spouse of the donor is given a partial interest in the property transferred, the gift-splitting privilege is available only for the value of the property

---

[1] Code Sec. 2513.

[2] Instructions for Form 709 (2004), p. 1.

transferred to persons other than the spouse and only to the extent that these persons' interests are ascertainable at the time the gift is reported.

¶ 2205 Gift Tax Returns

When gift-splitting is elected, the donor spouse must file a return if annual gifts to any one donee exceed the amount of the gift tax exclusion. However, the consenting spouse must file a return only if he or she made gifts to any one donee in excess of the gift tax exclusion, including gifts attributable to the consenting spouse under the gift-splitting provisions, or if any gifts made were of future interests.[3] The following examples illustrate this rule.

> *Example (1):* Gary Alto made gifts valued at $24,000 during 2004 to a third party, and his wife, Vicki, made no gifts during this time, but elects gift-splitting for this year. Each spouse is required to file a return for 2004. Gary is required to file a return because the amount of the gift exceeds the amount of the annual exclusion ($11,000) by $13,000. Vicki is required to file because she is considered as having made a gift of $12,000 to the third party, which exceeds the annual gift tax exclusion by $1,000.

> *Example (2):* Mimi Bradley made gifts valued at $16,000 during 2004 to a third party, and her husband, John, made no gifts. Only Mimi is required to file a return for 2004 because John is considered as having made a gift of $8,000, which does not exceed the annual gift tax exclusion.

To report gifts on Schedule A (Computation of Taxable Gifts) of Form 709 (United States Gift (and Generation-Skipping Transfer) Tax Return) whenever spouses elect to treat gifts to third parties as being made one-half by each of them, the following rules apply:[4]

> (1) If only one spouse makes gifts for which a return is required, the full value of all gifts made by the spouse filing the return must be entered in column F of part 1, 2, or 3, of Schedule A, even if the gift's value will be less than $11,000 after it is split in column G.

> (2) If split-gift treatment is elected and both spouses made gifts, the gifts made by the donor's spouse are listed in the space provided for "Gifts made by spouse" in Schedule A, part 1, 2, or 3, as appropriate.

Gifts entered in part 1 of Schedule A should be grouped into the following categories: (1) gifts to spouse; (2) gifts to third parties that are to be split; (3) gifts for charitable uses if gift-splitting is not elected; and (4) all other gifts.[5] Gifts entered in parts 2 and 3 of Schedule A should be listed in chronological order. In all cases in which it is not apparent how the amounts entered for Schedule A were computed, additional sheets of the same size as the return should be attached and the computations set forth thereon in detail. To avoid correspondence from the IRS, where both spouses must file a gift tax return, both returns should be filed together in the same envelope.[6]

¶ 2210 Exclusions and Exemptions

All exemptions and exclusions that are available to each spouse are applicable to a single gift when gift-splitting is elected, resulting in a doubling of the exemptions and exclusions applicable to the transfer. Gifts of present interests in the amount of $22,000 annually (for 2002 through 2004) may be made to each

---

[3] Reg. § 25.2513-1 and Reg. § 25.6019-2.

[4] Instructions for Form 709 (2004), p. 6.

[5] Instructions for Form 709 (2004), p. 8.

[6] Instructions for Form 709 (2004), p. 1.

donee without incurring a tax, because each spouse may claim an $11,000 exclusion with respect to each donee. The annual exclusion rose to $11,000 for the calendar year 2002 and beyond, as a result of inflation adjustments that had been in effect after 1998.

¶ 2215 Consent of Both Spouses

The privilege of dividing a gift between husband-and-wife donors is granted only if both signify their consent to such division. When one spouse consents to have gifts made by the other treated as having been made one-half by each of them, gifts made by the consenting spouse must also be treated as having been made one-half by each spouse.[7]

¶ 2220 Community Property

The gift-splitting privilege does not apply to gifts of community property. Gifts of community property are automatically treated as being made one-half from each spouse.[8] There is, consequently, no need to obtain consents with respect to gifts of community property.

¶ 2225 Time of Consent

Consent to split gifts must be given on or before April 15 of the year following the year in which the gifts were made.[9]

Consent to split-gift treatment may not be given after a deficiency notice with respect to tax in that year has been sent to either spouse.[10] Similarly, spouses may not consent to the election after the donor spouse has filed a gift tax return reporting the gifts and after the due date for the return has passed.[11] A consent, once given, may be revoked before the last day for filing the consent by filing a duplicate written notice with the IRS officer with whom the return was filed.[12]

The executor or administrator of the estate of a deceased spouse may give consent to gift-splitting treatment. The guardian or committee of a legally incompetent person may also give such consent.

¶ 2230 Form of Consent

In order to be effective, the consent to taxation to each spouse of one-half of the gifts must be signified by both husband and wife. The consent should be signified, by the spouse filing the return, by answering "Yes" on line 12, part 1, on the face of Form 709 (United States Gift (and Generation-Skipping Transfer) Tax Return) (reproduced in the Appendix at ¶3280) and, by the other spouse, by executing the "Consent of Spouse" appearing in part 1, line 18, of the same return.

---

[7] Rev. Rul. 146, 1953-2 CB 292.

[8] Instructions for Form 709 (2004), p. 1.

[9] Code Sec. 2513(b).

[10] Code Sec. 2513(b).

[11] Rev. Rul. 80-224, 1980-2 CB 281.

[12] Code Sec. 2513(c); Reg. § 25.2513-3.

Chapter 36
ANNUAL EXCLUSIONS

¶ 2250 Exclusions Available

The first $11,000 ($22,000 where gift-splitting is elected) of gifts of present interests made to any donee during the tax year is excluded in determining the amount of taxable gifts.[1] The annual exclusion is indexed for inflation after 1998. Under the indexing formula, indexed amounts are rounded to the next lowest multiple of $1,000. The aggregate yearly inflation adjustments raised the annual exclusion to $11,000 (from $10,000, which it had been since 1982) for gifts made in 2002 and later calendar years.[2] The annual exclusion is not limited in the number of donees for whom it may be taken or for the number of years in which it may be taken. However, it is limited to gifts of present, rather than future, interests (see ¶2265). Prior to 1982, the annual exclusion was $3,000.

In the case of gifts in trust, the trust beneficiaries, rather than the trust or trustees, are treated as the donees for the purpose of determining the number of annual exclusions allowable to the donor.

• ***Unlimited Educational and Medical Expense Exclusion***

An unlimited gift tax exclusion is available for amounts paid on behalf of a donee directly to an educational organization, provided that such amounts constitute tuition payments.[3] In addition, amounts paid to health care providers for medical services on behalf of a donee qualify for an unlimited exclusion. The exclusions for qualifying educational expenses and medical expenses are available without regard to the relationship between the donor and donee and are available in addition to the annual exclusion. Transfers to educational organizations and for medical expenses do not have to be reported as gifts on Schedule A (Computation of Taxable Gifts) of Form 709 (United States Gift (and Generation-Skipping Transfer) Tax Return) (2004).

Qualifying medical expenses, for purposes of the exclusion, are defined by reference to Code Sec. 213(d) (relating to the deductibility of medical and dental expenses for income tax purposes). The exclusion is not available to the extent that the amounts paid are reimbursed by insurance.

The IRS has privately ruled[4] that prepaid tuition payments qualified for the gift tax exclusion under Code Sec. 2503(c), where the payments were made directly to the educational institution in payment of specific tuition costs for designated individuals. Under the facts of the ruling, a donor transferred money

---

[1] Code Sec. 2503.

[2] Rev. Proc. 2001-59, 2001-2 CB 623; Rev. Proc. 2002-70, IRB 2002-46, 845; Rev. Proc. 2003-85, IRB 2003-49, 1184.

[3] Code Sec. 2503(e).

[4] Technical Advice Memorandum 199941013 (July 9, 1999).

to a private school pursuant to an agreement under which the money would be used exclusively for his two grandchildren. The donor agreed to pay any additional money in later years to reflect the costs of any increases in tuition, and agreed that if the grandchildren failed to attend the school in the specified years, the money would be forfeited to the school, rather than returned to the donor.

• ***Contributions to Qualified Tuition Programs***

Effective for transfers made after August 5, 1997, any contribution to a qualified tuition program (QTP) is treated as a completed gift of a present interest from the contributor to the beneficiary at the time of the contribution. Annual contributions are eligible for the gift tax exclusion (for 2004 it is $11,000 for an individual and $22,000 for a married couple electing gift-splitting).[5]

Contributions to a QTP are not considered qualifying transfers under the rules providing an unlimited annual exclusion with respect to payments for educational and medical expenses.[6] Effective for tax years beginning after December 31, 2001, a contribution made to a qualified private institution can also qualify for this treatment.

A contributor making a contribution in excess of the exclusion limit may elect to have the contribution treated as if it were made ratably over five years.[7] A gift tax return must be filed with respect to any contribution in excess of the annual gift tax exclusion limit (see ¶2052).

If a beneficiary's interest is rolled over to another beneficiary or there is a change in beneficiary, no gift tax consequences result, provided that the new beneficiary is assigned to the same generation as the old beneficiary.[8] Although the rollover of a beneficiary's interest to a beneficiary in a lower generation (e.g., parent to child or aunt to niece) will be treated as a taxable gift, the five-year averaging rule may be applied to exempt up to $55,000 ($110,000, if gift-splitting is elected) of the transfer.[9]

• ***Completion of Gift; Transfer by Check***

A gift tax annual exclusion is available only in the year that the gift is completed—that is, the year in which the donor effectively parts with dominion and control over the transferred property. Problems may arise when a donor makes a gift by check in one year, but the check is not paid by the donor's bank until the following year. The IRS has taken the position that completion of a gift of a check to a noncharitable donee will relate back to the earlier of the date on which the donor no longer has the power to change the disposition of the check or the date on which the donee deposited, cashed, or presented the check if (1) the drawee bank paid the check when it was first presented, (2) the donor was alive when the bank paid the check, (3) the donor intended to make a gift, (4) delivery was unconditional, and (5) the check was deposited, cashed, or presented by the donee in the year in which gift tax treatment is sought.[10]

---

[5] Code Sec. 529(b)(1), as amended by P.L. 107-16.

[6] Code Sec. 529(c)(2)(A).

[7] Code Sec. 529(c)(2)(B).

[8] Code Sec. 529(c)(5).

[9] Code Sec. 529(c)(2)(B).

[10] Rev. Rul. 96-56, 1996-2 CB 161, modifying Rev. Rul. 67-396, 1967-2 CB 351; *A. Metzger*, CA-4, 1994-2 USTC ¶60,179, aff'g 100 TC 204, CCH Dec. 48,910. However, see *S. Newman Est.*, CA-DC, 99-2 USTC ¶60,358, and *R. Rosano, Exr.*, CA-2, 2001-1 USTC ¶60,401, cert. denied Feb. 19, 2002, in which the relation-back doctrine was not applied to situations involving noncharitable donees where the decedent died before checks were presented.

¶ 2255 Gifts in Prior Years

The annual exclusion is available only for gifts made after 1981. From 1982 through 2001, the annual exclusion amount was $10,000. Although the annual exclusion was $3,000 for all years beginning with 1943 and ending with 1981, larger exclusions were allowed for 1942 and earlier years. These exclusions are sometimes important in determining the tax for a current year. Gifts of prior years play a part in determining the tax for the current years because of the cumulative nature of the tax.

¶ 2260 Gifts by Married Persons

When a husband and wife have agreed to treat gifts to third persons made by either of them as being made one-half by each, they double the number of annual exclusions available with respect to their gifts. Each may claim an exclusion for each third-party donee, provided, of course, that the gifts are of present interests (see ¶ 2200 through ¶ 2230).

¶ 2265 Future Interests

The annual exclusion is not allowed for gifts of future interests.[11] Denial of the exclusion results from difficulty in determining the number of eventual donees and the values of their respective shares. This difficulty is especially significant where contingent remainders are involved. Rather than attempt to set up many fine-line distinctions, Congress chose to deny the exclusion with respect to all gifts of future interests in property.

"Future interests" refers to the interest taken by the donee. They are interests, whether vested or contingent, "limited to commence in use, possession, or enjoyment at some future date or time."[12] Thus, all gifts of remainder interests, whether vested or contingent, are gifts of future interests. However, a gift in trust of a remainder interest in personal property to a donee who is an income beneficiary of the trust is a gift of a present interest. Such a gift qualifies for the exclusion in those states whose laws provide for the merger of the interests and the termination of the trust.[13]

Gifts of income that commence immediately are gifts of present interests. If, however, the income is to be accumulated and paid over at a later time, the gift of the income is a gift of a future interest. This is so even if, on some specified contingency, some portion or all of the income may be paid over earlier.[14] The IRS will not allow an exclusion for a gift of property in trust that provides that all income must be paid to a beneficiary, but permits corpus to be invested in nonincome-producing property and life insurance.[15] However, a gift to a minor is not a future interest if the property and its income may be expended for the benefit of the minor before the minor attains age 21 and may be distributed to the minor at that time or to the minor's estate if the minor dies before reaching age 21.[16]

The IRS has ruled that transfers by a donor of specified portions of real property equal in value to the annual exclusion constituted gifts of present interests that were eligible for the annual exclusion.[17] According to the IRS, the donees received the present, unrestricted right to the immediate use, possession and enjoyment of an ascertainable interest in the real property.

---

[11] Reg. § 25.2503-3.

[12] *A. Pelzer*, SCt, 41-1 USTC ¶ 10,027, 312 US 399; Reg. § 25.2503-3.

[13] Rev. Rul. 78-168, 1978-1 CB 298.

[14] *E.F. Fondren*, SCt, 45-1 USTC ¶ 10,164, 324 US 18.

[15] Rev. Rul. 69-344, 1969-1 CB 225.

[16] Code Sec. 2503(c).

[17] Rev. Rul. 83-180, 1983-2 CB 169.

A partner's gift to the partnership accounts of other partners has been held to qualify for the annual exclusion where the donee partners had the immediate and unrestricted right to possess and enjoy the transferred amounts.[18] Under the Uniform Partnership Act, as adopted in Indiana, each partner was entitled to receive amounts from his or her capital account on demand, since the underlying partnership agreement did not contain a provision to the contrary.

The IRS has also privately ruled[19] that gifts of limited partnership interests by parents to their children qualified for the annual exclusion. In concluding that the gifts constituted present interests, the IRS National Office noted that, under the terms of the partnership agreement and applicable state law, the limited partnership interests conferred the rights to receive distributions before withdrawal or dissolution of the partnership, the right to assign or sell the interest in whole or in part, and the right to bring a cause of action against the general partners personally for breach of fiduciary duty. These rights entitled the donee-children to any current economic benefits generated by the limited partnership interests and, accordingly, the interests qualified for the gift tax annual exclusion.

A husband and wife's annual exclusions were denied with respect to limited liability company (LLC) membership units transferred to their children, where the children did not derive a substantial economic benefit from the transfers. The Tax Court found a present economic benefit to be lacking because, under the terms of the LLC operating agreement, the donee-children could not (1) unilaterally withdraw their capital accounts, (2) sell or transfer their units without consent of the LLC manager, or (3) unilaterally effect a dissolution of the LLC.[20]

• ***Crummey Trusts***

A gift of the right to demand a portion of a trust corpus is a gift of a present interest,[21] so long as the donee-beneficiary is aware of the right to make the demand.[22] The Tax Court has held that transfers of property to a trust constituted a present interest where the trust beneficiaries (the grantor's grandchildren) had the right to withdraw an amount equal to the annual gift tax exclusion within 15 days of the transfer, even though the only other interests the grandchildren had in the trust were contingent remainder interests.[23] In so holding, the Tax Court applied the present interest test enunciated by the U.S. Court of Appeals for the Ninth Circuit in *D.C. Crummey*,[24] concluding that the grandchildren's withdrawal rights, if exercised, could not be legally resisted by the trustees.

¶ 2270 Gifts for the Benefit of a Minor

A gift of property to a minor in trust may qualify for the annual exclusion if certain statutory requirements are met. No part of a transfer for the benefit of a minor will be considered to be a future interest (which would not qualify for the exclusion) if the transfer meets the conditions specified in Code Sec. 2503(c):

(1) Both the property and its income may be expended by, or for the benefit of, the minor donee prior to his or her attaining the age of 21. To the

---

[18] *J.P. Wooley, Exr.*, DC Ind., 90-1 USTC ¶60,013.

[19] Technical Advice Memorandum 199944003 (July 2, 1999).

[20] *C. Hackl*, 118 TC 279, CCH Dec. 54,686, aff'd, CA-7, 2003-2 USTC ¶60,465, 335 F3d 664.

[21] Rev. Rul. 80-261, 1980-2 CB 279.

[22] Rev. Rul. 81-7, 1981-1 CB 474.

[23] *M. Cristofani Est.*, 97 TC 74, CCH Dec. 47,491 (Acq.), and *L. Kohlsaat Est.*, 73 TCM 2732, CCH Dec. 53,031(M), TC Memo. 1997-212. But see Technical Advice Memorandum 9628004 (Apr. 1, 1996) and Technical Advice Memorandum 9731004 (Apr. 21, 1997).

[24] *D.C. Crummey*, CA-9, 68-2 USTC ¶12,541, 397 F2d 82.

extent the property and income were not so expended, they will pass to the donee at that time.

(2) In the event of the donee's death prior to reaching 21 years of age, the property and income not expended will pass to the donee's estate or to persons appointed by him or her under the exercise of a general power of appointment.

Persons drafting trust provisions for minor beneficiaries should include both of the above conditions in the trust instrument. The absence of one of the above provisions will cause the loss of annual gift tax exclusions for the trusts, and the courts have not permitted the donors to change the trust provisions in a later year in order to obtain annual exclusions.[25] In addition, the right of the trustees to expend property and income for the benefit of the minor beneficiaries should not be limited to a specific purpose or subject to a substantial restriction.[26] For example, the courts have disallowed annual exclusions where the trustees could expend property or income for a minor beneficiary's medical care only. However, it would appear that a trust could limit categories of expenditure to those allowed guardians under the law of the state where the gift was made.

A gift of an income interest in a trust to a minor may qualify for the annual exclusion, even though the gift of the trust corpus does not qualify, or even though the minor does not have any interest in the corpus at all.[27] This is true because income interests payable to minor beneficiaries qualify as separate property interests apart from the corpus. An annual gift tax exclusion will be allowed for an income interest if (1) the income may be used for the beneficiary's benefit during minority, (2) the accumulated income will be distributed to him or her at age 21, and (3) the accumulated income is payable to the beneficiary's estate, or to persons designated in his or her will, if he or she dies before reaching age 21.[28] An annual exclusion for the income interest may be lost where the trustee has power to allocate income and expenses between corpus and income.

Example: Ron Kovak created a trust for his granddaughter, Cindy, who was to receive the income until she reached the age of 30, when she would receive the entire trust principal. The trustee was given discretion to use the principal for the benefit of the beneficiary and to accumulate income not used. The accumulated income was to be paid to Cindy when she reached majority or to her estate in the event of her death before that time. The gift property is separable into its several interests. In light of this division, the gift of a right to income until age 21 qualifies for the annual exclusion. The gifts of principal and income payable after majority to age 30 do not qualify.

The annual exclusion is available where a minor beneficiary has, on reaching age 21, either (1) a continuing right to compel immediate distribution of the trust corpus by giving written notice to the trustee, or to permit the trust to continue by its own terms, or (2) a right during a limited period to compel immediate distribution of the trust corpus by giving written notice to the trustee, a right which, if not exercised, will permit the trust to continue by its own terms.[29]

---

[25] *S.S. Davis*, 55 TC 416, CCH Dec. 30,455; *A. Van Den Wymelenberg*, CA-7, 68-2 USTC ¶12,537, 397 F2d 443, cert. denied; *E.D. Harris*, CA-5, 72-1 USTC ¶12,853, 461 F2d 554.

[26] *S.L. Faber*, CA-6, 71-1 USTC ¶12,760, 439 F2d 1189; *J.T. Pettus, Jr.*, 54 TC 112, CCH Dec. 29,926.

[27] *A.I. Herr*, 35 TC 732, CCH Dec. 24,652 (Acq.), aff'd by CA-3, 62-2 USTC ¶12,079, 303 F2d 780; Rev. Rul. 68-670, 1968-2 CB 413.

[28] Many states have lowered the age at which custodian property must be distributed to the minor from 21 to 18 years. The IRS has ruled that the annual exclusion still will be available in those states that have lowered the distribution age from 21 to 18 (Rev. Rul. 73-287, 1973-2 CB 321).

[29] Rev. Rul. 74-43, 1974-1 CB 285, revoking Rev. Rul. 60-218, 1960-1 CB 378.

¶ 2272 Uniform Transfers to Minors Act: Custodianship

A transfer of property for the benefit of a minor pursuant to the Uniform Transfers to Minors Act or one of its predecessors, the Uniform Gifts to Minors Act or the Model Gifts of Securities to Minors Act, is considered to be a complete gift of the full fair market value of the property. No taxable gift occurs by reason of a subsequent resignation of the custodian or termination of the custodianship for federal gift tax purposes. Such a gift also qualifies for the annual gift tax exclusion.

The value of the property transferred under the "Uniform" or the "Model" Act may be includible in the gross estate of the donor (with a credit against estate tax for prior gift taxes paid) if the donor appoints him- or herself as custodian of the property and dies while serving in that capacity before the minor donee attains majority. The income from such property, to the extent it is used for the support of the minor donee, is includible in the gross income of any person who is legally obligated to support the minor donee.[30]

¶ 2274 Reciprocal Transfers

The IRS will disallow annual exclusions that are artificially generated by reciprocal (cross) transfers, as illustrated below.

> ***Example:*** Brothers Allen, Brian, and Charlie Fox each have two children. The brothers agree that in 2004, each will give $11,000 to each of their two children, and each of their four nephews and nieces, for total transfers of $66,000 by each brother. If annual exclusions apply to all of the transfers, each of the brothers will, in effect, cause a transfer of $33,000 for each of their children, without incurring any gift tax.

Where the IRS applies the reciprocal transfer doctrine within the context of determining the allowance of gift tax annual exclusions, it will look beyond the form of the transfers, and attribute all monies coming to each donee to his or her respective donor.[31] Accordingly, in the above Example, Allen, Brian, and Charlie will each be limited to two $11,000 annual exclusions. The additional $22,000 that each brother will be deemed to transfer to his two children will be taxable gifts.

¶ 2275 Present Interest with Possibility of Reduction

If a donor makes a gift of a present interest in property, the possibility that the interest may be diminished by an exercise of a power is disregarded in determining whether the interest qualifies for the annual exclusion if no part of the interest will at any time pass to any other person.[32]

¶ 2280 Reporting Exclusions on Gift Tax Return

After reporting all gifts by the donor on the gift tax return form, subtracting the portion, if any, reported by the donor's spouse on a separate return, and adding the portion of the spouse's gifts being taxed to donor, the annual exclusions are subtracted from the resulting "Total gifts," resulting in the "Total included amount of gifts" (lines 1, 2, and 3, part 4 of Schedule A (Computation of Taxable Gifts) of Form 709 (United States Gift (and Generation-Skipping Transfer) Tax Return) (2004)) (see the Appendix at ¶3280).

---

[30] Rev. Rul. 59-357, 1959-2 CB 212.

[31] *J.A. Schultz*, CA-4, 74-1 USTC ¶12,997, 493 F2d 1225; Rev. Rul. 85-24, 1985-1 CB 329; *L. Sather*, CA-8, 2001-1 USTC ¶60,409, aff'g in part (this issue) and rev'g in part (on another issue), 78 TCM 456, CCH Dec. 53,548(M), TC Memo. 1999-309; *R. Schuler Est.*, CA-8, 2002-1 USTC ¶60,432, aff'g 80 TCM 934, CCH Dec. 54,171(M), TC Memo. 2000-392.

[32] Reg. §25.2503-3(b).

Chapter 37
DEDUCTIONS AND EXEMPTIONS

¶ 2300 Reductions to Taxable Amount

In addition to the annual exclusion (see ¶2250) available to a donor for gifts of present interests made to each donee, the gift tax law provides for various deductions. Their total serves to reduce the "Total included amount of gifts" (line 3, part 4 of Schedule A (Computation of Taxable Gifts) of Form 709 (United States Gift (and Generation-Skipping Transfer) Tax Return)) (2004) to the ultimate amount of taxable gifts for the calendar year on which the tax is to be paid. Allowable deductions include the deduction for charitable, public and similar gifts and the marital deduction.

For gifts made prior to 1977, a specific exemption of $30,000 was allowed, in addition to the above-noted reductions.

¶ 2305 Charitable, Public, and Religious Transfers

Various gifts for charitable, public, and religious purposes are deductible in determining net gifts subject to tax. Specifically, there may be deducted the value of gifts to or for the use of the following:

(1) The United States, any state, territory, or any political subdivision thereof, or the District of Columbia, for exclusively public purposes.

(2) Any corporation, trust, community chest, fund, or foundation, organized and operated exclusively for religious, charitable, scientific, literary, or educational purposes, including the encouragement of art and the prevention of cruelty to children or animals. No part of the net earnings of such organization may inure to the benefit of any private shareholder or individual. Furthermore, the organization may not attempt to influence legislation or participate in, or intervene in (including the publishing or distributing of statements), any political campaign on behalf of (or in opposition to) any candidate for public office.

(3) A fraternal society, order, or association, operating under the lodge system, provided such gifts are to be used by such fraternal society, order, or association exclusively for one or more of the purposes enumerated in (2), above.

(4) Any organization of war veterans or auxiliary unit or society thereof if such organization, auxiliary unit, or society thereof is organized in the United States or any of its possessions. No part of its net earnings may inure to the benefit of any private shareholder or individual.[1]

The charitable deduction is not limited to gifts for use within the United States, or to gifts to or for the use of domestic corporations, trusts, community chests, funds, or foundations, or fraternal societies, orders, or associations operating under the lodge system. The exercise or release of a power of appointment that results in the passing of the property subject to the power to or for the use of any of the organizations listed above is a transfer by gift for purposes of the deduction.

Contributions to a political party or to a candidate for public office do not constitute a gift "to or for the use of the United States, any State, Territory, or any political subdivision thereof" for "exclusively public purposes" and, therefore, do not qualify as deductible charitable contributions. Contributions to political organizations are not subject to the gift tax.[2]

• ***Disallowance of Deduction in Certain Cases***

Charitable deductions (both estate and gift tax) will be denied for otherwise deductible bequests and gifts to an organization on which the Code Sec. 507 private foundation termination tax has been imposed. General contributors will be denied deductions after the organization is notified of the loss of its private foundation status.[3] Substantial contributors (generally, persons contributing more than $5,000 and whose contributions exceed two percent of the fund's year-end total) will be denied deductions in the year when the IRS takes action to terminate the private foundation status of an organization. Deductions are also denied for bequests and gifts to any private foundation or split-interest trust if such an entity or organization fails to meet these requirements.

The governing instrument of a private foundation must require the organization to distribute income currently and prohibit it from engaging in self-dealing, from retaining any excess business holdings, from making any speculative investments and from making taxable expenditures to government officials (for propaganda purposes or to influence legislation). Violations of these requirements by a donor and the entity may also cause the disallowance of deductions.[4]

• ***Partial Interests in Property***

The allowance of gift tax deductions for split-interest gifts (where there are charitable and noncharitable donees) is limited to remainder interests in annuity trusts and unitrusts, to remainder interests in pooled income funds, to charitable lead trust interests (see ¶1123) that are payable in the form of a guaranteed annuity or a fixed percentage of the fair market value of the property distributed yearly, to remainder interests in nontrust transfers of residences and farms, and to nontrust transfers of an undivided portion of a donor's entire interest in property.

If the donor gives his or her entire interest to recognized charities, even though the interest is split among different charities, the gifts are not subject to the above rules and a charitable deduction may be claimed for the entire value of the property transferred[5] (see ¶1120 for further details).

---

[1] Reg. §25.2522(a)-1.
[2] Code Sec. 2501(a)(5).
[3] Reg. §25.2522(c)-2(a).
[4] Code Sec. 508(e).
[5] Code Sec. 2522(c); Reg. §25.2522(c)-3(c).

Whether a transfer to a pooled income fund (Code Sec. 642(c)(5)) or to an *inter vivos* charitable remainder trust (Code Sec. 664) qualifies for a charitable deduction under Code Sec. 2522(c)(2)(A) are questions on which the IRS ordinarily will not issue an advance ruling or determination.[6]

• ***Nonresidents Not Citizens***

If the donor is a nonresident who is not a U.S. citizen, the basic rules for determining whether a transfer qualifies for the charitable deduction are the same as those for citizens or residents.[7] In addition, the following requirements apply:

(1) If the gift is to or for the use of a corporation, such corporation must be one that is created or organized under the laws of the United States or of any state or Territory thereof.

(2) If the gift is made to or for the use of a trust, or community chest, fund, or foundation, or a fraternal society, order, or association, operating within the lodge system, the gift must be for use within the United States exclusively for religious, charitable, scientific, literary, or educational purposes, including the encouragement of art and the prevention of cruelty to children or animals.

The above requirements are, of course, subject to any special arrangements that may be made with the country of which such a donor is a citizen or resident.

• ***Claiming Deduction on Gift Tax Return***

The values of all charitable, public, and religious gifts listed in Schedule A (Computation of Taxable Gifts) of Form 709 (United States Gift (and Generation-Skipping Transfer) Tax Return) (2004) should be totaled and then reduced by the total exclusions claimed on Schedule A with respect to the gifts. The difference should then be entered on part 4, line 7 (see the Appendix at ¶3280).

¶ 2311 Unlimited Marital Deduction

The monetary ceiling on the gift tax marital deduction was eliminated for gifts made after 1981.[8] Thus, unlimited amounts of property, except for certain terminable interests (see ¶2318), may be transferred between spouses free of gift taxes. In accord with this unlimited deduction, the limitations on the marital deduction with respect to community property (see ¶2322) that applied to gifts made before 1982 have also been repealed.

• ***Alien Spouses***

The first $114,000 (for 2004, indexed) of gifts per year to an alien spouse will not be taxed.[9] (This amount was $112,000 for gifts in 2003, $110,000 for gifts in 2002, $106,000 for gifts in 2001, and $103,000 for gifts in 2000).[10] To the extent that gifts are made in excess of this amount, no marital deduction will apply to reduce the gift tax. However, the annual exclusion for transfers by gift to a noncitizen spouse is allowed only for transfers that would qualify for the marital deduction if the donee were a U.S. citizen. For example, a gift in trust would not qualify for the annual exclusion unless it fell within one of the exceptions to the terminable interest rule.

---

[6] Rev. Proc. 2004-3, IRB 2004-1, 114.

[7] Code Sec. 2522(b); Reg. §25.2522(b)-1.

[8] Code Sec. 2523(a).

[9] Rev. Proc. 2003-85, IRB 2003-49, 184.

[10] Code Sec. 2523(i); Rev. Proc. 98-61 (Section 3.16), 1998-2 CB 811; Rev. Proc. 99-42, IRB 1999-46, 568; Rev. Proc. 2001-13, 2001-1 CB 111; Rev. Proc. 2001-59, 2001-2 CB 623; Rev. Proc. 2002-70, IRB 2002-46, 845.

Effective for gifts made on or after July 14, 1988, it is no longer required that the donor spouse be a U.S. citizen or a resident in order for a gift to qualify for the marital deduction if the surviving spouse is a U.S. citizen. However, this does not change the rule stipulating that the gift tax marital deduction will apply only if the donee spouse is a U.S. citizen.[11] For further discussion of the availability of the marital deduction for property passing to non-U.S. citizen spouses, see ¶1000 and ¶1004.

¶2313 Qualified Terminable Interests

Generally, transfers of terminable interests (such as life estates, terms for years, annuities, etc.) do not qualify for the marital deduction (see ¶2318). However, there is a major exception to the terminable interest rule for qualified terminable interest property (QTIP).[12] This type of property is also eligible for the estate tax marital deduction. The definition of such property is discussed at ¶1002. Briefly, under these rules, a life interest granted to a spouse will not be treated as a terminable interest and the entire value of property in which the spouse is granted the interest will qualify for the marital deduction.

If a spouse disposes of all or part of a qualifying interest for life in QTIP property for which a marital deduction was allowed, that spouse is deemed to have made a transfer of all interest in the property, other than the qualifying income interest, that is subject to the gift tax.[13] Effective July 18, 2003, Reg. §25.2519-1 has been amended to provide that the amount of the donee spouse's transfer under Code Sec. 2519 is reduced by the amount of the gift tax that the spouse is entitled to recover from the recipient of the transferred property under Code Sec. 2207A(b). The amount of the recoverable gift tax and the amount of the remainder interest transferred under Code Sec. 2519 are determined by using the same interrelated computation applicable to other transfers in which the transferee assumes the gift tax liability.[14]

The IRS has ruled that a surviving spouse's purchase of the remainder interest in QTIP property for cash constituted a disposition of the spouse's income interest for purposes of Code Sec. 2519, resulting in a taxable gift of the remainder interest.[15] In so ruling, the IRS concluded that the spouse's purchase of the remainder interest was analogous to a commutation, that is, a proportionate distribution of the QTIP property between the income beneficiary (the spouse) and the remaindermen. (Commutations have been held to be taxable dispositions of the spouse's income interest in QTIP property.[16]) This similarity between a sale of the spouse's interest and a commutation is demonstrated by the fact that after paying cash for the value of the remainder interest, the spouse's income interest in the QTIP property is terminated, and the spouse receives outright ownership of the property having a net value equal to the value of the spouse's remainder interest. Thus, following the transaction, the spouse would be in essentially the same economic position as if a commutation of the interest had been effectuated.

In addition, the spouse making a transfer of QTIP property may recover the gift tax, including penalties and interest, on the remainder interest from the recipients of the property.[17] Reg. §25.2207A-1 has been amended to provide, effective July 18, 2003, that if the donee spouse fails to exercise the right to recover the gift tax, such failure constitutes a gift in the amount of the unrecovered gift tax to the person from whom recovery could have been made. Further,

---

[11] Reg. §25.2523(i)-1.

[12] Code Sec. 2523(f).

[13] Code Sec. 2519.

[14] Reg. §25.2519-1, amended by T.D. 9077.

[15] Rev. Rul. 98-8, 1998-1 CB 541.

[16] Reg. §25.2519-1(g), Example 2; *H. Novotny Est.*, 93 TC 12, CCH Dec. 45,822.

[17] Code Sec. 2207A(b).

any delay in the exercise of the right of recovery is a below-market loan that may be subject to imputation under Code Sec. 7872 (see ¶2161). The donee spouse may waive the right of recovery in writing, thereby causing the spouse's gift of the unrecovered amounts to be complete upon the later of the date of the waiver or the date of the gift tax payment.[18]

If QTIP property received by the surviving spouse is not transferred during the surviving spouse's lifetime, the entire value of the property is included in his or her gross estate at death.

Further, it should be noted that, generally, the transfer to a spouse of an interest in a joint and survivor annuity in which only the spouses have the right to receive payments prior to the death of the surviving spouse qualifies for the marital deduction. However, such a transfer does not qualify for a gift tax marital deduction if either the donor or the executor irrevocably elects out of QTIP treatment.[19] The donee's subsequent transfer of an interest in the annuity is treated as a transfer of all interest in the annuity other than the donor's interest. If the donee dies before the donor, no amount with respect to the annuity is includible in the estate of the donee.

¶2314 Split Gifts to Spouse and Charity

A special rule is provided for transfers of interests in the same property made after 1981 to a spouse and a qualifying charitable organization. If an individual creates a qualified charitable remainder annuity or unitrust and if the donor and his or her spouse are the only noncharitable beneficiaries, the prohibition on deduction of terminable interests (see ¶2318) does not apply. The individual receives a charitable deduction for the value of the remainder interest and a marital deduction for the value of the annuity or unitrust income interest, and no transfer tax is imposed.[20]

If the individual transfers a qualified income interest (see ¶1002 and ¶2313) to a spouse with a remainder to charity, the entire value of the property will be considered as passing to the spouse and will qualify for a marital deduction.

¶2316 Pre-1982 Gift Tax Marital Deduction

For gifts made after 1976 and before 1982, a marital deduction was allowed for the first $100,000 of lifetime gifts to the donor's spouse.[21] The next $100,000 of lifetime gifts was fully taxable (that is, gifts ranging from $100,001 to $200,000). A 50-percent deduction applied to lifetime gifts to a spouse in excess of $200,000. The $100,000 lifetime marital deduction was in addition to the $3,000 annual exclusion. Thus, an annual gift of $3,000 to the donor's spouse did not count for purposes of the $100,000 lifetime exclusion for transfers between spouses.

For gifts made prior to 1977, the gift tax marital deduction was limited to 50 percent of the value of the property transferred to the spouse.

¶2317 Income to One Other Than Spouse

A gift of a vested remainder interest in property to a donor's spouse qualifies for the marital deduction.[22] It qualifies, even though the income from the property is made payable to the donor or a third person. The two interests in the one property are separate and distinct.

---

[18] Reg. §25.2207A-1, as amended by T.D. 9077.

[19] Code Sec. 2523(f)(6).

[20] Code Sec. 2523(g) and Code Sec. 2056(b)(8).

[21] Code Sec. 2523(a), prior to amendment by P.L. 97-34.

[22] Rev. Rul. 54-470, 1954-2 CB 320.

¶ 2318 Life Estate or Other Terminable Interest

Except as discussed at ¶2314 for certain interests transferred after 1981, the gift tax marital deduction is not allowed for transfers of "terminable interests."[23] If the transfer is of an interest that will terminate or fail on lapse of time or the occurrence of an event or contingency, or on the failure of an event or contingency to occur, a deduction is not allowed if (1) the reversionary or remainder interest is in the donor or any transferee, other than the spouse, who has acquired the interest for less than an adequate and full consideration in money or money's worth, or (2) the donor or transferee may thereby possess or enjoy any part of the property after such termination or failure of the interest transferred to the spouse.[24]

An exercise or release at any time by the donor (either alone or in conjuction with any person) of a power to appoint an interest in property is deemed to be a transfer by the donor. If the exercise or release is made in favor of a person other than the donor's spouse, a marital deduction will not be allowed.

¶ 2319 Interest in Unidentified Assets

The marital deduction is reduced by the value of assets transferred in trust from which a marital gift may be satisfied and for which a marital deduction would not be allowed if they were transferred by gift to the donor's spouse.[25] This provision has particular application to gifts in trust under which the donor's spouse has the remainder interest or the trust income and a power to appoint to himself or his estate.

> *Example:* David Strom gave his wife, Shirley, an interest valued at $500,000 in a group of assets, most of which qualify for the marital deduction, but one of which does not. The item that does not qualify (an interest in the residual value of an estate) is worth $100,000. For purposes of computing the marital deduction, the value of the interest passing to Shirley is reduced by $100,000.

¶ 2320 Joint Ownership

Gifts by the donor to his or her spouse as joint tenant with the donor or as tenant by the entirety are exempt from the terminable interest provisions (see ¶2318) and will qualify for the marital deduction.[26] The possibility of the reacquisition of the property through survivorship or severance of the tenancy will not defeat the deduction.

¶ 2321 Power of Appointment

Life estates accompanied by certain powers of appointment are also exempt from terminable interest status.[27] If the donee spouse receives a power of appointment over property held in trust or otherwise, in addition to other interests in the transferred property, a deduction may be allowable. The donee spouse must be able to exercise the power in favor of him- or herself or his or her estate in all events. No one else may have the power to appoint any portion of the interest to anyone other than a donee spouse.

It is not essential that the life estate or the power exist with respect to the entire property involved. It is necessary only that the income be from all or a specific portion of the property transferred and that the power be coextensive

---

[23] Code Sec. 2523(b).
[24] Code Sec. 2523(b).
[25] Code Sec. 2523(c).
[26] Code Sec. 2523(d).
[27] Code Sec. 2523(e).

with the deductible amount. When the income and power relate only to a portion of the transferred property, only that portion qualifies for the deduction. These requirements are substantially the same as the estate tax requirements.

¶ 2322 Gifts of Community Property

A gift of a donor's interest in community property qualifies for the marital deduction in the case of gifts made after 1981. For gifts made before 1982, no marital deduction was allowable for gifts of such interests or of interests in certain separate property that was considered to be community property for marital deduction purposes.[28]

¶ 2323 Limits on Deductions

The gift tax charitable and marital deductions are allowable only to the extent that the gifts with respect to which those deductions are authorized are included in the total amount of gifts made during the calendar year.[29] This means that both deductions are determined after the annual exclusion is deducted.

> *Example:* In 2004, Lisa Lake makes a cash gift of $17,000 to charity. The entire $17,000 would qualify for the charitable deduction. However, the annual exclusion of $11,000 is deducted first, and, therefore, only $6,000 is included in the total amount of gifts. Lake is entitled to a charitable deduction of $6,000.

¶ 2330 Specific Exemption for Pre-1977 Gifts

In determining the amount of taxable gifts made before 1977 for the calendar quarter, donors who were U.S. citizens or residents at the time the gifts were made were entitled to a specific exemption of $30,000. This amount was reduced by the sum of the amounts claimed and allowed as an exemption in prior calendar years and quarters.[30]

The donor had the option of taking the exemption in its entirety in a single calendar quarter or spreading it over a period of calendar quarters in such amounts as he or she saw fit. However, after the limit had been reached, no further exemption was allowable.

¶ 2331 Reporting Deductions on Gift Tax Return

The marital and charitable deductions that are allowed to a donor are subtracted from "Total included amount of gifts" (lines 3 through 9 on part 4, Schedule A (Computation of Taxable Gifts) of Form 709 (United States Gift (and Generation-Skipping Transfer) Tax Return) (2004)) (see the Appendix at ¶ 3280).

---

[28] Code Sec. 2523(f), prior to repeal by P.L. 97-34.

[29] Code Sec. 2524.

[30] Code Sec. 2521, prior to repeal by P.L. 94-455.

Chapter 38
COMPUTATION AND PAYMENT OF TAX

¶ 2350 Cumulative Effect of Tax

The gift tax is cumulative in nature. As a result, prior years' and quarters' gifts push the current year's gifts into higher tax brackets.

The gift tax for each year (quarter for pre-1982 gifts) is determined by computing a tax on the taxable gifts made in that year (or quarter) plus taxable gifts made in all prior years beginning with June 6, 1932, and in all prior quarters beginning with the first quarter of calendar year 1971. In computing the tax on gifts made after 1981, gifts made in all years after 1981 and before the year for which the tax is being computed are also added. There is then subtracted from the resulting figure a tax computed only on the taxable gifts made in prior calendar periods (years and quarters). The unified transfer tax rate schedules (see ¶2600) are used in both of these computations for gifts made after 1976, but before January 1, 2010 (a separate rate schedule will apply to gifts made after December 31, 2009). The difference between the two amounts, as computed above, is the amount of gift tax payable for the year or quarter less the unified credit (see ¶2376) to the extent it has not been used in preceding calendar periods. For an example of the method of computing the gift tax and estate tax and of using the unified credit, see ¶1428.

Taxable gifts made after 1981 are reported on an annual return that is due April 15 of the year following the year of the gift.

Because of the method used to compute gift taxes for a given year, it is necessary on the gift tax return not only to determine the amount of taxable gifts for the year covered by the return but also to report the amount of taxable gifts determined for all prior calendar periods, beginning with 1932.

¶ 2355 Gifts for Prior Periods

Before the gift tax for a particular calendar year may actually be computed, it is necessary to take into account the taxable gifts made in prior calendar quarters and years. These gifts for prior quarters and years are recorded on Schedule B (Gifts From Prior Periods) of Form 709 (United States Gift (and Generation-Skipping Transfer) Tax Return) (2004) (see the Appendix at ¶3280).

The donor's name as used in each return previously filed should be shown on the current Schedule B if there has been a change in name on the current return or any prior return. Any variation in name (e.g., the use of the full given name instead of initials used previously) should be noted.

The amount of the specific exemption claimed for periods prior to 1977 must be entered in column D of Schedule B. The amount of unified credit claimed in prior quarters is entered in column C.

If a tax has been assessed and paid with respect to prior taxable gifts reported on a gift tax return, the IRS may not increase the valuation of such prior gifts once the statutory period of limitation for assessing a deficiency on the gifts has expired.[1] Although this rule does not apply when computing the amount of adjusted taxable gifts for estate tax purposes for gifts made after August 5, 1997, the IRS is not permitted to revalue a gift for estate tax purposes if the three-year statute of limitations has expired on an adequately disclosed gift[2] (see ¶1426).

¶ 2375 Unified Rate Schedule for Computing Gift Tax

The amount of gift tax payable on gifts made after 1976, but before January 1, 2010 (for any calendar quarter or year), is determined by applying the unified rate schedule to the cumulative lifetime taxable transfers and then subtracting the taxes payable on the lifetime transfers made for past tax periods (including pre-1977 taxable gifts). In computing the tax payable, the subtraction for taxes previously paid is based on the unified rate schedule.

The unified transfer tax rate schedule, which applies for both estate and gift tax purposes and the estates of decedents dying, and gifts made, before January 1, 2010, is reproduced at ¶1430. The rate schedule that applies only to gifts made after December 31, 2009 is reproduced at ¶2005.

¶ 2376 Unified Gift Tax Credit

For lifetime gifts made after 1976, but before January 1, 2010, and at-death transfers made after 1976, a single unified credit is subtracted after the determination of the taxpayer's gift or estate tax liability (see ¶1430 and ¶2375, above). The use of the unified credit against the tentative gift tax is mandatory.[3] In the case of gift taxes, the unified credit replaced the pre-1977 $30,000 specific exemption. A chart indicating the applicable credit and "exemption equivalent" for 1977 and later years follows.

Unified Credits and "Exemption Equivalents"

Year	*Unified Credit*	*Exemption Equivalent*
Jan. 1, 1977–June 30, 1977	$ 6,000	
July 1, 1977–Dec. 31, 1977	30,000	$120,666
1978	34,000	134,000
1979	38,000	147,333
1980	42,500	161,563
1981	47,000	175,225
1982	62,800	225,000
1983	79,300	275,000
1984	96,300	325,000
1985	121,800	400,000
1986	155,800	500,000
1987–1997	192,800	600,000

[1] Code Sec. 2504(c).

[2] *F.R. Smith Est.*, 94 TC 872, CCH Dec. 46,648 (Acq.); Code Sec. 2001(f) and Code Sec. 2504(c).

[3] Rev. Rul. 79-398, 1979-2 CB 338.

Beginning in 1998, the unified credit is determined by reference to the "applicable credit amount" and "the applicable exclusion amount" (formerly the exemption equivalent). The unified credit is as follows:

Year	*Applicable Credit Amount*	*Applicable Exclusion Amount*
1998	$202,050	$625,000
1999	211,300	650,000
2000 and 2001	220,550	675,000

• ***Impact of the 2001 Act***

The Economic Growth and Tax Relief Reconciliation Act of 2001 (P.L. 107-16) (2001 Act) increases the gift tax applicable exclusion amount to $1 million, beginning with gifts made in 2002. The 2001 Act also sets the estate tax applicable exclusion amount at $1 million for the estates of decedents dying in 2002 through 2009. The table below provides the applicable credit exclusion amounts for years 2002 through 2009:

Applicable Credit and Exclusion Amounts

Year	*Applicable Credit*	*Applicable Exclusion*
2002 through 2009	$345,800	$1,000,000

For years 2002 through 2009, the amount of the gift tax unified credit is equal to (1) the applicable credit amount in effect under Code Sec. 2010(c) for such calendar year, determined as if the applicable exclusion amount were $1 million, reduced by (2) the sum of the amounts allowable as a credit under Code Sec. 2505 for all preceding calendar periods.[4]

• ***Computation of Credit Following Estate Tax Repeal***

The 2001 Act retains the gift tax following estate tax repeal in 2010. Gift tax liability for years after 2009 is determined by using a rate schedule created by the 2001 Act. The credit allowed against the gift tax for such years will be equal to (1) the amount of the tentative tax that would be determined under the new gift tax-only rate schedule if the amount with respect to which such tentative tax is to be computed were $1 million, reduced by (2) the sum of the amounts allowable as a credit for all preceding calendar periods.[5]

Sunset provision. In order to comply with the Congressional Budget Act of 1974, the 2001 Act provides that all provisions of, and amendments made by, the 2001 Act will not apply to estates of decedents dying, gifts made, or generation-skipping transfers, after December 31, 2010. Unless Congress acts affirmatively in the interim, the Internal Revenue Code will thereafter be applied and administered as if these provisions had not been enacted (see ¶2595).

• ***Transitional Rule***

A special adjustment (transitional) rule applied with respect to gifts made during the period September 9, 1976, through December 31, 1976. To the extent that use was made of the $30,000 lifetime exemption during this period, the allowable unified gift tax credit is reduced by an amount equal to 20 percent of the exemption. Thus, if the full $30,000 exemption was used during this period, a maximum reduction of $6,000 would be made to the unified credit.

However, the amount of the credit allowed may not exceed the amount of the gift tax imposed on the donor for the particular calendar quarter or year. In

---

[4] Code Sec. 2505(a), as amended by P.L. 107-16.

[5] Code Sec. 2505(a)(1), as amended by P.L. 107-16.

addition, the amount of the credit that is available for gifts made in one of the above years must be reduced by the sum of the amounts allowable as a credit to the donor for all preceding calendar quarters or years.

> *Example:* Dawn Turner made taxable gifts in the years 1978, 1979, 1981, and 1982. Her tentative gift tax liabilities on these gifts amounted to $10,000 in 1978, $30,000 in 1979, $10,000 in 1981, and $20,000 in 1982. Turner's gift tax credit in 1978 would amount to $10,000—the amount of her gift tax liability.
>
> In 1979, Turner could claim a gift tax credit of $28,000 ($38,000 credit for 1979 less $10,000 credit claimed in 1978). In 1981, Turner could take a gift tax credit of $9,000 ($47,000 credit for 1981 less credits claimed in 1978 and 1979 of $38,000). In 1982, Turner could claim a credit of $15,800 ($62,800 credit for gifts made in 1982 less credits claimed in the years 1978–1979 and 1981 of $47,000). If Turner were to make no more gifts after 1982, $283,000 would be available to offset any gift tax liability incurred in 2004 ($345,800 applicable credit amount less $62,800).

Under Code Sec. 2504(c), the IRS may not, for gift tax purposes, revalue a prior taxable gift that was properly reported on a gift tax return once the statute of limitations for assessing a deficiency has expired on that prior gift. For this rule to apply, a gift tax must have been paid on the prior gift. However, for gifts made after December 31, 1996, recently adopted amendments to the regulations[6] state that the IRS will be barred from revaluing prior gifts only if such gifts were adequately disclosed (see ¶1426 for a discussion of what constitutes adequate disclosure). For gift tax returns covered by the adequate disclosure regulations, it is no longer necessary that a gift tax liability have been paid in order to block IRS revaluation of a time-expired prior gift. Thus, a gift tax return adequately disclosing gifts of present interests, each of which was shielded by the $10,000 annual exclusion (which, because of an inflation adjustment, rose to $11,000 for gifts made in 2002 and thereafter), could not be revalued by the IRS once the statute of limitations for assessing a deficiency on the gifts had expired.

See, also, ¶1426 regarding revaluation of prior gifts for estate tax purposes where the period of limitations has expired.

A husband and wife may each claim separate unified gift tax credits in the amounts specified above for gifts made by each of them, even though these gifts may have resulted from the gift-splitting provisions of Code Sec. 2513 (see ¶2013). Thus, married couples may give away substantial amounts to their children or other donees without incurring any gift tax liability.

¶ 2378 Benefits of Graduated Rates and Unified Credit Phased Out

For gifts made before January 1, 2002, the benefits of the graduated rates and the unified credit under the unified transfer tax system are phased out beginning with cumulative transfers rising above $10 million. This is accomplished by adding a surtax of five percent of the excess of any transfer over $10 million to the tentative tax computed in determining the ultimate transfer tax liability. The Economic Growth and Tax Relief Reconciliation Act of 2001 (P.L. 107-16) (2001

---

[6] Reg. §25.2504-2 and Reg. §301.6501(c)-1, as amended by T.D. 8845, Dec. 2, 1999; Rev. Proc. 2000-34, IRB 2000-34, 186.

Act) repealed the five-percent surtax for estates of decedents dying, and gifts made, after December 31, 2001.

For estates of decedents dying and gifts made after 1987 and before 1998, the tax is levied on amounts transferred in excess of $10 million but not exceeding $21,040,000, in order to recapture the benefit of any transfer tax rate below 55 percent as well as the unified credit.

Due to mistakes in the wording of the amendment to Code Sec. 2001(c)(2) by the Taxpayer Relief Act of 1997 (P.L. 105-34), the five-percent additional tax phases out the benefits of graduated rates, but not the benefits of the unified credit (applicable credit amount), for estates of decedents dying, and gifts made, after 1997. Therefore, the additional tax is levied on amounts transferred after 1997, but before January 1, 2002, in excess of $10 million, but not exceeding $17,184,000. The applicable credit amount is not recaptured.

Although the provision of the Revenue Act of 1987 (P.L. 100-203) that added the phaseout rules is effective with respect to transfers made after 1987, the Conference Committee Report to that Act states that pre-effective-date gifts are included in cumulative transfers for purposes of determining the adjustment for transfers made after the effective date; however, the tax rate on the earlier gifts remains unchanged. Thus, according to the Committee Report, if a person makes a $9 million gift before 1988, and an additional $4 million gift after 1987, $3 million of the latter transfer will be subject to the additional tax under the phaseout.

¶ 2380 Generation-Skipping Transfers

Generation-skipping transfers made during a calendar year are subject to the normal gift tax and to the generation-skipping transfer (GST) tax. The gift tax on such transfers is computed in the usual manner as described at ¶2350 through ¶2376, above.

However, the GST tax is computed separately from the gift tax and, if applicable, represents an additional tax that must be paid on Form 709 (United States Gift (and Generation-Skipping Transfer) Tax Return). The GST tax is computed on Schedule C (Computation of Generation-Skipping Transfer Tax) of Form 709.

¶ 2382 Gift Tax Treaties

Gift tax treaties are in force between the United States and Australia, Austria, Denmark, France, Germany, Japan, Sweden, and the United Kingdom. For specific information, the applicable treaty should be consulted. See CCH FEDERAL ESTATE AND GIFT TAX REPORTS for the text of such treaties.

¶ 2400 Due Date for Payment

The gift tax is generally paid at the same time the return is required to be filed.[7] The annual gift tax return is due by April 15 of the year following that in which the gifts were made. However, for the calendar year in which the donor dies, the gift tax return will be due on the earlier of the due date (with extensions) for filing the donor's estate tax return, or the "normal" due date with respect to the gifts (April 15 following the calendar year in which gifts were

[7] Code Sec. 6151.

made).[8] However, see ¶1650 for special extensions allowed those affected by terrorist attacks against the United States.

The gift tax should be paid to the IRS Service Center, Cincinnati, OH 45999, where the gift tax return is filed.

An extension of time to file an income tax return also is deemed to be an extension of time to file an annual gift tax return. In the Part II checkboxes of Form 4868 (Application for Automatic Extension of Time to File U.S. Individual Income Tax Return) (2004), a taxpayer requesting an extension of time to file an individual return indicates whether the taxpayer or the taxpayer's spouse plans to file a gift tax return for the year. The amount of gift or generation-skipping tax paid with the Form 4868 is then entered on lines 7 and 8. Payment in full of gift and generation-skipping taxes with the extension application avoids interest and penalties. If paying the taxes in full with Form 4868 would cause undue hardship, the taxpayer should attach an explanation to the completed form.

If a taxpayer does not request an income tax extension, new Form 8892, Payment of Gift/GST Tax and/or Application for Extension of Time To File Form 709, should be used to request an extension of time to file the taxpayer's gift tax return. This form must be used instead of writing a letter to the Cincinnati Service Center to request an extension of time to file Form 709. In addition to containing an extension request, Form 8892 also serves as a payment voucher for the gift tax balance due at the time of the extension.[9]

A donor who fails to pay the tax is liable for a penalty of one-half of one percent of the amount of such tax for each month that the tax remains unpaid up to a maximum of 25 percent.[10] In addition, a lien attaches to the transferred property and the donee may be held personally liable.[11]

¶ 2405 Form of Payment

Money orders and checks drawn on any bank or trust company incorporated under the laws of the United States, a state, territory or possession of the United States may be accepted by the appropriate IRS officer in payment of gift taxes. The check or money order in payment of the tax should be made payable to the "United States Treasury."[12] The donor's Social Security number, along with the number of the accompanying form and the applicable year, should be written on the check or money order.

Effective for tax payments made after December 31, 1998, the IRS is authorized to accept payment of taxes by credit or debit card. A payment by credit or debit card is deemed made when the card issuer authorizes the transaction, provided that the payment is actually received in the ordinary course of business. Although the IRS is prohibited from imposing a fee on individuals who pay their taxes by such methods, third-party service providers contracted to process the credit and debit card transactions are not prohibited from charging fees.[13]

• *Partial Payments*

If additional taxes, penalty, and interest have been assessed against a taxpayer and the taxpayer provides specific written directions as to how his or her partial payment is to be applied, the IRS will apply the payment in accordance with such directions. However, if the taxpayer does not provide such written

---

[8] Instructions for Form 709 (2004), p. 4.

[9] Instructions for Form 709 (2004), p. 4.

[10] Code Sec. 6651(a)(2).

[11] Code Sec. 6901 and Code Sec. 6902.

[12] Instructions for Form 709 (2004), p. 12.

[13] Reg. § 301.6311-2.

directions, the IRS will apply the payment to periods in the order of priority that will serve the "best interest" of the IRS. The payment will be applied to satisfy the liability for successive periods, in descending order of priority, until the payment is fully absorbed. If the amount applied is less than the liability, the amount will be applied to tax, penalty, and interest, in that order. Similar rules will apply for payments made pursuant to the terms of offers in compromise and collateral agreements.[14]

¶ 2410 Discount and Interest

No discount is allowed for payment of the gift tax in advance of the last day for payment of the tax. If the tax is not paid when due, interest and various penalties may be assessed. If the tax required to be shown on the return is simply not paid when due, interest at the current rate (see ¶ 1680) is charged from the last date for payment to the date when paid.[15] Under other circumstances, more serious penalties can apply.[16]

Extensions of time for payment of up to six months may be granted.[17]

---

[14] Rev. Proc. 2002-26, 2002-1 CB 746, superseding Rev. Rul. 73-304, 1973-2 CB 42, Rev. Rul. 73-305, 1973-2 CB 43, and Rev. Rul. 79-284, 1979-2 CB 83.

[15] Code Sec. 6601(a) and Code Sec. 6601(b).

[16] Code Sec. 6651.

[17] Code Sec. 6161(a).

GENERATION-SKIPPING TRANSFER TAX

Chapter 39

GENERAL RULES

¶ 2430 Purpose and Nature of the Tax

Property that is transferred to an heir or donee and eventually transferred to such person's own heirs or donees is generally exposed twice to federal estate or gift taxes. To avoid the second round of taxation, grantors sometimes have created life interests, with remainder interests reserved for members of subsequent generations. Generally, a generation-skipping transfer (GST) tax is imposed on such trusts or trust equivalents (see ¶2431). The GST tax is designed to tax this means of transferring accumulated wealth to successive generations in much the same way that a gift or estate tax would have taxed the outright transfer of the property by gift or inheritance.

The GST tax[1] attempts to simplify compliance and administration by applying the tax to direct beneficial interests only (powers over trust property are not subject to taxation). Additionally, the tax is applied to direct skips, as well as to taxable terminations and distributions (see ¶2433).

Like the estate tax, the tax on generation-skipping transfers was repealed by the Economic Growth and Tax Relief Reconciliation Act of 2001 (P.L. 107-16) (2001 Act), effective for generation-skipping transfers after December 31, 2009.

Sunset provision. In order to comply with the Congressional Budget Act of 1974, the 2001 Act provides that all provisions of, and amendments made by, the 2001 Act will not apply to estates of decedents dying, gifts made, or generation-skipping transfers, after December 31, 2010. Unless Congress acts affirmatively in the interim, the Internal Revenue Code will thereafter be applied and administered as if these provisions had not been enacted.

¶ 2431 What Is a Generation-Skipping Transfer?

The generation-skipping transfer (GST) tax applies to direct skips (for example, a transfer from a grandparent to a grandchild), as well as to taxable distributions and terminations (see ¶2433) of generation-skipping trust property.[2] The tax does not apply to any transfer (other than a direct skip) from a trust if the transfer was subject to estate or gift tax with respect to a person in the first generation below that of the grantor.

Gifts reported on Schedule A (Computation of Taxable Gifts) of Form 709 (United States Gift (and Generation-Skipping Transfer) Tax Return) (2004) that

[1] Code Sec. 2601 through Code Sec. 2664.

[2] Code Sec. 2611.

are also generation-skipping transfers may be subject to both gift and GST taxes. On the other hand, with one exception, if a transfer is excluded from the gift tax, then it is not subject to the GST tax. For example, an *inter vivos* transfer that is not subject to gift tax due to the exclusion from the gift tax of certain transfers for educational or medical expenses[3] is not a generation-skipping transfer. An exception exists where there is a nontaxable gift to a trust that is also a direct skip. In that situation, the transfer is subject to the GST tax unless no corpus or income may be distributed to anyone other than the beneficiary and the trust assets are includible in the beneficiary's estate if the beneficiary dies during the trust term.

• ***Property Subject to Tax Only Once***

Also excluded from the category of a taxable transfer is any transfer to the extent that the property transferred was previously subject to the GST tax.[4] However, the transferee in the prior transfer must have been a member of the same or a lower generation than the transferee in the later transfer. Additionally, the effect of the transfer must not be to avoid the GST tax entirely.

• ***Distributions from Trust Income Taxed***

Distributions from a trust that qualify as generation-skipping distributions are subject to tax whether the distributions are from the trust income or the trust corpus. However, where the distribution is from the trust income, the recipient is entitled to an income tax deduction[5] for the amount of the GST tax paid.

¶ 2433 Taxable Terminations and Distributions; Direct Skips

The terms "direct skip," "taxable distribution," and "taxable termination" have special meanings for generation-skipping transfer (GST) tax purposes. The occurrence of any of these three situations can result in the imposition of the GST tax. However, there is a $1,500,000 per-transferor exemption (for 2004; see ¶ 2455) for all these transfers.

• ***Direct Skip***

Two types of transfers considered direct skips are (1) a transfer outright for the benefit of a "skip person," and (2) a transfer of property to a trust exclusively for one or more such beneficiaries.[6] The transfer may occur during the transferor's lifetime or at death. Generally, a "skip person" is any beneficiary assigned to a generation that is two or more generations below that of the grantor. The term is further defined at ¶ 2435.

A $1,500,000 exemption is provided for each person making a generation-skipping transfer in 2004 and 2005. The exemption will rise to $2,000,000 for generation-skipping transfers made in 2006 through 2008. In 2009, the exemption will rise to $3,500,000.[7] Before 2004, the generation-skipping exemption was subject to an annual inflation adjustment. The exemption (indexed) was $1,120,000 for 2003, $1,100,000 for 2002, $1,060,000 for 2001, $1,030,000 for 2000, $1,010,000 for 1999, and $1 million for previous years (see ¶ 2455).[8]

---

[3] Code Sec. 529(c)(2), Code Sec. 2503(e), and Code Sec. 2611(b).

[4] Code Sec. 2611(b).

[5] Code Sec. 164(a)(4).

[6] Code Sec. 2612(c) and Code Sec. 2613.

[7] Code Sec. 2631.

[8] Rev. Proc. 98-61 (Section 3.16), 1998-2 CB 811; Rev. Proc. 99-42, 1999-2 CB 568; Rev. Proc. 2001-13, 2001-1 CB 337; Rev. Proc. 2001-59, 2001-2 CB 623; Rev. Proc. 2002-70, IRB 2002-46, 845.

• *Taxable Distribution*

A "taxable distribution" occurs whenever there is a distribution from a generation-skipping trust to a skip person.[9]

Example: Lorna Lane establishes a discretionary trust for the benefit of Lilly and Lorenzo, her daughter and grandson. Lorenzo is a "skip person" because he is two or more generations younger than Lorna. If the trustee makes a distribution of trust corpus to Lorenzo, it will be a taxable distribution.

• *Taxable Termination*

A "taxable termination" occurs on the termination of an interest in property held in trust. However, no taxable termination will occur if a nonskip person has an interest in the property immediately after such termination or if a distribution may not be made from the trust to a skip person at any time after the termination.[10] Such a termination usually occurs on the death of the person holding a life interest in the trust or on the lapse of time in a case where the grantor created an estate for years.

A partial termination of a trust is taxable if, on the termination of an interest in property held in a trust, a specified portion of the trust assets is distributed to skip persons who are lineal descendants of the holder of the interest (or to one or more trusts for the exclusive benefit of such persons).

¶ 2435 Skip Person and Nonskip Person Defined

A "skip person" is a natural person assigned to a generation that is two or more generations below the generation of the transferor.[11]

Example (1): Jim Feldman's grandchild, Sam, is a "skip person" for purposes of the generation-skipping transfer tax, as is his great-grandchild, Sally. Sam is in a generation that is two generations below that of his grandfather, Jim. Sally's generation is three generations below that of Jim. (See ¶ 2437 for a discussion of assignment of generations.)

The term "skip person" refers to a trust if (1) all interests in the trust are held by skip persons, or (2) there is no nonskip person holding an interest in such trust, and at no time after the generation-skipping transfer may a distribution be made from the trust to a nonskip person.

Example (2): Maria Jacobs creates a testamentary trust wherein income will be distributed to her husband for his life and, at his death, the remainder will be split between Maria's daughter and her grandson. The trust would not be a "skip person" because two "nonskip persons" hold an interest in the trust: Maria's husband and her daughter.

A direct skip (see ¶ 2433) transfer to a transferor's grandchild will not be taxable, however, if the child of the transferor who was that grandchild's parent is deceased at the time of the transfer (see ¶ 2437). In such a situation, the grandchild and all succeeding lineal descendants are "moved up" a generation.[12] A descendant who dies within 90 days after a transfer is treated as having predeceased the transferor, if state law or the governing instrument so provides.[13]

---

[9] Code Sec. 2612(b).
[10] Code Sec. 2612(a).
[11] Code Sec. 2613.
[12] Code Sec. 2612(c)(2).
[13] Reg. § 26.2612-1(a)(2)(i).

¶ 2437 Assignment of Generations

Generally, assignment of generations is determined along family lines. For example, a transferor, the transferor's spouse, and the transferor's brothers and sisters are one generation. Their children constitute the next generation, and the transferor's grandchildren are two generations below that of the transferor.

• *Predeceased Parent Rule*

A transfer to an individual who is a descendant of the parent of the transferor (or the transferor's spouse or former spouse) is moved up one generation if the individual's parent, who is a lineal descendant of the parent of the transferor (or the transferor's spouse or former spouse) is dead at the time of the transfer.[14] Thus, a transfer to a grandchild whose parent is dead is not considered a generation-skipping transfer. The Taxpayer Relief Act of 1997 (P.L. 105-34) extended the predeceased parent rule to collateral heirs of the transferor, such as grandnieces and grandnephews. However, in order for transfers to collateral heirs to qualify for the exception, the transferor must have no lineal descendants. The Act also extended the predeceased parent rule to taxable terminations and taxable distributions, provided that the parent of the relevant beneficiary was dead at the earliest time that the transfer (from which the beneficiary's interest in the property was established) was subject to the estate or gift tax. For transfers prior to 1998, the rule only applied to direct skips to the grandchildren of the transferor, or the transferor's spouse or former spouse. For purposes of the predeceased parent rule, a living descendant who dies within 90 days after a transfer is treated as having predeceased the transferor if applicable state law or the governing instrument so provides.[15]

Proposed regulations. Proposed regulations have been published that would provide rules and examples regarding the application of the predeceased parent rule of Code Sec. 2651(e).[16] Under these proposals, for example, an individual's interest in property or a trust would be established at the time that the transferor is subject to the estate or gift tax. However, the proposed regulations would provide an exception to this general rule for remainder interests in trusts for which a qualified terminable interest property (QTIP) election was made under Code Sec. 2056(b)(7). In the case of a QTIP election, the remainder beneficiary's interest would be deemed to have been established on the death of the transferor's spouse (the income beneficiary), rather than on the transferor's death.

In addition, the proposed regulations would address the situation where a transferor adopts a descendant of a parent of the transferor (or the transferor's spouse) who is a minor. Specifically, if an adoptive parent legally adopts an individual who is (1) a descendant of a parent of the adoptive parent (or the adoptive parent's spouse) and (2) under the age of 18 at the time of the adoption, then the adopted individual would be treated as a member of the generation that is one generation below that of the adoptive parent for GST purposes.

These proposed regulations will be applicable for terminations, distributions, and transfers occurring on or after the date the regulations are issued as final regulations in the *Federal Register*. However, taxpayers may generally rely on the proposed regulations for transfers occurring after December 31, 1997, until the publication of final regulations.

---

[14] Code Sec. 2651(e).

[15] Reg. § 26.2612-1(a)(2)(i).

[16] Proposed Reg. §§ 26.2651-1, 26.2651-2, and 26.2651-3, NPRM-REG-145988-03.

• ***Persons Who Are Not Lineal Descendants***

An individual who is not a lineal descendant is assigned to a generation on the basis of that individual's date of birth (subject, however, to the rules for treatment of legal adoptions, etc., discussed below).[17] An individual born within 12½ years of the date of the transferor's birth is assigned to the same generation as the transferor. An individual born more than 12½ years after but within 37½ years of the transferor's birth is assigned to the first generation younger than the transferor. Subsequent generation assignments are similarly made on the basis of 25-year periods.

• ***Marriage, Legal Adoptions, and Half-Blood Relationships***

For purposes of the generation-skipping transfer (GST) tax, a relationship by legal adoption or half-blood is equivalent to a relationship by whole-blood.[18] An individual who is married at any time to a transferor is assigned to the transferor's generation. Similarly, an individual who is married at any time to a lineal descendant of the transferor is assigned to the same generation as the descendant.[19] However, where, because of the application of the generation-skipping transfer predeceased parent rule, a grandchild was not deemed to be a skip person, the later adoption of the grandchild by his aunt did not alter his relationship to his grandparents for purposes of the GST tax. Accordingly, the adoption did not cause the grandchild to be reclassified as a skip person.[20]

• ***Other Special Rules***

Unless otherwise provided in regulations, an individual who could be assigned to more than one generation is assigned to the youngest such generation.[21]

If an estate, trust, partnership, corporation, or other entity has an interest in property, each individual having a beneficial interest in such entity is treated as having an interest in the property and is assigned to a generation as discussed above. A charitable organization or a charitable trust is assigned to the transferor's generation.[22]

¶ 2439 Other Definitions

The following definitions apply with respect to the generation-skipping transfer (GST) tax.

• ***"Interest"***

A person has an interest in property held in trust if (at the time the determination is made) that person is a mandatory or permissible recipient of distributions from the trust.[23] A beneficiary of a charitable remainder annuity trust, a charitable remainder unitrust,[24] or a pooled income fund[25] also has an interest in trust property. Certain "interests" used primarily to avoid the GST tax are disregarded.

Additionally, the fact that income or corpus of the trust may be used to satisfy an obligation of support arising under state law is disregarded in deter-

[17] Code Sec. 2651(d).

[18] Code Sec. 2651(b)(3).

[19] Code Sec. 2651(c).

[20] IRS Letter Ruling 199907015 (Nov. 20, 1998).

[21] Code Sec. 2651(f).

[22] Code Sec. 2651(f)(3).

[23] Code Sec. 2652(c).

[24] Code Sec. 664.

[25] Code Sec. 642(c)(5).

mining if a person has an interest in a trust, if (1) such use is discretionary, or (2) such use is pursuant to a state law substantially like the Uniform Gifts to Minors Act.[26]

• *"Transferor"*

A decedent is the "transferor," for purposes of the GST tax, when the transfer is of any property that would be subject to the estate tax. The donor is the transferor when the transfer is of any property that would be subject to the gift tax.[27] In addition, the Tax Court has held that the holder of a general power of appointment over property includible in the estate of the holder for estate tax purposes is a transferor for purposes of the GST tax.[28]

• *"Trust" and "Trustee"*

The term "trust" includes any arrangement (other than an estate) that has substantially the same effect as a trust.[29] In such a case, the "trustee" is the person in actual or constructive possession of the property subject to such an arrangement. Examples of arrangements to which these definitions apply include life estates and remainders, estates for years, and insurance and annuity contracts.[30]

• *Special Election Available*

If property qualifies for estate[31] or gift[32] tax qualified terminable interest property (QTIP) treatment, the estate of the decedent or the donor spouse may elect to treat such property as if the QTIP election had not been made, for purposes of the GST tax. Once made, however, this "reverse QTIP election" is irrevocable.[33] The effect of the reverse QTIP election is to permit the first spouse to die to be treated as the transferor of the GST tax-exempt QTIP trust. This election is necessary, because otherwise the surviving spouse would be deemed to be the transferor by reason of the inclusion of the QTIP trust in the survivor's estate under Code Sec. 2044.

Partial reverse QTIP elections may not be made. However, it may be possible to divide the QTIP trust into separate exempt and nonexempt trusts before the election is made.

Pursuant to Reg. §301.9100-1 and Reg. §301.9100-3, the IRS may grant an extension to file a reverse QTIP election on a showing that the taxpayer acted reasonably and in good faith, and that the interests of the government are not jeopardized. An executor who wishes to make a reverse QTIP after the deadline for doing so has expired can request relief by way of a letter ruling request under the rules of Rev. Proc. 2004-1[34] or its successor

• ***Alternate Simplified Procedure for Making Late Elections***

The IRS has detailed a simplified alternative method that may be used, effective August 9, 2004, to request an extension of time to make a reverse QTIP

---

[26] Code Sec. 2652(c)(3).

[27] Code Sec. 2652(a)(1).

[28] *E. Peterson Marital Trust*, CA-2, 96-1 USTC ¶60,225, aff'g TC, 102 TC 790, CCH Dec. 49,935. However, on similar facts the U.S. Court of Appeals for the Eighth Circuit reached an opposite result: *J. Simpson*, CA-8, 99-2 USTC ¶60,351, Nonacq., IRB 2000-9. Followed: *R. Bachler*, CA-9, 2002-1 USTC ¶60,430, rev'g DC Cal., 2000-2 USTC ¶60,390.

[29] Code Sec. 2652(b)(1).

[30] Code Sec. 2652(b)(3).

[31] Code Sec. 2056(b)(7).

[32] Code Sec. 2523(f).

[33] Reg. §26.2652-2.

[34] Rev. Proc. 2004-1, IRB 2004-32, 169.

election. Generally, an executor or trustee is eligible to use the alternative method in lieu of the letter ruling process if the following requirements are met:

(1) a valid Code Sec. 2056(b)(7) QTIP election was made for the property or trust on the decedent's federal estate tax return;

(2) the reverse QTIP election was not made on the return as filed because the qualified tax professional relied on by the taxpayer failed to advise the taxpayer of the need for making the election;

(3) the decedent has a sufficient amount of unused GST exemption, after the automatic allocation,[35] to result in a zero inclusion ratio for the reverse QTIP trust or property;

(4) the estate is not eligible for the automatic six-month extension;[36]

(5) the surviving spouse has not made a lifetime disposition of any part of the qualifying income interest for life in the QTIP property;

(6) the surviving surviving spouse is alive, or no more than six months have passed since the surviving spouse's death; and

(7) the procedural requirements set forth in section 4.03 of Rev. Proc. 2004-47 have been met.

This simplified alternative procedure may not be used where the permission to file a late reverse QTIP election is in connection with a late severance of a trust included in the decedent's gross estate, or in conjunction with an allocation of GST exemption. Such requests must be made through the letter ruling process.

If an executor has a letter ruling request pending with the IRS on August 9, 2004, the executor may withdraw the request and receive a refund of the user fee in certain circumstances.

¶ 2440 Applicable Provisions

All of the Internal Revenue Code provisions on procedure and administration, including penalties (Subtitle F), that apply to estate and gift taxation are applicable to the generation-skipping transfer tax.[37] Estate tax rules govern transfers occurring as a result of death; gift tax rules apply to *inter vivos* transfers.

¶ 2441 Effective Dates

The rules affecting generation-skipping transfers are generally applicable to transfers made after October 22, 1986. However, certain transfers from trusts that were irrevocable prior to that date are not subject to the generation-skipping transfer (GST) tax. Consequently, care must be taken when a transfer is contemplated from such a trust. In general, the following exceptions to the effective date rules apply:[38]

(1) The GST tax does not apply to any generation-skipping transfer under a trust that was irrevocable on September 25, 1985, but only to the extent that such transfer was not made out of corpus added to the trust after that date. This exception was amended by the Technical and Miscellaneous Revenue Act of 1988 (P.L. 100-647) to clarify that the exception regarding irrevocable trusts applies without regard to whether income received from corpus contributions made before September 26, 1985, is distributed or

[35] Code Sec. 2632(e); Reg. § 26.2632-1(d)(2).

[36] Reg. § 301.9100-2(b).

[37] Code Sec. 2661.

[38] Reg. § 26.2601-1(b).

accumulated.[39] The exercise of a limited power of appointment over a trust that was irrevocable on September 25, 1985, does not cause property subject to the power to lose its exemption from the GST tax if the power may not be exercised to postpone or suspend the vesting, absolute ownership, or power of alienation of an interest in the property for the longer of (1) 90 years as provided by the Uniform Rule Against Perpetuities, or (2) 21 years after the death of any life in being when the irrevocable trust was created.[40] However, assets that were transferred from a marital trust that was irrevocable prior to the effective date of the GST tax were subject to the GST tax because the transfer was treated as being made from property constructively added after the effective date of the GST tax, because of the lapse of a surviving spouse's testamentary general power of appointment over the property.[41]

(2) Any generation-skipping transfers occurring under wills or revocable trusts executed before October 22, 1986, are not subject to the tax, provided that the following conditions are met: (a) the document in existence on October 21, 1986, was not amended after that date in a manner that resulted in the creation of, or an increase in the amount of, a generation-skipping transfer; (b) in the case of a revocable trust, no addition was made to the trust after October 21, 1986, that resulted in the creation of, or increase in the amount of, a generation-skipping transfer; and (c) the decedent died before January 1, 1987.[42] Furthermore, revocable trusts that became irrevocable due to the transferor's death between September 25, 1985, and October 23, 1986, are also excluded from the category of taxable transfers.[43]

(3) Any generation-skipping transfer occurring under a trust (to the extent that such trust consists of property, or proceeds thereof, the value of which was included in a decedent's gross estate) or which is a direct skip occurring by reason of a decedent's death is not subject to the tax if the decedent was legally incompetent on October 22, 1986, and at all times thereafter until death. However, the exception does not apply to property transferred to such incompetent decedent (or to a trust) by gift or by reason of the death of another person, after August 3, 1990.[44]

The delays in effective dates were adopted to permit a reasonable period of time for individuals to re-execute their wills to reflect the extension of the GST tax to direct skips.

• ***Grandfathered Trusts***

In the following instances, the IRS has ruled that grandfathered status was not disturbed:

(1) the partition of a trust into two or more separate trusts, so long as the quality, value, or timing of the beneficial interests, rights, or expectancies provided in the original trust did not change;[45]

---

[39] Act Sec. 1014(h) of P.L. 100-647, amending Act Sec. 1433(b) of P.L. 99-514.

[40] Reg. §26.2601-1(b)(1)(v)(B)(2).

[41] *E. Peterson Marital Trust*, CA-2, 96-1 USTC ¶60,225, aff'g TC, 102 TC 790, CCH Dec. 49,935. However, on similar facts the U.S. Court of Appeals for the Eighth Circuit reached an opposite result: *J. Simpson*, CA-8, 99-2 USTC ¶60,351, Nonacq., IRB 2000-9. Followed: *R. Bachler*, CA-9, 2002-1 USTC ¶60,430, rev'g DC Cal., 2000-2 USTC ¶60,390.

[42] Reg. §26.2601-1(b)(2).

[43] Reg. §26.2601-1(a)(4).

[44] Act Sec. 11703(c) of P.L. 101-508; Reg. §26.2601-1(b)(3).

[45] IRS Letter Ruling 199920004 (Feb. 4, 1999), IRS Letter Ruling 9620016 (Feb. 15, 1996), and IRS Letter Ruling 9122027 (Feb. 28, 1991).

(2) the distribution of corpus to trust beneficiaries pursuant to a settlement agreement so long as each beneficiary received a terminating distribution that fairly reflected the value of the beneficiary's interest in the trust;[46]

(3) a settlement agreement among beneficiaries of a decedent's estate to transfer a portion of trust assets to a new trust where the settlement agreement was within the range of reasonable settlement agreements;[47]

(4) the merger of trusts with substantially identical terms;[48]

(5) the merger of two charitable annuity trusts and the loan back of some or all of the surviving trust's distributions to the surviving trust;[49]

(6) qualified disclaimers made after October 22, 1986, with respect to the estate of a decedent who died prior to that date;[50]

(7) the transfer of a beneficiary's contingent remainder interest in a trust created under the transferor's will, provided that the transfer did not (a) cause any change in the quality, value, or timing of any beneficiary's interest in the trust, (b) confer any additional powers or beneficial interests on any beneficiaries, (c) create any additional generation-skipping transfers or increase the amount of any generation-skipping transfer, or (d) change the number of younger generations provided for in the decedent's will;[51]

(8) the renunciation by the income beneficiary of an annuity interest in a trust and the purchase by the remainder beneficiaries of a commercial annuity of equal or greater value for the income beneficiary's benefit;[52]

(9) a spouse's power to appoint herself as trustee of a trust under which she was a beneficiary was not a general power of appointment because of a state statute limiting the exercise of this type of power. The state (Florida) statute prohibited the trustee from exercising discretionary powers in a manner other than for the trustee's health, support, maintenance, or education. The statute limiting the trustee's discretion in this manner was enacted after the spouse had already become a co-trustee. The IRS also found that the amendment did not constitute a lapse of a general power of appointment for gift tax purposes;[53]

(10) the division of a trust created for the settlor's seven grandchildren into seven separate trusts did not affect the trusts' GST tax-exempt status;[54]

(11) the division of a trust and the assets on a pro rata basis, those trusts being independently managed, and future division in the same format did not result in a material change in the kind or extent of the beneficiaries' entitlements;[55]

(12) judicial interpretation of the definition of the term "issue" in one trust to include adopted children and removal of a provision from another

---

[46] IRS Letter Ruling 9442018 (July 19, 1994).

[47] IRS Letter Ruling 9848009 (Aug. 4, 1998).

[48] IRS Letter Ruling 9348049 (Sept. 7, 1993) and IRS Letter Ruling 199912012 (Dec. 21, 1998).

[49] IRS Letter Ruling 9613014 (Dec. 27, 1995).

[50] IRS Letter Ruling 8725022 (Mar. 20, 1987).

[51] IRS Letter Ruling 9446024 (Aug. 17, 1994).

[52] IRS Letter Ruling 9221005 (Feb. 13, 1992).

[53] IRS Letter Ruling 199909016 (Nov. 30, 1998).

[54] IRS Letter Ruling 199909037 (Dec. 7, 1998).

[55] IRS Letter Ruling 199912034 (Dec. 28, 1998).

trust that was to equalize treatment between natural issue and adopted issue;[56]

(13) the exercise of a testamentary special power of appointment by the decedent's grandchildren to a trust for the benefit of such grandchildren's descendants;[57]

(14) the creation of a charitable subtrust funded with property from a grandfathered generation-skipping transfer trust and the subsequent revocation or termination of the subtrust, which would result in the assets being returned to the original grandfathered trust;[58]

(15) judicial reformation to correct a scrivener's error;[59]

(16) the consent of the trustee to allow the trust's primary asset, a corporation, to make a subchapter S election and an election to treat the trust as an electing small business trust;[60] and

(17) a change in the situs of the trust from the state where the former trustee conducted business to the state where the successor trustee conducted business.[61]

However, a trust lost its grandfathered status when a decedent's children renounced their rights of encroachment, during the surviving spouse's life, on the principal of a testamentary trust in order to satisfy the requirements for a qualified subchapter S trust. Because the renunciations were not made within a reasonable time (nine months) of the creation of the interests, the renunciations constituted a gift and the value of the gift was an addition to the trust for GST tax purposes. Accordingly, a proportionate amount of distributions from, and terminations of interests in property held in, the trust were subject to the provisions of the GST tax.[62]

• *Trust Modifications*

A modification of a generation-skipping trust that is otherwise exempt under the grandfather rules will generally cause a loss of exempt status only if the modification changes the quality, value, or timing of any powers, beneficial interests, rights, or expectancies originally provided for under the terms of the trust.[63]

In IRS Letter Ruling 9218053, the IRS was asked to rule on whether a construction of a 1962 trust would affect the trust's grandfathered status. Although the trust's purpose was to provide for the "security" of the income beneficiary, the beneficiary was unable to maintain her standard of living or pay her medical bills, and the trust's principal had increased to over $1 million. The proposed construction would authorize the trustee to make discretionary payments to the beneficiary and pay the beneficiary's medical bills. The IRS ruled that the construction would not cause the trust to be subject to the GST tax because it was a reasonable interpretation of the settlors' intent and did not alter

---

[56] IRS Letter Ruling 199915038 (Jan. 13, 1999).

[57] IRS Letter Ruling 199918006 (Nov. 28, 1998).

[58] IRS Letter Ruling 199939010 (June 24, 1999), IRS Letter Ruling 199939011 (June 24, 1999), and IRS Letter Ruling 199939012 (June 24, 1999).

[59] IRS Letter Ruling 199942016 (July 22, 1999).

[60] IRS Letter Rulings 200012003–200012044 (Nov. 15, 1999).

[61] IRS Letter Rulings 200012052-200012056 (Dec. 17, 1999).

[62] IRS Letter Ruling 9308007 (Nov. 24, 1992).

[63] IRS Letter Ruling 9508025 (Nov. 24, 1994).

the intended quality, quantity, or timing of the interests created by the trust. See IRS Letter Ruling 199917022, in which the IRS determined that the clarification of a trust provision to avoid the premature termination of the income interests of the spouses of decedent's children was reflective of the decedent's intent and did not cause the trust to be subject to GST tax.

Similarly, court orders modifying an exempt trust were ruled (1) to resolve the ambiguities that resulted from the liquidation of the closely held corporation whose stock was the primary asset of the trust, and (2) to be consistent with the grantor's intent to provide his grandchild with sufficient funds to finance his educational expenses.[64] Additionally, a court order allowing proceeds to be distributed as permitted under the original trust and the modification of the trust to follow state trustee investment rules outside those permitted in the original trust did not alter the trust's exempt status.[65]

By contrast, a proposed reformation of a 1967 trust whose annual income had increased from $9,000 to $270,000 would subject the trust to GST tax. The IRS ruled that the proposed reformation to eliminate the accumulation of surplus income and require the distribution of such income to the trust beneficiaries at least quarterly changed the quality, value, and timing of the beneficiaries' interests.[66]

Distribution of all trust income, at the trustee's discretion, among an incompetent beneficiary and his children and grandchildren was considered a reformation of a grandfathered trust that would cause the trust to lose its exemption from the GST tax.[67] Even if the applicable state (Minnesota) probate court were to construe the original trust instrument to allow such discretionary distributions, the IRS maintained that the instrument authorized distributions only to the extent necessary for the support and maintenance of the original beneficiary and his children. In IRS Letter Ruling 9544015, the IRS considered a proposed construction of a GST tax-exempt trust that gave each of the decedent's children the power to appoint trust income to family members, including the child's children, with unappointed income payable to the child's descendants. The IRS ruled that the proposed construction permitting the decedent's children to exercise their limited powers of appointment to create further limited powers of appointment and appoint income would not modify the terms of the trust. However, the proposed construction permitting distributions of principal and creating powers of appointment in succeeding income beneficiaries in the event a child does not exercise his limited power of appointment would modify the trust and cause it to lose its exempt status.

Trust modifications intended to qualify a trust as a shareholder of an S corporation were also ruled to cause loss of grandfathered status.[68] On the other hand, reorganization of a corporation in which two identical trusts held a controlling interest did not cause the combined trust to lose its grandfathered status.[69] Pursuant to the reorganization, shares of voting common stock were exchanged for virtually identical shares of a newly organized holding company. Moreover, a court decree provided that the exchange was not a sale or disposi-

---

[64] IRS Letter Ruling 9602016 (Oct. 11, 1995).

[65] IRS Letter Ruling 199907008 (Nov. 13, 1998), IRS Letter Ruling 199911026 (Dec. 17, 1998), and IRS Letter Ruling 199911027 (Dec. 17, 1998).

[66] IRS Letter Ruling 9449019 (Sept. 13, 1994).

[67] IRS Letter Ruling 9448024 (Aug. 31, 1994), as modified by IRS Letter Ruling 9522032 (Mar. 3, 1995).

[68] IRS Letter Ruling 8927026 (Apr. 6, 1989).

[69] IRS Letter Ruling 9507016 (Nov. 15, 1994).

tion and that the holding company shares were subject to the same rights and restrictions applicable, under the trust agreement, to the original stock.

• *Modification of Administrative Provisions*

Proposed modifications that relate exclusively to the administration of a trust will not cause that trust to lose its grandfathered status. However, in light of the numerous private letter rulings requested concerning the effect of proposed modifications or construction proceedings on the GST tax-exempt status of a trust, the IRS has promulgated amendments to Reg. §26.2600-1 and Reg. §26.2601-1. The amendments provide a more liberal standard with respect to changes that may be made to a trust without the trust losing its GST tax-exempt status. The amendments are intended to clarify the types of modifications allowable and are intended to reduce the need for private letter rulings in this area. Under the amended regulations, the exempt status of a trust would not be affected if the modification is pursuant to:

(1) the trustee's discretionary power to distribute principal to a new trust for the benefit of succeeding generations, provided that the vesting is not postponed beyond the perpetuities period of the original trust;

(2) a court-approved settlement produced from an arm's-length negotiation of a bona fide controversy relating to the administration of the trust or the construction of terms governing the trust;

(3) a court order in a construction proceeding to resolve an ambiguity or correct a scrivener's error; and

(4) a manner that does not shift a beneficial interest in the trust to any beneficiary that occupies a lower generation than the person who held the interest prior to modification and the time for vesting is not extended beyond the perpetuities period of the original trust.[70]

• *Powers of Appointment*

If property remains in a grandfathered trust that was irrevocable on September 25, 1985, after the release, exercise, or lapse of a power of appointment that is a taxable transfer for gift or estate tax purposes, the U.S. Court of Appeals for the Second Circuit in *E. Norman Peterson Marital Trust* held that the value of such property is treated as an addition to the trust.[71] For example, a general power of appointment marital deduction trust (or any other trust over which an individual has a general power of appointment) that is in existence on September 25, 1985, is not grandfathered from GST tax after the death of the power holder.

However, the above situation should be compared to that in *J. Simpson*,[72] in which the U.S. Court of Appeals for the Eighth Circuit held that an exercise of a general power of appointment was not subject to the GST tax because the power was created "under a trust" that was irrevocable prior to September 25, 1985. Although conceding that in both cases the transfer at issue would have been subject to the GST tax unless grandfathered by operation of the effective date provision of the tax, the Eighth Circuit noted that in *Peterson*, the generation-

---

[70] Reg. §26.2601-1(b)(4), as amended by T.D. 8912, Dec. 19, 2000.

[71] *E. Peterson Marital Trust*, CA-2, 96-1 USTC ¶60,225, aff'g 102 TC 790, CCH Dec. 49,935. See also, Reg. §26.2601-1(b)(1)(v)(A). However, on similar facts the U.S. Court of Appeals for the Eighth Circuit reached an opposite result: *J. Simpson*, CA-8, 99-2 USTC ¶60,351, Nonacq., IRB 2000-9. Followed: *R. Bachler*, CA-9, 2002-1 USTC ¶60,430, rev'g DC Cal., 2000-2 USTC ¶60,390.

[72] *J. Simpson*, CA-8, 99-2 USTC ¶60,351, Nonacq., IRB 2000-9.

skipping transfer came about as the result of a lapse of a general power of appointment rather than its exercise. Accordingly, the issue in *Peterson* was not whether the transfer effected by Mrs. Peterson's failure to exercise her power was "under the trust," but rather whether the transfer had been made "out of corpus added to the trust after September 25, 1985." The *Peterson* court held that the effective date provision did not protect a transfer involving the portion remaining in the trust after Mrs. Peterson's power of appointment had lapsed. In contrast, the power of appointment in *Simpson* was exercised with respect to the entire corpus leaving no remaining property in the trust. The IRS, however, has issued a nonacquiescence notice in *Simpson* regarding whether the transfer to the decedent's grandchildren as a result of the decedent's exercise of a power of appointment was exempt from GST tax under the effective date provisions.

The IRS has promulgated amendments to Reg. §26.2600-1 and Reg. §26.2601-1 that would clarify the application of the effective date provisions to transfers of property pursuant to the exercise, release, or lapse of a power of appointment. In its explanation of the regulations, the IRS concludes that there is no substantive difference between the transfer of property pursuant to the exercise of the power of appointment in *Simpson* and the lapse of the power of appointment in *Peterson*. The IRS reasons that the holder of the power of appointment has the equivalent of outright ownership in the property subject to the power and the value of such property is includible in the powerholder's estate. In addition, the powerholder in either *Simpson* or *Peterson* could avoid the GST tax by appointing the property to nonskip persons. Thus, the IRS agrees with the holding of the court in *Peterson* that the effective date provisions do not protect such transfers from the GST tax. Under the amended regulations, the transfer of property pursuant to the exercise, release, or lapse of a general power of appointment is not a transfer by the trust, but is a transfer by the holder of the power that becomes effective on such exercise, release, or lapse.[73]

If the release, exercise, or lapse of a general power over trust assets is not treated as a taxable transfer under the estate or gift tax provisions of the Internal Revenue Code, there is no deemed addition to the trust and no loss of grandfathered status. For example, in IRS Letter Ruling 9510009, a taxpayer proposed to release her pre-October 22, 1942 general power of appointment over a trust fund. The IRS pointed out that property subject to a pre-October 22, 1942, general power of appointment is includible in the gross estate only if the power is exercised and the release of a power is not treated as an exercise for this purpose. Therefore, the proposed release of the power was not subject to the estate tax. Similarly, it noted that Code Sec. 2514(a) provides that the complete release of a power created before this date is not deemed to be an exercise of the power for gift tax purposes. Because the transfer was not taxable under either the estate or gift tax provisions of the Code, the IRS concluded that there would be no deemed addition to the trust and no loss of grandfathered status.

By contrast, the release, exercise, or lapse of a special power of appointment is not treated as an addition to a trust if such power of appointment is created in an irrevocable trust that is not subject to the GST tax under Reg. §26.2601-1(b)(1) and, in the case of an exercise, the power is not exercised in a manner that may postpone or suspend the vesting, absolute ownership, or power of alienation of an interest in trust property for a period, measured from the date of creation of the trust, that extends beyond either (1) any life in being at the date of creation of

---

[73] Reg. §26.2601-1(b)(1)(i), as amended by T.D. 8912, Dec. 19, 2000.

the trust plus 21 years (the common law rule against perpetuities period), or (2) 90 years (the Uniform Statutory Rule Against Perpetuities period).[74] An exercise of a power of appointment that would exceed the applicable state law rule against perpetuities but is limited by the law is not a constructive addition.[75]

A power of appointment is a general power if it is exercisable in favor of the individual possessing the power, his estate, his creditors, or the creditors of his estate.[76] In contrast, a special power is one that is either (1) exercisable only in favor of one or more designated persons or classes other than the decedent or his creditors, or the decedent's estate or the creditors of his estate, or (2) expressly not exercisable in favor of the decedent or his creditors, or the decedent's estate or the creditors of his estate.[77] In IRS Letter Ruling 9511039, for example, modification of a trust agreement to allow beneficiaries to appoint the corpus of a trust only to their widows or children was not an addition to the trust because the power was a special power and was not exercised to improperly postpone or suspend vesting.

---

[74] Reg. § 26.2601-1(b)(1)(v)(B)(2).
[75] Reg. § 26.2601-1(b)(1)(v)(D), Ex. 7.
[76] Code Sec. 2041(b).
[77] Reg. § 20.2041-1(c)(1).

Chapter 40
COMPUTATION OF TAX

¶ 2450 Amount of Tax

In general, the generation-skipping transfer (GST) tax imposes a flat tax at the "applicable rate" (see ¶2459) on the taxable amount of a generation-skipping transfer. For purposes of determining the taxable amount of a direct skip, taxable distribution, or taxable termination, the following exemptions from the tax are provided: (1) a generation-skipping transfer exemption ($1,500,000 for 2004 and 2005) that may be allocated among several generation-skipping transfers (see ¶2455), and (2) an exemption that applies if the parent of the transferee is deceased at the time of the transfer (see ¶2437).

¶ 2451 Determination of Tax Base

In general, the method of computing the tax base or the taxable amount of a generation-skipping transfer depends on whether a taxable distribution, a taxable termination, or a direct skip is involved. Unless a trust instrument specifically referring to the generation-skipping transfer (GST) tax directs otherwise, the tax imposed on a generation-skipping transfer is charged to the property being transferred.[1]

• *Taxable Distributions*

In the case of taxable distributions, the amount subject to the GST tax is the amount received by the transferee.[2] This amount is reduced by any expenses incurred in connection with the determination, collection, or refund of the tax. As discussed at ¶2470, the transferee pays the tax on the taxable distribution. If the trustee pays any amount of the tax, the trustee is treated as having made an additional taxable distribution of that amount.[3]

• *Taxable Terminations*

In the case of a taxable termination, the amount subject to tax is the value of the property with respect to which the termination occurred.[4] A deduction is allowed for expenses, indebtedness, and taxes (similar to that discussed at ¶800 through ¶820) for amounts attributable to the property with respect to which the termination has occurred. The trustee pays any tax due on a taxable termination.

• *No Double Deductions for Expenses, Indebtedness, and Taxes*

Administration expenses, indebtedness, and taxes may be taken either as an income tax deduction on Form 1041 (U.S. Income Tax Return for Estates and Trusts) or as a deduction in determining taxable distributions and taxable termi-

---

[1] Code Sec. 2603(b).
[2] Code Sec. 2621.
[3] Code Sec. 2621(b).
[4] Code Sec. 2622.

nations for GST tax purposes. These amounts may not be deducted twice, however. To deduct them from an estate's taxable income, the fiduciary must file a waiver electing not to deduct the amounts for GST tax purposes.[5]

• ***Direct Skips***

The taxable amount on a direct skip is the value of the property received by the transferee.[6] If the direct skip is made from a trust, the tax is paid by the trustee; otherwise, it is paid by the transferor. This means that the tax base is the amount actually received by the skip person after reduction for the amount of GST tax paid on the transfer. This means that a direct skip is tax-exclusive.

To calculate the amount of GST tax payable, an interrelated computation is necessary. For 2004, the tax is 48 percent of the amount left after the amount of GST tax payable is removed from the tax base.

This tax-exclusive rate (TER) is calculated according to the following formula:

$$\text{TER} = \frac{\text{TIR (tax-inclusive rate)}}{1 + \text{TIR}}$$

Thus, for a 48-percent tax-inclusive rate, the tax-exclusive rate would be .48/1.48 = .324324. This rate is then applied to the amount subject to the GST tax to arrive at the amount of GST tax due. Form 706 (United States Estate (and Generation-Skipping Transfer) Tax Return), Schedule R (Generation-Skipping Transfer Tax) (Rev. Aug. 2004), part 2, line 8, accomplishes the same result by dividing the amount subject to the GST tax by 3.083333, to arrive at the amount of GST tax due.

> *Example (1):* David Green died, leaving all his assets to his grandson, Nick. Assume that, after payment of the estate tax, the amount left is $3.5 million. The full $3.5 million is not subject to the GST tax, but only the amount that Nick will receive after payment by the estate of the GST tax.
>
> Accordingly, under the facts of this Example, the GST tax would be .324324 × $3.5 million, which equals $1,135,134.

The rules applicable to a lifetime direct skip are the same as those applicable to a testamentary direct skip. The GST tax is paid by the transferor, and the transfer is tax-exclusive. However, the treatment of a lifetime direct skip resembles that of a tax-inclusive transfer because of the "gross-up" rule.[7] Under this rule, the amount of any taxable gift that is also a direct skip is increased by the amount of GST tax payable on the transaction.

> *Example (2):* Laura Green makes a gift of $3.5 million to her grandson, Paul. (Assume that the whole value of the gift is in the 48-percent marginal bracket and her unified credit of $555,800 and generation-skipping transfer exemption have been used up on $3.5 million of prior taxable gifts.) The GST tax on the gift is .48 times $3.5 million, which equals $1,680,000. This amount is then added to the amount of the tax base for purposes of calculating the gift tax. Thus, the gift tax base is $5,180,000, and the gift tax payable is $2,307,200. This means that the total transfer tax on a gift of $3.5 million is $3,987,200.

---

[5] Code Sec. 642(g).

[6] Code Sec. 2623.

[7] Code Sec. 2515.

Note that in the case of lifetime direct skips, the GST tax payable because of the gift is not itself subject to GST tax, but is subject to the gift tax. This makes the taxation of such transfers similar to a tax-inclusive treatment of taxable distributions and taxable terminations.

¶ 2453 Valuation

Generally, property is valued at the time of the generation-skipping transfer.[8] If property is transferred as a result of the death of a transferor, the value of the property, for generation-skipping transfer (GST) tax purposes, is its value for estate tax purposes. If an estate elects either alternate or special use valuation for the property, that value will be used to compute GST tax liability. Additionally, if one or more taxable terminations with respect to the same trust occur at the same time as, and as the result of, the death of an individual, an election may be made to value all of the property included in such terminations at its alternate value as set forth in Code Sec. 2032.[9]

For purposes of the valuation rules for generation-skipping transfers, the value of transferred property is reduced by the amount of any consideration provided by the transferee.[10]

¶ 2455 GST Exemption; Allocation

An exemption of $1,500,000 for 2004 and 2005 is provided for each person making generation-skipping transfers. The exemption may be allocated by a transferor (or the transferor's executor) to property transferred at any time but, once made, is irrevocable. The $1,500,000 exemption is not transferable between spouses; however, married couples may elect to split a transfer and treat it as made one-half by each spouse pursuant to the gift-splitting rules under Code Sec. 2513 (see ¶2013 and ¶2200).[11] For generation-skipping transfers made after 1998 and before January 1, 2004, the generation-skipping transfer (GST) tax exemption was indexed for inflation.[12] The inflation-adjusted figure for generation-skipping transfers in 2003 was $1,120,000, for transfers in 2002 it was $1,100,000, and for transfers in 2001 it was $1,060,000.[13] See the discussion below for the increase of the generation-skipping transfer exemption under the provisions of the Economic Growth and Tax Relief Reconciliation Act of 2001 (P.L. 107-16) (2001 Act).

• ***Increase in Exemption Amount Under the 2001 Act***

Effective for generation-skipping transfers after December 31, 2003, the 2001 Act provides that the amount of the GST tax exemption for any calendar year will be equal to the Code Sec. 2010(c) estate tax applicable exclusion amount in effect for such calendar year.[14] The estate tax applicable exclusion amount in effect for years after 2003 and prior to repeal of the estate and GST taxes in 2010 is as follows:

- $1.5 million in 2004 and 2005;
- $2 million in 2006, 2007, and 2008; and

---

[8] Code Sec. 2624.

[9] Code Sec. 2624(c).

[10] Code Sec. 2624(d).

[11] Code Sec. 2652(a)(2).

[12] Code Sec. 2631(c), as added by P.L. 105-34.

[13] Rev. Proc. 99-42, 1999-2 CB 568; Rev. Proc. 2001-13, 2001-1 CB 337; Rev. Proc. 2001-59, 2001-2 CB 623; Rev. Proc. 2002-70 IRB 2002-46, 845.

[14] Code Sec. 2631(c), as amended by P.L. 107-16.

- $3.5 million in 2009.[15]

Sunset provision. In order to comply with the Congressional Budget Act of 1974, the 2001 Act provides that all provisions of, and amendments made by, the 2001 Act will not apply to estates of decedents dying, gifts made, or generation-skipping transfers, after December 31, 2010. Unless Congress acts affirmatively in the interim, the Internal Revenue Code will thereafter be applied and administered as if these provisions had not been enacted.

Inflation adjustment stricken. The Code Sec. 2631(c) inflation adjustment provision added by the Taxpayer Relief Act of 1997 (P.L. 105-34) and clarified by the IRS Restructuring and Reform Act of 1998 (P.L. 105-206) is stricken with respect to generation-skipping transfers after December 31, 2003.[16]

• *Allocation of Exemption*

The GST tax exemption may be allocated by a transferor or the transferor's executor to property transferred at any time.[17] The election is irrevocable once made and must be made on or before the due date for filing an estate tax return (with extensions), regardless of whether a return is required to be filed.

If an allocation of GST tax exemption is made on a timely filed gift tax return or is deemed to have been made under the deemed allocation rules of Code Sec. 2632(b)(1), the value of the transferred property for purposes of determining the denominator of the applicable fraction is its value for gift tax purposes (and the allocation becomes effective on the date of the transfer).

Subject to relief provisions recently enacted (see below), if the transferor fails to make an election to allocate the GST tax exemption on a timely filed gift tax return, the transferor cannot use the value of the property as of the date of the transfer, but instead must use the value of the property as of the date of the allocation. Prior to enactment by the 2001 Act, there was no statutory provision that provided relief to taxpayers who inadvertently failed to make an election to allocate the GST tax exemption on a timely filed gift tax return. Under pre-2001 Act rules, the date the allocation is actually made must be used for valuation purposes, rather than an earlier date.[18]

• *Direct Skips*

If an individual makes a direct skip (as defined at ¶2433) during the individual's lifetime, any unused portion of the individual's exemption is deemed allocated to the transferred property to the extent necessary to reduce the inclusion ratio (as defined at ¶2461) for such property to zero.[19] If the amount of the direct skip exceeds the unused portion of the exemption, the entire unused portion is allocated to the property transferred. However, a transferor may elect to have these allocation rules not apply to a transfer. Once the election is made, it is irrevocable and cannot be modified after the date on which a timely filed Form 709 (United States Gift (and Generation-Skipping Transfer) Tax Return) is due.[20]

• *Late Elections*

Effective for requests pending on, or filed after, December 31, 2000, the IRS is directed to prescribe, by regulation, such circumstances and procedures under

---

[15] Code Sec. 2010(c), as amended by P.L. 107-16.

[16] Code Sec. 2631(c), as amended by P.L. 107-16.

[17] Code Sec. 2631.

[18] Code Sec. 2642(b)(3), prior to amendment by P.L. 107-16.

[19] Code Sec. 2632(b).

[20] Reg. §26.2632-1(b).

which extensions of time will be granted to make (1) allocations of GST tax exemption under Code Sec. 2642(b)(1) or Code Sec. 2642(b)(2), and (2) an election under Code Sec. 2632(b)(3) or Code Sec. 2632(c)(5).[21] Such regulations are to include procedures for requesting comparable relief with respect to transfers made before the enactment of the 2001 Act.

In determining whether to grant relief, the IRS is directed to take into account all relevant circumstances, including evidence of intent contained in the trust instrument or instrument of transfer.[22]

If relief is granted, thereby giving a taxpayer an extension of time to make an allocation of GST tax exemption with respect to a specific transfer, it would be possible for the taxpayer to use the date-of-transfer value for allocation purposes.

> ***Example (1):*** In 2004, Fred Miller transfers $1,500,000 of stock to a trust for the benefit of his grandchild, Marilyn Lee. If Miller's full GST tax exemption is allocated to the transfer on a timely filed gift tax return, then regardless of any future appreciation in the stock's value, no GST tax will be owed on a later trust distribution or termination. If, however, Miller does not allocate his GST tax exemption on a timely filed gift tax return and the value of the stock has grown to $1,880,000 by the time Miller makes the allocation, the allocation will fail to shelter the additional $380,000 (and any appreciation on that unsheltered amount) from future GST tax liability. If, instead, Miller were allowed to make a late election pursuant to Code Sec. 2642(g)(1), then Miller would be able to allocate his GST tax exemption based on the stock's value as of the transfer date ($1,500,000), as opposed to its later appreciated value.

The IRS has announced that taxpayers may seek an extension of time to make an election under Code Sec. 2632 or an allocation under Code Sec. 2642 under the rules of Reg. § 301.9100-3. Thus, relief will generally be granted if (1) the taxpayer has acted reasonably and in good faith, and (2) the relief will not prejudice the government's interests. These rules are effective with respect to requests for relief pending on, or filed after, December 31, 2000.[23] Taxpayers requesting relief are directed to follow the procedures for requesting a private letter ruling contained in § 5.02 of Rev. Proc. 2001-1,[24] or its successor revenue procedures.

• ***Alternate Method for Obtaining Extension to Allocate GST Exemption***

The IRS has detailed a simplified alternate method that may be used, effective August 2, 2004, to request an extension of time to make an allocation of the GST exemption.[25]

A taxpayer is eligible to use the alternate method in lieu of the letter ruling process to request an extension of time to allocate GST exemption if the following requirements are met:

> (1) prior to January 1, 2001, the taxpayer made a transfer by gift to a trust from which a GST could be made;
>
> (2) at the time the taxpayer files the request for relief under the alternate method, no taxable distributions had been made and no taxable terminations had occurred;

---

[21] Code Sec. 2642(g)(1)(A), as added by P.L. 107-16.

[22] Code Sec. 2642(g)(1)(B), as added by P.L. 107-16.

[23] Notice 2001-50, 2001-2 CB 189; modified by Rev. Proc. 2004-46, IRB 2004-31, 142.

[24] 2001-1 CB 1.

[25] Rev. Proc. 2004-46, IRB 2004-31, 142.

(3) the transfer qualified for the Code Sec. 2503(b) gift tax annual exclusion and the amount of the transfer (when combined with the value of all other gifts to the donee in that year) did not exceed the amount of the annual exclusion then in effect;

(4) no GST exemption was allocated to the transfer, whether or not a gift tax return was filed;

(5) at the time the taxpayer files the request, the taxpayer had unused GST exemption available to allocate to the transfer; and

(6) the procedural requirements detailed in Rev. Proc. 2004-46 are satisfied.

With respect to the procedural requirements, the taxpayer must file a Form 709 for the year of the transfer to the trust, regardless of whether a Form 709 had been previously filed. The taxpayer is directed to write "FILED PURSUANT TO REV. PROC. 2004-46" on the top of the Form 709. In addition to reporting the value of the transferred property as of the date of the transfer, the taxpayer must attach a "Notice of Allocation" statement containing several items of information, including the inclusion ratio of the trust after the allocation. The Form 709 must be filed on or before the due date for filing the taxpayer's federal estate tax return. Upon receipt of a request for relief using the alternate method, the IRS will determine whether the applicable requirements have been satisfied and will notify the taxpayer of the result of its determination. If the taxpayer satisfies the requirements, the allocation of GST exemption will be effective as of the date of the transfer.

No user fee is charged for requests filed under Rev. Proc. 2004-46. A taxpayer with a letter ruling request pending with the IRS on August 2, 2004, may withdraw the request and receive a refund of the user fee in certain circumstances

• ***Substantial Compliance***

Effective for transfers made after December 31, 2000, an allocation of GST tax exemption under Code Sec. 2632 that demonstrates an intent to have the lowest possible inclusion ratio with respect to a transfer or a trust is deemed to be an allocation of so much of the transferor's unused GST tax exemption as produces the lowest possible inclusion ratio.[26]

In determining whether there has been substantial compliance, all relevant circumstances are to be taken into account, including evidence of intent contained in the trust instrument or instrument of transfer.[27] The automatic allocation of GST tax exemption or election to prevent the allocation is irrevocable after the gift tax return due date, except that elections filed before January 27, 1996, became irrevocable on July 24, 1996.[28]

• ***Indirect Skips***

Effective for transfers made after December 31, 2000, if an individual makes a lifetime indirect skip, any unused portion of the individual's GST tax exemption is allocated to the property transferred to the extent necessary to make the inclusion ratio for such property equal to zero.[29] If the amount of the indirect skip

---

[26] Code Sec. 2642(g)(2), as added by P.L. 107-16.

[27] Code Sec. 2642(g)(2), as added by P.L. 107-16.

[28] Reg. §26.2632-1(b)(1).

[29] Code Sec. 2632(c)(1), as added by (P.L. 107-16).

exceeds the unused portion, then the entire unused portion is allocated to the property transferred.

Unused portion of GST tax exemption. For purposes of deemed allocations to lifetime indirect skips, the unused portion of an individual's GST tax exemption is the portion of the exemption that has not previously been (1) allocated by such individual, (2) treated as allocated under Code Sec. 2632(b) with respect to a direct skip occurring during or before the calendar year in which the indirect skip is made, *or* (3) treated as allocated under Code Sec. 2632(c)(1) with respect to a prior indirect skip.

Indirect skip. An "indirect skip" is defined as any transfer of property (other than a direct skip) subject to the gift tax made to a GST trust.[30]

GST trust. A "GST trust" is defined as a trust that could have a GST with respect to the transferor *unless*:

(1) the trust instrument provides that more than 25 percent of the trust corpus must be distributed to, or may be withdrawn by, one or more individuals who are nonskip persons (a) before the date that such individual attains age 46, (b) on or before one or more dates specified in the trust instrument that will occur before the date that such individual attains age 46, *or* (c) on the occurrence of an event that is reasonably expected to occur before the date that such individual attains age 46;

(2) the trust instrument provides that more than 25 percent of the trust corpus must be distributed to, or may be withdrawn by, one or more individuals who are nonskip persons *and* who are living on the date of death of another person identified in the instrument (either by name or by class) who is more than 10 years older than such individuals;

(3) the trust instrument provides that, if one or more individuals who are nonskip persons die on or before a date or event described in (1) or (2) above, more than 25 percent of the trust corpus (a) must be distributed to the estate or estates of one or more of such individuals, *or* (b) is subject to a general power of appointment exercisable by one or more of such individuals;

(4) any portion of the trust would be included in the gross estate of a nonskip person (other than the transferor) if such person died immediately after the transfer;

(5) the trust is a charitable lead annuity trust (per Code Sec. 2642(e)(3)(A)), a charitable remainder annuity trust, or a charitable remainder unitrust (per Code Sec. 664(d)); *or*

(6) a gift tax charitable deduction was allowed under Code Sec. 2522 with respect to the trust for the amount of an interest in the form of the right to receive annual payments of a fixed percentage of the net fair market value of the trust property (determined yearly) *and* which trust is required to pay principal to a nonskip person if such person is alive when the yearly payments for which the deduction was allowed terminate.[31]

Example (2): George Stack creates an irrevocable trust for the benefit of his lineal descendants. George has one child, Alice, who is age 21. The trust instrument provides that (1) all trust income is to be paid to Alice during her lifetime, and (2) one-third of the trust corpus is to be distributed to Alice

---

[30] Code Sec. 2632(c)(3)(A), as added by P.L. 107-16.

[31] Code Sec. 2632(c)(3)(B), as added by P.L. 107-16.

when she reaches age 25. At Alice's death, the remaining corpus is to be distributed to Alice's issue, *per stirpes*. The trust is not a generation-skipping transfer trust because more than 25 percent of the corpus must be distributed to a nonskip person, Alice, before she attains age 46.

Example (3): Gertrude Stack creates an irrevocable trust for the benefit of her lineal descendants. Gertrude has one child, Andrew, who is age 25. The trust instrument provides that (1) the trustee has discretion to distribute trust income to Andrew during his lifetime, and (2) one-fifth of the trust corpus is to be distributed to Andrew when he reaches age 45. At Andrew's death, the remaining corpus is to be distributed to Andrew's issue, *per stirpes*. The trust is a generation-skipping transfer trust because a generation-skipping transfer may occur with respect to Gertrude and the trust does not fall within any of the exceptions specified in (1)–(6) above.[32]

Right of withdrawal limited to annual exclusion amount. For purposes of determining whether a trust is a generation-skipping transfer trust, the value of transferred property is *not* considered to be includible in the gross estate of a nonskip person or subject to a right of withdrawal by reason of such person holding a right to withdraw an amount that does not exceed the Code Sec. 2503(b) gift tax annual exclusion amount ($11,000 per donee in 2002 through 2004) with respect to any transferor. In addition, it is assumed that powers of appointment held by nonskip persons will not be exercised.[33]

Estate tax inclusion period. An indirect skip to which Code Sec. 2642(f) applies is deemed to have been made only at the close of the estate tax inclusion period (ETIP). The value of such transfer is the fair market value of the trust property at the close of the ETIP.[34]

Election. An individual may opt out of the deemed allocation rule for lifetime indirect skips. An individual may elect to have Code Sec. 2632(c) *not* apply to (1) an indirect skip, or (2) any or all transfers made by the individual to a particular trust. In addition, an individual may elect to treat any trust as a generation-skipping transfer trust for purposes of Code Sec. 2632(c) with respect to any and all transfers made by the individual to the trust.[35]

An election to have Code Sec. 2632(c) not apply to an indirect skip is deemed to be timely if it is filed on a timely filed gift tax return for the calendar year in which the transfer was made or deemed to have been made under Code Sec. 2632(c)(4) (i.e., the close of the ETIP).[36] For other categories of elections permitted by Code Sec. 2632(c)(5)(A), the election may be made on a timely filed gift tax return for the calendar year for which the election is to become effective.[37]

Proposed regulations would provide procedures for electing out of the automatic allocation for indirect skips and for electing to treat a trust as a GST trust.[38] A transferor who wishes to elect out of the automatic rules would have the option of: (1) electing out for the specific transfer of the GST trust, or (2) making a single election that applies to the current transfer and all subsequent transfers made to the trust by that transferor. With respect to the second option,

---

[32] Code Sec. 2632(c)(3)(B)(i)-(vi), as added by P.L. 107-16.

[33] Code Sec. 2632(c)(3)(B), as added by P.L. 107-16.

[34] Code Sec. 2632(c)(4), as added by P.L. 107-16.

[35] Code Sec. 2632(c)(5)(A), as added by P.L. 107-16.

[36] Code Sec. 2632(c)(5)(B)(i), as added by P.L. 107-16.

[37] Code Sec. 2632(c)(5)(B)(ii), as added by P.L. 107-16.

[38] Proposed Reg. §26.2632-1, NPRM-REG-153841-02, July 13, 2004.

the election would remain effective until terminated by the transferor. A similar rule would apply with respect to the election to treat a trust as a GST under the proposed regulations. The election out of the automatic allocations rules for indirect skips and the election to treat any trust as a GST trust would be made by attaching a statement to a timely filed federal gift tax return for the applicable calendar year. If adopted, the proposed regulations would be applicable for elections made on or after July 13, 2004. However, any election under Code Sec. 2632(c)(5)(A) made before July 13, 2004, will be recognized if the election was made on a timely filed gift tax return in a manner that provided for adequate notice to the IRS that the transferor made the election.

Sunset provision. In order to comply with the Congressional Budget Act of 1974, the 2001 Act provides that all provisions of, and amendments made by, the 2001 Act will not apply to estates of decedents dying, gifts made, or generation-skipping transfers, after December 31, 2010. Unless Congress acts affirmatively in the interim, the Internal Revenue Code will thereafter be applied and administered as if these provisions had not been enacted.

• ***Retroactive Allocations of Unused GST Tax Exemption***

Effective for deaths of nonskip persons occurring after December 31, 2000, an individual may allocate unused GST tax exemption to any previous transfer(s) made to a trust, on a chronological basis.[39] This rule is designed to protect taxpayers when there is an "unnatural order of death" (such as when the second generation predeceases the first generation transferor) by allowing a transferor to allocate GST tax exemption retroactively to the date of the respective transfer to the trust.

Availability of retroactive allocation. An individual may make a retroactive allocation of GST tax exemption if (1) a nonskip person has an interest or a future interest in a trust to which any transfer has been made, (2) such person is a lineal descendant of a grandparent of the transferor or of a grandparent of the transferor's spouse or former spouse and such person is assigned to a generation below the generation assignment of the transferor, *and* (3) such person predeceases the transferor.[40]

Future interest. A person has a "future interest" in a trust if the trust permits income or corpus to be paid to such person on a future date or dates.[41]

Retroactive allocation made in calendar year within which nonskip person's death occurs. If a transferor's retroactive allocation is made on a gift tax return that is filed on or before the date prescribed by Code Sec. 6075(b) for gifts made within the calendar year within which the nonskip person's death occurred, then:

(1) for purposes of Code Sec. 2642(a), the value of such transfer(s) is determined as if such allocation had been made on a timely filed gift tax return for each calendar year within which each transfer was made;

(2) such allocation is effective immediately before such death; *and*

(3) the amount of the transferor's unused GST tax exemption that is available for allocation is determined immediately before such death.[42]

---

[39] Code Sec. 2632(d), as added by P.L. 107-16.

[40] Code Sec. 2632(d)(1), as added by P.L. 107-16.

[41] Code Sec. 2632(d)(3), as added by P.L. 107-16.

[42] Code Sec. 2632(d)(2), as added by P.L. 107-16.

Example (4): In 1999, Gary Stack creates an irrevocable trust for the primary benefit of his child, Anthony, who is age 21. The trust instrument provides that (1) the trustee has discretion to distribute trust income to Anthony during his lifetime, and (2) one-third of the trust corpus is to be distributed to Anthony at age 25, one-half of the remaining corpus at age 30, and the remainder of the corpus at age 35 (which will terminate the trust). If Anthony dies before reaching age 35, the corpus is to be distributed in equal shares to Anthony's children. Gary makes transfers to the trust in 1999 and 2000, but does not allocate any of his GST tax exemption to the transfers on the gift tax returns reporting the transfers. (Because of the effective date provisions, the deemed allocation rule of Code Sec. 2632(c), as added by the 2001 Act, does not apply to the 1999 or 2000 transfers). On September 1, 2004, before reaching age 25, Anthony dies, thus resulting in a taxable termination for GST tax purposes. Stack may retroactively allocate unused GST tax exemption to the transfers made in 1999 and 2000 and, thereby, exempt the trust property transferred to Anthony's children from the application of the GST tax.

• *Separate GST Exempt and GST Nonexempt Trust*

Although not required by the GST tax provisions of the Internal Revenue Code, it is usually a good idea from a tax planning viewpoint to have separate trusts for generation-skipping transfer exempt and generation-skipping transfer nonexempt assets. Where this is done, the generation-skipping transfer exempt trust will receive assets equal to the decedent's (or donor's) unused generation-skipping transfer exemption (or as much of it as he or she wishes to use). Because this trust will house only exempt assets—and will be drafted so as to not accept the receipt of nonexempt assets at a later date—the trust's inclusion ratio will always be zero (see ¶2461 for a discussion of the inclusion ratio rules). This means that no matter how much the assets in the trust appreciate after the initial transfer, no GST tax liability will be generated.

The second generation-skipping transfer trust in the typical two-generation-skipping transfer-trust arrangement will be the nonexempt trust, which will receive only assets against which the decedent's (grantor's) generation-skipping transfer exemption will not be allocated. Because this trust will have an inclusion ratio of one at all times (which means that all assets in the trust are subject to the GST tax), a recomputation of the inclusion ratio will not be required if additional assets are transferred into the trust at a later date.

Segregating completely exempt and completely nonexempt generation-skipping transfer assets can offer possible tax and cost savings:

(1) Funding the generation-skipping transfer exempt trust with assets that are expected to appreciate sharply will shield any increases in value from GST tax liability.

(2) The nonexempt trust should be funded with those assets that are not expected to appreciate as quickly. Even this trust can be a tax savings vehicle if it is used to make gift tax and GST tax deductible educational and medical payments. Since qualifying educational and medical payments are deductible in their own right, they should not be paid from the generation-skipping transfer exempt trust; doing so would waste a portion of the generation-skipping transfer exemption.

(3) The generation-skipping transfer exempt/nonexempt trusts arrangement is administratively less cumbersome than dealing with a par-

tially generation-skipping transfer exempt trust (that is, a trust with an inclusion ratio of greater than zero, and less than one). Particularly if a trust has multiple beneficiaries, makes frequent distributions, and will be accepting future contributions of trust property, the trustee of the trust will spend more time and effort computing tax liabilities of such a partially exempt trust, and recomputing the inclusion ratio whenever additional contributions into the trust are accepted.

• *Severing of Trusts*

Effective for severances after December 31, 2000, if a trust is severed in a "qualified severance," the resulting trusts will be treated as separate trusts thereafter for purposes of the GST tax.[43]

Qualified severance. A "qualified severance" is defined as the division of a single trust and the creation (by any means available under the governing instrument or local law) of two or more trusts if:

(1) the single trust was divided on a fractional basis; *and*

(2) the terms of the new trusts, in the aggregate, provide for the same succession of interests or beneficiaries as are provided for in the original trust.[44]

Proposed regulations. Proposed regulations have been published that would provide guidance on the qualified severance of a trust for GST tax purposes.[45] Under these proposals, each new trust must receive assets with a value equal to a fraction or percentage of the total value of the trust assets to satisfy the first requirement (relating to the division of a trust on a fractional basis). A severance of a trust based on a pecuniary amount, however, will not satisfy this requirement. Each separate trust does not need to be funded with a pro rata portion of each asset held by the original trust. However, if funding is done on a non-pro rata basis, it must be based on the total fair market value of the assets on the date of funding.

The proposed regulations provide that the second requirement (relating to the trust terms of the new trust) will be satisfied with respect to trusts from which discretionary, non-pro rata distributions may be made to beneficiaries if: (1) the terms of the separate trusts are the same as the terms of the original trust; (2) the severance does not shift a beneficial interest in the trust to any beneficiary in a lower generation than the person(s) who held the beneficial interest in the original trust; and (3) the severance does not extend the time for vesting of any beneficial interest in the trust beyond the period provided in the original trust. The IRS states that this rule regarding discretionary trusts is intended to facilitate the severance of trusts along family lines.

The proposed regulations specify that the applicability of Reg. §26.2654-1(b) is limited to severances occurring on or before December 31, 2000. The regulations will apply to severances occurring on or after the date that final regulations are published in the *Federal Register*. For severances occurring after December 31, 2000, and before the publication of final regulations, taxpayers are permitted to rely on any reasonable interpretation of Code Sec. 2642(a)(3), as long as reasonable notice is given to the IRS.

---

[43] Code Sec. 2642(a)(3), as added by P.L. 107-16.

[44] Code Sec. 2642(a)(3)(B)(i), as added by P.L. 107-16.

[45] Proposed Reg. §26.2642-6 and §26.2654-1, NPRM-REG-45987-03.

Trusts with an inclusion ratio greater than zero. A severance of a trust with an inclusion ratio of between zero and one is a "qualified severance" only if the single trust is divided into two trusts, one of which receives a fractional share of the total value of all trust assets equal to the applicable fraction of the single trust immediately before the severance. In such a case, the trust receiving the fractional share will have an inclusion ratio of zero and the other trust will have an inclusion ratio of one.[46]

> *Example (5):* George Stack creates an irrevocable trust for the benefit of his grandson, Albert. The trust instrument provides that the trustee has discretion to distribute trust income and corpus to Albert during his lifetime. At Albert's death, the corpus is to be distributed in equal shares to Albert's children. The trust instrument also gives the trustee the discretion to sever the trust for GST tax purposes. Based on the amount of GST tax exemption allocated to the trust and the value of the trust property, the trust's applicable fraction is 1/4, making the inclusion ratio equal to 3/4 (1 – 1/4 = 3/4). The trustee divides the trust into two trusts, each having terms identical to that of the original trust. One of the trusts receives a 1/4-fractional share of the total value of the trust assets. The severance is a "qualified severance," with the trust receiving the 1/4-fractional share having an inclusion ratio of zero, and the other trust having an inclusion ratio of one.

Timing and manner of severances. A severance under Code Sec. 2642(a)(3) may be made at any time. The Secretary is to prescribe the manner in which the qualified severance is to be reported.[47] Under proposed regulations, which would be effective on the date that they are published as final regulations, a qualified severance is reported by filing Form 706-GS(T), Generation-Skipping Transfer Tax Return for Terminations (or such other form that may be published by the IRS), and attaching a "Notice of Qualified Severance" to the return.[48]

Sunset provision. In order to comply with the Congressional Budget Act of 1974, the 2001 Act provides that all provisions of, and amendments made by, the 2001 Act will not apply to estates of decedents dying, gifts made, or generation-skipping transfers, after December 31, 2010. Unless Congress acts affirmatively in the interim, the Internal Revenue Code will thereafter be applied and administered as if these provisions and amendments had not been enacted.

• *Appreciation in Value of Exempt Property*

The House Ways and Means Committee Report to the Tax Reform Act of 1986 (P.L. 99-514) indicates that once the GST tax exemption is applied to a transfer of property, and the property (or a portion of it) is designated as exempt, all subsequent appreciation on the property (or that portion of it) is also exempt from tax. If only a portion of the property is initially exempt, any subsequent appreciation will be exempt in the same ratio as the initially exempt property bore to the total property.

> *Example (6):* In 2004, Elizabeth Davis establishes a $1,500,000 trust fund for the benefit of her grandchildren and great-grandchildren. Davis allocates her entire GST tax exemption to the trust. The assets in the trust appreciate

---

[46] Code Sec. 2642(a)(3)(B)(ii), as added by P.L. 107-16.

[47] Code Sec. 2642(a)(3)(C), as added by P.L. 107-16.

[48] Proposed Reg. § 26.2642-6, NPRM-REG-45987-03.

to $5 million. None of the appreciation is subject to tax because the initial transfer was fully exempt.

Example (7): Charles Duvall establishes a $2 million trust for the benefit of his children and grandchildren. Duvall allocates $500,000 of his GST tax exemption to the trust. The value of the trust appreciates to $8 million. Only one-quarter of the appreciation will be exempt because at the time of the transfer only one-quarter of the property qualified as exempt.

• ***Allocation of Unused Exemption at Death***

Any portion of a decedent's $1,500,000 GST tax exemption that has not been allocated at the decedent's death is allocated in the following order:

(1) to property that is the subject of a direct skip occurring at the decedent's death; and

(2) to trusts with respect to which the decedent is the transferor and from which a taxable distribution or termination may occur at or after the decedent's death.[49]

An allocation of the generation-skipping transfer exemption is ineffective with regard to a lifetime transfer of property that would be included in the transferor's estate (other than by virtue of Code Sec. 2035) if the transferor died immediately after the transfer until the end of the estate tax inclusion period (ETIP).[50] An allocation made during an ETIP is irrevocable, however.[51]

Example (8): Dale Ashwood sets up a 10-year grantor retained annuity trust for the benefit of his three grandchildren, reporting a taxable gift of $500,000 on his gift tax return and allocating $500,000 of his generation-skipping transfer exemption to the trust property. If Ashwood dies eight years later, the entire value of the trust property (then $800,000) will be included in his gross estate and will be subject to GST tax. Although Ashwood's allocation of the $500,000 generation-skipping transfer exemption was not effective when made on his gift tax return, it becomes effective at the end of the ETIP (here, his death) and will not shield the appreciation in the trust's value ($300,000) that will be subject to generation-skipping transfers. Although Ashwood's claimed generation-skipping transfer exemption was ineffective when made, it was, nonetheless, irrevocable, and his executor at death will not have the opportunity to undo the $500,000 generation-skipping transfer allocation and use it against other generation-skipping transfers.

An ETIP ends on the earlier of (1) the date on which the property would not be includible in the transferor's estate (other than under Code Sec. 2035), (2) the date on which there is a generation-skipping transfer with respect to the property, or (3) the transferor's death.[52] Transfers subject to an ETIP include transfers to qualified personal residence trusts, grantor retained annuity trusts, and grantor retained income trusts.

An ETIP also arises if, immediately after a transfer, the property would be includible in the estate of the transferor's spouse (other than under Code Sec. 2035). A spousal ETIP ends on the earlier of (1) the date on which the property would not be includible in the spouse's estate (other than under Code Sec. 2035), or (2) the spouse's death. Spousal ETIPs apply to transfers for which the spouse

---

[49] Code Sec. 2632(c).

[50] Reg. § 26.2632-1(c)(2).

[51] Reg. § 26.2632-1(c)(1).

[52] Reg. § 26.2632-1(c)(3).

is treated as a transferor because of a gift-splitting election, transfers to lifetime marital deduction trusts (other than trusts for which the reverse qualified terminable interest property election is made), and transfers to the extent the spouse has a withdrawal power.

There are two exceptions to application of the ETIP provisions. First, there is no ETIP when the possibility that the property will be included in the estate of the transferor or the transferor's spouse is so remote as to be negligible (less than five-percent probability determined by actuarial standards).[53] Second, there is no spousal ETIP if a power of withdrawal held by the transferor's spouse (1) is limited to the greater of $5,000 or five percent of trust principal, and (2) lapses within 60 days of the transfer to the trust.[54]

¶ 2457 GST Credit for State Taxes

If a generation-skipping transfer (other than a direct skip) occurs at the same time as, and as a result of, the death of an individual, a credit in the amount of the generation-skipping transfer (GST) tax paid to any state is permitted against the federal GST tax.[55] However, the credit is limited to five percent of the amount of federal GST tax imposed on the transfer.

• ***Impact of the 2001 Act***

The Economic Growth and Tax Relief Reconciliation Act of 2001 (P.L. 107-16) (2001 Act) repeals the credit for state GST taxes allowed for generation-skipping transfers occurring after December 31, 2004.[56] The 2001 Act repeals the Code Sec. 2011 state death tax credit, effective for the estates of decedents dying after 2004 (see ¶1370).

Sunset provision. In order to comply with the Congressional Budget Act of 1974, the 2001 Act provides that all provisions of, and amendments made by, the 2001 Act will not apply to estates of decedents dying, gifts made, or generation-skipping transfers, after December 31, 2010. Unless Congress acts affirmatively in the interim, the Internal Revenue Code will thereafter be applied and administered as if these provisions and amendments had not been enacted.

¶ 2459 Applicable Rate

All generation-skipping transfers are subject to tax at a flat rate equal to the product of the maximum estate tax rate (currently, 48 percent in 2004) and the "inclusion ratio" (as defined at ¶2461) with respect to the transfer.[57] The "maximum estate tax rate" is the maximum rate imposed by Code Sec. 2001 on the estates of decedents dying at the time of the taxable distribution, taxable termination or direct skip.

It should be noted, however, that, in the case of a direct skip occurring at death, the effective generation-skipping transfer tax rate will be considerably lower than the maximum estate tax rate in effect at the time. For any given rate, the tax exclusive, effective rate is calculated according to the following formula:

$$\frac{\text{Maximum Estate Tax Rate}}{1 + \text{Maximum Estate Tax Rate}}$$

A maximum estate tax rate of 48 percent (which is effective for generation-skipping transfers occurring in 2004; see below) yields the following result:

[53] Reg. §26.2632-1(c)(2)(ii)(A).

[54] Reg. §26.2632-1(c)(2)(ii)(B).

[55] Code Sec. 2604.

[56] Code Sec. 2604(c), as added by P.L. 107-16.

[57] Code Sec. 2641.

$$\frac{.48}{1.48} = .324324$$

Example: Harry West dies in 2004 and his will leaves his entire $5 million estate to his grandson, Jake.

Tax Base	$5,000,000
Tentative Estate Tax on above	2,220,800
Less: Unified Credit	(555,800)
Estate Tax	$1,665,000
GST Tax Base ($5,000,000 – $1,665,000)	$3,335,000
Less: GST Tax Exemption	(1,500,000)
Net GST Tax Base	$1,835,000
GST Tax Payable ($1,835,000 × .324324)	595,135
Total Transfer Tax	$2,260,135 *

* Note that the net GST tax base less the amount of GST tax paid times 48% is equal to the GST tax payable ($1,835,000 – $595,135 = $1,239,865; $1,239,865 × .48 = $595,135)

The Economic Growth and Tax Relief Reconciliation Act of 2001 (P.L. 107-16) (2001 Act) reduced the maximum estate tax rate from 55 percent (for 2001) to 50 percent, effective for estates of decedents dying after December 31, 2001.[58] The 2001 Act further reduces the maximum rate as follows:

- 49 percent for decedents dying in 2003;
- 48 percent in 2004;
- 47 percent in 2005;
- 46 percent in 2006; and
- 45 percent in 2007, 2008, and 2009.[59]

¶ 2461 Inclusion Ratio

The inclusion ratio for any property transferred in a generation-skipping transfer is the excess (if any) of one over the "applicable fraction" determined for the trust from which a generation-skipping transfer is made or, in the case of a direct skip, the applicable fraction determined for such a skip.[60] Stated differently, 1 – (applicable fraction) = inclusion ratio.

• *Applicable Fraction*

The applicable fraction is determined as follows: The numerator is the amount of the generation-skipping transfer exemption allocated to the trust or the property transferred in the direct skip. Its denominator is the value of the property transferred to the trust (or involved in the direct skip) reduced by the sum of any federal estate or state death tax attributable to the property that was recovered from the trust and any estate or gift tax charitable deductions allowed.[61]

$$\text{applicable fraction} = \frac{\text{amount of GST exemption allocated to trust or property}}{\text{(value of property transferred)} - \text{[state and federal estate taxes} + \text{charitable deductions allowed under Code Sec. 2055 or 2522]}}$$

[58] Code Sec. 2001(c)(1), as amended by P.L. 107-16.

[59] Code Sec. 2001(c)(2)(B), as added by P.L. 107-16.

[60] Code Sec. 2642(a).

[61] Code Sec. 2642(a)(2).

Example (1): Upon James Anderson's death in 2004, $3,245,000 is transferred to a trust for the benefit of his grandchildren. At the time of the transfer, the full $1,500,000 generation-skipping transfer (GST) tax exemption is allocated to this trust. Assuming that there are no estate/death tax and charitable deductions, the calculation of the GST tax would be as follows:

(1) Determination of the applicable fraction: $1,500,000 exemption divided by $3,245,000 in property equals applicable fraction of 0.462;

(2) Determination of the inclusion ratio: Subtract the applicable fraction from 1. Thus, the inclusion ratio is 1 minus 0.462, or 0.538.

The GST tax rate is the product of the inclusion ratio—in this case, 0.538—and the maximum federal estate tax rate at the time of the transfer—48%. Thus, the rate of tax on this transfer is 25.824%.

• ***Gift for Which Gift Tax Return Filed or Deemed Allocation Made***

For purposes of the GST tax, the value of property is generally determined at the time of a transfer to the trust or at the time of a direct skip. However, if an allocation of the GST tax exemption (see ¶2455) is made on a timely filed gift tax return[62] or is deemed to be made under Code Sec. 2632(b)(1), the value of the transferred property is its value for gift tax purposes (and the allocation becomes effective on the date of such transfer).[63]

If any allocation of the GST tax exemption to any property not transferred as a result of the death of the transferor is not made on a timely filed gift tax return and is not deemed to have been made under Code Sec. 2632(b)(1), the value of the property will be determined as of the time the allocation is filed with the IRS.[64] The Economic Growth and Tax Relief Reconciliation Act of 2001 (P.L. 107-16) (2001 Act) provides relief from this rule for certain late elections made with respect to generation-skipping transfer allocations (see ¶2455).

• ***QTIP Trusts***

If the value of the property is included in the gross estate of a spouse as qualified terminable interest property (QTIP) for which a marital deduction was previously allowed[65] and if the spouse was the transferor of the property, the value of the property (for GST tax purposes) will be the same as its value for estate tax purposes.[66]

• ***Treatment of Certain Nontaxable Gifts***

The inclusion ratio of a direct skip that is a nontaxable gift is zero. A nontaxable gift is one excluded from gift tax because of the annual exclusion or because it is a transfer for educational or medical expenses.[67] However, this rule does not apply to any transfer to a trust for the benefit of an individual unless (1) during the lifetime of that individual, no portion of the corpus or income of the trust may be distributed to (or for the benefit of) any other person, and (2) if the trust does not terminate before the individual dies, the assets of the trust will be includible in that individual's gross estate.

---

[62] Code Sec. 6075(b).

[63] Reg. §26.2632-1(b)(2)(ii)(A) and Reg. §26.2642-2(a)(1).

[64] Code Sec. 2642(b)(3).

[65] Code Sec. 2044.

[66] Code Sec. 2642(b)(4).

[67] Code Sec. 2642(c).

• ***Special Rules Where More Than One Transfer Is Made to a Trust***

If a transfer of property (other than a nontaxable gift) is made to a trust in existence before the transfer, the applicable fraction must be recomputed.[68] The numerator of this recomputed fraction is the sum of (1) the amount of the GST tax exemption allocated to the property involved in such a transfer, plus (2) the nontax portion of the trust (as defined below) immediately before such transfer. The denominator is the sum of (1) the value of the property involved in the transfer (reduced by the sum of (a) any federal estate or state death tax paid, and (b) any charitable deduction allowed), and (2) the value of all property in the trust immediately before the transfer.

For purposes of the special rule outlined above, the nontax portion of a trust is the product of the value of all of the property in the trust and the applicable fraction in effect for such trust.

Example (2): In 1998, Joseph Grant established a generation-skipping trust for the benefit of his descendants, which he initially funded with $1,000,000. However, he chose to allocate only $500,000 (or one-half) of his GST tax exemption ($1,000,000 in 1998) to the trust. Assuming that there were no allocable deductions, his initial applicable fraction was 0.5 and his inclusion ratio was also 0.5.

In 2004, Grant placed an additional $1,000,000 into the trust and allocated his remaining $1,000,000 GST tax exemption to it (the GST exemption is $1,500,000 for 2004). This necessitated the following recalculation. Assume that no deductions are allowable and that the initial trust corpus has not appreciated in value.

$$\frac{\left(\text{amount of GST tax exemption allocated to property involved in transfer}\right) + \left[\left(\text{value of all property in trust before transfer}\right)\left(\text{applicable fraction}\right)\right]}{\left[\left(\text{value of property involved in transfer}\right) - \text{federal estate or state death taxes recovered from trust attributable to such property and any charitable deductions}\right] + \left(\text{value of property in trust before transfer}\right)} =$$

$$\frac{(1{,}000{,}000) + [(1{,}000{,}000) \times (.5)]}{(\$1{,}000{,}000 - 0) + \$1{,}000{,}000} =$$

$$\frac{\$1{,}500{,}000}{\$2{,}000{,}000} = .750$$

Thus, the new applicable fraction is 0.750. The new inclusion ratio is 1 minus 0.750, which equals 0.250.

If any allocation of the GST tax exemption to property transferred to a trust is not made on a timely filed gift tax return and there was a previous allocation with respect to property transferred to the same trust, the applicable fraction for the trust must be recomputed at the time of the allocation.

---

[68] Code Sec. 2642(d).

¶ 2463 Taxation of Multiple Skips

If there is a generation-skipping transfer of any property and immediately after the transfer the property is held in trust, subsequent transfers from the portion of the trust attributable to that property are treated as if the transferor of the property were assigned to the first generation above the highest generation of any person who has an interest in such trust immediately after the transfer.[69] In general, the inclusion ratio of the trust will not be affected. However, Code Sec. 2653(b) specifically provides that, under regulations prescribed by the IRS, adjustments to the inclusion ratio are to be made to take into account any generation-skipping transfer (GST) tax borne by such a trust.

• *Pour-Over Trusts*

The inclusion ratio of a trust is affected if the generation-skipping transfer involves the transfer of property from one trust to another (i.e., a "pour-over" trust).[70] In such a case, the inclusion ratio for the pour-over trust is determined by treating the nontax portion of such distribution as if it were a part of a GST tax exemption allocated to such trust. The nontax portion of any distribution in this case is the amount of such distribution multiplied by the applicable fraction that applies to the distribution.

¶ 2465 Special Rules

The following special rules apply to the generation-skipping transfer (GST) tax.

• *Basis Adjustments*

If property is transferred in a generation-skipping transfer, the basis of the property in the hands of the transferee is stepped up (but not above fair market value) to reflect GST taxes attributable to appreciation.[71] For this purpose, the amount of GST tax imposed is computed without regard to the credit for state death taxes. The GST tax basis adjustment is applied after the basis adjustment for gift tax paid.[72] Thus, the two adjustments combined must not increase the basis of the property transferred above its fair market value.[73]

• *Certain Transfers at Death*

If the property is transferred in a taxable termination that occurs at the same time as, and as a result of, the death of an individual, the basis of the property is adjusted in a manner similar to that provided for in Code Sec. 1014(a) (relating to basis of property received from a decedent). However, if the inclusion ratio of the property is less than one, any increase or decrease in basis is limited by multiplying the increase by the inclusion ratio.[74] The stepped up basis adjustment under Code Sec. 1014 was repealed by the Economic Growth and Tax Relief Reconciliation Act of 2001 (P.L. 107-16), effective for estates of decedents dying after December 31, 2009.[75]

> *Example (1):* Ilsa Kuhn created an *inter vivos* trust funded with property with a basis of $2,000,000. Kuhn was to receive the income from the trust for her life and, upon her death, the remainder was directed to her grandson. When Kuhn died in 2004, the trust property had a fair market value of

---

[69] Code Sec. 2653.

[70] Code Sec. 2653(b)(2).

[71] Code Sec. 2654(a)(1).

[72] Code Sec. 1015(d).

[73] Code Sec. 2654(a).

[74] Code Sec. 2654(a)(2).

[75] Code Sec. 1014(g), as added by P.L. 107-16.

$3,500,000 million. Kuhn's estate allocates all of the $1,500,000 GST tax exemption to this taxable termination. The inclusion ratio would be .57 (1 – ($1,500,000 ÷ $3,500,000)). Thus, the adjusted basis of the property transferred to Kuhn's grandson would be $2,855,000 ([($3,500,000 – $2,000,000) × .57] + $2,000,000).

• ***Certain Trusts Treated as Separate Shares***

For purposes of the GST tax, the portions of a trust attributable to transfers from different transferors are treated as separate trusts. Similarly, substantially separate and independent shares of different beneficiaries in a trust are treated as separate trusts.[76]

Example (2): Tom Johnson and Julie Kelly created a trust for the benefit of Johnson's grandson and Kelly's son, Michael. Johnson contributed property worth $1.2 million and Kelly contributed property worth $2 million. For purposes of the GST tax, the trust would be treated as one trust containing $1.2 million with Johnson as the grantor and one trust containing $2 million with Kelly as the grantor.

Example (3): Larissa Jenkins created a trust to benefit her son, Manuel, and her granddaughter, Natalie, equally. She contributed $800,000 to the trust. The trust will be treated as two separate trusts containing $400,000 for each of Manuel and Natalie for purposes of the GST tax.

• ***Disclaimers***

For the effect of disclaimer, taxpayers are referred by statute[77] to Code Sec. 2518, which relates to gift tax disclaimers (see ¶2009). The triggering event for the nine-month disclaimer period is the direct skip, taxable termination, or taxable distribution.

• ***Limitation on Liability of Trustee***

A trustee is not personally liable for any increase in the GST tax that is attributable to the fact that the exemption of certain nontaxable gifts[78] does not apply to a transfer to the trust that was made during the life of the transferor and for which a gift tax return was not filed.[79]

The trustee is also not personally liable when the inclusion ratio (see ¶2461) with respect to the trust is greater than the amount of the ratio as computed on the basis of the return on which an allocation of the GST tax exemption to the property transferred to the trust was made (or deemed made under Code Sec. 2632).[80] The above exception, however, will not apply if the trustee has knowledge of facts sufficient to reasonably conclude that a gift tax return was required to be filed or that the inclusion ratio was erroneous.

• ***Nonresidents Not Citizens***

In the case of a generation-skipping transfer by a person who is neither a U.S. citizen nor a resident, the GST tax applies only to property that is subject to gift or estate tax at the time of a direct skip or transfer to a trust.[81] In other words, the GST tax applies only if the property is U.S. situs property (see ¶1620).

---

[76] Code Sec. 2654(b).
[77] Code Sec. 2654(c).
[78] Code Sec. 2642(c).
[79] Code Sec. 2654(d).
[80] Code Sec. 2654(d).
[81] Reg. §26.2663-2(b).

Chapter 41
RETURN REQUIREMENTS

¶ 2470 Liability for Tax

Which party is liable for generation-skipping transfer (GST) tax depends on the type of generation-skipping transfer.

The transferor is liable for GST tax resulting from a direct skip other than one from a trust, the trustee is liable for tax resulting from a direct skip from a trust or a taxable termination, and the transferee is liable for tax resulting from a taxable distribution.[1] If the trustee pays any amount of the tax on a taxable distribution, the trustee is treated as having made an additional taxable distribution of that amount (see ¶2451).

Generally, unless a trust instrument specifically directs otherwise, the GST tax is charged to the property constituting the transfer.[2] The estate and gift tax provisions with respect to transferee liability, liens, and related matters are applicable to the GST tax.[3] As a result, the donees of stock were liable as transferees for unpaid GST tax, even though no assessment of the tax had been asserted against the donor-transferor who was primarily liable for the tax.[4]

For an explanation of the limitations on the personal liability of a trustee, see ¶2465. See ¶2451 for an explanation of the amount of the transfer that is subject to tax.

¶ 2471 Persons Required to File Return; Required Returns

Regulations detail who is required to file generation-skipping transfer (GST) tax returns and the time and manner for filing such returns.[5] Generally, the person liable for the tax must file the return. The form of return is governed by the generation-skipping transfer involved.

• ***Direct Skips***

In the case of a lifetime direct skip, the donor is required to file Form 709 (United States Gift (and Generation-Skipping Transfer) Tax Return).

If the direct skip occurs at death, the executor must file the return unless the direct skip is from a trust or with respect to property that continues to be held in trust.[6] The executor must file Form 706 (United States Estate (and Generation-Skipping Transfer) Tax Return) (Rev. Aug. 2004) or Form 706-NA (United States Estate (and Generation-Skipping Transfer) Tax Return) (Rev. Jan. 2003). The GST

---

[1] Code Sec. 2603(a).

[2] Code Sec. 2603(b).

[3] Code Sec. 2661.

[4] *K. O'Neal II*, 102 TC 666, CCH Dec. 49,810.

[5] Reg. §26.2662-1.

[6] Reg. §26.2662-1(c)(1)(iv) and Reg. §26.2662-1(c)(1)(v).

tax payable by the estate is computed on Schedule R (Generation-Skipping Transfer Tax) of Form 706.

If a direct skip occurring at death is payable from a trust, the trustee is liable for the GST tax.[7] The executor must use Schedule R-1 (Generation-Skipping Transfer Tax, Direct Skips From a Trust, Payment Voucher) of Form 706 to notify the trustee that such a tax is due. Filled-in Schedule R appears at ¶3130, and Schedule R-1 appears at ¶3180. Instructions for completing these forms appear at ¶2473.

A special rule applies to direct skips occurring at death with respect to property held in a "trust arrangement."[8]

For decedents dying on or after June 24, 1996, if the total value of the property involved in direct skips with respect to the trustee of that trust arrangement is less than $250,000, the executor is liable for the GST tax on the direct skip and is required to file Form 706 or Form 706-NA (and not Schedule R-1 of Form 706).[9] For decedents dying before June 24, 1996, the executor is liable for the tax and required to file Form 706 or 706-NA if the property involved in the direct skip with respect to the trustee of the trust arrangement is, in the aggregate, less than $100,000.[10] In any event, the executor who is subject to such liability may recover the tax attributable to the transfer from the trustee of the trust arrangement if the property continues in trust or from the recipient of the property if the property is distributed.[11] The limits on the personal liability of a trustee are described at ¶2465.

• *Taxable Distributions*

The distributee is liable for the GST tax in the case of a taxable distribution and must file Form 706-GS(D) (Generation-Skipping Transfer Tax Return for Distributions) (Rev. Jan. 2003). The trustee of the trust involved in a taxable distribution must file Form 706-GS(D-1) (Notification of Distribution From a Generation-Skipping Trust) (Rev. Jan. 2003). The trustee must send a copy of this form to each distributee. Filled-in Forms 706-GS(D) and 706-GS(D-1) appear in the Appendix at ¶3230 and ¶3240, respectively. Instructions for completing each of these forms appear at ¶2479.

• *Taxable Terminations*

The trustee is liable for the GST tax in the case of a taxable termination and is required to file Form 706-GS(T) (Generation-Skipping Transfer Tax Return for Terminations) (Rev. Jan. 2003). A filled-in Form 706-GS(T) appears in the Appendix at ¶3250; instructions for filling in the form appear at ¶2487.

¶2473 Reporting Direct Skips Occurring at Death

Direct skips occurring at death are reported on Form 706 (United States Estate (and Generation-Skipping Transfer) Tax Return).

The entire estate and generation-skipping transfer (GST) tax must be paid on the due date of the return (within nine months of the decedent's date of death), unless an extension of time to pay has been granted.[12]

---

[7] Reg. §26.2662-1(c)(1)(iv).

[8] Reg. §26.2662-1(c)(2)(ii) states that the term "trust arrangement" includes any arrangement (other than an estate) which, although not an explicit trust, has the same effect as an explicit trust.

[9] Reg. §26.2662-1(c)(2)(iii).

[10] Reg. §26.2662-1(c)(2)(iv).

[11] Reg. §26.2662-1(c)(2)(v).

[12] Instructions for Form 706 (Rev. Aug. 2004), p. 2.

The estate tax is imposed on the value of the entire taxable estate regardless of who the distributees are. The GST tax is imposed on the value of property interests that actually pass to skip persons.

To report direct skips on Form 706, complete Schedules A through I in order to determine the property interests that are includible in the gross estate. Determine who the skip persons are. Then determine which skip persons are transferees of interests in property. Following these determinations, the direct skips to be reported must be divided between Schedule R (Generation-Skipping Transfer Tax) and Schedule R-1 (Generation-Skipping Transfer Tax), and these schedules must then be completed.[13]

Unless the Form 706 Instructions specifically provide otherwise, all generation-skipping transfers are reported on Schedule R.[14] For a direct skip to be reportable on Schedule R-1, the trust must be includible in the decedent's gross estate. The trustee, not the estate, is liable for the tax on direct skips from a trust. Schedule R-1 is to be used by the executor to notify the trustee that such a tax is due.

The estate tax value of the property interests subject to the direct skips are entered on Schedules R and R-1. If alternate valuation or special use valuation has been elected, those values must be entered on Schedules R and R-1. The allocation of the $1.5 million GST tax exemption applicable for 2004 and 2005 is calculated using lines 4, 5, and 6 in part 1 of Schedule R after completing parts 2 and 3 of Schedule R, and Schedule R-1.

Part 2 of Schedule R is used to compute the GST tax on direct skips in which the property interests transferred bear the GST tax on the transfers.[15] The tax on transfers in which the property interests transferred do not bear the GST tax on the transfers is reported on part 3.

¶ 2479 Reporting Distributions

Form 706-GS(D-1) (Notification of Distribution From a Generation-Skipping Trust) and Form 706-GS(D) (Generation-Skipping Transfer Tax Return for Distributions) must be filed for trust distributions that are subject to the generation-skipping transfer (GST) tax (see ¶ 3240 and ¶ 3230, respectively).

• ***Form 706-GS(D-1)***

Form 706-GS(D-1) is used by the trustee of a generation-skipping trust to report taxable distributions and to provide skip person distributees (see ¶ 2435) with information needed to compute the GST tax on the distribution. The form has two copies: Copy A (to be filed with the IRS) and Copy B (to be sent to the skip person distributee).

When to file. Form 706-GS(D-1) must be filed with the IRS (Copy A), and sent to the distributee (Copy B) no later than April 15 of the year following the calendar year in which the distributions were made.[16]

The distributee is to report on part II (Distributions) of Form 706-GS(D) all taxable distributions occurring in the year having an inclusion ratio greater than zero.

---

[13] Instructions for Form 706 (Rev. Aug. 2004), p. 23.

[14] Instructions for Form 706 (Rev. Aug. 2004), p. 23.

[15] Instructions for Form 706 (Rev. Aug. 2004), p. 25.

[16] Reg. § 26.2662-1(d).

Nonexplicit trusts. An arrangement that has substantially the same effect as a trust is treated as a trust for purposes of the GST tax even though it is not an explicit trust. Arrangements treated as nonexplicit trusts include insurance and annuity contracts, life estates, remainders, and estates for years. Decedents' estates are not classified as nonexplicit trusts for purposes of Form 706-GS(D-1).

The person in actual or constructive possession of the property held in a nonexplicit trust is considered to be the trustee and is liable for filing Form 706-GS(D-1).[17]

Separate trusts. Portions of a single trust must be treated as separate trusts for purposes of Form 706-GS(D-1) where:

(1) there are portions of the trust that are attributable to transfers from different transferors; or

(2) there are substantially separate and independent shares of different trust beneficiaries.[18]

• *Form 706-GS(D-1)—Line-by-Line Instructions*

Part I, General Instructions. The identifying number of the skip person distributee (whether an individual or a trust) is entered on line 1a of part I (General Information) of Form 706-GS(D-1) (see ¶3240). Enter the social security number of the individual distributee on line 1a; if the skip person distributee is a trust, the trust's employer identification number (EIN) is entered on line 1a. Enter the skip person distributee's name, address, and ZIP code on line 1b.

The employer identification number of the trust from which the distribution was made is entered on line 2a, and the trust's name, address, and ZIP code are entered on line 2b.

Part II, Distributions. Report all distributions from any given trust to a single skip person distributee during the calendar year on part II. The following information is entered under the columns of line 3 for each distribution:

(Column a) Item number: Consecutive numbers should be assigned to each distribution made during the year. Properties having different inclusion ratios are listed separately. Properties having the same inclusion ratio may be included under a single item number, even if they were distributed at different times.

(Column b) Description of property: Each parcel of real estate should be described in enough detail so that it may be located for inspection and valuation. If the parcel is improved, the improvements should be described. Any personal property distributed must be described in enough detail that the IRS can ascertain its value.

Stocks: For stocks, the following information should be supplied:

— Number of shares

— Classification of stock: common or preferred

— Issue

— Par value (where needed for valuation)

— Price per share

— Exact name of corporation

— Principal exchange upon which the stock is sold

[17] Instructions for Form 706-GS(D-1) (Rev. Jan. 2003), p. 1.

[18] Instructions for Form 706-GS(D-1) (Rev. Jan. 2003), p. 1.

— CUSIP number, if available

Bonds: For bonds, the following information should be supplied:

— Quantity and denomination

— Name of obligor

— Date of maturity

— Principal exchange upon which the bond is listed

— Interest rate

— Interest due date

— CUSIP number, if available

If a stock or bond is not listed on an exchange, the company's principal business office should be listed.

(Column c) Date of distribution: The trustee must disclose the date of distribution.

(Column d) Inclusion ratio: The trustee must provide an inclusion ratio (see ¶2461) for every distribution.

(Column e) Value: The trustee's responsibility with respect to valuing the property depends on the type of the property distributed. The trustee is required to provide the value of property having an objectively identifiable value, such as cash, stocks, or bonds. For other property, the trustee may provide a value but is only required to give the distributee all the information the trustee has that will help the distributee to determine the value of the distribution.

(Column f) Tentative transfer: The amount of the tentative transfer is the value, entered in column e, multiplied by the inclusion ratio, entered in column d.

Part III, Trust Information. Only Copy A (which goes to the IRS) contains part III, Trust Information, which requires the trustee to answer the questions on lines 4 through 7.

If the trust for which the Form 706-GS(D-1) is filed is a nonexplicit trust, the trustee filing the form must check the box on line 4 and attach a statement describing the trust arrangement that is substantially similar to an explicit trust.

If property has been contributed to the trust since the last Form 706-GS(T) (Generation-Skipping Transfer Tax Return For Terminations) or 706-GS(D-1) was filed, a schedule must be attached showing how the inclusion ratio was calculated (line 5).

Line 6 questions whether any contributions were made to the trust since the last Form 706-GS(T) or 706-GS(D-1) was filed that were not included in calculating the trust's inclusion ratio. If the answer is "Yes," a statement explaining why the contribution was not included must be attached.

If any exemption has been allocated to the trust by reason of the deemed allocation rules, this is indicated on line 7.

Signature required. Copy A of Form 706-GS(D-1) must be signed by the trustee or an authorized representative.

IRS Service Center. On Copy B of Form 706-GS(D-1), the copy sent to the skip person distributee, the trustee must enter the name and address of the IRS Service Center where the distributee should report the distribution on Form 706-GS(D). If the trust settlor was a resident U.S. citizen or resident alien, the form should be sent to the Internal Revenue Service Center at Cincinnati, OH 45999. If a private delivery service is used for the returns of U.S. residents, the return should be sent to the IRS at 201 W. Rivercenter Blvd., Covington, KY 41011. Returns of nonresident U.S. citizens or aliens should be sent to the Internal Revenue Service Center at Philadelphia, PA 19255, USA.[19] (A listing of the Internal Revenue Service Centers for returns filed before January 1, 2001, is reproduced at ¶2850.)

• *Form 706-GS(D)*

Form 706-GS(D) (see ¶3230) generally must be filed with respect to taxable trust distributions (see ¶2471).

The form is filed by the skip person (see ¶2435) recipients of the trust distributions. In preparing Form 706-GS(D), trust distributees will have to consult the applicable portions of the copy of the completed Form 706-GS(D-1) that the trustee of the generation-skipping trust is required to submit to them.

Time and place of filing. Form 706-GS(D) generally must be filed no later than April 15 of the year following the calendar year in which the distributions were made. Form 706-GS(D) should be filed at the IRS Service Center that the trustee has included at the bottom of Copy B, Form 706-GS(D-1), the distributee's copy (see the heading "IRS Service Center", above).[20]

• *Form 706-GS(D)—Line-by-Line Instructions*

Part I, General Information. The name of the skip person distributee (whether an individual or a trust) is entered on line 1a of part I, General Information, Form 706-GS(D). If the skip person distributee is an individual, that individual's Social Security number is entered on line 1b; if the skip person distributee is a trust, the trust's employer identification number (EIN) is entered on line 1c. In no case should numbers appear on both lines 1b and 1c.

The name and title of the person filing the return is entered on line 2a, but only if different from the name entered on line 1a. The trustee's name should be entered here if the skip person distributee is a trust. If the skip person distributee is a minor, or an adult under a disability that precludes the distributee from filing the return, the name of the person who is legally responsible for conducting the distributee's affairs, such as a parent or guardian, should be entered on line 2a. The parent's or guardian's title or relationship to the distributee should be included.

The address of the distributee or person filing the return is entered on line 2b.

Part II, Distributions. All taxable distributions with inclusion ratios greater than zero that the distributee received during the year are reported on part II of Form 706-GS(D). If additional space is required, the distributee should attach an additional sheet of the same size and use the same format that is used in part II to report any additional distributions.

(Column a) Trust EIN: The employer identification number of the distributing trust, from line 2a, Form 706-GS(D-1), is entered in column a of part II.

(Column b) Item number: The same item number that was used for the corresponding distribution on Form 706-GS(D-1), line 3, column a, should be

---

[19] Instructions for Form 706-GS(D-1) (Rev. Jan. 2003), p. 1.

[20] Instructions for Form 706-GS(D) (Rev. Jan. 2003), p. 1.

entered in column b. If the distributee receives distributions from more than one trust, the same item number may have to be repeated.

(Column c) Amount of transfer: The amount of transfer will usually be entered from line 3, column f, of Form 706-GS(D-1), unless the trustee has not entered any amount there or the distributee disagrees with the amount that the trustee has entered. If the distributee and the trustee disagree about the amount of the tentative transfer, the distributee should attach a statement to Form 706-GS(D) showing what the distributee considers the correct amounts and how they were computed.

The total tentative transfers from part II and from any continuation sheet should be entered on line 3 of part II. The distributee should also attach to Form 706-GS(D) a copy of each Form 706-GS(D-1) received during the year.

Part III, Tax Computation. Enter the amount of total transfers on line 3 of part II. Adjusted allowable expenses are deducted from the line 3 amount, and the resulting amount entered on line 5 which appears in part III. For purposes of this deduction, expenses incurred in connection with the preparation of Form 706-GS(D), or any other expenses incurred in connection with the determination, collection, or refund of the GST tax reported on the return are totalled and multiplied by the inclusion ratio. The resulting product is the amount of the "adjusted allowable expenses." A distributee who has more than one inclusion ratio to report on part II must prorate the total expense among them, based on the relative value of each distribution.

An expense item may be included in the total of line 4 allowable expenses even if it has not been paid at the time the return is filed, provided that the amount of the expense is clearly ascertainable at that time. If an additional allowable expense is incurred after Form 706-GS(D) is filed, a refund should be claimed on Form 843 (Claim for Refund and Request for Abatement) (Rev. Nov. 2002).[21]

A credit for state GST taxes paid may be claimed on line 8 if the taxable distribution occurred at the same time as, and as a result of, the death of an individual and the distribution is reported on the same Form 706-GS(D). However, the credit for the state GST tax paid is limited to a maximum of five percent of the federal gross GST tax reported on line 7.

Signature required. Form 706-GS(D) must be signed by the distributee or by the distributee's authorized representative.

¶ 2487 Reporting Terminations

Generation-skipping terminations are reported on Form 706-GS(T) (Generation-Skipping Transfer Tax Return for Terminations) (see ¶2471). The form is used by a trustee to compute and report the generation-skipping transfer (GST) tax due with respect to certain trust terminations (see ¶2433).

Form 706-GS(T) must be filed at the IRS Service Center for the state where an estate or gift tax is filed, no later than April 15 of the year following the calendar year in which the termination occurred.

---

[21] Instructions for Form 706-GS(D) (Rev. Jan. 2003), p. 2.

• *Nonexplicit Trust*

An arrangement that has substantially the same effect as a trust is treated as a trust for purposes of the GST tax even though it is not an explicit trust. Arrangements treated as nonexplicit trusts include insurance and annuity contracts, life estates, remainders, and estates for years. Decedents' estates are not classified as nonexplicit trusts for purposes of Form 706-GS(T) (see ¶2439). The person in actual or constructive possession of the property held in a nonexplicit trust is considered to be the trustee and is responsible for filing Form 706-GS.[22]

• *Separate Trusts*

Portions of a single trust must be treated as separate trusts for purposes of Form 706-GS(T) when:

(1) portions of the trust are attributable to transfers from different transferors; or

(2) substantially separate and independent shares are for different trust beneficiaries.

If a single trust is treated as separate trusts under the above rules, a single Form 706-GS(T) is filed, but a separate Schedule A (Taxable Terminations) must be filed with respect to each such separate trust.

• *Medical and Educational Exclusions*

Form 706-GS(T) need not be filed if the termination is not a generation-skipping transfer by reason of the gift tax exclusion for amounts paid for medical or educational expenses. This occurs if the property was distributed and used for medical or educational expenses of the transferee and would not have been subject to gift tax if the transfer had been made during an individual's lifetime.

• *Form 706-GS(T)—Line-by-Line Instructions*

The Form 706-GS(T) Instructions (Rev. Jan. 2003) (see ¶3250) indicate that the form is to be filled out in the following order: (1) parts I and II; (2) Schedule A (through line 4); (3) Schedule B(1) (General Trust Debts, Expenses, and Taxes), and Schedule B(2) (Specific Termination-Related Debts, Expenses, and Taxes); (4) Schedule A (lines 5 through 14); and (5) part III.

Part I, General Information. Enter the name of the trust and the trust's employer identification number (EIN) on lines 1a and 1b of part I, General Information, of Form 706-GS(T). Nonexplicit trusts, as well as explicit trusts, must have an EIN. The name and the address of the trustee (or the person who is considered to be the trustee under the nonexplicit trust rules) are entered on lines 2a and 2b.

Part II, Trust Information. The trustee is required to answer the questions on lines 3 through 8 of part II.

Line 3 questions whether any exemption has been allocated to the trust by reason of the deemed allocation rules of Code Sec. 2632 (see ¶2455). If the answer is "Yes," the allocation must be described on an attachment to Schedule A, line 7, showing how the inclusion ratio (see ¶2461) was calculated.

---

[22] Instructions for Form 706-GS(T) (Rev. Jan. 2003), p. 1.

If property has been contributed to the trust since the last Form 706-GS(T) or 706-GS(D-1) was filed, a schedule showing how the inclusion ratio was calculated should be attached (line 4).

If terminations occurred that were not reported because of payments relating to medical and educational exclusions or prior payment of the GST tax, check the "Yes" box on line 5, and attach a statement describing the termination.

Line 6 asks whether any contributions were made to the trust that were not included in calculating the trust's inclusion ratio. If the answer is "Yes," a statement explaining why the contribution was not included must be attached.

If the special qualified terminable interest property election (known as a "reverse QTIP" election) with respect to Code Sec. 2652(a)(3) has been made for the trust, this is indicated on line 7.

If the trust to which the Form 706-GS(T) is filed is a nonexplicit trust, check the box on line 8, and attach a statement describing the trust arrangement that makes it substantially similar to an explicit trust.

Schedule A. Separate copies of Schedule A will have to be filed for each terminating interest of a single trust that has a different inclusion ratio. Under line 1 are listed the names of the skip persons and their respective Social Security numbers, EINs, and the item number from line 4 of Schedule A in which the interest is held. The terminating power or interest is described in the space provided at line 2. If the trustee is reporting separate trusts, the reason for treating parts of the trust as separate trusts should be included here.

If the trustee wishes to elect alternate valuation, the election is made on line 3 of Schedule A.

The following information must be entered under the columns of line 4 for each taxable termination:

(Column a) Item number: All property having the same termination date, valuation date, and unit price may be combined under the same item number. Otherwise, a separate item number should be assigned to each article of property.

(Column b) Description of property subject to termination: Each parcel of real estate should be described in enough detail so that it may be located for inspection and valuation. If the parcel is improved, the improvements should be described. Personal property should be described in enough detail so that the IRS can ascertain its value.

Stocks: For stocks, the following information should be supplied:

— Number of shares

— Classification of stock: common or preferred

— Issue

— Par value (where needed for valuation)

— Price per share

— Exact name of corporation

— Principal exchange upon which stock is sold

— CUSIP number, if available

Bonds: For bonds, the following information should be supplied:

— Quantity and denomination

— Name of obligor
— Date of maturity
— Principal exchange, if listed on an exchange
— Interest rate
— Interest due date
— CUSIP number, if available

If a stock or bond is not listed on an exchange, the company's principal business office should be listed.

(Column c) Date of termination: The trustee must disclose the date of termination.

(Column d) Valuation date: Unless the trustee elected the alternate valuation date, this date should be the same as the termination date.

(Column e) Value: The value of property to be reported on Schedule A should be entered, reduced by the amount of any consideration that was provided by the skip person. An explanation of how the values were determined should be included, along with copies of any appraisals.

Deductible expenses. In determining the taxable amount for a taxable termination, certain expenses (under rules generally similar to those discussed at ¶780) may be deducted from the value of the property subject to the termination. These expenses are deducted on Schedule B(1) or Schedule B(2).

Schedule B(1). Enter the item number, description and amount of expenses that are related to the entire trust in columns a, b, and c, respectively, of Schedule B(1). In addition to a description of the nature of the expenses listed in column b, the name and address of the persons to whom the expenses were paid should be included.

The percentage of the expenses allocable to the property involved in the termination is to be entered on line 2. This percentage is determined by way of a two-step computation, as follows:

(1) the value of the interest that was terminated is divided by the total value of the trust at the time of the termination; and

(2) the amount determined under (1), above, is to be multiplied by a fraction, the numerator of which is the number of days in the year through the date of the termination, and the denominator of which is the total number of days in the year, or, if the entire trust was terminated during the year, the total number of days the trust was in existence during the year.

Schedule B(2). The item number, description, and amount of expenses that are related solely to the interest that has terminated are entered in columns a, b, and c, respectively, of Schedule B(2). If the expense entered relates to more property than is involved in the termination, but less than the entire trust, only the amount attributable to the property involved in the termination is to be entered in column c. This amount is determined by multiplying the total expense by a fraction, the numerator of which is the value of the property involved in the termination and to which the expense pertains, and the denominator of which is the total value of the property to which the expense pertains.

Schedule A, lines 5–14. The amount of the total deductions applicable to the Schedule A (carried over from the corresponding Schedule B, line 5) is entered on line 5. The inclusion ratio (see ¶2461) must be calculated with respect to every termination, and entered on line 7. All terminations, or any parts of a single termination that have different inclusion ratios must be shown on a separate Schedule A. The product of the amount shown on line 7 (inclusion ratio) and the maximum federal estate tax rate shown (line 8) is the applicable rate entered on line 9. That applicable rate is then multiplied by the taxable amount (line 6) to obtain the gross GST tax to be entered on line 10.

If the taxable termination occurs at the same time as, and as a result of, the death of an individual, the trustee may claim a credit for any state-imposed GST tax with regard to property that was also included as a termination reported on Form 706-GS(T). If applicable, enter this amount on line 11, although the allowable credit (line 13) is limited to the greater of the actual state GST taxes paid, and five percent of the gross GST tax computed on line 12. The net federal GST tax with respect to the termination reported on the Schedule A is computed by subtracting the amount on line 13 from the amount on line 10. This amount is entered on line 14 (and, in turn, entered also on line 9a, part III of Form 706-GS(T)).

Signature required. Form 706-GS(T) must be signed by the trustee or by his or her authorized representative.

SPECIAL VALUATION RULES

Chapter 42

ESTATE FREEZES

¶ 2500 Special Valuation Rules for Estate Freezes

The special valuation rules of Code Sec. 2701 through Code Sec. 2704 were enacted to prevent the transfer tax avoidance achieved by certain transfers to younger generations. In such transfers, the value of the transferred interest was determined by subtracting the value of the retained interest from the total value of the property. The value of the retained interest was overstated in order to reduce the value of the transferred interest and, consequently, the amount of the taxable gift.

In general, the special valuation rules preclude the undervaluation of gifts by providing rules for valuing retained interests. Code Sec. 2701 provides special rules for determining the amount of a gift when an individual transfers an equity interest in a corporation or a partnership to a family member while retaining an interest in the entity (see ¶2505). Code Sec. 2702 provides rules for determining the amount of a gift when an individual makes a transfer in trust to or for the benefit of a family member while retaining an interest in the trust (see ¶2550). Code Sec. 2703 disregards certain rights and restrictions for transfer tax valuation purposes (see ¶2580). Code Sec. 2704 forestalls the use of lapsing rights and restrictions to reduce transfer taxes (see ¶2590).

¶ 2505 Function of Code Sec. 2701

The classic estate freeze of a closely held business transferred the business's future appreciation to a younger generation in a manner that reduced or eliminated the transferor's gift tax cost.

> *Example (1):* Ben Thompson owns all of the common stock in Famco, which is valued at $50,000. As a result of a recapitalization, Ben receives common and preferred noncumulative voting stock. Because the preferred stock has a par value approximating the corporation's liquidation value and confers a right to put the stock at par value, Ben values the preferred stock

at $50,000. He then gives the common stock to his son, Chuck, and assigns no value to the gift. At Ben's death, the value of the preferred stock included in his gross estate is $50,000, but the value of Chuck's common stock has appreciated to $200,000.

Code Sec. 2701 addresses estate freezes by revaluing the older generation's retained interests. By assigning zero value or a lower value to the retained interest and using the subtraction method to value the gift, a higher value is assigned to the gifted interest for gift tax purposes. When the transferor dies, a special valuation adjustment may apply to lower the transferor's estate tax. Post-transfer appreciation, however, is not includible in the transferor's estate.

Example (2): Assume the same facts as in Example (1), except that Code Sec. 2701 applies. Ben's retained preferred stock is valued at zero, and the gift of common stock to Chuck is valued at $50,000. The $50,000 value of the preferred stock included in Ben's gross estate may be offset by a special valuation adjustment.

¶ 2510 Application of Code Sec. 2701

The Code Sec. 2701 valuation rules apply when (1) an interest in a corporation or a partnership is "transferred" to a "member of the family" of the transferor, and (2) the transferor or an "applicable family member" retains an "applicable retained interest."[1]

Members of the transferor's family. Members of the family of the transferor are generally members of the younger generation and include:

(1) the transferor's spouse;

(2) a lineal descendant of the transferor or the transferor's spouse; and

(3) the spouse of any such descendant.[2]

Applicable family members. Applicable family members are generally members of the older generation and include:

(1) the transferor's spouse;

(2) any ancestor of the transferor or the transferor's spouse; and

(3) the spouse of any such ancestor.[3]

• *Code Sec. 2701 Transfers*

The following types of transactions are transfers for purposes of Code Sec. 2701:

(1) transactions in which full and adequate consideration is given, but such consideration is less than the value of the transferred interest as determined under Code Sec. 2701 (such transactions would not otherwise be treated as taxable gifts under the gift tax provisions);[4]

(2) capital contributions to a new or existing entity;[5]

(3) changes in capital structure, including redemptions and recapitalizations, in which (a) the transferor or an applicable family member receives an applicable retained interest, (b) the transferor or applicable family member who holds an applicable retained interest before the transaction surrenders a junior equity interest and receives property other than an applicable

---

[1] Code Sec. 2701(a)(1); Reg. §25.2701-1(a)(1).

[2] Code Sec. 2701(e)(1); Reg. §25.2701-1(d)(1).

[3] Code Sec. 2701(e)(2); Reg. §25.2701-1(d)(2).

[4] Reg. §25.2701-1(b)(1).

[5] Reg. §25.2701-1(b)(2)(i)(A).

retained interest, or (c) the transferor or applicable family member who holds an applicable retained interest before the transaction surrenders an equity interest other than a junior interest and the fair market value of the applicable retained interest is increased;[6] and

(4) terminations of an indirect holding in an entity through a grantor trust, or, if through another type of trust, then to the extent the value of the indirectly held interest would have been included in the indirect holder's gross estate if the indirect holder died immediately prior to the termination.[7]

The following transactions are not treated as Code Sec. 2701 transfers:

(1) capital structure transactions that do not substantially change the interests held by the transferor, applicable family members, and members of the transferor's family (for example, an exchange of nonvoting common stock for common stock with nonvoting lapsing rights);

(2) the shift of rights resulting from the execution of a qualified disclaimer; and

(3) the shift of rights resulting from the exercise, release, or lapse of a power of appointment (other than a general power under Code Sec. 2514) except to the extent that such exercise, release, or lapse would constitute a transfer under the gift tax provisions.[8]

• *Applicable Retained Interests*

An applicable retained interest is either an extraordinary payment right or a distribution right in a family-controlled entity.[9]

Extraordinary payment rights include any put, call, or conversion right, any right to compel liquidation, or any similar right, the exercise or nonexercise of which affects the value of the transferred interest.[10] Extraordinary payment rights do not include (1) mandatory payment rights, (2) liquidation participation rights, (3) rights to Code Sec. 707(c) guaranteed payments, or (4) nonlapsing conversion rights.[11]

A distribution right is the right to receive distributions with respect to an equity interest.[12] Distribution rights do not include (1) rights to receive distributions with respect to an interest that is of the same class as, or junior to, the transferred interest, (2) extraordinary payment rights, (3) mandatory payment rights, (4) liquidation participation rights, (5) rights to Code Sec. 707(c) guaranteed payments, or (6) nonlapsing conversion rights.[13]

For a distribution right to be considered an applicable retained interest, the entity must be family controlled.[14] Such control exists if at least 50 percent of the total voting power or fair market value of the equity interests in a corporation (or at least 50 percent of the capital or profits interests in a partnership) are owned by the transferor, applicable family members, or any lineal descendants of the transferor or the transferor's spouse. In the case of a limited partnership, control means the holding of any interest as a general partner.[15]

---

[6] Reg. § 25.2701-1(b)(2)(i)(B).
[7] Reg. § 25.2701-1(b)(2)(i)(C).
[8] Reg. § 25.2701-1(b)(3).
[9] Code Sec. 2701(b)(1).
[10] Code Sec. 2701(c)(2)(A); Reg. § 25.2701-2(b)(2).
[11] Reg. § 25.2701-2(b)(4).
[12] Code Sec. 2701(c)(1)(A).
[13] Reg. § 25.2701-2(b)(3) -(4).
[14] Code Sec. 2701(b)(1)(A).
[15] Code Sec. 2701(b)(2); Reg. § 25.2701-2(b)(5).

• *Exceptions to Application of Code Sec. 2701*

Code Sec. 2701 does not apply under the following circumstances:

(1) market quotations on an established securities market are readily available for the value of an applicable retained interest or for the transferred interest;

(2) the retained interest is of the same class as the transferred interest;

(3) the rights in the retained interest are proportionally the same as all the rights in the transferred interest, without regard to nonlapsing differences in voting power (or, for a partnership, nonlapsing differences with respect to management and limitations on liability);[16] or

(4) the transfer results in a proportionate reduction of each class of equity interest held by the transferor and all applicable family members in the aggregate immediately before the transfer.[17]

For purposes of (3), above, a right that lapses by reason of federal or state law is treated as a nonlapsing right unless the IRS issues a contrary regulation or ruling.[18] Thus, for example, the IRS has ruled that the interest of a general partner who made a gift of limited partnership interests while retaining an interest as a general partner was not treated as an applicable retained interest since the retained rights were identical to the rights of the interest transferred except for nonlapsing differences with respect to management and limitations on liability.[19]

¶ 2515 Valuation of Applicable Retained Interests

Extraordinary payment rights are valued at zero. Distribution rights are also valued at zero unless they are qualified payment rights. (See ¶2510, "Applicable Retained Interests", for definitions of extraordinary payment rights and distribution rights.) If a qualified payment right exists in conjunction with one or more extraordinary payment rights, it is presumed that each extraordinary payment right is exercised in a way that results in the lowest value for all such rights.[20] If an applicable retained interest does not contain rights that are valued at zero or under the "lower of" rule, the retained interest is valued at its fair market value.[21]

• *Qualified Payments*

Qualified payments include the following:

(1) dividends payable on a periodic basis (at least annually) with respect to any cumulative preferred stock to the extent such dividends are determined at a fixed rate;

(2) other cumulative distributions payable on a periodic basis (at least annually) with respect to an equity interest to the extent they are determined at a fixed rate or as a fixed amount; and

(3) any distribution rights that the transferor has elected (or partially elected) to treat as qualified payments, provided that the amounts and times of payment specified in the election do not exceed the distributions authorized under the instrument.[22]

---

16 Code Sec. 2701(a)(2); Reg. §25.2701-1(c)(1)-(3).

17 Reg. §25.2701-1(c)(4).

18 Reg. §25.2701-1(c)(3).

19 IRS Letter Ruling 9415007 (Jan. 12, 1994).

20 Code Sec. 2701(a)(3).

21 Reg. §25.2701-2(a)(4).

22 Code Sec. 2701(c)(3); Reg. §25.2701-2(b)(6).

The IRS concluded that prepayment of annual distribution payments in accordance with the operating agreement of a limited liability company (LLC) constituted a qualified payment for purposes of Code Sec. 2701.[23] Under the operating agreement, which contemplated compliance with the special valuation rules, preferred LLC members were entitled to receive a specified percentage of that member's initial value in the entity. The prepayment was deemed to be a cumulative distribution payable on a periodic basis.[24]

A payment rate is determined at a fixed rate if it bears a fixed relationship to a specified market interest rate.

A transferor holding a qualified payment right may elect (or partially elect) to treat all rights of the same class as not being qualified payment rights.[25]

> ***Example:*** Betty Edson owns all of the common and preferred stock in Famco. Edson has the right to put all 200 shares of preferred stock having an annual cumulative dividend of $20 per share to Famco for $180,000. Assuming that the fair market value of Famco is $300,000 and the value of the cumulative dividend is $200,000, she transfers the common stock to her child and retains the preferred. Because Edson holds an extraordinary payment right (the put right) in conjunction with a qualified payment right (the right to cumulative dividends), the "lower of" rule applies and it is assumed that the put will be exercised immediately. The preferred stock is valued at $180,000 (lower of $180,000 or $200,000). Accordingly, the resulting gift is $120,000 ($300,000 minus $180,000). If Edson's put right did not exist, the applicable retained interest would consist only of a qualified payment right. Accordingly, the value of the preferred stock would be $200,000 and the resulting gift would be $100,000.

¶ 2520 Determination of Amount of Gift

After the amount of the retained interest has been determined, the subtraction method is used to determine the amount of the gift.[26] In general, the values of all family-held senior equity interests are subtracted from the fair market value of all family-held interests in the entity as determined immediately before the transfer. Although the values of senior equity interests are determined under the rules of Code Sec. 2701 if they are held by the transferor and applicable family members, other family- held senior equity interests are valued at their fair market value. The resulting balance is allocated among the transferred interests and other family-held junior interests. Certain discounts and other reductions are allowed under appropriate circumstances.[27] A 10-percent minimum value rule also applies to the valuation of gifts of junior equity interests.[28]

Family-held interests. Family-held interests are interests held directly or indirectly by the transferor, applicable family members, and any lineal descendants of the parents of the transferor or the transferor's spouse.[29]

Senior equity interests. Senior equity interests are interests that carry a right to distributions of income or capital that is preferred in comparison to the rights of the transferred interest.[30]

---

[23] IRS Letter Ruling 200114004 (Nov. 30, 2000).

[24] Code Sec. 2701(c)(3); Reg. § 25.2701-2(b)(6)(9)(B).

[25] Code Sec. 2701(c)(3)(C)(i); Reg. § 25.2701-2(c).

[26] Reg. § 25.2701-3.

[27] Reg. § 25.2701-3(a)(1).

[28] Code Sec. 2701(a)(4); Reg. § 25.2701-3(c).

[29] Reg. § 25.2701-3(a)(2)(i).

[30] Reg. § 25.2701-3(a)(2)(ii).

Junior (subordinate) equity interests. Junior equity interests are equity interests that are junior to the applicable retained interest.[31]

• *Four-Step Subtraction Method*

The amount of the gift is determined in the following four steps:

(1) **Value family-held interests.** In general, determine the value of all family-held equity interests in the entity immediately after the transfer (under the assumption that they are held by one individual). In the case of a contribution to capital, determine the fair market value of the contribution.

(2) **Subtract the value of senior equity interests.** Subtract from the amount determined in Step (1), (a) the sum of the fair market value of all family-held senior equity interests (other than applicable retained interests held by the transferor or applicable family members) *plus* the fair market value of any family-held interests of the same class or a junior class to transferred interests held by persons other than the transferor, applicable family members, and members of the transferor's family, and (b) the value of all applicable retained interests held by the transferor or applicable family members, as adjusted (see below).

If the value in Step (1) was determined under the special rule for contributions to capital, the value of any applicable retained interest received in exchange for the contribution must be subtracted from that value.

Adjustment. The percentage of any class of applicable retained interest held by the transferor and applicable family members that exceeds the "family interest percentage" is treated as a family-held interest that is not held by the transferor or an applicable family member. The family interest percentage is the highest ownership percentage (based on relative fair market values) of family-held interests in any class of junior equity interest or all junior equity interests, valued in the aggregate.

(3) **Allocate the remaining value.** The amount remaining after Step (2) is allocated among the transferred interests and the other junior equity interests held by the transferor, applicable family members, and members of the transferor's family. If there is more than one class of family-held junior equity interests, the allocation begins with the most senior class of junior equity interests in a manner that most fairly approximates their value if all the rights valued at zero did not exist. Any amount not appropriately allocated in this manner is allocated to the interests in proportion to their fair market values without regard to Code Sec. 2701.

(4) **Determine the amount of the gift.** The amount allocated to the transferred interests in Step (3) is reduced to make such of the following adjustments as are applicable:

(a) *Reduction for minority or similar discounts.* The amount of the gift is reduced by the excess, if any, of (1) a pro rata portion of the fair market value of the family-held interests of the same class (determined as if all voting rights conferred by family-held equity interests were held by one person), over (2) the value of the transferred interest (determined without regard to Code Sec. 2701).

(b) *Reduction for transfers with retained interest.* The amount of the gift is reduced by the amount, if any, of the reduction required under Code Sec. 2702 to reflect the value of a retained interest (see ¶2550).

---

[31] Reg. §25.2701-3(a)(2)(iii).

(c) *Reduction for consideration.* The amount of the gift is reduced up to the amount of the gift determined without regard to Code Sec. 2701 by the amount, if any, of consideration received by the transferor. Consideration in the form of an applicable retained interest is determined under Code Sec. 2701, except that in the case of a contribution to capital, the value of such an interest is zero.[32]

• ***Minimum Value Rule***

In addition to the four-step subtraction method, Code Sec. 2701 applies a minimum value rule in determining the amount of a gift. Under this rule, the value of a junior equity interest cannot be less than its pro rata portion of 10 percent of the sum of:

(1) the total value of all equity interests in the entity; and

(2) the total amount of any indebtedness the entity owes to the transferor and applicable family members.[33]

Example: Famco has 1,000 shares of nonvoting common stock and 1,000 shares of $1,000 par value voting preferred stock outstanding. Each share of preferred stock carries a cumulative annual dividend of 8% and a right to put the stock to Famco for its par value at any time. Jim Warner owns 60% of the preferred stock and 75% of the common stock. The balance of the preferred and common stock is owned by Mike Brooks, who is unrelated to Warner. Warner transfers all of his common stock to his daughter. Because the preferred stock confers both a qualified payment right and an extraordinary payment right, Warner's rights are valued under the "lower of" rule at $800 per share, taking into account Warner's voting rights.

The amount of Warner's gift is computed as follows:

Step 1: Assume that the value of all family-held interests in Famco, taking account of Warner's control of Famco, is $1 million.

Step 2: Subtract the value of the preferred stock held by Warner (.60 × $800,000 = $480,000, computed under the "lower of" rule of Reg. § 25.2701-2(a)(3)).

Step 3: The balance of $520,000 is allocated to the 750 shares of family-held common stock.

Step 4: No adjustments are made because no minority or similar discount is appropriate and no consideration was furnished for the transfer. The amount of the gift is $520,000.[34]

¶ 2525 Subsequent Valuations of Qualified Payment Rights

If a "taxable event" occurs with respect to any distribution right that was previously valued as a qualified payment interest (see ¶ 2515), the taxable estate or the taxable gifts of the individual holding the interest are increased.[35]

• ***Taxable Event***

A taxable event occurs if a qualified payment interest is transferred by the individual in whose hands the interest was originally valued under Code Sec. 2701 (or by certain individuals treated in the same manner as the original interest holder).[36] The transfer could be made either during life or at death.

---

[32] Reg. § 25.2701-3(b).

[33] Code Sec. 2701(a)(4); Reg. § 25.2701-3(c).

[34] Reg. § 25.2701-3(d), Example 1.

[35] Code Sec. 2701(d).

[36] Code Sec. 2701(d)(3); Reg. § 25.2701-4(b)(3).

A taxable event also occurs on the termination of an individual's rights with respect to a qualified payment interest.[37] A taxpayer also may elect to treat a late payment of certain qualified payments as a taxable event.[38] A qualified payment is late if it is paid more than four years after it is due. Qualified payments made during the four-year grace period are treated as having been made on the actual due date.[39]

A transfer is not a taxable event to the extent that a marital deduction (see ¶1000) is allowable for the transfer.[40] In such a case, the transferee or surviving spouse is treated as the holder of the interest from the time it is received.[41] In addition, if the interest holder transfers the qualified payment interest to an applicable family member in a taxable event, the transferee will be treated from that time on in the same manner as the transferor with respect to late or unpaid qualified payments that are first due after the taxable event.[42]

• ***Amount of Increase***

The taxable estate or taxable gifts of the interest holder are increased by the excess, if any, of:

(1) the amount of the qualified payments payable during the period beginning on the date of the transfer to which Code Sec. 2701 applied and ending on the date of the taxable event; and

(2) the earnings on such payments determined as if each payment were paid on its due date and reinvested on that date at a yield equal to the appropriate discount rate;

over the sum of:

(1) the amount of the qualified payments actually paid during the same period;

(2) the earnings on those payments determined as if each payment were reinvested as of the date actually paid at a rate equal to the appropriate discount rate; and

(3) to the extent necessary to prevent double inclusion, an amount equal to the sum of (a) the portion of the fair market value of the qualified payment interest solely attributable to the right to receive unpaid qualified payments (determined as of the date of the taxable event), (b) the fair market value of any equity interest received in lieu of qualified payments, and (c) the amount of any increase in the individual's aggregate taxable gifts by reason of the failure to enforce the right to receive qualified payments.[43]

The appropriate discount rate is the discount rate that was applied in determining the value of the qualified payment at the time of the original Code Sec. 2701 transfer.[44]

Limitation. Except in the case of an election to treat nonpayment of qualified payments as a taxable event, the amount of the increase in the individual's taxable estate or taxable gifts is limited to the "applicable percentage" of the excess, if any, of:

(1) the sum of:

---

[37] Reg. § 25.2701-4(b)(1).
[38] Code Sec. 2701(d)(3)(A)(iii).
[39] Code Sec. 2701(d)(2)(C).
[40] Code Sec. 2701(d)(3)(B).
[41] Code Sec. 2701(d)(3)(B)(iii).
[42] Reg. § 25.2701-4(b)(3).
[43] Reg. § 25.2701-4(c).
[44] Reg. § 25.2701-4(c)(3).

(a) the fair market value (determined as of the date of the taxable event) of all equity interests in the entity that are junior to any applicable retained interests; and

(b) any amounts expended by the entity to redeem or acquire any such junior interests; over

(2) the fair market value of such junior equity interests on the date of the original Code Sec. 2701 transfer.

The applicable percentage is equal to the number of shares of the applicable retained interest held by the interest holder on the date of the taxable event divided by the total number of shares of such interests in the business on the same date.[45]

¶ 2530 Attribution Rules

Under the attribution rules of Code Sec. 2701, an individual is treated as holding an equity interest to the extent that interest is held indirectly by that individual through ownership of a corporation, partnership, trust or other entity.[46] If an individual is deemed to hold an interest in more than one capacity, the interest is treated as held in a manner that attributes the largest ownership interest to the individual.[47]

Corporations. An individual is deemed to own any equity interest held by or for a corporation in the proportion that the fair market value of the stock held by the individual bears to the fair market value of all the stock of the corporation.[48]

Partnerships. An individual is deemed to own any equity interest held by or for a partnership in the proportion that the fair market value of the larger of the individual's profits interest or capital interest bears to the fair market value of the total profits interest or capital interest of the partnership.[49]

Trusts and estates. An individual is deemed to own any equity interest held by or for an estate or trust to the extent that the individual's beneficial interest may be satisfied by the equity interest or the income or proceeds from the equity interest. It is assumed that the fiduciary will exercise maximum discretion in favor of the individual. In the case of a grantor trust, the individual is deemed to hold 100 percent of any equity interest held by the trust. If the trust has multiple grantors, an individual grantor is deemed to own equity interests held by the trust to the extent of such individual's fractional share.[50]

¶ 2535 Mitigation of Double Taxation

If Code Sec. 2701 applies to reduce the value of a retained interest, double taxation would result if the retained interest were valued under generally applicable valuation rules when the transferor subsequently transfers the retained interest or the retained interest is included in the transferor's estate. Code Sec. 2701(e)(6) therefore provides that, if there is a subsequent transfer, or inclusion in the gross estate, of an applicable retained interest that was valued under Code Sec. 2701, appropriate adjustments are to be made for purposes of the transfer tax provisions to reflect the increase of amount of any prior taxable gift made by the transferor or decedent by reason of such valuation.

---

[45] Reg. § 25.2701-4(c)(6), and Reg. § 25.2701-4(d)(2).

[46] Code Sec. 2701(e)(3).

[47] Reg. § 25.2701-6(a)(1).

[48] Reg. § 25.2701-6(a)(2).

[49] Reg. § 25.2701-6(a)(3).

[50] Reg. § 25.2701-6(a)(4).

Regulations provide that, for purposes of determining the transferor's estate tax, the transferor's adjusted taxable gifts are reduced to reflect the increase of the transferor's taxable gifts under Code Sec. 2701.[51]

In general, the amount of the reduction is the lesser of (1) the amount by which the transferor's gifts are increased as a result of the application of Code Sec. 2701 to the transfer, or (2) the amount by which the individual's transfers are increased as a result of not applying the valuation rules to the later transfer of the applicable retained interest.

The regulations also provide an adjustment for split gifts that are generally consistent with the general principles of transfer taxation so that each spouse is treated as the transferor for one-half of the initial transfer and is entitled to mitigation under Code Sec. 2701(e)(6).

> ***Example:*** Ellen O'Brien owns 15,000 shares of $1,000 par value preferred stock of X Corp. and all of the 1,000 shares of common stock of X Corp. On January 15, 1998, when the fair market value of the common stock is $500,000 and the value of the preferred stock is $1.5 million, she transfers the common stock to her daughter, Sally. The fair market value of all of Ellen's interests prior to the transfer is $2 million. The Code Sec. 2701 value of the preferred interest is zero. The value of Ellen's taxable gift is $2.5 million (the Code Sec. 2701 transfer and Ellen's other taxable gifts). In 2004, when the preferred stock has a value of $1.4 million, Ellen transfers all of the preferred stock to Sally. She is entitled to reduce the amount on which her tax is computed by $1.4 million.

¶ 2540 Statute of Limitations

Although the statute of limitations on the assessment of gift tax is three years after the return was filed, special rules apply under the special valuation rules.

The statute of limitations for assessment of gift tax is modified so that it will not run on an undisclosed or inadequately disclosed transfer, regardless of whether a gift tax return was filed for other transfers in the year in which the Code Sec. 2701 transfer occurred.[52]

¶ 2545 Family Limited Partnerships

Family limited partnerships (FLPs) have become an extremely popular way to transfer assets to children and grandchildren. An FLP is typically created by transferring assets that are likely to appreciate rapidly to a newly created limited partnership under the limited partnership laws of the applicable state. In exchange for the assets, the transferor generally receives a very small general partnership interest (e.g., one or two percent) and a large limited partnership interest. The transferor retains the general partnership interest and transfers a portion of the limited partnership interest to the children. The interests received by the children are typically minority interests. The general partnership interest gives the transferor control over the operation of the business despite the fact that this interest represents only a small percentage of the value of the business.

• ***Nontax Advantages of FLPs***

Although the tax advantages associated with FLPs (discussed below) are usually the reasons most transferors create FLPs, there are other significant nontax advantages, including retained control over transferred assets, ease of

---

[51] Reg. § 25.2701-5.

[52] Code Sec. 6501(c)(9).

probate, ease of amendment, protection from creditors, and facilitation of annual exclusion gifts.

• *Tax Advantages*

Limited partnership interests transferred to children under an FLP are worth significantly less for transfer tax purposes than the same proportionate interest in the underlying assets would be worth. The holder of a minority limited partnership interest cannot make decisions about how the business is run, demand distributions, or force a liquidation of the partnership. In addition, an interest in an FLP may be far less marketable than an interest in the underlying assets of the business. As a result, minority interest and lack of marketability discounts are generally allowed on the transfer of interests in an FLP. The combined discount for a minority interest and lack of marketability is typically in the 20 percent to 40 percent range, but can be even higher.

• *IRS Attack on FLPs*

In addition to attacks on the tax advantages of FLPs based on application of the special valuation rules of the Code (discussed below), the IRS may well apply its "swing vote" theory to set aside valuation discounts claimed with respect to FLPs. Under this swing vote analysis, where family members can combine their voting power to create a collective swing vote, each member's interest must be considered to have a valuation premium.

Additionally, the IRS may invoke the investment company rule of Code Sec. 721(b) to require the recognition of gain upon contribution of appreciated securities to an FLP. Further, unless it can be shown that the children have a legitimate capital interest in the partnership, the IRS can disregard their partnership interests for income tax purposes. Finally, even if the FLP arrangement is successful in lowering transfer taxes, it will be at the cost of a loss of a Code Sec. 1014 stepped-up basis, which could lead to devastating income tax consequences, if the sharply appreciated assets were used to fund the FLP.

• *Application of Special Valuation Rules*

If a person transfers an interest in an FLP to or for the benefit of a family member and the transferor or an "applicable family member" retains an interest in the same partnership, the value of any partnership assets retained by the transferor will be zero (see ¶2510). However, if the interest retained by the transferor is proportionate to the transferred interest, without regard to nonlapsing differences with respect to management and limitations on liability, the zero value rule does not apply. Thus, to avoid the zero value rule, the FLP agreement will normally give the same proportionate rights to the transferor and transferees with respect to income, gain, loss, and deductions.

Code Sec. 2703 and the sham transaction doctrine. In IRS Technical Advice Memorandum 9719006[53], the IRS launched a major attack on FLPs. Under the facts of this ruling, assets were transferred from two trusts to an FLP that was created two days before a decedent's death. Immediately after the FLP received the assets, limited partnership interests were transferred to the transferor's children. The IRS ruled that valuation discounts claimed with respect to the FLP transaction should be disallowed under either of two theories. One theory was that, consistent with the sham transaction doctrine, the formation of the partner-

---

[53] IRS Technical Advice Memorandum 9719006 (Jan. 14, 1997).

ship interest should be treated as a single testamentary transaction and, therefore, the partnership should be disregarded for estate tax valuation purposes.

The IRS's alternative position was to apply Code Sec. 2703 (see ¶2580) to the transaction, with the result that, for transfer tax purposes, the value of the property is determined without regard to any option, agreement, or other restriction on the right to sell or use the property. The taxpayer argued that the property transferred was the partnership interests, and because there were no restrictions in the partnership agreement relating to the transferees' ability to sell, transfer, or use the interests, Code Sec. 2703 did not apply. The IRS disagreed, taking the position that what the children really received was the underlying assets subject to the partnership agreement. Thus, the partnership agreement was a restriction within the meaning of Code Sec. 2703, and any reduction in value caused by the partnership agreement was to be disregarded under Code Sec. 2703 unless the bona fide business arrangement exception of Code Sec. 2703(b) was applicable.

The IRS concluded that even if the steps of the transaction were not collapsed and the partnership interest, rather than the underlying assets, were treated as the subject of the transfers, Code Sec. 2703 would still apply, since under Reg. §25.2703-1(a)(3), a Code Sec. 2703 restriction can either be contained in a partnership agreement or implicit in the capital structure of the partnership.

In a recent case, a U.S. district court in Texas has concluded that a decedent's entering into an FLP agreement two days prior to her death was pursuant to a bona fide business arrangement, rather than an attempt to transfer property to members of her family for less than full and adequate consideration.[54] The court concluded that the transaction was a bona fide business transaction because (1) the primary purpose in forming the FLP was a desire to centralize management and preserve the family ranching operation, (2) the partnership was formed with the possibility of actively engaging in raising cattle in the future, (3) the partnership was not formed solely to reduce the decedent's estate tax, and (4) the decedent had no reason to believe she would die in the near future. Accordingly, the decedent's partnership interest was taxed under Code Sec. 2033 and came within the bona fide business transaction exception to Code Sec. 2703.

In another case involving Texas law, the Tax Court, in a decision reviewed by the entire Tax Court, rejected the IRS's attack against an FLP created by a donor two months before his death. The FLP was recognized as having sufficient substance for federal estate tax purposes because the partnership (1) was valid under Texas law, (2) changed the relationships between the decedent and his heirs and creditors, and (3) would not have been disregarded by potential purchasers of the decedent's assets. The court rejected the IRS's argument that, under Code Sec. 2703(a), the property to be valued was the partnership's underlying assets and that the partnership form was the restriction to be disregarded. According to the court, neither the language of, nor the intent behind, Code Sec. 2703(a) suggested that partnership assets were to be treated as the assets of a decedent's estate where the legal interest owned by the decedent at the time of death was a limited partnership interest.[55]

Code Sec. 2704. Citing the underlying Code and regulations, the IRS has published several Technical Advice Memoranda denying FLP valuation dis-

---

[54] *E. Church,* DC Tex., 2000-1 USTC ¶60,369, aff'd, CA-5, in an unpublished opinion, 2001-2 USTC ¶60,415.

[55] *A. Strangi Est.*, TC 478, CCH Dec. 54,135, aff'd, CA-5, on the issue of the property subject to the restriction, rev'd with respect to another issue, 2002-2 USTC ¶60,441.

counts that were deemed to relate to "applicable restrictions" (see ¶2590). With respect to an FLP, an applicable restriction is one that effectively limits the ability of the partnership to liquidate and with respect to which the transferor or any member of the transferor's family has the right after the transfer to remove the restriction. Reg. §25.2704-2(b) provides that a limitation on the ability to liquidate the partnership that is more restrictive than the limitations that would apply under state law in absence of the restriction will be deemed an applicable restriction for purposes of Code Sec. 2704. If an applicable restriction is disregarded, the transferred interest is valued as if the restriction did not exist and as if the rights of the transferor were determined under the state law that would apply in the absence of the restriction.

In a recent decision,[56] the Tax Court analyzed liquidation provisions of an FLP and found that the provisions were no more restrictive than those imposed under applicable state law (Texas). In so holding, the court rejected the IRS's argument that Texas law regarding the withdrawal from a partnership was germane to the analysis of the FLP liquidation provision.

¶2550 Function of Code Sec. 2702

Prior to the enactment of Code Sec. 2702, a transferor could transfer property and its future appreciation to younger family members at a fraction of the gift tax cost of an outright transfer by retaining various limited interests in the gifted property.

A popular form of transfer with a retained interest was the grantor retained interest trust (GRIT). In a typical GRIT, a grantor retains an income interest for a certain number of years, after which the remainder passes to specified beneficiaries. If the grantor dies during the term of the trust, the grantor's retained income interest causes the entire value of the trust property to be includible in the grantor's taxable estate, just as if the GRIT had never been created.[57]

The grantor is deemed to have made a taxable gift at the time the GRIT is funded. The GRIT lowers the value of the gift to the beneficiaries because the grantor retains an income interest in the gift property. There is the possibility that the property will not pass to the beneficiaries if the grantor dies before the end of the specified term, and the beneficiaries do not have use of the trust property before the end of the specified term. The value of the gift is equal to the present value of the actuarial value of the remainder interest, as determined under Code Sec. 7520 (see ¶530 and the Appendix at ¶2700).

> *Example (1):* Brian Foley, age 60, transfers $1 million to a 10-year GRIT. At the end of the 10 years, the trust will be distributed to his daughter, Jill. At the time of the transfer, the applicable interest rate under Code Sec. 7520 is 6.0%, which results in the retained interest being valued at $534,170 and the gift being valued at $465,830. If Brian survives the 10-year period, $1 million is removed from his estate at a gift tax cost of approximately four-tenths of the cost had $1 million been transferred outright.

Code Sec. 2702 limits the application of Code Sec. 7520 to the valuation of "qualified retained interests" and retained interests in personal residence trusts

---

[56] *B. Kerr*, 113 TC 450, Dec. 13, 2000, CCH Dec. 53,667, aff'd, CA-5, 2002-2 USTC ¶60,440. See also, *I. Knight*, 115 TC 506, CCH Dec. 54,136, a reviewed-by-the-court decision interpreting FLP restrictions as being no more restrictive than Texas law, and *M. Harper Est.*, 79 TCM 2232, CCH Dec. 53,939(M), TC Memo. 2000-202, following *Kerr*, and interpreting California law.

[57] Code Sec. 2036(a)(1).

(see ¶2570).[58] All other retained interests are valued at zero.[59] The subtraction method is used to determine the value of the gift. If the value of the retained interest is zero, the value of the gift is increased to equal the value of the property transferred in trust.

> *Example (2):* Assume the same facts as in Example (1), except that Code Sec. 2702 applies. Because Brian's retained interest is not a qualified retained interest, it is valued at zero and the gift to his daughter, Jill, is valued at $1 million.

¶ 2555 Application of Code Sec. 2702

Code Sec. 2702 applies when (1) an interest in trust is transferred to a "member of the transferor's family" and (2) the transferor or "applicable family member" retains an interest in the trust.[60]

Members of the transferor's family. Members of the transferor's family include:

(1) the transferor's spouse;

(2) any ancestor or lineal descendant of the transferor or the transferor's spouse;

(3) any brother or sister of the transferor; and

(4) any spouse of the persons described in (2) and (3).[61]

Applicable family members. Applicable family members are generally members of the older generation and include:

(1) the transferor's spouse;

(2) any ancestor of the transferor or the transferor's spouse; and

(3) the spouse of any such ancestor.[62]

• *Transfers of an Interest in Trust*

Transfers in trust include transfers to a new or existing trust and assignments of an interest in an existing trust. They do not include the exercise, release, or lapse of a power of appointment that is not a transfer under the gift tax provisions or the execution of a qualified disclaimer.[63] A transfer of an interest in trust includes a transfer of an interest in property that results in the creation of one or more term interests.[64] A term interest is one of a series of successive interests, which includes a life interest or an interest for a term of years.[65]

The following interests are not treated as term interests:

(1) concurrent fee interests, such as those held by tenants in common, tenants by the entireties, or joint tenants with right of survivorship; and

(2) leasehold interests to the extent the lease was acquired for adequate consideration, provided a good faith effort was made to determine the fair rental value of the property.[66]

The joint purchase of interests in the same property by a taxpayer and a member of the taxpayer's family is a transfer in trust if the taxpayer acquires only

---

58 Code Sec. 2702(a)(2)(B) and Code Sec. 2702(a)(3)(A)(ii).

59 Code Sec. 2702(a)(2)(A).

60 Code Sec. 2702(a)(1); Reg. § 25.2702-1(a).

61 Code Sec. 2702(e) and Code Sec. 2704(c)(2); Reg. § 25.2702-2(a)(1).

62 Code Sec. 2701(e)(2); Reg. § 25.2701-1(d)(2).

63 Reg. § 25.2702-2(a)(2).

64 Code Sec. 2702(c)(1).

65 Code Sec. 2702(c)(3).

66 Reg. § 25.2702-4(a) and Reg. § 25.2702-4(b).

a term interest in the property. The taxpayer will be treated as acquiring the entire property and transferring to the family members the interests they acquired. However, any consideration paid by the acquiring family members will be considered in determining the amount of any gifts deemed made by the taxpayer.[67]

Example: Arlene Ricci purchases a 15-year term interest in a commercial building, and her child, Carol, purchases the remainder interest. Arlene is treated as if she had acquired the entire property and then transferred the remainder interest to Carol.

• *Retained Interest*

A retained interest is an interest held by the same individual before and after a transfer in trust. If the transfer creates a term interest, the transferor is deemed to hold the interest both before and after the transfer[68] (see ¶2560).

• *Exceptions to Application*

Code Sec. 2702 does not apply to the following transfers:

(1) transfers treated as incomplete for gift tax purposes;

(2) transfers to a "personal residence trust" (see ¶2570);

(3) transfers to a charitable remainder trust;

(4) transfers to a charitable lead trust;

(5) transfers to a pooled income fund;

(6) transfers of a remainder interest if the only interest retained by the transferor or applicable family members is the right to income distributions in the sole discretion of an independent trustee; and

(7) transfers in trust incident to a divorce.[69]

¶ 2560 Valuation of Retained Interests

Retained interests are valued at zero unless:

(1) the interest is a "qualified retained interest" (see ¶2565);

(2) the interest is a retained interest in a personal residence trust or qualified personal residence trust (see ¶2570); or

(3) the interest is in certain nondepreciable tangible property.

• *Special Rule for Tangible Property*

A special valuation rule applies to interests in nondepreciable tangible property, such as land and works of art. The exception applies to transfers in trust of tangible property that would not be entitled to a depreciation or depletion deduction if the property were used in a trade or business or held for the production of income. In addition, the nonexercise of rights under a term interest must not increase the value of the remainder interest in the property. Depreciable improvements to property that would otherwise disqualify the property will be ignored if the fair market value of the improvements do not exceed five percent of the fair market value of the entire property.[70]

For such transfers, the value of the retained interest (other than a qualified interest) is the amount that the holder of the term interest establishes as the

---

[67] Code Sec. 2702(c)(2); Reg. § 25.2702-4(c).

[68] Reg. § 25.2702-2(a)(3).

[69] Reg. § 25.2702-1(c).

[70] Reg. § 25.2702-2(c)(2).

amount for which such interest could be sold to an unrelated party.[71] However, if the transferor cannot reasonably establish the value of the term interest, it will be valued at zero.[72] If tangible property is converted during the term of the interest into property that does not qualify for valuation under the special rule, for gift tax purposes, the conversion will be treated as a transfer of the value of the unexpired portion of the term interest for no consideration.[73]

• *Application to Flip Charitable Remainder Unitrusts*

Amendments to the regulations clarify the application of the zero value rule to flip charitable remainder unitrusts (CRUTs).[74] A flip CRUT is a CRUT that can be converted from one of the income exception methods of determining the unitrust amount to a fixed percentage method. The amended regulations allow the governing instrument of a CRUT to convert from one of the income exceptions to the fixed percentage method, provided that the date or event that triggers the conversion is outside the control of the trustees or any other person. Trustees had until June 30, 2000, to begin legal proceedings for special reformations of CRUTs to include a flip provision.[75]

The amended regulation clarifies that unitrust interests in an income-exception CRUT that are retained by the donor or any applicable family member will be valued at zero when a noncharitable beneficiary of the trust is someone other than (1) the donor, (2) the donor's U.S. citizen spouse, or (3) both the donor and the donor's U.S. citizen spouse. The zero value rule also applies both to CRUTs that use only the net income method and to a flip unitrust if it does not fall within one of the exemptions. The amended regulation clarifies that Code Sec. 2702 will not apply when there are only two consecutive noncharitable beneficial interests and the transferor holds the second of the two interests.

¶ 2565 Qualified Retained Interests

There are three types of qualified retained interests that are not valued at zero under Code Sec. 2702. The trusts that correspond to these interests are:

(1) a grantor retained annuity trust (GRAT), which makes fixed payments to the grantor at least annually;

(2) a grantor retained unitrust (GRUT), which makes payments to the grantor at least annually, but the amount of the payments is a fixed percentage of the trust's assets determined annually; or

(3) a noncontingent remainder interest if all the other interests in the trust consist of interests described in (1) and (2).[76]

• *Qualified Annuity Interest*

A qualified annuity interest is an irrevocable right to receive a fixed amount payable to, or for the benefit of, the holder of the interest for each taxable year of the term. A fixed amount is either (1) a stated dollar amount, or (2) a fixed fraction or percentage of the initial fair market value of the property transferred to the trust. The amount must be payable at least annually. In valuing a qualified annuity interest, an amount will be considered only to the extent that it does not exceed 120 percent of the stated dollar amount or the fixed fraction or percentage payable in the preceding year.[77]

---

[71] Code Sec. 2702(c)(4)(B).

[72] Reg. § 25.2702-2(c)(1).

[73] Reg. § 25.2702-2(c)(4)(i).

[74] T.D. 8791, amending Reg. § 25.2702-1, Dec. 9, 1998.

[75] Notice 99-31, 1999-1 CB 1185.

[76] Code Sec. 2702(b).

[77] Reg. § 25.2702-3(b)(1).

The governing instrument must:

(1) prohibit distributions to or for the benefit of any person other than the holder of the interest during the term of the interest;

(2) fix the term of the interest for the life of the holder, for a specific term of years, or for the shorter of those periods;

(3) prohibit prepayment of the income interest;[78]

(4) if the annuity is stated in terms of a fraction or percentage of the initial fair market value of the trust property, require payment adjustments or repayments as a result of any incorrect determination of the fair market value of the property;

(5) require the pro rata computation of the annuity amount in the case of a short taxable year and the last taxable year of the term; and

(6) prohibit additional contributions to the trust.[79]

The Court of Appeals for the Seventh Circuit has held that a husband's and wife's retained interests in four GRATs were not qualified interests and were valued as single-life annuities rather than dual-life annuities.[80] The interests retained in favor of the surviving spouses were not qualified interests under Code Sec. 2702(b) because (1) the spousal interests in each GRAT were not fixed or ascertainable at the inception of the GRAT, and (2) the retained interests could have extended beyond the death of the grantor. Therefore, the remainder interest (that is, the amount of the taxable gift) was increased. The Court of Appeals for the Ninth Circuit, however, has reached the opposite result in a case involving similar facts.[81] There, the court concluded that a two-life annuity retained by a husband and wife in each of their GRATs was a qualified interest. In reaching this result, the court reasoned that there was no difference between the annuity contained in each of the spouse's GRAT and the one described in Reg. § 25.2702(d)(1), Example 7, which was treated as a qualified interest. According to the court, the value of each spouse's gifts to the GRAT was ascertainable through the use of the two-life annuity table. The court distinguished the result in *W. Cook,* on the ground that that case involved the additional contingency that the grantor and the spouse be married at the time the annuity began. Because the spouses' retained annuities were qualified interests, the amount of the gifts to each GRAT was equal to the value of the property transferred to the GRAT, reduced by both the value of the grantor's qualified interest and the value of the qualified interest transferred to the grantor's spouse.

In response to the decision in *Schott,* the IRS has published proposed regulations that would clarify when a revocable spousal interest is a qualified interest. The exception treating a spouse's revocable successor interest as a qualified interest would apply only if the spouse's interest, standing alone, would constitute a qualified interest that meets the requirements of Reg. § 25.2702-3(d)(3), but for the grantor's revocation power. The IRS observes that a revocable spousal interest is contingent (and, therefore, not a qualified interest) if the spouse will not receive any payments if the transferor survives the fixed term

[78] Reg. § 25.2702-3(d)(2) -(4).

[79] Reg. § 25.2702-3(b)(2)-(4).

[80] *W. Cook,* CA-7, 2001-2 USTC ¶ 60,422, aff'g 115 TC 15, CCH Dec. 53,960. The appellate court in *W. Cook* cited Reg. § 25.2703-3(e), Example 6 for the proposition that the term of the annuity or unitrust interest must be fixed and ascertainable at the creation of the trust.

[81] *P. Schott,* CA-9, 2003-1 USTC ¶ 60,457, rev'g TC, 81 TCM 1600, CCH Dec. 54,331(M), TC Memo. 2001-110.

during which the transferor is the holder. The proposed amendments to the regulation would be effective for trusts created on or after July 26, 2004.[82]

• *Qualified Unitrust Interest*

A qualified unitrust interest is an irrevocable right to receive payment, at least annually, of a fixed percentage of the net fair market value of the trust assets, determined annually. The unitrust amount must be payable to, or for the benefit of, the holder of the unitrust interest for each taxable year of the term. In valuing a qualified unitrust interest, a percentage will be considered a fixed percentage only to the extent that it does not exceed 120 percent of the fixed fraction or percentage payable in the preceding year.[83]

The governing instrument must meet requirements (1)–(5) enumerated above for instruments creating qualified annuity interests.[84]

• *Payment of Annuity and Unitrust Amount*

The IRS has adopted amended regulations that prohibit the use of notes, other debt instruments, options, or similar financial arrangements that effectively delay the receipt by the grantor of a GRAT or GRUT of the annual payment necessary to satisfy the annuity or unitrust amount.[85] In the case of trusts created on or after September 20, 1999, the trust instrument must prohibit the trustee from issuing any of these delayed-payment instruments in satisfaction of an annuity or unitrust payment obligation. A transition rule provides that if a trust created before September 20, 1999, does not prohibit the above techniques, the retained interest is treated as a qualified interest under Code Sec. 2702(b) if the notes, other debt instruments, etc., are not issued after September 20, 1999, to satisfy the annuity or unitrust payments. In addition, any notes or other debt instruments issued on or before September 20, 1999, to satisfy the annual payment obligation must have been paid in full by December 31, 1999, and any option or similar financial arrangement must be terminated by such date, so that the grantor actually receives cash or other trust assets in satisfaction of the payment obligation.

• *Zeroed-Out GRATs*

In order to "zero out" a GRAT, the annuity payout rate must be set high enough so as to result in no gift. Simply put, this involves dividing the original principal amount by the appropriate factor for the corresponding term of years and Code Sec. 7520 rate in order to compute an annual payment that results in an annuity having a present value equal to the original trust principal.

> *Example:* If we assume the Code Sec. 7520 rate is 5.8% and the initial value of the trust principal is $1 million, in order to zero out a 10-year GRAT under those assumptions would require an annuity payment of $134,584.
>
> *Table B (IRS Publication 1457) annuity factor (5.8% and 10 years):* 7.4303
>
> *$1,000,000 ÷ 7.4303* = $134,584

The IRS has long taken the position that it is impossible to zero out a GRAT, stating "in a trust where the annuity amount will exhaust the funds of the trust precisely at the termination of the trust, the value of the retained interest cannot equal the amount transferred to the trust because of the possibility that the

---

[82] Proposed Reg. § 25.2702-3, NPRM-REG-163679-02.

[83] Reg. § 25.2702-3(c)(1).

[84] Reg. § 25.2702-3(c)(2) -(3) and Reg. § 25.2702-3(d)(2) -(4).

[85] Reg. § 25.2702-3, as amended by T.D. 8899, Sept. 1, 2000.

grantor may die before the expiration of the term of the trust."[86] Accordingly, under this analysis, an annuity stemming from a GRAT cannot be valued for a term certain, but must be valued for the shorter of a term certain or the prior death of the grantor.

The Tax Court has rejected the IRS's analysis in a unanimous reviewed-by-the-court opinion. In this case, a grantor's retained qualified interest in two GRATs was valued for gift tax purposes as an annuity for a specified term of years, rather than as an annuity for the shorter of a term certain or the period ending on the grantor's death.[87] In reaching its decision, the Tax Court also held that Reg. §25.2702-3(e), Example 5, was an invalid interpretation of Code Sec. 2702.

Under the facts of *Walton*, the grantor established two substantially identical GRATs, each of which had a term of two years and was funded by a transfer of common stock in a publicly traded corporation. Each GRAT proved that the grantor was to receive an annuity amount equal to 49.35 percent of the GRAT's initial value in the first year and 59.99 percent of such initial value in the second year. In the event the grantor died prior to the expiration of the two-year term, the unpaid annuity amounts were payable to the grantor's estate. After the completion of the two-year term, the remaining balance in the GRATs was to be distributed to the grantor's two daughters.

The Tax Court concluded that, for purposes of Code Sec. 2702, even if it viewed the GRATs as creating separate interests in favor of the grantor and her estate, both such interests were retained by the grantor because she could not, as a matter of law, make a gift to herself or to her estate. The GRATs, according to the court, created a single, noncontingent annuity interest payable for a specified term of years to the undifferentiated unit of the grantor or her estate. Such a result was consistent with Congressional intent to allow individuals to retain qualified annuity interests for a specified term of years, and the proper method for doing so was to make the balance of payments due after the grantor's death payable to the grantor's estate.

Arguing at the Tax Court, the IRS relied on Reg. §25.2702-3(e), Example 5, in support of the position that only the value of annuity payable for the shorter of two years or the period ending on the grantor's death could be subtracted from the fair market value of the gifted stock in calculating the taxable gift made by the grantor upon the creation of the GRATs. In rejecting the IRS's position, the court held that Example 5 was an unreasonable interpretation and an invalid extension of Code Sec. 2702. The court determined that the annuities at issue were more akin to the fixed-term interests cited with approval in the legislative history of Code Sec. 2702 than to the reversionary interests identified as leading to undervaluation.

Subsequently, the IRS announced its acquiescence to the Tax Court's *Walton* decision. As a result, in the fact situation described in Reg. §25.2702-3(e), Example 5, the IRS will treat the retained interest payable to the grantor or the grantor's estate as a qualified interest payable for a 10-year term.[88] The IRS has proposed amendments to the Reg. §25.2702-3(e), *Example 5* and *Example 6*, to conform the regulation to the *Walton* decision.[89] The proposed amendments would apply to trusts created on or after July 26, 2004. However, the IRS will not

---

[86] IRS Letter Ruling 9239015 (Jun. 25, 1992).

[87] *A. Walton*, 115 TC 589, CCH Dec. 54,165 (Acq.).

[88] Notice 2003-72.

[89] Proposed Reg. §25.2702-3, NPRM-REG-163679-02.

challenge any prior application of the changes to *Examples 5* and *6* in Reg. §25.2702-3(e).

• ***Qualified Remainder Interest***

A remainder interest (which includes a reversion) is the right to receive all or a fractional share of trust property on the termination of all or a fractional share of the trust. Therefore, a right to receive an amount that is a stated or pecuniary amount would not be a remainder interest.[90] A remainder interest is a qualified remainder interest if (1) it is payable to the beneficiary or the beneficiary's estate in all events, and (2) all interests in the trust, other than noncontingent remainder interests, are qualified annuity or unitrust interests. Therefore, the governing instrument cannot permit payment of income in excess of the annuity or unitrust amount to the holder of a qualified annuity or unitrust interest.[91]

• ***Intentionally Defective Grantor Trusts***

A planning technique that is increasingly being used as an alternative to a GRAT involves an installment sale to an intentionally defective grantor trust (hereinafter referred to as a "defective trust"). This technique offers possible tax advantages (discussed below), but it remains judicially untested.

Under the typical scenario, a grantor sets up an irrevocable trust (usually for the benefit of the grantor's children and/or grandchildren) and initially funds it with an amount of cash. The trust will be drafted so that sufficient trustee powers are retained so as to cause the property transfer to be deemed ineffective to shift ownership of trust assets for income tax purposes yet complete for transfer tax purposes. The grantor will thereafter enter into an installment sales agreement with the trust whereby the grantor will sell appreciated assets to the trust in exchange for the trust's installment note equal to the fair market value of the asset the trust receives. Interest will be paid by the trust to the grantor in an amount equal to the current AFR rate under Code Sec. 1274(d) for the term of the installment sale, with a balloon payment of principal due at the end of the installment term. If the trust document is properly structured and all the terms of the installment sale contract are carried out as if it were an arm's-length transaction between unrelated parties, there should be no income tax on the grantor's transfer of the property into the trust. This is so because, for income tax purposes, the trust will be a grantor trust, which has no independent tax standing apart from the grantor.[92] Although the initial cash transfer will be a completed gift, the installment sale between the grantor and the trust should have no gift tax consequences, since full and adequate consideration was exchanged.[93]

The installment sale to the defective trust effects an estate freeze by allowing the grantor to transfer appreciating assets in exchange for fixed assets in a transaction that will incur no gift tax consequences, yet shift future asset appreciation to the grantor's children/grandchildren estate tax free. Although the grantor's initial cash transfer into the trust will generate gift/generation-skipping transfer tax liability (or at least use up some of the grantor's unified credit and/or generation-skipping transfer exemption), this step is suggested by several tax planning commentators to ensure that the trust's existence is independent of the installment sales transaction that garners the tax advantages. Commentators

[90] Reg. §25.2702-3(f)(2).

[91] Reg. §25.2702-3(f)(1).

[92] Code Sec. 671 through Code Sec. 677.

[93] See IRS Letter Ruling 9535026 (May 31, 1995), where the IRS ruled that stock sold to a grantor trust in exchange for a promissory note was a sale and therefore not subject to Code Sec. 2701 or Code Sec. 2702.

suggest that the initial cash contribution be at least 10 percent of the value of the assets that will be the subject of the installment sale.

The defective trust technique certainly carries more risk potential than a GRAT transaction, which has predictable tax results if all rules specified in the Code are followed. However, the defective trust approach offers the possibility of several advantages over a GRAT:

(1) The defective trust can utilize an interest rate equal to 100 percent of the AFR rate, rather than 120 percent of the federal midterm rate, as required by for a GRAT. Therefore, more wealth is being removed from the grantor's estate for transfer tax purposes, since any income earned on the transferred appreciative assets will be retained by the trust, free of taxation in the grantor's gross estate.

(2) With a defective trust, the generation-skipping transfer lifetime exemption ($1,500,000 for 2004 and 2005) can be allocated when the transfer to the trust is made, thereby shielding any future appreciation from generation-skipping transfers. However, because a GRAT is subject to an estate tax inclusion period, the generation-skipping transfer exemption cannot be allocated at the funding of the trust, and more of the generation-skipping transfer exemption later may have to be used.

(3) With a defective trust, if the grantor dies before the end of the installment period, only the value of the unpaid note will be included in the grantor's gross estate. With a GRAT, the entire value of the trust assets must be included in the grantor's gross estate.

¶ 2570 Personal Residence Trusts

The zero valuation rule (see ¶ 2560) does not apply to retained interests in personal residence trusts and qualified personal residence trusts. Instead, such interests are valued under Code Sec. 7520. Grantor retained interest trusts, therefore, play a continued role in yielding transfer tax savings if they are used to transfer the grantor's personal residence.

• *Personal Residence Trust*

The governing instrument of a personal residence trust must prohibit the trust from holding any asset other than the personal residence of the term holder and "qualified proceeds" for the entire term of the trust.[94] Qualified proceeds refer to insurance proceeds received if the residence is damaged, destroyed, or involuntarily converted during the term of the trust. The trust instrument must require that the proceeds and income thereon are reinvested in a personal residence within two years of receipt.[95]

A personal residence is the principal residence or the second residence (within the meaning of Code Sec. 280A(d)(1)) of the term holder.[96] A personal residence may include appurtenant structures used by the term holder for residential purposes. It may also include adjacent land to the extent such land is reasonably appropriate for residential purposes, given the residence's size and location.[97] The amount of land that can be included under this provision can be substantial. For example, in one private letter ruling, the IRS allowed 10 acres of land surrounding a very large residence to be included,[98] and, in another, allowed the inclusion of two lots across the street from the personal residence

---

[94] Reg. § 25.2702-5(b)(1).

[95] Reg. § 25.2702-5(b)(3).

[96] Reg. § 25.2702-5(b)(2).

[97] Reg. § 25.2702-5(b)(2)(ii).

[98] IRS Letter Ruling 9442019 (Jul. 19, 1994).

that provided the term holder with access to a bay and a view of the bay.[99] The personal residence may not be used by anyone other than the term holder or the holder's spouse or dependent and may not be sold or transferred, directly or indirectly, to the grantor, the grantor's spouse, or an entity controlled by the grantor or the grantor's spouse.[100] A personal residence may not be used for purposes other than as a personal residence unless such use is secondary (such as a home office). Use as a hotel or as a bed and breakfast is not considered secondary.[101]

• ***Qualified Personal Residence Trust***

Unlike a personal residence trust, a qualified personal residence trust (QPRT) may hold property other than a personal residence. In other respects, the rules governing the definition of a personal residence and the use thereof with respect to QPRTs are substantially similar to those governing personal residence trusts.[102] Cash may be added to or held by the trust for the following limited purposes:

(1) to pay trust expenses (including mortgage payments) already incurred or expected to be incurred within the next six months;

(2) to pay for improvements to the residence within the next six months;

(3) to purchase the initial or replacement residence pursuant to a contract within the next three months.[103]

Governing instruments. The governing instrument of a qualified personal residence trust must require the following:

(1) any trust income must be distributed to the term holder at least annually;

(2) no principal may be distributed to a beneficiary other than the transferor during the term of the retained interest;

(3) the term holder's interest may not be prepaid;

(4) the trust may not hold any assets other than the personal residence of the term holder and the assets permitted by the regulations;

(5) the trustee must determine the amount of cash holdings allowed by the regulations and distribute the excess to the term holder at least quarterly and within 30 days of the termination of the term holder's interest;

(6) the trust will cease to be a qualified personal residence trust if the residence ceases to be used as a personal residence or if the residence is sold and the trust instrument prohibits the holding of sales proceeds;

(7) the trust will cease to be a QPRT if (a) the personal residence is sold, damaged or destroyed, and (b) a replacement residence is not acquired or the residence is not repaired within two years;

(8) if the trust ceases to be a qualified residence, the assets will be distributed to the term holder or converted into a qualified annuity interest for the benefit of the term holder within 30 days;[104] and

(9) the trust instrument must prohibit the trust from selling or transferring the residence, directly or indirectly, to the grantor, the grantor's

---

[99] IRS Letter Ruling 9503025 (Oct. 27, 1994).

[100] Reg. §25.2702-5(b)(1).

[101] Reg. §25.2702-5(b)(2)(iii).

[102] Reg. §25.2702-5(c)(1) and Reg. §25.2702-5(c)(2).

[103] Reg. §25.2702-5(c)(5)(ii)(A)(1).

[104] Reg. §25.2702-5(c)(5)(ii)(A)(2).

spouse, or an entity controlled by either of them during the retained term interest or at any time thereafter in which the trust is a grantor trust.[105]

Sample forms. The IRS has provided in Rev. Proc. 2003-42[106] a sample declaration of trust and alternate provisions that meet the requirements for a QPRT. The sample declaration of trust is designed for a QPRT with one transferor for a term equal to the lesser of the term holder's life or a term of years. The alternate provisions relate to additions to the trust to purchase a personal residence and to the disposition of trust assets on cessation of its qualification as a QPRT. The IRS will recognize a trust as meeting all of the QPRT requirements if: (1) the trust instrument is substantially similar to the sample declaration or properly integrates one or more of the alternate provisions in a document that is substantially similar to the sample declaration, and (2) the trust operates in a manner consistent with the terms of the trust instrument and is a valid trust under applicable local law.

A trust instrument that contains substantive provisions in addition to those provided in the sample declaration, or that omits any of the provisions contained in the sample declaration, will not be assured of QPRT qualification, but will not necessarily be disqualified from satisfying the QPRT requirements. The IRS generally will not issue a letter ruling on whether a trust with one term holder qualifies as a QPRT. However, the IRS will generally issue a letter ruling regarding the effect of substantive trust provisions on the qualification of a trust as a QPRT.[107]

¶ 2575 Mitigation of Double Taxation

If the value of a retained interest is reduced to zero under Code Sec. 2702, double taxation results if the retained interest is subsequently transferred by gift or at death. To mitigate double taxation, the transferor's taxable gifts are reduced at the time of the subsequent lifetime transfer or in determining the transferor's estate tax.[108]

The amount of the reduction is the lesser of:

(1) the increase in taxable gifts on the original transfer due to the application of Code Sec. 2702; or

(2) the increase in taxable gifts or gross estate on the subsequent transfer of the retained interest.[109]

¶ 2580 Rights and Restrictions Disregarded Under Code Sec. 2703

The purpose of Code Sec. 2703 is to prevent possible distortions in value that might result if a transferor retained certain rights or imposed certain restrictions with respect to the transferred property without intending to exercise the rights or restrictions. Unless the taxpayer establishes that the right or restriction qualifies for an exception to Code Sec. 2703, options, restrictive sale agreements and buy-sell agreements will be disregarded for transfer tax valuation purposes.

• ***Rights and Restrictions***

A right or restriction includes any option, agreement, or other right to acquire or use property at a price that is less than fair market value, or any

[105] Reg. § 25.2702-5(c)(9).

[106] IRB 2003-23, 993.

[107] Rev. Proc. 2003-42, IRB 2003-23, 993.

[108] Reg. § 25.2702-6(a).

[109] Reg. § 25.2702-6(b)(1).

restriction on the right to sell or use the property. For example, a lease entered into between a parent and child, the terms of which are not comparable to leases relating to similar property between unrelated parties, would be disregarded in valuing the leased property.

The right or restriction may be part of a partnership agreement, corporate bylaws, or articles of incorporation, or may be implicit in the capital structure of an entity. However, Code Sec. 2703 will not apply to a qualified easement under Code Sec. 2522(d) or Code Sec. 2055(f).[110]

• *Exceptions*

A right or restriction will not be disregarded for valuation purposes if the taxpayer can establish that it is:

(1) a bona fide arrangement;

(2) not a device to transfer property to family members for less than full and adequate consideration; and

(3) comparable to similar arrangements entered into by persons in arm's-length transactions.[111]

For purposes of the second requirement, family members include applicable family members, lineal descendants of the parents of the transferor or the transferor's spouse, and any other individual who is a natural object of the transferor's bounty.[112] Each of the above requirements must be satisfied independently.[113]

• *Application*

Code Sec. 2703 applies to rights or restrictions that are created or substantially modified after October 8, 1990. A substantial modification includes any discretionary modification of a right or restriction, whether or not authorized by the terms of an agreement, that results in anything more than a *de minimis* change in the quality, value, or timing of the rights of any party with respect to the property that is subject to the right or restriction. The addition of a family member as a party to a right or restriction is treated as a substantial modification unless the addition is required under the terms of the right or restriction or the person is assigned to a generation no lower than the lowest generation of individuals who already are parties to the right or restriction.[114]

The following items are not treated as substantial modifications:

(1) modifications required by the terms of a right or restriction;

(2) discretionary modifications that do not change the right or restriction;

(3) modifications of a capitalization rate with respect to a right or restriction, if done in such a way that the rate bears a fixed relationship to a specified market rate; and

(4) modifications that result in an option price that more closely approximates fair market value.[115]

---

[110] Reg. § 25.2703-1(a).

[111] Code Sec. 2703(b); Reg. § 25.2703-1(b)(1).

[112] Reg. § 25.2703-1(b)(3) and Reg. § 25.2701-2(b)(5).

[113] Reg. § 25.2703-1(b)(2).

[114] Reg. § 25.2703-1(c)(1).

[115] Reg. § 25.2703-1(c)(2).

¶ 2590 Treatment of Lapsing Rights and Restrictions

Code Sec. 2704 was enacted to reduce or eliminate the use of lapsing rights and restrictions as a way of reducing transfer taxes.

Example (1): During her life, Betty Smith owned 80% of the voting stock of Famco, and her children owned the remaining 20%. The bylaws of Famco provided that a shareholder's voting rights lapsed at death. Smith's will provided that, upon her death, all of her Famco stock would pass to her children. The value of Smith's stock with the voting rights is $750,000. However, the value of the same stock without the voting rights is $500,000. Prior to the enactment of Code Sec. 2704, Smith's estate would have been worth $250,000 less than it was when she was alive.

Under Code Sec. 2704(a), the lapse of a voting or liquidation right created after October 8, 1990, is treated as a transfer for transfer tax purposes if the holder of the lapsing right and members of the holder's family control the entity both before and after the lapse. The amount of the transfer is the excess, if any, of the value of the holder's interests in the entity immediately before the lapse over the value of such interests after the lapse.[116] Code Sec. 2704(b) covers the other side of lapsing rights—the restrictions placed on the transferor. Under Code Sec. 2704(b), if an interest in a corporation or partnership is transferred to, or for the benefit of, a member of the transferor's family, and the transferor and members of the transferor's family control the entity before the transfer, any "applicable restrictions" are disregarded in valuing the transferred interest.

Example (2): Assume the same facts as in Example (1), except that Code Sec. 2704(a) applies. Smith is deemed to have made a transfer of $250,000, the difference between the value of the stock with voting rights and the value of the stock without the voting rights. The amount of the transfer plus the $500,000 value of the stock in Smith's estate equals the value of Smith's stock before she died.

• *Lapse of Voting and Liquidation Rights*

For purposes of Code Sec. 2704(a), a voting right is the right to vote with respect to any matter of the entity. The right of a general partner to participate in partnership management is a voting right.[117] A liquidation right is the right to compel the entity to acquire all or a portion of the holder's interest in the entity. It is not necessary that the exercise of the right result in the complete liquidation of the entity.[118]

A voting or liquidation right lapses when a currently exercisable right is restricted or ceases to exist. The transfer of an interest conferring a right generally is not a lapse. However, a transfer that eliminates the transferor's right to compel the entity to acquire an interest retained by the transferor that is junior to the transferred interest is a lapse of a liquidation right with respect to the junior interest.[119]

A lapse of a liquidation right is not treated as a transfer (1) to the extent that the holder and members of the holder's family cannot, immediately after the lapse, liquidate an interest the holder could have liquidated before the lapse, (2) if the lapse was previously valued under Code Sec. 2701, or (3) if the lapse occurred by reason of a change in state law.[120]

---

116 Code Sec. 2704(a).

117 Reg. § 25.2704-1(a)(2)(iv).

118 Reg. § 25.2704-1(a)(2)(v).

119 Reg. § 25.2704-1(b) and Reg. § 25.2704-1(c)(1).

120 Reg. § 25.2704-1(c)(2).

• *Disregard of Applicable Restrictions*

An applicable restriction is a limitation on the ability to liquidate the entity that is more restrictive than the limitations that would apply under state law. Thus, a provision on liquidation that is no more restrictive than the corresponding state law should not be deemed to be an applicable restriction. To date, taxpayers have found this to be a winning argument in the Tax Court with respect to liquidation restrictions under Texas[121] and California[122] law.

A restriction is an applicable restriction only to the extent that (1) the restriction lapses after the transfer, or (2) the transferor or a member of the transferor's family has the right to remove the restriction immediately after the transfer.

Applicable restrictions do not include restrictions imposed by state or federal law or commercially reasonable restrictions on liquidation imposed by an unrelated person providing financing to the entity for trade of business operations. An unrelated person is any person who is not related to the transferor, the transferee, or any member of the family of either in a way specified by Code Sec. 267.[123] An option, right or agreement subject to Code Sec. 2703 is not an applicable restriction.[124]

• *Control Requirement*

Control has the same definition for purposes of Code Sec. 2704 as for purposes of Code Sec. 2701 (see ¶2510).[125] In the case of a corporation, it means at least 50 percent of the stock of the corporation, measured by vote or value. In the case of a partnership, it means at least 50 percent of the capital or profits interest and, in the case of a limited partnership, the holding of any interest as a general partner.[126]

Family member. For purposes of Code Sec. 2704, the following are family members with respect to any individual:

(1) the individual's spouse;

(2) an ancestor or lineal descendant of the individual or the individual's spouse;

(3) a brother or sister of the individual; and

(4) a spouse of any individual described in (2) or (3) above.[127]

The attribution rules of Code Sec. 2701(e)(3) apply in determining the interest held by any individual (see ¶2510).[128]

---

[121] *I. Knight*, 115 TC 506, CCH Dec. 54,136. *B. Kerr*, 113 TC 450, CCH Dec. 53,667, aff'd CA-5, 2002-1 USTC ¶60,440. Although affirming the Tax Court's holding, the U.S. Court of Appeals for the Fifth Circuit did so on the ground that the partnership agreement was not an applicable restriction because it did not allow family members, after the transfer, to remove the right to liquidate the partnership.

[122] *M. Harper Est.*, 79 TCM 2232, CCH Dec. 53,939(M), TC Memo. 2000-202.

[123] An individual's family, under Code Sec. 267, includes brothers, sisters (whether by whole or half-blood), spouse, ancestors, and lineal descendants.

[124] Reg. § 25.2704-2(b).

[125] Code Sec. 2704(c)(1).

[126] Code Sec. 2701(b)(2).

[127] Code Sec. 2704(c)(2).

[128] Code Sec. 2704(c)(3).

APPENDIX

RATES AND TABLES

¶ 2595 Repeal of Estate and GST Taxes: Impact of 2001 Act

The Economic Growth and Tax Relief Reconciliation Act of 2001 (P.L. 107-16) (2001 Act) provides that the estate tax will cease to apply to estates of decedents dying after December 31, 2009.[1] Further, the generation-skipping transfer (GST) tax is also repealed, effective for generation-skipping transfers after December 31, 2009.[2]

Sunset provision. In order to comply with the Congressional Budget Act of 1974, the 2001 Act provides that all provisions of, and amendments made by, the 2001 Act will not apply to estates of decedents dying, gifts made, or generation-skipping transfers, after December 31, 2010. Unless Congress acts affirmatively in the interim, the Internal Revenue Code will thereafter be applied and administered as if these provisions had not been enacted.

Prior to repeal, a number of modifications are made to the maximum estate and gift tax rate and the applicable exclusion amount. See the discussions at ¶ 10 and ¶ 15, respectively.

• ***Certain QDOT Distributions***

Under the 2001 Act, special rules will govern the application of Code Sec. 2056A with respect to the noncitizen surviving spouse of a decedent who dies before repeal. For decedents dying before January 1, 2010, the estate tax will continue to be imposed on any distribution from a qualified domestic trust (QDOT) made prior to January 1, 2021, that occurs before the date of the noncitizen surviving spouse's death.[3] In addition, there will continue to be an estate tax imposed on the value of the property remaining in a QDOT on the date of the noncitizen surviving spouse's death if such surviving spouse dies before January 1, 2010.[4] See ¶ 1004 for further discussion of the tax imposed by Code Sec. 2056A.

---

[1] Code Sec. 2210, as added by P.L. 107-16.

[2] Code Sec. 2664, as added by P.L. 107-16.

[3] Code Sec. 2210(b)(1), as added by P.L. 107-16.

[4] Code Sec. 2210(b)(2), as added by P.L. 107-16.

• *Estate Tax Recapture Provisions*

Both the House Ways and Means Committee Report accompanying the Death Tax Elimination Bill of 2001 (H.R. Rep. No. 107-37) and the Senate Finance Committee Report accompanying the Restoring Earnings to Lift Individuals and Empower Families (RELIEF) Bill of 2001 (S. Rep. No. 107-30) state that certain estate tax recapture provisions will continue to apply after repeal of the estate tax becomes effective. This language regarding tax recapture provisions would appear to be implicitly included in the Conference Committee Report's explanation of the 2001 Act, as the 2001 Act largely follows the Senate bill with respect to transfer tax provisions. However, it should be noted that there is *no* language in the 2001 Act that specifically addresses the continued applicability of such provisions following repeal.

The House and Senate Committee Reports cited above specifically identify the recapture rules applicable to the following Code provisions as being retained after repeal: (1) qualified conservation easements; (2) special use valuation; (3) qualified family-owned business interest (QFOBI) deduction; and (4) installment payment of estate tax for estates with an interest in a closely held business.

(1) *Qualified conservation easements.* According to the Committee Reports, the additional tax imposed under Code Sec. 2031(c)(5) as a result of the failure to implement an agreement to extinguish a donor's retained development rights in the conveyance of a qualified conservation easement will be retained after repeal of the estate tax. The provision is retained so that those persons with an interest in the land who fail to execute the agreement will remain liable for any additional tax that may be due following repeal. See ¶253 for further discussion of qualified conservation easements.

(2) *Special use valuation.* The recapture tax imposed under Code Sec. 2032A(c) if property ceases to qualify for special use valuation will be retained after repeal, according to the Committee Reports. The retention of this provision will ensure that those estates that claimed the benefit of special use valuation prior to repeal will be subject to recapture if a disqualifying event occurs after repeal. See ¶284 for further discussion of Code Sec. 2032A.

(3) *QFOBI deduction.* The Committee Reports state that the recapture tax imposed under Code Sec. 2057(f) if property ceases to qualify for the QFOBI deduction will be retained after repeal of the QFOBI deduction in 2004 and the repeal of the estate tax generally. The provision is retained so that estates that claimed the benefit of the deduction before repeal will be subject to recapture if a disqualifying event occurs following repeal. See ¶1150 for further discussion of the QFOBI deduction.

(4) *Installment payment of estate tax for estates with an interest in a closely held business.* According to the Committee Reports, the current estate tax installment payment rules under Code Sec. 6166 will be retained so that estates that entered into installment arrangements before repeal will continue to make their payments past the repeal date. In addition, the provisions of Code Sec. 6166(g), which require the payment of unpaid tax upon notice and demand if 50 percent or more of the value of the closely held business is disposed of, will be retained following repeal so that dispositions that occur after repeal will continue to subject the estate to the unpaid portion of the tax. See ¶1672 for further discussion of Code Sec. 6166.

• *Repeal of Stepped-Up Basis Rules*

In connection with the repeal of the estate and GST taxes, the long-standing stepped-up basis at death rules[5] are replaced by a carryover basis regime.[6] As a result, effective for property acquired from a decedent dying after December 31, 2009, the income tax basis of property acquired from a decedent will generally be carried over from the decedent. More specifically, the recipient of the property will receive a basis equal *to the lesser of* the adjusted basis of the property in the hands of the decedent, or the fair market value of the property on the date of the decedent's death.

As a partial replacement for the repealed step-up, the 2001 Act includes two separate basis increase provisions that are generally available for property passing from decedents (although special rules apply to property passing from nonresident decedents who were not U.S. citizens). First, the executor of the decedent's estate generally can step up the basis of assets of the executor's choosing by a total of $1.3 million.[7] The basis step-up available under this provision can be allocated to assets passing to any property recipient. Second, for properties passing to the decedent's surviving spouse, an additional $3 million in basis step-up is available.[8] Both of these basis increase provisions can be applied to property passing to a surviving spouse. Thus, up to $4.3 million in date-of-death basis step-up can be allocated to property received by a surviving spouse.

Like the estate and GST tax repeal, the repeal of the stepped-up basis at death rules is subject to a "sunset" provision for decedents dying after December 31, 2010.

¶ 2597 Transfer Tax Timeline

The Economic Growth and Tax Relief Reconciliation Act of 2001 (P.L. 107-16) (2001 Act) includes repeal of the federal estate and generation-skipping transfer (GST) taxes for decedents dying after 2009. However, the 2001 Act also makes numerous changes to the transfer tax system for decedents dying, and gifts made, during the years preceding repeal, as depicted in the following timeline:

2001

• Distance requirement for conservation easement exclusion lifted

• Deemed and retroactive allocations of GST tax exemption allowed

• Qualified severance of GST trusts available

• Valuation rules concerning date when allocation of GST tax exemption becomes final modified

• Relief provided for late elections to allocate GST tax exemption and for substantial compliance with regulations

2002

• Maximum estate, gift, and GST tax rate: 50 percent

• Surtax on large estates repealed

• Applicable exclusion amount for estate, gift, and GST tax: $1 million

---

[5] Code Sec. 1014, before repeal by P.L. 107-16.

[6] Code Sec. 1022, as added by P.L. 107-16.

[7] Code Sec. 1022(b), as added by P.L. 107-16.

[8] Code Sec. 1022(c), as added by P.L. 107-16.

- State death tax credit reduced to 75 percent of prior law amount
- Rules on installment payment of estate taxes liberalized

2003

- Maximum estate, gift, and GST tax rate: 49 percent
- Applicable exclusion amount for estate, gift, and GST tax: $1 million
- State death tax credit reduced to 50 percent of prior law amount

2004

- Maximum estate, gift, and GST tax rate: 48 percent
- Applicable exclusion amount for estate and GST tax: $1.5 million
- Inflation adjustment for GST tax exemption ends
- Exclusion amount for gift tax: $1 million
- State death tax credit reduced to 25 percent of prior law amount
- Deduction for qualified family-owned business interests (Code Sec. 2057) repealed

2005

- Maximum estate, gift, and GST tax rate: 47 percent
- Applicable exclusion amount for estate and GST tax: $1.5 million
- Exclusion amount for gift tax: $1 million
- State death tax credit becomes a deduction

2006

- Maximum estate, gift, and GST tax rate: 46 percent
- Applicable exclusion amount for estate and GST tax: $2 million
- Exclusion amount for gift tax: $1 million

2007–2008

- Maximum estate, gift, and GST tax rate: 45 percent
- Applicable exclusion amount for estate and GST tax: $2 million
- Exclusion amount for gift tax: $1 million

2009

- Maximum estate, gift, and GST tax rate: 45 percent
- Applicable exclusion amount for estate and GST tax: $3.5 million
- Exclusion amount for gift tax: $1 million

2010

- Estate and GST taxes repealed
- Gift tax remains in force with maximum rate of 35 percent and exclusion amount of $1 million
- Stepped-up basis for inherited assets repealed and replaced with "modified" carryover basis

2011

• "Sunset" provision forces return to pre-2001 Act law, absent Congressional action to the contrary

¶ 2600 Unified Rates and Credit

I. Estates of U.S. Citizens and Residents Dying, and Gifts Made, After 1976

Estate and gift tax rates are combined in a single rate schedule effective for the estates of decedents dying, and for gifts made, after December 31, 1976. For years prior to 2002, the rates are graduated from 37 percent for transfers in excess of $500,000 to 55 percent for transfers in excess of $3 million. Lifetime transfers and transfers made at death are cumulated for gift and estate tax purposes.

• ***Law Following the 2001 Act***

The enactment of the Economic Growth and Tax Relief Reconciliation Act of 2001 (P.L. 107-16) (2001 Act) brought significant change to the transfer tax system, the most notable being the repeal of the estate and generation-skipping transfer (GST) taxes in 2010. Prior to repeal, a number of modifications are made to the maximum estate tax rate and the estate tax applicable exclusion amount (discussed below). The 2001 Act reduces the top marginal rate to 50 percent for decedents dying, and gifts made, in 2002, with further reductions in later years, according to the following schedule: 49 percent for decedents dying (and gifts made) in 2003; 48 percent in 2004; 47 percent in 2005; 46 percent in 2006; and 45 percent in 2007, 2008, and 2009.

Sunset provision. It should be noted that the provisions of the 2001 Act will expire ("sunset") after December 31, 2010, meaning that the transfer tax laws in effect prior to the passage of the 2001 Act will be revived in 2011 unless Congress acts in the interim to extend the 2001 Act's effectiveness.

Prior to 1998, the benefits of the graduated rates and the unified credit under the unified transfer tax system were phased out beginning with cumulative transfers above $10 million. This was accomplished by adding five percent of the excess of any transfer over $10 million to the tentative tax computed in determining the ultimate transfer tax liability. For estates of decedents dying, and gifts made, after 1987 and before 1998, the additional tax was levied on transfers above $10 million, but not exceeding $21,040,000. Beginning in 1998, the five-percent additional tax phased out the benefits of the graduated rates, but not the benefits of the unified credit. Therefore, for years after 1997 and before 2002, the additional tax is levied on amounts transferred in excess of $10 million, but not exceeding $17,184,000.

• ***Law Following the 2001 Act***

The 2001 Act repeals the five-percent surtax for estates of decedents dying, and gifts made, after December 31, 2001.

The estate tax liability is determined by applying the unified rate schedule to the cumulated transfers and subtracting the gift taxes payable. The cumulated transfers to which the tentative tax applies is the sum of (1) the amount of the taxable estate, and (2) the amount of the taxable gifts made by the decedent after 1976, other than gifts includible in the gross estate. Gift taxes to be subtracted in computing the estate tax include the aggregate gift tax payable on gifts made after December 31, 1976. For this purpose, the amount of gift taxes paid by a decedent after 1976 is to be determined as if the rate schedule in effect in the year of death was in effect the year of the gift. However, with respect to certain gifts subsequently included in a decedent's gross estate, a credit is allowed (Code Sec. 2012) for gift taxes paid on pre-1977 gifts.

Gift tax liability for any calendar quarter (for gifts made after 1970 and before 1982) or year (for gifts made before 1971 and after 1981) is determined by applying the unified rate schedule to cumulative lifetime taxable transfers and subtracting the taxes payable for prior taxable periods. Preceding calendar periods are: (1) calendar year 1932 (after June 6) and 1970 and all intervening calendar years; (2) the first calendar quarter of 1971 and all quarters between that quarter and the first quarter of 1982; and (3) all calendar years after 1981 and before the year for which the tax is being computed. In computing cumulative taxable gifts for prior taxable periods, the donor's pre-1977 taxable gifts are to be taken into account, with the reduction for taxes previously paid to be based on the unified rate schedule.

• *Law Following the 2001 Act*

The 2001 Act retains the gift tax following estate tax repeal in 2010. Gift tax liability for years after 2009 is determined using a rate schedule created by the 2001 Act, which contains graduated rates ranging from 18 percent to 35 percent (for transfers in excess of $500,000).

The GST tax is applied at a flat rate derived from the maximum estate tax rate to direct skips, taxable distributions, and taxable terminations. The method for computing the taxable amount depends on whether a taxable distribution, a taxable termination, or a direct skip is involved. For a taxable distribution, as well as a direct skip, the amount received by the transferee is subject to the tax. In the case of a taxable termination, the tax is applied to the value of the property in which the interest terminates. Each transferor is provided with a $1 million exemption (adjusted for inflation occurring after 1997 and before 2004) that may be allocated among several generation-skipping transfers. A special $2 million per grandchild exemption was allowed for direct skips made prior to 1990. In addition, the GST tax does not apply to direct skips to a transferor's grandchildren (or the grandchildren of the transferor's spouse or former spouse) if the grandchild's parent, who is a lineal descendant of the transferor (or the transferor's spouse or former spouse), is deceased. Beginning in 1998, this deceased parent exception was expanded to include direct skips, taxable terminations, and distributions made to collateral heirs if the deceased parent was a descendant of the parent of the transferor (or of the transferor's spouse or former spouse). However, the deceased parent exception only applies to collateral heirs if the transferor has no living lineal descendants at the time of the transfer.

• *Law Following the 2001 Act*

The 2001 Act repeals the GST tax with respect to generation-skipping transfers made after December 31, 2009. The reductions in the maximum estate tax rate under the 2001 Act (discussed above) will cause corresponding reductions in the rate used to determine the GST tax for the years leading up to repeal. In addition, the 2001 Act provides that the amount of the GST tax exemption for any calendar year will be equal to the estate tax applicable exclusion amount in effect for such calendar year.

The unified rate schedule applying to estates of decedents dying, and gifts made, after 1983 and before 2002 appears below.

Unified Tax Rate Schedule

Column A *Taxable amount over*	Column B *Taxable amount not over*	Column C *Tax on amount in column A*	Column D *Rate of tax on excess over amount in column A Percent*
$ 0	$ 10,000	$ 0	18
10,000	20,000	1,800	20
20,000	40,000	3,800	22
40,000	60,000	8,200	24
60,000	80,000	13,000	26
80,000	100,000	18,200	28
100,000	150,000	23,800	30
150,000	250,000	38,800	32
250,000	500,000	70,800	34
500,000	750,000	155,800	37
750,000	1,000,000	248,300	39
1,000,000	1,250,000	345,800	41
1,250,000	1,500,000	448,300	43
1,500,000	2,000,000	555,800	45
2,000,000	2,500,000	780,800	49
2,500,000	3,000,000	1,025,800	53
3,000,000	....	1,290,800	55

Prior to 1984, different tax rates applied to cumulative lifetime and at-death transfers exceeding $3 million.

- **1983.** A 57-percent tax rate applied to transfers in the $3 to $3.5 million range and a 60-percent rate applied to amounts in excess of $3.5 million.

- **1982.** A 57-percent tax rate applied to transfers in the $3 to $3.5 million range; a 61-percent rate applied to transfers in the $3.5 to $4 million range; and a 65-percent rate applied to transfers in excess of $4 million.

- **1977–1981.** A 57-percent tax rate applied to transfers in the $3 to $3.5 million range; a 61-percent rate applied to transfers in the $3.5 to $4 million range; a 65-percent rate applied to transfers in the $4 to $4.5 million range; a 69-percent rate applied to transfers in the $4.5 to $5 million range; and a 70-percent rate applied to transfers in excess of $5 million.

In general, the amount of estate tax payable under the unified tax rate schedule is determined by applying the applicable rate to the aggregate of lifetime and at-death transfers, and then subtracting the gift taxes payable on gifts made after 1976. For this purpose, the amount of gift taxes paid by a decedent is to be determined as if the rate schedule in effect in the year of death was in effect in the year of the gift. See specific details at ¶1426 for computing the tax.

- ***Rate Schedule (2002–2009)***

The estate and gift tax rate schedule applicable to the estates of decedents dying, and gifts made, in 2002 through 2009 (the years prior to repeal of the estate tax in 2010) is as follows:

Transfer Tax Rate Schedule: 2002–2009*

(A) *Amount subject to tax more than—*	*(B)* *Amount subject to tax equal to or less than—*	*(C)* *Tax on amount in column (A)*	*(D)* *Rate of tax on excess over amount in column (A) Percent*
....	$ 10,000	....	18
$ 10,000	20,000	$ 1,800	20
20,000	40,000	3,800	22
40,000	60,000	8,200	24

Transfer Tax Rate Schedule: 2002–2009*

(A) Amount subject to tax more than—	*(B) Amount subject to tax equal to or less than—*	*(C) Tax on amount in column (A)*	*(D) Rate of tax on excess over amount in column (A) Percent*
60,000	80,000	13,000	26
80,000	100,000	18,200	28
100,000	150,000	23,800	30
150,000	250,000	38,800	32
250,000	500,000	70,800	34
500,000	750,000	155,800	37
750,000	1,000,000	248,300	39
1,000,000	1,250,000	345,800	41
1,250,000	1,500,000	448,300	43
1,500,000	2,000,000	555,800	45
2,000,000	2,500,000	780,800	49
2,500,000	....	1,025,800	50 *

* The 2001 Act reduces the top marginal rate for years after 2002, according to the following schedule:
- 49 percent for decedents dying, and gifts made, in 2003;
- 48 percent in 2004;
- 47 percent in 2005;
- 46 percent in 2006;
- 45 percent in 2007, 2008, and 2009.

For years 2003 through 2009, the tentative tax is to be determined by using a table prescribed by the IRS, which will be the same as the rate schedule shown above except for the adjustments necessary to reflect the reductions in the maximum rate.

• ***Benefits of Graduated Rates and Unified Credit Phased Out***

The benefits of the graduated rates and the unified credit under the unified transfer tax system are phased out for the estates of decedents dying before 1998 beginning with cumulative transfers above $10 million. This is accomplished by adding five percent of the excess of any transfer over $10 million to the tentative tax computed in determining the ultimate transfer tax liability. For estates of decedents dying, and gifts made, after 1987 and before 1998, the tax is levied on amounts transferred in excess of $10 million, but not exceeding $21,040,000, in order to recapture the benefit of any transfer tax rate below 55 percent, as well as the unified credit.

Due to mistakes in the wording of the amendment to Code Sec. 2001(c)(2) by the Taxpayer Relief Act of 1997 (P.L. 105-34), the five-percent additional tax phases out the benefits of the graduated rates, but not the benefits of the unified credit (applicable credit amount), for estates of decedents dying, and gifts made, after 1997 and before 2002. A provision in the Senate Committee Report on the IRS Restructuring and Reform Act of 1998 (P.L. 105-206) clarifying the phaseout range for the five-percent surtax to phase out the benefits of the unified credit was not included in the Conference Committee Report. Therefore, the additional tax is levied on amounts transferred after 1997 and before 2002 in excess of $10 million, but not exceeding $17,184,000. The applicable credit amount is not recaptured.

Although Code Sec. 2001(c)(2) was effective with respect to transfers made after 1987 under the Revenue Act of 1987 (P.L. 100-203), the Conference Committee Report for that Act states that pre-effective date gifts are included in cumulative transfers for purposes of determining the adjustment for transfers made after the effective date; however, the tax rate on the earlier gifts remains unchanged.

Thus, according to the Committee Report, if a person makes a $9 million gift before 1988, and an additional $4 million gift after 1987, $3 million of the latter transfer will be subject to the additional tax under the phase-out.

• ***Repeal of Five-Percent Surtax***

The 2001 Act repealed the five-percent surtax for the estates of decedents dying, and gifts made, after December 31, 2001.

• ***Unified Credit***

For estates of decedents dying after 1976 and gifts made after 1976, both the $60,000 estate tax exemption and the $30,000 lifetime gift tax exemption were replaced by a single unified credit. The amount of this credit is subtracted from the amount of the decedent's gross estate tax. In effect, the amount of the unified credit available at death will be reduced to the extent that any portion of the credit is used to offset gift taxes on lifetime transfers.

Amounts allowed as lifetime exemptions on gifts made after September 8, 1976, but before January 1, 1977, reduce the unified credit allowable by 20 percent of the exemption used, to a maximum of $6,000.

For estates of decedents dying in 1977 and thereafter, the credit was phased in as follows:

Year	*Amount of Credit*	*Amount of Exemption Equivalent*
1977	$ 30,000	$120,667
1978	34,000	134,000
1979	38,000	147,333
1980	42,500	161,563
1981	47,000	175,625
1982	62,800	225,000
1983	79,300	275,000
1984	96,300	325,000
1985	121,800	400,000
1986	155,800	500,000
1987–1997	192,800	600,000

The Taxpayer Relief Act of 1997 replaced the unified credit amount with an applicable credit amount, effective for the estates of decedents dying, and gifts made, after December 31, 1997. The applicable credit amount is defined as the amount of the tentative tax that would be determined under the Code Sec. 2001(c) rate schedule if the amount with respect to which the tentative tax is computed were the applicable exclusion amount. However, the amount of the credit cannot exceed the amount of estate tax imposed. The table below provides the applicable credit amount and the applicable exclusion amount for the period between 1998 and 2001.

Year	*Applicable Credit Amount*	*Applicable Exclusion Amount*
1998	$202,050	$625,000
1999	211,300	650,000
2000 and 2001	220,550	675,000

• ***Impact of the 2001 Act***

The enactment of the 2001 Act brought significant change to the transfer tax system, the most notable being the repeal of the estate and GST taxes in 2010. Prior to repeal, a number of modifications are made to the maximum estate tax rate and the estate and gift tax applicable exclusion amounts. The 2001 Act increases the *estate tax* applicable exclusion amount according to the following schedule:

- $1 million for decedents dying in 2002 and 2003;
- $1.5 million in 2004 and 2005;
- $2 million in 2006, 2007, and 2008; and
- $3.5 million in 2009.

The 2001 Act also increases the *gift tax* applicable exclusion amount to $1 million, beginning with gifts made in 2002. However, unlike the gradual increase in the estate tax applicable exclusion amount in the years leading up to repeal of the estate tax, the gift tax applicable exclusion amount remains at $1 million and is not indexed for inflation. For years 2002 through 2009, the amount of the gift tax unified credit is equal to (1) the applicable credit amount in effect under Code Sec. 2010(c) for such calendar year, determined as if the applicable exclusion amount were $1 million, reduced by (2) the sum of the amounts allowable as a credit under Code Sec. 2505 for all preceding calendar periods.[9]

The table below provides the applicable credit amount and the applicable exclusion amount for years 2002 and 2003.

Year	*Applicable Credit Amount*	*Applicable Exclusion Amount*
2002 and 2003	$345,800	$1,000,000

As a result of the 2001 Act, beginning in 2004, the unified credit will no longer be truly "unified," as the estate and gift tax applicable exclusion amounts will differ.

- ***Computation of Credit Following Estate Tax Repeal***

The 2001 Act retains the gift tax following estate tax repeal in 2010. Gift tax liability for years after 2009 is determined by using a rate schedule created by the 2001 Act.[10] The credit allowed against the gift tax for such years will be equal to (1) the amount of the tentative tax that would be determined under the new gift tax-only rate schedule if the amount with respect to which such tentative tax is to be computed was $1 million, reduced by (2) the sum of the amounts allowable as a credit for all preceding calendar periods.[11]

Sunset provision. In order to comply with the Congressional Budget Act of 1974, the 2001 Act provides that all provisions of, and amendments made by, the 2001 Act will not apply to estates of decedents dying, gifts made, or generation-skipping transfers, after December 31, 2010. Unless Congress acts affirmatively in the interim, the Internal Revenue Code will thereafter be applied and administered as if these provisions had not been enacted.

An illustration of the computation of federal gift and estate taxes under the unified transfer tax system is at ¶1428.

II. Estates of Nonresidents Not Citizens

Effective for the estates of decedents dying after November 10, 1988, estate and gift tax rates applicable to U.S. citizens are also applicable to the estates of nonresident aliens.

---

[9] Code Sec. 2505(a), as amended by P.L. 107-16.

[10] Code Sec. 2502(a), as amended by P.L. 107-16.

[11] Code Sec. 2505(a)(1), as amended by P.L. 107-16.

The gift tax applies to transfers made by nonresidents not U.S. citizens only with respect to transfers of tangible property situated within the United States.

A separate estate tax rate schedule applies in the case of nonresidents not U.S. citizens dying after December 31, 1976, and before November 11, 1988. The amount of estate tax is determined by applying the unified rate schedule below to the cumulative lifetime and deathtime transfers subject to United States transfer taxes and then subtracting gift taxes payable on the lifetime transfers made after December 31, 1976, but before January 1, 2010.

If the amount is:	The tentative tax is:
Not over $100,000	6% of the taxable estate.
Over $100,000 but not over $500,000	$6,000, plus 12% of excess over $100,000.
Over $500,000 but not over $1,000,000 . .	$54,000, plus 18% of excess over $500,000.
Over $1,000,000 but not over $2,000,000 .	$144,000, plus 24% of excess over $1,000,000.
Over $2,000,000	$348,000, plus 30% of excess over $2,000,000.

• ***Repeal of Estate Tax in 2010***

The 2001 Act repeals the estate tax with respect to the estates of decedents dying after December 31, 2009 (Code Sec. 2210, see ¶2595).

Sunset provision. In order to comply with the Congressional Budget Act of 1974, the 2001 Act provides that all provisions of, and amendments made by, the 2001 Act will not apply to estates of decedents dying, gifts made, or generation-skipping transfers, after December 31, 2010. Unless Congress acts affirmatively in the interim, the Internal Revenue Code will thereafter be applied and administered as if these provisions had not been enacted.

• ***Credit***

Effective for the estates of decedents dying after November 10, 1988, where permitted by treaty, the estate of a nonresident alien is allowed the same unified credit as a U.S. citizen multiplied by the percentage of the decedent's total gross estate situated in the United States. In other cases, the estate of a nonresident alien is allowed a unified credit of $13,000 (which exempts the first $60,000 of the estate from estate tax). The estate of a resident of a U.S. possession, dying after November 10, 1988, is entitled to a unified credit equal to the greater of (1) $13,000, or (2) $46,800 multiplied by the percentage of the decedent's gross estate situated in the United States.

A $30,000 estate tax exemption was available to the estates of nonresident aliens dying before January 1, 1977. Applicable for the estates of nonresident aliens dying after December 31, 1976, and before November 11, 1988, that exemption was eliminated and replaced by a credit of $3,600 that is allowed against the estate tax. In the case of residents of a possession of the United States (who are not considered citizens) dying after December 31, 1976, and before November 11, 1988, the credit allowable is the greater of $3,600 or that proportion of $15,075 that the value of that part of the decedent's property situated in the United States bears to the value of the entire gross estate wherever situated. The $15,075 figure was phased in over a five-year period.

¶ 2605 Rate Schedule Under Victims of Terrorism Tax Relief Act (P.L. 107-134) and Military Family Tax Relief Act (P.L. 108-121)

The following estate tax table applies only to members of the U.S. military who died in a combat zone (see ¶1560), to civilians who died as a result of certain terrorist attacks (see ¶1650), and to astronauts who died in the line of duty after December 31, 2002.[12]

(A) Amount subject to tax more than—	*(B) Amount subject to tax equal to or less than—*	*(C) Tax on amount in column (A)*	*(D) Rate of tax on excess over amount in column (A) Percent*
0	$100,000	0	0
$100,000	150,000	0	1
150,000	200,000	$500	2
200,000	300,000	1,500	3
300,000	500,000	4,500	4
500,000	700,000	12,500	5
700,000	900,000	22,500	6
900,000	1,100,000	34,500	7
1,100,000	1,600,000	48,500	8
1,600,000	2,100,000	88,500	9
2,100,000	2,600,000	133,500	10
2,600,000	3,100,000	183,500	11
3,100,000	3,600,000	238,500	12
3,600,000	4,100,000	298,500	13
4,100,000	5,100,000	363,500	14
5,100,000	6,100,000	503,500	15
6,100,000	7,100,000	653,500	16
7,100,000	8,100,000	813,500	17
8,100,000	9,100,000	983,500	18
9,100,000	10,100,000	1,163,500	19
10,100,000	....	1,353,500	20

¶ 2610 Postponement of Time-Sensitive Tax Acts

The IRS has issued[13] a list of time-sensitive acts, the performance of which may be postponed under Code Sec. 7508 (relating to individuals serving in the Armed Forces) and Code Sec. 7508A (relating to taxpayers affected by a Presidentially declared disaster). This IRS action does not, by itself, provide any postponements under Code Sec. 7508 and Code Sec. 7508A. In order for taxpayers to be entitled to a postponement of any act listed below, the IRS generally will publish a Notice or other guidance providing relief with respect to a specific combat zone or Presidentially declared disaster.

This revenue procedure is effective for acts that may be performed on or after September 11, 2001. It does not list acts specified in Code Sec. 7508, Code Sec. 7508A, or the regulations thereunder, such as the filing of tax returns or payment of taxes. Material not relevant to estate, gift, or generation-skipping transfer taxes has not been reproduced.

Section 6. Business and Individual Tax Issues

	Statute or Regulation	*Act Postponed*
		***
18.	Sec. 529(c)(3)(C)(i)	A rollover contribution to another qualified tuition program must be made no later than the 60th day after the date of a distribution from a qualified tuition program.
		***

[12] Code Sec. 2201, as amended by the Military Family Tax Relief Act of 2003.

[13] Rev. Proc. 2004-13, IRB 2004-335, superseding Rev. Proc. 2002-71, IRB 2002-46, 850, superseding Rev. Proc. 2001-53, IRB 2001-47, 506.

Section 6. Business and Individual Tax Issues

	Statute or Regulation	*Act Postponed*
28.	Treas. Reg. § 301.9100-2(a)(1)	An automatic extension of 12 months from the due date for making a regulatory election is granted to make certain elections, including the election to use other than the required taxable year under section 444, and the election to use LIFO under section 472.
29.	Treas. Reg. § 301.9100-2(b)-(d)	An automatic extension of 6 months from the due date of a return, excluding extensions, is granted to make the regulatory or statutory elections whose due dates are the due date of the return or the due date of the return including extension (for example, a taxpayer has an automatic 6-month extension to file an application to change a method of accounting under Rev. Proc. 2002-9), provided the taxpayer (a) timely filed its return for the year of election, (b) within that 6-month extension period, takes the required corrective action to file the election in accordance with the statute, regulations, revenue procedure, revenue ruling, notice or announcement permitting the election, and (c) writes at the top of the return, statement of election or other form "FILED PURSUANT TO § 301.9100-2."

Section 7. Corporate Issues

	Statute or Regulation	*Act Postponed*
		***
2.	Sec. 303 and Treas. Reg. § 1.303-2	A corporation must complete the distribution of property to a shareholder in redemption of all or part of the stock of the corporation which (for Federal estate tax purposes) is included in determining the estate of a decedent. Section 303 and Treas. Reg. § 1.303-2 require, among other things, that the distribution occur within the specified period.
		***

Section 9. Estate, Gift and Trust Issues

	Statute or Regulation	*Act Postponed*
1.	Sec. 643(g)	The trustee may elect to treat certain payments of estimated tax as paid by the beneficiary. The election shall be made on or before the 65th day after the close of the taxable year of the trust.
2.	Sec. 2011(c)	The executor of a decedent's estate must file a claim for a credit for state estate, inheritance, legacy or succession taxes by filing a claim within 4 years of filing Form 706, United States Estate (and Generation Skipping Transfer) Tax Return. (Section 2011 is amended effective for estates of decedents dying after 12/31/04).
3.	Sec. 2014(e)	The executor of a decedent's estate must file a claim for foreign death taxes within 4 years of filing Form 706, United States Estate (and Generation Skipping Transfer) Tax Return.

Section 9. Estate, Gift and Trust Issues

	Statute or Regulation	*Act Postponed*
4.	Sec. 2016 and Treas. Reg. §20.2016-1	If an executor of a decedent's estate (or any other person) receives a refund of any state or foreign death taxes claimed as a credit on Form 706, the IRS must be notified within 30 days of receipt. (Section 2016 is amended effective for estates of decedents dying after 12/31/04).
5.	Sec. 2031(c)	If an executor of a decedent's estate elects on Form 706 to exclude a portion of the value of land that is subject to a qualified conservation easement, agreements relating to development rights must be implemented within 2 years after the date of the decedent's death.
6.	Sec. 2032(d)	The executor of a decedent's estate may elect an alternate valuation on a late filed Form 706 if the Form 706 is not filed later than 1 year after the due date.
7.	Sec. 2032A(c)(7)	A qualified heir, with respect to specially valued property, is provided a two-year grace period immediately following the date of the decedent's death in which the failure by the qualified heir to begin using the property in a qualified use will not be considered a cessation of qualified use and therefore will not trigger additional estate tax.
8.	Sec. 2032A(d)(3)	The executor of a decedent's estate has 90 days after notification of incomplete information/signatures to provide the information/signatures to the IRS regarding an election on Form 706 with respect to specially valued property.
9.	Sec. 2046	A taxpayer may make a qualified disclaimer no later than 9 months after the date on which the transfer creating the interest is made, or the date the person attains age 21.
10.	Sec. 2053(d) and Treas. Reg. §§20.2053-9(c) and 10(c)	If the executor of a decedent's estate elects to take a deduction for state and foreign death tax imposed upon a transfer for charitable or other uses, the executor must file a written notification to that effect with the IRS before expiration of the period of limitations on assessments (generally 3 years). (Section 2053 is amended effective for estates of decedents dying after 12/31/04).
11.	Sec. 2055(e)(3)	A party in interest must commence a judicial proceeding to change an interest into a qualified interest no later than the 90th day after the estate tax return (Form 706) is required to be filed or, if no return is required, the last date for filing the income tax return for the first taxable year of the trust.

Section 9. Estate, Gift and Trust Issues

	Statute or Regulation	*Act Postponed*
12.	Sec. 2056(d)	A qualified domestic trust (QDOT) election must be made on Form 706, Schedule M, and the property must be transferred to the trust before the date on which the return is made. Any reformation to determine if a trust is a QDOT requires that the judicial proceeding be commenced on or before the due date for filing the return.
13.	Sec. 2056A(b)(2)	The trustee of a QDOT must file a claim for refund of excess tax no later than 1 year after the date of final determination of the decedent's estate tax liability.
14.	Sec. 2057(i)(3)(G)	A qualified heir, with respect to qualified family owned business, has a two-year grace period immediately following the date of the decedent's death in which the failure by the qualified heir to begin using the property in a qualified use will not be considered a cessation of qualified use and therefore will not trigger additional estate tax. (The section 2057 election is not available to estates of decedents dying after 12/31/03).
15.	Sec. 2057(i)(3)(H)	The executor of a decedent's estate has 90 days after notification of incomplete information/ signatures to provide the information/ signatures to the IRS regarding an election on Form 706 with respect to specially valued property.
16.	Sec. 2516	The IRS will treat certain transfers as made for full and adequate consideration in money or money's worth where husband and wife enter into a written agreement relative to their marital and property rights and divorce actually occurs within the 3-year period beginning on the date 1 year before such agreement is entered into.
17.	Sec. 2518(b)	A taxpayer may make a qualified disclaimer no later than 9 months after the date on which the transfer creating the interest is made, or the date the person attains age 21.

***

Section 14. Procedure and Administration Issues

	Statute or Regulation	*Act Postponed*
1.	Treas. Reg. § 301.6036-1(a)(2) and (3)	A court-appointed receiver or fiduciary in a non-bankruptcy receivership, a fiduciary in aid of foreclosure who takes possession of substantially all of the debtor's assets, or an assignee for benefit of creditors, must give written notice within ten days of his appointment to the IRS as to where the debtor will file his tax return.

***

Section 14. Procedure and Administration Issues

	Statute or Regulation	*Act Postponed*
4.	Sec. 6331(k)(1) and Treas. Reg. §301.7122-1T(f)(2)(ii)	If a taxpayer submits a good-faith revision of a rejected offer in compromise within 30 days after the rejection, the Service will not levy to collect the liability before deciding whether to accept the revised offer.
5.	Sec. 6331(k)(2) and Treas. Reg. §301.6331-4(a)(1)	If, within 30 days following the rejection or termination of an installment agreement, the taxpayer files an appeal with the IRS Office of Appeals, no levy may be made while the rejection or termination is being considered by Appeals.
6.	Sec. 7122(d)(2) and Treas. Reg. §301.7122-1T(f)(5)(i)	A taxpayer must request administrative review of a rejected offer in compromise within 30 days after the date on the letter of rejection.

¶ 2630 State Death Tax Credit Table

A credit is allowed against the federal estate tax for any estate, inheritance, legacy, or succession taxes actually paid to any state of the United States or the District of Columbia with respect to any property included in the decedent's gross estate. The credit is applied against the adjusted taxable estate, which for this purpose is the taxable estate reduced by $60,000. The credit is available only if it does not exceed the estate's tax liability after reduction by the unified credit. (The following table may not be used in computing taxes on estates of certain members of the Armed Forces.)

Estates of Decedents Dying After 1976

Adjusted Taxable Estate ("Adjusted Taxable Estate" is the decedent's taxable estate less $60,000) From	*To*	*Credit =*	*+ %*	*Of Excess Over*
0	$40,000	0	0.0	0
$40,000	90,000	0	0.8	$40,000
90,000	140,000	$400	1.6	90,000
140,000	240,000	1,200	2.4	140,000
240,000	440,000	3,600	3.2	240,000
440,000	640,000	10,000	4.0	440,000
640,000	840,000	18,000	4.8	640,000
840,000	1,040,000	27,600	5.6	840,000
1,040,000	1,540,000	38,800	6.4	1,040,000
1,540,000	2,040,000	70,800	7.2	1,540,000
2,040,000	2,540,000	106,800	8.0	2,040,000
2,540,000	3,040,000	146,800	8.8	2,540,000
3,040,000	3,540,000	190,800	9.6	3,040,000
3,540,000	4,040,000	238,800	10.4	3,540,000
4,040,000	5,040,000	290,800	11.2	4,040,000
5,040,000	6,040,000	402,800	12.0	5,040,000
6,040,000	7,040,000	522,800	12.8	6,040,000
7,040,000	8,040,000	650,800	13.6	7,040,000
8,040,000	9,040,000	786,800	14.4	8,040,000
9,040,000	10,040,000	930,800	15.2	9,040,000
10,040,000	....	1,082,800	16.0	10,040,000

• *Phaseout and Repeal of Credit*

The 2001 Act gradually phases out the state death tax credit between 2002 and 2004, with the credit repealed for the estates of decedents dying after December 31, 2004. Beginning in 2005, the state death tax credit is replaced by a deduction for state death taxes paid until the repeal of the estate tax in 2010[14] (see ¶1380). The credit is reduced by 25 percent for the estates of decedents dying in 2002, 50 percent for the estates of decedents dying in 2003, and 75 percent for the estates of decedents dying in 2004.

Sunset provision. In order to comply with the Congressional Budget Act of 1974, the 2001 Act provides that all provisions of, and amendments made by, the 2001 Act will not apply to estates of decedents dying, gifts made, or generation-skipping transfers, after December 31, 2010. Unless Congress acts affirmatively in the interim, the Internal Revenue Code will thereafter be applied and administered as if these provisions had not been enacted.

¶ 2640 Pre-1977 Estate Tax Rates

I. Effective for Estates of U.S. Citizens and Residents Dying Before 1977

The federal estate tax on estates of U.S. citizens and residents is computed on a "taxable estate," after deduction of a $60,000 exemption, at the rates below. This amount is further reduced by a state death tax credit computed under the table at "III. State Death Tax Credit" below, or by the actual amount of state death taxes, whichever is less. Credits are also available for foreign death taxes, certain gift taxes, and federal estate taxes on prior transfers. (The following table may not be used in computing taxes on estates of certain members of the Armed Forces.[15])

Taxable Estate (After deducting the $60,000 exemption) From	To	*Tax =*	*+*	*%*	*Of Excess Over*
0	$5,000	0		3	0
$5,000	10,000	$150		7	$5,000
10,000	20,000	500		11	10,000
20,000	30,000	1,600		14	20,000
30,000	40,000	3,000		18	30,000
40,000	50,000	4,800		22	40,000
50,000	60,000	7,000		25	50,000
60,000	100,000	9,500		28	60,000
100,000	250,000	20,700		30	100,000
250,000	500,000	65,700		32	250,000
500,000	750,000	145,700		35	500,000
750,000	1,000,000	233,200		37	750,000
1,000,000	1,250,000	325,700		39	1,000,000
1,250,000	1,500,000	423,200		42	1,250,000
1,500,000	2,000,000	528,200		45	1,500,000
2,000,000	2,500,000	753,200		49	2,000,000
2,500,000	3,000,000	998,200		53	2,500,000
3,000,000	3,500,000	1,263,200		56	3,000,000
3,500,000	4,000,000	1,543,200		59	3,500,000
4,000,000	5,000,000	1,838,200		63	4,000,000
5,000,000	6,000,000	2,468,200		67	5,000,000
6,000,000	7,000,000	3,138,200		70	6,000,000

[14] Code Sec. 2058, as added by P.L. 107-16.

[15] See Code Sec. 2011(d) and Code Sec. 2201.

Taxable Estate (After deducting the $60,000 exemption) From	To	Tax =	+ %	Of Excess Over
7,000,000	8,000,000	3,838,200	73	7,000,000
8,000,000	10,000,000	4,568,200	76	8,000,000
10,000,000	....	6,088,200	77	10,000,000

II. Estates of Nonresidents Not Citizens Dying After November 13, 1966 and Before January 1, 1977

The federal estate tax on estates of nonresidents not citizens dying after November 13, 1966 and before January 1, 1977, after deduction of the $30,000 exemption, but prior to any credit for state death taxes, gift taxes or taxes on prior transfers, is computed at the rates below.

Taxable Estate (After deducting the $30,000 exemption) From	To	Tax =	+ %	Of Excess Over
0	$100,000	0	5	0
$100,000	500,000	$5,000	10	$100,000
500,000	1,000,000	45,000	15	500,000
1,000,000	2,000,000	120,000	20	1,000,000
2,000,000	....	320,000	25	2,000,000

III. State Death Tax Credit

Taxable Estate (After deducting the applicable exemption) From	To	Credit =	+ %	Of Excess Over
0	$40,000	0	0.0	0
$40,000	90,000	0	0.8	$40,000
90,000	140,000	$400	1.6	90,000
140,000	240,000	1,200	2.4	140,000
240,000	440,000	3,600	3.2	240,000
440,000	640,000	10,000	4.0	440,000
640,000	840,000	18,000	4.8	640,000
840,000	1,040,000	27,600	5.6	840,000
1,040,000	1,540,000	38,800	6.4	1,040,000
1,540,000	2,040,000	70,800	7.2	1,540,000
2,040,000	2,540,000	106,800	8.0	2,040,000
2,540,000	3,040,000	146,800	8.8	2,540,000
3,040,000	3,540,000	190,800	9.6	3,040,000
3,540,000	4,040,000	238,800	10.4	3,540,000
4,040,000	5,040,000	290,800	11.2	4,040,000
5,040,000	6,040,000	402,800	12.0	5,040,000
6,040,000	7,040,000	522,800	12.8	6,040,000
7,040,000	8,040,000	650,800	13.6	7,040,000
8,040,000	9,040,000	786,800	14.4	8,040,000
9,040,000	10,040,000	930,800	15.2	9,040,000
10,040,000	....	1,082,800	16.0	10,040,000

¶ 2650 Pre-1977 Gift Tax Rates

The rate table below is applicable for gifts made in 1976 and prior years. See ¶2600 for unified rate table for gifts made after 1976. Gifts made prior to 1977 will be taken into account in the computation of the unified transfer tax generated by post-1976 gifts. In computing the tax payable on post-1976 gifts, the reduction for taxes paid previously is to be based on the unified rate schedule. See the illustration at ¶2008.

"Taxable gifts," as noted in the table below, are determined by deducting the $30,000 specific exemption (allowed only once, but cumulative until used up) and by deducting an annual exclusion of $3,000 per donee of gifts of present interests. The $30,000 specific exemption is eliminated for post-1976 gifts.

Taxable Gifts				
From	*To*	*Tax =*	*+ %*	*Of Excess Over*
....	$5,000	0.00	2¼%	....
$5,000	10,000	$112.50	5¼%	$5,000
10,000	20,000	375.00	8¼%	10,000
20,000	30,000	1,200.00	10½%	20,000
30,000	40,000	2,250.00	13½%	30,000
40,000	50,000	3,600.00	16½%	40,000
50,000	60,000	5,250.00	18¾%	50,000
60,000	100,000	7,125.00	21%	60,000
100,000	250,000	15,525.00	22½%	100,000
250,000	500,000	49,275.00	24%	250,000
500,000	750,000	109,275.00	26¼%	500,000
750,000	1,000,000	174,900.00	27¾%	750,000
1,000,000	1,250,000	244,275.00	29¼%	1,000,000
1,250,000	1,500,000	317,400.00	31½%	1,250,000
1,500,000	2,000,000	396,150.00	33¾%	1,500,000
2,000,000	2,500,000	564,900.00	36¾%	2,000,000
2,500,000	3,000,000	748,650.00	39¾%	2,500,000
3,000,000	3,500,000	947,400.00	42%	3,000,000
3,500,000	4,000,000	1,157,400.00	44¼%	3,500,000
4,000,000	5,000,000	1,378,650.00	47¼%	4,000,000
5,000,000	6,000,000	1,851,150.00	50¼%	5,000,000
6,000,000	7,000,000	2,353,650.00	52½%	6,000,000
7,000,000	8,000,000	2,878,650.00	54¾%	7,000,000
8,000,000	10,000,000	3,426,150.00	57%	8,000,000
10,000,000	....	4,566,150.00	57¾%	10,000,000

¶ 2700 Code Sec. 7520 Valuation Tables

Reproduced below are the tables containing actuarial factors to be used in determining the present value of certain limited interests of decedents dying after April 30, 1999, and to gifts of such interests made after that date. The tables are arranged in the following order:

Table 90CM	Life Table
Table S	Single Life
Table J	Adjustment Factors
Table K	Adjustment Factors
Table B	Term Certain
Table U(1)	Single Life Unitrust
Table D	Term Certain Unitrust
Table F	Payout Factors

• *Gifts Made After April 30, 1989, and Before May 1, 1999*

The following tables applicable to decedents dying, and gifts made, after April 30, 1989, and before May 1, 1999, are also reproduced. Tables S, J, K, B, D, and F, above, also apply to decedents dying, and gifts made, after April 30, 1989, and before May 1, 1999.

Table 80CNSMT	Life Table
Table S	Single Life
Table U(1)	Single Life Unitrust

LIFE TABLE
TABLE 90CM
APPLICABLE AFTER
APRIL 30, 1999

Age x	l(x)
(1)	(2)
0	100000
1	99064
2	98992
3	98944
4	98907
5	98877
6	98850
7	98826
8	98803
9	98783
10	98766
11	98750
12	98734
13	98713
14	98681
15	98635
16	98573
17	98497
18	98409
19	98314
20	98215
21	98113
22	98006
23	97896
24	97784
25	97671
26	97556
27	97441
28	97322
29	97199
30	97070
31	96934
32	96791
33	96642
34	96485
35	96322
36	96150
37	95969
38	95780
39	95581
40	95373
41	95156
42	94928
43	94687
44	94431
45	94154
46	93855
47	93528
48	93173
49	92787
50	92370
51	91918
52	91424
53	90885
54	90297
55	89658
56	88965
57	88214
58	87397
59	86506
60	85537
61	84490
62	83368
63	82169
64	80887
65	79519
66	78066
67	76531
68	74907
69	73186
70	71357
71	69411
72	67344
73	65154
74	62852
75	60449
76	57955
77	55373
78	52704
79	49943
80	47084
81	44129
82	41091
83	37994
84	34876
85	31770
86	28687
87	25638
88	22658
89	19783
90	17046
91	14466
92	12066
93	9884
94	7951
95	6282
96	4868
97	3694
98	2745
99	1999
100	1424
101	991
102	672
103	443
104	284
105	175
106	105
107	60
108	33
109	17
110	0

TABLE S
BASED ON LIFE TABLE 90CM
SINGLE LIFE REMAINDER FACTORS
APPLICABLE AFTER APRIL 30, 1999
INTEREST RATE

AGE	4.2%	4.4%	4.6%	4.8%	5.0%	5.2%	5.4%	5.6%	5.8%	6.0%
0	.06752	.06130	.05586	.05109	.04691	.04322	.03998	.03711	.03458	.03233
1	.06137	.05495	.04932	.04438	.04003	.03620	.03283	.02985	.02721	.02487
2	.06325	.05667	.05088	.04580	.04132	.03737	.03388	.03079	.02806	.02563
3	.06545	.05869	.05275	.04752	.04291	.03883	.03523	.03203	.02920	.02668
4	.06784	.06092	.05482	.04944	.04469	.04048	.03676	.03346	.03052	.02791
5	.07040	.06331	.05705	.05152	.04662	.04229	.03845	.03503	.03199	.02928
6	.07310	.06583	.05941	.05372	.04869	.04422	.04025	.03672	.03357	.03076
7	.07594	.06849	.06191	.05607	.05089	.04628	.04219	.03854	.03528	.03236
8	.07891	.07129	.06453	.05853	.05321	.04846	.04424	.04046	.03709	.03407
9	.08203	.07423	.06731	.06115	.05567	.05079	.04643	.04253	.03904	.03592
10	.08532	.07734	.07024	.06392	.05829	.05326	.04877	.04474	.04114	.03790
11	.08875	.08059	.07331	.06683	.06104	.05587	.05124	.04709	.04336	.04002
12	.09233	.08398	.07653	.06989	.06394	.05862	.05385	.04957	.04572	.04226
13	.09601	.08748	.07985	.07304	.06693	.06146	.05655	.05214	.04816	.04458
14	.09974	.09102	.08322	.07624	.06997	.06435	.05929	.05474	.05064	.04694
15	.10350	.09460	.08661	.07946	.07303	.06725	.06204	.05735	.05312	.04930
16	.10728	.09818	.09001	.08268	.07608	.07014	.06479	.05996	.05559	.05164
17	.11108	.10179	.09344	.08592	.07916	.07306	.06755	.06257	.05807	.05399
18	.11494	.10545	.09691	.08921	.08227	.07601	.07034	.06521	.06057	.05636
19	.11889	.10921	.10047	.09259	.08548	.07904	.07322	.06794	.06315	.05880
20	.12298	.11310	.10417	.09610	.08881	.08220	.07622	.07078	.06584	.06135
21	.12722	.11713	.10801	.09976	.09228	.08550	.07935	.07375	.06866	.06403
22	.13159	.12130	.11199	.10354	.09588	.08893	.08260	.07685	.07160	.06682
23	.13613	.12563	.11612	.10748	.09964	.09250	.08601	.08009	.07468	.06975
24	.14084	.13014	.12043	.11160	.10357	.09625	.08958	.08349	.07793	.07284
25	.14574	.13484	.12493	.11591	.10768	.10018	.09334	.08708	.08135	.07611
26	.15084	.13974	.12963	.12041	.11199	.10431	.09728	.09085	.08496	.07956
27	.15615	.14485	.13454	.12513	.11652	.10865	.10144	.09484	.08878	.08322
28	.16166	.15016	.13965	.13004	.12124	.11319	.10580	.09901	.09279	.08706
29	.16737	.15567	.14497	.13516	.12617	.11792	.11035	.10339	.09699	.09109
30	.17328	.16138	.15048	.14047	.13129	.12286	.11510	.10796	.10138	.09532
31	.17938	.16728	.15618	.14599	.13661	.12799	.12004	.11272	.10597	.09974
32	.18568	.17339	.16210	.15171	.14214	.13333	.12520	.11769	.11076	.10435
33	.19220	.17972	.16824	.15766	.14790	.13889	.13058	.12289	.11578	.10920
34	.19894	.18627	.17460	.16383	.15388	.14468	.13618	.12831	.12102	.11426
35	.20592	.19307	.18121	.17025	.16011	.15073	.14204	.13399	.12652	.11958
36	.21312	.20010	.18805	.17691	.16658	.15701	.14814	.13990	.13225	.12514
37	.22057	.20737	.19514	.18382	.17331	.16356	.15450	.14608	.13825	.13096
38	.22827	.21490	.20251	.19100	.18031	.17038	.16113	.15253	.14452	.13705
39	.23623	.22270	.21013	.19845	.18759	.17747	.16805	.15927	.15108	.14344
40	.24446	.23078	.21805	.20620	.19516	.18487	.17527	.16631	.15795	.15013
41	.25298	.23915	.22626	.21425	.20305	.19259	.18282	.17368	.16514	.15715
42	.26178	.24782	.23478	.22262	.21125	.20062	.19069	.18138	.17267	.16450
43	.27087	.25678	.24360	.23129	.21977	.20898	.19888	.18941	.18053	.17220
44	.28025	.26603	.25273	.24027	.22860	.21766	.20740	.19777	.18873	.18023
45	.28987	.27555	.26212	.24953	.23772	.22664	.21622	.20644	.19724	.18858
46	.29976	.28533	.27179	.25908	.24714	.23591	.22536	.21542	.20606	.19725

TABLE S
BASED ON LIFE TABLE 90CM
SINGLE LIFE REMAINDER FACTORS
APPLICABLE AFTER APRIL 30, 1999
INTEREST RATE

AGE	4.2%	4.4%	4.6%	4.8%	5.0%	5.2%	5.4%	5.6%	5.8%	6.0%
47	.30987	.29535	.28171	.26889	.25682	.24546	.23476	.22468	.21518	.20621
48	.32023	.30563	.29190	.27897	.26678	.25530	.24447	.23425	.22460	.21549
49	.33082	.31615	.30234	.28931	.27702	.26543	.25447	.24412	.23434	.22509
50	.34166	.32694	.31306	.29995	.28756	.27586	.26479	.25432	.24441	.23502
51	.35274	.33798	.32404	.31085	.29838	.28658	.27541	.26482	.25479	.24528
52	.36402	.34924	.33525	.32200	.30946	.29757	.28630	.27561	.26547	.25584
53	.37550	.36070	.34668	.33339	.32078	.30882	.29746	.28667	.27643	.26669
54	.38717	.37237	.35833	.34500	.33234	.32031	.30888	.29801	.28766	.27782
55	.39903	.38424	.37019	.35683	.34413	.33205	.32056	.30961	.29918	.28925
56	.41108	.39631	.38227	.36890	.35617	.34405	.33250	.32149	.31099	.30097
57	.42330	.40857	.39455	.38118	.36844	.35629	.34469	.33363	.32306	.31297
58	.43566	.42098	.40699	.39364	.38089	.36873	.35710	.34600	.33538	.32522
59	.44811	.43351	.41956	.40623	.39350	.38133	.36968	.35855	.34789	.33768
60	.46066	.44613	.43224	.41896	.40624	.39408	.38243	.37127	.36058	.35033
61	.47330	.45887	.44505	.43182	.41914	.40699	.39535	.38418	.37347	.36318
62	.48608	.47175	.45802	.44485	.43223	.42011	.40848	.39732	.38660	.37629
63	.49898	.48478	.47115	.45807	.44550	.43343	.42184	.41069	.39997	.38966
64	.51200	.49793	.48442	.47143	.45895	.44694	.43539	.42427	.41357	.40326
65	.52512	.51121	.49782	.48495	.47255	.46062	.44912	.43805	.42738	.41709
66	.53835	.52461	.51137	.49862	.48634	.47449	.46307	.45206	.44143	.43118
67	.55174	.53818	.52511	.51250	.50034	.48860	.47727	.46633	.45576	.44556
68	.56524	.55188	.53899	.52654	.51452	.50291	.49168	.48083	.47034	.46020
69	.57882	.56568	.55299	.54071	.52885	.51737	.50627	.49552	.48513	.47506
70	.59242	.57951	.56703	.55495	.54325	.53193	.52096	.51034	.50004	.49007
71	.60598	.59332	.58106	.56918	.55767	.54651	.53569	.52520	.51503	.50516
72	.61948	.60707	.59504	.58338	.57206	.56108	.55043	.54009	.53004	.52029
73	.63287	.62073	.60895	.59751	.58640	.57561	.56513	.55495	.54505	.53543
74	.64621	.63435	.62282	.61162	.60073	.59015	.57985	.56984	.56009	.55061
75	.65953	.64796	.63671	.62575	.61510	.60473	.59463	.58480	.57523	.56591
76	.67287	.66160	.65063	.63995	.62954	.61940	.60952	.59989	.59050	.58135
77	.68622	.67526	.66459	.65419	.64404	.63415	.62450	.61509	.60590	.59694
78	.69954	.68892	.67856	.66845	.65858	.64895	.63955	.63036	.62140	.61264
79	.71278	.70250	.69246	.68265	.67308	.66372	.65457	.64563	.63690	.62836
80	.72581	.71588	.70618	.69668	.68740	.67833	.66945	.66077	.65227	.64396
81	.73857	.72899	.71962	.71045	.70147	.69268	.68408	.67566	.66741	.65933
82	.75101	.74178	.73274	.72389	.71522	.70672	.69840	.69024	.68225	.67441
83	.76311	.75423	.74553	.73700	.72864	.72044	.71240	.70451	.69678	.68919
84	.77497	.76645	.75809	.74988	.74183	.73393	.72618	.71857	.71110	.70377
85	.78665	.77848	.77047	.76260	.75487	.74728	.73982	.73250	.72530	.71823
86	.79805	.79025	.78258	.77504	.76764	.76036	.75320	.74617	.73925	.73245
87	.80904	.80159	.79427	.78706	.77998	.77301	.76615	.75940	.75277	.74624
88	.81962	.81251	.80552	.79865	.79188	.78521	.77865	.77220	.76584	.75958
89	.82978	.82302	.81636	.80980	.80335	.79699	.79072	.78455	.77847	.77248
90	.83952	.83309	.82676	.82052	.81437	.80831	.80234	.79645	.79064	.78492
91	.84870	.84260	.83658	.83064	.82479	.81902	.81332	.80771	.80217	.79671
92	.85716	.85136	.84563	.83998	.83441	.82891	.82348	.81812	.81283	.80761
93	.86494	.85942	.85396	.84858	.84326	.83801	.83283	.82771	.82266	.81767
94	.87216	.86690	.86170	.85657	.85149	.84648	.84153	.83664	.83181	.82704

TABLE S
BASED ON LIFE TABLE 90CM
SINGLE LIFE REMAINDER FACTORS
APPLICABLE AFTER APRIL 30, 1999
INTEREST RATE

AGE	*4.2%*	*4.4%*	*4.6%*	*4.8%*	*5.0%*	*5.2%*	*5.4%*	*5.6%*	*5.8%*	*6.0%*
95	.87898	.87397	.86902	.86412	.85928	.85450	.84977	.84510	.84049	.83592
96	.88537	.88060	.87587	.87121	.86659	.86203	.85751	.85305	.84864	.84427
97	.89127	.88672	.88221	.87775	.87335	.86898	.86467	.86040	.85618	.85200
98	.89680	.89245	.88815	.88389	.87968	.87551	.87138	.86730	.86326	.85926
99	.90217	.89803	.89393	.88987	.88585	.88187	.87793	.87402	.87016	.86633
100	.90738	.90344	.89953	.89567	.89183	.88804	.88428	.88056	.87687	.87322
101	.91250	.90876	.90504	.90137	.89772	.89412	.89054	.88699	.88348	.88000
102	.91751	.91396	.91045	.90696	.90350	.90007	.89668	.89331	.88997	.88666
103	.92247	.91912	.91579	.91249	.90922	.90598	.90276	.89957	.89640	.89326
104	.92775	.92460	.92148	.91839	.91532	.91227	.90924	.90624	.90326	.90031
105	.93290	.92996	.92704	.92415	.92127	.91841	.91558	.91276	.90997	.90719
106	.93948	.93680	.93415	.93151	.92889	.92628	.92370	.92113	.91857	.91604
107	.94739	.94504	.94271	.94039	.93808	.93579	.93351	.93124	.92899	.92675
108	.95950	.95767	.95585	.95404	.95224	.95045	.94867	.94689	.94512	.94336
109	.97985	.97893	.97801	.97710	.97619	.97529	.97438	.97348	.97259	.97170

TABLE S
BASED ON LIFE TABLE 90CM
SINGLE LIFE REMAINDER FACTORS
APPLICABLE AFTER APRIL 30, 1999
INTEREST RATE

AGE	6.2%	6.4%	6.6%	6.8%	7.0%	7.2%	7.4%	7.6%	7.8%	8.0%
0	.03034	.02857	.02700	.02559	.02433	.02321	.02220	.02129	.02047	.01973
1	.02279	.02094	.01929	.01782	.01650	.01533	.01427	.01331	.01246	.01168
2	.02347	.02155	.01983	.01829	.01692	.01569	.01458	.01358	.01268	.01187
3	.02444	.02243	.02065	.01905	.01761	.01632	.01516	.01412	.01317	.01232
4	.02558	.02349	.02163	.01996	.01846	.01712	.01590	.01481	.01382	.01292
5	.02686	.02469	.02275	.02101	.01945	.01804	.01677	.01562	.01458	.01364
6	.02825	.02600	.02398	.02217	.02053	.01906	.01773	.01653	.01544	.01445
7	.02976	.02742	.02532	.02343	.02172	.02019	.01880	.01754	.01640	.01536
8	.03137	.02894	.02675	.02479	.02301	.02140	.01995	.01864	.01744	.01635
9	.03311	.03059	.02832	.02627	.02442	.02274	.02122	.01985	.01859	.01745
10	.03499	.03237	.03001	.02788	.02595	.02420	.02262	.02118	.01987	.01867
11	.03700	.03428	.03183	.02961	.02760	.02578	.02413	.02262	.02125	.02000
12	.03913	.03632	.03377	.03146	.02937	.02748	.02575	.02418	.02275	.02144
13	.04135	.03843	.03579	.03339	.03122	.02924	.02744	.02580	.02431	.02294
14	.04359	.04057	.03783	.03534	.03308	.03102	.02915	.02744	.02587	.02444
15	.04584	.04270	.03986	.03728	.03493	.03279	.03083	.02905	.02742	.02593
16	.04806	.04482	.04187	.03919	.03674	.03452	.03248	.03063	.02892	.02736
17	.05029	.04692	.04387	.04108	.03855	.03623	.03411	.03218	.03040	.02877
18	.05253	.04905	.04588	.04299	.04036	.03795	.03574	.03373	.03187	.03017
19	.05484	.05124	.04796	.04496	.04222	.03972	.03742	.03532	.03339	.03161
20	.05726	.05354	.05013	.04702	.04418	.04158	.03919	.03700	.03498	.03313
21	.05980	.05595	.05242	.04920	.04625	.04354	.04105	.03877	.03667	.03473
22	.06246	.05847	.05482	.05147	.04841	.04559	.04301	.04063	.03844	.03642
23	.06524	.06112	.05734	.05387	.05069	.04777	.04508	.04260	.04032	.03821
24	.06819	.06392	.06001	.05642	.05312	.05008	.04728	.04470	.04232	.04012
25	.07131	.06690	.06285	.05913	.05570	.05255	.04964	.04695	.04447	.04218
26	.07460	.07005	.06586	.06200	.05845	.05518	.05215	.04936	.04677	.04438
27	.07810	.07340	.06907	.06508	.06140	.05800	.05485	.05195	.04925	.04676
28	.08179	.07693	.07246	.06833	.06451	.06098	.05772	.05469	.05189	.04929
29	.08566	.08065	.07603	.07176	.06780	.06414	.06075	.05761	.05469	.05198
30	.08973	.08456	.07978	.07536	.07127	.06748	.06396	.06069	.05766	.05483
31	.09398	.08865	.08372	.07915	.07491	.07098	.06733	.06394	.06078	.05785
32	.09843	.09294	.08785	.08313	.07875	.07468	.07089	.06737	.06409	.06103
33	.10310	.09745	.09220	.08732	.08279	.07858	.07466	.07100	.06759	.06441
34	.10799	.10217	.09676	.09173	.08705	.08269	.07862	.07483	.07129	.06798
35	.11314	.10715	.10157	.09638	.09155	.08704	.08283	.07890	.07522	.07179
36	.11852	.11236	.10662	.10127	.09628	.09162	.08726	.08319	.07938	.07581
37	.12416	.11783	.11193	.10641	.10126	.09645	.09194	.08772	.08377	.08006
38	.13009	.12359	.11751	.11183	.10652	.10155	.09689	.09253	.08843	.08459
39	.13629	.12962	.12338	.11753	.11206	.10693	.10212	.09761	.09337	.08938
40	.14281	.13597	.12955	.12355	.11791	.11262	.10766	.10299	.09860	.09447
41	.14966	.14264	.13606	.12989	.12409	.11864	.11352	.10870	.10417	.09989
42	.15685	.14966	.14291	.13657	.13061	.12500	.11972	.11475	.11006	.10564
43	.16437	.15702	.15010	.14360	.13747	.13171	.12627	.12115	.11631	.11174
44	.17224	.16472	.15764	.15098	.14469	.13876	.13317	.12789	.12290	.11819
45	.18042	.17274	.16550	.15867	.15223	.14615	.14040	.13496	.12982	.12496
46	.18893	.18110	.17370	.16671	.16011	.15387	.14796	.14238	.13708	.13207

TABLE S
BASED ON LIFE TABLE 90CM
SINGLE LIFE REMAINDER FACTORS
APPLICABLE AFTER APRIL 30, 1999
INTEREST RATE

AGE	*6.2%*	*6.4%*	*6.6%*	*6.8%*	*7.0%*	*7.2%*	*7.4%*	*7.6%*	*7.8%*	*8.0%*
47	.19775	.18975	.18220	.17505	.16830	.16190	.15584	.15010	.14466	.13950
48	.20688	.19873	.19102	.18373	.17682	.17027	.16406	.15817	.15258	.14727
49	.21633	.20804	.20018	.19274	.18568	.17898	.17262	.16658	.16084	.15539
50	.22612	.21769	.20969	.20210	.19490	.18805	.18155	.17536	.16948	.16388
51	.23625	.22769	.21955	.21182	.20448	.19749	.19084	.18452	.17849	.17275
52	.24669	.23799	.22973	.22186	.21438	.20726	.20047	.19400	.18784	.18196
53	.25742	.24861	.24022	.23222	.22461	.21735	.21043	.20383	.19753	.19151
54	.26845	.25952	.25101	.24290	.23516	.22777	.22072	.21399	.20756	.20140
55	.27978	.27074	.26212	.25389	.24604	.23853	.23136	.22450	.21793	.21166
56	.29140	.28227	.27355	.26522	.25725	.24963	.24233	.23535	.22867	.22227
57	.30333	.29411	.28529	.27686	.26879	.26106	.25365	.24656	.23976	.23324
58	.31551	.30621	.29731	.28878	.28061	.27278	.26528	.25807	.25116	.24453
59	.32790	.31854	.30956	.30095	.29269	.28477	.27716	.26986	.26284	.25610
60	.34050	.33107	.32202	.31334	.30500	.29699	.28929	.28190	.27478	.26794
61	.35331	.34384	.33473	.32598	.31757	.30948	.30170	.29422	.28701	.28007
62	.36639	.35688	.34772	.33892	.33044	.32229	.31443	.30687	.29958	.29255
63	.37974	.37020	.36101	.35216	.34363	.33542	.32750	.31986	.31250	.30539
64	.39334	.38378	.37456	.36568	.35711	.34884	.34087	.33317	.32574	.31857
65	.40718	.39761	.38838	.37947	.37087	.36257	.35455	.34681	.33932	.33208
66	.42128	.41172	.40249	.39357	.38496	.37663	.36858	.36079	.35326	.34597
67	.43569	.42616	.41694	.40803	.39941	.39107	.38299	.37518	.36761	.36028
68	.45038	.44089	.43170	.42281	.41419	.40585	.39777	.38994	.38235	.37499
69	.46531	.45587	.44672	.43786	.42927	.42094	.41286	.40503	.39743	.39006
70	.48040	.47103	.46194	.45312	.44456	.43626	.42820	.42038	.41278	.40540
71	.49558	.48629	.47727	.46851	.46000	.45174	.44371	.43591	.42832	.42095
72	.51082	.50162	.49268	.48399	.47554	.46733	.45934	.45157	.44401	.43666
73	.52607	.51697	.50813	.49952	.49114	.48299	.47506	.46733	.45981	.45249
74	.54139	.53241	.52367	.51515	.50686	.49879	.49092	.48325	.47578	.46849
75	.55683	.54798	.53936	.53095	.52276	.51477	.50698	.49938	.49197	.48474
76	.57243	.56373	.55524	.54696	.53888	.53100	.52330	.51579	.50846	.50130
77	.58819	.57965	.57132	.56318	.55523	.54747	.53988	.53247	.52523	.51815
78	.60408	.59572	.58755	.57957	.57177	.56414	.55668	.54939	.54225	.53527
79	.62001	.61184	.60385	.59604	.58840	.58092	.57360	.56644	.55943	.55256
80	.63582	.62786	.62007	.61244	.60497	.59765	.59048	.58347	.57659	.56985
81	.65142	.64367	.63608	.62864	.62135	.61421	.60721	.60034	.59361	.58701
82	.66673	.65920	.65182	.64458	.63748	.63052	.62368	.61698	.61041	.60395
83	.68175	.67444	.66728	.66024	.65334	.64656	.63991	.63338	.62696	.62066
84	.69657	.68950	.68256	.67574	.66904	.66246	.65599	.64964	.64340	.63727
85	.71128	.70446	.69775	.69116	.68467	.67830	.67204	.66587	.65982	.65386
86	.72576	.71919	.71272	.70636	.70010	.69394	.68789	.68193	.67606	.67029
87	.73981	.73349	.72726	.72114	.71511	.70917	.70333	.69757	.69190	.68632
88	.75342	.74735	.74137	.73548	.72968	.72396	.71833	.71279	.70732	.70194
89	.76658	.76076	.75503	.74938	.74381	.73832	.73290	.72757	.72231	.71712
90	.77928	.77371	.76823	.76281	.75748	.75221	.74702	.74190	.73684	.73186
91	.79131	.78600	.78075	.77557	.77046	.76542	.76044	.75553	.75068	.74589
92	.80246	.79737	.79235	.78740	.78250	.77767	.77290	.76818	.76353	.75893
93	.81274	.80788	.80307	.79832	.79363	.78899	.78441	.77989	.77542	.77100
94	.82232	.81766	.81306	.80850	.80401	.79956	.79517	.79082	.78653	.78228

TABLE S
BASED ON LIFE TABLE 90CM
SINGLE LIFE REMAINDER FACTORS
APPLICABLE AFTER APRIL 30, 1999
INTEREST RATE

AGE	6.2%	6.4%	6.6%	6.8%	7.0%	7.2%	7.4%	7.6%	7.8%	8.0%
95	.83141	.82695	.82254	.81818	.81387	.80961	.80539	.80122	.79710	.79302
96	.83996	.83569	.83147	.82729	.82316	.81907	.81503	.81103	.80707	.80315
97	.84787	.84378	.83973	.83573	.83176	.82784	.82396	.82012	.81632	.81255
98	.85530	.85138	.84750	.84366	.83985	.83609	.83236	.82867	.82502	.82140
99	.86255	.85880	.85508	.85140	.84776	.84415	.84057	.83703	.83353	.83005
100	.86960	.86601	.86246	.85894	.85546	.85200	.84858	.84519	.84183	.83849
101	.87655	.87313	.86974	.86638	.86305	.85975	.85648	.85324	.85003	.84684
102	.88338	.88012	.87689	.87369	.87052	.86738	.86426	.86116	.85809	.85505
103	.89015	.88706	.88399	.88095	.87793	.87494	.87197	.86903	.86611	.86321
104	.89737	.89446	.89157	.88871	.88586	.88304	.88024	.87745	.87469	.87195
105	.90443	.90170	.89898	.89628	.89360	.89094	.88830	.88568	.88307	.88049
106	.91351	.91101	.90852	.90605	.90359	.90115	.89873	.89632	.89392	.89154
107	.92452	.92230	.92010	.91791	.91573	.91356	.91141	.90927	.90714	.90502
108	.94161	.93987	.93814	.93641	.93469	.93298	.93128	.92958	.92790	.92622
109	.97081	.96992	.96904	.96816	.96729	.96642	.96555	.96468	.96382	.96296

TABLE S
BASED ON LIFE TABLE 90CM
SINGLE LIFE REMAINDER FACTORS
APPLICABLE AFTER APRIL 30, 1999
INTEREST RATE

AGE	8.2%	8.4%	8.6%	8.8%	9.0%	9.2%	9.4%	9.6%	9.8%	10.0%
0	.01906	.01845	.01790	.01740	.01694	.01652	.01613	.01578	.01546	.01516
1	.01098	.01034	.00977	.00924	.00876	.00833	.00793	.00756	.00722	.00691
2	.01113	.01046	.00986	.00930	.00880	.00834	.00791	.00753	.00717	.00684
3	.01155	.01084	.01020	.00962	.00909	.00860	.00816	.00775	.00737	.00702
4	.01211	.01137	.01069	.01008	.00952	.00900	.00853	.00810	.00770	.00733
5	.01279	.01201	.01130	.01065	.01006	.00952	.00902	.00856	.00814	.00775
6	.01356	.01274	.01199	.01131	.01068	.01011	.00959	.00910	.00865	.00824
7	.01442	.01356	.01277	.01205	.01140	.01079	.01023	.00972	.00925	.00881
8	.01536	.01446	.01363	.01287	.01218	.01154	.01096	.01041	.00991	.00945
9	.01641	.01546	.01460	.01380	.01307	.01240	.01178	.01120	.01068	.01019
10	.01758	.01659	.01567	.01484	.01407	.01336	.01270	.01210	.01154	.01103
11	.01886	.01781	.01686	.01598	.01517	.01442	.01373	.01310	.01251	.01196
12	.02024	.01915	.01814	.01721	.01636	.01558	.01485	.01419	.01357	.01299
13	.02168	.02054	.01948	.01851	.01762	.01679	.01603	.01533	.01467	.01407
14	.02313	.02193	.02083	.01981	.01887	.01801	.01721	.01646	.01578	.01514
15	.02456	.02330	.02214	.02107	.02009	.01918	.01834	.01756	.01684	.01617
16	.02593	.02462	.02340	.02229	.02126	.02030	.01942	.01860	.01785	.01714
17	.02728	.02590	.02463	.02346	.02238	.02138	.02046	.01960	.01880	.01806
18	.02861	.02717	.02584	.02462	.02348	.02243	.02146	.02056	.01972	.01894
19	.02998	.02847	.02708	.02580	.02461	.02351	.02249	.02154	.02066	.01984
20	.03142	.02984	.02839	.02704	.02580	.02465	.02357	.02258	.02165	.02079
21	.03295	.03130	.02978	.02837	.02706	.02585	.02473	.02368	.02271	.02180
22	.03455	.03283	.03124	.02976	.02839	.02712	.02594	.02484	.02382	.02286
23	.03626	.03446	.03279	.03124	.02981	.02847	.02723	.02608	.02500	.02400
24	.03809	.03620	.03446	.03283	.03133	.02993	.02863	.02741	.02628	.02522
25	.04005	.03808	.03625	.03456	.03298	.03151	.03014	.02887	.02768	.02656
26	.04216	.04010	.03819	.03641	.03476	.03322	.03178	.03044	.02919	.02802
27	.04444	.04229	.04029	.03843	.03670	.03508	.03357	.03217	.03085	.02962
28	.04687	.04463	.04254	.04059	.03877	.03708	.03550	.03402	.03263	.03133
29	.04946	.04712	.04493	.04289	.04099	.03922	.03756	.03600	.03455	.03318
30	.05221	.04976	.04748	.04534	.04335	.04149	.03975	.03812	.03659	.03515
31	.05511	.05255	.05017	.04794	.04585	.04390	.04208	.04037	.03876	.03725
32	.05818	.05551	.05302	.05069	.04851	.04647	.04455	.04276	.04107	.03948
33	.06144	.05866	.05606	.05363	.05135	.04921	.04720	.04532	.04355	.04188
34	.06489	.06200	.05928	.05674	.05436	.05212	.05002	.04805	.04619	.04444
35	.06857	.06555	.06273	.06007	.05758	.05524	.05304	.05097	.04902	.04718
36	.07246	.06932	.06638	.06361	.06101	.05856	.05626	.05409	.05205	.05012
37	.07659	.07332	.07025	.06737	.06466	.06210	.05969	.05742	.05528	.05325
38	.08098	.07758	.07439	.07138	.06855	.06588	.06336	.06099	.05874	.05662
39	.08563	.08210	.07878	.07565	.07270	.06992	.06729	.06480	.06245	.06023
40	.09059	.08692	.08347	.08021	.07714	.07423	.07149	.06889	.06643	.06411
41	.09586	.09206	.08848	.08509	.08189	.07886	.07600	.07329	.07072	.06828
42	.10147	.09753	.09381	.09029	.08696	.08381	.08083	.07800	.07531	.07277
43	.10742	.10334	.09948	.09583	.09237	.08909	.08598	.08304	.08024	.07758
44	.11373	.10950	.10551	.10172	.09813	.09472	.09148	.08841	.08549	.08272
45	.12035	.11599	.11185	.10792	.10420	.10066	.09730	.09410	.09106	.08817
46	.12732	.12281	.11853	.11447	.11061	.10694	.10345	.10013	.09696	.09395

TABLE S
BASED ON LIFE TABLE 90CM
SINGLE LIFE REMAINDER FACTORS
APPLICABLE AFTER APRIL 30, 1999
INTEREST RATE

AGE	8.2%	8.4%	8.6%	8.8%	9.0%	9.2%	9.4%	9.6%	9.8%	10.0%
47	.13460	.12995	.12553	.12133	.11733	.11353	.10991	.10646	.10317	.10004
48	.14223	.13743	.13287	.12853	.12439	.12046	.11671	.11313	.10972	.10646
49	.15020	.14526	.14056	.13608	.13181	.12774	.12385	.12015	.11661	.11322
50	.15855	.15347	.14862	.14401	.13960	.13540	.13138	.12754	.12388	.12037
51	.16727	.16205	.15707	.15232	.14777	.14344	.13929	.13532	.13153	.12789
52	.17634	.17098	.16587	.16097	.15630	.15183	.14755	.14345	.13953	.13577
53	.18576	.18027	.17501	.16999	.16518	.16057	.15616	.15194	.14789	.14400
54	.19552	.18990	.18451	.17935	.17441	.16968	.16514	.16078	.15661	.15260
55	.20564	.19989	.19437	.18908	.18402	.17915	.17449	.17001	.16571	.16157
56	.21613	.21025	.20461	.19919	.19400	.18901	.18422	.17962	.17519	.17093
57	.22698	.22098	.21522	.20968	.20436	.19925	.19434	.18961	.18507	.18069
58	.23816	.23204	.22616	.22051	.21507	.20984	.20481	.19996	.19530	.19080
59	.24962	.24339	.23740	.23163	.22608	.22073	.21558	.21062	.20584	.20123
60	.26136	.25502	.24892	.24304	.23738	.23192	.22666	.22158	.21669	.21196
61	.27339	.26695	.26075	.25477	.24900	.24343	.23806	.23288	.22787	.22304
62	.28578	.27925	.27295	.26687	.26100	.25533	.24985	.24456	.23945	.23451
63	.29854	.29192	.28553	.27935	.27339	.26762	.26205	.25666	.25145	.24641
64	.31164	.30494	.29846	.29221	.28615	.28030	.27463	.26915	.26384	.25870
65	.32508	.31831	.31177	.30543	.29930	.29336	.28761	.28203	.27663	.27140
66	.33891	.33208	.32547	.31906	.31285	.30684	.30101	.29536	.28987	.28456
67	.35318	.34630	.33963	.33316	.32689	.32081	.31491	.30918	.30363	.29823
68	.36785	.36093	.35422	.34770	.34138	.33524	.32928	.32349	.31787	.31240
69	.38290	.37595	.36920	.36265	.35628	.35009	.34408	.33824	.33256	.32703
70	.39823	.39127	.38450	.37791	.37151	.36529	.35924	.35335	.34762	.34204
71	.41378	.40681	.40003	.39343	.38701	.38076	.37467	.36875	.36298	.35736
72	.42950	.42253	.41575	.40914	.40271	.39644	.39034	.38438	.37858	.37293
73	.44535	.43840	.43162	.42502	.41858	.41231	.40619	.40022	.39440	.38872
74	.46139	.45446	.44771	.44112	.43469	.42842	.42230	.41632	.41049	.40479
75	.47769	.47080	.46408	.45752	.45111	.44485	.43874	.43277	.42693	.42123
76	.49430	.48747	.48079	.47427	.46790	.46167	.45558	.44963	.44380	.43811
77	.51123	.50447	.49786	.49139	.48506	.47888	.47282	.46690	.46111	.45543
78	.52845	.52177	.51523	.50884	.50257	.49645	.49044	.48457	.47881	.47317
79	.54584	.53926	.53282	.52650	.52032	.51426	.50833	.50251	.49681	.49122
80	.56325	.55678	.55044	.54423	.53813	.53216	.52630	.52056	.51492	.50939
81	.58054	.57419	.56797	.56186	.55587	.54999	.54422	.53856	.53300	.52754
82	.59762	.59140	.58530	.57931	.57343	.56766	.56198	.55641	.55094	.54557
83	.61448	.60840	.60243	.59657	.59081	.58515	.57958	.57411	.56874	.56346
84	.63124	.62531	.61949	.61376	.60813	.60259	.59715	.59179	.58652	.58134
85	.64800	.64224	.63657	.63099	.62550	.62010	.61478	.60955	.60441	.59934
86	.66461	.65902	.65351	.64810	.64276	.63751	.63233	.62724	.62222	.61728
87	.68083	.67541	.67008	.66483	.65965	.65455	.64953	.64458	.63970	.63489
88	.69663	.69140	.68624	.68116	.67615	.67121	.66634	.66154	.65680	.65213
89	.71201	.70696	.70199	.69708	.69224	.68747	.68276	.67811	.67353	.66900
90	.72694	.72209	.71730	.71257	.70791	.70330	.69876	.69427	.68984	.68547
91	.74117	.73650	.73190	.72735	.72286	.71842	.71404	.70972	.70545	.70123
92	.75439	.74991	.74548	.74110	.73678	.73251	.72829	.72412	.72000	.71593
93	.76664	.76233	.75806	.75385	.74969	.74557	.74150	.73748	.73350	.72957

TABLE S
BASED ON LIFE TABLE 90CM
SINGLE LIFE REMAINDER FACTORS
APPLICABLE AFTER APRIL 30, 1999
INTEREST RATE

AGE	*8.2%*	*8.4%*	*8.6%*	*8.8%*	*9.0%*	*9.2%*	*9.4%*	*9.6%*	*9.8%*	*10.0%*
94	.77809	.77394	.76983	.76578	.76177	.75780	.75388	.75000	.74616	.74237
95	.78899	.78500	.78106	.77715	.77329	.76947	.76569	.76195	.75826	.75460
96	.79928	.79544	.79165	.78790	.78418	.78050	.77686	.77326	.76970	.76617
97	.80883	.80514	.80149	.79787	.79430	.79075	.78725	.78377	.78033	.77693
98	.81781	.81427	.81075	.80727	.80382	.80041	.79703	.79368	.79036	.78708
99	.82661	.82320	.81982	.81648	.81316	.80988	.80662	.80340	.80020	.79704
100	.83519	.83192	.82868	.82547	.82228	.81913	.81600	.81290	.80982	.80678
101	.84368	.84055	.83744	.83437	.83131	.82829	.82529	.82231	.81936	.81643
102	.85203	.84904	.84607	.84313	.84021	.83731	.83444	.83159	.82876	.82596
103	.86034	.85748	.85465	.85184	.84906	.84629	.84355	.84082	.83812	.83544
104	.86923	.86653	.86385	.86119	.85855	.85593	.85333	.85074	.84818	.84563
105	.87792	.87537	.87283	.87032	.86782	.86534	.86287	.86042	.85799	.85557
106	.88918	.88683	.88450	.88218	.87987	.87758	.87530	.87304	.87079	.86855
107	.90291	.90082	.89873	.89666	.89460	.89255	.89051	.88849	.88647	.88447
108	.92455	.92288	.92123	.91958	.91794	.91630	.91468	.91306	.91145	.90984
109	.96211	.96125	.96041	.95956	.95872	.95788	.95704	.95620	.95537	.95455

TABLE S
BASED ON LIFE TABLE 90CM
SINGLE LIFE REMAINDER FACTORS
APPLICABLE AFTER APRIL 30, 1999
INTEREST RATE

AGE	10.2%	10.4%	10.6%	10.8%	11.0%	11.2%	11.4%	11.6%	11.8%	12.0%
0	.01488	.01463	.01439	.01417	.01396	.01377	.01359	.01343	.01327	.01312
1	.00662	.00636	.00612	.00589	.00568	.00548	.00530	.00513	.00497	.00482
2	.00654	.00626	.00600	.00576	.00554	.00533	.00514	.00496	.00479	.00463
3	.00670	.00641	.00613	.00588	.00564	.00542	.00522	.00502	.00484	.00468
4	.00699	.00668	.00639	.00612	.00587	.00563	.00542	.00521	.00502	.00484
5	.00739	.00706	.00675	.00646	.00620	.00595	.00571	.00550	.00529	.00510
6	.00786	.00751	.00718	.00687	.00659	.00633	.00608	.00585	.00563	.00543
7	.00841	.00803	.00769	.00736	.00706	.00678	.00652	.00627	.00604	.00582
8	.00902	.00863	.00826	.00791	.00759	.00730	.00702	.00675	.00651	.00628
9	.00973	.00931	.00892	.00856	.00822	.00790	.00760	.00733	.00706	.00682
10	.01055	.01010	.00969	.00930	.00894	.00861	.00829	.00799	.00772	.00746
11	.01146	.01099	.01055	.01014	.00976	.00940	.00907	.00875	.00846	.00818
12	.01246	.01196	.01150	.01106	.01066	.01028	.00993	.00960	.00928	.00899
13	.01351	.01298	.01249	.01204	.01161	.01121	.01084	.01049	.01016	.00985
14	.01455	.01400	.01348	.01300	.01255	.01213	.01173	.01136	.01102	.01069
15	.01555	.01497	.01443	.01392	.01345	.01300	.01259	.01220	.01183	.01148
16	.01648	.01587	.01530	.01477	.01427	.01380	.01336	.01295	.01257	.01220
17	.01737	.01673	.01612	.01556	.01504	.01455	.01408	.01365	.01324	.01286
18	.01822	.01754	.01691	.01632	.01576	.01525	.01476	.01430	.01387	.01347
19	.01908	.01837	.01770	.01708	.01650	.01595	.01544	.01495	.01450	.01407
20	.01999	.01924	.01854	.01788	.01726	.01669	.01615	.01564	.01516	.01471
21	.02096	.02017	.01943	.01874	.01809	.01748	.01691	.01637	.01586	.01539
22	.02197	.02114	.02036	.01963	.01895	.01830	.01770	.01713	.01660	.01610
23	.02306	.02218	.02136	.02059	.01987	.01919	.01855	.01795	.01739	.01686
24	.02424	.02331	.02245	.02163	.02087	.02016	.01948	.01885	.01825	.01769
25	.02552	.02455	.02364	.02278	.02197	.02122	.02051	.01984	.01920	.01861
26	.02692	.02589	.02493	.02403	.02318	.02238	.02162	.02091	.02025	.01961
27	.02846	.02738	.02636	.02541	.02451	.02367	.02287	.02212	.02141	.02074
28	.03012	.02898	.02791	.02690	.02595	.02506	.02422	.02342	.02267	.02196
29	.03190	.03070	.02957	.02851	.02751	.02656	.02567	.02483	.02404	.02329
30	.03381	.03254	.03135	.03023	.02917	.02817	.02723	.02634	.02551	.02471
31	.03583	.03450	.03324	.03206	.03094	.02989	.02890	.02796	.02707	.02623
32	.03799	.03659	.03527	.03402	.03284	.03173	.03068	.02968	.02874	.02785
33	.04031	.03883	.03744	.03612	.03488	.03371	.03260	.03155	.03055	.02961
34	.04279	.04123	.03976	.03838	.03707	.03583	.03465	.03354	.03249	.03149
35	.04545	.04382	.04227	.04081	.03943	.03812	.03688	.03571	.03459	.03354
36	.04830	.04658	.04495	.04341	.04196	.04058	.03927	.03803	.03685	.03573
37	.05134	.04953	.04782	.04620	.04467	.04321	.04183	.04052	.03928	.03809
38	.05462	.05272	.05092	.04921	.04760	.04606	.04461	.04322	.04191	.04066
39	.05812	.05613	.05424	.05245	.05075	.04913	.04760	.04614	.04475	.04343
40	.06190	.05981	.05782	.05594	.05415	.05245	.05083	.04929	.04783	.04643
41	.06597	.06378	.06170	.05972	.05784	.05605	.05435	.05272	.05118	.04970
42	.07035	.06806	.06587	.06380	.06182	.05994	.05815	.05644	.05481	.05326
43	.07505	.07265	.07036	.06818	.06611	.06414	.06225	.06045	.05874	.05710
44	.08008	.07757	.07518	.07290	.07072	.06865	.06667	.06478	.06298	.06125
45	.08542	.08279	.08029	.07791	.07563	.07346	.07138	.06940	.06750	.06569
46	.09108	.08834	.08573	.08324	.08085	.07858	.07640	.07432	.07233	.07043

TABLE S
BASED ON LIFE TABLE 90CM
SINGLE LIFE REMAINDER FACTORS
APPLICABLE AFTER APRIL 30, 1999
INTEREST RATE

AGE	10.2%	10.4%	10.6%	10.8%	11.0%	11.2%	11.4%	11.6%	11.8%	12.0%
47	.09705	.09419	.09147	.08886	.08637	.08399	.08172	.07954	.07745	.07545
48	.10335	.10038	.09754	.09482	.09222	.08973	.08735	.08507	.08288	.08078
49	.10999	.10690	.10394	.10111	.09840	.09581	.09332	.09093	.08864	.08644
50	.11701	.11380	.11073	.10778	.10496	.10225	.09965	.09716	.09477	.09247
51	.12441	.12108	.11789	.11482	.11189	.10907	.10636	.10376	.10126	.09886
52	.13217	.12871	.12540	.12222	.11916	.11623	.11341	.11071	.10810	.10560
53	.14028	.13670	.13327	.12997	.12680	.12375	.12082	.11801	.11529	.11268
54	.14875	.14505	.14150	.13808	.13480	.13163	.12859	.12566	.12284	.12012
55	.15760	.15378	.15011	.14657	.14317	.13989	.13674	.13370	.13077	.12794
56	.16684	.16290	.15911	.15546	.15194	.14855	.14528	.14213	.13909	.13615
57	.17648	.17242	.16851	.16474	.16111	.15760	.15422	.15096	.14781	.14477
58	.18647	.18229	.17827	.17438	.17064	.16702	.16353	.16015	.15689	.15374
59	.19678	.19249	.18835	.18435	.18049	.17676	.17316	.16968	.16631	.16305
60	.20740	.20300	.19875	.19464	.19066	.18682	.18311	.17952	.17604	.17268
61	.21837	.21385	.20949	.20527	.20119	.19724	.19341	.18971	.18613	.18266
62	.22973	.22511	.22064	.21631	.21212	.20807	.20414	.20033	.19664	.19306
63	.24152	.23680	.23222	.22779	.22350	.21934	.21530	.21139	.20760	.20392
64	.25372	.24890	.24422	.23969	.23529	.23103	.22690	.22289	.21899	.21521
65	.26633	.26141	.25664	.25201	.24752	.24316	.23893	.23482	.23083	.22695
66	.27940	.27439	.26953	.26481	.26023	.25577	.25145	.24724	.24316	.23918
67	.29299	.28790	.28296	.27815	.27348	.26894	.26453	.26024	.25606	.25200
68	.30709	.30193	.29691	.29202	.28728	.28265	.27816	.27378	.26952	.26537
69	.32166	.31643	.31134	.30639	.30157	.29687	.29230	.28785	.28351	.27928
70	.33661	.33133	.32618	.32116	.31628	.31152	.30688	.30235	.29794	.29364
71	.35188	.34654	.34134	.33627	.33133	.32651	.32181	.31722	.31275	.30838
72	.36742	.36204	.35679	.35168	.34668	.34181	.33706	.33241	.32788	.32345
73	.38317	.37776	.37248	.36733	.36229	.35738	.35257	.34788	.34330	.33882
74	.39923	.39380	.38849	.38330	.37823	.37328	.36844	.36370	.35908	.35455
75	.41566	.41021	.40489	.39968	.39459	.38961	.38474	.37997	.37531	.37074
76	.43254	.42709	.42176	.41655	.41144	.40645	.40156	.39677	.39208	.38749
77	.44988	.44444	.43912	.43391	.42880	.42380	.41891	.41411	.40940	.40479
78	.46765	.46224	.45694	.45174	.44665	.44166	.43677	.43197	.42726	.42265
79	.48574	.48037	.47510	.46993	.46487	.45990	.45502	.45024	.44554	.44094
80	.50397	.49865	.49343	.48830	.48327	.47834	.47349	.46873	.46406	.45947
81	.52219	.51693	.51176	.50669	.50171	.49682	.49201	.48729	.48265	.47809
82	.54029	.53510	.53000	.52499	.52007	.51523	.51047	.50580	.50120	.49667
83	.55826	.55315	.54813	.54319	.53834	.53356	.52886	.52424	.51969	.51522
84	.57624	.57123	.56629	.56144	.55666	.55195	.54732	.54277	.53828	.53386
85	.59435	.58944	.58460	.57984	.57516	.57054	.56599	.56151	.55710	.55275
86	.61241	.60762	.60289	.59824	.59365	.58913	.58468	.58029	.57596	.57170
87	.63015	.62548	.62087	.61633	.61185	.60744	.60309	.59880	.59456	.59039
88	.64753	.64299	.63851	.63409	.62973	.62543	.62118	.61700	.61287	.60879
89	.66454	.66013	.65579	.65150	.64726	.64308	.63895	.63488	.63086	.62689
90	.68115	.67689	.67268	.66853	.66442	.66037	.65637	.65241	.64851	.64465
91	.69706	.69294	.68887	.68486	.68089	.67696	.67309	.66925	.66547	.66173
92	.71190	.70792	.70399	.70011	.69627	.69247	.68872	.68501	.68134	.67771
93	.72569	.72184	.71804	.71429	.71057	.70689	.70326	.69967	.69611	.69259
94	.73861	.73490	.73123	.72759	.72400	.72044	.71692	.71344	.71000	.70659

TABLE S
BASED ON LIFE TABLE 90CM
SINGLE LIFE REMAINDER FACTORS
APPLICABLE AFTER APRIL 30, 1999
INTEREST RATE

AGE	*10.2%*	*10.4%*	*10.6%*	*10.8%*	*11.0%*	*11.2%*	*11.4%*	*11.6%*	*11.8%*	*12.0%*
95	.75097	.74739	.74384	.74033	.73686	.73342	.73002	.72665	.72331	.72001
96	.76267	.75922	.75579	.75240	.74905	.74572	.74243	.73917	.73595	.73275
97	.77356	.77022	.76691	.76363	.76039	.75718	.75399	.75084	.74772	.74463
98	.78382	.78059	.77740	.77423	.77110	.76799	.76491	.76186	.75884	.75584
99	.79390	.79079	.78771	.78465	.78162	.77862	.77565	.77270	.76978	.76688
100	.80376	.80076	.79779	.79485	.79193	.78904	.78617	.78333	.78051	.77771
101	.81353	.81066	.80780	.80497	.80217	.79938	.79662	.79388	.79117	.78847
102	.82318	.82042	.81768	.81496	.81227	.80960	.80694	.80431	.80170	.79911
103	.83278	.83014	.82752	.82491	.82233	.81977	.81723	.81470	.81220	.80971
104	.84310	.84059	.83810	.83563	.83317	.83073	.82831	.82591	.82352	.82115
105	.85318	.85079	.84843	.84607	.84374	.84142	.83911	.83682	.83455	.83229
106	.86633	.86413	.86193	.85975	.85758	.85543	.85329	.85116	.84904	.84694
107	.88247	.88049	.87852	.87656	.87460	.87266	.87073	.86881	.86690	.86500
108	.90825	.90666	.90507	.90350	.90193	.90037	.89881	.89727	.89572	.89419
109	.95372	.95290	.95208	.95126	.95045	.94964	.94883	.94803	.94723	.94643

TABLE S
BASED ON LIFE TABLE 90CM
SINGLE LIFE REMAINDER FACTORS
APPLICABLE AFTER APRIL 30, 1999
INTEREST RATE

AGE	12.2%	12.4%	12.6%	12.8%	13.0%	13.2%	13.4%	13.6%	13.8%	14.0%
0	.01298	.01285	.01273	.01261	.01250	.01240	.01230	.01221	.01212	.01203
1	.00468	.00455	.00443	.00431	.00420	.00410	.00400	.00391	.00382	.00374
2	.00448	.00435	.00421	.00409	.00398	.00387	.00376	.00366	.00357	.00348
3	.00452	.00437	.00423	.00410	.00398	.00386	.00375	.00365	.00355	.00345
4	.00468	.00452	.00437	.00423	.00410	.00397	.00386	.00375	.00364	.00354
5	.00493	.00476	.00460	.00445	.00431	.00418	.00405	.00393	.00382	.00371
6	.00524	.00506	.00489	.00473	.00458	.00444	.00430	.00418	.00406	.00394
7	.00562	.00543	.00525	.00508	.00492	.00477	.00462	.00449	.00436	.00423
8	.00606	.00586	.00566	.00548	.00531	.00515	.00499	.00485	.00471	.00458
9	.00659	.00637	.00616	.00597	.00579	.00561	.00545	.00529	.00514	.00500
10	.00721	.00698	.00676	.00655	.00636	.00617	.00600	.00583	.00567	.00552
11	.00792	.00767	.00744	.00722	.00701	.00682	.00663	.00645	.00628	.00612
12	.00871	.00845	.00821	.00797	.00775	.00754	.00735	.00716	.00698	.00681
13	.00955	.00928	.00902	.00877	.00854	.00831	.00810	.00790	.00771	.00753
14	.01038	.01009	.00981	.00955	.00930	.00907	.00885	.00864	.00843	.00824
15	.01116	.01085	.01056	.01028	.01002	.00977	.00954	.00932	.00910	.00890
16	.01186	.01153	.01123	.01094	.01066	.01040	.01015	.00992	.00969	.00948
17	.01250	.01215	.01183	.01152	.01124	.01096	.01070	.01045	.01022	.00999
18	.01308	.01272	.01238	.01206	.01175	.01147	.01119	.01093	.01068	.01044
19	.01367	.01329	.01293	.01259	.01227	.01196	.01167	.01140	.01113	.01088
20	.01428	.01388	.01350	.01314	.01280	.01248	.01217	.01188	.01161	.01134
21	.01494	.01451	.01411	.01373	.01337	.01303	.01271	.01240	.01211	.01183
22	.01562	.01517	.01475	.01435	.01397	.01361	.01326	.01294	.01263	.01233
23	.01635	.01588	.01543	.01501	.01460	.01422	.01386	.01351	.01319	.01287
24	.01716	.01665	.01618	.01573	.01530	.01489	.01451	.01415	.01380	.01347
25	.01804	.01751	.01701	.01653	.01608	.01565	.01524	.01485	.01448	.01413
26	.01902	.01845	.01792	.01741	.01693	.01648	.01604	.01563	.01524	.01487
27	.02011	.01951	.01895	.01841	.01790	.01742	.01696	.01652	.01610	.01571
28	.02129	.02066	.02006	.01949	.01895	.01844	.01795	.01748	.01704	.01662
29	.02258	.02191	.02127	.02067	.02009	.01955	.01903	.01853	.01806	.01762
30	.02396	.02325	.02257	.02193	.02132	.02074	.02019	.01966	.01916	.01869
31	.02543	.02467	.02396	.02328	.02263	.02201	.02143	.02087	.02034	.01983
32	.02701	.02621	.02545	.02472	.02404	.02338	.02276	.02217	.02160	.02106
33	.02871	.02786	.02706	.02629	.02556	.02487	.02420	.02357	.02297	.02240
34	.03054	.02964	.02879	.02797	.02720	.02646	.02576	.02509	.02445	.02383
35	.03253	.03158	.03067	.02981	.02898	.02820	.02745	.02674	.02606	.02541
36	.03467	.03366	.03269	.03178	.03090	.03007	.02928	.02852	.02779	.02710
37	.03697	.03590	.03488	.03391	.03298	.03209	.03125	.03044	.02967	.02893
38	.03947	.03833	.03725	.03622	.03524	.03430	.03340	.03254	.03172	.03094
39	.04217	.04096	.03982	.03873	.03768	.03669	.03573	.03482	.03395	.03312
40	.04510	.04383	.04262	.04146	.04035	.03930	.03828	.03732	.03639	.03550
41	.04830	.04695	.04567	.04445	.04327	.04215	.04108	.04005	.03907	.03812
42	.05177	.05035	.04900	.04770	.04646	.04527	.04413	.04304	.04200	.04100
43	.05553	.05404	.05261	.05123	.04992	.04866	.04746	.04630	.04520	.04413
44	.05960	.05802	.05651	.05506	.05368	.05235	.05107	.04985	.04867	.04754
45	.06395	.06229	.06069	.05917	.05770	.05630	.05495	.05365	.05241	.05121
46	.06860	.06685	.06517	.06356	.06202	.06053	.05911	.05774	.05643	.05516

TABLE S
BASED ON LIFE TABLE 90CM
SINGLE LIFE REMAINDER FACTORS
APPLICABLE AFTER APRIL 30, 1999
INTEREST RATE

AGE	12.2%	12.4%	12.6%	12.8%	13.0%	13.2%	13.4%	13.6%	13.8%	14.0%
47	.07353	.07169	.06992	.06823	.06660	.06504	.06353	.06209	.06070	.05936
48	.07877	.07684	.07498	.07320	.07149	.06984	.06826	.06673	.06527	.06385
49	.08433	.08231	.08036	.07849	.07669	.07495	.07329	.07168	.07013	.06864
50	.09026	.08814	.08609	.08413	.08224	.08042	.07867	.07698	.07535	.07378
51	.09655	.09433	.09219	.09013	.08815	.08624	.08440	.08262	.08091	.07926
52	.10318	.10086	.09863	.09647	.09439	.09239	.09046	.08860	.08680	.08506
53	.11017	.10774	.10541	.10315	.10098	.09888	.09686	.09491	.09302	.09120
54	.11750	.11498	.11254	.11019	.10792	.10572	.10361	.10156	.09958	.09767
55	.12522	.12258	.12005	.11759	.11522	.11294	.11072	.10859	.10652	.10451
56	.13332	.13059	.12794	.12539	.12292	.12054	.11823	.11599	.11383	.11174
57	.14183	.13899	.13624	.13359	.13102	.12853	.12613	.12380	.12154	.11936
58	.15070	.14775	.14490	.14215	.13948	.13689	.13439	.13197	.12962	.12734
59	.15990	.15685	.15389	.15103	.14826	.14558	.14298	.14046	.13801	.13564
60	.16942	.16626	.16321	.16024	.15737	.15459	.15189	.14927	.14673	.14426
61	.17929	.17603	.17287	.16981	.16684	.16395	.16115	.15844	.15580	.15324
62	.18960	.18623	.18297	.17980	.17673	.17375	.17085	.16803	.16530	.16264
63	.20035	.19688	.19352	.19025	.18708	.18400	.18100	.17809	.17525	.17250
64	.21154	.20797	.20451	.20114	.19787	.19469	.19159	.18859	.18566	.18281
65	.22318	.21951	.21595	.21249	.20912	.20584	.20265	.19955	.19652	.19358
66	.23532	.23156	.22790	.22434	.22088	.21751	.21422	.21102	.20791	.20487
67	.24804	.24419	.24044	.23679	.23324	.22977	.22640	.22311	.21990	.21678
68	.26133	.25740	.25356	.24983	.24618	.24263	.23917	.23579	.23250	.22929
69	.27516	.27114	.26723	.26341	.25969	.25605	.25251	.24905	.24567	.24237
70	.28945	.28536	.28137	.27747	.27367	.26996	.26633	.26279	.25934	.25596
71	.30412	.29996	.29590	.29193	.28806	.28427	.28057	.27696	.27343	.26998
72	.31913	.31491	.31078	.30675	.30281	.29895	.29519	.29150	.28790	.28438
73	.33444	.33016	.32597	.32188	.31788	.31396	.31013	.30638	.30271	.29913
74	.35012	.34579	.34155	.33741	.33335	.32938	.32549	.32168	.31795	.31430
75	.36628	.36190	.35762	.35343	.34932	.34530	.34136	.33750	.33372	.33001
76	.38299	.37858	.37427	.37004	.36589	.36183	.35784	.35394	.35011	.34636
77	.40028	.39585	.39151	.38725	.38307	.37898	.37496	.37103	.36716	.36337
78	.41812	.41368	.40933	.40506	.40086	.39675	.39271	.38874	.38485	.38103
79	.43641	.43198	.42762	.42334	.41914	.41502	.41096	.40698	.40308	.39924
80	.45496	.45054	.44619	.44192	.43772	.43360	.42954	.42556	.42164	.41779
81	.47360	.46920	.46487	.46061	.45643	.45231	.44827	.44429	.44038	.43653
82	.49223	.48785	.48355	.47932	.47516	.47106	.46703	.46307	.45916	.45532
83	.51081	.50648	.50221	.49802	.49388	.48982	.48581	.48187	.47799	.47416
84	.52951	.52523	.52101	.51686	.51277	.50874	.50477	.50086	.49701	.49321
85	.54847	.54425	.54009	.53600	.53196	.52798	.52406	.52019	.51638	.51262
86	.56749	.56335	.55926	.55523	.55126	.54734	.54348	.53966	.53591	.53220
87	.58627	.58221	.57820	.57425	.57035	.56650	.56270	.55895	.55526	.55161
88	.60477	.60079	.59688	.59301	.58919	.58542	.58170	.57802	.57439	.57081
89	.62297	.61909	.61527	.61149	.60776	.60408	.60044	.59685	.59330	.58979
90	.64084	.63707	.63335	.62968	.62604	.62246	.61891	.61540	.61194	.60851
91	.65803	.65437	.65076	.64719	.64366	.64017	.63672	.63330	.62993	.62659
92	.67412	.67058	.66707	.66360	.66017	.65678	.65342	.65010	.64682	.64357
93	.68911	.68567	.68227	.67890	.67557	.67227	.66901	.66578	.66258	.65942
94	.70321	.69988	.69657	.69330	.69006	.68686	.68369	.68055	.67744	.67437

TABLE S
BASED ON LIFE TABLE 90CM
SINGLE LIFE REMAINDER FACTORS
APPLICABLE AFTER APRIL 30, 1999
INTEREST RATE

AGE	12.2%	12.4%	12.6%	12.8%	13.0%	13.2%	13.4%	13.6%	13.8%	14.0%
95	.71674	.71351	.71031	.70713	.70399	.70088	.69781	.69476	.69174	.68875
96	.72959	.72646	.72335	.72028	.71724	.71422	.71123	.70828	.70534	.70244
97	.74156	.73853	.73552	.73254	.72959	.72666	.72376	.72089	.71804	.71522
98	.75287	.74993	.74702	.74413	.74126	.73842	.73561	.73282	.73006	.72732
99	.76401	.76117	.75834	.75555	.75277	.75002	.74730	.74459	.74191	.73926
100	.77494	.77219	.76946	.76676	.76408	.76142	.75878	.75616	.75357	.75099
101	.78580	.78315	.78052	.77791	.77532	.77275	.77021	.76768	.76517	.76268
102	.79654	.79399	.79146	.78894	.78645	.78397	.78152	.77908	.77666	.77426
103	.80724	.80479	.80236	.79994	.79755	.79517	.79280	.79046	.78813	.78582
104	.81879	.81646	.81413	.81183	.80954	.80726	.80501	.80276	.80054	.79832
105	.83005	.82782	.82560	.82340	.82121	.81904	.81688	.81474	.81260	.81049
106	.84485	.84277	.84071	.83866	.83662	.83459	.83257	.83057	.82857	.82659
107	.86311	.86124	.85937	.85751	.85566	.85382	.85199	.85017	.84835	.84655
108	.89266	.89114	.88963	.88812	.88662	.88513	.88364	.88216	.88068	.87922
109	.94563	.94484	.94405	.94326	.94248	.94170	.94092	.94014	.93937	.93860

TABLE J
ADJUSTMENT FACTORS FOR TERM CERTAIN ANNUITIES
PAYABLE AT THE BEGINNING OF EACH INTERVAL
APPLICABLE AFTER APRIL 30, 1989
FREQUENCY OF PAYMENTS

INTEREST RATE	*ANNUALLY*	*SEMI ANNUALLY*	*QUARTERLY*	*MONTHLY*	*WEEKLY*
4.2	1.0420	1.0314	1.0261	1.0226	1.0213
4.4	1.0440	1.0329	1.0274	1.0237	1.0223
4.6	1.0460	1.0344	1.0286	1.0247	1.0233
4.8	1.0480	1.0359	1.0298	1.0258	1.0243
5.0	1.0500	1.0373	1.0311	1.0269	1.0253
5.2	1.0520	1.0388	1.0323	1.0279	1.0263
5.4	1.0540	1.0403	1.0335	1.0290	1.0273
5.6	1.0560	1.0418	1.0348	1.0301	1.0283
5.8	1.0580	1.0433	1.0360	1.0311	1.0293
6.0	1.0600	1.0448	1.0372	1.0322	1.0303
6.2	1.0620	1.0463	1.0385	1.0333	1.0313
6.4	1.0640	1.0478	1.0397	1.0343	1.0323
6.6	1.0660	1.0492	1.0409	1.0354	1.0333
6.8	1.0680	1.0507	1.0422	1.0365	1.0343
7.0	1.0700	1.0522	1.0434	1.0375	1.0353
7.2	1.0720	1.0537	1.0446	1.0386	1.0363
7.4	1.0740	1.0552	1.0458	1.0396	1.0373
7.6	1.0760	1.0567	1.0471	1.0407	1.0383
7.8	1.0780	1.0581	1.0483	1.0418	1.0393
8.0	1.0800	1.0596	1.0495	1.0428	1.0403
8.2	1.0820	1.0611	1.0507	1.0439	1.0413
8.4	1.0840	1.0626	1.0520	1.0449	1.0422
8.6	1.0860	1.0641	1.0532	1.0460	1.0432
8.8	1.0880	1.0655	1.0544	1.0471	1.0442
9.0	1.0900	1.0670	1.0556	1.0481	1.0452
9.2	1.0920	1.0685	1.0569	1.0492	1.0462
9.4	1.0940	1.0700	1.0581	1.0502	1.0472
9.6	1.0960	1.0715	1.0593	1.0513	1.0482
9.8	1.0980	1.0729	1.0605	1.0523	1.0492
10.0	1.1000	1.0744	1.0618	1.0534	1.0502
10.2	1.1020	1.0759	1.0630	1.0544	1.0512
10.4	1.1040	1.0774	1.0642	1.0555	1.0521
10.6	1.1060	1.0788	1.0654	1.0565	1.0531
10.8	1.1080	1.0803	1.0666	1.0576	1.0541
11.0	1.1100	1.0818	1.0679	1.0586	1.0551
11.2	1.1120	1.0833	1.0691	1.0597	1.0561
11.4	1.1140	1.0847	1.0703	1.0607	1.0571
11.6	1.1160	1.0862	1.0715	1.0618	1.0581
11.8	1.1180	1.0877	1.0727	1.0628	1.0590
12.0	1.1200	1.0892	1.0739	1.0639	1.0600
12.2	1.1220	1.0906	1.0752	1.0649	1.0610
12.4	1.1240	1.0921	1.0764	1.0660	1.0620
12.6	1.1260	1.0936	1.0776	1.0670	1.0630
12.8	1.1280	1.0950	1.0788	1.0681	1.0639
13.0	1.1300	1.0965	1.0800	1.0691	1.0649
13.2	1.1320	1.0980	1.0812	1.0701	1.0659

TABLE J
ADJUSTMENT FACTORS FOR TERM CERTAIN ANNUITIES
PAYABLE AT THE BEGINNING OF EACH INTERVAL
APPLICABLE AFTER APRIL 30, 1989
FREQUENCY OF PAYMENTS

INTEREST RATE	*ANNUALLY*	*SEMI ANNUALLY*	*QUARTERLY*	*MONTHLY*	*WEEKLY*
13.4	1.1340	1.0994	1.0824	1.0712	1.0669
13.6	1.1360	1.1009	1.0836	1.0722	1.0679
13.8	1.1380	1.1024	1.0849	1.0733	1.0688
14.0	1.1400	1.1039	1.0861	1.0743	1.0698

TABLE K
ADJUSTMENT FACTORS FOR ANNUITIES
PAYABLE AT THE END OF EACH INTERVAL
APPLICABLE AFTER APRIL 30, 1989
FREQUENCY OF PAYMENTS

INTEREST RATE	*ANNUALLY*	*SEMI ANNUALLY*	*QUARTERLY*	*MONTHLY*	*WEEKLY*
4.2	1.0000	1.0104	1.0156	1.0191	1.0205
4.4	1.0000	1.0109	1.0164	1.0200	1.0214
4.6	1.0000	1.0114	1.0171	1.0209	1.0224
4.8	1.0000	1.0119	1.0178	1.0218	1.0234
5.0	1.0000	1.0123	1.0186	1.0227	1.0243
5.2	1.0000	1.0128	1.0193	1.0236	1.0253
5.4	1.0000	1.0133	1.0200	1.0245	1.0262
5.6	1.0000	1.0138	1.0208	1.0254	1.0272
5.8	1.0000	1.0143	1.0215	1.0263	1.0282
6.0	1.0000	1.0148	1.0222	1.0272	1.0291
6.2	1.0000	1.0153	1.0230	1.0281	1.0301
6.4	1.0000	1.0158	1.0237	1.0290	1.0311
6.6	1.0000	1.0162	1.0244	1.0299	1.0320
6.8	1.0000	1.0167	1.0252	1.0308	1.0330
7.0	1.0000	1.0172	1.0259	1.0317	1.0339
7.2	1.0000	1.0177	1.0266	1.0326	1.0349
7.4	1.0000	1.0182	1.0273	1.0335	1.0358
7.6	1.0000	1.0187	1.0281	1.0344	1.0368
7.8	1.0000	1.0191	1.0288	1.0353	1.0378
8.0	1.0000	1.0196	1.0295	1.0362	1.0387
8.2	1.0000	1.0201	1.0302	1.0370	1.0397
8.4	1.0000	1.0206	1.0310	1.0379	1.0406
8.6	1.0000	1.0211	1.0317	1.0388	1.0416
8.8	1.0000	1.0215	1.0324	1.0397	1.0425
9.0	1.0000	1.0220	1.0331	1.0406	1.0435
9.2	1.0000	1.0225	1.0339	1.0415	1.0444
9.4	1.0000	1.0230	1.0346	1.0424	1.0454
9.6	1.0000	1.0235	1.0353	1.0433	1.0463
9.8	1.0000	1.0239	1.0360	1.0442	1.0473
10.0	1.0000	1.0244	1.0368	1.0450	1.0482
10.2	1.0000	1.0249	1.0375	1.0459	1.0492
10.4	1.0000	1.0254	1.0382	1.0468	1.0501
10.6	1.0000	1.0258	1.0389	1.0477	1.0511
10.8	1.0000	1.0263	1.0396	1.0486	1.0520
11.0	1.0000	1.0268	1.0404	1.0495	1.0530
11.2	1.0000	1.0273	1.0411	1.0503	1.0539
11.4	1.0000	1.0277	1.0418	1.0512	1.0549
11.6	1.0000	1.0282	1.0425	1.0521	1.0558
11.8	1.0000	1.0287	1.0432	1.0530	1.0568
12.0	1.0000	1.0292	1.0439	1.0539	1.0577
12.2	1.0000	1.0296	1.0447	1.0548	1.0587
12.4	1.0000	1.0301	1.0454	1.0556	1.0596
12.6	1.0000	1.0306	1.0461	1.0565	1.0605
12.8	1.0000	1.0310	1.0468	1.0574	1.0615
13.0	1.0000	1.0315	1.0475	1.0583	1.0624
13.2	1.0000	1.0320	1.0482	1.0591	1.0634
13.4	1.0000	1.0324	1.0489	1.0600	1.0643

TABLE K
ADJUSTMENT FACTORS FOR ANNUITIES
PAYABLE AT THE END OF EACH INTERVAL
APPLICABLE AFTER APRIL 30, 1989
FREQUENCY OF PAYMENTS

INTEREST RATE	*ANNUALLY*	*SEMI ANNUALLY*	*QUARTERLY*	*MONTHLY*	*WEEKLY*
13.6	1.0000	1.0329	1.0496	1.0609	1.0652
13.8	1.0000	1.0334	1.0504	1.0618	1.0662
14.0	1.0000	1.0339	1.0511	1.0626	1.0671

TABLE B
TERM CERTAIN REMAINDER FACTORS
APPLICABLE AFTER APRIL 30, 1989
INTEREST RATE

YEARS	*4.2%*	*4.4%*	*4.6%*	*4.8%*	*5.0%*	*5.2%*	*5.4%*	*5.6%*	*5.8%*	*6.0%*
1	.959693	.957854	.956023	.954198	.952381	.950570	.948767	.946970	.945180	.943396
2	.921010	.917485	.913980	.910495	.907029	.903584	.900158	.896752	.893364	.889996
3	.883887	.878817	.873786	.868793	.863838	.858920	.854040	.849197	.844390	.839619
4	.848260	.841779	.835359	.829001	.822702	.816464	.810285	.804163	.798100	.792094
5	.814069	.806302	.798623	.791031	.783526	.776106	.768771	.761518	.754348	.747258
6	.781257	.772320	.763501	.754801	.746215	.737744	.729384	.721135	.712994	.704961
7	.749766	.739770	.729925	.720230	.710681	.701277	.692015	.682893	.673908	.665057
8	.719545	.708592	.697825	.687242	.676839	.666613	.656561	.646679	.636964	.627412
9	.690543	.678728	.667137	.655765	.644609	.633663	.622923	.612385	.602045	.591898
10	.662709	.650122	.637798	.625730	.613913	.602341	.591009	.579910	.569041	.558395
11	.635997	.622722	.609750	.597071	.584679	.572568	.560729	.549157	.537846	.526788
12	.610362	.596477	.582935	.569724	.556837	.544266	.532001	.520035	.508361	.496969
13	.585760	.571339	.557299	.543630	.530321	.517363	.504745	.492458	.480492	.468839
14	.562150	.547259	.532790	.518731	.505068	.491790	.478885	.466343	.454151	.442301
15	.539491	.524195	.509360	.494972	.481017	.467481	.454350	.441612	.429255	.417265
16	.517746	.502102	.486960	.472302	.458112	.444374	.431072	.418194	.405723	.393646
17	.496877	.480941	.465545	.450670	.436297	.422408	.408987	.396017	.383481	.371364
18	.476849	.460671	.445071	.430028	.415521	.401529	.388033	.375016	.362458	.350344
19	.457629	.441256	.425498	.410332	.395734	.381681	.368153	.355129	.342588	.330513
20	.439183	.422659	.406786	.391538	.376889	.362815	.349291	.336296	.323807	.311805
21	.421481	.404846	.388897	.373605	.358942	.344881	.331396	.318462	.306056	.294155
22	.404492	.387783	.371794	.356494	.341850	.327834	.314417	.301574	.289278	.277505
23	.388188	.371440	.355444	.340166	.325571	.311629	.298309	.285581	.273420	.261797
24	.372542	.355785	.339813	.324586	.310068	.296225	.283025	.270437	.258431	.246979
25	.357526	.340791	.324869	.309719	.295303	.281583	.268525	.256096	.244263	.232999
26	.343115	.326428	.310582	.295533	.281241	.267664	.254768	.242515	.230873	.219810
27	.329285	.312670	.296923	.281998	.267848	.254434	.241715	.229654	.218216	.207368
28	.316012	.299493	.283866	.269082	.255094	.241857	.229331	.217475	.206253	.195630
29	.303275	.286870	.271382	.256757	.242946	.229902	.217582	.205943	.194947	.184557
30	.291051	.274780	.259447	.244997	.231377	.218538	.206434	.195021	.184260	.174110
31	.279319	.263199	.248038	.233776	.220359	.207736	.195858	.184679	.174158	.164255
32	.268061	.252106	.237130	.223069	.209866	.197468	.185823	.174886	.164611	.154957
33	.257256	.241481	.226702	.212852	.199873	.187707	.176303	.165612	.155587	.146186
34	.246887	.231304	.216732	.203103	.190355	.178429	.167270	.156829	.147058	.137912
35	.236935	.221556	.207201	.193801	.181290	.169609	.158701	.148512	.138996	.130105
36	.227385	.212218	.198089	.184924	.172657	.161225	.150570	.140637	.131376	.122741
37	.218220	.203274	.189377	.176454	.164436	.153256	.142856	.133179	.124174	.115793
38	.209424	.194707	.181049	.168373	.156605	.145681	.135537	.126116	.117367	.109239
39	.200983	.186501	.173087	.160661	.149148	.138480	.128593	.119428	.110933	.103056
40	.192882	.178641	.165475	.153302	.142046	.131635	.122004	.113095	.104851	.097222
41	.185107	.171112	.158198	.146281	.135282	.125128	.115754	.107098	.099103	.091719
42	.177646	.163900	.151241	.139581	.128840	.118943	.109823	.101418	.093670	.086527
43	.170486	.156992	.144590	.133188	.122704	.113064	.104197	.096040	.088535	.081630
44	.163614	.150376	.138231	.127088	.116861	.107475	.098858	.090947	.083682	.077009
45	.157019	.144038	.132152	.121267	.111297	.102163	.093793	.086124	.079094	.072650
46	.150690	.137968	.126340	.115713	.105997	.097113	.088988	.081557	.074758	.068538
47	.144616	.132153	.120784	.110413	.100949	.092312	.084429	.077232	.070660	.064658
48	.138787	.126583	.115473	.105356	.096142	.087749	.080103	.073136	.066786	.060998

TABLE B
TERM CERTAIN REMAINDER FACTORS
APPLICABLE AFTER APRIL 30, 1989
INTEREST RATE

YEARS	*4.2%*	*4.4%*	*4.6%*	*4.8%*	*5.0%*	*5.2%*	*5.4%*	*5.6%*	*5.8%*	*6.0%*
49	.133193	.121248	.110395	.100530	.091564	.083412	.075999	.069258	.063125	.057546
50	.127824	.116138	.105540	.095926	.087204	.079289	.072106	.065585	.059665	.054288
51	.122672	.111243	.100898	.091532	.083051	.075370	.068411	.062107	.056394	.051215
52	.117728	.106555	.096461	.087340	.079096	.071644	.064907	.058813	.053302	.048316
53	.112982	.102064	.092219	.083340	.075330	.068103	.061581	.055695	.050380	.045582
54	.108428	.097763	.088164	.079523	.071743	.064737	.058426	.052741	.047618	.043001
55	.104058	.093642	.084286	.075880	.068326	.061537	.055433	.049944	.045008	.040567
56	.099864	.089696	.080580	.072405	.065073	.058495	.052593	.047296	.042541	.038271
57	.095839	.085916	.077036	.069089	.061974	.055604	.049898	.044787	.040208	.036105
58	.091976	.082295	.073648	.065924	.059023	.052855	.047342	.042412	.038004	.034061
59	.088268	.078826	.070409	.062905	.056212	.050243	.044916	.040163	.035921	.032133
60	.084710	.075504	.067313	.060024	.053536	.047759	.042615	.038033	.033952	.030314

TABLE B
TERM CERTAIN REMAINDER FACTORS
APPLICABLE AFTER APRIL 30, 1989
INTEREST RATE

YEARS	*6.2%*	*6.4%*	*6.6%*	*6.8%*	*7.0%*	*7.2%*	*7.4%*	*7.6%*	*7.8%*	*8.0%*
1	.941620	.939850	.938086	.936330	.934579	.932836	.931099	.929368	.927644	.925926
2	.886647	.883317	.880006	.876713	.873439	.870183	.866945	.863725	.860523	.857339
3	.834885	.830185	.825521	.820892	.816298	.811738	.807211	.802718	.798259	.793832
4	.786144	.780249	.774410	.768626	.762895	.757218	.751593	.746021	.740500	.735030
5	.740248	.733317	.726464	.719687	.712986	.706360	.699808	.693328	.686920	.680583
6	.697032	.689208	.681486	.673864	.666342	.658918	.651590	.644357	.637217	.630170
7	.656339	.647752	.639292	.630959	.622750	.614662	.606694	.598845	.591111	.583490
8	.618022	.608789	.599711	.590786	.582009	.573379	.564892	.556547	.548340	.540269
9	.581942	.572170	.562581	.553170	.543934	.534868	.525971	.517237	.508664	.500249
10	.547968	.537754	.527750	.517950	.508349	.498944	.489731	.480704	.471859	.463193
11	.515977	.505408	.495075	.484972	.475093	.465433	.455987	.446750	.437717	.428883
12	.485854	.475007	.464423	.454093	.444012	.434173	.424569	.415196	.406046	.397114
13	.457490	.446436	.435669	.425181	.414964	.405012	.395316	.385870	.376666	.367698
14	.430781	.419582	.408695	.398109	.387817	.377810	.368078	.358615	.349412	.340461
15	.405632	.394344	.383391	.372762	.362446	.352434	.342717	.333285	.324130	.315242
16	.381951	.370624	.359654	.349028	.338735	.328763	.319103	.309745	.300677	.291890
17	.359653	.348331	.337386	.326805	.316574	.306682	.297117	.287867	.278921	.270269
18	.338656	.327379	.316498	.305997	.295864	.286084	.276645	.267534	.258739	.250249
19	.318885	.307687	.296902	.286514	.276508	.266870	.257584	.248638	.240018	.231712
20	.300268	.289179	.278520	.268272	.258419	.248946	.239836	.231076	.222651	.214548
21	.282739	.271785	.261276	.251191	.241513	.232225	.223311	.214755	.206541	.198656
22	.266232	.255437	.245099	.235197	.225713	.216628	.207925	.199586	.191596	.183941
23	.250689	.240073	.229924	.220222	.210947	.202078	.193598	.185489	.177733	.170315
24	.236054	.225632	.215689	.206201	.197147	.188506	.180259	.172387	.164873	.157699
25	.222273	.212060	.202334	.193072	.184249	.175845	.167839	.160211	.152943	.146018
26	.209297	.199305	.189807	.180779	.172195	.164035	.156275	.148895	.141877	.135202
27	.197078	.187317	.178056	.169269	.160930	.153017	.145507	.138379	.131611	.125187
28	.185572	.176049	.167031	.158491	.150402	.142740	.135482	.128605	.122088	.115914
29	.174739	.165460	.156690	.148400	.140563	.133153	.126147	.119521	.113255	.107328
30	.164537	.155507	.146989	.138951	.131367	.124210	.117455	.111079	.105060	.099377
31	.154932	.146154	.137888	.130104	.122773	.115868	.109362	.103233	.097458	.092016
32	.145887	.137362	.129351	.121820	.114741	.108085	.101827	.095942	.090406	.085200
33	.137370	.129100	.121342	.114064	.107235	.100826	.094811	.089165	.083865	.078889
34	.129350	.121335	.113830	.106802	.100219	.094054	.088278	.082867	.077797	.073045
35	.121798	.114036	.106782	.100001	.093663	.087737	.082196	.077014	.072168	.067635
36	.114688	.107177	.100171	.093634	.087535	.081844	.076532	.071574	.066946	.062625
37	.107992	.100730	.093969	.087673	.081809	.076347	.071259	.066519	.062102	.057986
38	.101688	.094671	.088151	.082090	.076457	.071219	.066349	.061821	.057609	.053690
39	.095751	.088977	.082693	.076864	.071455	.066436	.061778	.057454	.053440	.049713
40	.090161	.083625	.077573	.071970	.066780	.061974	.057521	.053396	.049573	.046031
41	.084897	.078595	.072770	.067387	.062412	.057811	.053558	.049625	.045987	.042621
42	.079941	.073867	.068265	.063097	.058329	.053929	.049868	.046120	.042659	.039464
43	.075274	.069424	.064038	.059079	.054513	.050307	.046432	.042862	.039572	.036541
44	.070880	.065248	.060074	.055318	.050946	.046928	.043233	.039835	.036709	.033834
45	.066742	.061323	.056354	.051796	.047613	.043776	.040254	.037021	.034053	.031328
46	.062845	.057635	.052865	.048498	.044499	.040836	.037480	.034406	.031589	.029007
47	.059176	.054168	.049592	.045410	.041587	.038093	.034898	.031976	.029303	.026859
48	.055722	.050910	.046522	.042519	.038867	.035535	.032493	.029717	.027183	.024869

TABLE B
TERM CERTAIN REMAINDER FACTORS
APPLICABLE AFTER APRIL 30, 1989
INTEREST RATE

YEARS	6.2%	6.4%	6.6%	6.8%	7.0%	7.2%	7.4%	7.6%	7.8%	8.0%
49	.052469	.047848	.043641	.039812	.036324	.033148	.030255	.027618	.025216	.023027
50	.049405	.044970	.040939	.037277	.033948	.030922	.028170	.025668	.023392	.021321
51	.046521	.042265	.038405	.034903	.031727	.028845	.026229	.023855	.021699	.019742
52	.043805	.039722	.036027	.032681	.029651	.026907	.024422	.022170	.020129	.018280
53	.041248	.037333	.033796	.030600	.027711	.025100	.022739	.020604	.018673	.016925
54	.038840	.035087	.031704	.028652	.025899	.023414	.021172	.019149	.017322	.015672
55	.036572	.032977	.029741	.026828	.024204	.021842	.019714	.017796	.016068	.014511
56	.034437	.030993	.027900	.025119	.022621	.020375	.018355	.016539	.014906	.013436
57	.032427	.029129	.026172	.023520	.021141	.019006	.017091	.015371	.013827	.012441
58	.030534	.027377	.024552	.022023	.019758	.017730	.015913	.014285	.012827	.011519
59	.028751	.025730	.023032	.020620	.018465	.016539	.014817	.013276	.011899	.010666
60	.027073	.024183	.021606	.019307	.017257	.015428	.013796	.012339	.011038	.009876

TABLE B
TERM CERTAIN REMAINDER FACTORS
APPLICABLE AFTER APRIL 30, 1989
INTEREST RATE

YEARS	8.2%	8.4%	8.6%	8.8%	9.0%	9.2%	9.4%	9.6%	9.8%	10.0%
1	.924214	.922509	.920810	.919118	.917431	.915751	.914077	.912409	.910747	.909091
2	.854172	.851023	.847892	.844777	.841680	.838600	.835536	.832490	.829460	.826446
3	.789438	.785077	.780747	.776450	.772183	.767948	.763744	.759571	.755428	.751315
4	.729610	.724241	.718920	.713649	.708425	.703250	.698121	.693039	.688003	.683013
5	.674316	.668119	.661989	.655927	.649931	.644001	.638136	.632335	.626597	.620921
6	.623213	.616346	.609566	.602874	.596267	.589745	.583305	.576948	.570671	.564474
7	.575982	.568585	.561295	.554112	.547034	.540059	.533186	.526412	.519737	.513158
8	.532331	.524524	.516846	.509294	.501866	.494560	.487373	.480303	.473349	.466507
9	.491988	.483879	.475917	.468101	.460428	.452894	.445496	.438233	.431101	.424098
10	.454703	.446383	.438230	.430240	.422411	.414738	.407218	.399848	.392624	.385543
11	.420243	.411792	.403526	.395441	.387533	.379797	.372228	.364824	.357581	.350494
12	.388394	.379882	.371571	.363457	.355535	.347799	.340245	.332869	.325666	.318631
13	.358960	.350445	.342147	.334060	.326179	.318497	.311010	.303713	.296599	.289664
14	.331756	.323288	.315052	.307040	.299246	.291664	.284287	.277110	.270127	.263331
15	.306613	.298236	.290103	.282206	.274538	.267092	.259860	.252838	.246017	.239392
16	.283376	.275126	.267130	.259381	.251870	.244589	.237532	.230691	.224059	.217629
17	.261901	.253806	.245976	.238401	.231073	.223983	.217123	.210485	.204061	.197845
18	.242052	.234139	.226497	.219119	.211994	.205113	.198467	.192048	.185848	.179859
19	.223708	.215995	.208561	.201396	.194490	.187832	.181414	.175226	.169260	.163508
20	.206754	.199257	.192045	.185107	.178431	.172007	.165826	.159878	.154153	.148644
21	.191085	.183817	.176837	.170135	.163698	.157516	.151578	.145874	.140395	.135131
22	.176604	.169573	.162834	.156374	.150182	.144245	.138554	.133097	.127864	.122846
23	.163220	.156432	.149939	.143726	.137781	.132093	.126649	.121439	.116452	.111678
24	.150850	.144310	.138065	.132101	.126405	.120964	.115767	.110802	.106058	.101526
25	.139418	.133128	.127132	.121416	.115968	.110773	.105820	.101097	.096592	.092296
26	.128852	.122811	.117064	.111596	.106393	.101441	.096727	.092241	.087971	.083905
27	.119087	.113295	.107794	.102570	.097608	.092894	.088416	.084162	.080119	.076278
28	.110062	.104515	.099258	.094274	.089548	.085068	.080819	.076790	.072968	.069343
29	.101721	.096416	.091398	.086649	.082155	.077901	.073875	.070064	.066456	.063039
30	.094012	.088945	.084160	.079640	.075371	.071338	.067527	.063927	.060524	.057309
31	.086887	.082053	.077495	.073199	.069148	.065328	.061725	.058327	.055122	.052099
32	.080302	.075694	.071358	.067278	.063438	.059824	.056422	.053218	.050202	.047362
33	.074216	.069829	.065708	.061837	.058200	.054784	.051574	.048557	.045722	.043057
34	.068592	.064418	.060504	.056835	.053395	.050168	.047142	.044304	.041641	.039143
35	.063394	.059426	.055713	.052238	.048986	.045942	.043092	.040423	.037924	.035584
36	.058589	.054821	.051301	.048013	.044941	.042071	.039389	.036882	.034539	.032349
37	.054149	.050573	.047239	.044130	.041231	.038527	.036005	.033652	.031457	.029408
38	.050045	.046654	.043498	.040560	.037826	.035281	.032911	.030704	.028649	.026735
39	.046253	.043039	.040053	.037280	.034703	.032309	.030083	.028015	.026092	.024304
40	.042747	.039703	.036881	.034264	.031838	.029587	.027498	.025561	.023763	.022095
41	.039508	.036627	.033961	.031493	.029209	.027094	.025136	.023322	.021642	.020086
42	.036514	.033789	.031271	.028946	.026797	.024811	.022976	.021279	.019711	.018260
43	.033746	.031170	.028795	.026605	.024584	.022721	.021002	.019415	.017951	.016600
44	.031189	.028755	.026515	.024453	.022555	.020807	.019197	.017715	.016349	.015091
45	.028825	.026527	.024415	.022475	.020692	.019054	.017548	.016163	.014890	.013719
46	.026641	.024471	.022482	.020657	.018984	.017449	.016040	.014747	.013561	.012472
47	.024622	.022575	.020701	.018986	.017416	.015978	.014662	.013456	.012351	.011338
48	.022756	.020825	.019062	.017451	.015978	.014632	.013402	.012277	.011248	.010307

TABLE B
TERM CERTAIN REMAINDER FACTORS
APPLICABLE AFTER APRIL 30, 1989
INTEREST RATE

YEARS	*8.2%*	*8.4%*	*8.6%*	*8.8%*	*9.0%*	*9.2%*	*9.4%*	*9.6%*	*9.8%*	*10.0%*
49	.021031	.019212	.017552	.016039	.014659	.013400	.012250	.011202	.010244	.009370
50	.019437	.017723	.016163	.014742	.013449	.012271	.011198	.010221	.009330	.008519
51	.017964	.016350	.014883	.013550	.012338	.011237	.010236	.009325	.008497	.007744
52	.016603	.015083	.013704	.012454	.011319	.010290	.009356	.008508	.007739	.007040
53	.015345	.013914	.012619	.011446	.010385	.009423	.008552	.007763	.007048	.006400
54	.014182	.012836	.011620	.010521	.009527	.008629	.007817	.007083	.006419	.005818
55	.013107	.011841	.010699	.009670	.008741	.007902	.007146	.006463	.005846	.005289
56	.012114	.010923	.009852	.008888	.008019	.007237	.006532	.005897	.005324	.004809
57	.011196	.010077	.009072	.008169	.007357	.006627	.005971	.005380	.004849	.004371
58	.010347	.009296	.008354	.007508	.006749	.006069	.005458	.004909	.004416	.003974
59	.009563	.008576	.007692	.006901	.006192	.005557	.004989	.004479	.004022	.003613
60	.008838	.007911	.007083	.006343	.005681	.005089	.004560	.004087	.003663	.003284

TABLE B
TERM CERTAIN REMAINDER FACTORS
APPLICABLE AFTER APRIL 30, 1989
INTEREST RATE

YEARS	10.2%	10.4%	10.6%	10.8%	11.0%	11.2%	11.4%	11.6%	11.8%	12.0%
1	.907441	.905797	.904159	.902527	.900901	.899281	.897666	.896057	.894454	.892857
2	.823449	.820468	.817504	.814555	.811622	.808706	.805804	.802919	.800049	.797194
3	.747232	.743178	.739153	.735158	.731191	.727253	.723343	.719461	.715607	.711780
4	.678069	.673168	.668312	.663500	.658731	.654005	.649321	.644679	.640078	.635518
5	.615307	.609754	.604261	.598827	.593451	.588134	.582873	.577669	.572520	.567427
6	.558355	.552313	.546348	.540457	.534641	.528897	.523225	.517625	.512093	.506631
7	.506674	.500284	.493985	.487777	.481658	.475627	.469682	.463821	.458044	.452349
8	.459777	.453156	.446641	.440232	.433926	.427722	.421617	.415610	.409700	.403883
9	.417221	.410467	.403835	.397322	.390925	.384642	.378472	.372411	.366458	.360610
10	.378603	.371800	.365131	.358593	.352184	.345901	.339741	.333701	.327780	.321973
11	.343560	.336775	.330137	.323640	.317283	.311062	.304974	.299016	.293184	.287476
12	.311760	.305050	.298496	.292094	.285841	.279732	.273765	.267935	.262240	.256675
13	.282904	.276313	.269888	.263623	.257514	.251558	.245749	.240085	.234561	.229174
14	.256719	.250284	.244022	.237927	.231995	.226221	.220601	.215130	.209804	.204620
15	.232957	.226706	.220634	.214735	.209004	.203436	.198026	.192769	.187661	.182696
16	.211395	.205350	.199489	.193804	.188292	.182946	.177761	.172732	.167854	.163122
17	.191828	.186005	.180369	.174914	.169633	.164520	.159570	.154778	.150138	.145644
18	.174073	.168483	.163083	.157864	.152822	.147950	.143241	.138690	.134291	.130040
19	.157961	.152612	.147453	.142477	.137678	.133048	.128582	.124274	.120117	.116107
20	.143340	.138235	.133321	.128589	.124034	.119648	.115424	.111357	.107439	.103667
21	.130073	.125213	.120543	.116055	.111742	.107597	.103612	.099782	.096100	.092560
22	.118033	.113418	.108990	.104743	.100669	.096760	.093009	.089410	.085957	.082643
23	.107108	.102733	.098544	.094533	.090693	.087014	.083491	.080117	.076884	.073788
24	.097195	.093056	.089100	.085319	.081705	.078250	.074947	.071789	.068770	.065882
25	.088198	.084289	.080560	.077003	.073608	.070369	.067278	.064327	.061511	.058823
26	.080035	.076349	.072839	.069497	.066314	.063281	.060393	.057641	.055019	.052521
27	.072627	.069157	.065858	.062723	.059742	.056908	.054213	.051650	.049212	.046894
28	.065905	.062642	.059547	.056609	.053822	.051176	.048665	.046281	.044018	.041869
29	.059804	.056741	.053840	.051091	.048488	.046022	.043685	.041470	.039372	.037383
30	.054269	.051396	.048680	.046111	.043683	.041386	.039214	.037160	.035216	.033378
31	.049246	.046554	.044014	.041617	.039354	.037218	.035201	.033297	.031500	.029802
32	.044688	.042169	.039796	.037560	.035454	.033469	.031599	.029836	.028175	.026609
33	.040552	.038196	.035982	.033899	.031940	.030098	.028365	.026735	.025201	.023758
34	.036798	.034598	.032533	.030595	.028775	.027067	.025463	.023956	.022541	.021212
35	.033392	.031339	.029415	.027613	.025924	.024341	.022857	.021466	.020162	.018940
36	.030301	.028387	.026596	.024921	.023355	.021889	.020518	.019235	.018034	.016910
37	.027497	.025712	.024047	.022492	.021040	.019684	.018418	.017236	.016131	.015098
38	.024952	.023290	.021742	.020300	.018955	.017702	.016533	.015444	.014428	.013481
39	.022642	.021096	.019658	.018321	.017077	.015919	.014841	.013839	.012905	.012036
40	.020546	.019109	.017774	.016535	.015384	.014316	.013323	.012400	.011543	.010747
41	.018645	.017309	.016071	.014923	.013860	.012874	.011959	.011111	.010325	.009595
42	.016919	.015678	.014531	.013469	.012486	.011577	.010735	.009956	.009235	.008567
43	.015353	.014201	.013138	.012156	.011249	.010411	.009637	.008922	.008260	.007649
44	.013932	.012864	.011879	.010971	.010134	.009362	.008651	.007994	.007389	.006830
45	.012642	.011652	.010740	.009902	.009130	.008419	.007765	.007163	.006609	.006098
46	.011472	.010554	.009711	.008937	.008225	.007571	.006971	.006419	.005911	.005445
47	.010410	.009560	.008780	.008065	.007410	.006809	.006257	.005752	.005287	.004861
48	.009447	.008659	.007939	.007279	.006676	.006123	.005617	.005154	.004729	.004340

TABLE B
TERM CERTAIN REMAINDER FACTORS
APPLICABLE AFTER APRIL 30, 1989
INTEREST RATE

YEARS	*10.2%*	*10.4%*	*10.6%*	*10.8%*	*11.0%*	*11.2%*	*11.4%*	*11.6%*	*11.8%*	*12.0%*
49	.008572	.007844	.007178	.006570	.006014	.005506	.005042	.004618	.004230	.003875
50	.007779	.007105	.006490	.005929	.005418	.004952	.004526	.004138	.003784	.003460
51	.007059	.006435	.005868	.005351	.004881	.004453	.004063	.003708	.003384	.003089
52	.006406	.005829	.005306	.004830	.004397	.004005	.003647	.003322	.003027	.002758
53	.005813	.005280	.004797	.004359	.003962	.003601	.003274	.002977	.002708	.002463
54	.005275	.004783	.004337	.003934	.003569	.003238	.002939	.002668	.002422	.002199
55	.004786	.004332	.003922	.003551	.003215	.002912	.002638	.002390	.002166	.001963
56	.004343	.003924	.003546	.003205	.002897	.002619	.002368	.002142	.001938	.001753
57	.003941	.003554	.003206	.002892	.002610	.002355	.002126	.001919	.001733	.001565
58	.003577	.003220	.002899	.002610	.002351	.002118	.001908	.001720	.001550	.001398
59	.003246	.002916	.002621	.002356	.002118	.001905	.001713	.001541	.001387	.001248
60	.002945	.002642	.002370	.002126	.001908	.001713	.001538	.001381	.001240	.001114

TABLE B
TERM CERTAIN REMAINDER FACTORS
APPLICABLE AFTER APRIL 30, 1989
INTEREST RATE

YEARS	12.2%	12.4%	12.6%	12.8%	13.0%	13.2%	13.4%	13.6%	13.8%	14.0%
1	.891266	.889680	.888099	.886525	.884956	.883392	.881834	.880282	.878735	.877193
2	.794354	.791530	.788721	.785926	.783147	.780382	.777632	.774896	.772175	.769468
3	.707981	.704208	.700462	.696743	.693050	.689383	.685742	.682127	.678536	.674972
4	.630999	.626520	.622080	.617680	.613319	.608996	.604711	.600464	.596254	.592080
5	.562388	.557402	.552469	.547589	.542760	.537982	.533255	.528577	.523949	.519369
6	.501237	.495909	.490648	.485451	.480319	.475249	.470242	.465297	.460412	.455587
7	.446735	.441200	.435744	.430364	.425061	.419831	.414676	.409592	.404580	.399637
8	.398160	.392527	.386984	.381529	.376160	.370876	.365675	.360557	.355518	.350559
9	.354866	.349223	.343680	.338235	.332885	.327629	.322465	.317391	.312406	.307508
10	.316280	.310697	.305222	.299853	.294588	.289425	.284361	.279394	.274522	.269744
11	.281889	.276421	.271068	.265827	.260698	.255676	.250759	.245945	.241232	.236617
12	.251238	.245926	.240735	.235663	.230706	.225862	.221128	.216501	.211979	.207559
13	.223920	.218795	.213797	.208921	.204165	.199525	.194998	.190582	.186273	.182069
14	.199572	.194658	.189873	.185213	.180677	.176258	.171956	.167766	.163685	.159710
15	.177872	.173183	.168626	.164196	.159891	.155705	.151637	.147681	.143835	.140096
16	.158531	.154077	.149757	.145564	.141496	.137549	.133718	.130001	.126393	.122892
17	.141293	.137080	.132999	.129046	.125218	.121510	.117917	.114438	.111066	.107800
18	.125930	.121957	.118116	.114403	.110812	.107341	.103984	.100737	.097598	.094561
19	.112237	.108503	.104899	.101421	.098064	.094824	.091696	.088677	.085762	.082948
20	.100033	.096533	.093161	.089912	.086782	.083767	.080861	.078061	.075362	.072762
21	.089156	.085883	.082736	.079709	.076798	.073999	.071306	.068716	.066224	.063826
22	.079462	.076408	.073478	.070664	.067963	.065370	.062880	.060489	.058193	.055988
23	.070821	.067979	.065255	.062646	.060144	.057747	.055450	.053247	.051136	.049112
24	.063121	.060480	.057953	.055537	.053225	.051014	.048898	.046873	.044935	.043081
25	.056257	.053807	.051468	.049235	.047102	.045065	.043119	.041261	.039486	.037790
26	.050140	.047871	.045709	.043648	.041683	.039810	.038024	.036321	.034698	.033149
27	.044688	.042590	.040594	.038695	.036888	.035168	.033531	.031973	.030490	.029078
28	.039829	.037892	.036052	.034304	.032644	.031067	.029569	.028145	.026793	.025507
29	.035498	.033711	.032017	.030411	.028889	.027444	.026075	.024776	.023544	.022375
30	.031638	.029992	.028435	.026960	.025565	.024244	.022994	.021810	.020689	.019627
31	.028198	.026684	.025253	.023901	.022624	.021417	.020277	.019199	.018180	.017217
32	.025132	.023740	.022427	.021189	.020021	.018920	.017881	.016900	.015975	.015102
33	.022399	.021121	.019917	.018785	.017718	.016714	.015768	.014877	.014038	.013248
34	.019964	.018791	.017689	.016653	.015680	.014765	.013905	.013096	.012336	.011621
35	.017793	.016718	.015709	.014763	.013876	.013043	.012261	.011528	.010840	.010194
36	.015858	.014873	.013951	.013088	.012279	.011522	.010813	.010148	.009525	.008942
37	.014134	.013233	.012390	.011603	.010867	.010178	.009535	.008933	.008370	.007844
38	.012597	.011773	.011004	.010286	.009617	.008992	.008408	.007864	.007355	.006880
39	.011227	.010474	.009772	.009119	.008510	.007943	.007415	.006922	.006463	.006035
40	.010007	.009319	.008679	.008084	.007531	.007017	.006538	.006093	.005679	.005294
41	.008919	.008291	.007708	.007167	.006665	.006199	.005766	.005364	.004991	.004644
42	.007949	.007376	.006845	.006354	.005898	.005476	.005085	.004722	.004386	.004074
43	.007084	.006562	.006079	.005633	.005219	.004837	.004484	.004157	.003854	.003573
44	.006314	.005838	.005399	.004993	.004619	.004273	.003954	.003659	.003386	.003135
45	.005628	.005194	.004795	.004427	.004088	.003775	.003487	.003221	.002976	.002750
46	.005016	.004621	.004258	.003924	.003617	.003335	.003075	.002835	.002615	.002412
47	.004470	.004111	.003782	.003479	.003201	.002946	.002711	.002496	.002298	.002116
48	.003984	.003658	.003359	.003084	.002833	.002602	.002391	.002197	.002019	.001856

TABLE B
TERM CERTAIN REMAINDER FACTORS
APPLICABLE AFTER APRIL 30, 1989
INTEREST RATE

YEARS	12.2%	12.4%	12.6%	12.8%	13.0%	13.2%	13.4%	13.6%	13.8%	14.0%
49	.003551	.003254	.002983	.002734	.002507	.002299	.002108	.001934	.001774	.001628
50	.003165	.002895	.002649	.002424	.002219	.002031	.001859	.001702	.001559	.001428
51	.002821	.002576	.002353	.002149	.001963	.001794	.001640	.001499	.001370	.001253
52	.002514	.002292	.002089	.001905	.001737	.001585	.001446	.001319	.001204	.001099
53	.002241	.002039	.001856	.001689	.001538	.001400	.001275	.001161	.001058	.000964
54	.001997	.001814	.001648	.001497	.001361	.001237	.001124	.001022	.000930	.000846
55	.001780	.001614	.001463	.001327	.001204	.001093	.000991	.000900	.000817	.000742
56	.001586	.001436	.001300	.001177	.001066	.000965	.000874	.000792	.000718	.000651
57	.001414	.001277	.001154	.001043	.000943	.000853	.000771	.000697	.000631	.000571
58	.001260	.001136	.001025	.000925	.000835	.000753	.000680	.000614	.000554	.000501
59	.001123	.001011	.000910	.000820	.000739	.000665	.000600	.000540	.000487	.000439
60	.001001	.000900	.000809	.000727	.000654	.000588	.000529	.000476	.000428	.000385

TABLE U(1)
BASED ON LIFE TABLE 90CM
UNITRUST SINGLE LIFE REMAINDER FACTORS
APPLICABLE FOR TRANSFERS AFTER APRIL 30, 1999
ADJUSTED PAYOUT RATE

AGE	4.2%	4.4%	4.6%	4.8%	5.0%	5.2%	5.4%	5.6%	5.8%	6.0%
0	.06177	.05580	.05061	.04609	.04215	.03871	.03570	.03307	.03075	.02872
1	.05543	.04925	.04388	.03919	.03509	.03151	.02838	.02563	.02321	.02109
2	.05716	.05081	.04528	.04045	.03622	.03252	.02927	.02642	.02391	.02170
3	.05920	.05268	.04699	.04201	.03765	.03382	.03046	.02750	.02490	.02260
4	.06143	.05475	.04889	.04376	.03926	.03530	.03182	.02876	.02605	.02366
5	.06384	.05697	.05095	.04567	.04103	.03694	.03334	.03016	.02735	.02487
6	.06637	.05933	.05315	.04771	.04292	.03870	.03497	.03168	.02876	.02618
7	.06905	.06183	.05547	.04987	.04494	.04058	.03673	.03332	.03029	.02761
8	.07186	.06445	.05792	.05216	.04708	.04258	.03859	.03506	.03192	.02914
9	.07482	.06722	.06052	.05460	.04936	.04471	.04060	.03694	.03369	.03079
10	.07793	.07015	.06327	.05718	.05179	.04700	.04274	.03896	.03559	.03259
11	.08120	.07323	.06617	.05991	.05435	.04942	.04502	.04111	.03762	.03450
12	.08461	.07645	.06920	.06277	.05706	.05197	.04744	.04339	.03978	.03655
13	.08812	.07976	.07234	.06574	.05985	.05461	.04993	.04576	.04202	.03867
14	.09168	.08313	.07552	.06874	.06269	.05729	.05247	.04815	.04428	.04081
15	.09527	.08652	.07872	.07176	.06554	.05999	.05501	.05055	.04655	.04296
16	.09886	.08991	.08192	.07478	.06839	.06267	.05754	.05294	.04880	.04508
17	.10249	.09334	.08515	.07782	.07126	.06537	.06008	.05533	.05105	.04720
18	.10616	.09680	.08842	.08090	.07415	.06809	.06264	.05774	.05332	.04933
19	.10994	.10037	.09178	.08407	.07714	.07091	.06529	.06023	.05566	.05153
20	.11384	.10406	.09527	.08737	.08025	.07383	.06805	.06283	.05811	.05384
21	.11790	.10790	.09891	.09080	.08349	.07690	.07094	.06555	.06068	.05626
22	.12208	.11188	.10267	.09436	.08686	.08008	.07395	.06839	.06336	.05879
23	.12643	.11601	.10659	.09808	.09038	.08342	.07710	.07138	.06618	.06146
24	.13095	.12031	.11069	.10197	.09408	.08692	.08042	.07452	.06915	.06427
25	.13567	.12481	.11497	.10605	.09795	.09060	.08392	.07784	.07230	.06726
26	.14058	.12950	.11945	.11032	.10202	.09447	.08760	.08134	.07563	.07042
27	.14571	.13442	.12415	.11481	.10631	.09856	.09149	.08505	.07916	.07379
28	.15104	.13953	.12904	.11949	.11078	.10284	.09558	.08895	.08288	.07733
29	.15656	.14484	.13414	.12438	.11546	.10731	.09986	.09304	.08679	.08106
30	.16229	.15034	.13943	.12946	.12034	.11198	.10433	.09732	.09089	.08498
31	.16821	.15605	.14493	.13474	.12541	.11685	.10900	.10179	.09517	.08909
32	.17433	.16196	.15063	.14023	.13069	.12193	.11387	.10647	.09966	.09339
33	.18068	.16810	.15655	.14595	.13620	.12723	.11897	.11137	.10437	.09791
34	.18724	.17446	.16270	.15189	.14193	.13275	.12430	.11650	.10930	.10265
35	.19405	.18107	.16910	.15808	.14791	.13853	.12987	.12187	.11448	.10764
36	.20109	.18791	.17574	.16451	.15414	.14456	.13569	.12749	.11990	.11287
37	.20838	.19500	.18263	.17120	.16062	.15083	.14177	.13337	.12558	.11835
38	.21593	.20236	.18979	.17816	.16739	.15739	.14813	.13953	.13154	.12412
39	.22374	.20998	.19723	.18540	.17443	.16423	.15477	.14597	.13779	.13017
40	.23183	.21789	.20496	.19294	.18177	.17138	.16172	.15272	.14434	.13653
41	.24021	.22611	.21299	.20079	.18943	.17885	.16899	.15980	.15123	.14322
42	.24889	.23463	.22134	.20896	.19741	.18665	.17660	.16721	.15845	.15025
43	.25786	.24344	.23000	.21744	.20572	.19477	.18453	.17496	.16601	.15762
44	.26712	.25257	.23896	.22625	.21435	.20322	.19281	.18305	.17391	.16534
45	.27665	.26196	.24821	.23534	.22328	.21198	.20139	.19145	.18213	.17338
46	.28644	.27163	.25774	.24472	.23251	.22105	.21028	.20018	.19068	.18174

TABLE U(1)
BASED ON LIFE TABLE 90CM
UNITRUST SINGLE LIFE REMAINDER FACTORS
APPLICABLE FOR TRANSFERS AFTER APRIL 30, 1999
ADJUSTED PAYOUT RATE

AGE	4.2%	4.4%	4.6%	4.8%	5.0%	5.2%	5.4%	5.6%	5.8%	6.0%
47	.29647	.28155	.26754	.25438	.24201	.23040	.21947	.20919	.19952	.19041
48	.30676	.29173	.27760	.26431	.25181	.24004	.22896	.21852	.20868	.19941
49	.31729	.30217	.28794	.27453	.26190	.24999	.23876	.22817	.21817	.20873
50	.32808	.31289	.29856	.28505	.27229	.26026	.24889	.23814	.22799	.21839
51	.33912	.32387	.30946	.29585	.28299	.27083	.25933	.24845	.23815	.22840
52	.35038	.33507	.32060	.30691	.29395	.28168	.27005	.25904	.24861	.23872
53	.36185	.34651	.33198	.31821	.30517	.29280	.28106	.26993	.25937	.24934
54	.37352	.35815	.34358	.32976	.31664	.30418	.29234	.28110	.27042	.26026
55	.38539	.37002	.35542	.34155	.32836	.31583	.30390	.29256	.28177	.27149
56	.39746	.38209	.36748	.35358	.34034	.32774	.31574	.30431	.29342	.28303
57	.40971	.39437	.37976	.36584	.35257	.33992	.32785	.31634	.30536	.29488
58	.42212	.40682	.39222	.37829	.36500	.35231	.34019	.32862	.31756	.30699
59	.43464	.41939	.40482	.39090	.37759	.36488	.35272	.34109	.32996	.31932
60	.44726	.43207	.41754	.40364	.39034	.37761	.36542	.35375	.34257	.33186
61	.45999	.44488	.43041	.41655	.40326	.39053	.37833	.36662	.35540	.34463
62	.47286	.45785	.44345	.42964	.41639	.40367	.39146	.37974	.36848	.35767
63	.48589	.47098	.45667	.44293	.42972	.41703	.40484	.39311	.38184	.37100
64	.49903	.48426	.47005	.45638	.44324	.43060	.41843	.40671	.39544	.38458
65	.51229	.49766	.48357	.47001	.45694	.44435	.43223	.42054	.40927	.39841
66	.52568	.51121	.49726	.48381	.47084	.45833	.44626	.43461	.42337	.41252
67	.53924	.52495	.51115	.49784	.48498	.47256	.46056	.44898	.43778	.42696
68	.55293	.53883	.52521	.51205	.49932	.48701	.47511	.46360	.45246	.44169
69	.56671	.55283	.53940	.52640	.51382	.50165	.48985	.47844	.46738	.45666
70	.58052	.56687	.55365	.54084	.52843	.51639	.50473	.49342	.48245	.47181
71	.59431	.58091	.56791	.55529	.54306	.53118	.51966	.50847	.49761	.48707
72	.60804	.59490	.58213	.56973	.55768	.54598	.53461	.52357	.51283	.50239
73	.62168	.60881	.59629	.58411	.57227	.56076	.54955	.53866	.52806	.51774
74	.63528	.62268	.61042	.59848	.58686	.57555	.56453	.55380	.54335	.53316
75	.64887	.63657	.62458	.61290	.60151	.59041	.57959	.56904	.55875	.54872
76	.66249	.65049	.63880	.62739	.61625	.60538	.59478	.58443	.57432	.56446
77	.67612	.66446	.65307	.64194	.63108	.62046	.61009	.59995	.59005	.58037
78	.68975	.67843	.66736	.65654	.64596	.63561	.62548	.61558	.60590	.59643
79	.70330	.69233	.68160	.67109	.66081	.65074	.64088	.63123	.62178	.61253
80	.71666	.70605	.69566	.68548	.67550	.66573	.65615	.64676	.63755	.62853
81	.72975	.71950	.70946	.69961	.68995	.68047	.67117	.66205	.65310	.64433
82	.74250	.73263	.72293	.71342	.70407	.69490	.68589	.67705	.66837	.65984
83	.75493	.74542	.73608	.72690	.71788	.70902	.70031	.69175	.68333	.67506
84	.76712	.75798	.74900	.74016	.73147	.72292	.71451	.70624	.69810	.69010
85	.77913	.77037	.76175	.75326	.74491	.73668	.72859	.72061	.71276	.70503
86	.79086	.78248	.77423	.76610	.75808	.75019	.74241	.73474	.72719	.71974
87	.80218	.79418	.78628	.77850	.77083	.76326	.75580	.74844	.74118	.73402
88	.81307	.80544	.79790	.79047	.78313	.77589	.76874	.76169	.75473	.74786
89	.82355	.81628	.80909	.80200	.79500	.78808	.78125	.77450	.76783	.76125
90	.83360	.82668	.81985	.81309	.80642	.79982	.79330	.78685	.78048	.77418
91	.84308	.83650	.83000	.82357	.81721	.81092	.80470	.79855	.79246	.78645
92	.85182	.84556	.83937	.83325	.82718	.82119	.81525	.80937	.80356	.79780
93	.85985	.85390	.84800	.84215	.83637	.83064	.82497	.81936	.81379	.80829
94	.86732	.86164	.85601	.85044	.84491	.83944	.83402	.82865	.82333	.81806

TABLE U(1)
BASED ON LIFE TABLE 90CM
UNITRUST SINGLE LIFE REMAINDER FACTORS
APPLICABLE FOR TRANSFERS AFTER APRIL 30, 1999
ADJUSTED PAYOUT RATE

AGE	4.2%	4.4%	4.6%	4.8%	5.0%	5.2%	5.4%	5.6%	5.8%	6.0%
95	.87437	.86895	.86359	.85827	.85300	.84778	.84260	.83746	.83237	.82733
96	.88097	.87582	.87070	.86563	.86060	.85561	.85066	.84575	.84088	.83605
97	.88708	.88216	.87727	.87243	.86762	.86285	.85811	.85341	.84875	.84413
98	.89280	.88810	.88343	.87880	.87420	.86964	.86511	.86061	.85614	.85171
99	.89836	.89388	.88943	.88501	.88062	.87626	.87193	.86763	.86336	.85911
100	.90375	.89948	.89525	.89103	.88685	.88269	.87856	.87445	.87037	.86632
101	.90905	.90500	.90097	.89696	.89298	.88902	.88509	.88118	.87729	.87342
102	.91424	.91040	.90658	.90278	.89900	.89524	.89150	.88778	.88408	.88040
103	.91939	.91575	.91214	.90854	.90496	.90139	.89785	.89432	.89081	.88732
104	.92485	.92144	.91805	.91467	.91131	.90796	.90463	.90131	.89800	.89471
105	.93020	.92701	.92383	.92067	.91751	.91437	.91125	.90813	.90502	.90193
106	.93701	.93411	.93122	.92834	.92546	.92260	.91974	.91689	.91405	.91122
107	.94522	.94268	.94013	.93760	.93507	.93254	.93002	.92750	.92499	.92249
108	.95782	.95583	.95385	.95187	.94989	.94791	.94593	.94396	.94199	.94002
109	.97900	.97800	.97700	.97600	.97500	.97400	.97300	.97200	.97100	.97000

TABLE U(1)
BASED ON LIFE TABLE 90CM
UNITRUST SINGLE LIFE REMAINDER FACTORS
APPLICABLE FOR TRANSFERS AFTER APRIL 30, 1999
ADJUSTED PAYOUT RATE

AGE	6.2%	6.4%	6.6%	6.8%	7.0%	7.2%	7.4%	7.6%	7.8%	8.0%
0	.02693	.02534	.02395	.02271	.02161	.02063	.01976	.01898	.01828	.01765
1	.01922	.01756	.01610	.01480	.01365	.01263	.01171	.01090	.01017	.00951
2	.01975	.01802	.01650	.01514	.01393	.01286	.01190	.01104	.01028	.00959
3	.02056	.01876	.01717	.01575	.01449	.01336	.01235	.01145	.01064	.00992
4	.02155	.01967	.01800	.01652	.01520	.01401	.01296	.01201	.01116	.01039
5	.02266	.02071	.01896	.01741	.01603	.01479	.01368	.01269	.01179	.01098
6	.02389	.02184	.02003	.01841	.01696	.01566	.01450	.01345	.01251	.01166
7	.02522	.02309	.02120	.01950	.01799	.01663	.01540	.01431	.01332	.01242
8	.02665	.02444	.02246	.02069	.01910	.01768	.01640	.01524	.01420	.01326
9	.02821	.02590	.02384	.02199	.02033	.01884	.01750	.01629	.01520	.01421
10	.02990	.02750	.02535	.02342	.02169	.02013	.01872	.01745	.01631	.01526
11	.03172	.02922	.02698	.02497	.02316	.02153	.02006	.01872	.01752	.01643
12	.03365	.03106	.02872	.02663	.02474	.02303	.02149	.02010	.01884	.01769
13	.03566	.03297	.03054	.02835	.02638	.02460	.02299	.02154	.02021	.01901
14	.03770	.03490	.03237	.03010	.02804	.02619	.02450	.02298	.02159	.02033
15	.03973	.03682	.03419	.03182	.02968	.02775	.02599	.02439	.02294	.02162
16	.04173	.03871	.03598	.03352	.03129	.02926	.02743	.02576	.02424	.02286
17	.04372	.04059	.03775	.03519	.03287	.03076	.02884	.02710	.02551	.02406
18	.04573	.04248	.03953	.03686	.03444	.03224	.03024	.02842	.02676	.02524
19	.04780	.04443	.04137	.03859	.03607	.03378	.03169	.02978	.02804	.02646
20	.04997	.04647	.04329	.04040	.03778	.03539	.03321	.03122	.02940	.02773
21	.05226	.04862	.04532	.04232	.03958	.03709	.03481	.03274	.03083	.02909
22	.05465	.05088	.04745	.04432	.04148	.03888	.03650	.03433	.03234	.03052
23	.05716	.05325	.04969	.04645	.04348	.04077	.03830	.03603	.03394	.03203
24	.05983	.05578	.05208	.04871	.04562	.04280	.04021	.03784	.03566	.03367
25	.06266	.05846	.05463	.05112	.04791	.04497	.04227	.03980	.03752	.03543
26	.06566	.06131	.05734	.05369	.05035	.04729	.04448	.04189	.03951	.03732
27	.06887	.06436	.06024	.05646	.05298	.04979	.04686	.04416	.04168	.03939
28	.07225	.06758	.06331	.05938	.05577	.05245	.04940	.04658	.04398	.04159
29	.07581	.07099	.06656	.06248	.05873	.05528	.05210	.04916	.04645	.04394
30	.07956	.07457	.06998	.06575	.06186	.05827	.05495	.05189	.04906	.04644
31	.08348	.07833	.07358	.06920	.06515	.06142	.05797	.05478	.05182	.04908
32	.08761	.08228	.07736	.07282	.06863	.06475	.06116	.05783	.05475	.05189
33	.09195	.08645	.08136	.07666	.07231	.06828	.06454	.06108	.05786	.05488
34	.09651	.09082	.08557	.08070	.07619	.07200	.06812	.06452	.06117	.05805
35	.10131	.09545	.09002	.08498	.08030	.07596	.07193	.06818	.06469	.06144
36	.10635	.10031	.09470	.08949	.08465	.08015	.07596	.07206	.06842	.06503
37	.11165	.10542	.09963	.09424	.08923	.08457	.08022	.07617	.07238	.06885
38	.11722	.11081	.10484	.09927	.09409	.08926	.08475	.08054	.07661	.07293
39	.12308	.11648	.11032	.10458	.09922	.09422	.08955	.08518	.08109	.07726
40	.12925	.12246	.11612	.11020	.10466	.09949	.09465	.09011	.08587	.08189
41	.13575	.12877	.12225	.11614	.11043	.10508	.10007	.09537	.09097	.08683
42	.14259	.13542	.12871	.12243	.11654	.11101	.10583	.10097	.09640	.09210
43	.14977	.14242	.13552	.12905	.12298	.11729	.11193	.10690	.10217	.09771
44	.15731	.14976	.14269	.13604	.12979	.12391	.11838	.11318	.10828	.10367
45	.16516	.15743	.15017	.14334	.13691	.13086	.12516	.11979	.11472	.10994
46	.17334	.16544	.15800	.15099	.14438	.13816	.13228	.12674	.12150	.11656

TABLE U(1)
BASED ON LIFE TABLE 90CM
UNITRUST SINGLE LIFE REMAINDER FACTORS
APPLICABLE FOR TRANSFERS AFTER APRIL 30, 1999
ADJUSTED PAYOUT RATE

AGE	6.2%	6.4%	6.6%	6.8%	7.0%	7.2%	7.4%	7.6%	7.8%	8.0%
47	.18184	.17375	.16613	.15895	.15217	.14576	.13972	.13400	.12860	.12349
48	.19066	.18240	.17461	.16724	.16029	.15371	.14749	.14161	.13604	.13077
49	.19981	.19138	.18342	.17588	.16875	.16201	.15562	.14956	.14383	.13839
50	.20931	.20072	.19259	.18489	.17759	.17067	.16412	.15790	.15199	.14639
51	.21917	.21042	.20212	.19426	.18679	.17971	.17299	.16660	.16054	.15477
52	.22933	.22043	.21198	.20395	.19633	.18909	.18220	.17566	.16943	.16350
53	.23981	.23076	.22216	.21399	.20621	.19881	.19176	.18506	.17867	.17258
54	.25060	.24141	.23267	.22434	.21642	.20886	.20166	.19480	.18826	.18201
55	.26171	.25239	.24351	.23504	.22697	.21927	.21192	.20491	.19821	.19182
56	.27313	.26369	.25468	.24608	.23787	.23003	.22254	.21538	.20854	.20199
57	.28487	.27531	.26618	.25746	.24912	.24114	.23351	.22621	.21923	.21254
58	.29688	.28722	.27798	.26914	.26067	.25257	.24481	.23738	.23025	.22343
59	.30913	.29937	.29002	.28107	.27249	.26427	.25639	.24882	.24157	.23461
60	.32159	.31175	.30231	.29325	.28457	.27623	.26823	.26055	.25317	.24608
61	.33429	.32437	.31485	.30571	.29692	.28848	.28037	.27257	.26507	.25786
62	.34728	.33730	.32770	.31847	.30960	.30106	.29285	.28495	.27734	.27001
63	.36057	.35053	.34087	.33157	.32262	.31400	.30569	.29769	.28998	.28255
64	.37412	.36404	.35433	.34498	.33596	.32726	.31887	.31078	.30298	.29545
65	.38794	.37783	.36809	.35868	.34961	.34085	.33239	.32422	.31633	.30871
66	.40205	.39193	.38216	.37272	.36361	.35479	.34628	.33804	.33008	.32238
67	.41650	.40639	.39661	.38715	.37800	.36915	.36059	.35230	.34428	.33651
68	.43126	.42117	.41139	.40193	.39277	.38390	.37530	.36697	.35890	.35108
69	.44628	.43622	.42648	.41703	.40787	.39898	.39037	.38201	.37391	.36604
70	.46150	.45149	.44178	.43236	.42321	.41433	.40571	.39735	.38922	.38132
71	.47683	.46689	.45723	.44785	.43873	.42987	.42126	.41290	.40476	.39685
72	.49225	.48238	.47279	.46346	.45439	.44556	.43697	.42862	.42048	.41257
73	.50770	.49793	.48841	.47915	.47013	.46135	.45280	.44447	.43635	.42844
74	.52324	.51358	.50416	.49498	.48603	.47731	.46880	.46051	.45242	.44454
75	.53894	.52939	.52008	.51100	.50214	.49349	.48505	.47681	.46877	.46092
76	.55483	.54543	.53624	.52728	.51852	.50996	.50160	.49344	.48546	.47766
77	.57091	.56167	.55263	.54380	.53516	.52671	.51845	.51038	.50247	.49475
78	.58716	.57809	.56922	.56053	.55203	.54372	.53557	.52760	.51980	.51216
79	.60346	.59459	.58590	.57738	.56904	.56086	.55286	.54501	.53732	.52978
80	.61969	.61102	.60252	.59419	.58601	.57800	.57014	.56243	.55487	.54745
81	.63571	.62726	.61897	.61082	.60283	.59499	.58729	.57974	.57232	.56503
82	.65146	.64324	.63515	.62722	.61942	.61176	.60423	.59683	.58957	.58242
83	.66693	.65893	.65108	.64335	.63575	.62828	.62093	.61371	.60660	.59962
84	.68222	.67447	.66684	.65934	.65195	.64468	.63753	.63049	.62356	.61674
85	.69742	.68993	.68255	.67528	.66812	.66106	.65411	.64727	.64053	.63389
86	.71241	.70517	.69805	.69102	.68410	.67727	.67054	.66390	.65736	.65091
87	.72696	.72000	.71313	.70635	.69967	.69307	.68656	.68014	.67381	.66756
88	.74108	.73438	.72777	.72125	.71480	.70845	.70217	.69597	.68985	.68380
89	.75475	.74832	.74198	.73571	.72951	.72339	.71734	.71137	.70547	.69963
90	.76796	.76180	.75572	.74971	.74376	.73788	.73207	.72633	.72065	.71503
91	.78049	.77460	.76878	.76302	.75732	.75168	.74610	.74058	.73512	.72972
92	.79211	.78647	.78089	.77537	.76990	.76449	.75913	.75383	.74858	.74338
93	.80283	.79743	.79208	.78679	.78154	.77634	.77119	.76610	.76105	.75604
94	.81283	.80765	.80253	.79744	.79240	.78741	.78247	.77756	.77270	.76789

TABLE U(1)
BASED ON LIFE TABLE 90CM
UNITRUST SINGLE LIFE REMAINDER FACTORS
APPLICABLE FOR TRANSFERS AFTER APRIL 30, 1999
ADJUSTED PAYOUT RATE

AGE	6.2%	6.4%	6.6%	6.8%	7.0%	7.2%	7.4%	7.6%	7.8%	8.0%
95	.82233	.81737	.81245	.80757	.80274	.79795	.79320	.78849	.78382	.77918
96	.83126	.82651	.82180	.81712	.81248	.80788	.80332	.79880	.79431	.78985
97	.83953	.83498	.83046	.82597	.82152	.81710	.81271	.80836	.80404	.79976
98	.84731	.84294	.83860	.83429	.83002	.82577	.82155	.81737	.81321	.80908
99	.85490	.85071	.84656	.84243	.83832	.83425	.83020	.82618	.82219	.81822
100	.86229	.85828	.85431	.85035	.84642	.84252	.83864	.83478	.83095	.82714
101	.86958	.86575	.86195	.85818	.85442	.85069	.84698	.84329	.83962	.83597
102	.87674	.87310	.86947	.86587	.86229	.85873	.85518	.85166	.84815	.84466
103	.88384	.88038	.87694	.87351	.87010	.86671	.86334	.85998	.85663	.85331
104	.89143	.88817	.88492	.88169	.87847	.87526	.87207	.86889	.86573	.86258
105	.89885	.89578	.89272	.88967	.88664	.88361	.88060	.87760	.87461	.87163
106	.90840	.90559	.90278	.89999	.89720	.89442	.89165	.88888	.88613	.88338
107	.91999	.91750	.91501	.91253	.91005	.90758	.90511	.90265	.90019	.89774
108	.93805	.93609	.93412	.93216	.93020	.92824	.92629	.92434	.92239	.92044
109	.96900	.96800	.96700	.96600	.96500	.96400	.96300	.96200	.96100	.96000

TABLE U(1)
BASED ON LIFE TABLE 90CM
UNITRUST SINGLE LIFE REMAINDER FACTORS
APPLICABLE FOR TRANSFERS AFTER APRIL 30, 1999
ADJUSTED PAYOUT RATE

AGE	8.2%	8.4%	8.6%	8.8%	9.0%	9.2%	9.4%	9.6%	9.8%	10.0%
0	.01709	.01658	.01612	.01570	.01532	.01497	.01466	.01437	.01410	.01386
1	.00892	.00839	.00791	.00747	.00708	.00672	.00639	.00609	.00582	.00557
2	.00896	.00840	.00790	.00744	.00702	.00664	.00629	.00598	.00569	.00542
3	.00926	.00867	.00814	.00765	.00721	.00681	.00644	.00611	.00580	.00552
4	.00970	.00908	.00851	.00800	.00753	.00711	.00672	.00636	.00604	.00574
5	.01026	.00960	.00900	.00846	.00796	.00751	.00710	.00672	.00637	.00606
6	.01089	.01019	.00956	.00899	.00846	.00799	.00755	.00715	.00678	.00644
7	.01161	.01088	.01021	.00960	.00905	.00854	.00808	.00765	.00726	.00690
8	.01241	.01163	.01093	.01029	.00970	.00917	.00867	.00822	.00781	.00743
9	.01331	.01249	.01175	.01107	.01045	.00988	.00936	.00889	.00845	.00804
10	.01432	.01346	.01268	.01196	.01131	.01071	.01016	.00965	.00918	.00875
11	.01543	.01453	.01370	.01295	.01226	.01162	.01104	.01051	.01001	.00956
12	.01664	.01569	.01482	.01403	.01330	.01263	.01202	.01145	.01093	.01045
13	.01791	.01691	.01600	.01516	.01440	.01369	.01304	.01245	.01190	.01139
14	.01918	.01813	.01717	.01629	.01548	.01474	.01406	.01343	.01285	.01231
15	.02041	.01931	.01831	.01738	.01653	.01576	.01504	.01437	.01376	.01320
16	.02160	.02044	.01938	.01841	.01752	.01670	.01595	.01525	.01460	.01401
17	.02274	.02152	.02041	.01940	.01846	.01760	.01680	.01607	.01539	.01476
18	.02386	.02258	.02142	.02035	.01936	.01846	.01762	.01685	.01613	.01547
19	.02500	.02367	.02245	.02132	.02029	.01933	.01845	.01764	.01689	.01619
20	.02621	.02481	.02353	.02235	.02126	.02025	.01933	.01847	.01768	.01694
21	.02749	.02603	.02468	.02344	.02229	.02124	.02026	.01936	.01852	.01774
22	.02884	.02730	.02589	.02458	.02338	.02227	.02124	.02029	.01940	.01859
23	.03028	.02867	.02718	.02581	.02454	.02337	.02229	.02128	.02035	.01949
24	.03183	.03013	.02857	.02713	.02580	.02456	.02342	.02236	.02138	.02047
25	.03350	.03172	.03008	.02857	.02717	.02587	.02467	.02355	.02251	.02155
26	.03530	.03344	.03172	.03013	.02865	.02729	.02602	.02484	.02375	.02273
27	.03727	.03532	.03351	.03183	.03028	.02885	.02751	.02627	.02511	.02404
28	.03937	.03732	.03543	.03367	.03204	.03052	.02911	.02780	.02658	.02545
29	.04162	.03947	.03748	.03564	.03392	.03233	.03084	.02946	.02818	.02698
30	.04401	.04176	.03967	.03773	.03593	.03425	.03269	.03124	.02988	.02861
31	.04654	.04419	.04200	.03996	.03807	.03630	.03466	.03312	.03169	.03035
32	.04923	.04676	.04447	.04233	.04034	.03849	.03676	.03514	.03363	.03221
33	.05210	.04952	.04711	.04487	.04278	.04083	.03901	.03731	.03571	.03422
34	.05515	.05245	.04993	.04758	.04538	.04333	.04142	.03962	.03794	.03637
35	.05841	.05558	.05295	.05048	.04818	.04603	.04401	.04212	.04035	.03869
36	.06187	.05892	.05616	.05358	.05116	.04890	.04678	.04480	.04293	.04118
37	.06555	.06247	.05958	.05688	.05435	.05198	.04975	.04766	.04570	.04385
38	.06949	.06627	.06325	.06043	.05777	.05528	.05295	.05075	.04868	.04674
39	.07368	.07032	.06717	.06421	.06143	.05882	.05637	.05406	.05189	.04984
40	.07816	.07465	.07137	.06827	.06537	.06263	.06006	.05764	.05535	.05320
41	.08295	.07930	.07587	.07264	.06960	.06674	.06405	.06150	.05910	.05683
42	.08807	.08427	.08069	.07733	.07415	.07116	.06833	.06567	.06315	.06077
43	.09352	.08957	.08585	.08233	.07902	.07589	.07294	.07014	.06750	.06500
44	.09932	.09521	.09134	.08768	.08423	.08096	.07787	.07495	.07218	.06956
45	.10543	.10117	.09715	.09334	.08974	.08634	.08311	.08005	.07716	.07441
46	.11189	.10747	.10329	.09933	.09559	.09204	.08867	.08548	.08245	.07958

TABLE U(1)
BASED ON LIFE TABLE 90CM
UNITRUST SINGLE LIFE REMAINDER FACTORS
APPLICABLE FOR TRANSFERS AFTER APRIL 30, 1999
ADJUSTED PAYOUT RATE

AGE	8.2%	8.4%	8.6%	8.8%	9.0%	9.2%	9.4%	9.6%	9.8%	10.0%
47	.11866	.11408	.10974	.10564	.10174	.09805	.09454	.09121	.08805	.08504
48	.12577	.12103	.11654	.11228	.10823	.10439	.10074	.09727	.09397	.09083
49	.13323	.12833	.12368	.11926	.11506	.11107	.10728	.10366	.10022	.09695
50	.14107	.13601	.13120	.12663	.12228	.11813	.11419	.11043	.10685	.10344
51	.14928	.14407	.13910	.13437	.12987	.12558	.12149	.11758	.11386	.11031
52	.15785	.15248	.14735	.14247	.13781	.13337	.12913	.12508	.12122	.11752
53	.16678	.16124	.15597	.15093	.14612	.14153	.13714	.13294	.12893	.12509
54	.17606	.17037	.16493	.15974	.15478	.15004	.14550	.14116	.13700	.13302
55	.18570	.17986	.17428	.16893	.16382	.15893	.15424	.14976	.14546	.14134
56	.19573	.18974	.18400	.17851	.17325	.16821	.16338	.15875	.15430	.15004
57	.20613	.20000	.19412	.18848	.18307	.17789	.17291	.16814	.16355	.15914
58	.21688	.21060	.20458	.19880	.19325	.18792	.18280	.17788	.17316	.16861
59	.22793	.22151	.21535	.20943	.20374	.19827	.19301	.18795	.18309	.17840
60	.23927	.23272	.22642	.22036	.21454	.20893	.20354	.19834	.19334	.18851
61	.25092	.24425	.23782	.23163	.22567	.21993	.21440	.20907	.20393	.19898
62	.26295	.25616	.24961	.24329	.23721	.23134	.22568	.22021	.21494	.20985
63	.27538	.26847	.26180	.25537	.24916	.24316	.23738	.23179	.22639	.22117
64	.28817	.28116	.27438	.26783	.26150	.25539	.24949	.24377	.23825	.23291
65	.30134	.29423	.28735	.28069	.27426	.26803	.26201	.25618	.25054	.24508
66	.31493	.30772	.30075	.29399	.28746	.28113	.27500	.26906	.26331	.25774
67	.32899	.32170	.31464	.30780	.30118	.29475	.28852	.28248	.27663	.27095
68	.34349	.33614	.32901	.32209	.31538	.30887	.30256	.29643	.29047	.28469
69	.35841	.35100	.34381	.33683	.33005	.32346	.31707	.31085	.30481	.29894
70	.37366	.36620	.35896	.35193	.34509	.33844	.33197	.32568	.31957	.31362
71	.38916	.38167	.37440	.36732	.36043	.35372	.34720	.34084	.33466	.32864
72	.40486	.39736	.39006	.38295	.37602	.36927	.36270	.35629	.35005	.34396
73	.42074	.41323	.40591	.39878	.39182	.38504	.37843	.37198	.36568	.35955
74	.43685	.42934	.42202	.41488	.40791	.40110	.39446	.38798	.38165	.37547
75	.45326	.44577	.43846	.43132	.42435	.41754	.41088	.40438	.39802	.39181
76	.47004	.46259	.45530	.44818	.44122	.43442	.42776	.42125	.41488	.40865
77	.48718	.47979	.47255	.46547	.45853	.45175	.44511	.43861	.43225	.42601
78	.50467	.49735	.49017	.48314	.47626	.46951	.46290	.45643	.45008	.44386
79	.52239	.51515	.50806	.50110	.49427	.48758	.48102	.47459	.46828	.46209
80	.54018	.53304	.52603	.51916	.51242	.50580	.49930	.49292	.48666	.48052
81	.55788	.55085	.54396	.53718	.53053	.52399	.51757	.51126	.50507	.49898
82	.57540	.56851	.56173	.55506	.54851	.54207	.53574	.52951	.52339	.51737
83	.59274	.58598	.57933	.57279	.56635	.56001	.55378	.54765	.54161	.53567
84	.61002	.60341	.59690	.59049	.58418	.57796	.57184	.56582	.55988	.55403
85	.62734	.62090	.61454	.60828	.60211	.59603	.59004	.58414	.57832	.57258
86	.64455	.63828	.63210	.62600	.61999	.61406	.60821	.60244	.59675	.59113
87	.66139	.65531	.64930	.64337	.63752	.63175	.62605	.62043	.61488	.60939
88	.67783	.67194	.66612	.66037	.65469	.64908	.64354	.63807	.63267	.62733
89	.69387	.68817	.68254	.67698	.67148	.66605	.66068	.65537	.65012	.64493
90	.70947	.70398	.69855	.69318	.68786	.68261	.67742	.67228	.66719	.66217
91	.72437	.71908	.71385	.70867	.70354	.69847	.69345	.68848	.68357	.67870
92	.73823	.73314	.72810	.72310	.71816	.71326	.70841	.70361	.69886	.69415
93	.75109	.74618	.74132	.73650	.73173	.72700	.72232	.71768	.71308	.70852
94	.76312	.75839	.75370	.74905	.74445	.73988	.73536	.73087	.72643	.72202

TABLE U(1)
BASED ON LIFE TABLE 90CM
UNITRUST SINGLE LIFE REMAINDER FACTORS
APPLICABLE FOR TRANSFERS AFTER APRIL 30, 1999
ADJUSTED PAYOUT RATE

AGE	*8.2%*	*8.4%*	*8.6%*	*8.8%*	*9.0%*	*9.2%*	*9.4%*	*9.6%*	*9.8%*	*10.0%*
95	.77459	.77004	.76552	.76104	.75660	.75220	.74783	.74350	.73920	.73494
96	.78543	.78105	.77670	.77238	.76810	.76386	.75964	.75546	.75131	.74720
97	.79550	.79128	.78709	.78293	.77880	.77470	.77063	.76659	.76258	.75860
98	.80498	.80091	.79687	.79286	.78888	.78492	.78099	.77709	.77322	.76937
99	.81428	.81036	.80647	.80261	.79877	.79496	.79117	.78741	.78367	.77995
100	.82336	.81959	.81586	.81214	.80845	.80478	.80113	.79751	.79390	.79032
101	.83234	.82873	.82515	.82158	.81804	.81451	.81101	.80753	.80406	.80062
102	.84119	.83774	.83431	.83089	.82750	.82412	.82076	.81742	.81409	.81078
103	.84999	.84670	.84342	.84016	.83691	.83368	.83046	.82726	.82408	.82091
104	.85944	.85632	.85321	.85011	.84703	.84396	.84090	.83786	.83483	.83182
105	.86866	.86570	.86276	.85982	.85690	.85399	.85109	.84820	.84532	.84245
106	.88065	.87792	.87520	.87248	.86978	.86708	.86440	.86172	.85905	.85638
107	.89530	.89286	.89042	.88799	.88557	.88315	.88073	.87833	.87592	.87352
108	.91849	.91654	.91460	.91266	.91072	.90879	.90685	.90492	.90299	.90106
109	.95900	.95800	.95700	.95600	.95500	.95400	.95300	.95200	.95100	.95000

TABLE U(1)
BASED ON LIFE TABLE 90CM
UNITRUST SINGLE LIFE REMAINDER FACTORS
APPLICABLE FOR TRANSFERS AFTER APRIL 30, 1999
ADJUSTED PAYOUT RATE

AGE	10.2%	10.4%	10.6%	10.8%	11.0%	11.2%	11.4%	11.6%	11.8%	12.0%
0	.01363	.01342	.01323	.01305	.01288	.01272	.01258	.01244	.01231	.01219
1	.00534	.00512	.00493	.00474	.00458	.00442	.00427	.00414	.00401	.00389
2	.00518	.00495	.00474	.00455	.00437	.00421	.00405	.00391	.00377	.00365
3	.00526	.00502	.00480	.00459	.00440	.00422	.00406	.00391	.00376	.00363
4	.00546	.00521	.00497	.00475	.00455	.00436	.00419	.00402	.00387	.00373
5	.00576	.00549	.00524	.00501	.00479	.00459	.00440	.00423	.00406	.00391
6	.00613	.00584	.00557	.00532	.00509	.00488	.00468	.00449	.00432	.00415
7	.00657	.00626	.00598	.00571	.00547	.00524	.00502	.00482	.00464	.00446
8	.00707	.00675	.00644	.00616	.00590	.00565	.00542	.00521	.00501	.00482
9	.00766	.00732	.00699	.00669	.00641	.00615	.00591	.00568	.00547	.00527
10	.00835	.00798	.00764	.00732	.00702	.00675	.00649	.00624	.00602	.00580
11	.00913	.00874	.00838	.00804	.00772	.00743	.00715	.00689	.00665	.00642
12	.01000	.00959	.00920	.00884	.00851	.00819	.00790	.00762	.00737	.00712
13	.01091	.01048	.01007	.00969	.00933	.00900	.00869	.00840	.00813	.00787
14	.01181	.01135	.01092	.01052	.01014	.00979	.00947	.00916	.00887	.00860
15	.01267	.01218	.01173	.01130	.01091	.01054	.01019	.00987	.00956	.00928
16	.01345	.01294	.01246	.01201	.01160	.01121	.01084	.01050	.01018	.00988
17	.01418	.01364	.01313	.01266	.01222	.01181	.01143	.01107	.01073	.01041
18	.01486	.01429	.01375	.01326	.01279	.01236	.01196	.01158	.01122	.01088
19	.01554	.01494	.01438	.01385	.01336	.01291	.01248	.01208	.01170	.01135
20	.01626	.01562	.01503	.01448	.01396	.01348	.01303	.01260	.01220	.01183
21	.01702	.01635	.01573	.01514	.01460	.01409	.01361	.01316	.01274	.01235
22	.01782	.01711	.01645	.01584	.01526	.01472	.01422	.01374	.01330	.01288
23	.01868	.01793	.01724	.01658	.01597	.01540	.01487	.01437	.01390	.01345
24	.01962	.01883	.01809	.01740	.01675	.01615	.01558	.01505	.01455	.01408
25	.02065	.01981	.01903	.01830	.01762	.01698	.01638	.01581	.01528	.01478
26	.02178	.02089	.02006	.01929	.01856	.01789	.01725	.01665	.01609	.01556
27	.02303	.02209	.02122	.02040	.01963	.01891	.01824	.01760	.01700	.01644
28	.02439	.02339	.02247	.02160	.02079	.02002	.01931	.01863	.01800	.01740
29	.02585	.02480	.02382	.02290	.02204	.02123	.02047	.01976	.01908	.01845
30	.02742	.02631	.02527	.02430	.02339	.02253	.02172	.02096	.02025	.01957
31	.02910	.02793	.02683	.02579	.02482	.02391	.02306	.02225	.02149	.02077
32	.03089	.02965	.02849	.02739	.02636	.02540	.02449	.02363	.02282	.02206
33	.03282	.03151	.03028	.02912	.02803	.02701	.02604	.02513	.02427	.02346
34	.03489	.03350	.03220	.03097	.02982	.02873	.02771	.02674	.02583	.02497
35	.03713	.03567	.03429	.03299	.03177	.03061	.02953	.02850	.02753	.02661
36	.03953	.03798	.03653	.03515	.03386	.03263	.03148	.03039	.02936	.02838
37	.04211	.04048	.03894	.03748	.03611	.03481	.03359	.03243	.03134	.03030
38	.04490	.04318	.04155	.04001	.03856	.03719	.03589	.03466	.03350	.03239
39	.04791	.04609	.04437	.04274	.04120	.03975	.03837	.03707	.03583	.03466
40	.05116	.04924	.04742	.04571	.04408	.04254	.04108	.03970	.03839	.03714
41	.05469	.05267	.05075	.04894	.04722	.04559	.04405	.04258	.04119	.03987
42	.05851	.05638	.05436	.05245	.05063	.04891	.04728	.04573	.04425	.04285
43	.06263	.06039	.05827	.05625	.05433	.05252	.05079	.04915	.04759	.04610
44	.06707	.06472	.06248	.06035	.05834	.05642	.05459	.05286	.05121	.04963
45	.07180	.06933	.06698	.06474	.06262	.06059	.05867	.05684	.05509	.05342
46	.07685	.07425	.07178	.06943	.06720	.06507	.06304	.06110	.05926	.05750

TABLE U(1)
BASED ON LIFE TABLE 90CM
UNITRUST SINGLE LIFE REMAINDER FACTORS
APPLICABLE FOR TRANSFERS AFTER APRIL 30, 1999
ADJUSTED PAYOUT RATE

AGE	10.2%	10.4%	10.6%	10.8%	11.0%	11.2%	11.4%	11.6%	11.8%	12.0%
47	.08218	.07946	.07687	.07440	.07205	.06981	.06768	.06564	.06369	.06183
48	.08784	.08499	.08228	.07969	.07722	.07487	.07262	.07047	.06842	.06646
49	.09382	.09085	.08801	.08530	.08271	.08024	.07788	.07562	.07346	.07140
50	.10018	.09707	.09410	.09127	.08856	.08597	.08349	.08112	.07885	.07667
51	.10691	.10367	.10057	.09761	.09477	.09206	.08946	.08697	.08459	.08231
52	.11399	.11061	.10738	.10429	.10132	.09849	.09577	.09316	.09066	.08826
53	.12142	.11791	.11454	.11132	.10823	.10526	.10242	.09969	.09707	.09456
54	.12921	.12556	.12206	.11870	.11548	.11239	.10942	.10657	.10383	.10120
55	.13738	.13359	.12995	.12646	.12311	.11989	.11679	.11382	.11096	.10820
56	.14595	.14202	.13824	.13462	.13113	.12778	.12456	.12146	.11847	.11560
57	.15491	.15084	.14693	.14317	.13955	.13607	.13272	.12949	.12638	.12338
58	.16424	.16004	.15599	.15209	.14834	.14473	.14125	.13789	.13465	.13153
59	.17390	.16955	.16537	.16134	.15746	.15371	.15010	.14662	.14325	.14001
60	.18387	.17939	.17507	.17091	.16689	.16302	.15927	.15566	.15217	.14880
61	.19420	.18958	.18513	.18084	.17669	.17268	.16881	.16506	.16145	.15795
62	.20494	.20020	.19561	.19119	.18691	.18277	.17877	.17490	.17115	.16753
63	.21613	.21126	.20654	.20199	.19758	.19331	.18918	.18518	.18131	.17757
64	.22774	.22274	.21791	.21322	.20869	.20429	.20004	.19592	.19192	.18805
65	.23979	.23467	.22971	.22490	.22025	.21573	.21135	.20710	.20299	.19899
66	.25233	.24709	.24202	.23709	.23231	.22767	.22318	.21881	.21457	.21045
67	.26543	.26009	.25489	.24985	.24496	.24021	.23560	.23111	.22676	.22252
68	.27908	.27363	.26833	.26319	.25819	.25332	.24860	.24400	.23954	.23519
69	.29324	.28769	.28230	.27705	.27195	.26699	.26216	.25746	.25288	.24843
70	.30783	.30219	.29671	.29137	.28618	.28112	.27619	.27139	.26672	.26216
71	.32277	.31706	.31150	.30608	.30079	.29564	.29063	.28573	.28096	.27631
72	.33803	.33225	.32661	.32112	.31575	.31052	.30542	.30044	.29559	.29084
73	.35356	.34772	.34201	.33645	.33101	.32571	.32053	.31547	.31053	.30571
74	.36943	.36354	.35778	.35215	.34666	.34129	.33604	.33091	.32590	.32100
75	.38574	.37980	.37400	.36833	.36278	.35735	.35205	.34686	.34178	.33681
76	.40256	.39660	.39076	.38505	.37947	.37400	.36864	.36340	.35827	.35324
77	.41991	.41394	.40808	.40235	.39674	.39124	.38585	.38056	.37539	.37032
78	.43777	.43180	.42594	.42020	.41457	.40906	.40365	.39834	.39314	.38803
79	.45602	.45007	.44422	.43849	.43287	.42735	.42193	.41661	.41139	.40627
80	.47449	.46856	.46275	.45704	.45143	.44592	.44051	.43519	.42997	.42484
81	.49300	.48712	.48134	.47566	.47008	.46460	.45921	.45391	.44870	.44357
82	.51145	.50563	.49990	.49427	.48873	.48328	.47792	.47265	.46746	.46235
83	.52983	.52407	.51841	.51284	.50735	.50195	.49663	.49139	.48624	.48116
84	.54828	.54261	.53702	.53151	.52609	.52075	.51549	.51030	.50519	.50015
85	.56693	.56135	.55586	.55044	.54510	.53983	.53464	.52952	.52447	.51949
86	.58560	.58013	.57474	.56943	.56418	.55901	.55390	.54886	.54389	.53898
87	.60398	.59864	.59337	.58817	.58303	.57795	.57294	.56799	.56310	.55828
88	.62206	.61685	.61170	.60662	.60159	.59663	.59173	.58688	.58209	.57736
89	.63980	.63474	.62972	.62477	.61987	.61503	.61024	.60551	.60083	.59620
90	.65719	.65227	.64741	.64259	.63783	.63312	.62846	.62385	.61928	.61477
91	.67388	.66912	.66440	.65973	.65511	.65053	.64600	.64152	.63708	.63269
92	.68949	.68487	.68030	.67577	.67129	.66685	.66245	.65809	.65378	.64950
93	.70401	.69954	.69511	.69072	.68637	.68205	.67778	.67355	.66935	.66519
94	.71765	.71332	.70902	.70477	.70055	.69636	.69222	.68810	.68403	.67998

TABLE U(1)
BASED ON LIFE TABLE 90CM
UNITRUST SINGLE LIFE REMAINDER FACTORS
APPLICABLE FOR TRANSFERS AFTER APRIL 30, 1999
ADJUSTED PAYOUT RATE

AGE	10.2%	10.4%	10.6%	10.8%	11.0%	11.2%	11.4%	11.6%	11.8%	12.0%
95	.73072	.72653	.72237	.71825	.71416	.71010	.70608	.70209	.69813	.69421
96	.74311	.73906	.73504	.73105	.72709	.72316	.71926	.71539	.71155	.70774
97	.75465	.75073	.74684	.74297	.73914	.73533	.73155	.72780	.72407	.72037
98	.76555	.76175	.75798	.75424	.75052	.74683	.74317	.73953	.73591	.73232
99	.77626	.77260	.76895	.76534	.76174	.75817	.75462	.75109	.74759	.74411
100	.78676	.78323	.77971	.77622	.77274	.76929	.76586	.76245	.75906	.75569
101	.79719	.79379	.79040	.78703	.78368	.78035	.77704	.77375	.77048	.76722
102	.80749	.80422	.80096	.79772	.79450	.79130	.78811	.78494	.78178	.77864
103	.81775	.81461	.81149	.80838	.80529	.80221	.79914	.79609	.79306	.79003
104	.82881	.82582	.82284	.81988	.81693	.81399	.81106	.80815	.80525	.80236
105	.83959	.83674	.83391	.83108	.82826	.82546	.82267	.81988	.81711	.81435
106	.85373	.85108	.84844	.84581	.84319	.84058	.83797	.83537	.83278	.83020
107	.87113	.86875	.86636	.86399	.86161	.85925	.85689	.85453	.85218	.84984
108	.89913	.89721	.89529	.89337	.89145	.88953	.88762	.88571	.88380	.88189
109	.94900	.94800	.94700	.94600	.94500	.94400	.94300	.94200	.94100	.94000

TABLE U(1)
BASED ON LIFE TABLE 90CM
UNITRUST SINGLE LIFE REMAINDER FACTORS
APPLICABLE FOR TRANSFERS AFTER APRIL 30, 1999
ADJUSTED PAYOUT RATE

AGE	12.2%	12.4%	12.6%	12.8%	13.0%	13.2%	13.4%	13.6%	13.8%	14.0%
0	.01208	.01197	.01187	.01177	.01168	.01159	.01151	.01143	.01135	.01128
1	.00378	.00367	.00358	.00348	.00340	.00331	.00323	.00316	.00309	.00302
2	.00353	.00342	.00331	.00322	.00312	.00304	.00295	.00288	.00280	.00273
3	.00350	.00339	.00327	.00317	.00307	.00298	.00289	.00281	.00273	.00265
4	.00359	.00347	.00335	.00324	.00313	.00303	.00294	.00285	.00276	.00268
5	.00377	.00363	.00351	.00339	.00327	.00317	.00306	.00297	.00288	.00279
6	.00400	.00386	.00372	.00359	.00347	.00335	.00325	.00314	.00305	.00295
7	.00430	.00414	.00400	.00386	.00373	.00360	.00349	.00338	.00327	.00317
8	.00465	.00448	.00432	.00417	.00403	.00390	.00378	.00366	.00354	.00344
9	.00508	.00490	.00473	.00457	.00442	.00428	.00414	.00402	.00389	.00378
10	.00560	.00541	.00523	.00506	.00490	.00475	.00460	.00446	.00433	.00421
11	.00620	.00600	.00581	.00563	.00546	.00529	.00514	.00499	.00485	.00472
12	.00689	.00668	.00647	.00628	.00610	.00593	.00576	.00560	.00545	.00531
13	.00763	.00740	.00718	.00698	.00678	.00660	.00642	.00626	.00610	.00595
14	.00834	.00810	.00787	.00766	.00745	.00726	.00707	.00689	.00673	.00657
15	.00901	.00875	.00851	.00828	.00807	.00786	.00767	.00748	.00730	.00714
16	.00959	.00932	.00907	.00883	.00860	.00839	.00818	.00799	.00780	.00762
17	.01011	.00983	.00956	.00930	.00907	.00884	.00862	.00842	.00822	.00804
18	.01057	.01027	.00999	.00972	.00947	.00923	.00900	.00879	.00858	.00839
19	.01101	.01070	.01040	.01012	.00985	.00960	.00936	.00914	.00892	.00871
20	.01148	.01115	.01083	.01054	.01026	.00999	.00974	.00950	.00927	.00905
21	.01197	.01162	.01129	.01098	.01068	.01040	.01014	.00988	.00964	.00941
22	.01249	.01211	.01176	.01143	.01112	.01082	.01054	.01027	.01002	.00978
23	.01304	.01264	.01227	.01192	.01159	.01127	.01098	.01069	.01042	.01017
24	.01364	.01322	.01283	.01246	.01210	.01177	.01145	.01115	.01087	.01060
25	.01431	.01387	.01345	.01306	.01268	.01233	.01199	.01168	.01137	.01109
26	.01506	.01459	.01415	.01373	.01333	.01295	.01260	.01226	.01194	.01163
27	.01591	.01541	.01494	.01449	.01407	.01367	.01329	.01293	.01259	.01226
28	.01684	.01631	.01580	.01533	.01488	.01445	.01405	.01367	.01330	.01296
29	.01785	.01728	.01675	.01624	.01577	.01531	.01488	.01447	.01408	.01372
30	.01893	.01833	.01776	.01723	.01672	.01623	.01578	.01534	.01493	.01453
31	.02010	.01946	.01885	.01828	.01773	.01722	.01673	.01627	.01582	.01540
32	.02134	.02066	.02002	.01940	.01883	.01828	.01776	.01726	.01679	.01634
33	.02270	.02197	.02128	.02063	.02002	.01943	.01887	.01835	.01784	.01736
34	.02415	.02338	.02265	.02195	.02130	.02067	.02008	.01951	.01897	.01846
35	.02574	.02492	.02414	.02340	.02270	.02203	.02140	.02080	.02022	.01967
36	.02746	.02658	.02575	.02496	.02422	.02350	.02283	.02218	.02157	.02098
37	.02932	.02838	.02750	.02666	.02586	.02510	.02438	.02369	.02303	.02241
38	.03135	.03035	.02941	.02851	.02766	.02685	.02608	.02534	.02464	.02397
39	.03355	.03249	.03149	.03053	.02962	.02876	.02793	.02715	.02640	.02568
40	.03596	.03484	.03377	.03275	.03178	.03086	.02998	.02914	.02833	.02757
41	.03861	.03742	.03628	.03520	.03416	.03318	.03224	.03134	.03048	.02966
42	.04152	.04025	.03903	.03788	.03678	.03573	.03473	.03377	.03285	.03198
43	.04468	.04333	.04205	.04082	.03965	.03853	.03746	.03644	.03546	.03453
44	.04813	.04670	.04533	.04403	.04278	.04159	.04045	.03936	.03832	.03732
45	.05183	.05032	.04887	.04748	.04616	.04489	.04368	.04252	.04141	.04034
46	.05582	.05421	.05267	.05121	.04980	.04846	.04717	.04593	.04475	.04362

TABLE U(1)
BASED ON LIFE TABLE 90CM
UNITRUST SINGLE LIFE REMAINDER FACTORS
APPLICABLE FOR TRANSFERS AFTER APRIL 30, 1999
ADJUSTED PAYOUT RATE

AGE	12.2%	12.4%	12.6%	12.8%	13.0%	13.2%	13.4%	13.6%	13.8%	14.0%
47	.06006	.05836	.05673	.05518	.05369	.05226	.05089	.04958	.04832	.04711
48	.06459	.06279	.06107	.05943	.05785	.05634	.05488	.05349	.05216	.05087
49	.06942	.06752	.06571	.06397	.06230	.06070	.05916	.05768	.05626	.05490
50	.07459	.07259	.07068	.06884	.06708	.06538	.06376	.06219	.06069	.05924
51	.08012	.07801	.07599	.07406	.07220	.07041	.06869	.06703	.06544	.06391
52	.08596	.08375	.08163	.07959	.07763	.07574	.07392	.07218	.07049	.06887
53	.09214	.08982	.08759	.08544	.08338	.08139	.07948	.07763	.07586	.07415
54	.09867	.09623	.09389	.09164	.08946	.08737	.08536	.08342	.08154	.07974
55	.10556	.10301	.10055	.09819	.09591	.09371	.09159	.08955	.08757	.08567
56	.11283	.11016	.10759	.10511	.10272	.10042	.09819	.09605	.09397	.09197
57	.12050	.11771	.11502	.11243	.10993	.10751	.10518	.10293	.10075	.09864
58	.12852	.12562	.12281	.12011	.11749	.11496	.11252	.11016	.10787	.10567
59	.13687	.13385	.13092	.12810	.12537	.12273	.12017	.11770	.11531	.11299
60	.14554	.14240	.13935	.13641	.13356	.13080	.12813	.12555	.12305	.12063
61	.15457	.15130	.14813	.14507	.14210	.13923	.13644	.13375	.13113	.12860
62	.16402	.16063	.15734	.15415	.15107	.14808	.14518	.14237	.13964	.13699
63	.17393	.17042	.16700	.16370	.16049	.15738	.15437	.15144	.14860	.14584
64	.18429	.18065	.17712	.17369	.17036	.16714	.16400	.16096	.15800	.15513
65	.19511	.19135	.18769	.18415	.18070	.17735	.17410	.17094	.16787	.16488
66	.20645	.20257	.19880	.19513	.19157	.18810	.18473	.18146	.17827	.17517
67	.21841	.21441	.21052	.20673	.20305	.19947	.19599	.19259	.18929	.18608
68	.23096	.22685	.22284	.21895	.21515	.21146	.20786	.20436	.20094	.19762
69	.24409	.23987	.23575	.23175	.22784	.22404	.22033	.21672	.21320	.20976
70	.25772	.25339	.24918	.24507	.24106	.23715	.23333	.22961	.22598	.22244
71	.27178	.26735	.26304	.25882	.25471	.25070	.24679	.24296	.23923	.23559
72	.28622	.28170	.27729	.27298	.26877	.26467	.26065	.25673	.25290	.24915
73	.30100	.29639	.29189	.28749	.28320	.27899	.27489	.27087	.26694	.26310
74	.31621	.31152	.30694	.30246	.29807	.29378	.28959	.28548	.28146	.27753
75	.33195	.32719	.32253	.31797	.31351	.30914	.30486	.30067	.29657	.29255
76	.34832	.34350	.33877	.33415	.32961	.32517	.32082	.31656	.31238	.30828
77	.36535	.36047	.35570	.35101	.34642	.34192	.33750	.33317	.32892	.32475
78	.38302	.37811	.37329	.36856	.36392	.35937	.35490	.35051	.34621	.34198
79	.40124	.39630	.39145	.38669	.38201	.37742	.37291	.36848	.36413	.35985
80	.41980	.41485	.40998	.40520	.40050	.39588	.39134	.38688	.38249	.37818
81	.43854	.43358	.42871	.42392	.41921	.41457	.41001	.40553	.40112	.39678
82	.45733	.45238	.44752	.44273	.43802	.43338	.42881	.42431	.41989	.41553
83	.47616	.47123	.46638	.46161	.45690	.45227	.44770	.44320	.43877	.43441
84	.49519	.49030	.48548	.48073	.47604	.47143	.46688	.46239	.45797	.45361
85	.51458	.50974	.50496	.50025	.49560	.49102	.48650	.48204	.47763	.47329
86	.53413	.52935	.52463	.51998	.51538	.51084	.50636	.50194	.49758	.49327
87	.55351	.54881	.54416	.53957	.53503	.53055	.52613	.52176	.51744	.51317
88	.57268	.56806	.56349	.55898	.55451	.55010	.54574	.54144	.53718	.53296
89	.59162	.58710	.58262	.57819	.57382	.56949	.56520	.56097	.55678	.55263
90	.61030	.60588	.60151	.59718	.59290	.58866	.58447	.58032	.57621	.57214
91	.62834	.62403	.61977	.61554	.61136	.60722	.60312	.59907	.59505	.59107
92	.64527	.64107	.63692	.63280	.62872	.62468	.62068	.61672	.61279	.60890
93	.66107	.65699	.65294	.64893	.64495	.64101	.63711	.63323	.62940	.62559
94	.67597	.67200	.66806	.66415	.66027	.65643	.65262	.64884	.64509	.64138

TABLE U(1)
BASED ON LIFE TABLE 90CM
UNITRUST SINGLE LIFE REMAINDER FACTORS
APPLICABLE FOR TRANSFERS AFTER APRIL 30, 1999
ADJUSTED PAYOUT RATE

AGE	*12.2%*	*12.4%*	*12.6%*	*12.8%*	*13.0%*	*13.2%*	*13.4%*	*13.6%*	*13.8%*	*14.0%*
95	.69031	.68645	.68262	.67881	.67504	.67130	.66759	.66390	.66025	.65662
96	.70396	.70021	.69648	.69279	.68912	.68548	.68186	.67828	.67471	.67118
97	.71670	.71305	.70943	.70584	.70227	.69872	.69520	.69171	.68824	.68480
98	.72875	.72521	.72169	.71819	.71472	.71127	.70784	.70444	.70106	.69770
99	.74065	.73721	.73379	.73040	.72703	.72368	.72035	.71704	.71375	.71048
100	.75234	.74901	.74570	.74241	.73914	.73589	.73265	.72944	.72625	.72307
101	.76399	.76077	.75757	.75438	.75122	.74807	.74494	.74183	.73873	.73565
102	.77552	.77241	.76932	.76625	.76319	.76015	.75712	.75411	.75111	.74813
103	.78703	.78404	.78106	.77809	.77514	.77221	.76929	.76638	.76348	.76060
104	.79948	.79662	.79377	.79093	.78810	.78528	.78248	.77969	.77691	.77414
105	.81159	.80885	.80612	.80340	.80069	.79799	.79530	.79262	.78995	.78729
106	.82763	.82506	.82250	.81995	.81741	.81488	.81235	.80983	.80732	.80482
107	.84749	.84516	.84283	.84051	.83819	.83587	.83356	.83126	.82896	.82666
108	.87999	.87808	.87618	.87428	.87238	.87049	.86859	.86670	.86481	.86293
109	.93900	.93800	.93700	.93600	.93500	.93400	.93300	.93200	.93100	.93000

TABLE D
SHOWING THE PRESENT WORTH OF A REMAINDER INTEREST
POSTPONED FOR A TERM CERTAIN IN A
CHARITABLE REMAINDER UNITRUST
APPLICABLE AFTER APRIL 30, 1989
ADJUSTED PAYOUT RATE

YEARS	*4.2%*	*4.4%*	*4.6%*	*4.8%*	*5.0%*	*5.2%*	*5.4%*	*5.6%*	*5.8%*	*6.0%*
1	.958000	.956000	.954000	.952000	.950000	.948000	.946000	.944000	.942000	.940000
2	.917764	.913936	.910116	.906304	.902500	.898704	.894916	.891136	.887364	.883600
3	.879218	.873723	.868251	.862801	.857375	.851971	.846591	.841232	.835897	.830584
4	.842291	.835279	.828311	.821387	.814506	.807669	.800875	.794123	.787415	.780749
5	.806915	.798527	.790209	.781960	.773781	.765670	.757627	.749652	.741745	.733904
6	.773024	.763392	.753859	.744426	.735092	.725855	.716716	.707672	.698724	.689870
7	.740557	.729802	.719182	.708694	.698337	.688111	.678013	.668042	.658198	.648478
8	.709454	.697691	.686099	.674677	.663420	.652329	.641400	.630632	.620022	.609569
9	.679657	.666993	.654539	.642292	.630249	.618408	.606765	.595317	.584061	.572995
10	.651111	.637645	.624430	.611462	.598737	.586251	.573999	.561979	.550185	.538615
11	.623764	.609589	.595706	.582112	.568800	.555766	.543003	.530508	.518275	.506298
12	.597566	.582767	.568304	.554170	.540360	.526866	.513681	.500800	.488215	.475920
13	.572469	.557125	.542162	.527570	.513342	.499469	.485942	.472755	.459898	.447365
14	.548425	.532611	.517222	.502247	.487675	.473496	.459701	.446281	.433224	.420523
15	.525391	.509177	.493430	.478139	.463291	.448875	.434878	.421289	.408097	.395292
16	.503325	.486773	.470732	.455188	.440127	.425533	.411394	.397697	.384427	.371574
17	.482185	.465355	.449079	.433339	.418120	.403405	.389179	.375426	.362131	.349280
18	.461933	.444879	.428421	.412539	.397214	.382428	.368163	.354402	.341127	.328323
19	.442532	.425304	.408714	.392737	.377354	.362542	.348282	.334555	.321342	.308624
20	.423946	.406591	.389913	.373886	.358486	.343690	.329475	.315820	.302704	.290106

TABLE D
SHOWING THE PRESENT WORTH OF A REMAINDER INTEREST
POSTPONED FOR A TERM CERTAIN IN A
CHARITABLE REMAINDER UNITRUST
APPLICABLE AFTER APRIL 30, 1989
ADJUSTED PAYOUT RATE

YEARS	*6.2%*	*6.4%*	*6.6%*	*6.8%*	*7.0%*	*7.2%*	*7.4%*	*7.6%*	*7.8%*	*8.0%*
1	.938000	.936000	.934000	.932000	.930000	.928000	.926000	.924000	.922000	.920000
2	.879844	.876096	.872356	.868624	.864900	.861184	.857476	.853776	.850084	.846400
3	.825294	.820026	.814781	.809558	.804357	.799179	.794023	.788889	.783777	.778688
4	.774125	.767544	.761005	.754508	.748052	.741638	.735265	.728933	.722643	.716393
5	.726130	.718421	.710779	.703201	.695688	.688240	.680855	.673535	.666277	.659082
6	.681110	.672442	.663867	.655383	.646990	.638687	.630472	.622346	.614307	.606355
7	.638881	.629406	.620052	.610817	.601701	.592701	.583817	.575048	.566391	.557847
8	.599270	.589124	.579129	.569282	.559582	.550027	.540615	.531344	.522213	.513219
9	.562115	.551420	.540906	.530571	.520411	.510425	.500609	.490962	.481480	.472161
10	.527264	.516129	.505206	.494492	.483982	.473674	.463564	.453649	.443925	.434388
11	.494574	.483097	.471863	.460866	.450104	.439570	.429260	.419171	.409298	.399637
12	.463910	.452179	.440720	.429527	.418596	.407921	.397495	.387314	.377373	.367666
13	.435148	.423239	.411632	.400320	.389295	.378550	.368081	.357879	.347938	.338253
14	.408169	.396152	.384465	.373098	.362044	.351295	.340843	.330680	.320799	.311193
15	.382862	.370798	.359090	.347727	.336701	.326002	.315620	.305548	.295777	.286297
16	.359125	.347067	.335390	.324082	.313132	.302529	.292264	.282326	.272706	.263394
17	.336859	.324855	.313254	.302044	.291213	.280747	.270637	.260870	.251435	.242322
18	.315974	.304064	.292579	.281505	.270828	.260533	.250610	.241044	.231823	.222936
19	.296383	.284604	.273269	.262363	.251870	.241775	.232065	.222724	.213741	.205101
20	.278008	.266389	.255233	.244522	.234239	.224367	.214892	.205797	.197069	.188693

TABLE D
SHOWING THE PRESENT WORTH OF A REMAINDER INTEREST
POSTPONED FOR A TERM CERTAIN IN A
CHARITABLE REMAINDER UNITRUST
APPLICABLE AFTER APRIL 30, 1989
ADJUSTED PAYOUT RATE

YEARS	*8.2%*	*8.4%*	*8.6%*	*8.8%*	*9.0%*	*9.2%*	*9.4%*	*9.6%*	*9.8%*	*10.0%*
1	.918000	.916000	.914000	.912000	.910000	.908000	.906000	.904000	.902000	.900000
2	.842724	.839056	.835396	.831744	.828100	.824464	.820836	.817216	.813604	.810000
3	.773621	.768575	.763552	.758551	.753571	.748613	.743677	.738763	.733871	.729000
4	.710184	.704015	.697886	.691798	.685750	.679741	.673772	.667842	.661951	.656100
5	.651949	.644878	.637868	.630920	.624032	.617205	.610437	.603729	.597080	.590490
6	.598489	.590708	.583012	.575399	.567869	.560422	.553056	.545771	.538566	.531441
7	.549413	.541089	.532873	.524764	.516761	.508863	.501069	.493377	.485787	.478297
8	.504361	.495637	.487046	.478585	.470253	.462048	.453968	.446013	.438180	.430467
9	.463003	.454004	.445160	.436469	.427930	.419539	.411295	.403196	.395238	.387420
10	.425037	.415867	.406876	.398060	.389416	.380942	.372634	.364489	.356505	.348678
11	.390184	.380934	.371885	.363031	.354369	.345895	.337606	.329498	.321567	.313811
12	.358189	.348936	.339902	.331084	.322475	.314073	.305871	.297866	.290054	.282430
13	.328817	.319625	.310671	.301949	.293453	.285178	.277119	.269271	.261628	.254187
14	.301854	.292777	.283953	.275377	.267042	.258942	.251070	.243421	.235989	.228768
15	.277102	.268184	.259533	.251144	.243008	.235119	.227469	.220053	.212862	.205891
16	.254380	.245656	.237213	.229043	.221137	.213488	.206087	.198928	.192001	.185302
17	.233521	.225021	.216813	.208887	.201235	.193847	.186715	.179830	.173185	.166772
18	.214372	.206119	.198167	.190505	.183124	.176013	.169164	.162567	.156213	.150095
19	.196794	.188805	.181125	.173741	.166643	.159820	.153262	.146960	.140904	.135085
20	.180657	.172946	.165548	.158452	.151645	.145117	.138856	.132852	.127096	.121577

TABLE D
SHOWING THE PRESENT WORTH OF A REMAINDER INTEREST
POSTPONED FOR A TERM CERTAIN IN A
CHARITABLE REMAINDER UNITRUST
APPLICABLE AFTER APRIL 30, 1989
ADJUSTED PAYOUT RATE

YEARS	*10.2%*	*10.4%*	*10.6%*	*10.8%*	*11.0%*	*11.2%*	*11.4%*	*11.6%*	*11.8%*	*12.0%*
1	.898000	.896000	.894000	.892000	.890000	.888000	.886000	.884000	.882000	.880000
2	.806404	.802816	.799236	.795664	.792100	.788544	.784996	.781456	.777924	.774400
3	.724151	.719323	.714517	.709732	.704969	.700227	.695506	.690807	.686129	.681472
4	.650287	.644514	.638778	.633081	.627422	.621802	.616219	.610673	.605166	.599695
5	.583958	.577484	.571068	.564708	.558406	.552160	.545970	.539835	.533756	.527732
6	.524394	.517426	.510535	.503720	.496981	.490318	.483729	.477214	.470773	.464404
7	.470906	.463613	.456418	.449318	.442313	.435402	.428584	.421858	.415222	.408676
8	.422874	.415398	.408038	.400792	.393659	.386637	.379726	.372922	.366226	.359635
9	.379741	.372196	.364786	.357506	.350356	.343334	.336437	.329663	.323011	.316478
10	.341007	.333488	.326118	.318896	.311817	.304881	.298083	.291422	.284896	.278501
11	.306224	.298805	.291550	.284455	.277517	.270734	.264102	.257617	.251278	.245081
12	.274989	.267729	.260645	.253734	.246990	.240412	.233994	.227734	.221627	.215671
13	.246941	.239886	.233017	.226331	.219821	.213486	.207319	.201317	.195475	.189791
14	.221753	.214937	.208317	.201887	.195641	.189575	.183684	.177964	.172409	.167016
15	.199134	.192584	.186236	.180083	.174121	.168343	.162744	.157320	.152065	.146974
16	.178822	.172555	.166495	.160634	.154967	.149488	.144191	.139071	.134121	.129337
17	.160582	.154609	.148846	.143286	.137921	.132746	.127754	.122939	.118295	.113817
18	.144203	.138530	.133069	.127811	.122750	.117878	.113190	.108678	.104336	.100159
19	.129494	.124123	.118963	.114007	.109247	.104676	.100286	.096071	.092024	.088140
20	.116286	.111214	.106353	.101694	.097230	.092952	.088853	.084927	.081166	.077563

TABLE D
SHOWING THE PRESENT WORTH OF A REMAINDER INTEREST
POSTPONED FOR A TERM CERTAIN IN A
CHARITABLE REMAINDER UNITRUST
APPLICABLE AFTER APRIL 30, 1989
ADJUSTED PAYOUT RATE

YEARS	*12.2%*	*12.4%*	*12.6%*	*12.8%*	*13.0%*	*13.2%*	*13.4%*	*13.6%*	*13.8%*	*14.0%*
1	.878000	.876000	.874000	.872000	.870000	.868000	.866000	.864000	.862000	.860000
2	.770884	.767376	.763876	.760384	.756900	.753424	.749956	.746496	.743044	.739600
3	.676836	.672221	.667628	.663055	.658503	.653972	.649462	.644973	.640504	.636056
4	.594262	.588866	.583507	.578184	.572898	.567648	.562434	.557256	.552114	.547008
5	.521762	.515847	.509985	.504176	.498421	.492718	.487068	.481469	.475923	.470427
6	.458107	.451882	.445727	.439642	.433626	.427679	.421801	.415990	.410245	.404567
7	.402218	.395848	.389565	.383368	.377255	.371226	.365279	.359415	.353631	.347928
8	.353147	.346763	.340480	.334297	.328212	.322224	.316332	.310535	.304830	.299218
9	.310063	.303764	.297579	.291507	.285544	.279690	.273944	.268302	.262764	.257327
10	.272236	.266098	.260084	.254194	.248423	.242771	.237235	.231813	.226502	.221302
11	.239023	.233102	.227314	.221657	.216128	.210725	.205446	.200286	.195245	.190319
12	.209862	.204197	.198672	.193285	.188032	.182910	.177916	.173047	.168301	.163675
13	.184259	.178877	.173640	.168544	.163588	.158766	.154075	.149513	.145076	.140760
14	.161779	.156696	.151761	.146971	.142321	.137809	.133429	.129179	.125055	.121054
15	.142042	.137266	.132639	.128158	.123819	.119618	.115550	.111611	.107798	.104106
16	.124713	.120245	.115927	.111754	.107723	.103828	.100066	.096432	.092922	.089531
17	.109498	.105334	.101320	.097450	.093719	.090123	.086657	.083317	.080098	.076997
18	.096139	.092273	.088554	.084976	.081535	.078227	.075045	.071986	.069045	.066217
19	.084410	.080831	.077396	.074099	.070936	.067901	.064989	.062196	.059517	.056947
20	.074112	.070808	.067644	.064614	.061714	.058938	.056280	.053737	.051303	.048974

TABLE F(4.2)
WITH INTEREST AT 4.2 PERCENT,
SHOWING FACTORS FOR COMPUTATION
OF THE ADJUSTED PAYOUT RATE FOR
CERTAIN VALUATIONS APPLICABLE AFTER APRIL 30, 1989

1		2			
NUMBER OF MONTHS BY WHICH THE VALUATION DATE FOR THE FIRST FULL TAXABLE YEAR OF THE TRUST PRECEDES THE FIRST PAYOUT		FACTORS FOR PAYOUT AT THE END OF EACH PERIOD			
AT LEAST	*BUT LESS THAN*	*ANNUAL PERIOD*	*SEMIANNUAL PERIOD*	*QUARTERLY PERIOD*	*MONTHLY PERIOD*
...	1	1.000000	.989820	.984755	.981389
1	2	.996577	.986432	.981385	.978030
2	3	.993166	.983056	.978026	
3	4	.989767	.979691	.974679	
4	5	.986380	.976338		
5	6	.983004	.972996		
6	7	.979639	.969666		
7	8	.976286			
8	9	.972945			
9	10	.969615			
10	11	.966296			
11	12	.962989			
12	...	.959693			

TABLE F(4.4)
WITH INTEREST AT 4.4 PERCENT,
SHOWING FACTORS FOR COMPUTATION
OF THE ADJUSTED PAYOUT RATE FOR
CERTAIN VALUATIONS APPLICABLE AFTER APRIL 30, 1989

1		2			
NUMBER OF MONTHS BY WHICH THE VALUATION DATE FOR THE FIRST FULL TAXABLE YEAR OF THE TRUST PRECEDES THE FIRST PAYOUT		FACTORS FOR PAYOUT AT THE END OF EACH PERIOD			
AT LEAST	*BUT LESS THAN*	*ANNUAL PERIOD*	*SEMIANNUAL PERIOD*	*QUARTERLY PERIOD*	*MONTHLY PERIOD*
...	1	1.000000	.989350	.984054	.980533
1	2	.996418	.985806	.980529	.977021
2	3	.992849	.982275	.977017	
3	4	.989293	.978757	.973517	
4	5	.985749	.975251		
5	6	.982219	.971758		
6	7	.978700	.968277		
7	8	.975195			
8	9	.971702			
9	10	.968221			
10	11	.964753			
11	12	.961298			
12	...	.957854			

TABLE F(4.6)
WITH INTEREST AT 4.6 PERCENT,
SHOWING FACTORS FOR COMPUTATION
OF THE ADJUSTED PAYOUT RATE FOR
CERTAIN VALUATIONS APPLICABLE AFTER APRIL 30, 1989

1 NUMBER OF MONTHS BY WHICH THE VALUATION DATE FOR THE FIRST FULL TAXABLE YEAR OF THE TRUST PRECEDES THE FIRST PAYOUT		2 FACTORS FOR PAYOUT AT THE END OF EACH PERIOD			
AT LEAST	*BUT LESS THAN*	*ANNUAL PERIOD*	*SEMIANNUAL PERIOD*	*QUARTERLY PERIOD*	*MONTHLY PERIOD*
...	1	1.000000	.988882	.983354	.979680
1	2	.996259	.985183	.979676	.976015
2	3	.992532	.981498	.976011	
3	4	.988820	.977826	.972360	
4	5	.985121	.974168		
5	6	.981436	.970524		
6	7	.977764	.966894		
7	8	.974107			
8	9	.970463			
9	10	.966832			
10	11	.963216			
11	12	.959613			
12	...	.956023			

TABLE F(4.8)
WITH INTEREST AT 4.8 PERCENT,
SHOWING FACTORS FOR COMPUTATION
OF THE ADJUSTED PAYOUT RATE FOR
CERTAIN VALUATIONS APPLICABLE AFTER APRIL 30, 1989

1 NUMBER OF MONTHS BY WHICH THE VALUATION DATE FOR THE FIRST FULL TAXABLE YEAR OF THE TRUST PRECEDES THE FIRST PAYOUT		2 FACTORS FOR PAYOUT AT THE END OF EACH PERIOD			
AT LEAST	*BUT LESS THAN*	*ANNUAL PERIOD*	*SEMIANNUAL PERIOD*	*QUARTERLY PERIOD*	*MONTHLY PERIOD*
...	1	1.000000	.988415	.982657	.978830
1	2	.996101	.984561	.978825	.975013
2	3	.992217	.980722	.975008	
3	4	.988348	.976898	.971206	
4	5	.984494	.973089		
5	6	.980655	.969294		
6	7	.976831	.965515		
7	8	.973022			
8	9	.969228			
9	10	.965448			
10	11	.961684			
11	12	.957934			
12	...	.954198			

**TABLE F(5.0)
WITH INTEREST AT 5.0 PERCENT,
SHOWING FACTORS FOR COMPUTATION
OF THE ADJUSTED PAYOUT RATE FOR
CERTAIN VALUATIONS APPLICABLE AFTER APRIL 30, 1989**

1 NUMBER OF MONTHS BY WHICH THE VALUATION DATE FOR THE FIRST FULL TAXABLE YEAR OF THE TRUST PRECEDES THE FIRST PAYOUT		2 FACTORS FOR PAYOUT AT THE END OF EACH PERIOD			
AT LEAST	*BUT LESS THAN*	*ANNUAL PERIOD*	*SEMIANNUAL PERIOD*	*QUARTERLY PERIOD*	*MONTHLY PERIOD*
...	1	1.000000	.987950	.981961	.977982
1	2	.995942	.983941	.977977	.974014
2	3	.991901	.979949	.974009	
3	4	.987877	.975973	.970057	
4	5	.983868	.972013		
5	6	.979876	.968069		
6	7	.975900	.964141		
7	8	.971940			
8	9	.967997			
9	10	.964069			
10	11	.960157			
11	12	.956261			
12	...	.952381			

**TABLE F(5.2)
WITH INTEREST AT 5.2 PERCENT,
SHOWING FACTORS FOR COMPUTATION
OF THE ADJUSTED PAYOUT RATE FOR
CERTAIN VALUATIONS APPLICABLE AFTER APRIL 30, 1989**

1 NUMBER OF MONTHS BY WHICH THE VALUATION DATE FOR THE FIRST FULL TAXABLE YEAR OF THE TRUST PRECEDES THE FIRST PAYOUT		2 FACTORS FOR PAYOUT AT THE END OF EACH PERIOD			
AT LEAST	*BUT LESS THAN*	*ANNUAL PERIOD*	*SEMIANNUAL PERIOD*	*QUARTERLY PERIOD*	*MONTHLY PERIOD*
...	1	1.000000	.987486	.981268	.977137
1	2	.995784	.983323	.977132	.973018
2	3	.991587	.979178	.973012	
3	4	.987407	.975050	.968911	
4	5	.983244	.970940		
5	6	.979099	.966847		
6	7	.974972	.962771		
7	8	.970862			
8	9	.966769			
9	10	.962694			
10	11	.958636			
11	12	.954594			
12	...	.950570			

TABLE F(5.4)
WITH INTEREST AT 5.4 PERCENT,
SHOWING FACTORS FOR COMPUTATION
OF THE ADJUSTED PAYOUT RATE FOR
CERTAIN VALUATIONS APPLICABLE AFTER APRIL 30, 1989

1		2			
NUMBER OF MONTHS BY WHICH THE VALUATION DATE FOR THE FIRST FULL TAXABLE YEAR OF THE TRUST PRECEDES THE FIRST PAYOUT		FACTORS FOR PAYOUT AT THE END OF EACH PERIOD			
AT LEAST	*BUT LESS THAN*	*ANNUAL PERIOD*	*SEMIANNUAL PERIOD*	*QUARTERLY PERIOD*	*MONTHLY PERIOD*
...	1	1.000000	.987023	.980577	.976295
1	2	.995627	.982707	.976289	.972026
2	3	.991273	.978409	.972019	
3	4	.986938	.974131	.967769	
4	5	.982622	.969871		
5	6	.978325	.965629		
6	7	.974047	.961407		
7	8	.969787			
8	9	.965546			
9	10	.961323			
10	11	.957119			
11	12	.952934			
12	...	.948767			

TABLE F(5.6)
WITH INTEREST AT 5.6 PERCENT,
SHOWING FACTORS FOR COMPUTATION
OF THE ADJUSTED PAYOUT RATE FOR
CERTAIN VALUATIONS APPLICABLE AFTER APRIL 30, 1989

1		2			
NUMBER OF MONTHS BY WHICH THE VALUATION DATE FOR THE FIRST FULL TAXABLE YEAR OF THE TRUST PRECEDES THE FIRST PAYOUT		FACTORS FOR PAYOUT AT THE END OF EACH PERIOD			
AT LEAST	*BUT LESS THAN*	*ANNUAL PERIOD*	*SEMIANNUAL PERIOD*	*QUARTERLY PERIOD*	*MONTHLY PERIOD*
...	1	1.000000	.986562	.979888	.975455
1	2	.995470	.982092	.975449	.971036
2	3	.990960	.977643	.971029	
3	4	.986470	.973214	.966630	
4	5	.982001	.968805		
5	6	.977552	.964416		
6	7	.973124	.960047		
7	8	.968715			
8	9	.964326			
9	10	.959958			
10	11	.955609			
11	12	.951279			
12	...	.946970			

TABLE F(5.8)
WITH INTEREST AT 5.8 PERCENT,
SHOWING FACTORS FOR COMPUTATION
OF THE ADJUSTED PAYOUT RATE FOR
CERTAIN VALUATIONS APPLICABLE AFTER APRIL 30, 1989

1 NUMBER OF MONTHS BY WHICH THE VALUATION DATE FOR THE FIRST FULL TAXABLE YEAR OF THE TRUST PRECEDES THE FIRST PAYOUT		2 FACTORS FOR PAYOUT AT THE END OF EACH PERIOD			
AT LEAST	*BUT LESS THAN*	*ANNUAL PERIOD*	*SEMIANNUAL PERIOD*	*QUARTERLY PERIOD*	*MONTHLY PERIOD*
...	1	1.000000	.986102	.979201	.974618
1	2	.995313	.981480	.974611	.970050
2	3	.990647	.976879	.970043	
3	4	.986004	.972300	.965496	
4	5	.981382	.967743		
5	6	.976782	.963206		
6	7	.972203	.958692		
7	8	.967646			
8	9	.963111			
9	10	.958596			
10	11	.954103			
11	12	.949631			
12	...	.945180			

TABLE F(6.0)
WITH INTEREST AT 6.0 PERCENT,
SHOWING FACTORS FOR COMPUTATION
OF THE ADJUSTED PAYOUT RATE FOR
CERTAIN VALUATIONS APPLICABLE AFTER APRIL 30, 1989

1 NUMBER OF MONTHS BY WHICH THE VALUATION DATE FOR THE FIRST FULL TAXABLE YEAR OF THE TRUST PRECEDES THE FIRST PAYOUT		2 FACTORS FOR PAYOUT AT THE END OF EACH PERIOD			
AT LEAST	*BUT LESS THAN*	*ANNUAL PERIOD*	*SEMIANNUAL PERIOD*	*QUARTERLY PERIOD*	*MONTHLY PERIOD*
...	1	1.000000	.985643	.978516	.973784
1	2	.995156	.980869	.973776	.969067
2	3	.990336	.976117	.969059	
3	4	.985538	.971389	.964365	
4	5	.980764	.966684		
5	6	.976014	.962001		
6	7	.971286	.957341		
7	8	.966581			
8	9	.961899			
9	10	.957239			
10	11	.952603			
11	12	.947988			
12	...	.943396			

TABLE F(6.2)
WITH INTEREST AT 6.2 PERCENT,
SHOWING FACTORS FOR COMPUTATION
OF THE ADJUSTED PAYOUT RATE FOR
CERTAIN VALUATIONS APPLICABLE AFTER APRIL 30, 1989

1 NUMBER OF MONTHS BY WHICH THE VALUATION DATE FOR THE FIRST FULL TAXABLE YEAR OF THE TRUST PRECEDES THE FIRST PAYOUT		2 FACTORS FOR PAYOUT AT THE END OF EACH PERIOD			
AT LEAST	*BUT LESS THAN*	*ANNUAL PERIOD*	*SEMIANNUAL PERIOD*	*QUARTERLY PERIOD*	*MONTHLY PERIOD*
...	1	1.000000	.985185	.977833	.972952
1	2	.995000	.980259	.972944	.968087
2	3	.990024	.975358	.968079	
3	4	.985074	.970481	.963238	
4	5	.980148	.965628		
5	6	.975247	.960799		
6	7	.970371	.955995		
7	8	.965519			
8	9	.960691			
9	10	.955887			
10	11	.951107			
11	12	.946352			
12	...	.941620			

TABLE F(6.4)
WITH INTEREST AT 6.4 PERCENT,
SHOWING FACTORS FOR COMPUTATION
OF THE ADJUSTED PAYOUT RATE FOR
CERTAIN VALUATIONS APPLICABLE AFTER APRIL 30, 1989

1 NUMBER OF MONTHS BY WHICH THE VALUATION DATE FOR THE FIRST FULL TAXABLE YEAR OF THE TRUST PRECEDES THE FIRST PAYOUT		2 FACTORS FOR PAYOUT AT THE END OF EACH PERIOD			
AT LEAST	*BUT LESS THAN*	*ANNUAL PERIOD*	*SEMIANNUAL PERIOD*	*QUARTERLY PERIOD*	*MONTHLY PERIOD*
...	1	1.000000	.984729	.977152	.972122
1	2	.994844	.979652	.972114	.967110
2	3	.989714	.974600	.967101	
3	4	.984611	.969575	.962115	
4	5	.979534	.964576		
5	6	.974483	.959602		
6	7	.969458	.954654		
7	8	.964460			
8	9	.959487			
9	10	.954539			
10	11	.949617			
11	12	.944721			
12	...	.939850			

TABLE F(6.6)
WITH INTEREST AT 6.6 PERCENT,
SHOWING FACTORS FOR COMPUTATION
OF THE ADJUSTED PAYOUT RATE FOR
CERTAIN VALUATIONS APPLICABLE AFTER APRIL 30, 1989

1 NUMBER OF MONTHS BY WHICH THE VALUATION DATE FOR THE FIRST FULL TAXABLE YEAR OF THE TRUST PRECEDES THE FIRST PAYOUT		2 FACTORS FOR PAYOUT AT THE END OF EACH PERIOD			
AT LEAST	*BUT LESS THAN*	*ANNUAL PERIOD*	*SEMIANNUAL PERIOD*	*QUARTERLY PERIOD*	*MONTHLY PERIOD*
...	1	1.000000	.984274	.976473	.971295
1	2	.994688	.979046	.971286	.966136
2	3	.989404	.973845	.966127	
3	4	.984149	.968672	.960995	
4	5	.978921	.963527		
5	6	.973721	.958408		
6	7	.968549	.953317		
7	8	.963404			
8	9	.958286			
9	10	.953196			
10	11	.948132			
11	12	.943096			
12	...	.938086			

TABLE F(6.8)
WITH INTEREST AT 6.8 PERCENT,
SHOWING FACTORS FOR COMPUTATION
OF THE ADJUSTED PAYOUT RATE FOR
CERTAIN VALUATIONS APPLICABLE AFTER APRIL 30, 1989

1 NUMBER OF MONTHS BY WHICH THE VALUATION DATE FOR THE FIRST FULL TAXABLE YEAR OF THE TRUST PRECEDES THE FIRST PAYOUT		2 FACTORS FOR PAYOUT AT THE END OF EACH PERIOD			
AT LEAST	*BUT LESS THAN*	*ANNUAL PERIOD*	*SEMIANNUAL PERIOD*	*QUARTERLY PERIOD*	*MONTHLY PERIOD*
...	1	1.000000	.983821	.975796	.970471
1	2	.994533	.978442	.970461	.965165
2	3	.989095	.973092	.965156	
3	4	.983688	.967772	.959879	
4	5	.978309	.962481		
5	6	.972961	.957219		
6	7	.967641	.951985		
7	8	.962351			
8	9	.957089			
9	10	.951857			
10	11	.946653			
11	12	.941477			
12	...	.936330			

TABLE F(7.0)
WITH INTEREST AT 7.0 PERCENT,
SHOWING FACTORS FOR COMPUTATION
OF THE ADJUSTED PAYOUT RATE FOR
CERTAIN VALUATIONS APPLICABLE AFTER APRIL 30, 1989

1		2			
NUMBER OF MONTHS BY WHICH THE VALUATION DATE FOR THE FIRST FULL TAXABLE YEAR OF THE TRUST PRECEDES THE FIRST PAYOUT		FACTORS FOR PAYOUT AT THE END OF EACH PERIOD			
AT LEAST	*BUT LESS THAN*	*ANNUAL PERIOD*	*SEMIANNUAL PERIOD*	*QUARTERLY PERIOD*	*MONTHLY PERIOD*
...	1	1.000000	.983368	.975122	.969649
1	2	.994378	.977839	.969639	.964198
2	3	.988787	.972342	.964187	
3	4	.983228	.966875	.958766	
4	5	.977700	.961439		
5	6	.972203	.956033		
6	7	.966736	.950658		
7	8	.961301			
8	9	.955896			
9	10	.950522			
10	11	.945178			
11	12	.939864			
12	...	.934579			

TABLE F(7.2)
WITH INTEREST AT 7.2 PERCENT,
SHOWING FACTORS FOR COMPUTATION
OF THE ADJUSTED PAYOUT RATE FOR
CERTAIN VALUATIONS APPLICABLE AFTER APRIL 30, 1989

1		2			
NUMBER OF MONTHS BY WHICH THE VALUATION DATE FOR THE FIRST FULL TAXABLE YEAR OF THE TRUST PRECEDES THE FIRST PAYOUT		FACTORS FOR PAYOUT AT THE END OF EACH PERIOD			
AT LEAST	*BUT LESS THAN*	*ANNUAL PERIOD*	*SEMIANNUAL PERIOD*	*QUARTERLY PERIOD*	*MONTHLY PERIOD*
...	1	1.000000	.982917	.974449	.968830
1	2	.994223	.977239	.968819	.963233
2	3	.988479	.971593	.963222	
3	4	.982769	.965980	.957658	
4	5	.977091	.960400		
5	6	.971446	.954851		
6	7	.965834	.949335		
7	8	.960255			
8	9	.954707			
9	10	.949192			
10	11	.943708			
11	12	.938256			
12	...	.932836			

TABLE F(7.4)
WITH INTEREST AT 7.4 PERCENT,
SHOWING FACTORS FOR COMPUTATION
OF THE ADJUSTED PAYOUT RATE FOR
CERTAIN VALUATIONS APPLICABLE AFTER APRIL 30, 1989

1 NUMBER OF MONTHS BY WHICH THE VALUATION DATE FOR THE FIRST FULL TAXABLE YEAR OF THE TRUST PRECEDES THE FIRST PAYOUT		2 FACTORS FOR PAYOUT AT THE END OF EACH PERIOD			
AT LEAST	*BUT LESS THAN*	*ANNUAL PERIOD*	*SEMIANNUAL PERIOD*	*QUARTERLY PERIOD*	*MONTHLY PERIOD*
...	1	1.000000	.982467	.973778	.968013
1	2	.994068	.976640	.968002	.962271
2	3	.988172	.970847	.962260	
3	4	.982311	.965088	.956552	
4	5	.976484	.959364		
5	6	.970692	.953673		
6	7	.964935	.948017		
7	8	.959211			
8	9	.953521			
9	10	.947866			
10	11	.942243			
11	12	.936654			
12	...	.931099			

TABLE F(7.6)
WITH INTEREST AT 7.6 PERCENT,
SHOWING FACTORS FOR COMPUTATION
OF THE ADJUSTED PAYOUT RATE FOR
CERTAIN VALUATIONS APPLICABLE AFTER APRIL 30, 1989

1 NUMBER OF MONTHS BY WHICH THE VALUATION DATE FOR THE FIRST FULL TAXABLE YEAR OF THE TRUST PRECEDES THE FIRST PAYOUT		2 FACTORS FOR PAYOUT AT THE END OF EACH PERIOD			
AT LEAST	*BUT LESS THAN*	*ANNUAL PERIOD*	*SEMIANNUAL PERIOD*	*QUARTERLY PERIOD*	*MONTHLY PERIOD*
...	1	1.000000	.982019	.973109	.967199
1	2	.993914	.976042	.967187	.961313
2	3	.987866	.970103	.961301	
3	4	.981854	.964199	.955451	
4	5	.975879	.958331		
5	6	.969940	.952499		
6	7	.964037	.946703		
7	8	.958171			
8	9	.952340			
9	10	.946544			
10	11	.940784			
11	12	.935058			
12	...	.929368			

TABLE F(7.8)
WITH INTEREST AT 7.8 PERCENT,
SHOWING FACTORS FOR COMPUTATION
OF THE ADJUSTED PAYOUT RATE FOR
CERTAIN VALUATIONS APPLICABLE AFTER APRIL 30, 1989

1 NUMBER OF MONTHS BY WHICH THE VALUATION DATE FOR THE FIRST FULL TAXABLE YEAR OF THE TRUST PRECEDES THE FIRST PAYOUT		2 FACTORS FOR PAYOUT AT THE END OF EACH PERIOD			
AT LEAST	*BUT LESS THAN*	*ANNUAL PERIOD*	*SEMIANNUAL PERIOD*	*QUARTERLY PERIOD*	*MONTHLY PERIOD*
...	1	1.000000	.981571	.972442	.966387
1	2	.993761	.975447	.966374	.960357
2	3	.987560	.969361	.960345	
3	4	.981398	.963312	.954353	
4	5	.975275	.957302		
5	6	.969190	.951329		
6	7	.963143	.945393		
7	8	.957133			
8	9	.951161			
9	10	.945227			
10	11	.939329			
11	12	.933468			
12	...	.927644			

TABLE F(8.0)
WITH INTEREST AT 8.0 PERCENT,
SHOWING FACTORS FOR COMPUTATION
OF THE ADJUSTED PAYOUT RATE FOR
CERTAIN VALUATIONS APPLICABLE AFTER APRIL 30, 1989

1 NUMBER OF MONTHS BY WHICH THE VALUATION DATE FOR THE FIRST FULL TAXABLE YEAR OF THE TRUST PRECEDES THE FIRST PAYOUT		2 FACTORS FOR PAYOUT AT THE END OF EACH PERIOD			
AT LEAST	*BUT LESS THAN*	*ANNUAL PERIOD*	*SEMIANNUAL PERIOD*	*QUARTERLY PERIOD*	*MONTHLY PERIOD*
...	1	1.000000	.981125	.971777	.965578
1	2	.993607	.974853	.965564	.959405
2	3	.987255	.968621	.959392	
3	4	.980944	.962429	.953258	
4	5	.974673	.956276		
5	6	.968442	.950162		
6	7	.962250	.944088		
7	8	.956099			
8	9	.949987			
9	10	.943913			
10	11	.937879			
11	12	.931883			
12	...	.925926			

TABLE F(8.2)
WITH INTEREST AT 8.2 PERCENT,
SHOWING FACTORS FOR COMPUTATION
OF THE ADJUSTED PAYOUT RATE FOR
CERTAIN VALUATIONS APPLICABLE AFTER APRIL 30, 1989

1		2			
NUMBER OF MONTHS BY WHICH THE VALUATION DATE FOR THE FIRST FULL TAXABLE YEAR OF THE TRUST PRECEDES THE FIRST PAYOUT		FACTORS FOR PAYOUT AT THE END OF EACH PERIOD			
AT LEAST	*BUT LESS THAN*	*ANNUAL PERIOD*	*SEMIANNUAL PERIOD*	*QUARTERLY PERIOD*	*MONTHLY PERIOD*
...	1	1.000000	.980680	.971114	.964771
1	2	.993454	.974261	.964757	.958455
2	3	.986951	.967883	.958441	
3	4	.980490	.961547	.952167	
4	5	.974072	.955253		
5	6	.967695	.949000		
6	7	.961361	.942788		
7	8	.955068			
8	9	.948816			
9	10	.942605			
10	11	.936434			
11	12	.930304			
12	...	.924214			

TABLE F(8.4)
WITH INTEREST AT 8.4 PERCENT,
SHOWING FACTORS FOR COMPUTATION
OF THE ADJUSTED PAYOUT RATE FOR
CERTAIN VALUATIONS APPLICABLE AFTER APRIL 30, 1989

1		2			
NUMBER OF MONTHS BY WHICH THE VALUATION DATE FOR THE FIRST FULL TAXABLE YEAR OF THE TRUST PRECEDES THE FIRST PAYOUT		FACTORS FOR PAYOUT AT THE END OF EACH PERIOD			
AT LEAST	*BUT LESS THAN*	*ANNUAL PERIOD*	*SEMIANNUAL PERIOD*	*QUARTERLY PERIOD*	*MONTHLY PERIOD*
...	1	1.000000	.980237	.970453	.963966
1	2	.993301	.973670	.963952	.957509
2	3	.986647	.967148	.957494	
3	4	.980037	.960669	.951080	
4	5	.973472	.954233		
5	6	.966951	.947841		
6	7	.960473	.941491		
7	8	.954039			
8	9	.947648			
9	10	.941300			
10	11	.934994			
11	12	.928731			
12	...	.922509			

TABLE F(8.6)
WITH INTEREST AT 8.6 PERCENT,
SHOWING FACTORS FOR COMPUTATION
OF THE ADJUSTED PAYOUT RATE FOR
CERTAIN VALUATIONS APPLICABLE AFTER APRIL 30, 1989

1 NUMBER OF MONTHS BY WHICH THE VALUATION DATE FOR THE FIRST FULL TAXABLE YEAR OF THE TRUST PRECEDES THE FIRST PAYOUT		2 FACTORS FOR PAYOUT AT THE END OF EACH PERIOD			
AT LEAST	*BUT LESS THAN*	*ANNUAL PERIOD*	*SEMIANNUAL PERIOD*	*QUARTERLY PERIOD*	*MONTHLY PERIOD*
...	1	1.000000	.979794	.969794	.963164
1	2	.993148	.973081	.963149	.956565
2	3	.986344	.966414	.956550	
3	4	.979586	.959793	.949996	
4	5	.972874	.953217		
5	6	.966209	.946686		
6	7	.959589	.940199		
7	8	.953014			
8	9	.946484			
9	10	.940000			
10	11	.933559			
11	12	.927163			
12	...	.920810			

TABLE F(8.8)
WITH INTEREST AT 8.8 PERCENT,
SHOWING FACTORS FOR COMPUTATION
OF THE ADJUSTED PAYOUT RATE FOR
CERTAIN VALUATIONS APPLICABLE AFTER APRIL 30, 1989

1 NUMBER OF MONTHS BY WHICH THE VALUATION DATE FOR THE FIRST FULL TAXABLE YEAR OF THE TRUST PRECEDES THE FIRST PAYOUT		2 FACTORS FOR PAYOUT AT THE END OF EACH PERIOD			
AT LEAST	*BUT LESS THAN*	*ANNUAL PERIOD*	*SEMIANNUAL PERIOD*	*QUARTERLY PERIOD*	*MONTHLY PERIOD*
...	1	1.000000	.979353	.969136	.962364
1	2	.992996	.972494	.962349	.955624
2	3	.986041	.965683	.955609	
3	4	.979135	.958919	.948916	
4	5	.972278	.952203		
5	6	.965468	.945534		
6	7	.958706	.938912		
7	8	.951992			
8	9	.945324			
9	10	.938703			
10	11	.932129			
11	12	.925600			
12	...	.919118			

TABLE F(9.0)
WITH INTEREST AT 9.0 PERCENT,
SHOWING FACTORS FOR COMPUTATION
OF THE ADJUSTED PAYOUT RATE FOR
CERTAIN VALUATIONS APPLICABLE AFTER APRIL 30, 1989

1 NUMBER OF MONTHS BY WHICH THE VALUATION DATE FOR THE FIRST FULL TAXABLE YEAR OF THE TRUST PRECEDES THE FIRST PAYOUT		2 FACTORS FOR PAYOUT AT THE END OF EACH PERIOD			
AT LEAST	*BUT LESS THAN*	*ANNUAL PERIOD*	*SEMIANNUAL PERIOD*	*QUARTERLY PERIOD*	*MONTHLY PERIOD*
...	1	1.000000	.978913	.968481	.961567
1	2	.992844	.971908	.961551	.954686
2	3	.985740	.964954	.954670	
3	4	.978686	.958049	.947839	
4	5	.971683	.951193		
5	6	.964730	.944387		
6	7	.957826	.937629		
7	8	.950972			
8	9	.944167			
9	10	.937411			
10	11	.930703			
11	12	.924043			
12	...	.917431			

TABLE F(9.2)
WITH INTEREST AT 9.2 PERCENT,
SHOWING FACTORS FOR COMPUTATION
OF THE ADJUSTED PAYOUT RATE FOR
CERTAIN VALUATIONS APPLICABLE AFTER APRIL 30, 1989

1 NUMBER OF MONTHS BY WHICH THE VALUATION DATE FOR THE FIRST FULL TAXABLE YEAR OF THE TRUST PRECEDES THE FIRST PAYOUT		2 FACTORS FOR PAYOUT AT THE END OF EACH PERIOD			
AT LEAST	*BUT LESS THAN*	*ANNUAL PERIOD*	*SEMIANNUAL PERIOD*	*QUARTERLY PERIOD*	*MONTHLY PERIOD*
...	1	1.000000	.978474	.967827	.960772
1	2	.992693	.971324	.960755	.953752
2	3	.985439	.964226	.953734	
3	4	.978238	.957180	.946765	
4	5	.971089	.950186		
5	6	.963993	.943242		
6	7	.956949	.936350		
7	8	.949956			
8	9	.943014			
9	10	.936123			
10	11	.929283			
11	12	.922492			
12	...	.915751			

TABLE F(9.4)
WITH INTEREST AT 9.4 PERCENT,
SHOWING FACTORS FOR COMPUTATION
OF THE ADJUSTED PAYOUT RATE FOR
CERTAIN VALUATIONS APPLICABLE AFTER APRIL 30, 1989

1 NUMBER OF MONTHS BY WHICH THE VALUATION DATE FOR THE FIRST FULL TAXABLE YEAR OF THE TRUST PRECEDES THE FIRST PAYOUT		2 FACTORS FOR PAYOUT AT THE END OF EACH PERIOD			
AT LEAST	*BUT LESS THAN*	*ANNUAL PERIOD*	*SEMIANNUAL PERIOD*	*QUARTERLY PERIOD*	*MONTHLY PERIOD*
...	1	1.000000	.978037	.967176	.959980
1	2	.992541	.970742	.959962	.952820
2	3	.985138	.963501	.952802	
3	4	.977790	.956315	.945695	
4	5	.970497	.949182		
5	6	.963258	.942102		
6	7	.956074	.935075		
7	8	.948942			
8	9	.941865			
9	10	.934839			
10	11	.927867			
11	12	.920946			
12	...	.914077			

TABLE F(9.6)
WITH INTEREST AT 9.6 PERCENT,
SHOWING FACTORS FOR COMPUTATION
OF THE ADJUSTED PAYOUT RATE FOR
CERTAIN VALUATIONS APPLICABLE AFTER APRIL 30, 1989

1 NUMBER OF MONTHS BY WHICH THE VALUATION DATE FOR THE FIRST FULL TAXABLE YEAR OF THE TRUST PRECEDES THE FIRST PAYOUT		2 FACTORS FOR PAYOUT AT THE END OF EACH PERIOD			
AT LEAST	*BUT LESS THAN*	*ANNUAL PERIOD*	*SEMIANNUAL PERIOD*	*QUARTERLY PERIOD*	*MONTHLY PERIOD*
...	1	1.000000	.977600	.966526	.959190
1	2	.992390	.970161	.959171	.951890
2	3	.984838	.962778	.951872	
3	4	.977344	.955452	.944628	
4	5	.969906	.948181		
5	6	.962526	.940965		
6	7	.955201	.933805		
7	8	.947932			
8	9	.940718			
9	10	.933560			
10	11	.926455			
11	12	.919405			
12	...	.912409			

TABLE F(9.8)
WITH INTEREST AT 9.8 PERCENT,
SHOWING FACTORS FOR COMPUTATION
OF THE ADJUSTED PAYOUT RATE FOR
CERTAIN VALUATIONS APPLICABLE AFTER APRIL 30, 1989

1 NUMBER OF MONTHS BY WHICH THE VALUATION DATE FOR THE FIRST FULL TAXABLE YEAR OF THE TRUST PRECEDES THE FIRST PAYOUT		2 FACTORS FOR PAYOUT AT THE END OF EACH PERIOD			
AT LEAST	*BUT LESS THAN*	*ANNUAL PERIOD*	*SEMIANNUAL PERIOD*	*QUARTERLY PERIOD*	*MONTHLY PERIOD*
...	1	1.000000	.977165	.965878	.958402
1	2	.992239	.969582	.958382	.950964
2	3	.984539	.962057	.950945	
3	4	.976898	.954591	.943565	
4	5	.969317	.947183		
5	6	.961795	.939832		
6	7	.954331	.932539		
7	8	.946924			
8	9	.939576			
9	10	.932284			
10	11	.925049			
11	12	.917870			
12	...	.910747			

TABLE F(10.0)
WITH INTEREST AT 10.0 PERCENT,
SHOWING FACTORS FOR COMPUTATION
OF THE ADJUSTED PAYOUT RATE FOR
CERTAIN VALUATIONS APPLICABLE AFTER APRIL 30, 1989

1 NUMBER OF MONTHS BY WHICH THE VALUATION DATE FOR THE FIRST FULL TAXABLE YEAR OF THE TRUST PRECEDES THE FIRST PAYOUT		2 FACTORS FOR PAYOUT AT THE END OF EACH PERIOD			
AT LEAST	*BUT LESS THAN*	*ANNUAL PERIOD*	*SEMIANNUAL PERIOD*	*QUARTERLY PERIOD*	*MONTHLY PERIOD*
...	1	1.000000	.976731	.965232	.957616
1	2	.992089	.969004	.957596	.950041
2	3	.984240	.961338	.950021	
3	4	.976454	.953733	.942505	
4	5	.968729	.946188		
5	6	.961066	.938703		
6	7	.953463	.931277		
7	8	.945920			
8	9	.938436			
9	10	.931012			
10	11	.923647			
11	12	.916340			
12	...	.909091			

TABLE F(10.2)
WITH INTEREST AT 10.2 PERCENT,
SHOWING FACTORS FOR COMPUTATION
OF THE ADJUSTED PAYOUT RATE FOR
CERTAIN VALUATIONS APPLICABLE AFTER APRIL 30, 1989

1 NUMBER OF MONTHS BY WHICH THE VALUATION DATE FOR THE FIRST FULL TAXABLE YEAR OF THE TRUST PRECEDES THE FIRST PAYOUT		2 FACTORS FOR PAYOUT AT THE END OF EACH PERIOD			
AT LEAST	*BUT LESS THAN*	*ANNUAL PERIOD*	*SEMIANNUAL PERIOD*	*QUARTERLY PERIOD*	*MONTHLY PERIOD*
...	1	1.000000	.976298	.964588	.956833
1	2	.991939	.968428	.956812	.949120
2	3	.983943	.960622	.949099	
3	4	.976011	.952878	.941448	
4	5	.968143	.945196		
5	6	.960338	.937577		
6	7	.952597	.930019		
7	8	.944918			
8	9	.937301			
9	10	.929745			
10	11	.922250			
11	12	.914816			
12	...	.907441			

TABLE F(10.4)
WITH INTEREST AT 10.4 PERCENT,
SHOWING FACTORS FOR COMPUTATION
OF THE ADJUSTED PAYOUT RATE FOR
CERTAIN VALUATIONS APPLICABLE AFTER APRIL 30, 1989

1 NUMBER OF MONTHS BY WHICH THE VALUATION DATE FOR THE FIRST FULL TAXABLE YEAR OF THE TRUST PRECEDES THE FIRST PAYOUT		2 FACTORS FOR PAYOUT AT THE END OF EACH PERIOD			
AT LEAST	*BUT LESS THAN*	*ANNUAL PERIOD*	*SEMIANNUAL PERIOD*	*QUARTERLY PERIOD*	*MONTHLY PERIOD*
...	1	1.000000	.975867	.963946	.956052
1	2	.991789	.967854	.956031	.948202
2	3	.983645	.959907	.948181	
3	4	.975568	.952025	.940395	
4	5	.967558	.944208		
5	6	.959613	.936455		
6	7	.951734	.928765		
7	8	.943919			
8	9	.936168			
9	10	.928481			
10	11	.920858			
11	12	.913296			
12	...	.905797			

TABLE F(10.6)
WITH INTEREST AT 10.6 PERCENT,
SHOWING FACTORS FOR COMPUTATION
OF THE ADJUSTED PAYOUT RATE FOR
CERTAIN VALUATIONS APPLICABLE AFTER APRIL 30, 1989

1 NUMBER OF MONTHS BY WHICH THE VALUATION DATE FOR THE FIRST FULL TAXABLE YEAR OF THE TRUST PRECEDES THE FIRST PAYOUT		2 FACTORS FOR PAYOUT AT THE END OF EACH PERIOD			
AT LEAST	*BUT LESS THAN*	*ANNUAL PERIOD*	*SEMIANNUAL PERIOD*	*QUARTERLY PERIOD*	*MONTHLY PERIOD*
...	1	1.000000	.975436	.963305	.955274
1	2	.991639	.967281	.955252	.947287
2	3	.983349	.959194	.947265	
3	4	.975127	.951174	.939345	
4	5	.966974	.943222		
5	6	.958890	.935336		
6	7	.950873	.927516		
7	8	.942923			
8	9	.935039			
9	10	.927222			
10	11	.919470			
11	12	.911782			
12	...	.904159			

TABLE F(10.8)
WITH INTEREST AT 10.8 PERCENT,
SHOWING FACTORS FOR COMPUTATION
OF THE ADJUSTED PAYOUT RATE FOR
CERTAIN VALUATIONS APPLICABLE AFTER APRIL 30, 1989

1 NUMBER OF MONTHS BY WHICH THE VALUATION DATE FOR THE FIRST FULL TAXABLE YEAR OF THE TRUST PRECEDES THE FIRST PAYOUT		2 FACTORS FOR PAYOUT AT THE END OF EACH PERIOD			
AT LEAST	*BUT LESS THAN*	*ANNUAL PERIOD*	*SEMIANNUAL PERIOD*	*QUARTERLY PERIOD*	*MONTHLY PERIOD*
...	1	1.000000	.975007	.962667	.954498
1	2	.991490	.966710	.954475	.946375
2	3	.983052	.958483	.946352	
3	4	.974687	.950327	.938299	
4	5	.966392	.942239		
5	6	.958168	.934221		
6	7	.950014	.926271		
7	8	.941930			
8	9	.933914			
9	10	.925966			
10	11	.918086			
11	12	.910273			
12	...	.902527			

TABLE F(11.0)
WITH INTEREST AT 11.0 PERCENT,
SHOWING FACTORS FOR COMPUTATION
OF THE ADJUSTED PAYOUT RATE FOR
CERTAIN VALUATIONS APPLICABLE AFTER APRIL 30, 1989

1		2			
NUMBER OF MONTHS BY WHICH THE VALUATION DATE FOR THE FIRST FULL TAXABLE YEAR OF THE TRUST PRECEDES THE FIRST PAYOUT		FACTORS FOR PAYOUT AT THE END OF EACH PERIOD			
AT LEAST	*BUT LESS THAN*	*ANNUAL PERIOD*	*SEMIANNUAL PERIOD*	*QUARTERLY PERIOD*	*MONTHLY PERIOD*
...	1	1.000000	.974579	.962030	.953724
1	2	.991341	.966140	.953700	.945466
2	3	.982757	.957774	.945442	
3	4	.974247	.949481	.937255	
4	5	.965811	.941260		
5	6	.957449	.933109		
6	7	.949158	.925029		
7	8	.940939			
8	9	.932792			
9	10	.924715			
10	11	.916708			
11	12	.908770			
12	...	.900901			

TABLE F(11.2)
WITH INTEREST AT 11.2 PERCENT,
SHOWING FACTORS FOR COMPUTATION
OF THE ADJUSTED PAYOUT RATE FOR
CERTAIN VALUATIONS APPLICABLE AFTER APRIL 30, 1989

1		2			
NUMBER OF MONTHS BY WHICH THE VALUATION DATE FOR THE FIRST FULL TAXABLE YEAR OF THE TRUST PRECEDES THE FIRST PAYOUT		FACTORS FOR PAYOUT AT THE END OF EACH PERIOD			
AT LEAST	*BUT LESS THAN*	*ANNUAL PERIOD*	*SEMIANNUAL PERIOD*	*QUARTERLY PERIOD*	*MONTHLY PERIOD*
...	1	1.000000	.974152	.961395	.952952
1	2	.991192	.965572	.952927	.944559
2	3	.982462	.957068	.944534	
3	4	.973809	.948638	.936215	
4	5	.965232	.940283		
5	6	.956731	.932001		
6	7	.948304	.923792		
7	8	.939952			
8	9	.931673			
9	10	.923467			
10	11	.915333			
11	12	.907272			
12	...	.899281			

TABLE F(11.4)
WITH INTEREST AT 11.4 PERCENT,
SHOWING FACTORS FOR COMPUTATION
OF THE ADJUSTED PAYOUT RATE FOR
CERTAIN VALUATIONS APPLICABLE AFTER APRIL 30, 1989

1 NUMBER OF MONTHS BY WHICH THE VALUATION DATE FOR THE FIRST FULL TAXABLE YEAR OF THE TRUST PRECEDES THE FIRST PAYOUT		2 FACTORS FOR PAYOUT AT THE END OF EACH PERIOD			
AT LEAST	*BUT LESS THAN*	*ANNUAL PERIOD*	*SEMIANNUAL PERIOD*	*QUARTERLY PERIOD*	*MONTHLY PERIOD*
...	1	1.000000	.973726	.960762	.952183
1	2	.991044	.965005	.952157	.943655
2	3	.982168	.956363	.943630	
3	4	.973372	.947798	.935178	
4	5	.964654	.939309		
5	6	.956015	.930896		
6	7	.947452	.922559		
7	8	.938967			
8	9	.930557			
9	10	.922223			
10	11	.913964			
11	12	.905778			
12	...	.897666			

TABLE F(11.6)
WITH INTEREST AT 11.6 PERCENT,
SHOWING FACTORS FOR COMPUTATION
OF THE ADJUSTED PAYOUT RATE FOR
CERTAIN VALUATIONS APPLICABLE AFTER APRIL 30, 1989

1 NUMBER OF MONTHS BY WHICH THE VALUATION DATE FOR THE FIRST FULL TAXABLE YEAR OF THE TRUST PRECEDES THE FIRST PAYOUT		2 FACTORS FOR PAYOUT AT THE END OF EACH PERIOD			
AT LEAST	*BUT LESS THAN*	*ANNUAL PERIOD*	*SEMIANNUAL PERIOD*	*QUARTERLY PERIOD*	*MONTHLY PERIOD*
...	1	1.000000	.973302	.960130	.951416
1	2	.990896	.964440	.951389	.942754
2	3	.981874	.955660	.942728	
3	4	.972935	.946959	.934145	
4	5	.964077	.938338		
5	6	.955300	.929795		
6	7	.946603	.921330		
7	8	.937985			
8	9	.929445			
9	10	.920984			
10	11	.912599			
11	12	.904290			
12	...	.896057			

TABLE F(11.8)
WITH INTEREST AT 11.8 PERCENT,
SHOWING FACTORS FOR COMPUTATION
OF THE ADJUSTED PAYOUT RATE FOR
CERTAIN VALUATIONS APPLICABLE AFTER APRIL 30, 1989

1 NUMBER OF MONTHS BY WHICH THE VALUATION DATE FOR THE FIRST FULL TAXABLE YEAR OF THE TRUST PRECEDES THE FIRST PAYOUT		2 FACTORS FOR PAYOUT AT THE END OF EACH PERIOD			
AT LEAST	*BUT LESS THAN*	*ANNUAL PERIOD*	*SEMIANNUAL PERIOD*	*QUARTERLY PERIOD*	*MONTHLY PERIOD*
...	1	1.000000	.972878	.959501	.950651
1	2	.990748	.963877	.950624	.941855
2	3	.981582	.954959	.941828	
3	4	.972500	.946124	.933114	
4	5	.963502	.937370		
5	6	.954588	.928698		
6	7	.945756	.920105		
7	8	.937006			
8	9	.928337			
9	10	.919748			
10	11	.911238			
11	12	.902807			
12	...	.894454			

TABLE F(12.0)
WITH INTEREST AT 12.0 PERCENT,
SHOWING FACTORS FOR COMPUTATION
OF THE ADJUSTED PAYOUT RATE FOR
CERTAIN VALUATIONS APPLICABLE AFTER APRIL 30, 1989

1 NUMBER OF MONTHS BY WHICH THE VALUATION DATE FOR THE FIRST FULL TAXABLE YEAR OF THE TRUST PRECEDES THE FIRST PAYOUT		2 FACTORS FOR PAYOUT AT THE END OF EACH PERIOD			
AT LEAST	*BUT LESS THAN*	*ANNUAL PERIOD*	*SEMIANNUAL PERIOD*	*QUARTERLY PERIOD*	*MONTHLY PERIOD*
...	1	1.000000	.972456	.958873	.949888
1	2	.990600	.963315	.949860	.940960
2	3	.981289	.954260	.940932	
3	4	.972065	.945290	.932087	
4	5	.962928	.936405		
5	6	.953877	.927603		
6	7	.944911	.918884		
7	8	.936029			
8	9	.927231			
9	10	.918515			
10	11	.909882			
11	12	.901329			
12	...	.892857			

TABLE F(12.2)
WITH INTEREST AT 12.2 PERCENT,
SHOWING FACTORS FOR COMPUTATION
OF THE ADJUSTED PAYOUT RATE FOR
CERTAIN VALUATIONS APPLICABLE AFTER APRIL 30, 1989

1 NUMBER OF MONTHS BY WHICH THE VALUATION DATE FOR THE FIRST FULL TAXABLE YEAR OF THE TRUST PRECEDES THE FIRST PAYOUT		2 FACTORS FOR PAYOUT AT THE END OF EACH PERIOD			
AT LEAST	*BUT LESS THAN*	*ANNUAL PERIOD*	*SEMIANNUAL PERIOD*	*QUARTERLY PERIOD*	*MONTHLY PERIOD*
...	1	1.000000	.972034	.958247	.949128
1	2	.990453	.962754	.949099	.940067
2	3	.980997	.953563	.940038	
3	4	.971632	.944460	.931063	
4	5	.962356	.935443		
5	6	.953168	.926512		
6	7	.944069	.917667		
7	8	.935056			
8	9	.926129			
9	10	.917287			
10	11	.908530			
11	12	.899856			
12	...	.891266			

TABLE F(12.4)
WITH INTEREST AT 12.4 PERCENT,
SHOWING FACTORS FOR COMPUTATION
OF THE ADJUSTED PAYOUT RATE FOR
CERTAIN VALUATIONS APPLICABLE AFTER APRIL 30, 1989

1 NUMBER OF MONTHS BY WHICH THE VALUATION DATE FOR THE FIRST FULL TAXABLE YEAR OF THE TRUST PRECEDES THE FIRST PAYOUT		2 FACTORS FOR PAYOUT AT THE END OF EACH PERIOD			
AT LEAST	*BUT LESS THAN*	*ANNUAL PERIOD*	*SEMIANNUAL PERIOD*	*QUARTERLY PERIOD*	*MONTHLY PERIOD*
...	1	1.000000	.971614	.957623	.948370
1	2	.990306	.962195	.948340	.939176
2	3	.980706	.952868	.939147	
3	4	.971199	.943631	.930043	
4	5	.961785	.934484		
5	6	.952461	.925425		
6	7	.943228	.916454		
7	8	.934085			
8	9	.925030			
9	10	.916063			
10	11	.907183			
11	12	.898389			
12	...	.889680			

TABLE F(12.6)
WITH INTEREST AT 12.6 PERCENT,
SHOWING FACTORS FOR COMPUTATION
OF THE ADJUSTED PAYOUT RATE FOR
CERTAIN VALUATIONS APPLICABLE AFTER APRIL 30, 1989

1 NUMBER OF MONTHS BY WHICH THE VALUATION DATE FOR THE FIRST FULL TAXABLE YEAR OF THE TRUST PRECEDES THE FIRST PAYOUT		2 FACTORS FOR PAYOUT AT THE END OF EACH PERIOD			
AT LEAST	*BUT LESS THAN*	*ANNUAL PERIOD*	*SEMIANNUAL PERIOD*	*QUARTERLY PERIOD*	*MONTHLY PERIOD*
...	1	1.000000	.971195	.957000	.947614
1	2	.990159	.961638	.947583	.938289
2	3	.980416	.952175	.938258	
3	4	.970768	.942805	.929025	
4	5	.961215	.933527		
5	6	.951756	.924341		
6	7	.942390	.915245		
7	8	.933117			
8	9	.923934			
9	10	.914842			
10	11	.905840			
11	12	.896926			
12	...	.888099			

TABLE F(12.8)
WITH INTEREST AT 12.8 PERCENT,
SHOWING FACTORS FOR COMPUTATION
OF THE ADJUSTED PAYOUT RATE FOR
CERTAIN VALUATIONS APPLICABLE AFTER APRIL 30, 1989

1 NUMBER OF MONTHS BY WHICH THE VALUATION DATE FOR THE FIRST FULL TAXABLE YEAR OF THE TRUST PRECEDES THE FIRST PAYOUT		2 FACTORS FOR PAYOUT AT THE END OF EACH PERIOD			
AT LEAST	*BUT LESS THAN*	*ANNUAL PERIOD*	*SEMIANNUAL PERIOD*	*QUARTERLY PERIOD*	*MONTHLY PERIOD*
...	1	1.000000	.970777	.956379	.946860
1	2	.990013	.961082	.946828	.937403
2	3	.980126	.951484	.937372	
3	4	.970337	.941981	.928011	
4	5	.960647	.932574		
5	6	.951053	.923260		
6	7	.941554	.914040		
7	8	.932151			
8	9	.922842			
9	10	.913625			
10	11	.904501			
11	12	.895468			
12	...	.886525			

TABLE F(13.0)
WITH INTEREST AT 13.0 PERCENT,
SHOWING FACTORS FOR COMPUTATION
OF THE ADJUSTED PAYOUT RATE FOR
CERTAIN VALUATIONS APPLICABLE AFTER APRIL 30, 1989

1		2			
NUMBER OF MONTHS BY WHICH THE VALUATION DATE FOR THE FIRST FULL TAXABLE YEAR OF THE TRUST PRECEDES THE FIRST PAYOUT		FACTORS FOR PAYOUT AT THE END OF EACH PERIOD			
AT LEAST	*BUT LESS THAN*	*ANNUAL PERIOD*	*SEMIANNUAL PERIOD*	*QUARTERLY PERIOD*	*MONTHLY PERIOD*
...	1	1.000000	.970360	.955760	.946108
1	2	.989867	.960528	.946075	.936521
2	3	.979836	.950795	.936489	
3	4	.969908	.941160	.926999	
4	5	.960079	.931623		
5	6	.950351	.922183		
6	7	.940721	.912838		
7	8	.931188			
8	9	.921753			
9	10	.912412			
10	11	.903167			
11	12	.894015			
12	...	.884956			

TABLE F(13.2)
WITH INTEREST AT 13.2 PERCENT,
SHOWING FACTORS FOR COMPUTATION
OF THE ADJUSTED PAYOUT RATE FOR
CERTAIN VALUATIONS APPLICABLE AFTER APRIL 30, 1989

1		2			
NUMBER OF MONTHS BY WHICH THE VALUATION DATE FOR THE FIRST FULL TAXABLE YEAR OF THE TRUST PRECEDES THE FIRST PAYOUT		FACTORS FOR PAYOUT AT THE END OF EACH PERIOD			
AT LEAST	*BUT LESS THAN*	*ANNUAL PERIOD*	*SEMIANNUAL PERIOD*	*QUARTERLY PERIOD*	*MONTHLY PERIOD*
...	1	1.000000	.969945	.955143	.945359
1	2	.989721	.959975	.945325	.935641
2	3	.979548	.950107	.935608	
3	4	.969479	.940341	.925991	
4	5	.959514	.930675		
5	6	.949651	.921109		
6	7	.939889	.911641		
7	8	.930228			
8	9	.920667			
9	10	.911203			
10	11	.901837			
11	12	.892567			
12	...	.883392			

TABLE F(13.4)
WITH INTEREST AT 13.4 PERCENT,
SHOWING FACTORS FOR COMPUTATION
OF THE ADJUSTED PAYOUT RATE FOR
CERTAIN VALUATIONS APPLICABLE AFTER APRIL 30, 1989

1 NUMBER OF MONTHS BY WHICH THE VALUATION DATE FOR THE FIRST FULL TAXABLE YEAR OF THE TRUST PRECEDES THE FIRST PAYOUT		2 FACTORS FOR PAYOUT AT THE END OF EACH PERIOD			
AT LEAST	*BUT LESS THAN*	*ANNUAL PERIOD*	*SEMIANNUAL PERIOD*	*QUARTERLY PERIOD*	*MONTHLY PERIOD*
...	1	1.000000	.969530	.954527	.944611
1	2	.989575	.959423	.944577	.934764
2	3	.979260	.949422	.934730	
3	4	.969051	.939524	.924986	
4	5	.958949	.929730		
5	6	.948953	.920038		
6	7	.939060	.910447		
7	8	.929271			
8	9	.919584			
9	10	.909998			
10	11	.900511			
11	12	.891124			
12	...	.881834			

TABLE F(13.6)
WITH INTEREST AT 13.6 PERCENT,
SHOWING FACTORS FOR COMPUTATION
OF THE ADJUSTED PAYOUT RATE FOR
CERTAIN VALUATIONS APPLICABLE AFTER APRIL 30, 1989

1 NUMBER OF MONTHS BY WHICH THE VALUATION DATE FOR THE FIRST FULL TAXABLE YEAR OF THE TRUST PRECEDES THE FIRST PAYOUT		2 FACTORS FOR PAYOUT AT THE END OF EACH PERIOD			
AT LEAST	*BUT LESS THAN*	*ANNUAL PERIOD*	*SEMIANNUAL PERIOD*	*QUARTERLY PERIOD*	*MONTHLY PERIOD*
...	1	1.000000	.969117	.953913	.943866
1	2	.989430	.958873	.943831	.933890
2	3	.978972	.948738	.933854	
3	4	.968624	.938710	.923984	
4	5	.958386	.928788		
5	6	.948256	.918971		
6	7	.938233	.909257		
7	8	.928316			
8	9	.918504			
9	10	.908796			
10	11	.899190			
11	12	.889686			
12	..	.880282			

TABLE F(13.8)
WITH INTEREST AT 13.8 PERCENT,
SHOWING FACTORS FOR COMPUTATION
OF THE ADJUSTED PAYOUT RATE FOR
CERTAIN VALUATIONS APPLICABLE AFTER APRIL 30, 1989

1 NUMBER OF MONTHS BY WHICH THE VALUATION DATE FOR THE FIRST FULL TAXABLE YEAR OF THE TRUST PRECEDES THE FIRST PAYOUT		2 FACTORS FOR PAYOUT AT THE END OF EACH PERIOD			
AT LEAST	*BUT LESS THAN*	*ANNUAL PERIOD*	*SEMIANNUAL PERIOD*	*QUARTERLY PERIOD*	*MONTHLY PERIOD*
...	1	1.000000	.968704	.953301	.943123
1	2	.989285	.958325	.943087	.933018
2	3	.978685	.948056	.932982	
3	4	.968199	.937898	.922985	
4	5	.957824	.927849		
5	6	.947561	.917907		
6	7	.937408	.908072		
7	8	.927364			
8	9	.917428			
9	10	.907598			
10	11	.897873			
11	12	.888252			
12	...	.878735			

TABLE F(14.0)
WITH INTEREST AT 14.0 PERCENT,
SHOWING FACTORS FOR COMPUTATION
OF THE ADJUSTED PAYOUT RATE FOR
CERTAIN VALUATIONS APPLICABLE AFTER APRIL 30, 1989

1 NUMBER OF MONTHS BY WHICH THE VALUATION DATE FOR THE FIRST FULL TAXABLE YEAR OF THE TRUST PRECEDES THE FIRST PAYOUT		2 FACTORS FOR PAYOUT AT THE END OF EACH PERIOD			
AT LEAST	*BUT LESS THAN*	*ANNUAL PERIOD*	*SEMIANNUAL PERIOD*	*QUARTERLY PERIOD*	*MONTHLY PERIOD*
...	1	1.000000	.968293	.952691	.942382
1	2	.989140	.957778	.942345	.932148
2	3	.978399	.947377	.932111	
3	4	.967774	.937088	.921989	
4	5	.957264	.926912		
5	6	.946868	.916846		
6	7	.936586	.906889		
7	8	.926415			
8	9	.916354			
9	10	.906403			
10	11	.896560			
11	12	.886824			
12	...	.877193			

TABLE 80CNSMT
APPLICABLE AFTER APRIL 30, 1989, AND BEFORE MAY 1, 1999

Age x	*1(x)*	*Age x*	*1(x)*	*Age x*	*1(x)*
(1)	(2)	(1)	(2)	(1)	(2)
0	100000	37	95492	74	59279
1	98740	38	95317	75	56799
2	98648	39	95129	76	54239
3	98584	40	94926	77	51599
4	98535	41	94706	78	48878
5	98495	42	94465	79	46071
6	98459	43	94201	80	43180
7	98426	44	93913	81	40208
8	98396	45	93599	82	37172
9	98370	46	93256	83	34095
10	98347	47	92882	84	31012
11	98328	48	92472	85	27960
12	98309	49	92021	86	24961
13	98285	50	91526	87	22038
14	98248	51	90986	88	19235
15	98196	52	90402	89	16598
16	98129	53	89771	90	14154
17	98047	54	89087	91	11908
18	97953	55	88348	92	9863
19	97851	56	87551	93	8032
20	97741	57	86695	94	6424
21	97623	58	85776	95	5043
22	97499	59	84789	96	3884
23	97370	60	83726	97	2939
24	97240	61	82581	98	2185
25	97110	62	81348	99	1598
26	96982	63	80024	100	1150
27	96856	64	78609	101	815
28	96730	65	77107	102	570
29	96604	66	75520	103	393
30	96477	67	73846	104	267
31	96350	68	72082	105	179
32	96220	69	70218	106	119
33	96088	70	68248	107	78
34	95951	71	66165	108	51
35	95808	72	63972	109	33
36	95655	73	61673	110	0

TABLE S
BASED ON LIFE TABLE 80CNSMT
SINGLE LIFE REMAINDER FACTORS
APPLICABLE AFTER APRIL 30, 1989, AND BEFORE MAY 1, 1999
INTEREST RATE

AGE	4.2%	4.4%	4.6%	4.8%	5.0%	5.2%	5.4%	5.6%	5.8%	6.0%
0	.07389	.06749	.06188	.05695	.05261	.04879	.04541	.04243	.03978	.03744
1	.06494	.05832	.05250	.04738	.04287	.03889	.03537	.03226	.02950	.02705
2	.06678	.05999	.05401	.04874	.04410	.03999	.03636	.03314	.03028	.02773
3	.06897	.06200	.05587	.05045	.04567	.04143	.03768	.03435	.03139	.02875
4	.07139	.06425	.05796	.05239	.04746	.04310	.03922	.03578	.03271	.02998
5	.07401	.06669	.06023	.05451	.04944	.04494	.04094	.03738	.03421	.03137
6	.07677	.06928	.06265	.05677	.05156	.04692	.04279	.03911	.03583	.03289
7	.07968	.07201	.06521	.05918	.05381	.04903	.04477	.04097	.03757	.03453
8	.08274	.07489	.06792	.06172	.05621	.05129	.04689	.04297	.03945	.03630
9	.08597	.07794	.07079	.06443	.05876	.05370	.04917	.04511	.04148	.03821
10	.08936	.08115	.07383	.06730	.06147	.05626	.05159	.04741	.04365	.04027
11	.09293	.08453	.07704	.07035	.06436	.05900	.05419	.04988	.04599	.04250
12	.09666	.08807	.08040	.07354	.06739	.06188	.05693	.05248	.04847	.04486
13	.10049	.09172	.08387	.07684	.07053	.06487	.05977	.05518	.05104	.04731
14	.10437	.09541	.08738	.08017	.07370	.06788	.06263	.05791	.05364	.04978
15	.10827	.09912	.09090	.08352	.07688	.07090	.06551	.06064	.05623	.05225
16	.11220	.10285	.09445	.08689	.08008	.07394	.06839	.06337	.05883	.05472
17	.11615	.10661	.09802	.09028	.08330	.07699	.07129	.06612	.06144	.05719
18	.12017	.11043	.10165	.09373	.08656	.08009	.07422	.06890	.06408	.05969
19	.12428	.11434	.10537	.09726	.08992	.08327	.07724	.07177	.06679	.06226
20	.12850	.11836	.10919	.10089	.09337	.08654	.08035	.07471	.06959	.06492
21	.13282	.12248	.11311	.10462	.09692	.08991	.08355	.07775	.07247	.06765
22	.13728	.12673	.11717	.10848	.10059	.09341	.08686	.08090	.07546	.07049
23	.14188	.13113	.12136	.11248	.10440	.09703	.09032	.08418	.07858	.07345
24	.14667	.13572	.12575	.11667	.10839	.10084	.09395	.08764	.08187	.07659
25	.15167	.14051	.13034	.12106	.11259	.10486	.09778	.09130	.08536	.07991
26	.15690	.14554	.13517	.12569	.11703	.10910	.10184	.09518	.08907	.08346
27	.16237	.15081	.14024	.13056	.12171	.11359	.10614	.09930	.09302	.08724
28	.16808	.15632	.14555	.13567	.12662	.11831	.11068	.10366	.09720	.09125
29	.17404	.16208	.15110	.14104	.13179	.12329	.11547	.10827	.10163	.09551
30	.18025	.16808	.15692	.14665	.13721	.12852	.12051	.11313	.10631	.10002
31	.18672	.17436	.16300	.15255	.14291	.13403	.12584	.11827	.11127	.10480
32	.19344	.18090	.16935	.15870	.14888	.13980	.13142	.12367	.11650	.10985
33	.20044	.18772	.17598	.16514	.15513	.14587	.13730	.12936	.12201	.11519
34	.20770	.19480	.18287	.17185	.16165	.15221	.14345	.13533	.12780	.12080
35	.21522	.20215	.19005	.17884	.16846	.15883	.14989	.14159	.13388	.12670
36	.22299	.20974	.19747	.18609	.17552	.16571	.15660	.14812	.14022	.13287
37	.23101	.21760	.20516	.19360	.18286	.17288	.16358	.15492	.14685	.13933
38	.23928	.22572	.21311	.20139	.19048	.18032	.17085	.16201	.15377	.14607
39	.24780	.23409	.22133	.20945	.19837	.18804	.17840	.16939	.16097	.15310
40	.25658	.24273	.22982	.21778	.20654	.19605	.18624	.17706	.16847	.16043
41	.26560	.25163	.23858	.22639	.21499	.20434	.19436	.18502	.17627	.16806
42	.27486	.26076	.24758	.23525	.22370	.21289	.20276	.19326	.18434	.17597
43	.28435	.27013	.25683	.24436	.23268	.22172	.21143	.20177	.19270	.18416
44	.29407	.27975	.26633	.25373	.24191	.23081	.22038	.21057	.20134	.19265
45	.30402	.28961	.27608	.26337	.25142	.24019	.22962	.21966	.21028	.20144
46	.31420	.29970	.28608	.27326	.26120	.24983	.23913	.22904	.21951	.21053

TABLE S
BASED ON LIFE TABLE 80CNSMT
SINGLE LIFE REMAINDER FACTORS
APPLICABLE AFTER APRIL 30, 1989, AND BEFORE MAY 1, 1999
INTEREST RATE

AGE	*4.2%*	*4.4%*	*4.6%*	*4.8%*	*5.0%*	*5.2%*	*5.4%*	*5.6%*	*5.8%*	*6.0%*
47	.32460	.31004	.29632	.28341	.27123	.25975	.24892	.23870	.22904	.21991
48	.33521	.32058	.30679	.29379	.28151	.26992	.25897	.24862	.23883	.22957
49	.34599	.33132	.31746	.30438	.29201	.28032	.26926	.25879	.24888	.23949
50	.35695	.34224	.32833	.31518	.30273	.29094	.27978	.26921	.25918	.24966
51	.36809	.35335	.33940	.32619	.31367	.30180	.29055	.27987	.26973	.26010
52	.37944	.36468	.35070	.33744	.32486	.31292	.30158	.29081	.28057	.27083
53	.39098	.37622	.36222	.34892	.33629	.32429	.31288	.30203	.29170	.28186
54	.40269	.38794	.37393	.36062	.34795	.33590	.32442	.31349	.30308	.29316
55	.41457	.39985	.38585	.37252	.35983	.34774	.33621	.32522	.31474	.30473
56	.42662	.41194	.39796	.38464	.37193	.35981	.34824	.33720	.32666	.31658
57	.43884	.42422	.41028	.39697	.38426	.37213	.36053	.34945	.33885	.32872
58	.45123	.43668	.42279	.40951	.39682	.38468	.37307	.36196	.35132	.34114
59	.46377	.44931	.43547	.42224	.40958	.39745	.38584	.37471	.36405	.35383
60	.47643	.46206	.44830	.43513	.42250	.41040	.39880	.38767	.37699	.36674
61	.48916	.47491	.46124	.44814	.43556	.42350	.41192	.40080	.39012	.37985
62	.50196	.48783	.47427	.46124	.44874	.43672	.42518	.41408	.40340	.39314
63	.51480	.50081	.48736	.47444	.46201	.45006	.43856	.42749	.41684	.40658
64	.52770	.51386	.50054	.48773	.47540	.46352	.45208	.44105	.43043	.42019
65	.54069	.52701	.51384	.50115	.48892	.47713	.46577	.45480	.44422	.43401
66	.55378	.54029	.52727	.51472	.50262	.49093	.47965	.46876	.45824	.44808
67	.56697	.55368	.54084	.52845	.51648	.50491	.49373	.48293	.47248	.46238
68	.58026	.56717	.55453	.54231	.53049	.51905	.50800	.49729	.48694	.47691
69	.59358	.58072	.56828	.55624	.54459	.53330	.52238	.51179	.50154	.49160
70	.60689	.59427	.58205	.57021	.55874	.54762	.53683	.52638	.51624	.50641
71	.62014	.60778	.59578	.58415	.57287	.56193	.55131	.54100	.53099	.52126
72	.63334	.62123	.60948	.59808	.58700	.57624	.56579	.55563	.54577	.53617
73	.64648	.63465	.62315	.61198	.60112	.59056	.58029	.57030	.56059	.55113
74	.65961	.64806	.63682	.62590	.61527	.60492	.59485	.58504	.57550	.56620
75	.67274	.66149	.65054	.63987	.62948	.61936	.60950	.59990	.59053	.58140
76	.68589	.67495	.66429	.65390	.64377	.63390	.62427	.61487	.60570	.59676
77	.69903	.68841	.67806	.66796	.65811	.64849	.63910	.62993	.62097	.61223
78	.71209	.70182	.69179	.68199	.67242	.66307	.65393	.64501	.63628	.62775
79	.72500	.71507	.70537	.69588	.68660	.67754	.66867	.65999	.65151	.64321
80	.73768	.72809	.71872	.70955	.70058	.69180	.68320	.67479	.66655	.65849
81	.75001	.74077	.73173	.72288	.71422	.70573	.69741	.68926	.68128	.67345
82	.76195	.75306	.74435	.73582	.72746	.71926	.71123	.70335	.69562	.68804
83	.77346	.76491	.75654	.74832	.74026	.73236	.72460	.71699	.70952	.70219
84	.78456	.77636	.76831	.76041	.75265	.74503	.73756	.73021	.72300	.71592
85	.79530	.78743	.77971	.77212	.76466	.75733	.75014	.74306	.73611	.72928
86	.80560	.79806	.79065	.78337	.77621	.76917	.76225	.75544	.74875	.74216
87	.81535	.80813	.80103	.79404	.78717	.78041	.77375	.76720	.76076	.75442
88	.82462	.81771	.81090	.80420	.79760	.79111	.78472	.77842	.77223	.76612
89	.83356	.82694	.82043	.81401	.80769	.80147	.79533	.78929	.78334	.77747
90	.84225	.83593	.82971	.82357	.81753	.81157	.80570	.79991	.79420	.78857
91	.85058	.84455	.83861	.83276	.82698	.82129	.81567	.81013	.80466	.79927
92	.85838	.85263	.84696	.84137	.83585	.83040	.82503	.81973	.81449	.80933
93	.86557	.86009	.85467	.84932	.84405	.83884	.83370	.82862	.82360	.81865

TABLE S
BASED ON LIFE TABLE 80CNSMT
SINGLE LIFE REMAINDER FACTORS
APPLICABLE AFTER APRIL 30, 1989, AND BEFORE MAY 1, 1999
INTEREST RATE

AGE	*4.2%*	*4.4%*	*4.6%*	*4.8%*	*5.0%*	*5.2%*	*5.4%*	*5.6%*	*5.8%*	*6.0%*
94	.87212	.86687	.86169	.85657	.85152	.84653	.84160	.83673	.83192	.82717
95	.87801	.87298	.86801	.86310	.85825	.85345	.84872	.84404	.83941	.83484
96	.88322	.87838	.87360	.86888	.86420	.85959	.85502	.85051	.84605	.84165
97	.88795	.88328	.87867	.87411	.86961	.86515	.86074	.85639	.85208	.84782
98	.89220	.88769	.88323	.87883	.87447	.87016	.86589	.86167	.85750	.85337
99	.89612	.89176	.88745	.88318	.87895	.87478	.87064	.86656	.86251	.85850
100	.89977	.89555	.89136	.88722	.88313	.87908	.87506	.87109	.86716	.86327
101	.90326	.89917	.89511	.89110	.88712	.88318	.87929	.87543	.87161	.86783
102	.90690	.90294	.89901	.89513	.89128	.88746	.88369	.87995	.87624	.87257
103	.91076	.90694	.90315	.89940	.89569	.89200	.88835	.88474	.88116	.87760
104	.91504	.91138	.90775	.90415	.90058	.89704	.89354	.89006	.88661	.88319
105	.92027	.91681	.91337	.90996	.90658	.90322	.89989	.89659	.89331	.89006
106	.92763	.92445	.92130	.91816	.91506	.91197	.90890	.90586	.90284	.89983
107	.93799	.93523	.93249	.92977	.92707	.92438	.92170	.91905	.91641	.91378
108	.95429	.95223	.95018	.94814	.94611	.94409	.94208	.94008	.93809	.93611
109	.97985	.97893	.97801	.97710	.97619	.97529	.97438	.97348	.97259	.97170

TABLE S
BASED ON LIFE TABLE 80CNSMT
SINGLE LIFE REMAINDER FACTORS
APPLICABLE AFTER APRIL 30, 1989, AND BEFORE MAY 1, 1999
INTEREST RATE

AGE	6.2%	6.4%	6.6%	6.8%	7.0%	7.2%	7.4%	7.6%	7.8%	8.0%
0	.03535	.03349	.03183	.03035	.02902	.02783	.02676	.02579	.02492	.02413
1	.02486	.02292	.02119	.01963	.01824	.01699	.01587	.01486	.01395	.01312
2	.02547	.02345	.02164	.02002	.01857	.01727	.01609	.01504	.01408	.01321
3	.02640	.02429	.02241	.02073	.01921	.01785	.01662	.01552	.01451	.01361
4	.02753	.02535	.02339	.02163	.02005	.01863	.01735	.01619	.01514	.01418
5	.02883	.02656	.02453	.02269	.02105	.01956	.01822	.01700	.01590	.01490
6	.03026	.02790	.02578	.02387	.02215	.02060	.01919	.01792	.01677	.01572
7	.03180	.02935	.02714	.02515	.02336	.02174	.02027	.01894	.01773	.01664
8	.03347	.03092	.02863	.02656	.02469	.02300	.02146	.02007	.01881	.01766
9	.03528	.03263	.03025	.02810	.02615	.02438	.02278	.02133	.02000	.01880
10	.03723	.03449	.03201	.02977	.02774	.02590	.02423	.02271	.02133	.02006
11	.03935	.03650	.03393	.03160	.02949	.02757	.02583	.02424	.02279	.02147
12	.04160	.03865	.03598	.03356	.03136	.02936	.02755	.02589	.02438	.02299
13	.04394	.04088	.03811	.03560	.03331	.03123	.02934	.02761	.02603	.02458
14	.04629	.04312	.04025	.03764	.03527	.03311	.03113	.02933	.02768	.02617
15	.04864	.04536	.04238	.03968	.03721	.03496	.03290	.03103	.02930	.02773
16	.05099	.04759	.04451	.04170	.03913	.03679	.03466	.03270	.03090	.02926
17	.05333	.04982	.04662	.04370	.04104	.03861	.03638	.03434	.03247	.03075
18	.05570	.05207	.04875	.04573	.04296	.04044	.03812	.03599	.03404	.03225
19	.05814	.05438	.05095	.04781	.04494	.04231	.03990	.03769	.03565	.03378
20	.06065	.05677	.05321	.04996	.04698	.04424	.04173	.03943	.03731	.03535
21	.06325	.05922	.05554	.05217	.04907	.04623	.04362	.04122	.03901	.03697
22	.06594	.06178	.05797	.05447	.05126	.04831	.04559	.04309	.04078	.03865
23	.06876	.06446	.06051	.05688	.05355	.05048	.04766	.04505	.04265	.04042
24	.07174	.06729	.06321	.05945	.05599	.05281	.04987	.04715	.04465	.04233
25	.07491	.07031	.06609	.06219	.05861	.05530	.05224	.04941	.04680	.04438
26	.07830	.07355	.06918	.06515	.06142	.05799	.05481	.05187	.04915	.04662
27	.08192	.07702	.07250	.06832	.06446	.06090	.05759	.05454	.05170	.04906
28	.08577	.08071	.07603	.07171	.06772	.06402	.06059	.05740	.05445	.05170
29	.08986	.08464	.07981	.07534	.07120	.06736	.06380	.06049	.05742	.05456
30	.09420	.08882	.08383	.07921	.07492	.07095	.06725	.06381	.06061	.05763
31	.09881	.09327	.08812	.08335	.07891	.07479	.07095	.06738	.06405	.06095
32	.10369	.09797	.09267	.08774	.08315	.07888	.07491	.07120	.06774	.06451
33	.10885	.10297	.09750	.09241	.08767	.08325	.07913	.07529	.07170	.06834
34	.11430	.10824	.10261	.09736	.09246	.08790	.08363	.07964	.07592	.07243
35	.12002	.11380	.10800	.10259	.09754	.09282	.08841	.08428	.08041	.07679
36	.12602	.11963	.11366	.10809	.10288	.09800	.09344	.08917	.08516	.08140
37	.13230	.12574	.11961	.11387	.10850	.10347	.09876	.09433	.09018	.08628
38	.13887	.13214	.12584	.11994	.11441	.10922	.10436	.09978	.09549	.09145
39	.14573	.13883	.13237	.12630	.12061	.11527	.11025	.10553	.10109	.09690
40	.15290	.14583	.13920	.13297	.12712	.12162	.11644	.11157	.10698	.10266
41	.16036	.15312	.14633	.13994	.13393	.12827	.12294	.11792	.11318	.10871
42	.16810	.16071	.15375	.14720	.14103	.13522	.12973	.12456	.11967	.11505
43	.17614	.16858	.16146	.15475	.14842	.14245	.13682	.13149	.12645	.12169
44	.18447	.17675	.16948	.16261	.15613	.15000	.14421	.13873	.13355	.12864
45	.19310	.18524	.17780	.17078	.16414	.15787	.15192	.14630	.14096	.13591

TABLE S
BASED ON LIFE TABLE 80CNSMT
SINGLE LIFE REMAINDER FACTORS
APPLICABLE AFTER APRIL 30, 1989, AND BEFORE MAY 1, 1999
INTEREST RATE

AGE	6.2%	6.4%	6.6%	6.8%	7.0%	7.2%	7.4%	7.6%	7.8%	8.0%
46	.20204	.19402	.18644	.17926	.17247	.16604	.15995	.15418	.14870	.14350
47	.21128	.20311	.19538	.18806	.18112	.17454	.16830	.16238	.15676	.15141
48	.22080	.21249	.20462	.19716	.19007	.18335	.17696	.17090	.16513	.15964
49	.23059	.22214	.21413	.20653	.19930	.19244	.18591	.17970	.17379	.16816
50	.24063	.23206	.22391	.21617	.20881	.20180	.19514	.18879	.18274	.17697
51	.25095	.24225	.23398	.22610	.21861	.21147	.20466	.19818	.19199	.18609
52	.26157	.25275	.24436	.23636	.22874	.22147	.21453	.20791	.20159	.19556
53	.27249	.26357	.25505	.24694	.23919	.23180	.22474	.21799	.21154	.20537
54	.28369	.27466	.26604	.25782	.24995	.24244	.23526	.22839	.22181	.21552
55	.29518	.28605	.27734	.26900	.26103	.25341	.24611	.23912	.23243	.22601
56	.30695	.29774	.28893	.28050	.27242	.26469	.25728	.25019	.24338	.23685
57	.31902	.30973	.30084	.29232	.28415	.27632	.26881	.26161	.25469	.24805
58	.33138	.32203	.31306	.30446	.29621	.28829	.28069	.27339	.26637	.25962
59	.34402	.33461	.32558	.31691	.30859	.30059	.29290	.28550	.27839	.27155
60	.35690	.34745	.33836	.32963	.32124	.31317	.30540	.29792	.29073	.28379
61	.36999	.36050	.35137	.34259	.33414	.32601	.31817	.31062	.30334	.29633
62	.38325	.37374	.36458	.35576	.34726	.33907	.33117	.32356	.31621	.30912
63	.39669	.38717	.37799	.36913	.36060	.35236	.34441	.33674	.32933	.32217
64	.41031	.40078	.39159	.38272	.37415	.36588	.35789	.35016	.34270	.33548
65	.42416	.41464	.40545	.39656	.38798	.37968	.37166	.36390	.35639	.34912
66	.43825	.42876	.41958	.41070	.40211	.39380	.38576	.37797	.37043	.36312
67	.45260	.44315	.43399	.42513	.41655	.40824	.40019	.39238	.38482	.37749
68	.46720	.45779	.44868	.43985	.43129	.42299	.41494	.40713	.39956	.39221
69	.48197	.47263	.46357	.45478	.44625	.43798	.42995	.42215	.41458	.40722
70	.49686	.48760	.47861	.46988	.46140	.45316	.44516	.43738	.42983	.42248
71	.51182	.50265	.49374	.48508	.47666	.46847	.46051	.45276	.44523	.43790
72	.52685	.51778	.50896	.50038	.49203	.48390	.47599	.46829	.46079	.45349
73	.54194	.53298	.52426	.51578	.50751	.49946	.49161	.48397	.47652	.46926
74	.55714	.54832	.53972	.53134	.52317	.51520	.50744	.49986	.49247	.48527
75	.57250	.56382	.55536	.54710	.53904	.53118	.52351	.51601	.50870	.50156
76	.58803	.57951	.57120	.56308	.55515	.54740	.53984	.53245	.52522	.51817
77	.60369	.59535	.58720	.57923	.57144	.56383	.55639	.54912	.54200	.53504
78	.61942	.61126	.60329	.59549	.58787	.58040	.57310	.56596	.55896	.55212
79	.63508	.62713	.61935	.61174	.60428	.59698	.58983	.58283	.57597	.56925
80	.65059	.64285	.63527	.62785	.62058	.61345	.60646	.59961	.59290	.58632
81	.66579	.65827	.65090	.64368	.63659	.62965	.62283	.61615	.60959	.60316
82	.68061	.67332	.66616	.65914	.65226	.64550	.63886	.63235	.62595	.61968
83	.69499	.68793	.68099	.67418	.66749	.66092	.65447	.64813	.64191	.63579
84	.70896	.70213	.69541	.68881	.68233	.67595	.66969	.66353	.65748	.65153
85	.72256	.71596	.70947	.70308	.69681	.69063	.68456	.67859	.67271	.66693
86	.73569	.72931	.72305	.71688	.71081	.70484	.69896	.69318	.68748	.68188
87	.74818	.74204	.73599	.73003	.72417	.71839	.71271	.70711	.70159	.69616
88	.76011	.75419	.74836	.74261	.73695	.73137	.72588	.72046	.71512	.70986
89	.77169	.76599	.76037	.75484	.74938	.74400	.73870	.73347	.72831	.72323
90	.78302	.77755	.77215	.76683	.76158	.75640	.75129	.74625	.74128	.73638
91	.79395	.78870	.78352	.77842	.77337	.76840	.76349	.75864	.75385	.74913
92	.80423	.79920	.79423	.78933	.78449	.77971	.77499	.77033	.76572	.76118

TABLE S
BASED ON LIFE TABLE 80CNSMT
SINGLE LIFE REMAINDER FACTORS
APPLICABLE AFTER APRIL 30, 1989, AND BEFORE MAY 1, 1999
INTEREST RATE

AGE	*6.2%*	*6.4%*	*6.6%*	*6.8%*	*7.0%*	*7.2%*	*7.4%*	*7.6%*	*7.8%*	*8.0%*
93	.81377	.80894	.80417	.79946	.79481	.79022	.78568	.78120	.77677	.77239
94	.82247	.81784	.81325	.80873	.80425	.79983	.79547	.79115	.78688	.78266
95	.83033	.82586	.82145	.81709	.81278	.80852	.80431	.80014	.79602	.79195
96	.83729	.83298	.82872	.82451	.82034	.81622	.81215	.80812	.80414	.80019
97	.84361	.83944	.83532	.83124	.82721	.82322	.81927	.81537	.81151	.80769
98	.84929	.84525	.84126	.83730	.83339	.82952	.82569	.82190	.81815	.81443
99	.85454	.85062	.84674	.84290	.83910	.83534	.83161	.82792	.82427	.82066
100	.85942	.85561	.85184	.84810	.84440	.84074	.83711	.83352	.82997	.82644
101	.86408	.86037	.85670	.85306	.84946	.84589	.84236	.83886	.83539	.83196
102	.86894	.86534	.86177	.85823	.85473	.85126	.84782	.84442	.84104	.83770
103	.87408	.87060	.86714	.86371	.86032	.85695	.85362	.85031	.84703	.84378
104	.87980	.87644	.87311	.86980	.86653	.86328	.86005	.85686	.85369	.85054
105	.88684	.88363	.88046	.87731	.87418	.87108	.86800	.86494	.86191	.85890
106	.89685	.89389	.89095	.88804	.88514	.88226	.87940	.87656	.87374	.87094
107	.91117	.90858	.90600	.90344	.90089	.89836	.89584	.89334	.89085	.88838
108	.93414	.93217	.93022	.92828	.92634	.92442	.92250	.92060	.91870	.91681
109	.97081	.96992	.96904	.96816	.96729	.96642	.96555	.96468	.96382	.96296

TABLE S
BASED ON LIFE TABLE 80CNSMT
SINGLE LIFE REMAINDER FACTORS
APPLICABLE AFTER APRIL 30, 1989, AND BEFORE MAY 1, 1999
INTEREST RATE

AGE	8.2%	8.4%	8.6%	8.8%	9.0%	9.2%	9.4%	9.6%	9.8%	10.0%
0	.02341	.02276	.02217	.02163	.02114	.02069	.02027	.01989	.01954	.01922
1	.01237	.01170	.01108	.01052	.01000	.00953	.00910	.00871	.00834	.00801
2	.01243	.01172	.01107	.01048	.00994	.00944	.00899	.00857	.00819	.00784
3	.01278	.01203	.01135	.01073	.01016	.00964	.00916	.00872	.00832	.00795
4	.01332	.01253	.01182	.01116	.01056	.01001	.00951	.00904	.00862	.00822
5	.01400	.01317	.01241	.01172	.01109	.01051	.00998	.00949	.00904	.00862
6	.01477	.01390	.01310	.01238	.01171	.01110	.01054	.01002	.00954	.00910
7	.01563	.01472	.01389	.01312	.01242	.01178	.01118	.01064	.01013	.00966
8	.01660	.01564	.01477	.01396	.01322	.01254	.01192	.01134	.01081	.01031
9	.01770	.01669	.01577	.01492	.01414	.01342	.01276	.01216	.01159	.01107
10	.01891	.01785	.01688	.01599	.01517	.01442	.01372	.01308	.01249	.01194
11	.02026	.01915	.01814	.01720	.01634	.01555	.01481	.01414	.01351	.01293
12	.02173	.02056	.01950	.01852	.01761	.01678	.01601	.01529	.01463	.01402
13	.02326	.02204	.02092	.01989	.01895	.01807	.01726	.01651	.01582	.01517
14	.02478	.02351	.02234	.02126	.02027	.01935	.01850	.01771	.01698	.01630
15	.02628	.02495	.02372	.02259	.02155	.02058	.01969	.01886	.01810	.01738
16	.02774	.02635	.02507	.02388	.02279	.02178	.02084	.01997	.01917	.01842
17	.02917	.02772	.02637	.02513	.02399	.02293	.02194	.02103	.02018	.01940
18	.03059	.02907	.02767	.02637	.02517	.02406	.02302	.02207	.02118	.02035
19	.03205	.03046	.02899	.02763	.02637	.02521	.02412	.02312	.02218	.02131
20	.03355	.03188	.03035	.02892	.02760	.02638	.02524	.02419	.02320	.02229
21	.03509	.03334	.03173	.03024	.02886	.02758	.02638	.02527	.02424	.02328
22	.03669	.03487	.03318	.03162	.03017	.02882	.02757	.02640	.02532	.02430
23	.03837	.03646	.03470	.03306	.03154	.03013	.02881	.02759	.02644	.02538
24	.04018	.03819	.03634	.03463	.03303	.03155	.03016	.02888	.02767	.02655
25	.04214	.04006	.03812	.03633	.03465	.03309	.03164	.03029	.02902	.02784
26	.04428	.04210	.04008	.03820	.03644	.03481	.03328	.03186	.03052	.02928
27	.04662	.04434	.04223	.04025	.03841	.03670	.03509	.03360	.03219	.03088
28	.04915	.04677	.04456	.04249	.04056	.03876	.03708	.03550	.03403	.03264
29	.05189	.04941	.04709	.04493	.04291	.04102	.03925	.03760	.03604	.03458
30	.05485	.05226	.04984	.04757	.04546	.04348	.04162	.03988	.03825	.03671
31	.05805	.05535	.05282	.05045	.04824	.04616	.04421	.04238	.04067	.03905
32	.06149	.05867	.05603	.05356	.05124	.04906	.04702	.04510	.04329	.04160
33	.06520	.06226	.05950	.05692	.05449	.05221	.05007	.04806	.04616	.04438
34	.06916	.06609	.06322	.06052	.05799	.05560	.05336	.05125	.04926	.04738
35	.07339	.07020	.06720	.06439	.06174	.05925	.05690	.05469	.05260	.05063
36	.07787	.07455	.07143	.06850	.06573	.06313	.06068	.05836	.05617	.05411
37	.08262	.07917	.07593	.07287	.06999	.06727	.06470	.06228	.05999	.05783
38	.08765	.08407	.08069	.07751	.07451	.07167	.06899	.06646	.06407	.06180
39	.09296	.08925	.08574	.08243	.07931	.07635	.07356	.07092	.06841	.06604
40	.09858	.09472	.09109	.08765	.08440	.08132	.07841	.07565	.07303	.07055
41	.10449	.10050	.09673	.09316	.08978	.08658	.08355	.08067	.07794	.07535
42	.11069	.10656	.10265	.09895	.09544	.09212	.08896	.08596	.08312	.08041
43	.11718	.11291	.10887	.10503	.10140	.09794	.09466	.09154	.08858	.08576
44	.12399	.11958	.11540	.11143	.10766	.10407	.10067	.09743	.09434	.09141
45	.13111	.12656	.12224	.11814	.11423	.11052	.10699	.10362	.10042	.09736
46	.13856	.13387	.12941	.12516	.12113	.11728	.11362	.11013	.10680	.10363

TABLE S
BASED ON LIFE TABLE 80CNSMT
SINGLE LIFE REMAINDER FACTORS
APPLICABLE AFTER APRIL 30, 1989, AND BEFORE MAY 1, 1999
INTEREST RATE

AGE	8.2%	8.4%	8.6%	8.8%	9.0%	9.2%	9.4%	9.6%	9.8%	10.0%
47	.14633	.14150	.13690	.13252	.12835	.12438	.12059	.11697	.11352	.11022
48	.15442	.14945	.14471	.14020	.13589	.13179	.12787	.12412	.12055	.11713
49	.16280	.15769	.15281	.14816	.14373	.13949	.13544	.13157	.12787	.12433
50	.17147	.16622	.16121	.15643	.15186	.14749	.14331	.13931	.13548	.13182
51	.18045	.17507	.16993	.16501	.16030	.15580	.15150	.14737	.14342	.13963
52	.18979	.18427	.17899	.17394	.16911	.16448	.16004	.15579	.15172	.14780
53	.19947	.19383	.18842	.18324	.17828	.17352	.16896	.16458	.16038	.15635
54	.20950	.20372	.19819	.19288	.18779	.18291	.17822	.17372	.16940	.16524
55	.21986	.21397	.20831	.20288	.19767	.19266	.18785	.18322	.17878	.17450
56	.23058	.22457	.21879	.21324	.20791	.20278	.19785	.19310	.18854	.18414
57	.24167	.23554	.22965	.22399	.21854	.21329	.20824	.20338	.19870	.19419
58	.25314	.24690	.24090	.23512	.22956	.22420	.21904	.21407	.20927	.20464
59	.26497	.25863	.25252	.24664	.24097	.23550	.23023	.22515	.22024	.21551
60	.27712	.27068	.26448	.25849	.25272	.24716	.24178	.23659	.23158	.22674
61	.28956	.28304	.27674	.27067	.26480	.25913	.25366	.24837	.24325	.23831
62	.30228	.29567	.28929	.28312	.27717	.27141	.26584	.26045	.25524	.25020
63	.31525	.30857	.30211	.29586	.28982	.28397	.27832	.27284	.26754	.26240
64	.32851	.32176	.31522	.30890	.30278	.29685	.29111	.28555	.28016	.27493
65	.34209	.33528	.32868	.32229	.31610	.31010	.30429	.29865	.29317	.28787
66	.35604	.34918	.34253	.33609	.32983	.32377	.31788	.31217	.30663	.30124
67	.37037	.36347	.35678	.35028	.34398	.33786	.33191	.32614	.32053	.31508
68	.38508	.37815	.37142	.36489	.35854	.35237	.34638	.34055	.33488	.32937
69	.40008	.39313	.38638	.37982	.37344	.36724	.36120	.35533	.34961	.34405
70	.41533	.40838	.40162	.39504	.38864	.38241	.37634	.37043	.36468	.35907
71	.43076	.42382	.41705	.41047	.40405	.39780	.39171	.38578	.38000	.37436
72	.44638	.43945	.43269	.42611	.41969	.41344	.40733	.40138	.39558	.38991
73	.46218	.45527	.44854	.44197	.43556	.42931	.42321	.41725	.41143	.40575
74	.47823	.47137	.46466	.45812	.45173	.44549	.43940	.43345	.42763	.42195
75	.49459	.48777	.48112	.47462	.46826	.46205	.45598	.45004	.44424	.43856
76	.51127	.50452	.49793	.49148	.48517	.47900	.47297	.46706	.46129	.45563
77	.52823	.52157	.51505	.50867	.50243	.49632	.49033	.48447	.47873	.47311
78	.54541	.53885	.53242	.52613	.51996	.51392	.50800	.50220	.49652	.49094
79	.56267	.55621	.54989	.54369	.53762	.53166	.52582	.52009	.51448	.50897
80	.57987	.57354	.56733	.56125	.55527	.54941	.54366	.53802	.53248	.52705
81	.59685	.59065	.58457	.57860	.57274	.56699	.56134	.55579	.55035	.54499
82	.61351	.60746	.60151	.59567	.58993	.58429	.57875	.57331	.56796	.56270
83	.62978	.62387	.61806	.61236	.60675	.60123	.59581	.59047	.58523	.58007
84	.64567	.63992	.63426	.62869	.62321	.61783	.61253	.60731	.60218	.59713
85	.66125	.65565	.65014	.64472	.63938	.63413	.62896	.62387	.61886	.61392
86	.67636	.67092	.66557	.66030	.65511	.65000	.64496	.64000	.63511	.63030
87	.69081	.68554	.68034	.67522	.67018	.66520	.66031	.65548	.65071	.64602
88	.70468	.69957	.69453	.68956	.68466	.67983	.67507	.67037	.66574	.66117
89	.71821	.71326	.70838	.70357	.69882	.69414	.68952	.68495	.68045	.67601
90	.73153	.72676	.72204	.71739	.71280	.70827	.70379	.69938	.69502	.69071
91	.74447	.73986	.73532	.73083	.72640	.72202	.71770	.71343	.70921	.70504
92	.75669	.75225	.74787	.74354	.73927	.73504	.73087	.72674	.72267	.71864
93	.76807	.76379	.75957	.75540	.75127	.74719	.74317	.73918	.73524	.73135

TABLE S
BASED ON LIFE TABLE 80CNSMT
SINGLE LIFE REMAINDER FACTORS
APPLICABLE AFTER APRIL 30, 1989, AND BEFORE MAY 1, 1999
INTEREST RATE

AGE	8.2%	8.4%	8.6%	8.8%	9.0%	9.2%	9.4%	9.6%	9.8%	10.0%
94	.77849	.77437	.77030	.76627	.76229	.75835	.75446	.75061	.74680	.74303
95	.78792	.78394	.78001	.77611	.77226	.76845	.76468	.76096	.75727	.75362
96	.79630	.79244	.78863	.78485	.78112	.77742	.77377	.77015	.76657	.76303
97	.80391	.80016	.79646	.79280	.78917	.78559	.78203	.77852	.77504	.77160
98	.81076	.80712	.80352	.79996	.79643	.79294	.78948	.78606	.78267	.77931
99	.81709	.81354	.81004	.80657	.80313	.79972	.79635	.79302	.78971	.78644
100	.82296	.81950	.81609	.81270	.80934	.80602	.80273	.79947	.79624	.79304
101	.82855	.82518	.82185	.81854	.81526	.81201	.80880	.80561	.80245	.79932
102	.83438	.83110	.82785	.82462	.82142	.81826	.81512	.81200	.80892	.80586
103	.84056	.83737	.83420	.83106	.82795	.82487	.82181	.81878	.81577	.81279
104	.84743	.84433	.84127	.83822	.83521	.83221	.82924	.82630	.82338	.82048
105	.85591	.85295	.85001	.84709	.84419	.84132	.83846	.83563	.83282	.83003
106	.86816	.86540	.86266	.85993	.85723	.85454	.85187	.84922	.84659	.84397
107	.88592	.88348	.88105	.87863	.87623	.87384	.87147	.86911	.86676	.86443
108	.91493	.91306	.91119	.90934	.90749	.90566	.90383	.90201	.90020	.89840
109	.96211	.96125	.96041	.95956	.95872	.95788	.95704	.95620	.95537	.95455

TABLE S
BASED ON LIFE TABLE 80CNSMT
SINGLE LIFE REMAINDER FACTORS
APPLICABLE AFTER APRIL 30, 1989, AND BEFORE MAY 1, 1999
INTEREST RATE

AGE	10.2%	10.4%	10.6%	10.8%	11.0%	11.2%	11.4%	11.6%	11.8%	12.0%
0	.01891	.01864	.01838	.01814	.01791	.01770	.01750	.01732	.01715	.01698
1	.00770	.00741	.00715	.00690	.00667	.00646	.00626	.00608	.00590	.00574
2	.00751	.00721	.00693	.00667	.00643	.00620	.00600	.00580	.00562	.00544
3	.00760	.00728	.00699	.00671	.00646	.00622	.00600	.00579	.00560	.00541
4	.00786	.00752	.00721	.00692	.00665	.00639	.00616	.00594	.00573	.00554
5	.00824	.00788	.00755	.00724	.00695	.00668	.00643	.00620	.00598	.00578
6	.00869	.00832	.00796	.00764	.00733	.00705	.00678	.00654	.00630	.00608
7	.00923	.00883	.00846	.00811	.00779	.00749	.00720	.00694	.00669	.00646
8	.00986	.00943	.00904	.00867	.00833	.00801	.00771	.00743	.00716	.00692
9	.01059	.01014	.00972	.00933	.00897	.00863	.00831	.00801	.00773	.00747
10	.01142	.01095	.01051	.01009	.00971	.00935	.00901	.00869	.00840	.00812
11	.01239	.01189	.01142	.01098	.01057	.01019	.00983	.00950	.00918	.00889
12	.01345	.01292	.01243	.01197	.01154	.01113	.01075	.01040	.01007	.00975
13	.01457	.01401	.01349	.01300	.01255	.01212	.01172	.01135	.01100	.01067
14	.01567	.01508	.01453	.01402	.01354	.01309	.01267	.01227	.01190	.01155
15	.01672	.01610	.01552	.01498	.01448	.01400	.01356	.01314	.01275	.01238
16	.01772	.01707	.01646	.01589	.01536	.01486	.01439	.01396	.01354	.01315
17	.01866	.01798	.01734	.01674	.01618	.01566	.01516	.01470	.01427	.01386
18	.01958	.01886	.01818	.01755	.01697	.01641	.01590	.01541	.01495	.01452
19	.02050	.01974	.01903	.01837	.01775	.01717	.01662	.01611	.01563	.01517
20	.02143	.02064	.01989	.01919	.01854	.01793	.01735	.01681	.01630	.01582
21	.02238	.02154	.02075	.02002	.01933	.01868	.01807	.01750	.01696	.01646
22	.02336	.02247	.02164	.02087	.02014	.01946	.01882	.01821	.01764	.01711
23	.02438	.02345	.02257	.02176	.02099	.02027	.01959	.01895	.01835	.01778
24	.02550	.02451	.02359	.02273	.02192	.02115	.02044	.01976	.01913	.01853
25	.02673	.02569	.02472	.02381	.02295	.02214	.02138	.02067	.01999	.01936
26	.02811	.02701	.02598	.02502	.02411	.02326	.02246	.02170	.02098	.02031
27	.02965	.02849	.02741	.02639	.02543	.02452	.02367	.02287	.02211	.02140
28	.03134	.03013	.02898	.02790	.02689	.02593	.02503	.02418	.02338	.02262
29	.03322	.03193	.03072	.02958	.02851	.02750	.02654	.02564	.02479	.02398
30	.03527	.03391	.03264	.03143	.03030	.02923	.02821	.02726	.02635	.02550
31	.03753	.03610	.03475	.03348	.03228	.03115	.03008	.02907	.02811	.02720
32	.04000	.03849	.03707	.03573	.03446	.03326	.03213	.03105	.03004	.02907
33	.04269	.04111	.03961	.03819	.03685	.03558	.03438	.03325	.03217	.03115
34	.04561	.04394	.04236	.04087	.03946	.03812	.03685	.03565	.03451	.03342
35	.04877	.04702	.04535	.04378	.04229	.04087	.03953	.03826	.03706	.03591
36	.05215	.05031	.04856	.04690	.04533	.04384	.04242	.04108	.03980	.03859
37	.05578	.05384	.05200	.05025	.04860	.04703	.04553	.04411	.04276	.04148
38	.05965	.05761	.05568	.05385	.05211	.05045	.04888	.04738	.04595	.04460
39	.06379	.06165	.05962	.05770	.05587	.05412	.05247	.05089	.04939	.04795
40	.06820	.06596	.06383	.06181	.05989	.05806	.05631	.05465	.05307	.05155
41	.07288	.07054	.06832	.06620	.06418	.06226	.06042	.05868	.05701	.05541
42	.07784	.07539	.07306	.07085	.06873	.06671	.06479	.06295	.06119	.05952
43	.08308	.08052	.07808	.07576	.07355	.07143	.06941	.06748	.06564	.06387
44	.08861	.08594	.08340	.08097	.07865	.07644	.07432	.07230	.07036	.06851
45	.09445	.09167	.08901	.08648	.08406	.08174	.07953	.07741	.07538	.07343
46	.10060	.09770	.09494	.09230	.08977	.08735	.08503	.08281	.08068	.07865

TABLE S
BASED ON LIFE TABLE 80CNSMT
SINGLE LIFE REMAINDER FACTORS
APPLICABLE AFTER APRIL 30, 1989, AND BEFORE MAY 1, 1999
INTEREST RATE

AGE	10.2%	10.4%	10.6%	10.8%	11.0%	11.2%	11.4%	11.6%	11.8%	12.0%
47	.10707	.10406	.10119	.09843	.09579	.09327	.09085	.08853	.08630	.08417
48	.11386	.11073	.10774	.10487	.10213	.09949	.09697	.09455	.09222	.08999
49	.12094	.11769	.11458	.11160	.10874	.10600	.10337	.10084	.09842	.09609
50	.12831	.12494	.12172	.11862	.11565	.11280	.11006	.10743	.10490	.10247
51	.13600	.13251	.12917	.12596	.12288	.11991	.11706	.11432	.11169	.10915
52	.14405	.14044	.13698	.13366	.13046	.12738	.12442	.12157	.11883	.11619
53	.15247	.14875	.14517	.14172	.13841	.13522	.13215	.12919	.12635	.12360
54	.16124	.15740	.15370	.15014	.14671	.14341	.14023	.13717	.13421	.13136
55	.17039	.16642	.16261	.15893	.15539	.15198	.14868	.14551	.14244	.13948
56	.17991	.17583	.17190	.16811	.16445	.16092	.15752	.15423	.15106	.14799
57	.18984	.18564	.18160	.17769	.17392	.17029	.16677	.16338	.16010	.15692
58	.20018	.19587	.19172	.18770	.18382	.18007	.17645	.17295	.16956	.16628
59	.21093	.20652	.20225	.19812	.19414	.19028	.18655	.18294	.17945	.17606
60	.22206	.21753	.21316	.20893	.20483	.20087	.19703	.19332	.18972	.18624
61	.23353	.22890	.22442	.22009	.21589	.21182	.20788	.20407	.20037	.19678
62	.24532	.24059	.23601	.23158	.22728	.22311	.21907	.21515	.21135	.20767
63	.25742	.25260	.24793	.24339	.23900	.23473	.23060	.22658	.22268	.21890
64	.26987	.26495	.26019	.25556	.25107	.24671	.24248	.23837	.23438	.23050
65	.28271	.27771	.27286	.26815	.26357	.25912	.25480	.25059	.24651	.24254
66	.29601	.29093	.28600	.28120	.27654	.27200	.26760	.26331	.25913	.25507
67	.30978	.30462	.29961	.29474	.29000	.28539	.28090	.27653	.27227	.26813
68	.32401	.31879	.31371	.30877	.30396	.29927	.29471	.29027	.28593	.28171
69	.33863	.33336	.32822	.32322	.31835	.31359	.30896	.30445	.30005	.29576
70	.35361	.34829	.34310	.33804	.33311	.32830	.32361	.31903	.31457	.31021
71	.36886	.36349	.35826	.35316	.34818	.34332	.33858	.33394	.32942	.32500
72	.38439	.37899	.37373	.36858	.36356	.35866	.35387	.34919	.34461	.34015
73	.40021	.39479	.38950	.38432	.37927	.37433	.36950	.36478	.36016	.35565
74	.41639	.41096	.40565	.40046	.39538	.39042	.38556	.38081	.37616	.37161
75	.43301	.42758	.42226	.41706	.41198	.40699	.40212	.39734	.39267	.38809
76	.45009	.44467	.43937	.43417	.42908	.42410	.41921	.41443	.40974	.40514
77	.46761	.46221	.45693	.45175	.44667	.44170	.43682	.43203	.42734	.42274
78	.48548	.48013	.47488	.46973	.46468	.45972	.45486	.45009	.44541	.44082
79	.50356	.49826	.49306	.48795	.48294	.47802	.47319	.46845	.46379	.45922
80	.52171	.51647	.51133	.50628	.50132	.49644	.49166	.48695	.48233	.47779
81	.53974	.53457	.52950	.52451	.51961	.51479	.51006	.50541	.50083	.49633
82	.55753	.55245	.54745	.54254	.53771	.53296	.52828	.52369	.51917	.51472
83	.57500	.57001	.56510	.56026	.55551	.55083	.54623	.54170	.53724	.53285
84	.59216	.58726	.58245	.57770	.57304	.56844	.56391	.55945	.55506	.55074
85	.60906	.60428	.59956	.59492	.59034	.58583	.58139	.57702	.57270	.56845
86	.62555	.62088	.61627	.61173	.60725	.60284	.59849	.59420	.58997	.58580
87	.64139	.63683	.63233	.62790	.62352	.61921	.61495	.61076	.60661	.60253
88	.65666	.65221	.64783	.64350	.63923	.63502	.63086	.62675	.62270	.61871
89	.67163	.66730	.66304	.65882	.65466	.65055	.64650	.64249	.63854	.63463
90	.68646	.68226	.67812	.67402	.66998	.66599	.66204	.65814	.65430	.65049
91	.70093	.69686	.69285	.68888	.68496	.68108	.67725	.67347	.66973	.66604
92	.71466	.71073	.70684	.70300	.69920	.69545	.69173	.68806	.68444	.68085
93	.72750	.72370	.71994	.71622	.71254	.70890	.70530	.70174	.69822	.69474

TABLE S
BASED ON LIFE TABLE 80CNSMT
SINGLE LIFE REMAINDER FACTORS
APPLICABLE AFTER APRIL 30, 1989, AND BEFORE MAY 1, 1999
INTEREST RATE

AGE	*10.2%*	*10.4%*	*10.6%*	*10.8%*	*11.0%*	*11.2%*	*11.4%*	*11.6%*	*11.8%*	*12.0%*
94	.73931	.73562	.73198	.72838	.72481	.72129	.71780	.71434	.71093	.70755
95	.75001	.74644	.74291	.73941	.73595	.73253	.72914	.72579	.72247	.71919
96	.75953	.75606	.75262	.74923	.74586	.74253	.73924	.73598	.73275	.72955
97	.76819	.76481	.76147	.75816	.75489	.75165	.74844	.74526	.74211	.73899
98	.77599	.77270	.76944	.76621	.76302	.75986	.75672	.75362	.75054	.74750
99	.78319	.77998	.77680	.77365	.77053	.76744	.76437	.76134	.75833	.75535
100	.78987	.78673	.78362	.78054	.77748	.77446	.77146	.76849	.76555	.76263
101	.79622	.79315	.79010	.78708	.78409	.78113	.77819	.77528	.77239	.76953
102	.80283	.79983	.79685	.79390	.79097	.78807	.78519	.78234	.77951	.77671
103	.80983	.80690	.80399	.80111	.79825	.79541	.79260	.78981	.78705	.78430
104	.81760	.81475	.81192	.80912	.80633	.80357	.80083	.79810	.79541	.79273
105	.82726	.82451	.82178	.81907	.81638	.81371	.81106	.80843	.80582	.80322
106	.84137	.83879	.83623	.83368	.83115	.82863	.82614	.82366	.82119	.81874
107	.86211	.85981	.85751	.85523	.85297	.85071	.84847	.84624	.84403	.84182
108	.89660	.89481	.89304	.89127	.88950	.88775	.88601	.88427	.88254	.88081
109	.95372	.95290	.95208	.95126	.95045	.94964	.94883	.94803	.94723	.94643

TABLE S
BASED ON LIFE TABLE 80CNSMT
SINGLE LIFE REMAINDER FACTORS
APPLICABLE AFTER APRIL 30, 1989, AND BEFORE MAY 1, 1999
INTEREST RATE

AGE	12.2%	12.4%	12.6%	12.8%	13.0%	13.2%	13.4%	13.6%	13.8%	14.0%
0	.01683	.01669	.01655	.01642	.01630	.01618	.01607	.01596	.01586	.01576
1	.00559	.00544	.00531	.00518	.00506	.00494	.00484	.00473	.00464	.00454
2	.00528	.00513	.00499	.00485	.00473	.00461	.00449	.00439	.00428	.00419
3	.00524	.00508	.00493	.00479	.00465	.00453	.00441	.00429	.00419	.00408
4	.00536	.00519	.00503	.00488	.00473	.00460	.00447	.00435	.00423	.00412
5	.00558	.00540	.00523	.00507	.00492	.00477	.00464	.00451	.00439	.00427
6	.00588	.00569	.00550	.00533	.00517	.00502	.00487	.00473	.00460	.00448
7	.00624	.00604	.00584	.00566	.00549	.00532	.00517	.00502	.00488	.00475
8	.00668	.00646	.00626	.00606	.00588	.00570	.00554	.00538	.00523	.00509
9	.00722	.00699	.00677	.00656	.00636	.00617	.00600	.00583	.00567	.00552
10	.00785	.00761	.00737	.00715	.00694	.00674	.00655	.00637	.00620	.00604
11	.00861	.00835	.00810	.00786	.00764	.00743	.00723	.00704	.00686	.00668
12	.00946	.00918	.00891	.00866	.00843	.00820	.00799	.00779	.00760	.00741
13	.01035	.01006	.00978	.00951	.00927	.00903	.00880	.00859	.00839	.00819
14	.01122	.01091	.01061	.01034	.01007	.00982	.00958	.00936	.00914	.00894
15	.01203	.01171	.01140	.01110	.01082	.01056	.01031	.01007	.00985	.00963
16	.01279	.01244	.01211	.01181	.01151	.01123	.01097	.01072	.01048	.01025
17	.01347	.01311	.01276	.01244	.01213	.01184	.01156	.01130	.01104	.01081
18	.01411	.01373	.01336	.01302	.01270	.01239	.01210	.01182	.01155	.01130
19	.01474	.01434	.01396	.01359	.01325	.01293	.01262	.01233	.01205	.01178
20	.01537	.01494	.01454	.01415	.01379	.01345	.01313	.01282	.01252	.01224
21	.01598	.01553	.01510	.01470	.01432	.01396	.01361	.01329	.01298	.01268
22	.01660	.01613	.01568	.01525	.01485	.01446	.01410	.01375	.01343	.01312
23	.01725	.01674	.01627	.01581	.01539	.01498	.01460	.01423	.01388	.01355
24	.01796	.01742	.01692	.01644	.01599	.01556	.01515	.01476	.01439	.01404
25	.01876	.01819	.01765	.01714	.01666	.01621	.01577	.01536	.01497	.01460
26	.01967	.01907	.01850	.01796	.01745	.01696	.01650	.01606	.01565	.01525
27	.02072	.02008	.01948	.01890	.01836	.01784	.01735	.01688	.01644	.01601
28	.02190	.02122	.02057	.01996	.01938	.01883	.01831	.01781	.01734	.01689
29	.02322	.02249	.02181	.02116	.02054	.01996	.01940	.01887	.01836	.01788
30	.02469	.02392	.02319	.02250	.02184	.02122	.02062	.02006	.01952	.01900
31	.02634	.02552	.02475	.02401	.02331	.02264	.02201	.02140	.02083	.02028
32	.02816	.02729	.02647	.02568	.02494	.02423	.02355	.02291	.02229	.02170
33	.03018	.02926	.02838	.02755	.02675	.02600	.02528	.02459	.02393	.02331
34	.03239	.03142	.03048	.02960	.02875	.02795	.02718	.02645	.02575	.02508
35	.03482	.03378	.03279	.03185	.03095	.03009	.02928	.02850	.02775	.02704
36	.03743	.03633	.03528	.03428	.03333	.03242	.03155	.03072	.02992	.02916
37	.04026	.03909	.03798	.03692	.03591	.03494	.03401	.03313	.03228	.03147
38	.04330	.04207	.04089	.03977	.03869	.03767	.03668	.03574	.03484	.03398
39	.04658	.04528	.04403	.04284	.04170	.04061	.03957	.03857	.03762	.03670
40	.05011	.04873	.04741	.04615	.04495	.04379	.04269	.04163	.04061	.03964
41	.05389	.05244	.05104	.04971	.04844	.04721	.04604	.04492	.04384	.04281
42	.05791	.05638	.05491	.05350	.05216	.05086	.04962	.04844	.04729	.04620
43	.06219	.06057	.05902	.05754	.05612	.05475	.05344	.05218	.05098	.04981
44	.06673	.06503	.06340	.06184	.06034	.05890	.05752	.05619	.05491	.05368
45	.07157	.06978	.06806	.06642	.06484	.06332	.06186	.06046	.05911	.05781
46	.07669	.07481	.07301	.07128	.06962	.06802	.06649	.06501	.06358	.06221

TABLE S
BASED ON LIFE TABLE 80CNSMT
SINGLE LIFE REMAINDER FACTORS
APPLICABLE AFTER APRIL 30, 1989, AND BEFORE MAY 1, 1999
INTEREST RATE

AGE	12.2%	12.4%	12.6%	12.8%	13.0%	13.2%	13.4%	13.6%	13.8%	14.0%
47	.08212	.08015	.07826	.07645	.07470	.07302	.07140	.06984	.06834	.06690
48	.08784	.08578	.08380	.08190	.08006	.07830	.07660	.07496	.07338	.07186
49	.09384	.09169	.08961	.08762	.08570	.08384	.08206	.08034	.07868	.07708
50	.10013	.09787	.09570	.09361	.09160	.08966	.08779	.08598	.08424	.08256
51	.10671	.10436	.10209	.09991	.09780	.09577	.09381	.09192	.09009	.08832
52	.11365	.11120	.10883	.10655	.10435	.10222	.10017	.09819	.09628	.09442
53	.12095	.11840	.11593	.11355	.11126	.10904	.10689	.10482	.10282	.10088
54	.12860	.12595	.12338	.12090	.11851	.11619	.11396	.11179	.10970	.10767
55	.13663	.13386	.13120	.12862	.12613	.12372	.12138	.11912	.11694	.11482
56	.14503	.14217	.13940	.13672	.13413	.13162	.12919	.12683	.12456	.12235
57	.15385	.15089	.14801	.14523	.14254	.13994	.13741	.13496	.13259	.13029
58	.16311	.16004	.15706	.15418	.15139	.14868	.14606	.14352	.14105	.13866
59	.17279	.16961	.16654	.16355	.16066	.15786	.15514	.15250	.14994	.14745
60	.18286	.17958	.17640	.17332	.17033	.16743	.16462	.16188	.15922	.15664
61	.19330	.18992	.18665	.18347	.18038	.17738	.17447	.17164	.16889	.16622
62	.20409	.20061	.19724	.19396	.19078	.18768	.18467	.18175	.17891	.17614
63	.21522	.21165	.20818	.20480	.20152	.19833	.19523	.19221	.18928	.18642
64	.22672	.22306	.21949	.21602	.21265	.20937	.20617	.20306	.20003	.19708
65	.23867	.23491	.23125	.22769	.22423	.22085	.21757	.21437	.21125	.20821
66	.25112	.24727	.24353	.23988	.23632	.23286	.22948	.22619	.22299	.21986
67	.26409	.26016	.25633	.25260	.24896	.24541	.24195	.23857	.23528	.23206
68	.27760	.27359	.26968	.26586	.26214	.25851	.25497	.25151	.24814	.24484
69	.29157	.28748	.28350	.27961	.27581	.27211	.26849	.26495	.26150	.25812
70	.30596	.30181	.29775	.29379	.28992	.28614	.28245	.27884	.27532	.27187
71	.32069	.31648	.31236	.30833	.30440	.30055	.29679	.29312	.28952	.28600
72	.33578	.33151	.32733	.32325	.31925	.31535	.31152	.30778	.30412	.30054
73	.35123	.34691	.34269	.33855	.33450	.33054	.32666	.32286	.31914	.31550
74	.36715	.36279	.35852	.35434	.35024	.34623	.34230	.33845	.33468	.33098
75	.38360	.37921	.37491	.37069	.36656	.36250	.35853	.35464	.35082	.34708
76	.40064	.39623	.39190	.38765	.38349	.37941	.37540	.37148	.36762	.36384
77	.41823	.41381	.40947	.40521	.40103	.39692	.39290	.38895	.38507	.38126
78	.43632	.43189	.42755	.42329	.41910	.41499	.41095	.40698	.40309	.39926
79	.45473	.45032	.44599	.44173	.43755	.43344	.42940	.42543	.42153	.41770
80	.47333	.46894	.46463	.46040	.45623	.45213	.44811	.44414	.44025	.43642
81	.49191	.48755	.48328	.47907	.47493	.47085	.46684	.46290	.45902	.45520
82	.51034	.50603	.50179	.49762	.49351	.48947	.48549	.48157	.47772	.47392
83	.52852	.52427	.52008	.51595	.51189	.50788	.50394	.50006	.49623	.49246
84	.54648	.54228	.53815	.53407	.53006	.52610	.52221	.51836	.51458	.51084
85	.56426	.56013	.55606	.55205	.54810	.54420	.54035	.53656	.53282	.52913
86	.58169	.57764	.57364	.56970	.56581	.56197	.55818	.55445	.55076	.54713
87	.59850	.59452	.59060	.58673	.58291	.57913	.57541	.57174	.56811	.56453
88	.61476	.61086	.60702	.60322	.59947	.59577	.59212	.58851	.58494	.58142
89	.63078	.62697	.62321	.61950	.61583	.61220	.60862	.60508	.60159	.59813
90	.64674	.64302	.63935	.63573	.63215	.62861	.62511	.62165	.61823	.61485
91	.66238	.65877	.65520	.65167	.64819	.64474	.64133	.63795	.63462	.63132
92	.67730	.67379	.67032	.66689	.66350	.66014	.65682	.65354	.65029	.64708
93	.69130	.68789	.68452	.68119	.67789	.67463	.67140	.66820	.66504	.66191

TABLE S
BASED ON LIFE TABLE 80CNSMT
SINGLE LIFE REMAINDER FACTORS
APPLICABLE AFTER APRIL 30, 1989, AND BEFORE MAY 1, 1999
INTEREST RATE

AGE	*12.2%*	*12.4%*	*12.6%*	*12.8%*	*13.0%*	*13.2%*	*13.4%*	*13.6%*	*13.8%*	*14.0%*
94	.70421	.70090	.69762	.69438	.69118	.68800	.68486	.68175	.67867	.67563
95	.71594	.71272	.70954	.70639	.70326	.70017	.69712	.69409	.69109	.68812
96	.72638	.72325	.72014	.71707	.71403	.71101	.70803	.70507	.70215	.69925
97	.73590	.73285	.72982	.72682	.72385	.72090	.71799	.71510	.71224	.70941
98	.74448	.74149	.73853	.73560	.73269	.72981	.72696	.72414	.72134	.71856
99	.75240	.74948	.74658	.74371	.74086	.73805	.73525	.73248	.72974	.72702
100	.75974	.75687	.75403	.75121	.74842	.74566	.74292	.74020	.73751	.73484
101	.76669	.76388	.76109	.75833	.75559	.75287	.75018	.74751	.74486	.74223
102	.77393	.77117	.76844	.76573	.76304	.76037	.75773	.75511	.75251	.74993
103	.78158	.77888	.77620	.77355	.77091	.76830	.76571	.76313	.76058	.75805
104	.79007	.78743	.78482	.78222	.77964	.77709	.77455	.77203	.76953	.76705
105	.80065	.79809	.79556	.79304	.79054	.78805	.78559	.78314	.78071	.77829
106	.81631	.81389	.81149	.80911	.80674	.80438	.80204	.79972	.79741	.79511
107	.83963	.83745	.83529	.83313	.83099	.82886	.82674	.82463	.82254	.82045
108	.87910	.87739	.87569	.87400	.87232	.87064	.86897	.86731	.86566	.86401
109	.94563	.94484	.94405	.94326	.94248	.94170	.94092	.94014	.93937	.93860

TABLE U(1)
BASED ON LIFE TABLE 80CNSMT
UNITRUST SINGLE LIFE REMAINDER FACTORS
APPLICABLE AFTER APRIL 30, 1989, AND BEFORE MAY 1, 1999
ADJUSTED PAYOUT RATE

AGE	4.2%	4.4%	4.6%	4.8%	5.0%	5.2%	5.4%	5.6%	5.8%	6.0%
0	.06797	.06181	.05645	.05177	.04768	.04410	.04096	.03820	.03578	.03364
1	.05881	.05243	.04686	.04199	.03773	.03400	.03072	.02784	.02531	.02308
2	.06049	.05394	.04821	.04319	.03880	.03494	.03155	.02856	.02593	.02361
3	.06252	.05579	.04990	.04473	.04020	.03621	.03270	.02961	.02688	.02446
4	.06479	.05788	.05182	.04650	.04183	.03771	.03408	.03087	.02804	.02553
5	.06724	.06016	.05393	.04845	.04363	.03937	.03562	.03230	.02936	.02675
6	.06984	.06257	.05618	.05054	.04557	.04117	.03729	.03385	.03080	.02809
7	.07259	.06513	.05856	.05276	.04764	.04310	.03909	.03552	.03236	.02954
8	.07548	.06784	.06109	.05513	.04985	.04517	.04102	.03733	.03405	.03113
9	.07854	.07071	.06378	.05765	.05221	.04738	.04310	.03928	.03588	.03285
10	.08176	.07374	.06663	.06033	.05473	.04976	.04533	.04138	.03786	.03471
11	.08517	.07695	.06966	.06319	.05743	.05230	.04772	.04364	.04000	.03673
12	.08872	.08031	.07284	.06619	.06026	.05498	.05026	.04604	.04227	.03889
13	.09238	.08378	.07612	.06929	.06320	.05776	.05289	.04853	.04463	.04113
14	.09608	.08728	.07943	.07243	.06616	.06056	.05554	.05104	.04701	.04338
15	.09981	.09081	.08276	.07557	.06914	.06337	.05820	.05356	.04938	.04563
16	.10356	.09435	.08612	.07874	.07213	.06619	.06086	.05607	.05176	.04787
17	.10733	.09792	.08949	.08192	.07513	.06902	.06353	.05858	.05413	.05010
18	.11117	.10155	.09291	.08515	.07817	.07189	.06623	.06113	.05652	.05236
19	.11509	.10526	.09642	.08847	.08130	.07484	.06901	.06375	.05899	.05469
20	.11913	.10908	.10003	.09188	.08452	.07788	.07188	.06645	.06154	.05708
21	.12326	.11300	.10375	.09539	.08784	.08101	.07483	.06923	.06416	.05955
22	.12753	.11705	.10758	.09902	.09127	.08426	.07789	.07212	.06688	.06212
23	.13195	.12125	.11156	.10279	.09484	.08763	.08109	.07514	.06973	.06481
24	.13655	.12563	.11573	.10675	.09860	.09119	.08446	.07833	.07274	.06766
25	.14136	.13022	.12010	.11091	.10255	.09495	.08802	.08171	.07595	.07069
26	.14640	.13504	.12471	.11530	.10674	.09893	.09181	.08531	.07937	.07394
27	.15169	.14011	.12956	.11994	.11117	.10316	.09584	.08915	.08302	.07742
28	.15721	.14542	.13465	.12482	.11583	.10762	.10010	.09322	.08691	.08112
29	.16299	.15097	.13999	.12994	.12075	.11233	.10461	.09753	.09104	.08507
30	.16901	.15678	.14559	.13533	.12592	.11729	.10937	.10210	.09541	.08926
31	.17531	.16287	.15146	.14099	.13137	.12254	.11441	.10694	.10006	.09372
32	.18186	.16921	.15759	.14691	.13709	.12804	.11972	.11205	.10497	.09844
33	.18869	.17584	.16401	.15312	.14309	.13384	.12531	.11744	.11017	.10345
34	.19578	.18273	.17070	.15961	.14937	.13992	.13119	.12312	.11565	.10874
35	.20315	.18990	.17767	.16637	.15593	.14628	.13735	.12908	.12142	.11431
36	.21076	.19732	.18490	.17340	.16276	.15291	.14377	.13531	.12745	.12016
37	.21863	.20501	.19239	.18071	.16987	.15982	.15049	.14182	.13377	.12628
38	.22676	.21296	.20016	.18828	.17725	.16701	.15748	.14862	.14037	.13269
39	.23515	.22118	.20820	.19614	.18492	.17448	.16476	.15571	.14727	.13940
40	.24379	.22967	.21652	.20428	.19288	.18225	.17234	.16310	.15447	.14641
41	.25270	.23842	.22511	.21270	.20112	.19031	.18021	.17078	.16197	.15372
42	.26184	.24742	.23395	.22137	.20962	.19864	.18836	.17875	.16975	.16132
43	.27123	.25666	.24305	.23031	.21840	.20724	.19679	.18700	.17782	.16921
44	.28085	.26616	.25241	.23952	.22745	.21613	.20551	.19554	.18618	.17739
45	.29072	.27591	.26203	.24901	.23678	.22530	.21452	.20438	.19485	.18589
46	.30082	.28591	.27191	.25875	.24639	.23476	.22381	.21352	.20382	.19468

TABLE U(1)
BASED ON LIFE TABLE 80CNSMT
UNITRUST SINGLE LIFE REMAINDER FACTORS
APPLICABLE AFTER APRIL 30, 1989, AND BEFORE MAY 1, 1999
ADJUSTED PAYOUT RATE

AGE	4.2%	4.4%	4.6%	4.8%	5.0%	5.2%	5.4%	5.6%	5.8%	6.0%
47	.31116	.29616	.28204	.26877	.25626	.24449	.23340	.22295	.21309	.20379
48	.32171	.30663	.29241	.27902	.26640	.25449	.24326	.23265	.22264	.21318
49	.33245	.31730	.30300	.28950	.27676	.26473	.25336	.24262	.23246	.22285
50	.34338	.32816	.31379	.30020	.28735	.27521	.26371	.25283	.24253	.23277
51	.35449	.33923	.32479	.31112	.29818	.28593	.27431	.26331	.25287	.24297
52	.36582	.35053	.33603	.32230	.30927	.29692	.28520	.27408	.26352	.25349
53	.37736	.36205	.34751	.33372	.32063	.30819	.29637	.28514	.27446	.26431
54	.38909	.37376	.35921	.34537	.33221	.31970	.30780	.29647	.28569	.27542
55	.40099	.38568	.37111	.35724	.34404	.33146	.31949	.30807	.29719	.28681
56	.41308	.39779	.38322	.36934	.35610	.34348	.33143	.31994	.30898	.29851
57	.42536	.41011	.39555	.38167	.36841	.35575	.34366	.33210	.32106	.31051
58	.43781	.42262	.40810	.39422	.38096	.36828	.35615	.34454	.33344	.32281
59	.45043	.43530	.42083	.40698	.39373	.38104	.36888	.35724	.34609	.33540
60	.46318	.44813	.43372	.41992	.40668	.39400	.38183	.37017	.35898	.34824
61	.47602	.46107	.44674	.43299	.41979	.40713	.39497	.38329	.37207	.36129
62	.48893	.47410	.45986	.44617	.43303	.42039	.40825	.39657	.38534	.37454
63	.50190	.48720	.47306	.45946	.44638	.43379	.42168	.41001	.39878	.38796
64	.51494	.50038	.48636	.47286	.45986	.44733	.43526	.42362	.41240	.40158
65	.52808	.51368	.49980	.48641	.47350	.46104	.44903	.43743	.42624	.41544
66	.54134	.52711	.51338	.50013	.48733	.47496	.46302	.45148	.44033	.42956
67	.55471	.54068	.52712	.51401	.50134	.48908	.47723	.46577	.45467	.44394
68	.56820	.55437	.54100	.52805	.51552	.50339	.49165	.48027	.46925	.45858
69	.58172	.56812	.55495	.54219	.52982	.51783	.50620	.49494	.48401	.47341
70	.59526	.58190	.56894	.55637	.54417	.53234	.52086	.50971	.49889	.48838
71	.60874	.59564	.58291	.57055	.55854	.54687	.53554	.52453	.51382	.50342
72	.62218	.60934	.59685	.58471	.57291	.56143	.55026	.53939	.52882	.51854
73	.63557	.62301	.61078	.59887	.58728	.57600	.56501	.55431	.54389	.53373
74	.64896	.63669	.62472	.61307	.60171	.59064	.57985	.56932	.55906	.54906
75	.66237	.65040	.63872	.62733	.61622	.60538	.59480	.58447	.57439	.56455
76	.67581	.66416	.65279	.64168	.63083	.62023	.60988	.59977	.58989	.58023
77	.68925	.67793	.66688	.65606	.64550	.63516	.62506	.61517	.60551	.59605
78	.70263	.69166	.68093	.67044	.66016	.65010	.64026	.63062	.62119	.61195
79	.71585	.70525	.69486	.68468	.67471	.66495	.65538	.64600	.63681	.62780
80	.72885	.71860	.70856	.69872	.68906	.67959	.67031	.66120	.65227	.64350
81	.74150	.73162	.72193	.71242	.70308	.69392	.68492	.67609	.66742	.65890
82	.75376	.74425	.73490	.72572	.71671	.70785	.69915	.69059	.68219	.67393
83	.76559	.75643	.74744	.73859	.72989	.72134	.71293	.70466	.69652	.68852
84	.77700	.76821	.75955	.75104	.74266	.73441	.72629	.71831	.71044	.70270
85	.78805	.77961	.77130	.76311	.75505	.74711	.73929	.73158	.72399	.71652
86	.79866	.79056	.78258	.77472	.76697	.75933	.75180	.74438	.73707	.72985
87	.80870	.80094	.79329	.78574	.77829	.77095	.76370	.75656	.74951	.74255
88	.81825	.81081	.80348	.79623	.78908	.78202	.77506	.76818	.76139	.75469
89	.82746	.82035	.81332	.80638	.79952	.79275	.78606	.77945	.77292	.76647
90	.83643	.82963	.82291	.81627	.80971	.80322	.79681	.79047	.78420	.77801
91	.84503	.83854	.83212	.82578	.81950	.81330	.80716	.80109	.79509	.78915
92	.85308	.84689	.84076	.83470	.82870	.82276	.81689	.81107	.80532	.79963
93	.86052	.85460	.84875	.84295	.83721	.83152	.82590	.82033	.81481	.80935

TABLE U(1)
BASED ON LIFE TABLE 80CNSMT
UNITRUST SINGLE LIFE REMAINDER FACTORS
APPLICABLE AFTER APRIL 30, 1989, AND BEFORE MAY 1, 1999
ADJUSTED PAYOUT RATE

AGE	4.2%	4.4%	4.6%	4.8%	5.0%	5.2%	5.4%	5.6%	5.8%	6.0%
94	.86729	.86163	.85602	.85046	.84496	.83951	.83412	.82877	.82348	.81823
95	.87338	.86795	.86257	.85723	.85195	.84672	.84153	.83639	.83129	.82624
96	.87877	.87354	.86836	.86323	.85814	.85309	.84809	.84313	.83822	.83334
97	.88365	.87861	.87362	.86867	.86375	.85888	.85405	.84926	.84450	.83979
98	.88805	.88318	.87835	.87356	.86880	.86409	.85941	.85477	.85016	.84559
99	.89210	.88739	.88271	.87807	.87347	.86890	.86436	.85986	.85539	.85095
100	.89588	.89131	.88678	.88227	.87780	.87337	.86896	.86459	.86024	.85593
101	.89949	.89506	.89066	.88629	.88195	.87764	.87336	.86911	.86488	.86069
102	.90325	.89897	.89471	.89047	.88627	.88209	.87794	.87381	.86971	.86564
103	.90724	.90311	.89900	.89491	.89085	.88681	.88279	.87880	.87484	.87089
104	.91167	.90770	.90376	.89983	.89593	.89205	.88819	.88435	.88053	.87673
105	.91708	.91333	.90959	.90587	.90217	.89848	.89481	.89116	.88752	.88391
106	.92470	.92126	.91782	.91440	.91100	.90760	.90422	.90085	.89749	.89414
107	.93545	.93246	.92948	.92650	.92353	.92057	.91762	.91467	.91173	.90880
108	.95239	.95016	.94792	.94569	.94346	.94123	.93900	.93678	.93456	.93234
109	.97900	.97800	.97700	.97600	.97500	.97400	.97300	.97200	.97100	.97000

TABLE U(1)
BASED ON LIFE TABLE 80CNSMT
UNITRUST SINGLE LIFE REMAINDER FACTORS
APPLICABLE AFTER APRIL 30, 1989, AND BEFORE MAY 1, 1999
ADJUSTED PAYOUT RATE

AGE	*6.2%*	*6.4%*	*6.6%*	*6.8%*	*7.0%*	*7.2%*	*7.4%*	*7.6%*	*7.8%*	*8.0%*
0	.03176	.03009	.02861	.02730	.02613	.02509	.02416	.02333	.02258	.02191
1	.02110	.01936	.01781	.01644	.01522	.01413	.01316	.01229	.01150	.01080
2	.02156	.01974	.01812	.01669	.01541	.01427	.01325	.01234	.01152	.01078
3	.02233	.02043	.01875	.01725	.01591	.01471	.01364	.01268	.01182	.01105
4	.02330	.02132	.01956	.01800	.01660	.01535	.01422	.01322	.01231	.01149
5	.02443	.02237	.02054	.01890	.01743	.01612	.01494	.01389	.01293	.01208
6	.02568	.02353	.02162	.01990	.01837	.01700	.01576	.01465	.01365	.01275
7	.02704	.02480	.02280	.02102	.01941	.01798	.01668	.01552	.01446	.01351
8	.02852	.02619	.02411	.02224	.02057	.01906	.01770	.01648	.01537	.01437
9	.03014	.02772	.02554	.02360	.02184	.02027	.01885	.01756	.01640	.01535
10	.03190	.02938	.02711	.02508	.02325	.02160	.02012	.01877	.01755	.01645
11	.03381	.03119	.02883	.02672	.02481	.02308	.02153	.02012	.01884	.01768
12	.03585	.03313	.03068	.02847	.02648	.02468	.02305	.02157	.02023	.01902
13	.03798	.03515	.03260	.03030	.02822	.02635	.02464	.02310	.02170	.02042
14	.04012	.03718	.03453	.03213	.02997	.02801	.02623	.02462	.02315	.02181
15	.04225	.03919	.03644	.03395	.03169	.02965	.02779	.02611	.02457	.02317
16	.04436	.04120	.03833	.03574	.03339	.03126	.02932	.02756	.02595	.02449
17	.04647	.04319	.04021	.03752	.03507	.03285	.03082	.02898	.02730	.02577
18	.04860	.04519	.04210	.03930	.03675	.03443	.03232	.03040	.02864	.02703
19	.05079	.04725	.04404	.04113	.03847	.03606	.03386	.03185	.03001	.02833
20	.05304	.04938	.04604	.04301	.04025	.03773	.03543	.03333	.03141	.02965
21	.05537	.05157	.04811	.04495	.04208	.03945	.03705	.03486	.03285	.03101
22	.05779	.05385	.05025	.04698	.04398	.04125	.03874	.03645	.03435	.03242
23	.06032	.05623	.05250	.04910	.04598	.04313	.04052	.03812	.03592	.03390
24	.06302	.05878	.05491	.05136	.04812	.04515	.04242	.03992	.03762	.03550
25	.06589	.06150	.05748	.05380	.05042	.04733	.04448	.04187	.03946	.03725
26	.06897	.06442	.06025	.05643	.05292	.04969	.04673	.04400	.04148	.03916
27	.07228	.06757	.06325	.05928	.05563	.05227	.04917	.04632	.04369	.04126
28	.07582	.07094	.06646	.06234	.05854	.05504	.05182	.04884	.04609	.04355
29	.07958	.07454	.06990	.06562	.06167	.05804	.05468	.05157	.04870	.04604
30	.08360	.07838	.07357	.06913	.06504	.06125	.05775	.05452	.05152	.04874
31	.08788	.08249	.07751	.07291	.06866	.06472	.06108	.05771	.05457	.05167
32	.09242	.08685	.08170	.07694	.07252	.06844	.06465	.06113	.05786	.05483
33	.09724	.09149	.08617	.08124	.07666	.07242	.06848	.06482	.06141	.05824
34	.10234	.09641	.09091	.08581	.08107	.07667	.07257	.06876	.06521	.06191
35	.10773	.10161	.09594	.09066	.08575	.08119	.07694	.07298	.06928	.06583
36	.11338	.10708	.10122	.09577	.09070	.08597	.08156	.07744	.07360	.07001
37	.11932	.11283	.10680	.10117	.09592	.09102	.08645	.08217	.07818	.07444
38	.12554	.11887	.11265	.10685	.10142	.09636	.09162	.08719	.08304	.07915
39	.13206	.12521	.11880	.11282	.10722	.10198	.09708	.09249	.08818	.08414
40	.13888	.13184	.12526	.11909	.11332	.10791	.10284	.09808	.09361	.08942
41	.14601	.13878	.13201	.12567	.11972	.11414	.10890	.10398	.09935	.09499
42	.15342	.14601	.13906	.13254	.12641	.12066	.11525	.11016	.10537	.10086
43	.16112	.15353	.14640	.13970	.13340	.12747	.12189	.11663	.11168	.10701
44	.16913	.16136	.15406	.14718	.14070	.13460	.12885	.12342	.11830	.11347
45	.17745	.16951	.16202	.15497	.14832	.14204	.13612	.13053	.12525	.12025
46	.18608	.17796	.17030	.16308	.15625	.14981	.14372	.13796	.13251	.12735

TABLE U(1)
BASED ON LIFE TABLE 80CNSMT
UNITRUST SINGLE LIFE REMAINDER FACTORS
APPLICABLE AFTER APRIL 30, 1989, AND BEFORE MAY 1, 1999
ADJUSTED PAYOUT RATE

AGE	6.2%	6.4%	6.6%	6.8%	7.0%	7.2%	7.4%	7.6%	7.8%	8.0%
47	.19501	.18673	.17890	.17150	.16451	.15790	.15164	.14571	.14010	.13478
48	.20425	.19579	.18780	.18024	.17308	.16630	.15987	.15378	.14800	.14252
49	.21375	.20514	.19698	.18926	.18193	.17499	.16840	.16214	.15620	.15056
50	.22352	.21476	.20644	.19856	.19107	.18396	.17721	.17080	.16470	.15890
51	.23358	.22467	.21620	.20816	.20051	.19325	.18634	.17976	.17350	.16755
52	.24396	.23490	.22628	.21809	.21030	.20288	.19581	.18908	.18267	.17655
53	.25465	.24545	.23670	.22836	.22042	.21285	.20563	.19875	.19218	.18592
54	.26563	.25631	.24742	.23895	.23086	.22315	.21579	.20876	.20204	.19562
55	.27692	.26747	.25846	.24986	.24164	.23379	.22628	.21911	.21225	.20568
56	.28850	.27895	.26982	.26109	.25275	.24476	.23712	.22981	.22281	.21611
57	.30041	.29076	.28152	.27267	.26421	.25610	.24833	.24089	.23376	.22691
58	.31263	.30288	.29355	.28460	.27602	.26780	.25991	.25234	.24508	.23811
59	.32515	.31532	.30590	.29685	.28817	.27984	.27184	.26416	.25677	.24968
60	.33793	.32803	.31853	.30940	.30062	.29219	.28409	.27630	.26880	.26159
61	.35093	.34098	.33141	.32220	.31335	.30483	.29663	.28873	.28113	.27381
62	.36414	.35414	.34451	.33524	.32631	.31771	.30942	.30144	.29374	.28631
63	.37754	.36750	.35783	.34850	.33951	.33084	.32247	.31440	.30661	.29910
64	.39115	.38108	.37137	.36200	.35296	.34422	.33579	.32765	.31978	.31217
65	.40500	.39493	.38519	.37579	.36670	.35792	.34943	.34122	.33328	.32560
66	.41914	.40906	.39932	.38990	.38079	.37197	.36343	.35517	.34717	.33943
67	.43355	.42350	.41376	.40434	.39521	.38636	.37780	.36950	.36145	.35365
68	.44824	.43822	.42851	.41909	.40996	.40111	.39252	.38419	.37611	.36827
69	.46313	.45316	.44348	.43409	.42498	.41613	.40754	.39919	.39109	.38322
70	.47818	.46827	.45864	.44929	.44020	.43137	.42279	.41445	.40634	.39845
71	.49331	.48348	.47391	.46461	.45557	.44677	.43821	.42988	.42177	.41388
72	.50853	.49879	.48930	.48007	.47108	.46233	.45380	.44550	.43741	.42952
73	.52384	.51421	.50482	.49566	.48674	.47805	.46957	.46130	.45324	.44538
74	.53930	.52979	.52050	.51145	.50261	.49399	.48557	.47736	.46934	.46152
75	.55495	.54557	.53641	.52747	.51873	.51020	.50187	.49372	.48577	.47799
76	.57079	.56157	.55256	.54374	.53513	.52670	.51847	.51041	.50253	.49483
77	.58680	.57775	.56890	.56024	.55176	.54346	.53534	.52739	.51960	.51198
78	.60291	.59405	.58537	.57687	.56855	.56040	.55241	.54458	.53691	.52940
79	.61898	.61032	.60184	.59353	.58537	.57738	.56954	.56185	.55431	.54691
80	.63491	.62647	.61819	.61007	.60210	.59428	.58660	.57907	.57167	.56441
81	.65054	.64234	.63427	.62636	.61858	.61094	.60344	.59606	.58882	.58170
82	.66582	.65784	.65000	.64229	.63472	.62727	.61994	.61274	.60566	.59870
83	.68065	.67291	.66530	.65781	.65044	.64319	.63605	.62903	.62212	.61532
84	.69508	.68758	.68020	.67293	.66577	.65872	.65178	.64495	.63821	.63158
85	.70915	.70190	.69475	.68770	.68076	.67392	.66718	.66054	.65399	.64754
86	.72274	.71573	.70882	.70200	.69528	.68865	.68212	.67567	.66931	.66304
87	.73569	.72892	.72224	.71565	.70915	.70273	.69639	.69014	.68397	.67788
88	.74807	.74154	.73509	.72872	.72243	.71622	.71009	.70403	.69805	.69214
89	.76010	.75381	.74759	.74144	.73537	.72937	.72344	.71758	.71179	.70607
90	.77189	.76584	.75985	.75394	.74809	.74230	.73659	.73093	.72534	.71981
91	.78327	.77746	.77171	.76603	.76040	.75484	.74933	.74388	.73850	.73316
92	.79399	.78841	.78289	.77743	.77202	.76667	.76137	.75613	.75093	.74579
93	.80394	.79858	.79328	.78803	.78283	.77768	.77258	.76753	.76252	.75757

TABLE U(1)
BASED ON LIFE TABLE 80CNSMT
UNITRUST SINGLE LIFE REMAINDER FACTORS
APPLICABLE AFTER APRIL 30, 1989, AND BEFORE MAY 1, 1999
ADJUSTED PAYOUT RATE

AGE	*6.2%*	*6.4%*	*6.6%*	*6.8%*	*7.0%*	*7.2%*	*7.4%*	*7.6%*	*7.8%*	*8.0%*
94	.81303	.80788	.80278	.79773	.79272	.78776	.78284	.77797	.77315	.76837
95	.82124	.81628	.81136	.80649	.80166	.79687	.79213	.78742	.78276	.77814
96	.82851	.82372	.81897	.81426	.80959	.80496	.80036	.79581	.79129	.78682
97	.83512	.83048	.82588	.82132	.81679	.81230	.80785	.80343	.79905	.79471
98	.84106	.83656	.83210	.82767	.82328	.81892	.81459	.81030	.80604	.80181
99	.84655	.84218	.83785	.83354	.82927	.82503	.82082	.81664	.81249	.80837
100	.85165	.84740	.84318	.83899	.83483	.83070	.82660	.82252	.81848	.81446
101	.85652	.85238	.84827	.84419	.84013	.83611	.83210	.82813	.82418	.82026
102	.86159	.85757	.85358	.84960	.84566	.84174	.83784	.83397	.83012	.82630
103	.86697	.86307	.85920	.85535	.85152	.84771	.84392	.84016	.83642	.83270
104	.87295	.86919	.86544	.86172	.85802	.85434	.85068	.84704	.84341	.83981
106	.89081	.88749	.88418	.88088	.87760	.87433	.87106	.86782	.86458	.86135
107	.90588	.90296	.90005	.89715	.89425	.89137	.88849	.88561	.88275	.87989
108	.93013	.92791	.92570	.92350	.92129	.91909	.91689	.91469	.91250	.91031
109	.96900	.96800	.96700	.96600	.96500	.96400	.96300	.96200	.96100	.96000

TABLE U(1)
BASED ON LIFE TABLE 80CNSMT
UNITRUST SINGLE LIFE REMAINDER FACTORS
APPLICABLE AFTER APRIL 30, 1989, AND BEFORE MAY 1, 1999
ADJUSTED PAYOUT RATE

AGE	*8.2%*	*8.4%*	*8.6%*	*8.8%*	*9.0%*	*9.2%*	*9.4%*	*9.6%*	*9.8%*	*10.0%*
0	.02130	.02075	.02025	.01980	.01939	.01901	.01867	.01835	.01806	.01779
1	.01017	.00960	.00908	.00861	.00819	.00780	.00745	.00712	.00683	.00655
2	.01011	.00951	.00897	.00848	.00803	.00762	.00725	.00690	.00659	.00630
3	.01035	.00971	.00914	.00862	.00815	.00771	.00732	.00696	.00663	.00632
4	.01076	.01009	.00948	.00894	.00843	.00798	.00756	.00718	.00683	.00650
5	.01130	.01059	.00996	.00938	.00885	.00836	.00792	.00752	.00714	.00680
6	.01193	.01119	.01051	.00990	.00934	.00883	.00836	.00793	.00754	.00717
7	.01265	.01187	.01116	.01051	.00992	.00938	.00888	.00842	.00800	.00762
8	.01347	.01264	.01189	.01121	.01058	.01001	.00948	.00900	.00856	.00815
9	.01440	.01353	.01274	.01201	.01135	.01075	.01019	.00968	.00921	.00877
10	.01544	.01453	.01369	.01293	.01223	.01159	.01101	.01046	.00997	.00950
11	.01662	.01566	.01478	.01398	.01324	.01257	.01195	.01137	.01085	.01036
12	.01791	.01690	.01597	.01513	.01435	.01364	.01298	.01238	.01182	.01131
13	.01926	.01820	.01722	.01634	.01552	.01477	.01408	.01344	.01285	.01231
14	.02059	.01948	.01846	.01752	.01667	.01588	.01515	.01448	.01386	.01328
15	.02189	.02072	.01965	.01867	.01777	.01694	.01617	.01547	.01481	.01421
16	.02315	.02192	.02080	.01977	.01882	.01795	.01714	.01640	.01572	.01508
17	.02436	.02308	.02190	.02082	.01982	.01891	.01806	.01728	.01656	.01589
18	.02556	.02422	.02298	.02184	.02080	.01983	.01894	.01812	.01736	.01665
19	.02679	.02537	.02408	.02288	.02178	.02077	.01983	.01897	.01817	.01742
20	.02804	.02656	.02519	.02394	.02278	.02172	.02073	.01982	.01898	.01819
21	.02932	.02776	.02633	.02501	.02380	.02268	.02164	.02068	.01979	.01896
22	.03065	.02902	.02751	.02613	.02485	.02367	.02258	.02157	.02063	.01976
23	.03204	.03033	.02876	.02730	.02595	.02471	.02356	.02249	.02150	.02058
24	.03356	.03176	.03010	.02857	.02716	.02585	.02463	.02351	.02246	.02149
25	.03520	.03332	.03158	.02997	.02848	.02710	.02582	.02463	.02352	.02249
26	.03702	.03504	.03321	.03152	.02995	.02850	.02714	.02589	.02472	.02363
27	.03902	.03695	.03502	.03324	.03159	.03006	.02863	.02730	.02607	.02492
28	.04120	.03902	.03700	.03513	.03339	.03178	.03027	.02887	.02757	.02635
29	.04358	.04129	.03917	.03720	.03537	.03367	.03208	.03061	.02923	.02794
30	.04616	.04376	.04154	.03947	.03754	.03575	.03408	.03251	.03106	.02969
31	.04897	.04646	.04413	.04195	.03993	.03804	.03627	.03463	.03309	.03165
32	.05200	.04938	.04693	.04465	.04252	.04053	.03867	.03693	.03531	.03378
33	.05529	.05254	.04998	.04758	.04534	.04325	.04130	.03946	.03775	.03614
34	.05883	.05595	.05326	.05075	.04840	.04620	.04414	.04221	.04040	.03870
35	.06262	.05961	.05680	.05417	.05170	.04939	.04723	.04520	.04329	.04149
36	.06665	.06351	.06057	.05781	.05523	.05280	.05053	.04839	.04638	.04449
37	.07094	.06766	.06459	.06171	.05900	.05646	.05407	.05182	.04971	.04771
38	.07550	.07208	.06888	.06586	.06303	.06037	.05786	.05550	.05327	.05118
39	.08034	.07678	.07344	.07029	.06733	.06454	.06191	.05943	.05709	.05489
40	.08547	.08177	.07828	.07499	.07190	.06898	.06623	.06363	.06118	.05886
41	.09090	.08704	.08341	.07998	.07675	.07371	.07083	.06811	.06553	.06310
42	.09661	.09260	.08882	.08525	.08188	.07870	.07569	.07284	.07015	.06760
43	.10260	.09844	.09451	.09080	.08729	.08397	.08083	.07785	.07503	.07236
44	.10891	.10459	.10051	.09666	.09300	.08954	.08626	.08316	.08021	.07741
45	.11553	.11106	.10683	.10282	.09902	.09542	.09201	.08876	.08568	.08276
46	.12247	.11784	.11346	.10930	.10536	.10161	.09806	.09468	.09146	.08841

TABLE U(1)
BASED ON LIFE TABLE 80CNSMT
UNITRUST SINGLE LIFE REMAINDER FACTORS
APPLICABLE AFTER APRIL 30, 1989, AND BEFORE MAY 1, 1999
ADJUSTED PAYOUT RATE

AGE	8.2%	8.4%	8.6%	8.8%	9.0%	9.2%	9.4%	9.6%	9.8%	10.0%
47	.12974	.12496	.12042	.11611	.11202	.10813	.10443	.10091	.09756	.09438
48	.13732	.13238	.12769	.12323	.11899	.11495	.11111	.10745	.10397	.10065
49	.14520	.14011	.13526	.13064	.12625	.12207	.11809	.11429	.11066	.10721
50	.15338	.14812	.14312	.13836	.13381	.12948	.12535	.12141	.11765	.11405
51	.16187	.15646	.15130	.14639	.14169	.13721	.13294	.12885	.12495	.12121
52	.17072	.16516	.15985	.15478	.14993	.14531	.14088	.13665	.13261	.12873
53	.17993	.17422	.16876	.16353	.15854	.15377	.14920	.14482	.14064	.13662
54	.18949	.18362	.17801	.17264	.16750	.16258	.15787	.15335	.14902	.14486
55	.19940	.19339	.18763	.18212	.17683	.17176	.16690	.16224	.15777	.15348
56	.20968	.20353	.19762	.19196	.18654	.18132	.17632	.17152	.16691	.16247
57	.22035	.21406	.20802	.20222	.19665	.19129	.18615	.18121	.17646	.17189
58	.23142	.22499	.21881	.21287	.20717	.20168	.19640	.19132	.18643	.18172
59	.24286	.23630	.23000	.22393	.21809	.21247	.20705	.20184	.19682	.19198
60	.25465	.24797	.24154	.23534	.22938	.22363	.21808	.21274	.20759	.20262
61	.26676	.25996	.25341	.24710	.24101	.23513	.22946	.22399	.21871	.21361
62	.27916	.27225	.26559	.25916	.25295	.24695	.24117	.23557	.23017	.22495
63	.29184	.28483	.27806	.27152	.26520	.25909	.25319	.24748	.24196	.23661
64	.30483	.29772	.29085	.28421	.27779	.27157	.26555	.25973	.25409	.24863
65	.31817	.31098	.30402	.29729	.29076	.28444	.27832	.27240	.26665	.26108
66	.33192	.32466	.31762	.31079	.30418	.29777	.29155	.28552	.27968	.27400
67	.34609	.33876	.33164	.32474	.31805	.31156	.30525	.29913	.29319	.28742
68	.36066	.35328	.34610	.33914	.33238	.32581	.31943	.31323	.30720	.30134
69	.37558	.36815	.36093	.35391	.34709	.34045	.33400	.32773	.32163	.31569
70	.39078	.38332	.37606	.36900	.36213	.35545	.34894	.34260	.33643	.33042
71	.40620	.39872	.39144	.38435	.37744	.37071	.36415	.35776	.35153	.34547
72	.42184	.41435	.40706	.39994	.39301	.38625	.37965	.37322	.36694	.36082
73	.43771	.43023	.42293	.41581	.40886	.40207	.39545	.38899	.38267	.37651
74	.45387	.44641	.43912	.43201	.42505	.41826	.41163	.40514	.39881	.39261
75	.47039	.46296	.45570	.44861	.44167	.43488	.42824	.42175	.41541	.40920
76	.48729	.47991	.47269	.46563	.45872	.45196	.44534	.43886	.43251	.42630
77	.50452	.49722	.49006	.48305	.47619	.46946	.46287	.45642	.45009	.44389
78	.52203	.51481	.50773	.50079	.49399	.48732	.48078	.47437	.46808	.46191
79	.53966	.53254	.52556	.51870	.51198	.50538	.49891	.49255	.48632	.48019
80	.55728	.55028	.54340	.53665	.53002	.52351	.51712	.51083	.50466	.49860
81	.57471	.56784	.56109	.55445	.54792	.54151	.53521	.52901	.52292	.51692
82	.59186	.58512	.57850	.57199	.56558	.55927	.55307	.54697	.54097	.53506
83	.60863	.60204	.59556	.58918	.58289	.57671	.57062	.56462	.55872	.55290
84	.62505	.61862	.61228	.60604	.59989	.59383	.58786	.58198	.57618	.57047
85	.64118	.63491	.62873	.62263	.61663	.61070	.60486	.59911	.59343	.58783
86	.65685	.65075	.64473	.63879	.63294	.62716	.62145	.61583	.61027	.60479
87	.67187	.66594	.66008	.65430	.64859	.64296	.63739	.63190	.62647	.62112
88	.68631	.68054	.67485	.66923	.66367	.65818	.65276	.64740	.64211	.63688
89	.70042	.69483	.68930	.68384	.67845	.67311	.66784	.66262	.65747	.65237
90	.71434	.70894	.70359	.69830	.69307	.68790	.68278	.67772	.67271	.66775
91	.72789	.72266	.71750	.71239	.70733	.70232	.69736	.69246	.68760	.68280
92	.74070	.73567	.73068	.72574	.72085	.71601	.71121	.70647	.70176	.69711
93	.75266	.74780	.74298	.73821	.73348	.72880	.72417	.71957	.71502	.71051

TABLE U(1)
BASED ON LIFE TABLE 80CNSMT
UNITRUST SINGLE LIFE REMAINDER FACTORS
APPLICABLE AFTER APRIL 30, 1989, AND BEFORE MAY 1, 1999
ADJUSTED PAYOUT RATE

AGE	*8.2%*	*8.4%*	*8.6%*	*8.8%*	*9.0%*	*9.2%*	*9.4%*	*9.6%*	*9.8%*	*10.0%*
94	.76363	.75893	.75428	.74967	.74510	.74057	.73608	.73163	.72722	.72285
95	.77356	.76901	.76451	.76005	.75562	.75123	.74688	.74257	.73829	.73405
96	.78237	.77797	.77360	.76927	.76497	.76071	.75648	.75229	.74813	.74401
97	.79039	.78612	.78187	.77766	.77348	.76934	.76523	.76115	.75710	.75308
98	.79762	.79345	.78932	.78522	.78115	.77711	.77310	.76913	.76518	.76126
99	.80429	.80023	.79620	.79220	.78823	.78429	.78038	.77649	.77264	.76881
100	.81047	.80651	.80258	.79867	.79479	.79094	.78712	.78332	.77955	.77580
101	.81636	.81249	.80865	.80483	.80104	.79727	.79352	.78981	.78611	.78244
102	.82250	.81872	.81497	.81124	.80754	.80386	.80020	.79656	.79295	.78936
103	.82900	.82532	.82167	.81804	.81442	.81083	.80726	.80371	.80018	.79667
104	.83622	.83266	.82911	.82558	.82207	.81858	.81510	.81165	.80821	.80479
106	.85814	.85494	.85175	.84857	.84540	.84225	.83911	.83598	.83286	.82975
107	.87704	.87420	.87136	.86853	.86571	.86290	.86009	.85729	.85450	.85171
108	.90812	.90593	.90375	.90156	.89939	.89721	.89504	.89286	.89070	.88853
109	.95900	.95800	.95700	.95600	.95500	.95400	.95300	.95200	.95100	.95000

TABLE U(1)
BASED ON LIFE TABLE 80CNSMT
UNITRUST SINGLE LIFE REMAINDER FACTORS
APPLICABLE AFTER APRIL 30, 1989, AND BEFORE MAY 1, 1999
ADJUSTED PAYOUT RATE

AGE	*10.2%*	*10.4%*	*10.6%*	*10.8%*	*11.0%*	*11.2%*	*11.4%*	*11.6%*	*11.8%*	*12.0%*
0	.01754	.01731	.01710	.01690	.01671	.01654	.01638	.01622	.01608	.01594
1	.00630	.00607	.00585	.00565	.00547	.00530	.00514	.00499	.00485	.00472
2	.00604	.00579	.00557	.00536	.00516	.00498	.00481	.00465	.00451	.00437
3	.00604	.00578	.00554	.00532	.00511	.00492	.00474	.00458	.00442	.00427
4	.00621	.00593	.00568	.00544	.00522	.00502	.00483	.00465	.00448	.00433
5	.00648	.00619	.00592	.00567	.00544	.00522	.00502	.00483	.00465	.00449
6	.00684	.00653	.00624	.00597	.00572	.00549	.00528	.00507	.00489	.00471
7	.00726	.00693	.00663	.00634	.00608	.00583	.00560	.00539	.00518	.00499
8	.00777	.00742	.00709	.00679	.00651	.00624	.00600	.00577	.00555	.00535
9	.00837	.00800	.00765	.00733	.00703	.00675	.00649	.00625	.00602	.00580
10	.00908	.00868	.00832	.00797	.00765	.00736	.00708	.00682	.00657	.00634
11	.00991	.00949	.00910	.00874	.00840	.00808	.00779	.00751	.00725	.00700
12	.01083	.01039	.00997	.00959	.00923	.00890	.00858	.00829	.00801	.00775
13	.01181	.01134	.01090	.01049	.01012	.00976	.00943	.00912	.00883	.00855
14	.01275	.01226	.01180	.01137	.01097	.01060	.01025	.00992	.00961	.00932
15	.01365	.01313	.01264	.01219	.01177	.01138	.01101	.01066	.01034	.01003
16	.01449	.01394	.01343	.01295	.01251	.01209	.01171	.01134	.01100	.01068
17	.01526	.01469	.01415	.01365	.01318	.01274	.01233	.01195	.01159	.01125
18	.01600	.01539	.01482	.01430	.01380	.01334	.01291	.01251	.01213	.01177
19	.01673	.01609	.01550	.01494	.01442	.01393	.01348	.01305	.01265	.01227
20	.01747	.01679	.01616	.01557	.01502	.01451	.01403	.01358	.01316	.01276
21	.01820	.01748	.01682	.01620	.01562	.01508	.01457	.01409	.01365	.01323
22	.01895	.01819	.01749	.01683	.01622	.01565	.01511	.01461	.01414	.01369
23	.01972	.01893	.01818	.01749	.01684	.01624	.01567	.01514	.01464	.01417
24	.02058	.01974	.01895	.01822	.01753	.01689	.01629	.01572	.01519	.01469
25	.02154	.02064	.01981	.01903	.01830	.01762	.01698	.01638	.01582	.01529
26	.02262	.02167	.02079	.01996	.01919	.01847	.01779	.01715	.01655	.01599
27	.02385	.02284	.02191	.02103	.02021	.01944	.01872	.01804	.01740	.01680
28	.02521	.02415	.02316	.02222	.02135	.02053	.01977	.01904	.01836	.01772
29	.02673	.02561	.02455	.02357	.02264	.02177	.02095	.02018	.01946	.01877
30	.02842	.02723	.02611	.02506	.02407	.02315	.02227	.02146	.02068	.01996
31	.03030	.02903	.02784	.02673	.02568	.02470	.02377	.02290	.02207	.02130
32	.03235	.03101	.02976	.02857	.02746	.02641	.02543	.02450	.02362	.02279
33	.03463	.03321	.03188	.03062	.02944	.02833	.02728	.02629	.02535	.02447
34	.03711	.03561	.03419	.03286	.03161	.03043	.02931	.02826	.02726	.02632
35	.03981	.03822	.03672	.03531	.03398	.03273	.03154	.03042	.02936	.02836
36	.04271	.04103	.03945	.03796	.03655	.03522	.03396	.03277	.03164	.03057
37	.04584	.04407	.04239	.04081	.03932	.03791	.03657	.03531	.03411	.03297
38	.04920	.04733	.04556	.04389	.04231	.04082	.03940	.03806	.03679	.03558
39	.05280	.05083	.04897	.04721	.04554	.04396	.04246	.04103	.03968	.03840
40	.05667	.05459	.05263	.05077	.04901	.04733	.04575	.04424	.04280	.04144
41	.06080	.05861	.05655	.05459	.05272	.05096	.04928	.04768	.04617	.04472
42	.06518	.06289	.06071	.05864	.05668	.05482	.05305	.05136	.04975	.04822
43	.06982	.06742	.06513	.06296	.06089	.05893	.05706	.05528	.05358	.05196
44	.07475	.07223	.06983	.06754	.06537	.06330	.06133	.05945	.05766	.05595
45	.07998	.07733	.07481	.07242	.07014	.06796	.06588	.06390	.06202	.06021
46	.08550	.08273	.08010	.07758	.07519	.07290	.07072	.06864	.06665	.06474

TABLE U(1)
BASED ON LIFE TABLE 80CNSMT
UNITRUST SINGLE LIFE REMAINDER FACTORS
APPLICABLE AFTER APRIL 30, 1989, AND BEFORE MAY 1, 1999
ADJUSTED PAYOUT RATE

AGE	10.2%	10.4%	10.6%	10.8%	11.0%	11.2%	11.4%	11.6%	11.8%	12.0%
47	.09134	.08845	.08569	.08306	.08055	.07815	.07586	.07367	.07157	.06957
48	.09748	.09446	.09158	.08882	.08619	.08368	.08128	.07898	.07678	.07467
49	.10391	.10076	.09775	.09487	.09212	.08949	.08697	.08456	.08225	.08003
50	.11062	.10734	.10420	.10120	.09832	.09557	.09293	.09041	.08798	.08566
51	.11764	.11423	.11096	.10783	.10483	.10195	.09919	.09655	.09401	.09158
52	.12503	.12148	.11807	.11481	.11168	.10868	.10581	.10304	.10039	.09784
53	.13278	.12909	.12556	.12216	.11891	.11578	.11278	.10989	.10712	.10445
54	.14088	.13706	.13339	.12986	.12648	.12322	.12009	.11709	.11419	.11141
55	.14936	.14540	.14159	.13793	.13442	.13103	.12778	.12464	.12163	.11872
56	.15821	.15412	.15018	.14639	.14274	.13923	.13584	.13258	.12944	.12642
57	.16749	.16326	.15918	.15526	.15148	.14784	.14433	.14094	.13768	.13453
58	.17719	.17282	.16862	.16456	.16065	.15688	.15324	.14973	.14634	.14306
59	.18731	.18281	.17847	.17429	.17025	.16634	.16258	.15894	.15543	.15203
60	.19782	.19319	.18872	.18440	.18023	.17621	.17231	.16855	.16491	.16139
61	.20869	.20393	.19934	.19489	.19060	.18644	.18242	.17854	.17477	.17113
62	.21990	.21502	.21029	.20573	.20131	.19703	.19289	.18887	.18499	.18123
63	.23144	.22644	.22159	.21690	.21236	.20796	.20370	.19956	.19556	.19167
64	.24335	.23823	.23326	.22845	.22379	.21927	.21489	.21063	.20651	.20250
65	.25568	.25045	.24537	.24044	.23566	.23103	.22653	.22216	.21791	.21379
66	.26850	.26316	.25797	.25293	.24804	.24329	.23868	.23420	.22984	.22560
67	.28182	.27637	.27108	.26594	.26095	.25609	.25137	.24678	.24231	.23797
68	.29565	.29011	.28472	.27949	.27439	.26943	.26461	.25991	.25534	.25089
69	.30991	.30429	.29882	.29349	.28830	.28325	.27833	.27354	.26887	.26432
70	.32457	.31887	.31332	.30791	.30264	.29750	.29249	.28760	.28284	.27820
71	.33955	.33378	.32816	.32267	.31732	.31210	.30701	.30204	.29719	.29246
72	.35485	.34902	.34333	.33778	.33236	.32707	.32190	.31686	.31193	.30711
73	.37049	.36461	.35887	.35326	.34778	.34242	.33719	.33207	.32707	.32218
74	.38656	.38064	.37485	.36920	.36366	.35825	.35296	.34778	.34272	.33776
75	.40312	.39717	.39136	.38566	.38009	.37464	.36930	.36407	.35895	.35394
76	.42022	.41426	.40842	.40271	.39711	.39163	.38625	.38099	.37583	.37077
77	.43782	.43187	.42603	.42031	.41470	.40920	.40380	.39851	.39332	.38823
78	.45586	.44992	.44410	.43839	.43278	.42728	.42188	.41658	.41138	.40627
79	.47418	.46828	.46248	.45679	.45120	.44572	.44033	.43503	.42983	.42472
80	.49264	.48679	.48103	.47538	.46982	.46436	.45900	.45372	.44853	.44343
81	.51103	.50524	.49954	.49394	.48843	.48301	.47768	.47243	.46727	.46219
82	.52925	.52352	.51789	.51235	.50690	.50153	.49624	.49104	.48591	.48087
83	.54718	.54154	.53598	.53051	.52512	.51981	.51459	.50943	.50436	.49936
84	.56484	.55930	.55383	.54844	.54313	.53789	.53273	.52764	.52262	.51767
85	.58231	.57686	.57149	.56619	.56096	.55581	.55072	.54571	.54076	.53588
86	.59939	.59405	.58878	.58358	.57845	.57339	.56839	.56346	.55858	.55377
87	.61583	.61061	.60545	.60035	.59532	.59035	.58545	.58060	.57581	.57108
88	.63171	.62661	.62156	.61658	.61165	.60678	.60196	.59721	.59251	.58786
89	.64733	.64235	.63742	.63255	.62774	.62298	.61827	.61361	.60900	.60444
90	.66285	.65801	.65321	.64847	.64377	.63913	.63453	.62998	.62548	.62103
91	.67804	.67334	.66868	.66407	.65950	.65498	.65050	.64607	.64169	.63735
92	.69250	.68793	.68341	.67893	.67450	.67011	.66575	.66144	.65718	.65295
93	.70604	.70162	.69723	.69288	.68858	.68431	.68008	.67589	.67174	.66762

TABLE U(1)
BASED ON LIFE TABLE 80CNSMT
UNITRUST SINGLE LIFE REMAINDER FACTORS
APPLICABLE AFTER APRIL 30, 1989, AND BEFORE MAY 1, 1999
ADJUSTED PAYOUT RATE

AGE	*10.2%*	*10.4%*	*10.6%*	*10.8%*	*11.0%*	*11.2%*	*11.4%*	*11.6%*	*11.8%*	*12.0%*
94	.71852	.71422	.70997	.70575	.70156	.69742	.69331	.68923	.68519	.68119
95	.72984	.72567	.72154	.71744	.71337	.70934	.70534	.70137	.69744	.69354
96	.73992	.73586	.73183	.72784	.72388	.71995	.71605	.71218	.70835	.70454
97	.74910	.74514	.74122	.73733	.73346	.72963	.72582	.72205	.71830	.71458
98	.75737	.75351	.74967	.74587	.74209	.73835	.73463	.73093	.72727	.72363
99	.76501	.76123	.75748	.75376	.75007	.74640	.74276	.73914	.73555	.73198
100	.77208	.76838	.76471	.76107	.75745	.75385	.75028	.74673	.74321	.73971
101	.77879	.77517	.77157	.76800	.76444	.76092	.75741	.75392	.75046	.74702
102	.78579	.78224	.77871	.77521	.77173	.76827	.76483	.76141	.75801	.75463
103	.79318	.78971	.78626	.78283	.77942	.77604	.77266	.76931	.76598	.76267
104	.80139	.79801	.79464	.79129	.78796	.78465	.78136	.77808	.77482	.77157
106	.82665	.82357	.82049	.81743	.81438	.81134	.80831	.80530	.80229	.79930
107	.84893	.84616	.84340	.84064	.83789	.83515	.83241	.82969	.82696	.82425
108	.88637	.88421	.88205	.87989	.87774	.87559	.87344	.87129	.86915	.86701
109	.94900	.94800	.94700	.94600	.94500	.94400	.94300	.94200	.94100	.94000

TABLE U(1)
BASED ON LIFE TABLE 80CNSMT)
UNITRUST SINGLE LIFE REMAINDER FACTORS)
APPLICABLE AFTER APRIL 30, 1989, AND BEFORE MAY 1, 1999
ADJUSTED PAYOUT RATE

AGE	12.2%	12.4%	12.6%	12.8%	13.0%	13.2%	13.4%	13.6%	13.8%	14.0%
0	.01581	.01569	.01557	.01546	.01536	.01526	.01516	.01507	.01499	.01490
1	.00459	.00448	.00437	.00426	.00417	.00407	.00399	.00390	.00382	.00375
2	.00424	.00412	.00400	.00389	.00379	.00369	.00360	.00352	.00343	.00335
3	.00414	.00401	.00389	.00377	.00366	.00356	.00346	.00337	.00328	.00320
4	.00418	.00404	.00391	.00379	.00368	.00357	.00347	.00337	.00327	.00319
5	.00433	.00418	.00405	.00391	.00379	.00368	.00357	.00346	.00336	.00327
6	.00454	.00439	.00424	.00410	.00397	.00384	.00372	.00361	.00351	.00341
7	.00482	.00465	.00449	.00434	.00420	.00407	.00394	.00382	.00371	.00360
8	.00516	.00498	.00481	.00465	.00450	.00436	.00422	.00410	.00397	.00386
9	.00560	.00541	.00523	.00505	.00489	.00474	.00459	.00446	.00433	.00420
10	.00613	.00592	.00573	.00555	.00537	.00521	.00505	.00491	.00477	.00463
11	.00677	.00655	.00635	.00615	.00597	.00580	.00563	.00547	.00532	.00518
12	.00751	.00728	.00706	.00685	.00666	.00647	.00629	.00613	.00597	.00581
13	.00829	.00805	.00782	.00760	.00739	.00719	.00701	.00683	.00666	.00650
14	.00905	.00879	.00854	.00831	.00809	.00789	.00769	.00750	.00732	.00715
15	.00974	.00947	.00921	.00897	.00874	.00852	.00831	.00811	.00793	.00775
16	.01037	.01009	.00982	.00956	.00932	.00909	.00887	.00866	.00846	.00827
17	.01093	.01063	.01034	.01007	.00982	.00958	.00935	.00913	.00892	.00873
18	.01143	.01112	.01082	.01053	.01027	.01001	.00977	.00954	.00933	.00912
19	.01192	.01159	.01127	.01097	.01069	.01043	.01017	.00993	.00970	.00949
20	.01239	.01204	.01170	.01139	.01109	.01081	.01055	.01029	.01005	.00983
21	.01283	.01246	.01211	.01178	.01147	.01117	.01089	.01063	.01037	.01013
22	.01328	.01288	.01251	.01216	.01183	.01152	.01122	.01094	.01067	.01042
23	.01372	.01331	.01292	.01254	.01219	.01186	.01155	.01125	.01097	.01070
24	.01422	.01378	.01336	.01297	.01260	.01225	.01191	.01160	.01130	.01101
25	.01479	.01432	.01388	.01346	.01306	.01269	.01233	.01200	.01168	.01138
26	.01545	.01495	.01448	.01404	.01362	.01322	.01284	.01248	.01214	.01182
27	.01623	.01570	.01520	.01472	.01427	.01385	.01344	.01306	.01270	.01235
28	.01712	.01655	.01601	.01551	.01503	.01457	.01414	.01373	.01334	.01298
29	.01813	.01752	.01695	.01641	.01589	.01541	.01494	.01451	.01409	.01370
30	.01927	.01862	.01801	.01743	.01688	.01635	.01586	.01539	.01495	.01452
31	.02056	.01987	.01922	.01859	.01801	.01745	.01692	.01642	.01594	.01548
32	.02201	.02127	.02057	.01990	.01927	.01868	.01811	.01757	.01706	.01657
33	.02363	.02284	.02209	.02138	.02071	.02007	.01946	.01888	.01833	.01781
34	.02543	.02458	.02378	.02302	.02230	.02162	.02096	.02034	.01975	.01919
35	.02741	.02651	.02565	.02484	.02407	.02333	.02264	.02197	.02134	.02073
36	.02956	.02859	.02768	.02681	.02599	.02520	.02446	.02374	.02307	.02242
37	.03189	.03087	.02990	.02897	.02809	.02725	.02645	.02569	.02496	.02427
38	.03443	.03334	.03230	.03131	.03037	.02948	.02862	.02781	.02703	.02628
39	.03718	.03602	.03491	.03386	.03285	.03190	.03099	.03011	.02928	.02849
40	.04015	.03891	.03774	.03662	.03555	.03453	.03355	.03262	.03173	.03088
41	.04335	.04204	.04079	.03959	.03846	.03737	.03633	.03534	.03439	.03348
42	.04677	.04538	.04405	.04278	.04157	.04042	.03931	.03825	.03724	.03627
43	.05042	.04894	.04754	.04619	.04491	.04368	.04250	.04138	.04030	.03926
44	.05432	.05276	.05127	.04984	.04848	.04718	.04593	.04473	.04358	.04248
45	.05849	.05684	.05526	.05375	.05231	.05092	.04960	.04832	.04710	.04593
46	.06292	.06118	.05952	.05792	.05639	.05492	.05352	.05217	.05087	.04963

TABLE U(1)
BASED ON LIFE TABLE 80CNSMT)
UNITRUST SINGLE LIFE REMAINDER FACTORS)
APPLICABLE AFTER APRIL 30, 1989, AND BEFORE MAY 1, 1999
ADJUSTED PAYOUT RATE

AGE	12.2%	12.4%	12.6%	12.8%	13.0%	13.2%	13.4%	13.6%	13.8%	14.0%
47	.06765	.06581	.06405	.06237	.06075	.05920	.05771	.05628	.05491	.05359
48	.07265	.07071	.06886	.06708	.06537	.06373	.06216	.06064	.05919	.05779
49	.07791	.07587	.07392	.07204	.07024	.06851	.06685	.06525	.06371	.06223
50	.08343	.08129	.07923	.07726	.07536	.07354	.07178	.07009	.06847	.06690
51	.08924	.08699	.08483	.08276	.08076	.07884	.07699	.07520	.07349	.07183
52	.09539	.09303	.09076	.08858	.08648	.08446	.08251	.08064	.07883	.07708
53	.10189	.09942	.09704	.09475	.09255	.09043	.08838	.08640	.08450	.08266
54	.10872	.10614	.10365	.10126	.09894	.09672	.09456	.09249	.09049	.08855
55	.11592	.11322	.11062	.10811	.10569	.10335	.10110	.09892	.09682	.09478
56	.12350	.12068	.11796	.11534	.11281	.11036	.10800	.10571	.10350	.10137
57	.13148	.12855	.12572	.12298	.12033	.11777	.11530	.11291	.11060	.10836
58	.13990	.13685	.13389	.13104	.12828	.12561	.12303	.12053	.11811	.11576
59	.14875	.14557	.14250	.13953	.13665	.13387	.13118	.12856	.12604	.12359
60	.15799	.15469	.15150	.14841	.14542	.14253	.13972	.13700	.13436	.13180
61	.16761	.16419	.16088	.15768	.15457	.15156	.14864	.14580	.14305	.14039
62	.17758	.17404	.17062	.16729	.16407	.16094	.15791	.15496	.15210	.14932
63	.18791	.18425	.18071	.17726	.17392	.17068	.16753	.16447	.16150	.15861
64	.19862	.19484	.19118	.18762	.18417	.18081	.17754	.17437	.17129	.16829
65	.20979	.20590	.20212	.19845	.19487	.19140	.18802	.18474	.18154	.17843
66	.22149	.21748	.21359	.20980	.20612	.20253	.19904	.19564	.19233	.18911
67	.23374	.22962	.22562	.22172	.21792	.21423	.21062	.20712	.20370	.20037
68	.24656	.24234	.23822	.23422	.23031	.22651	.22280	.21919	.21566	.21222
69	.25988	.25556	.25134	.24724	.24323	.23932	.23551	.23179	.22816	.22461
70	.27367	.26925	.26493	.26073	.25662	.25261	.24870	.24488	.24115	.23750
71	.28784	.28333	.27892	.27462	.27042	.26631	.26230	.25839	.25456	.25082
72	.30241	.29781	.29332	.28893	.28464	.28044	.27634	.27233	.26841	.26457
73	.31740	.31272	.30815	.30368	.29930	.29502	.29084	.28674	.28273	.27880
74	.33291	.32817	.32352	.31897	.31452	.31016	.30589	.30171	.29762	.29361
75	.34903	.34422	.33951	.33490	.33038	.32595	.32161	.31735	.31318	.30909
76	.36581	.36095	.35619	.35152	.34694	.34245	.33805	.33373	.32949	.32533
77	.38324	.37835	.37354	.36883	.36420	.35966	.35520	.35083	.34654	.34232
78	.40126	.39634	.39150	.38676	.38210	.37752	.37302	.36861	.36427	.36001
79	.41970	.41476	.40992	.40515	.40047	.39587	.39135	.38690	.38253	.37823
80	.43842	.43348	.42864	.42387	.41918	.41456	.41002	.40556	.40117	.39685
81	.45719	.45228	.44744	.44267	.43799	.43337	.42883	.42436	.41996	.41562
82	.47590	.47101	.46619	.46145	.45677	.45217	.44764	.44317	.43877	.43443
83	.49443	.48957	.48478	.48007	.47542	.47084	.46632	.46187	.45748	.45315
84	.51279	.50798	.50324	.49856	.49394	.48939	.48490	.48048	.47611	.47180
85	.53106	.52630	.52161	.51698	.51241	.50790	.50345	.49906	.49473	.49045
86	.54902	.54434	.53971	.53514	.53062	.52616	.52176	.51741	.51312	.50888
87	.56640	.56178	.55722	.55271	.54826	.54386	.53951	.53521	.53097	.52677
88	.58326	.57872	.57423	.56979	.56541	.56107	.55678	.55254	.54834	.54420
89	.59994	.59548	.59107	.58671	.58240	.57813	.57391	.56973	.56560	.56152
90	.61662	.61226	.60794	.60367	.59944	.59526	.59112	.58702	.58296	.57894
91	.63305	.62879	.62457	.62040	.61627	.61217	.60812	.60411	.60013	.59619
92	.64876	.64461	.64050	.63643	.63239	.62839	.62443	.62051	.61662	.61277
93	.66355	.65950	.65550	.65153	.64759	.64369	.63983	.63600	.63220	.62843

TABLE U(1)
BASED ON LIFE TABLE 80CNSMT)
UNITRUST SINGLE LIFE REMAINDER FACTORS)
APPLICABLE AFTER APRIL 30, 1989, AND BEFORE MAY 1, 1999
ADJUSTED PAYOUT RATE

AGE	*12.2%*	*12.4%*	*12.6%*	*12.8%*	*13.0%*	*13.2%*	*13.4%*	*13.6%*	*13.8%*	*14.0%*
94	.67722	.67328	.66938	.66551	.66167	.65786	.65409	.65035	.64664	.64296
95	.68967	.68583	.68203	.67825	.67451	.67079	.66711	.66345	.65983	.65623
96	.70076	.69701	.69330	.68961	.68595	.68231	.67871	.67513	.67158	.66806
97	.71089	.70722	.70359	.69998	.69640	.69284	.68931	.68581	.68234	.67888
98	.72001	.71642	.71286	.70933	.70582	.70233	.69887	.69544	.69203	.68864
99	.72844	.72492	.72143	.71796	.71452	.71110	.70770	.70433	.70098	.69765
100	.73623	.73278	.72935	.72594	.72256	.71920	.71586	.71254	.70924	.70597
101	.74361	.74021	.73684	.73349	.73016	.72685	.72356	.72029	.71704	.71382
102	.75128	.74794	.74463	.74133	.73806	.73480	.73157	.72835	.72515	.72198
103	.75938	.75610	.75284	.74961	.74639	.74319	.74000	.73684	.73369	.73056
104	.76835	.76514	.76194	.75877	.75561	.75246	.74934	.74623	.74313	.74005
105	.77956	.77643	.77332	.77023	.76714	.76408	.76102	.75798	.75496	.75195
106	.79632	.79334	.79038	.78743	.78449	.78157	.77865	.77575	.77285	.76997
107	.82154	.81884	.81615	.81346	.81079	.80811	.80545	.80279	.80014	.79750
108	.86487	.86274	.86061	.85848	.85635	.85423	.85210	.84998	.84787	.84575
109	.93900	.93800	.93700	.93600	.93500	.93400	.93300	.93200	.93100	.93000

¶ 2800 Applicable Federal Rates

The present value of an annuity, interest for life or for a term of years, or a remainder or reversionary interest is generally determined by using the IRS valuation tables if the valuation date is after April 30, 1989. The interest rate component of the valuation tables is based on the applicable federal rate (AFR) as described under Code Sec. 7520. This rate is equal to 120 percent of the federal mid-term rate issued monthly by the Secretary of the Treasury, rounded to the nearest even tenth of a percent (see ¶ 530).

The following interest rate table provides the Code Sec. 7520 120-percent AFR mid-term valuation interest rate factors, beginning with January 1997.

Month	*Interest factor*
November 2004	4.2%
October 2004	4.4%
September 2004	4.6%
August 2004	4.8%
July 2004	5.0%
June 2004	4.6%
May 2004	3.8%
April 2004	3.8%
March 2004	4.0%
February 2004	4.2%
January 2004	4.2%
December 2003	4.2%
November 2003	4.0%
October 2003	4.4%
September 2003	4.2%
August 2003	3.2%
July 2003	3.0%
June 2003	3.6%
May 2003	3.8%
April 2003	3.6%
March 2003	3.8%
February 2003	4.0%
January 2003	4.2%
December 2002	4.0%
November 2002	3.6%
October 2002	4.2%
September 2002	4.6%
August 2002	5.2%
July 2002	5.6%
June 2002	5.8%
May 2002	6.0%
April 2002	5.6%
March 2002	5.4%
February 2002	5.6%
January 2002	5.4%
December 2001	4.8%
November 2001	5.0%
October 2001	5.6%
September 2001	5.8%
August 2001	6.0%
July 2001	6.2%
June 2001	6.0%
May 2001	5.8%
April 2001	6.0%
March 2001	6.2%
February 2001	6.2%
January 2001	6.8%
December 2000	7.0%
November 2000	7.2%
October 2000	7.4%
September 2000	7.6%
August 2000	7.6%
July 2000	8.0%
June 2000	8.0%
May 2000	7.8%
April 2000	8.0%
March 2000	8.2%
February 2000	8.0%
January 2000	7.4%
December 1999	7.4%
November 1999	7.4%
October 1999	7.2%
September 1999	7.2%
August 1999	7.2%
July 1999	7.0%
June 1999	6.4%
May 1999	6.2%
April 1999	6.4%
March 1999	5.8%
February 1999	5.6%
January 1999	5.6%
December 1998	5.4%
November 1998	5.4%
October 1998	6.2%
September 1998	6.6%
August 1998	6.8%
July 1998	6.8%
June 1998	7.0%
May 1998	6.8%
April 1998	6.8%
March 1998	6.8%
February 1998	6.8%
January 1998	7.2%
December 1997	7.2%
November 1997	7.4%
October 1997	7.6%
September 1997	7.6%
August 1997	7.6%
July 1997	8.0%
June 1997	8.2%
May 1997	8.2%
April 1997	7.8%
March 1997	7.8%

Month	Interest factor
February 1997	7.6%
January 1997	7.4%

¶ 2850 Locations for Filing Estate, Gift, and GST Tax Forms

The place for filing Forms 706, 706-CE, 706-GS(D), 706-GS(D-1), 706-GS(T), and 709 will differ depending on the filing date of the return. The IRS Service Centers for filing these returns are listed below for return due dates before 2001, during 2001, and beginning January 1, 2002.

Place for Filing Returns Before January 1, 2001

For estates of decedents domiciled in, donors residing in, and settlors (now or at the time of death) residing in	*Use the following Internal Revenue Service address — For returns filed*
	Before January 1, 2001
Florida, Georgia, South Carolina	Atlanta, GA 39901
Illinois, Iowa, Minnesota, Missouri, Wisconsin	Kansas City, MO 64999
New Jersey, New York (New York City and counties of Nassau, Rockland, Suffolk, and Westchester)	Holtsville, NY 00501
New York (all other counties), Connecticut, Maine, Massachusetts, New Hampshire, Rhode Island, Vermont	Andover, MA 05501
Delaware, District of Columbia, Maryland, Pennsylvania, Virginia (as well as nonresident U.S. citizens)	Philadelphia, PA 19255
Indiana, Kentucky, Michigan, Ohio, West Virginia	Cincinnati, OH 45999
Kansas, New Mexico, Oklahoma, Texas	Austin, TX 73301
Alaska, Arizona, California (counties of Alpine, Amador, Butte, Calaveras, Colusa, Contra Costa, Del Norte, El Dorado, Glenn, Humboldt, Lake, Lassen, Marin, Mendocino, Modoc, Napa, Nevada, Placer, Plumas, Sacramento, San Joaquin, Shasta, Sierra, Siskiyou, Solona, Sonoma, Sutter, Tehama, Trinity, Yolo, and Yuba), Colorado, Idaho, Montana, Nebraska, Nevada, North Dakota, Oregon, South Dakota, Utah, Washington, Wyoming	Ogden, UT 84201
California (all other counties), Hawaii	Fresno, CA 93888

For estates of decedents domiciled in, donors residing in, and settlors (now or at the time of death) residing in	*Use the following Internal Revenue Service address — For returns filed*
Alabama, Arkansas, Louisiana, Mississippi, North Carolina, Tennessee	Memphis, TN 37501

Place for Filing Returns During, and After, 2001

For estates of decedents domiciled in, donors residing in, and settlors (now or at the time ofdeath) residing in	*Use the following Internal Revenue Service address — For returns filed*	
	During 2001	*Beginning January 1, 2002*[1]
New York (New York City and counties of Nassau, Rockland, Suffolk, and Westchester)	Brookhaven Service Center Holtsville, NY 00501	Cincinnati, OH 45999
New York (all other counties), Connecticut, Maine, Massachusetts, New Hampshire, Rhode Island, Vermont	Andover, MA 05501	Cincinnati, OH 45999
Florida, Georgia	Atlanta, GA 39901	Cincinnati, OH 45999
Arkansas, Delaware, District of Columbia, Hawaii, Indiana, Iowa, Kentucky, Louisiana, Maryland, Michigan, Minnesota, Mississippi, Missouri, New Jersey, North Carolina, Ohio, Pennsylvania, South Carolina, Texas, West Virginia, Wisconsin	Cincinnati, OH 45999	Cincinnati, OH 45999
Kansas, New Mexico, Oklahoma	Austin, TX 73301	Cincinnati, OH 45999
Alaska, Arizona, California (counties of Alpine, Amador, Butte, Calaveras, Colusa, Contra Costa, Del Norte, El Dorado, Glenn, Humboldt, Lake, Lassen, Marin, Mendocino, Modoc, Napa, Nevada, Placer, Plumas, Sacramento, San Joaquin, Shasta, Sierra, Siskiyou, Solona, Sonoma, Sutter, Tehama, Trinity, Yolo, and Yuba), Colorado, Idaho, Montana, Nebraska, Nevada, North Dakota, Oregon, South Dakota, Utah, Washington, Wyoming	Ogden, UT 84201	Cincinnati, OH 45999
California (all other counties)	Fresno, CA 93888	Cincinnati, OH 45999
Illinois	Kansas City, MO 64999	Cincinnati, OH 45999

[1] Announcement 2001-74, 2001-2 CB 40.

	During 2001	*Beginning January 1, 2002*[1]
Alabama, Tennessee	Memphis, TN 37501	Cincinnati, OH 45999
Virginia	Philadelphia, PA 19255	Cincinnati, OH 45999
American Samoa, Guam, the U.S. Virgin Islands, Puerto Rico, a foreign address, or have an APO or FPO address	Philadelphia, PA 19255	Philadelphia, PA 19255

Any return filed before July 9, 2001, will be deemed filed correctly if it was filed according to the instructions for the particular form at the time it was filed. Returns delivered after December 31, 2001, by courier services should be sent to: 201 W. Rivercenter Blvd., Covington, KY 41015.

¶ 2900

FILLED-IN FORMS TABLE OF CONTENTS

¶ 2910 Fact Situation for Form 706

The following example illustrates a timely filed federal estate tax return with respect to the estate of James X. Diversey, who died on January 1, 2004, while a resident of Cook County, Illinois. Mr. Diversey, a retired vice president of a siding manufacturing company, is survived by his wife, Carrie, two sons (Robert and Richard Diversey), two sisters (Martha Diversey and Ann Fagan), and a granddaughter (Katherine Diversey, the daughter of Robert).

After several specific devises, Diversey's will provides that the residuary estate is to pour over into his revocable trust that had been set up during his lifetime. After payment of all taxes and expenses (without contribution from marital property, property specifically devised, or property passing outside of the probate estate), the trust residue is to be distributed as follows: one-half to the decedent's sister, Ann Fagan, and one-fourth to each of his two sons.

The decedent's wife, Carrie M. Diversey, has substantial wealth apart from the assets that she held with her husband. Because of this, James chose to limit marital bequests to her to about $610,000 (out of a gross estate exceeding $2,850,000).

¶ 2920 Form 706 (Page One)

The filled-in page one of Form 706 relates to the James X. Diversey estate. See the fact situation at ¶2910.

Form **706** (Rev. August 2004) Department of the Treasury Internal Revenue Service

United States Estate (and Generation-Skipping Transfer) Tax Return

Estate of a citizen or resident of the United States (see separate instructions). To be filed for decedents dying after December 31, 2003, and before January 1, 2005. For Paperwork Reduction Act Notice, see the separate instructions.

OMB No. 1545-0015

Part 1.—Decedent and Executor

1a Decedent's first name and middle initial (and maiden name, if any): James X.	1b Decedent's last name: Diversey		2 Decedent's Social Security No.: 241-24-3049
3a County, state, and ZIP code, or foreign country of legal residence (domicile) at time of death: Cook Co.,IL,60430	3b Year domicile established: 1949	4 Date of birth: 11-14-19	5 Date of death: 1-1-2004
6a Name of executor (see page 3 of the instructions): Carrie M. Diversey	6b Executor's address (number and street including apartment or suite no. or rural route; city, town, or post office; state; and ZIP code) and phone no.: 54 Fir Street, Homewood, IL 60430, Phone no. 847-123-9876		
6c Executor's social security number (see page 3 of the instructions): 322-43-8143			
7a Name and location of court where will was probated or estate administered: Probate Court, Cook County, IL			7b Case number: 04-xx-xxxx
8 If decedent died testate, check here ▶ ☒ and attach a certified copy of the will.		9 If Form 4768 is attached, check here ▶ ☐	
10 If Schedule R-1 is attached, check here ▶ ☐			

Part 2.—Tax Computation

Line	Description		Amount
1	Total gross estate less exclusion (from Part 5, Recapitulation, page 3, item 12)		2,850,550
2	Total allowable deductions (from Part 5, Recapitulation, page 3, item 22)		1,064,214
3	Taxable estate (subtract line 2 from line 1)		1,786,336
4	Adjusted taxable gifts (total taxable gifts (within the meaning of section 2503) made by the decedent after December 31, 1976, other than gifts that are includible in decedent's gross estate (section 2001(b)))		0
5	Add lines 3 and 4		1,786,336
6	Tentative tax on the amount on line 5 from Table A on page 4 of the instructions		684,651
7	Total gift tax payable with respect to gifts made by the decedent after December 31, 1976. Include gift taxes by the decedent's spouse for such spouse's share of split gifts (section 2513) only if the decedent was the donor of these gifts and they are includible in the decedent's gross estate (see instructions)		0
8	Gross estate tax (subtract line 7 from line 6)		684,651
9	Maximum unified credit (applicable credit amount) against estate tax	555,800	
10	Adjustment to unified credit (applicable credit amount). (This adjustment may not exceed $6,000. See page 5 of the instructions.)	0	
11	Allowable unified credit (applicable credit amount) (subtract line 10 from line 9)		555,800
12	Subtract line 11 from line 8 (but do not enter less than zero)		128,851
13	Credit for state death taxes (cannot exceed line 12). **Attach credit evidence** (see instructions). Figure the credit by using the amount on line 3 less $60,000. See Table B in the instructions. Enter the amount here from Table B ▶ 84,216 ☐ .25		21,054
14	Subtract line 13 from line 12		107,797
15	Credit for Federal gift taxes on pre-1977 gifts (section 2012) (attach computation)	0	
16	Credit for foreign death taxes (from Schedule(s) P). (Attach Form(s) 706-CE.)	0	
17	Credit for tax on prior transfers (from Schedule Q)	8,160	
18	Total (add lines 15, 16, and 17)		8,160
19	Net estate tax (subtract line 18 from line 14)		99,637
20	Generation-skipping transfer taxes (from Schedule R, Part 2, line 10)		0
21	Total transfer taxes (add lines 19 and 20)		99,637
22	Prior payments. Explain in an attached statement	0	
23	United States Treasury bonds redeemed in payment of estate tax	0	
24	Total (add lines 22 and 23)		0
25	Balance due (or overpayment) (subtract line 24 from line 21)		99,637

Under penalties of perjury, I declare that I have examined this return, including accompanying schedules and statements, and to the best of my knowledge and belief, it is true, correct, and complete. Declaration of preparer other than the executor is based on all information of which preparer has any knowledge.

Carrie M. Diversey — 10-1-2004
Signature(s) of executor(s) — Date

William S. Oaks — 542 James St. Homewood, IL 60430 — 10-1-2004
Signature of preparer other than executor — Address (and ZIP code) — Date

¶ 2930 Form 706 (Page Two)

The filled-in page two of Form 706 relates to the James X. Diversey estate. See the fact situation at ¶2910.

Form 706 (Rev. 8-2004)

Estate of: James X. Diversey

Part 3 — Elections by the Executor

Please check the "Yes" or "No" box for each question. (See instructions beginning on page 6.)		Yes	No
1 Do you elect alternate valuation?	1		X
2 Do you elect special use valuation? If "Yes," you must complete and attach Schedule A-1.	2		X
3 Do you elect to pay the taxes in installments as described in section 6166? If "Yes," you must attach the additional information described on page 10 of the instructions.	3		X
4 Do you elect to postpone the part of the taxes attributable to a reversionary or remainder interest as described in section 6163?	4		X

Part 4 — General Information (**Note:** *Please attach the necessary supplemental documents.* **You must attach the death certificate.**) *(See instructions on page 10.)*

Authorization to receive confidential tax information under Regs. sec. 601.504(b)(2)(i); to act as the estate's representative before the IRS; and to make written or oral presentations on behalf of the estate if return prepared by an attorney, accountant, or enrolled agent for the executor:

Name of representative (print or type)	State	Address (number, street, and room or suite no., city, state, and ZIP code)
William S. Oaks	IL	542 James St., Homewood, IL 60430

I declare that I am the ☒ attorney/ ☐ certified public accountant/ ☐ enrolled agent (you must check the applicable box) for the executor and prepared this return for the executor. I am not under suspension or disbarment from practice before the Internal Revenue Service and am qualified to practice in the state shown above.

Signature	CAF number	Date	Telephone number
		10-1-2004	(708) 940-4600

1 Death certificate number and issuing authority (attach a copy of the death certificate to this return).
CX-12345 Cook County, IL

2 Decedent's business or occupation. If retired, check here ☐ ☒ and state decedent's former business or occupation.
Vice President, Siding Manufacturing Co., Inc., Homewood, IL 60430

3 Marital status of the decedent at time of death:

☒ Married

☐ Widow or widower — Name, SSN, and date of death of deceased spouse ☐

☐ Single

☐ Legally separated

☐ Divorced — Date divorce decree became final ☐

4a Surviving spouse's name	4b Social security number	4c Amount received (see page 10 of the instructions)
Carrie M. Diversey	322-43-8143	609,455

5 Individuals (other than the surviving spouse), trusts, or other estates who receive benefits from the estate (do not include charitable beneficiaries shown in Schedule O) (see instructions). For Privacy Act Notice (applicable to individual beneficiaries only), see the Instructions for Form 1040.

Name of individual, trust, or estate receiving $5,000 or more	Identifying number	Relationship to decedent	Amount (see instructions)
Robert Diversey	497-86-4763	Son	373,911
Richard Diversey	358-76-0957	Son	373,911
Ann Fagan	343-44-6123	Sister	747,823
Martha Diversey	279-60-2763	Sister	65,000
Katherine Diversey	352-54-6197	Granddaughter	105,000
All unascertainable beneficiaries and those who receive less than $5,000 ☐			
Total			1,665,645

Please check the "Yes" or "No" box for each question.	Yes	No
6 Does the gross estate contain any section 2044 property (qualified terminable interest property (QTIP) from a prior gift or estate) (see page 11 of the instructions)?		X

(continued on next page) **Page 2**

¶ 2940 Form 706 (Recapitulation)

The filled-in page three of Form 706, containing the Recapitulation, relates to the James X. Diversey estate. See the fact situation at ¶2910.

Form 706 (Rev. 8-2004)

Part 4 — General Information *(continued)*

	Please check the "Yes" or "No" box for each question.	Yes	No
7a	Have Federal gift tax returns ever been filed? If "Yes," please attach copies of the returns, if available, and furnish the following information:		X
7b	Period(s) covered — 7c Internal Revenue office(s) where filed		
	If you answer "Yes" to any of questions 8 - 16, you must attach additional information as described in the instructions.		
8a	Was there any insurance on the decedent's life that is not included on the return as part of the gross estate?	X	
b	Did the decedent own any insurance on the life of another that is not included in the gross estate?		X
9	Did the decedent, at the time of death, own any property as a joint tenant with right of survivorship in which (a) one or more of the other joint tenants was someone other than the decedent's spouse, and (b) less than the full value of the property is included on the return as part of the gross estate? If "Yes," you must complete and attach Schedule E	X	
10	Did the decedent, at the time of death, own any interest in a partnership or unincorporated business or any stock in an inactive or closely held corporation?	X	
11	Did the decedent make any transfer described in section 2035, 2036, 2037, or 2038 (see the instructions for Schedule G beginning on page 13 of the separate instructions)? If "Yes," you must complete and attach Schedule G	X	
12	Were there in existence at the time of the decedent's death:		
a	Any trusts created by the decedent during his or her lifetime?	X	
b	Any trusts not created by the decedent under which the decedent possessed any power, beneficial interest, or trusteeship?	X	
13	Did the decedent ever possess, exercise, or release any general power of appointment? If "Yes," you must complete and attach Schedule H	X	
14	Was the marital deduction computed under the transitional rule of Public Law 97-34, section 403(e)(3) (Economic Recovery Tax Act of 1981)?		X
	If "Yes," attach a separate computation of the marital deduction, enter the amount on item 20 of the Recapitulation, and note on item 20 "computation attached."		
15	Was the decedent, immediately before death, receiving an annuity described in the "General" paragraph of the instructions for Schedule I? If "Yes," you must complete and attach Schedule I	X	
16	Was the decedent ever the beneficiary of a trust for which a deduction was claimed by the estate of a pre-deceased spouse under section 2056(b)(7) and which is not reported on this return? If "Yes," attach an explanation		X

Part 5 — Recapitulation

Item number	Gross estate		Alternate value	Value at date of death
1	Schedule A — Real Estate	1		1,442,150
2	Schedule B — Stocks and Bonds	2		177,800
3	Schedule C — Mortgages, Notes, and Cash	3		195,969
4	Schedule D — Insurance on the Decedent's Life (attach Form(s) 712)	4		61,120
5	Schedule E — Jointly Owned Property (attach Form(s) 712 for life insurance)	5		294,693
6	Schedule F — Other Miscellaneous Property (attach Form(s) 712 for life insurance)	6		369,150
7	Schedule G — Transfers During Decedent's Life (att. Form(s) 712 for life insurance)	7		252,368
8	Schedule H — Powers of Appointment	8		20,000
9	Schedule I — Annuities	9		37,300
10	Total gross estate (add items 1 through 9)	10		2,850,550
11	Schedule U — Qualified Conservation Easement Exclusion	11		0
12	Total gross estate less exclusion (subtract item 11 from item 10). Enter here and on line 1 of Part 2 — Tax Computation	12		2,850,550

Item number	Deductions		Amount
13	Schedule J — Funeral Expenses and Expenses Incurred in Administering Property Subject to Claims	13	65,675
14	Schedule K — Debts of the Decedent	14	31,145
15	Schedule K — Mortgages and Liens	15	331,680
16	Total of items 13 through 15	16	428,500
17	Allowable amount of deductions from item 16 (see the instructions for item 17 of the Recapitulation)	17	428,500
18	Schedule L — Net Losses During Administration	18	3,294
19	Schedule L — Expenses Incurred in Administering Property Not Subject to Claims	19	1,875
20	Schedule M — Bequests, etc., to Surviving Spouse	20	609,455
21	Schedule O — Charitable, Public, and Similar Gifts and Bequests	21	21,090
22	Total allowable deductions (add items 17 through 21). Enter here and on line 2 of the Tax Computation	22	1,064,214

Page 3

¶ 2950 Filled-In Schedule A

Example Where Alternate Valuation Was Not Elected

The filled-in examples of Schedule A, Form 706 (Rev. August 2004), relate to the James X. Diversey estate. See the fact situation at ¶2910.

Form 706 (Rev. 8-2004)

Estate of: James X. Diversey

SCHEDULE A — Real Estate

- ☐ *For jointly owned property that must be disclosed on Schedule E, see the instructions on the reverse side of Schedule E.*
- ☐ *Real estate that is part of a sole proprietorship should be shown on Schedule F.*
- ☐ *Real estate that is included in the gross estate under section 2035, 2036, 2037, or 2038 should be shown on Schedule G.*
- ☐ *Real estate that is included in the gross estate under section 2041 should be shown on Schedule H.*
- ☐ *If you elect section 2032A valuation, you must complete Schedule A and Schedule A-1.*

Item number	Description	Alternate valuation date	Alternate value	Value at date of death
1	House and lot, 121 Oleander Ave., Tampa, FL (Lot 8, Square 492). Rent of $5,400 due at the end of each quarter: Feb. 1, May 1, Aug. 1, and Nov. 1. Value based on attached appraisal.			336,000
	Rent due, Item 1 for quarter ending Nov. 2003, but not collected at date of death.			5,400
	Rent accrued, Item 1 for Nov. and Dec. 2003, and collected on Feb. 1, 2004.			3,600
2	House and lot, 402 Oceanside Dr., Tampa, FL (Lot 18, Square 40). Rent of $4,750 payable monthly. Value based on attached appraisal.			888,000
	Rent due, Item 2 for Dec. 2003, but not collected at date of death.			4,750
3	Unimproved Lot, Elgin, IL (Township 41, Range 10). Value based on attached appraisal.			99,400
4	Unimproved Lot, Schaumburg, IL (Township 57, Range 3). Value based on attached appraisal.			105,000
	Total from continuation schedules or additional sheets attached to this schedule...........			
	TOTAL. (Also enter on Part 5, Recapitulation, page 3, at item 1.)........................			1,442,150

(If more space is needed, attach the continuation schedule from the end of this package or additional sheets of the same size.)
(See the instructions.)

Schedule A — Page 4

Example Where Estate Qualified for and Elected Alternate Valuation

The amounts shown in the following Schedule are not entered in example of the Recapitulation at ¶2930, because the alternate valuation method was not elected by the estate of the hypothetical decedent, James X. Diversey.

Form 706 (Rev. 8-2004)

Estate of: James X. Diversey

SCHEDULE A — Real Estate

- *For jointly owned property that must be disclosed on Schedule E, see the instructions on the reverse side of Schedule E.*
- *Real estate that is part of a sole proprietorship should be shown on Schedule F.*
- *Real estate that is included in the gross estate under section 2035, 2036, 2037, or 2038 should be shown on Schedule G.*
- *Real estate that is included in the gross estate under section 2041 should be shown on Schedule H.*
- *If you elect section 2032A valuation, you must complete Schedule A and Schedule A-1.*

Item number	Description	Alternate valuation date	Alternate value	Value at date of death
1	House and lot, 121 Oleander Ave.,Tampa, FL (Lot 8, Sq. 492). Rent of $5,400 due at end of each qtr:Feb 1, May 1, Aug 1, and Nov. 1.Value based on appraisal. Not disposed with 6 mon. of death.	7-1-2004	340,000	336,000
	Rent due, Item 1 for quarter ending Nov. 2003, but not collected until Feb. 1, 2004.	2-1-2004	5,400	5,400
	Rent accrued, Item 1 for Nov. and Dec. 2003, and collected on Feb. 1, 2004.	2-1-2004	3,600	3,600
2	House and lot, 402 Oceanside Dr, Tampa,FL, (Lot 18, Square 40). Rent of $4,750 payable monthly. Value based on appraisal. Property exchanged for farm on May 1, 2004.	5-1-2004	882,500	888,000
	Rent due, Item 2 for Dec. 2003, but not collected until Feb. 1, 2004.	2-1-2004	4,750	4,750
3	Unimproved lot, Elgin, IL (Township 41, Range 10). Property sold on Mar. 1, 2004.	3-1-2004	99,400	99,400
4	Unimproved lot, Schaumburg, IL (Township 57, Range 3). Property sold on April 5, 2004.	4-5-2004	102,500	105,000
	Total from continuation schedules or additional sheets attached to this schedule			
	TOTAL. (Also enter on Part 5, Recapitulation, page 3, at item 1.)		1,438,150	1,442,150

(If more space is needed, attach the continuation schedule from the end of this package or additional sheets of the same size.) (See the instructions.)

Schedule A — Page 4

¶ 2960 Filled-In Schedule B

The filled-in Schedule B of Form 706 relates to the James X. Diversey estate. See the fact situation at ¶2910.

Form 706 (Rev. 8-2004)

Estate of: James X. Diversey

SCHEDULE B — Stocks and Bonds

(For jointly owned property that must be disclosed on Schedule E, see the instructions for Schedule E.)

Item number	Description including face amount of bonds or number of shares and par value where needed for identification. Give 9-digit CUSIP number.	CUSIP number	Unit value	Alternate valuation date	Alternate value	Value at date of death
1	$60,000 - Midwest Mining Co., First Mort. 8% 20-yr. bonds, due 2006. Interest payable quarterly Feb. 1, May 1, Aug. 1, and Nov. 1.	123456789	108			64,800
	Interest coupons attached to Item 1, due and payable Nov.1,2003, but not cashed at date of death.					1,200
	Interest accrued on Item 1, Nov. 1, 2003, to Jan. 1, 2004.					800
2	1,000 shares Public Service Corp., common, Traded on NYSE.	987654321	109			109,000
	Dividend on Item 2 of $2.00 per share, declared Dec. 10, 2003, payable on Jan. 10, 2004 to shareholders of record on Dec. 31, 2003.					2,000
	Total from continuation schedules (or additional sheets) attached to this schedule					
	TOTAL. (Also enter on Part 5, Recapitulation, page 3, at item 2.)........................					177,800

(If more space is needed, attach the continuation schedule from the end of this package or additional sheets of the same size.)
(The instructions to Schedule B are in the separate instructions.)

Schedule B — Page 12

The amounts shown in the following Schedule are not entered in example of the Recapitulation at ¶2930, because the alternate valuation method was not elected by the estate of the hypothetical decedent, James X. Diversey.

Form 706 (Rev. 8-2004)

Estate of: James X. Diversey

SCHEDULE B — Stocks and Bonds

(For jointly owned property that must be disclosed on Schedule E, see the instructions for Schedule E.)

Item number	Description including face amount of bonds or number of shares and par value where needed for identification. Give 9-digit CUSIP number.	CUSIP number	Unit value	Alternate valuation date	Alternate value	Value at date of death
1	$60,000-Midwest Mining Co, first mort.8% 20-year bonds due 2006. Interest payable quarterly on Feb. 1, May 1, Aug. 1, and Nov. 1.	123456789	108			64,800
	$30,000 of Item 1 distributed to legatee on Apr.1, 2004.		106	4/1/2004	31,800	
	$30,000 of Item 1 sold by executor on May 1, 2004.		106	5/1/2004	31,800	
	Interest coupons attached to Item 1 due and payable Nov. 1,2003,but not cashed at DOD, cashed by executor Feb. 1, 2004.			2/1/2004	1,200	1,200
	Interest accrued on Item 1, Nov 1, 2003, to Jan 1, 2004.			2/1/2004	800	800
2	1000 sh.Public Service Corp common stock traded on NYSE.	987654321	109			109,000
	Not disposed of within 6 months of death.		102	7/1/2004	102,000	
3	Dividend on Item 2, $2 per share declared Dec. 10, 2003, payable Jan. 10, 2004 to shareholders of record on Dec. 31, 2003.			1/10/2004	2,000	2,000
	Total from continuation schedules (or additional sheets) attached to this schedule					
	TOTAL. (Also enter on Part 5, Recapitulation, page 3, at item 2.)........................				169,600	177,800

(If more space is needed, attach the continuation schedule from the end of this package or additional sheets of the same size.)

(The instructions to Schedule B are in the separate instructions.)

Schedule B — Page 12

¶ 2970 Filled-In Schedule C

The filled-in Schedule C of Form 706 relates to the James X. Diversey estate. See the fact situation at ¶2910.

Form 706 (Rev. 8-2004)

Estate of: James X. Diversey

SCHEDULE C — Mortgages, Notes, and Cash

(For jointly owned property that must be disclosed on Schedule E, see the instructions for Schedule E.)

Item number	Description	Alternate valuation date	Alternate value	Value at date of death
1	Mortgage of $200,000 unpaid balance of $177,240, dated Jan. 1, 1996; Edward Hansen to James X. Diversey; premises 18742 James St., payable in monthly installments of $2,028.60 during first 10 days of each month; interest at 9% per annum, payable out of each installment on unpaid balance; interest to Dec. 31, 2003, paid with last installment on Dec. 3, 2003.			177,240
2	Note for $1,000; unpaid balance of $1,000; given Dec. 1, 2003 by Robert Diversey, 54 Fir St., Homewood IL to James X. Diversey, payable Dec. 1, 2004 with interest at 8% per annum at maturity.			1,000
	Interest on Item 2 accrued at date of decedent's death.			7
3	Cash in decedent's home			1,562
4	Cash on deposit in savings account in decedent's name. Acct. No. 21-738-0 at State National Bank, Peterson and Pulaski Aves., Chicago, IL.			15,410
5	Cash in safe deposit box held in name of decedent at State National Bank, Peterson and Pulaski Aves., Chicago, IL.			750
	Total from continuation schedules (or additional sheets) attached to this schedule			
	TOTAL. (Also enter on Part 5, Recapitulation, page 3, at item 3.)			195,969

(If more space is needed, attach the continuation schedule from the end of this package or additional sheets of the same size.)
(See the instructions.)

Schedule C — Page 13

¶ 2980 Filled-In Schedule D

The filled-in Schedule D of Form 706 relates to the James X. Diversey estate. See the fact situation at ¶2910.

Form 706 (Rev. 8-2004)

Estate of: James X. Diversey

SCHEDULE D — Insurance on the Decedent's Life

You must list **all** policies on the life of the decedent and attach a Form 712 for each policy.

Item number	Description	Alternate valuation date	Alternate value	Value at date of death
1	$10,000 term policy No. N41713643, Union Life Ins. Co., payable to Carrie Diversey, as named beneficiary, proceeds of $10,000 payable in one lump sum, per attached Form 712.			10,000
	Accrued dividends on Item 1: None.			
2	$50,000 20-pay life policy 10-612-5,Boston Life Ins.Co.,proceeds payable in lump sum to decedent's estate,per attached Form 712.			50,000
	$1,120 additional paid-up insurance purchased with dividends on policy in Item 2.			1,120
	INSURANCE PROCEEDS NOT INCLUDIBLE IN GROSS ESTATE:			
	$50,000 20-pay life policy No. 86325, taken out in Jan. 1947 with Met. Life Ins. Co., and paid up in Jan. 1966; proceeds irrevocably payable to Carrie Diversey, named beneficiary, in installments for life or for 20 years certain; proceeds not includible because the insured retained no incidents of ownership and because premiums costs were paid by beneficiary Carrie Diversey,who became owner of the policy by reason of irrevocable assignment of rights for love and affection(Form 712 attached).			
Total from continuation schedules (or additional sheets) attached to this schedule				
TOTAL. (Also enter on Part 5, Recapitulation, page 3, at item 4.)				61,120

(If more space is needed, attach the continuation schedule from the end of this package or additional sheets of the same size.)
(See the instructions.)

Schedule D — Page 15

¶ 2990 Filled-In Schedule E

The filled-in Schedule E of Form 706 relates to the James X. Diversey estate. See the fact situation at ¶2910.

Form 706 (Rev. 8-2004)

Estate of: James X. Diversey

SCHEDULE E — Jointly Owned Property

(If you elect section 2032A valuation, you must complete Schedule E and Schedule A-1.)

PART 1. — Qualified Joint Interests — Interests Held by the Decedent and His or Her Spouse as the Only Joint Tenants (Section 2040(b)(2))

Item number	Description For securities, give CUSIP number.	Alternate valuation date	Alternate value	Value at date of death
1	Residence, 54 Fir Street, Homewood, IL. Single family dwelling on 1/2 acre lot (Plot 68, page 3, Lot 16, square 10).Value per appraisal (copy attached).			355,000
2	Checking account No. 46835, State National Bank, Peterson and Pulaski Aves., Chicago IL.			4,386
	Total from continuation schedules (or additional sheets) attached to this schedule			
1a	Totals	1a		359,386
1b	Amounts included in gross estate (one-half of line 1a)	1b		179,693

PART 2. — All Other Joint Interests

2a State the name and address of each surviving co-tenant. If there are more than three surviving co-tenants, list the additional co-tenants on an attached sheet.

Name	Address (number and street, city, state, and ZIP code)
A. Martha Diversey	54 Fir Street, Homewood, IL 60430
B.	
C.	

Item number	Enter letter for co-tenant	Description (including alternate valuation date if any) For securities, give CUSIP number.	Percentage includible	Includible alternate value	Includible value at date of death
1	A	Rental building and lot 8141 Sangmar, Chicago, IL (Plot 6, page 2, Lot 48, sq. 48). Two-story brick single family dwelling. Value based on appraisal (attached).One half of the value is includible because Martha Diversey contributed one-half of the purchase price of $10,000 in 1957. Property is titled in joint tenancy with right of survivorship.	50%		115,000
		Total from continuation schedules (or additional sheets) attached to this schedule			
2b		Total other joint interests	2b		115,000
3		**Total includible joint interests** (add lines 1b and 2b). Also enter on Part 5, Recapitulation, page 3, at item 5	3		294,693

(If more space is needed, attach the continuation schedule from the end of this package or additional sheets of the same size.)

(See the instructions.) **Schedule E — Page 17**

¶ 3000 Filled-In Schedule F

The filled-in Schedule F of Form 706 relates to the James X. Diversey estate. See the fact situation at ¶2910.

Form 706 (Rev. 8-2004)

Estate of: James X. Diversey

SCHEDULE F — Other Miscellaneous Property Not Reportable Under Any Other Schedule

(For jointly owned property that must be disclosed on Schedule E, see the instructions for Schedule E.)
(If you elect section 2032A valuation, you must complete Schedule F and Schedule A-1.)

		Yes	No
1	Did the decedent at the time of death own any articles of artistic or collectible value in excess of $3,000 or any collections whose artistic or collectible value combined at date of death exceeded $10,000? . . . . If "Yes," submit full details on this schedule and attach appraisals.		X
2	Has the decedent's estate, spouse, or any other person, received (or will receive) any bonus or award as a result of the decedent's employment or death? . . . . If "Yes," submit full details on this schedule.		X
3	Did the decedent at the time of death have, or have access to, a safe deposit box? . . . . If "Yes," state location, and if held in joint names of decedent and another, state name and relationship of joint depositor. If any of the contents of the safe deposit box are omitted from the schedules in this return, explain fully why omitted.	X	

Item number	Description For securities, give CUSIP number.	Alternate valuation date	Alternate value	Value at date of death
1	Household goods and effects, including clothing, all located at 54 Fir Street, Homewood, IL. Value per appraisal (copy attached).			17,650
2	50% interest in City Windows Company, located at 175th and Park Ave., Homewood IL. Partnership business operated by Robert Diversey. Value per appraisal (copy attached).			325,000
3	2002 Cadillac DeVille, 8-cyl., 4-door sedan,18,000 miles. VIN #1G6JD45YZYU807991. Value per appraisal (copy attached).			26,500
	Total from continuation schedules (or additional sheets) attached to this schedule			
	TOTAL. (Also enter on Part 5, Recapitulation, page 3, at item 6.).			369,150

(If more space is needed, attach the continuation schedule from the end of this package or additional sheets of the same size.)
(See the instructions.)

Schedule F — Page 19

¶ 3010 Filled-In Schedule G

The filled-in Schedule G of Form 706 relates to the James X. Diversey estate. See the fact situation at ¶2910.

Form 706 (Rev. 8-2004)

Estate of: James X. Diversey

SCHEDULE G — Transfers During Decedent's Life

(If you elect section 2032A valuation, you must complete Schedule G and Schedule A-1.)

Item number	Description For securities, give CUSIP number.	Alternate valuation date	Alternate value	Value at date of death
A.	Gift tax paid by the decedent or the estate for all gifts made by the decedent or his or her spouse within 3 years before the decedent's death (section 2035(b))	XXXXX		0
B.	Transfers includible under section 2035(a), 2036, 2037, or 2038:			
1	On Feb. 1999, the decedent created the Diversey Revocable Trust with 1st Bank, Ina IL, as successor Trustee. The decedent retained right to trust income for life. At his death, trust corpus was to be paid 1/2 to his sister (Ann Fagan) and 1/4 to each of his sons (copy of Trust Agreement attached). On the date of the decedent's death, the following assets were held in the Trust (See Continuation Schedule G):			
	Total from continuation schedules (or additional sheets) attached to this schedule			252,368
	TOTAL. (Also enter on Part 5, Recapitulation, page 3, at item 7.)			252,368

¶ 3020 Filled-In Continuation Schedule for Schedule G

The filled-in Continuation Schedule for Schedule G of Form 706 relates to the James X. Diversey estate. See the fact situation at ¶2910.

Form 706 (Rev. 8-2004) (Make copies of this schedule before completing it if you will need more than one schedule.)

Estate of: James X. Diversey

CONTINUATION SCHEDULE

Continuation of Schedule G
(Enter letter of schedule you are continuing.)

Item number	Description For securities, give CUSIP number.	Unit value (Sch. B, E, or G only)	Alternate valuation date	Alternate value	Value at date of death or amount deductible
	Item B. 1, Continued:				
	ASSETS HELD IN TRUST:				
a	4,000 shares GTW common stock CUSIP 876543210. Traded OTC.	7.500			30,000
b	$150,000 United States Treasury Note dated 10/31/1998, maturity 10/31/2013; 5.75%, dealer quote, CUSIP 765432109.	99.875			149,813
	Interest accrued on Item b, Oct. 31, 2003, to Jan. 2004.				1,441
c	23,400 shares Oakbrook-Burnbrook Moving Co., common stock, CUSIP 678901234. Traded OTC.	2.500			58,500
d	Cash held in trust on date of death.				12,614
	TOTAL. (Carry forward to main schedule.)				252,368

See the instructions.

Continuation Schedule — Page 39

¶ 3030 Filled-In Schedule H

The filled-in Schedule H of Form 706 relates to the James X. Diversey estate. See the fact situation at ¶2910.

SCHEDULE H — Powers of Appointment

(Include "5 and 5 lapsing" powers (section 2041(b)(2)) held by the decedent.)

(If you elect section 2032A valuation, you must complete Schedule H and Schedule A-1.)

Item number	Description	Alternate valuation date	Alternate value	Value at date of death
1	Securities held by the Sixth National Bank of Chicago, IL, in a testamentary trust created by William Diversey, the decedent's father, who died 11/10/64. The decedent was granted a general power of appointment that he still possessed, unexercised, on the date of his death. Assets held in trust subject to his power are listed on the attached supplement.			20,000
	Total from continuation schedules (or additional sheets) attached to this schedule			
	TOTAL. (Also enter on Part 5, Recapitulation, page 3, at item 8.)			20,000

(If more space is needed, attach the continuation schedule from the end of this package or additional sheets of the same size.)

(The instructions to Schedules G and H are in the separate instructions.) **Schedules G and H — Page 21**

¶ 3040 Filled-In Schedule I

The filled-in Schedule I of Form 706 relates to the James X. Diversey estate. See the fact situation at ¶2910.

Form 706 (Rev. 8-2004)

Estate of: James X. Diversey

SCHEDULE I — Annuities

Note: *Generally, no exclusion is allowed for the estates of decedents dying after December 31, 1984 (see page 15 of the instructions).*

		Yes	No
A	Are you excluding from the decedent's gross estate the value of a lump-sum distribution described in section 2039(f)(2) (as in effect before its repeal by the Deficit Reduction Act of 1984)? . . . . If "Yes," you must attach the information required by the instructions.		X

Item number	Description Show the entire value of the annuity before any exclusions.	Alternate valuation date	Includible alternate value	Includible value at date of death
1	Annuity contract X-16304 issued by Reliable Ins.Co.,Jefferson City, MO, Jan. 15, 1965, payable in monthly installments of $100.00 to the decedent for life,then to his widow, Carrie Diversey, for life. On the death of the survivor, the excess cost over annuity payments is to be refunded to their son, Robert Diversey. Carrie Diversey was born on January 3, 1927. The decedent paid the entire cost of the annuity. Value obtained from company that issued the contract.			12,300
2	Lump-sum death benefit paid to decedent's widow, Carrie Diversey, under terms of employees' trust qualified under Code Sec. 401(a) to which the decedent's former employer, Siding Mfg. Co., Homewood, IL, contributed one-half of the cost, while decedent contributed the other one-half.			25,000
3	United Annuities of America, Inc., policy No. 355950-492. During his lifetime, the decedent was receiving monthly payment of $125.00 under the policy. No value is included in the decedent's gross estate because all payments under the policy ceased upon his death. (Letter of Issuer attached).			0
	Total from continuation schedules (or additional sheets) attached to this schedule			
	TOTAL. (Also enter on Part 5, Recapitulation, page 3, at item 9.)			37,300

(If more space is needed, attach the continuation schedule from the end of this package or additional sheets of the same size.)

Schedule I — Page 22 (The instructions to Schedule I are in the separate instructions.)

¶ 3050 Filled-In Schedule J

The filled-in Schedule J of Form 706 relates to the James X. Diversey estate. See the fact situation at ¶2910.

Form 706 (Rev. 8-2004)

Estate of: James X. Diversey

SCHEDULE J — Funeral Expenses and Expenses Incurred in Administering Property Subject to Claims

Note: *Do not list on this schedule expenses of administering property not subject to claims. For those expenses, see the instructions for Schedule L.*

If executors' commissions, attorney fees, etc., are claimed and allowed as a deduction for estate tax purposes, they are not allowable as a deduction in computing the taxable income of the estate for federal income tax purposes. They are allowable as an income tax deduction on Form 1041 if a waiver is filed to waive the deduction on Form 706 (see the Form 1041 instructions).

Item number	Description	Expense amount	Total amount
	A. Funeral expenses:		
1	a. Homewood Funeral Home, Homewood, IL: Funeral and incidental expenses.	8,000	8,000
	b. Oak Ridge Cemetery, Oak Park, IL: Burial plot and marker.	2,275	2,275
	Total funeral expenses ▶		10,275
	B. Administration expenses:		
	1 Executors' commissions — amount estimated/~~agreed upon/paid~~. (Strike out the words that do not apply.)		22,000
	2 Attorney fees — amount estimated/~~agreed upon/paid~~. (Strike out the words that do not apply.)		19,500
	3 Accountant fees — amount estimated/~~agreed upon/paid~~. (Strike out the words that do not apply.)		6,500
	4 Miscellaneous expenses:	Expense amount	
	a. Roberts and Oaks, 542 James St., Homewood, IL: Appraisal of Illinois real estate and personal effects.	1,500	
	b. Hillsborough Realty Appraisals, 410 Ashley Dr., Tampa, FL, Appraisal of Florida real estate.	2,850	
	c. Jordan Business Consultants, 100 N. Michigan Ave., Chicago, IL: Appraisal of partnership interest.	2,500	
	d. Probate Court, Cook County, IL: Probate fees and incidental expenses.	250	
	e. Other administration expenses: Hiring of clerk, collection and storage of assets, etc.	300	
	Total miscellaneous expenses from continuation schedules (or additional sheets) attached to this schedule		
	Total miscellaneous expenses ▶		7,400
	TOTAL. (Also enter on Part 5, Recapitulation, page 3, at item 13.) ▶		65,675

(If more space is needed, attach the continuation schedule from the end of this package or additional sheets of the same size.)
(See the instructions.) **Schedule J — Page 23**

¶ 3060 Filled-In Schedule K

The filled-in Schedule K of Form 706 relates to the James X. Diversey estate. See the fact situation at ¶2910.

Form 706 (Rev. 8-2004)

Estate of: James X. Diversey

SCHEDULE K — Debts of the Decedent, and Mortgages and Liens

Item number	Debts of the Decedent — Creditor and nature of claim, and allowable death taxes	Amount unpaid to date	Amount in contest	Amount claimed as a deduction
1	Richard LaForge,M.D.,63 E. 8th St., Chicago,IL. Medical services for decedent's last illness (Nov. 26,2003 to Jan. 1, 2004.			3,200
2	St. Luke's Hosp., Chicago, IL. Hospitalization from Dec. 28, 2003 to to Jan. 1,2004 for decedent's last illness.			27,295
3	Telco Co., phone service from Nov. 26, 2003 to Jan. 1, 2004.			150
4	All Energy, Inc., Gas,electric service, Nov. 24, 2003 to Jan. 1, 2004.			500
	Total from continuation schedules (or additional sheets) attached to this schedule			
	TOTAL. (Also enter on Part 5, Recapitulation, page 3, at item 14.)			31,145

Item number	Mortgages and Liens — Description	Amount
1	Mortgage secured by house and lot, 402 Oceanside Drive, Tampa, FL (Schedule A, Item 2). The decedent was personally liable. The mortgagee is Home Mortgage Co., Hillsborough and Florida Aves., Tampa, FL. The mortgage is for 20 years, dated March 13, 1997, with a face amount of $416,000; interest at 7% per annum. Interest paid through Dec. 31, 2003, prior to decedent's death.	331,680
	Total from continuation schedules (or additional sheets) attached to this schedule	
	TOTAL. (Also enter on Part 5, Recapitulation, page 3, at item 15.)	331,680

(If more space is needed, attach the continuation schedule from the end of this package or additional sheets of the same size.)
(The instructions to Schedule K are in the separate instructions.) Schedule K — Page 25

¶ 3070 Filled-In Schedule L

The filled-in Schedule L of Form 706 relates to the James X. Diversey estate. See the fact situation at ¶2910.

Form 706 (Rev. 8-2004)

Estate of: James X. Diversey

SCHEDULE L — Net Losses During Administration and Expenses Incurred in Administering Property Not Subject to Claims

Item number	Net losses during administration (Note: *Do not deduct losses claimed on a Federal income tax return.*)	Amount
1	Damage to house listed on Schedule A, Item 2, resulting from high winds on August 30, 2004. Five windows were broken and siding on a portion of the upper half of the house required patching and repainting. Loss was not covered by insurance.	3,294
	Total from continuation schedules (or additional sheets) attached to this schedule	
	TOTAL. (Also enter on Part 5, Recapitulation, page 3, at item 18.)	3,294

Item number	Expenses incurred in administering property not subject to claims (Indicate whether estimated, agreed upon, or paid.)	Amount
1	Trustee commissions paid to the 1st Bank, Ina, IL, with respect to the James X. Diversey Revocable Trust, listed on Schedule G, Item 1.	1,875
	Total from continuation schedules (or additional sheets) attached to this schedule	
	TOTAL. (Also enter on Part 5, Recapitulation, page 3, at item 19.)	1,875

(If more space is needed, attach the continuation schedule from the end of this package or additional sheets of the same size.)

Schedule L — Page 26 (The instructions to Schedule L are in the separate instructions.)

¶ 3080 Filled-In Schedule M

The filled-in Schedule M of Form 706 relates to the James X. Diversey estate. See the fact situation at ¶2910.

Form 706 (Rev. 8-2004)

Estate of: James X. Diversey

SCHEDULE M — Bequests, etc., to Surviving Spouse

Election To Deduct Qualified Terminable Interest Property Under Section 2056(b)(7). If a trust (or other property) meets the requirements of qualified terminable interest property under section 2056(b)(7), and

a. The trust or other property is listed on Schedule M, and

b. The value of the trust (or other property) is entered in whole or in part as a deduction on Schedule M, then unless the executor specifically identifies the trust (all or a fractional portion or percentage) or other property to be excluded from the election, the executor shall be deemed to have made an election to have such trust (or other property) treated as qualified terminable interest property under section 2056(b)(7).

If less than the entire value of the trust (or other property) that the executor has included in the gross estate is entered as a deduction on Schedule M, the executor shall be considered to have made an election only as to a fraction of the trust (or other property). The numerator of this fraction is equal to the amount of the trust (or other property) deducted on Schedule M. The denominator is equal to the total value of the trust (or other property).

Election To Deduct Qualified Domestic Trust Property Under Section 2056A. If a trust meets the requirements of a qualified domestic trust under section 2056A(a) and this return is filed no later than 1 year after the time prescribed by law (including extensions) for filing the return, and

a. The entire value of a trust or trust property is listed on Schedule M, and

b. The entire value of the trust or trust property is entered as a deduction on Schedule M,

then unless the executor specifically identifies the trust to be excluded from the election, the executor shall be deemed to have made an election to have the entire trust treated as qualified domestic trust property.

			Yes	No
1	Did any property pass to the surviving spouse as a result of a qualified disclaimer? *If "Yes," attach a copy of the written disclaimer required by section 2518(b).*	1		X
2a	In what country was the surviving spouse born? United States			
b	What is the surviving spouse's date of birth? January 3, 1927			
c	Is the surviving spouse a U.S. citizen?	2c	X	
d	If the surviving spouse is a naturalized citizen, when did the surviving spouse acquire citizenship?			
e	If the surviving spouse is not a U.S. citizen, of what country is the surviving spouse a citizen?			
3	**Election Out of QTIP Treatment of Annuities** — Do you elect under section 2056(b)(7)(C)(ii) **not** to treat as qualified terminable interest property any joint and survivor annuities that are included in the gross estate and would otherwise be treated as qualified terminable interest property under section 2056(b)(7)(C)? (see instructions)	3		X

Item number	Description of property interests passing to surviving spouse	Amount
1	House and lot, 121 Oleander Ave., Tampa, FL, subject to devise in Paragraph 8 of decedent's Will (Schedule A, Item 1).	336,000
2	Cadillac DeVille (Schedule F, Item 3).	26,500
3	Cash (Schedule C, aggregate of items 3 and 5).	2,312
4	Life insurance proceeds from Union Life Ins. Co., policy no. N41713643 (Schedule D, Item 1).	10,000
	Total from continuation schedules (or additional sheets) attached to this schedule	234,643

4	**Total** amount of property interests listed on Schedule M			4	609,455
5a	Federal estate taxes payable out of property interests listed on Schedule M	5a	0		
b	Other death taxes payable out of property interests listed on Schedule M	5b	0		
c	Federal and state GST taxes payable out of property interests listed on Schedule M	5c	0		
d	Add items 5a, b, and c			5d	0
6	Net amount of property interests listed on Schedule M (subtract 5d from 4). Also enter on Part 5, Recapitulation, page 3, at item 20			6	609,455

(If more space is needed, attach the continuation schedule from the end of this package or additional sheets of the same size.) (See the instructions.)

Schedule M — Page 27

¶ 3090 Filled-In Continuation Schedule for Schedule M

The filled-in Continuation Schedule for Schedule M of Form 706 relates to the James X. Diversey estate. See the fact situation at ¶2910.

Form 706 (Rev. 8-2004) (Make copies of this schedule before completing it if you will need more than one schedule.)

Estate of: James X. Diversey

CONTINUATION SCHEDULE

Continuation of Schedule M
(Enter letter of schedule you are continuing.)

Item number	Description For securities, give CUSIP number.	Unit value (Sch. B, E, or G only)	Alternate valuation date	Alternate value	Value at date of death or amount deductible
5	Checking account No.46835, State National Bank (1/2 of the amount listed on Schedule E, Part 1, Item 2).				2,193
6	Death Benefit from qualified plan (Schedule I, Item 2).				25,000
7	Bequest under Para. 3 of Will, of household goods and personalty (Schedule F, Item 1).				17,650
8	Residence, 54 Fir Street, Homewood, IL (1/2 of the value listed on Schedule E, Part 1, Item 1).				177,500
9	Annuity contract No. X-16304 (Schedule I, Item 1).				12,300
TOTAL. (Carry forward to main schedule.)					234,643

See the instructions.

Continuation Schedule — Page 39

¶ 3100 Filled-In Schedule O

The filled-in Schedule O of Form 706 relates to the James X. Diversey estate. See the fact situation at ¶2910.

Form 706 (Rev. 8-2004)

Estate of: James X. Diversey

SCHEDULE O — Charitable, Public, and Similar Gifts and Bequests

		Yes	No
1a	If the transfer was made by will, has any action been instituted to have interpreted or to contest the will or any of its provisions affecting the charitable deductions claimed in this schedule? . . . . . If "Yes," full details must be submitted with this schedule.		X
b	According to the information and belief of the person or persons filing this return, is any such action planned? . . . . If "Yes," full details must be submitted with this schedule.		X
2	Did any property pass to charity as the result of a qualified disclaimer? . . . . . If "Yes," attach a copy of the written disclaimer required by section 2518(b).		X

Item number	Name and address of beneficiary	Character of institution	Amount
1	American Heart Assn., Chicago, IL, 10 shares Public Service Corp., common stock (Schedule B, Item 2).	Medical Research	1,090
2	1st Bank, Ina, IL, in trust for the purpose of providing scholarships for worthy graduates of Homewood-Flossmor High School in accordance with paragraph 8 of the decedent's Will.	Trust Co.	20,000

	Total from continuation schedules (or additional sheets) attached to this schedule			
3	Total		**3**	21,090
4a	Federal estate tax payable out of property interests listed above	**4a** 0		
b	Other death taxes payable out of property interests listed above	**4b** 0		
c	Federal and state GST taxes payable out of property interests listed above	**4c** 0		
d	Add items 4a, b, and c		**4d**	0
5	Net value of property interests listed above (subtract 4d from 3). Also enter on Part 5, Recapitulation, page 3, at item 21		**5**	21,090

(If more space is needed, attach the continuation schedule from the end of this package or additional sheets of the same size.)
(The instructions to Schedule O are in the separate instructions.)

Schedule O — Page 31

¶ 3110 Filled-In Worksheet for Schedule Q

The filled-in Worksheet for Schedule Q of Form 706 relates to the James X. Diversey estate. See the fact situation at ¶2910.

Worksheet for Schedule Q — Credit for Tax on Prior Transfers

Part I Transferor's tax on prior transfers

Item	Transferor (From Schedule Q) A	B	C	Total for all transfers (line 8 only)
1. Gross value of prior transfer to this transferee	109,000			
2. Death taxes payable from prior transfer	0			
3. Encumbrances allocable to prior transfer	0			
4. Obligations allocable to prior transfer	0			
5. Marital deduction applicable to line 1 above, as shown on transferor's Form 706	0			
6. TOTAL *(Add lines 2, 3, 4, and 5)*	0.00			
7. **Net value of transfers** *(Subtract line 6 from line 1)*	109,000.00			
8. **Net value of transfers** *(Add columns A, B, and C of line 7)*	109,000			109,000.00
9. Transferor's taxable estate	1,200,000			
10. Federal estate tax paid	82,000			
11. State death taxes paid	22,600			
12. Foreign death taxes paid	0			
13. Other death taxes paid	0			
14. TOTAL taxes paid *(Add lines 10, 11, 12 and 13)*	104,600.00			
15. **Value of transferor's estate** *(Subtract line 14 from line 9)*	1,095,400.00			
16. Net Federal estate tax paid on transferor's estate	82,000			
17. Credit for gift tax paid on transferor's estate with respect to pre-1977 gifts (section 2012)	0			
18. Credit allowed transferor's estate for tax on prior transfers from prior transferor(s) who died within 10 years before death of decedent	0			
19. Tax on transferor's estate *(Add lines 16, 17, and 18)*	82,000.00			
20. Transferor's tax on prior transfers (Line 7 ÷ line 15) × line 19 of respective estates)	8,159.58			

Part II Transferee's tax on prior transfers

Item						Amount
21. Transferee's actual tax before allowance of credit for prior transfers *(see instructions)*					21	107,797
22. Total gross estate of transferee *(from line 1 of the Tax Computation, page 1, Form 706)*					22	2,850,550
23. Net value of all transfers *(from line 8 of this worksheet)*					23	109,000
24. Transferee's reduced gross estate *(subtract line 23 from line 22)*					24	27,415,500
25. Total debts and deductions (not including marital and charitable deductions) *(items 17, 18, and 19 of the Recapitulation, page 3, Form 706)*			25	433,669		
26. Marital and Qualified Family-Owned Business Interest deduction *(from item 20 and 22, Recapitulation, page 3, Form 706) (see instructions)*			26	609,455		
27. Charitable bequests *(from item 21, Recapitulation, page 3, Form 706)*			27	21,090		
28. Charitable deduction proportion ([line 23 ÷ (line 22 − line 25)] × line 27)			28	951.15		
29. Reduced charitable deduction *(subtract line 28 from line 27)*			29	20,138.85		
30. Transferee's deduction as adjusted *(add lines 25, 26, and 29)*					30	1,063,263
31. (a) Transferee's reduced taxable estate *(subtract line 30 from line 24)*					31(a)	1,678,287
(b) Adjusted taxable gifts					31(b)	0
(c) Total reduced taxable estate *(add lines 31(a) and 31(b))*					31(c)	1,678,287
32. Tentative tax on reduced taxable estate			32	636,029		
33. (a) Post-1976 gift taxes paid	33(a)	0				
(b) Unified credit (applicable credit amount)	33(b)	555,800				
(c) Section 2011 state death tax credit	33(c)	19,109				
(d) Section 2012 gift tax credit	33(d)	0				
(e) Section 2014 foreign death tax credit	33(e)	0				
(f) Total credits *(add lines 33(a) through 33(e))*			33(f)	574,909		
34. Net tax on reduced taxable estate *(subtract line 33(f) from line 32)*					34	61,120
35. Transferee's tax on prior transfers *(subtract line 34 from line 21)*					35	46,677

-30- **Instructions for Schedules**

¶ 3120 Filled-In Schedule Q

The filled-in Schedule Q of Form 706 relates to the James X. Diversey estate. See the fact situation at ¶2910.

SCHEDULE Q — Credit for Tax on Prior Transfers

Part 1 — Transferor Information

	Name of transferor	Social security number	IRS office where estate tax return was filed	Date of death
A	Albert Smith	335-05-1234	Cincinnati, OH	2-2-2003
B				
C				

Check here ▶ ☐ if section 2013(f) (special valuation of farm, etc., real property) adjustments to the computation of the credit were made (see page 21 of the instructions).

Part 2 — Computation of Credit (see instructions beginning on page 20)

Item	Transferor A	Transferor B	Transferor C	Total A, B, & C
1 Transferee's tax as apportioned (from worksheet, (line 7 ÷ line 8) × line 35 for each column)	46,677			
2 Transferor's tax (from each column of worksheet, line 20)	8,160			
3 Maximum amount before percentage requirement (for each column, enter amount from line 1 or 2, whichever is smaller)	8,160			
4 Percentage allowed (each column) (see instructions)	100 %	%	%	
5 Credit allowable (line 3 × line 4 for each column)	8,160			
6 TOTAL credit allowable (add columns A, B, and C of line 5). Enter here and on line 17 of Part 2, Tax Computation				8,160

Schedules P and Q — Page 32 (The instructions to Schedules P and Q are in the separate instructions.)

¶ 3130 Filled-In Schedule R

The filled-in Schedule R of Form 706 relates to the James X. Diversey estate. See the fact situation at ¶2910.

Form 706 (Rev. 8-2004)

SCHEDULE R — Generation-Skipping Transfer Tax

Note: *To avoid application of the deemed allocation rules, Form 706 and Schedule R should be filed to allocate the GST exemption to trusts that may later have taxable terminations or distributions under section 2612 even if the form is not required to be filed to report estate or GST tax.*

The GST tax is imposed on taxable transfers of interests in property located **outside the United States** *as well as property located inside the United States.*

See instructions beginning on page 21.

Part 1 — GST Exemption Reconciliation (Section 2631) and Section 2652(a)(3) (Special QTIP) Election

You no longer need to check a box to make a section 2652(a)(3) (special QTIP) election. If you list qualifying property in Part 1, line 9, below, you will be considered to have made this election. See page 24 of the separate instructions for details.

1	Maximum allowable GST exemption	1	1,500,000
2	Total GST exemption allocated by the decedent against decedent's lifetime transfers	2	0
3	Total GST exemption allocated by the executor, using Form 709, against decedent's lifetime transfers	3	0
4	GST exemption allocated on line 6 of Schedule R, Part 2	4	0
5	GST exemption allocated on line 6 of Schedule R, Part 3	5	105,000
6	Total GST exemption allocated on line 4 of Schedule(s) R-1	6	0
7	Total GST exemption allocated to inter vivos transfers and direct skips (add lines 2 - 6)	7	105,000
8	GST exemption available to allocate to trusts and section 2032A interests (subtract line 7 from line 1)	8	1,395,000

9 Allocation of GST exemption to trusts (as defined for GST tax purposes):

A Name of trust	B Trust's EIN (if any)	C GST exemption allocated on lines 2 - 6, above (see instructions)	D Additional GST exemption allocated (see instructions)	E Trust's inclusion ratio (optional — see instructions)
9D Total. May not exceed line 8, above		9D		

10 GST exemption available to allocate to section 2032A interests received by individual beneficiaries (subtract line 9D from line 8). You must attach special use allocation schedule (see instructions) . . . 10 1,395,000

(The instructions to Schedule R are in the separate instructions.) **Schedule R — Page 33**

Form 706 (Rev. 8-2004)

Estate of: James X. Diversey

Part 2 — Direct Skips Where the Property Interests Transferred Bear the GST Tax on the Direct Skips

Name of skip person	Description of property interest transferred	Estate tax value

1	Total estate tax values of all property interests listed above	1	
2	Estate taxes, state death taxes, and other charges borne by the property interests listed above	2	
3	GST taxes borne by the property interests listed above but imposed on direct skips other than those shown on this Part 2 (see instructions)	3	
4	Total fixed taxes and other charges (add lines 2 and 3)	4	
5	Total tentative maximum direct skips (subtract line 4 from line 1)	5	
6	GST exemption allocated	6	
7	Subtract line 6 from line 5	7	
8	GST tax due (divide line 7 by 3.083333)	8	
9	Enter the amount from line 8 of Schedule R, Part 3	9	0
10	**Total GST taxes payable by the estate** (add lines 8 and 9). Enter here and on line 20 of Part 2 — Tax Computation, on page 1	10	0

Schedule R — Page 34

Form 706 (Rev. 8-2004)

Estate of: James X. Diversey

Part 3 — Direct Skips Where the Property Interests Transferred Do Not Bear the GST Tax on the Direct Skips

Name of skip person	Description of property interest transferred	Estate tax value
Katherine Diversey	Unimproved lot, Schaumburg, IL (Schedule A, Item 4). Under Paragraph 10 of the decedent's Will, all federal estate and generation-skipping transfer taxes are payable from the residue.	105,000

1	Total estate tax values of all property interests listed above	1	105,000
2	Estate taxes, state death taxes, and other charges borne by the property interests listed above	2	0
3	GST taxes borne by the property interests listed above but imposed on direct skips other than those shown on this Part 3 (see instructions)	3	0
4	Total fixed taxes and other charges (add lines 2 and 3)	4	0
5	Total tentative maximum direct skips (subtract line 4 from line 1)	5	105,000
6	GST exemption allocated	6	105,000
7	Subtract line 6 from line 5	7	0
8	GST tax due (multiply line 7 by .48). Enter here and on Schedule R, Part 2, line 9	8	0

Schedule R — Page 35

¶ 3140 Fact Situation for Form 706, Schedule A

James X. Diversey, the hypothetical decedent in the main Form 706 example (see ¶2910), did not own property that would have qualified his estate for the special use deduction (reported on Schedule A-1). The following filled-in Schedule A-1, Form 706 (Rev. Aug. 2004), relates to the fact pattern below.

Donald Whitecliffe died with a gross estate of $2,175,000, and total deductions of $140,000. He had owned and operated a farm in Antioch, Illinois, until his death on March 15, 2004. The farm has been in the Whitecliffe family since 1949. Whitecliffe, a widower, is survived by his son, Brad, and two grandchildren, John and Randy (Brad's sons). Because Brad had no interest in continuing to operate the farm, Whitecliffe's will devised the farm to the grandchildren, who will jointly run the farm.

Although the farm property has a value of $600,000 as a farm, its highest and best use would be as a residential development valued at $850,000. Because the estate met all qualifications for doing so, and the qualified heirs agreed to sign all required agreements, the estate elected special use valuation (see ¶280 and following).

The $600,000 value of the farm transferred to the two grandchildren is a generation-skipping transfer that the decedent's executor would report on Form 706, Schedule R. In order to avoid GST tax liability, a portion of Donald Whitecliffe's $1,500,000 GST exemption, if still unused at the time of his death, would have to be allocated to the transfer.

¶ 3150 Filled-In Schedule A-1

Form 706 (Rev. 8-2004)

Checklist for Section 2032A Election. *If you are going to make the special use valuation election on Schedule A-1, please use this checklist to ensure that you are providing everything necessary to make a valid election.*

To have a valid special use valuation election under section 2032A, you must file, in addition to the Federal estate tax return, **(a)** a notice of election (Schedule A-1, Part 2), and **(b)** a fully executed agreement (Schedule A-1, Part 3). You must include certain information in the notice of election. To ensure that the notice of election includes all of the information required for a valid election, use the following checklist. The checklist is for your use only. Do not file it with the return.

1. Does the notice of election include the decedent's name and social security number as they appear on the estate tax return?

2. Does the notice of election include the relevant qualified use of the property to be specially valued?

3. Does the notice of election describe the items of real property shown on the estate tax return that are to be specially valued and identify the property by the Form 706 schedule and item number?

4. Does the notice of election include the fair market value of the real property to be specially valued and also include its value based on the qualified use (determined without the adjustments provided in section 2032A(b)(3)(B))?

5. Does the notice of election include the adjusted value (as defined in section 2032A(b)(3)(B)) of **(a)** all real property that both passes from the decedent and is used in a qualified use, without regard to whether it is to be specially valued, and **(b)** all real property to be specially valued?

6. Does the notice of election include **(a)** the items of personal property shown on the estate tax return that pass from the decedent to a qualified heir and that are used in qualified use and **(b)** the total value of such personal property adjusted under section 2032A(b)(3)(B)?

7. Does the notice of election include the adjusted value of the gross estate? (See section 2032A(b)(3)(A).)

8. Does the notice of election include the method used to determine the special use value?

9. Does the notice of election include copies of written appraisals of the fair market value of the real property?

10. Does the notice of election include a statement that the decedent and/or a member of his or her family has owned all of the specially valued property for at least 5 years of the 8 years immediately preceding the date of the decedent's death?

11. Does the notice of election include a statement as to whether there were any periods during the 8-year period preceding the decedent's date of death during which the decedent or a member of his or her family did not **(a)** own the property to be specially valued, **(b)** use it in a qualified use, or **(c)** materially participate in the operation of the farm or other business? (See section 2032A(e)(6).)

12. Does the notice of election include, for each item of specially valued property, the name of every person taking an interest in that item of specially valued property and the following information about each such person: **(a)** the person's address, **(b)** the person's taxpayer identification number, **(c)** the person's relationship to the decedent, and **(d)** the value of the property interest passing to that person based on both fair market value and qualified use?

13. Does the notice of election include affidavits describing the activities constituting material participation and the identity of the material participants?

14. Does the notice of election include a legal description of each item of specially valued property?

(In the case of an election made for qualified woodlands, the information included in the notice of election must include the reason for entitlement to the woodlands election.)

Any election made under section 2032A will not be valid unless a properly executed agreement (Schedule A-1, Part 3) is filed with the estate tax return. To ensure that the agreement satisfies the requirements for a valid election, use the following checklist.

1. Has the agreement been signed by each and every qualified heir having an interest in the property being specially valued?

2. Has every qualified heir expressed consent to personal liability under section 2032A(c) in the event of an early disposition or early cessation of qualified use?

3. Is the agreement that is actually signed by the qualified heirs in a form that is binding on all of the qualified heirs having an interest in the specially valued property?

4. Does the agreement designate an agent to act for the parties to the agreement in all dealings with the IRS on matters arising under section 2032A?

5. Has the agreement been signed by the designated agent and does it give the address of the agent?

Page 7

Form 706 (Rev. 8-2004)

Estate of: Donald Whitecliffe | Decedent's Social Security Number 020-30-4050

SCHEDULE A-1 — Section 2032A Valuation

Part 1. Type of Election (Before making an election, see the checklist on page 7.):

☐ **Protective election (Regulations section 20.2032A-8(b)).** Complete Part 2, line 1, and column A of lines 3 and 4. (See instructions.)

☒ **Regular election.** Complete all of Part 2 (including line 11, if applicable) and Part 3. (See instructions.)

Before completing Schedule A-1, see the checklist on page 7 for the information and documents that must be included to make a valid election.

The election is not valid unless the agreement (i.e., Part 3 — Agreement to Special Valuation Under Section 2032A) —

- Is signed by each and every qualified heir with an interest in the specially valued property, and
- Is attached to this return when it is filed.

Part 2. Notice of Election (Regulations section 20.2032A-8(a)(3))

Note: *All real property entered on lines 2 and 3 must also be entered on Schedules A, E, F, G, or H, as applicable.*

1 Qualified use — check one ▶ ☒ Farm used for farming, or
▶ ☐ Trade or business other than farming

2 Real property used in a qualified use, passing to qualified heirs, and to be specially valued on this Form 706.

A Schedule and item number from Form 706	B Full value (without section 2032A(b)(3)(B) adjustment)	C Adjusted value (with section 2032A(b)(3)(B) adjustment)	D Value based on qualified use (without section 2032A(b)(3)(B) adjustment)
Schedule A, Item 1.	850,000	600,000	600,000
Totals	850,000	600,000	600,000

Attach a legal description of all property listed on line 2.
Attach copies of appraisals showing the column B values for all property listed on line 2.

3 Real property used in a qualified use, passing to qualified heirs, but not specially valued on this Form 706.

A Schedule and item number from Form 706	B Full value (without section 2032A(b)(3)(B) adjustment)	C Adjusted value (with section 2032A(b)(3)(B) adjustment)	D Value based on qualified use (without section 2032A(b)(3)(B) adjustment)
Totals			

If you checked "Regular election," you must attach copies of appraisals showing the column B values for all property listed on line 3.

(continued on next page)

Schedule A-1 — Page 8

Form 706 (Rev. 8-2004)

4 Personal property used in a qualified use and passing to qualified heirs.

A Schedule and item number from Form 706	B Adjusted value (with section 2032A(b)(3)(B) adjustment)	A (continued) Schedule and item number from Form 706	B (continued) Adjusted value (with section 2032A(b)(3)(B) adjustment)
		"Subtotal" from Col. B, below left	
Subtotal		Total adjusted value	

5 Enter the value of the total gross estate as adjusted under section 2032A(b)(3)(A). ▶ 2,175,000

6 **Attach a description of the method used to determine the special value based on qualified use.**

7 Did the decedent and/or a member of his or her family own all property listed on line 2 for at least 5 of the 8 years immediately preceding the date of the decedent's death? ☒ **Yes** ☐ **No**

8 Were there any periods during the 8-year period preceding the date of the decedent's death during which the decedent or a member of his or her family:

	Yes	No
a Did not own the property listed on line 2 above?		X
b Did not use the property listed on line 2 above in a qualified use?		X
c Did not materially participate in the operation of the farm or other business within the meaning of section 2032A(e)(6)?		X

If "Yes" to any of the above, you must attach a statement listing the periods. If applicable, describe whether the exceptions of sections 2032A(b)(4) or (5) are met.

9 **Attach affidavits describing the activities constituting material participation and the identity and relationship to the decedent of the material participants.**

10 Persons holding interests. Enter the requested information for each party who received any interest in the specially valued property. **(Each of the qualified heirs receiving an interest in the property must sign the agreement, and the agreement must be filed with this return.)**

	Name	Address
A	John Whitecliffe	104 Basswood Way, Fox Lake, IL
B	Randy Whitecliffe	18150 Gaither Road, Addison, IL
C		
D		
E		
F		
G		
H		

	Identifying number	Relationship to decedent	Fair market value	Special use value
A	341-34-1341	Grandson	425,000	300,000
B	341-41-3413	Grandson	425,000	300,000
C				
D				
E				
F				
G				
H				

You must attach a computation of the GST tax savings attributable to direct skips for each person listed above who is a skip person. (See instructions.)

11 **Woodlands election.** Check here ▶ ☐ if you wish to make a woodlands election as described in section 2032A(e)(13). Enter the Schedule and item numbers from Form 706 of the property for which you are making this election ▶ ______

You must attach a statement explaining why you are entitled to make this election. The IRS may issue regulations that require more information to substantiate this election. You will be notified by the IRS if you must supply further information.

Schedule A-1 — Page 9

Form 706 (Rev. 8-2004)

Part 3. Agreement to Special Valuation Under Section 2032A

Estate of:	Date of Death	Decedent's Social Security Number
Donald Whitecliffe	03/15/2004	020-30-4050

There cannot be a valid election unless:

- The agreement is executed by each and every one of the qualified heirs, and
- The agreement is included with the estate tax return when the estate tax return is filed.

We (list all qualified heirs and other persons having an interest in the property required to sign this agreement)

John Whitecliffe

Randy Whilecliffe ,

being all the qualified heirs and ______________________________

______________________________ ,

being all other parties having interests in the property which is qualified real property and which is valued under section 2032A of the Internal Revenue Code, do hereby approve of the election made by Flournoy Lombard , Executor/Administrator of the estate of Donald Whitecliffe , pursuant to section 2032A to value said property on the basis of the qualified use to which the property is devoted and do hereby enter into this agreement pursuant to section 2032A(d).

The undersigned agree and consent to the application of subsection (c) of section 2032A of the Code with respect to all the property described on line 2 of Part 2 of Schedule A-1 of Form 706, attached to this agreement. More specifically, the undersigned heirs expressly agree and consent to personal liability under subsection (c) of 2032A for the additional estate and GST taxes imposed by that subsection with respect to their respective interests in the above-described property in the event of certain early dispositions of the property or early cessation of the qualified use of the property. It is understood that if a qualified heir disposes of any interest in qualified real property to any member of his or her family, such member may thereafter be treated as the qualified heir with respect to such interest upon filing a Form 706-A and a new agreement.

The undersigned interested parties who are not qualified heirs consent to the collection of any additional estate and GST taxes imposed under section 2032A(c) of the Code from the specially valued property.

If there is a disposition of any interest which passes, or has passed to him or her, or if there is a cessation of the qualified use of any specially valued property which passes or passed to him or her, each of the undersigned heirs agrees to file a **Form 706-A,** United States Additional Estate Tax Return, and pay any additional estate and GST taxes due within 6 months of the disposition or cessation.

It is understood by all interested parties that this agreement is a condition precedent to the election of special use valuation under section 2032A of the Code and must be executed by every interested party even though that person may not have received the estate (or GST) tax benefits or be in possession of such property.

Each of the undersigned understands that by making this election, a lien will be created and recorded pursuant to section 6324B of the Code on the property referred to in this agreement for the adjusted tax differences with respect to the estate as defined in section 2032A(c)(2)(C).

As the interested parties, the undersigned designate the following individual as their agent for all dealings with the Internal Revenue Service concerning the continued qualification of the specially valued property under 2032A of the Code and on all issues regarding the special lien under section 6324B. The agent is authorized to act for the parties with respect to all dealings with the Service on matters affecting the qualified real property described earlier. This authority includes the following:

- To receive confidential information on all matters relating to continued qualification under section 2032A of the specially valued real property and on all matters relating to the special lien arising under section 6324B.
- To furnish the Internal Revenue Service with any requested information concerning the property.
- To notify the Internal Revenue Service of any disposition or cessation of qualified use of any part of the property.
- To receive, but not to endorse and collect, checks in payment of any refund of Internal Revenue taxes, penalties, or interest.
- To execute waivers (including offers of waivers) of restrictions on assessment or collection of deficiencies in tax and waivers of notice of disallowance of a claim for credit or refund.
- To execute closing agreements under section 7121.

(continued on next page)

Schedule A-1 — Page 10

Form 706 (Rev. 8-2004)

Part 3. Agreement to Special Valuation Under Section 2032A *(Continued)*

Estate of:	Date of Death	Decedent's Social Security Number
Donald Whitecliffe	03/15/2004	020-30-4050

- Other acts (specify) ▶

By signing this agreement, the agent agrees to provide the Internal Revenue Service with any requested information concerning this property and to notify the Internal Revenue Service of any disposition or cessation of the qualified use of any part of this property.

Flournoy Lombard — Flournoy Lombard — 990 S. Ridgeland, Oak Park, II

Name of Agent — Signature — Address

The property to which this agreement relates is listed in Form 706, United States Estate (and Generation-Skipping Transfer) Tax Return, and in the Notice of Election, along with its fair market value according to section 2031 of the Code and its special use value according to section 2032A. The name, address, social security number, and interest (including the value) of each of the undersigned in this property are as set forth in the attached Notice of Election.

IN WITNESS WHEREOF, the undersigned have hereunto set their hands at Oak Park, IL,

this 10th day of July 2004.

SIGNATURES OF EACH OF THE QUALIFIED HEIRS:

John Whitecliffe	Randy Whitecliffe
Signature of qualified heir	Signature of qualified heir
Signature of qualified heir	Signature of qualified heir
Signature of qualified heir	Signature of qualified heir
Signature of qualified heir	Signature of qualified heir
Signature of qualified heir	Signature of qualified heir
Signature of qualified heir	Signature of qualified heir

Signatures of other interested parties

Signatures of other interested parties

Schedule A-1 — Page 11

¶ 3170 Filled-In Schedule P

James X. Diversey, the hypothetical decedent in the main Form 706 example (see ¶ 2910), did not own property that would have generated a credit for foreign death taxes paid. The following filled-in Schedule P, Form 706 (Rev. Aug. 2004), relates to the fact situation below.

Tom Wilson was a citizen of, and domiciled in, the United States at the time of his death in 2004. His gross estate consisted of real property in Finland valued at $100,000; stocks of U.S. corporations, $1,600,000; bonds of corporations organized under the laws of Finland, $90,000; and stocks of corporations organized under the laws of Finland, $150,000. Debts and administration expenses totaled $40,000.

The Finnish real property, which is valued at $100,000, and $100,000 of the U.S. stock were the only items that passed to Wilson's surviving spouse, and qualified for the marital deduction. The amount of the federal estate tax, less the unified credit and the credit for state inheritance taxes, was $70,500. The amount of the Finnish inheritance tax imposed on the surviving spouse's inheritance of $100,000 was $30,000. The stock in Finnish corporations, valued at $150,000, passed to Wilson's daughter, and the amount of Finnish inheritance tax imposed was $45,000. Finland did not impose an inheritance tax on the bonds issued by Finnish corporations.

Form 706 (Rev. 8-2004)

Estate of: Tom Wilson

SCHEDULE P — Credit for Foreign Death Taxes

List all foreign countries to which death taxes have been paid and for which a credit is claimed on this return.
Finland

If a credit is claimed for death taxes paid to more than one foreign country, compute the credit for taxes paid to one country on this sheet and attach a separate copy of Schedule P for each of the other countries.

The credit computed on this sheet is for the Finnish Inheritance Tax
(Name of death tax or taxes)

imposed in Finland
(Name of country)

Credit is computed under the U.S. - Finland Death Tax Convention
(Insert title of treaty or "statute")

Citizenship (nationality) of decedent at time of death U.S.A.

(All amounts and values must be entered in United States money.)		
1 Total of estate, inheritance, legacy, and succession taxes imposed in the country named above attributable to property situated in that country, subjected to these taxes, and included in the gross estate (as defined by statute)	1	75,000
2 Value of the gross estate (adjusted, if necessary, according to the instructions for item 2)	2	1,700,000
3 Value of property situated in that country, subjected to death taxes imposed in that country, and included in the gross estate (adjusted, if necessary, according to the instructions for item 3)	3	150,000
4 Tax imposed by section 2001 reduced by the total credits claimed under sections 2010, 2011, and 2012 (see instructions)	4	70,500
5 Amount of Federal estate tax attributable to property specified at item 3. (Divide item 3 by item 2 and multiply the result by item 4.)	5	6,221
6 Credit for death taxes imposed in the country named above (the smaller of item 1 or item 5). Also enter on line 16 of Part 2, Tax Computation	6	6,221

¶ 3180 Filled-In Schedule R-1

James X. Diversey, the hypothetical decedent in the main Form 706 example (see ¶ 2910), did not make a generation-skipping transfer reportable on Schedule R-1. The following filled-in Schedule R-1, Form 706 (Rev. Aug. 2004), relates to the fact pattern below.

Howard Buckner died the owner of a life insurance policy on his own life, with his granddaughter, Mellisa Buckner, as sole beneficiary. Under Buckner's irrevocable election, at his death, the insurer would pay out the proceeds as an annuity for the life of the beneficiary. Because this insurance policy is deemed to be a "trust arrangement" under Reg. § 26.2662-1(c)(2)(ii), with a value exceeding $250,000, the direct skip to the grandchild is reported on Schedule R-1, rather than Schedule R (Instructions to Form 706 (Rev. Aug. 2004), p. 23).

SCHEDULE R-1 (Form 706) (Rev. August 2004) Department of the Treasury Internal Revenue Service	**Generation-Skipping Transfer Tax** Direct Skips From a Trust Payment Voucher	OMB No. 1545-0015

Executor: File one copy with Form 706 and send two copies to the fiduciary. Do not pay the tax shown. See the separate instructions.
Fiduciary: See instructions on the following page. Pay the tax shown on line 6.

Name of trust Insurance Trust (Non-explicit trust)		Trust's EIN 56-1234567
Name and title of fiduciary Total Life Co. of Louisiana	Name of decedent Howard Buckner	
Address of fiduciary (number and street) 4500 Rue Rivage	Decedent's SSN 120-01-1212	Service Center where Form 706 was filed Cincinnati, Ohio
City, state, and ZIP code New Orleans, LA	Name of executor First National Bank of Atlanta, N.A.	
Address of executor (number and street) 101 First Street	City, state, and ZIP code Cincinnati, Ohio	
Date of decedent's death 6/14/2004	Filing due date of Schedule R, Form 706 (with extensions) 3/14/2005	

Part 1 — Computation of the GST Tax on the Direct Skip

Description of property interests subject to the direct skip	Estate tax value
Total Life Co. of Louisiana Universal Variable Life Insurance Policy #4124399-UV. Value as listed on Schedule D, Item 1. Proceeds payable under settlement option #4 as an annuity for the life of the beneficiary, the decedent's granddaughter, Mellisa Buckner.	510,434

1	Total estate tax value of all property interests listed above	1	510,434
2	Estate taxes, state death taxes, and other charges borne by the property interests listed above	2	
3	Tentative maximum direct skip from trust (subtract line 2 from line 1)	3	510,434
4	GST exemption allocated	4	
5	Subtract line 4 from line 3	5	510,434
6	**GST tax due from fiduciary** (divide line 5 by 3.083333) **(See instructions if property will not bear the GST tax.)**	6	165,546

Under penalties of perjury, I declare that I have examined this return, including accompanying schedules and statements, and to the best of my knowledge and belief, it is true, correct, and complete.

Virginia M. Buckner — 3/14/2005

Signature(s) of executor(s) — Date

___ — Date

Signature of fiduciary or officer representing fiduciary — Date

Schedule R-1 (Form 706) — Page 36

¶ 3190 Filled-in Schedule U

James X. Diversey, the hypothetical decedent in the main Form 706 example (see ¶ 2910), did not own property that would have generated a qualified conservation easement exclusion. The following filled-in Schedule U, Form 706 (Rev. Aug. 2004), relates to the fact situation below.

Pursuant to her will, Dee Jones conveyed a qualified conservation easement for open space with respect to 160 acres of land proximate to the Everglades National Park, Collier County, Florida. The fair market value of the property on the date of Jones' death in 2004 was $400,000 without the conservation easement and $150,000 with the easement. The decedent's children, who will receive the property, will retain no development rights in the property.

Form 706 (Rev. 8-2004)

Estate of: Dee Jones

SCHEDULE U — Qualified Conservation Easement Exclusion

Part 1 — Election

Note: *The executor is deemed to have made the election under section 2031(c)(6) if he or she files Schedule U and excludes any qualifying conservation easements from the gross estate.*

Part 2 — General Qualifications

1 Describe the land subject to the qualified conservation easement (see separate instructions) 160 acres of undeveloped pasture and marshland in Collier County, Florida.

2 Did the decedent or a member of the decedent's family own the land described above during the 3-year period ending on the date of the decedent's death? .... ☒ Yes ☐ No

3 Describe the conservation easement with regard to which the exclusion is being claimed (see separate instructions).
Perpetual easement for open space to Everglades Preservation Fund, Inc.

Part 3 — Computation of Exclusion

4	Estate tax value of the land subject to the qualified conservation easement (see separate instructions)			4	400,000
5	Date of death value of any easements granted prior to decedent's death and included on line 10 below (see instructions)	5	0		
6	Add lines 4 and 5	6	400,000		
7	Value of retained development rights on the land (see instructions)	7	0		
8	Subtract line 7 from line 6	8	400,000		
9	Multiply line 8 by 30% (.30)	9	120,000		
10	Value of qualified conservation easement for which the exclusion is being claimed (see instructions) **Note:** *If line 10 is less than line 9, continue with line 11. If line 10 is equal to or more than line 9, skip lines 11 through 13, enter ".40" on line 14, and complete the schedule.*	10	150,000		
11	Divide line 10 by line 8. Figure to 3 decimal places (e.g., .123) *If line 11 is equal to or less than .100, stop here; the estate does not qualify for the conservation easement exclusion.*	11			
12	Subtract line 11 from .300. Enter the answer in hundredths by rounding any thousandths up to the next higher hundredth (i.e., .030 = .03; but .031 = .04)	12			
13	Multiply line 12 by 2	13			
14	Subtract line 13 from .40	14	0.40		
15	Deduction under section 2055(f) for the conservation easement (see separate instructions)	15	0		
16	Amount of indebtedness on the land (see separate instructions)	16	0		
17	Total reductions in value (add lines 7, 15, and 16)			17	0
18	Net value of land (subtract line 17 from line 4)			18	400,000
19	Multiply line 18 by line 14			19	160,000
20	Enter the smaller of line 19 or the exclusion limitation (see instructions). Also enter this amount on item 11, Part 5, Recapitulation, Page 3			20	160,000

Schedule U — Page 38

¶ 3200 Filled-In Form 706-A

James X. Diversey, the hypothetical decedent in the main Form 706 example (see ¶ 2910), did not have special use valuation property. The following filled-in Form 706-A (Rev. Sept. 2004) relates to the fact situation below.

Helen Gower, qualified heir of Henry Gower, who died on May 1, 1998, continued the qualified use of the family farm until it was acquired by eminent domain by the county airport authority on February 21, 2004. At the date of Henry Gower's death, the farm property, valued at its highest and best use, was worth $1,400,000. Operating as a farm, the farm property had a fair market value of $450,000. However, in the year of Henry's death (1998), the special use valuation election could reduce the value of special use valuation property by a maximum of $750,000. Accordingly, the value of the farm property entered on Henry's Form 706 (which is not reproduced herein) was $650,000 ($1,400,000 – $750,000), rather than $450,000.

Electing the special use valuation, the estate of Henry Gower computed its federal estate tax liability as follows:

Taxable estate	$1,950,000
Tentative tax on above	$ 758,300
Less: Applicable credit amount	$ 202,050
Less: Credit for state death taxes	$ 96,000
Estate tax reported on Form 706	$ 460,250

As required by Form 706-A, Part II, Line 3b, Helen Gower recomputed the federal estate tax on Henry Gower's estate, without the benefit of the reduced value of the farm based on its special use value:

Taxable estate	$2,700,000
Tentative tax on above	$1,131,800
Less: Applicable credit amount	$ 202,050
Less: Credit for state death taxes	$ 155,600
Recomputed federal estate tax	$ 774,150

Gower received compensation in the amount of $1,435,000 from the airport authority; she reinvested $500,000 in the acquisition of a replacement farm property on July 9, 2004.

Form **706-A** (Rev. September 2004) Department of the Treasury Internal Revenue Service

United States Additional Estate Tax Return

(To report dispositions or cessations of qualified use under section 2032A of the Internal Revenue Code)

For Privacy Act and Paperwork Reduction Act Notice, see page 4 of the separate instructions.

OMB No. 1545-0016

Part I General Information

1a Name of qualified heir: Helen Gower	2 Heir's social security number: 279-33-1234
1b Address of qualified heir (number and street, including apartment number, P.O. Box, or rural route): 124 South Elmwood	3 Commencement date (see instructions): 5-30-1999
1c City, town or post office, state, and ZIP code: Twin Lakes, WI 51534	

4 Decedent's name reported on Form 706	5 Decedent's social security number	6 Date of death
Henry Gower	315-71-4711	5-1-1998

Part II Tax Computation (First complete Schedules A and B—see instructions.)

1	Value at date of death (or alternate valuation date) of all specially valued property that passed from decedent to qualified heir:				
a	Without section 2032A election	1a	1,400,000		
b	With section 2032A election	1b	650,000		
c	Balance (subtract line 1b from line 1a)			1c	750,000
2	Value at date of death (or alternate valuation date) of all specially valued property in decedent's estate:				
a	Without section 2032A election	2a	1,400,000		
b	With section 2032A election	2b	650,000		
c	Balance (subtract line 2b from line 2a)			2c	750,000
3	Decedent's estate tax:				
a	Recomputed without section 2032A election (attach computation)	3a	774,150		
b	Reported on Form 706 with section 2032A election	3b	460,250		
c	Balance (subtract line 3b from line 3a)			3c	313,900
4	Divide line 1c by line 2c and enter the result as a percentage			4	100.00%
5	Total estate tax saved (multiply line 3c by percentage on line 4)			5	313,900
6	Value, without section 2032A election, at date of death (or alternate valuation date) of specially valued property shown on Schedule A of this Form 706-A	6	1,400,000		
7	Divide line 6 by line 1a and enter the result as a percentage			7	100.00%
8	Multiply line 5 by percentage on line 7			8	313,900
9	Total estate tax recaptured on previous Form(s) 706-A (attach copies of 706-A)			9	
10	Remaining estate tax savings (subtract line 9 from line 5) (do not enter less than zero)			10	313,900
11	Enter the lesser of line 8 or line 10			11	313,900
12	Enter the total of column D, Schedule A, page 2	12	1,435,000		
13	Enter the total of column E, Schedule A, page 2	13	650,000		
14	Balance (subtract line 13 from line 12) (but enter the line 12 amount in the case of a disposition of standing timber on qualified woodland)			14	785,000
15	Enter the lesser of line 11 or line 14			15	313,900

If you completed Schedule B, complete lines 16–19. If you did not complete Schedule B, skip lines 16–18 and enter the amount from line 15 on line 19.

16	Enter the total cost (or FMV) from Schedule B	16	500,000
17	Divide line 16 by line 12 and enter the result as a percentage (do not enter more than 100%)	17	34.84%
18	Multiply line 15 by percentage on line 17	18	109,363
19	**Additional estate tax,** subtract line 18 from line 15 (do not enter less than zero)	19	204,537

Under penalties of perjury, I declare that I have examined this return, and to the best of my knowledge and belief, it is true, correct, and complete. Declaration of preparer other than taxpayer is based on all information of which preparer has any knowledge.

Helen Gower — Signature of taxpayer/qualified heir — Date: 8-21-2004

Signature of preparer other than taxpayer/qualified heir — Date

Address (and ZIP code)

Form **706-A** (Rev. 9-2004)

Form 706-A (Rev. 9-2004) Page **2**

Schedule A.—Disposition of Specially Valued Property or Cessation of Qualified Use

List property in chronological order of disposition or cessation

A Item number	B Description of specially valued property and schedule and item number where reported on the decedent's Form 706	C Date of disposition (or date qualified use ceased)	D Amount received (or fair market value if applicable) (see instructions)	E Special use value (see instructions)
1	Form 706, Schedule A, Item 1 Description— Farm, Kenosha Co., WI	2-21-2004	1,435,000	650,000
Totals: Enter total of column D on line 12 of the Tax Computation, and total of column E on line 13 of the Tax Computation.			1,435,000	650,000

Form 706-A (Rev. 9-2004) Page 3

Schedule B.—Involuntary Conversions or Exchanges Check if for: [X] Involuntary conversion [ ] Exchange

Qualified replacement (or exchange) property

A Item	B Description of qualified replacement (or exchange) property	C Cost (or FMV)
1	Farm, R.R. 6, Box 15, Kenosha Corners, WI (Northeast quarter, Section 12, Kenosha County, WI). This farm was acquired on July 9, 2004, as replacement property for the involuntarily converted property listed on Schedule A, Item 1.	500,000
Total cost (or FMV) (enter here and on line 16 of the Tax Computation)		500,000

Form **706-A** (Rev. 9-2004)

Form 706-A (Rev. 9-2004) Page 4

Schedule C.—Dispositions to Family Members of the Qualified Heir

Each transferee must enter into an agreement to be personally liable for any additional taxes imposed by section 2032A(c) and the agreement must be attached to this Form 706-A. (See instructions.)

Transferee #1:	Last name	First name	Middle initial
	Social security number	Relationship to the qualified heir	

Description of property transferred

A Item number	B Description of specially valued property and schedule and item number where reported on the decedent's Form 706	C Date of disposition
1	Form 706, Schedule ________, Item ________ Description—	

Transferee #2:	Last name	First name	Middle initial
	Social security number	Relationship to the qualified heir	

Description of property transferred

A Item number	B Description of specially valued property and schedule and item number where reported on the decedent's Form 706	C Date of disposition
1	Form 706, Schedule ________, Item ________ Description—	

If there are more than two transferees, attach additional sheets using the same format. Form **706-A** (Rev. 9-2004)

¶ 3210 Filled-In Form 706-D

The filled-in Form 706-D, United States Additional Estate Tax Return Under Code Section 2057 (October 2003), illustrates a disposition of a qualified family-owned business interest (QFOBI) for which a deduction under Code Sec. 2057 was taken with respect to the deceased ancestor's Form 706. Although the deduction for qualified family-owned business interests was repealed for estates of decedents dying after December 31, 2003 (see ¶1150), the recapture imposed under Code Sec. 2057(f) will continue to apply after this date if a disqualifying event occurs.

Fred Willins, a farmer, died on February 1, 2001. Primarily because of his shrewd investments made over the years, Willins died with a federal gross estate of $1,875,000, which included the farm business valued at $950,000. Willins' farm was bequeathed to his son, Bob (also a farmer), who intended to continue to operate the business after his father's death. Willins' executor had two categories of deductions that he claimed on the Form 706: $50,000 for administration expenses, and $675,000 as the maximum qualified family-owned business interest deduction. After credit for $42,000 in state death taxes paid, the Willins estate paid federal estate taxes of $163,250.

On July 2, 2004, the state of Illinois acquired the farm by eminent domain under a plan to develop a state park. Bob Willins received compensation in the amount of $985,000 for his farm. Three months later, Bob acquired a replacement farm for $600,000 in McHenry County, Illinois.

As required by Form 706-D, part II, line 3a, Bob Willins recomputed the federal estate tax on his father's estate, without the deduction for the qualified family-owned business interest:

Federal gross estate:	$1,875,000
Less: Administrative expenses	50,000
Taxable estate	$1,825,000
Tentative tax on above	$702,050
Less: Applicable credit amount	220,550
Less: Credit for state death taxes	87,000
Recomputed federal estate tax	$394,500

Using Form 706-D, Bob figured that he owed additional estate tax of $90,387. Because he did not want to incur additional interest assessments, he paid interest that he estimated would be due for the period beginning on the date that the original estate tax liability under Code Sec. 2001 was due (from November 1, 2001, the due date of Fred Willins' estate tax return) until the filing date, when he submitted with the return a check for $105,464 (a total of $90,387 tax and $15,077 interest). Note that, in conformance to the Form 706-D Instructions (page 2), the amount of the estimated interest due was entered on the dotted line to the left of the entry space for line 15, and was not included in the amount of tax entered on line 15.

Form **706-D** (Rev. October 2003) Department of the Treasury Internal Revenue Service

United States Additional Estate Tax Return Under Code Section 2057

OMB No. 1545-1680

Part I General Information

1a Name of qualified heir Bob Willins	2 Qualified heir's social security number 098-12-4567
1b Address of qualified heir (number and street, including apt. no., P.O. box, or rural route) 1800 Gilmore Road	3 Commencement date (see instructions) 7-1-2001
1c City, town or post office, state, and ZIP code Richmond, IL 60071	

4 Decedent's name reported on Form 706	5 Decedent's social security number	6 Date of death
Fred Willins	098-12-5678	2-1-2001

Part II Tax Computation (First complete Schedules A and B — see instructions.)

1	Qualified heir's share of the total qualified family-owned business interests (from line 4, Schedule T, of the decedent's estate tax return)		1	950,000
2	Total reported value of qualified family-owned business interests (from line 6, Schedule T, of the decedent's estate tax return)		2	950,000
3	Decedent's estate tax:			
a	Recomputed without the qualified family-owned business interest deduction (attach computation)	3a 394,500		
b	Reported on Form 706 (or as finally agreed to)	3b 163,250		
c	Gross additional estate tax (subtract line 3b from line 3a)		3c	231,250
4	Qualified heir's percentage of qualified family-owned business interests. Divide line 1 by line 2. Enter result as a percentage (carry out your answer to at least the nearest tenth of a percent)		4	100.0000 %
5	Qualified heir's share of total reduction in estate tax. Multiply line 3c by line 4		5	231,250
6	Enter the **Total** from column (E), Schedule A, page 2		6	950,000
7	Divide line 6 by line 1. Enter the result as a percentage (carry out your answer to at least the nearest tenth of a percent)		7	100.0000 %
8	Multiply line 5 by the percentage on line 7		8	231,250
9	Applicable percentage (see instructions)		9	100 %
10	**Total additional estate tax.** Multiply line 8 by the percentage on line 9		10	231,250

If you completed Schedule B, complete lines 11 through 15. If you did not complete Schedule B, skip lines 11 through 14 and enter the amount from line 10 on line 15.

11	Enter the total cost or fair market value (FMV) from column (C), Schedule B, page 2		11	600,000
12	Enter the total of column (D), Schedule A, page 2		12	985,000
13	Divide line 11 by line 12. Enter the result as a percentage (carry out your answer to at least the nearest tenth of a percent) (do not enter more than 100%)		13	60.9137 %
14	Multiply line 10 by the percentage on line 13		14	140,863
15	**Additional estate tax due.** Subtract line 14 from line 10 (do not enter less than zero)	15,077	15	90,387

Under penalties of perjury, I declare that I have examined this return, including accompanying schedules and statements, and to the best of my knowledge and belief, it is true, correct, and complete. Declaration of preparer (other than taxpayer) is based on all information of which preparer has any knowledge.

Sign Here	Bob Willins Signature of taxpayer or person filing on behalf of taxpayer	1-2-2005 Date
Paid Preparer's Use Only	Preparer's signature	Date
	Preparer's name and address	ZIP code

Form **706-D** (Rev. 10-2003)

Form 706-D (Rev. 10-2003) Page 2

Schedule A. Disposition of Qualified Family-Owned Business Interest, Failure to Materially Participate, or Disqualifying Act (Taxable Under Section 2057(f)(1))

(A) Item number	(B) Description of property and explanation of disqualifying act	(C) Date of disposition, failure to materially participate, or disqualifying act (see instructions)	(D) Amount realized or fair market value (FMV) if applicable (see instructions)	(E) Date of death value (see instructions)
1	Form 706, Schedule F, Item 1 Description — 300-acre farm, 4601 Fulkner Road, Antioh, Lake County, IL.	7-2-2004	985,000	950,000
Total. Enter the total of column (D) on line 12 of Part II, Tax Computation, page 1, and the total of column (E) on line 6 of the Tax Computation			985,000	950,000

Schedule B. Involuntary Conversions or Exchanges

Check if for ☒ Involuntary Conversion ☐ Exchange

(A) Item	(B) Description of qualified replacement (or exchange) property	(C) Cost or fair market value (FMV)
1	200-acre farm, 1800 Gilmore Road, Richmond, McHenry Co., IL.	600,000
Total. Enter the total of column (C) on line 11 of Part II, Tax Computation, page 1.		600,000

Schedule C. Nontaxable Transfers

Transferee	Last name	First name	Middle Initial
	Social security number	Relationship to the qualified heir	

Check if for ☐ Disposition to Family Member ☐ Qualified Conservation Contribution ☐ Loss of U.S. Citizenship

(A) Item	(B) Description of property and explanation of nontaxable transfers	(C) Date of disposition, contribution, trust agreement, or bond
1	Form 706, Schedule ____, Item ____ Description —	

Form 706-D (Rev. 10-2003)

¶ 3220 Fact Situation for Forms 706-GS(D) and 706-GS(D-1)

For purposes of the filled-in Forms 706-GS(D), Generation-Skipping Transfer Tax Return for Distributions (Rev. Jan. 2003), and 706-GS(D-1), Notification of Distribution From a Generation-Skipping Trust (Rev. Jan. 2003), the following facts are assumed:

On his death, Able Smith's will established the Able Smith GST Trust for the benefit of his son, Brian, his grandson, Charles, and his granddaughter, Donna. The trust provides that the income from the $3.7 million trust corpus is to go to Brian for life, with the remainder to go to Charles and Donna at Brian's death. In addition, the trustee is given the power to invade trust corpus for the benefit of Charles and/or Donna. Ten months later, the trustee exercises the power, transferring $100,000 in cash to Charles.

No Schedule R or R-1 was filed with Able Smith's Form 706 because the transfer was to a trust having at least one nonskip person beneficiary, thus making the trust a nonskip person.

¶ 3230 Filled-In Form 706-GS(D)

Form **706-GS(D)** (Rev. January 2003) Department of the Treasury Internal Revenue Service

Generation-Skipping Transfer Tax Return For Distributions

For calendar year 2004

OMB No. 1545-1144

Attach a copy of all Forms 706-GS(D-1) to this return.

Part I General Information

1a Name of skip person distributee	1b Social security number of individual distributee (see instructions)
Charles Smith	123-40-6789
2a Name and title of person filing return (if different from 1a, see instructions)	1c Employer identification number of trust distributee (see instructions)

2b Address of distributee or person filing return (see instructions) (number and street or P.O. box; city, town, or post office; state; and ZIP code)
1310 South Harvey Ave.
Oak Park, IL 60304

Part II Distributions

a Trust EIN (from line 2a, Form 706-GS(D-1))	b Item no. (from line 3, column a, Form 706-GS(D-1))	c Amount of Transfer (from Tentative transfer, line 3, column f, Form 706-GS(D-1))
77-6654321		71,400

3	Total transfers (add amounts in column c)	3	71,400

Part III Tax Computation

4	Adjusted allowable expenses (see instructions)			4	178
5	Taxable amount (subtract line 4 from line 3)			5	71,222
6	Maximum Federal estate tax rate (see instructions)			6	48 %
7	Gross GST tax (multiply line 5 by line 6)			7	34,187
8	Creditable state GST tax (if any)	8	0		
9	Multiply line 7 by 5% (.05)	9	1,709		
10	Allowable credit (enter the smaller of line 8 or line 9)			10	0
11	Net GST tax (subtract line 10 from line 7)			11	34,187
12	Payment, if any, made with Form 2758			12	0
13	**Tax due**—if line 11 is larger than line 12, enter amount owed ▶ *(Make the check payable to the United States Treasury.)*			13	34,187
14	**Overpayment**—if line 12 is larger than line 11, enter amount to be refunded ▶			14	0

Under penalties of perjury, I declare that I have examined this return, including accompanying schedules and statements, and to the best of my knowledge and belief, it is true, correct, and complete. Declaration of preparer other than taxpayer is based on all information of which preparer has any knowledge.

Sign Here	▶ Charles Smith — Signature of taxpayer or person filing on behalf of taxpayer	Date 4-15-2005
Paid Preparer's Use Only	Preparer's signature ▶ Gunderson Cuyler III	Date 4-15-2005
	Firm's name (or yours if self-employed) and address ▶ Gunderson Cuyler III, 1419 Granger Ave., Elk Grove, IL	ZIP code ▶ 60007

For Privacy Act and Paperwork Reduction Act Notice, see page 3 of separate instructions. Form **706-GS(D)** (Rev. 1-2003)

¶ 3240 Filled-In Form 706-GS(D-1)

Form **706-GS(D-1)**
(Rev. January 2003)
Department of the Treasury
Internal Revenue Service

Notification of Distribution From a Generation-Skipping Trust
(Complete for each skip person distributee — see separate instructions.)
For calendar year 2004

OMB No. 1545-1143

Copy A — Send to IRS

Part I General Information

1a Skip person distributee's identifying number (see instructions)	**2a Trust's employer identification number** (see instructions)
123-40-6789	77-6654321
1b Skip person distributee's name, address, and ZIP code	**2b** Trust's name, address, and ZIP code
Charles Smith 1310 South Harvey Avenue Oak Park, IL 60304	Able Smith GST Trust Southern Trust Company 100 South Lake Street Oak Park, IL 60302

Part II Distributions

3 Describe each distribution below (see instructions).

a Item no.	b Description of property	c Date of distribution	d Inclusion ratio	e Value (see instructions)	f Tentative transfer (multiply col. **e** by col. **d**)
1	Cash; distribution from corpus of Able Smith GST Trust.	12-28-2004	.7140	100,000	71,400

Part III Trust Information (see instructions)

4 If this is not an explicit trust, check the box and attach a statement describing the arrangement that makes its effect substantially similar to an explicit trust ▶ ☐

		Yes	No
5	Has any property been contributed to this trust since the last Form 706-GS(T) or (D-1) was filed? If "Yes," attach a schedule showing how the trust's inclusion ratio has been refigured		X
6	Have any contributions been made to this trust since the last Form 706-GS(T) or (D-1) was filed that were not included in calculating the trust's inclusion ratio? If "Yes," attach a statement explaining why the contributions were not included		X
7	Has any exemption been allocated to this trust by reason of the deemed allocation rules?		X

Under penalties of perjury, I declare that I have examined this return, including accompanying schedules and statements, and to the best of my knowledge and belief, it is true, correct, and complete. Declaration of preparer other than trustee is based on all information of which preparer has any knowledge.

Signature of trustee ▶ *Charles Smith* **Date** ▶ 4-15-2005

Signature of preparer other than trustee ▶ *Gunderson Cuyler III* **Date** ▶ 4-15-2005

Address ▶ 1419 Granger Road, Elk Grove, IL 60007

For Paperwork Reduction Act Notice, see page 5 of the separate trustee's instructions. Form **706-GS(D-1)** (Rev. 1-2003)

Form **706-GS(D-1)**
(Rev. January 2003)
Department of the Treasury
Internal Revenue Service

Notification of Distribution From a Generation-Skipping Trust

(Complete for each skip person distributee — see separate instructions.)
For calendar year 2004

OMB No. 1545-1143

Copy B — For Distributee

Part I General Information

1a Skip person distributee's identifying number (see instructions)	**2a Trust's employer identification number** (see instructions)
123-40-6789	77-6654321
1b Skip person distributee's name, address, and ZIP code	**2b** Trust's name, address, and ZIP code
Charles Smith 1310 South Harvey Avenue Oak Park, IL 60304	Able Smith GST Trust Southern Trust Company 100 South Lake Street Oak Park, IL 60302

Part II Distributions

3 Describe each distribution below (see instructions).

a Item no.	**b** Description of property	**c** Date of distribution	**d** Inclusion ratio	**e** Value (see instructions)	**f** Tentative transfer (multiply col. **e** by col. **d**)
1	Cash; distribution from corpus of Able Smith GST Trust.	12-28-2004	.7140	100,000	71,400

Skip Person Distributee — To report this distribution, you must file Form 706-GS(D), Generation-Skipping Transfer Tax Return for Distributions, at the following Internal Revenue Service Center. ▫ Cincinnati, OH 45999

For Paperwork Reduction Act Notice, see page 5 of the separate trustee's instructions. Form **706-GS(D-1)** (Rev. 1-2003)

¶ 3250 Filled-In Form 706-GS(T)

For purposes of the filled-in Form 706-GS(T), Generation-Skipping Transfer Tax Return for Terminations (Rev. Jan. 2003), below, the following facts are assumed:

Frank Wood established the Frank Wood Trust on January 1, 1992, funded with $4 million. The trust was irrevocable, and the grantor retained no interests in, or powers to alter or amend, the trust. Frank's son, Sanford, was to receive the trust income for life, with trust remainder to go to Glenn (Frank's grandson) at Sanford's death. Upon Sanford's death on November 15, 2004, the trust corpus, then having a value of $6,735,950, was distributed to Glenn.

At the time that Frank Wood set up the trust, he filed a gift tax return (Form 709) upon which he properly and timely elected to apply the full amount of his then-available $1 million generation-skipping transfer tax exemption to the $4 million transferred into the trust. Accordingly, the inclusion ratio reported on Form 706-GS(T) is computed as:

$$1 - \frac{1{,}000{,}000}{4{,}000{,}000} = \quad 1 - 1/4 = 3/4, \text{ or } .75$$

In 2001, 2002, 2003, and early in 2004, Frank Wood made direct cash gifts of $10,000, $20,000, $30,000, and $40,000, respectively, to Glenn, and allocated GST exemption amounts with respect to these gifts ($10,000 for the 2001 transfer, $20,000 for the 2002 transfer, $30,000 for the 2003 transfer, and $40,000 for the 2004 transfer).

Form **706-GS(T)**
(Rev. January 2003)
Department of the Treasury
Internal Revenue Service

Generation-Skipping Transfer Tax Return For Terminations

For calendar year 2004

OMB No. 1545-1145

Part I **General Information**

1a Name of trust	1b Trust's employer identification number (see instructions)
Frank Wood Trust	58-4343434

2a Name of trustee
Aldridge State Bank

2b Trustee's address (number and street or P.O. box; apt. or suite no.; city, town or post office; state and ZIP code)
1234 Ridgeview, Oak Park, IL 60304

Part II **Trust Information** (see page 3 of the instructions)

		Yes	No	Sch. A number(s)
3	Has any exemption been allocated to this trust by reason of the deemed allocation rules of section 2632? If "Yes," describe the allocation on the line 7, Schedule A attachment showing how the inclusion ratio was calculated		X	
4	Has property been contributed to this trust since the last Form 706-GS(T) or 706-GS(D-1) was filed? If "Yes," attach a schedule showing how the inclusion ratio was calculated		X	
5	Have any terminations occurred that are not reported on this return because of the exceptions in section 2611(b)(1) or (2) relating to medical and educational exclusions and prior payment of GST tax? If "Yes," attach a statement describing the termination		X	
6	Have any contributions been made to this trust that were not included in calculating the trust's inclusion ratio? If "Yes," attach a statement explaining why the contribution was not included		X	
7	Has the special QTIP election in section 2652(a)(3) been made for this trust?			

8 If this is not an explicit trust (see page 1 of the instructions under **Who Must File**), check box and attach a statement describing the trust arrangement that makes its effect substantially similar to an explicit trust ▶ ☐

Part III **Tax Computation**

9a Summary of attached Schedules A (see instructions for line 9b on page 6)

Schedule A No.		Net GST tax (from Sch. A, line 14)
1	9a1	2,400,696
2	9a2	
3	9a3	
4	9a4	
5	9a5	
6	9a6	
9b Total from all additional Schedules A attached to this form ▶	9b	
10 **Total** net GST tax (add lines 9a1 - 9b)	10	2,400,696
11 Payment, if any, made with Form 2758	11	
12 **Tax due** — if line 10 is larger than line 11, enter amount owed	12	2,400,696
13 **Overpayment** — if line 11 is larger than line 10, enter amount to be refunded	13	0

Sign Here

Under penalties of perjury, I declare that I have examined this return, including accompanying schedules and statements, and to the best of my knowledge and belief, it is true, correct, and complete. Declaration of preparer other than fiduciary is based on all information of which preparer has any knowledge.

▶ Amy S. Wolcott — Signature of fiduciary or officer representing fiduciary — Date 4-15-2005

Paid Preparer's Use Only

Preparer's signature ▶ — Date

Firm's name (or yours if self-employed) and address ▶ — ZIP code

For Paperwork Reduction Act Notice, see page 6 of separate instructions. Form **706-GS(T)** (Rev. 1-2003)

Form 706-GS(T) (Rev. 1-2003) Page **2**

Name of trust	EIN of trust
Frank Wood Trust	58-4343434

Schedule A No.

Note: *Make copies of this schedule before completing it if you will need more than one Schedule A.*

Schedule A — Taxable Terminations

(See page 3 of the instructions before completing this schedule.)

1 a Name of skip persons	b SSN or EIN of skip person	c Item no. from line 4 below in which interest held
Glenn Wood	321-45-9876	1

2 Describe the terminating power or interest. If you need more space, attach an additional sheet.

Glenn Wood had the sole remainder interest in the Frank Wood Trust, created on January 1, 1992, by Frank Wood, who is Glenn's grandfather. Upon the death of the income beneficiary (Sanford Wood, Glenn's father) on November 15, 2004, all trust assets ($6,735,950) were distributed to Glenn.

3 If you elect alternate valuation, check here (see page 4 of the instructions) ▶ ☐

4 Describe each taxable termination below (see page 4 of the instructions)

a Item no.	b Description of property subject to termination	c Date of termination	d Valuation date	e Value
1	Cash from Frank Wood Trust.	11-15-2004	11-15-2004	6,735,950

	Total ▶	4	6,735,950
5	Total deductions applicable to this Schedule A (from attached Schedule B, line 5)	5	67,350
6	Taxable amount (subtract line 5 from line 4)	6	6,668,600
7	Inclusion ratio (attach separate schedule showing computation)	7	.7500
8	Maximum Federal estate tax rate (see **Table** on page 6 of the instructions)	8	48 %
9	Applicable rate (multiply line 7 by line 8)	9	0.360000
10	Gross GST tax (multiply line 6 by line 9)	10	2,400,696
11	Creditable state GST tax, if any (attach credit evidence) — 11: 0		
12	Multiply line 10 by 5% (.05) — 12: 120,035		
13	Allowable credit (enter the smaller of line 11 or line 12)	13	0
14	Net GST tax (subtract line 13 from line 10) (enter here and on line 9, Part III, page 1)	14	2,400,696

Schedule A (Form 706-GS(T)) (Rev. 1-2003)

Form 706-GS(T) (Rev. 1-2003) Page 3

Name of trust	Schedule A No. ▶
Frank Wood Trust	EIN of trust 58-4343434

Note: *Make copies of this schedule before completing it if you will need more than one Schedule B.*

Schedule B(1) — General Trust Debts, Expenses, and Taxes
(Section 2622(b)) (Enter only items related to the entire trust; see page 4 of the instructions.)

a Item no.	b Description	c Amount
1	Trustee fee paid Aldridge State Bank, Oak Park, IL	67,350

1	Total of Schedule B(1)	1	67,350
2	Percentage allocated to corresponding Schedule A	2	100 %
3	Net deduction (multiply line 1 by line 2)	3	67,350

Schedule B(2) — Specific Termination-Related Debts, Expenses, and Taxes
(Section 2622(b)) (Enter only items related solely to terminations appearing on corresponding Schedule A; see page 5 of the instructions.)

a Item no.	b Description	c Amount
1		

4	Total of Schedule B(2)	4	
5	**Total** — Add lines 3 and 4 (enter here and on line 5 of the corresponding Schedule A)	5	67,350

Schedules B(1) and B(2) (Form 706-GS(T)) (Rev. 1-2003)

¶ 3260 Filled-In Form 706-NA

The following filled-in Form 706-NA, United States Estate (and Generation-Skipping Transfer) Tax Return—Estate of nonresident not a citizen of the United States (Rev. Jan. 2003), is based on the hypothetical fact situation of Rodney M. Lodge, a Canadian citizen. Mr. Lodge died owning a U.S. gross estate of $657,774 and a gross estate outside the United States of $1,738,870. By reason of a 1995 Protocol amending the applicable treaty between the United States and Canada, Mr. Lodge is entitled to a unified credit amount of $152,545, computed as follows:

	$657,774		(Gross estate in United States)
	2,396,644		(Entire gross estate, wherever located)
=	.27446	×	$555,800 (Applicable credit amount for U.S. citizens in 2004)
=	$152,545		

Form **706-NA** (Rev. January 2003) Department of the Treasury Internal Revenue Service

United States Estate (and Generation-Skipping Transfer) Tax Return
Estate of nonresident not a citizen of the United States
(To be filed for decedents dying after December 31, 2001.)
(See separate instructions. Section references are to the Internal Revenue Code.)

OMB No. 1545-0531

Attach supplemental documents and translations. Show amounts in U.S. dollars.

Part I — Decedent, Executor, and Attorney

1a Decedent's first (given) name and middle initial	Rodney M.
b Decedent's last (family) name	Lodge
2 U.S. social security number (if any)	
3 Place of death	Washington D.C., U.S.A.
4 Domicile at time of death	Ontario, Canada
5 Citizenship (nationality)	Canadian
6 Date of death	2-1-2004
7a Date of birth	1-4-1945
b Place of birth	Ontario, Canada
8 Business or occupation	Television Reporter
In United States — 9a Name of executor	Martin Lodge
b Address	44 West Elm Street Albany, NY 12207
10a Name of attorney for estate	Michelle K. Murphy
b Address	120 Ohio Avenue Washington, D.C. 20036
Outside United States — 11a Name of executor	Phillip Lodge
b Address	224 Foxmoor Drive Ontario, Canada
12a Name of attorney for estate	Rutherford Harvey
b Address	422 Covington Road Ontario, Canada

Part II — Tax Computation

Line	Description			Line	Amount
1	Taxable estate (from Schedule B, line 8)			1	641,990
2	Total taxable gifts of tangible or intangible property located in the U.S., transferred (directly or indirectly) by the decedent after December 31, 1976, and not included in the gross estate (see section 2511)			2	0
3	Total (add lines 1 and 2)			3	641,990
4	Tentative tax on the amount on line 3 (see page 4 of instructions)			4	208,336
5	Tentative tax on the amount on line 2 (see page 4 of instructions)			5	0
6	Gross estate tax (subtract line 5 from line 4)			6	208,336
7	Unified credit — enter smaller of line 6 amount or maximum allowed (see page 4 of instructions)			7	152,545
8	Balance (subtract line 7 from line 6)			8	55,791
9	Credit for state death taxes (see page 4 of instructions and attach credit evidence)			9	0
10	Balance (subtract line 9 from line 8)			10	55,791
11	Other credits (see page 4 of instructions)	11	0		
12	Credit for tax on prior transfers (attach Schedule Q, Form 706)	12	0		
13	Total (add lines 11 and 12)			13	0
14	Net estate tax (subtract line 13 from line 10)			14	55,791
15	Total generation-skipping transfer tax (attach Schedule R, Form 706)			15	0
16	**Total transfer taxes** (add lines 14 and 15)			16	55,791
17	Earlier payments (see page 4 of instructions and attach explanation)	17	0		
18	U.S. Treasury bonds redeemed to pay estate tax	18	0		
19	Total (add lines 17 and 18)			19	0
20	Balance due (subtract line 19 from line 16) (see page 4 of instructions)			20	55,791

Under penalties of perjury, I declare that I have examined this return, including any additional sheets attached, and to the best of my knowledge and belief, it is true, correct, and complete. I understand that a complete return requires listing all property constituting the part of the decedent's gross estate (as defined by the statute) situated in the United States.

Martin Lodge — 11-2-2004
(Signature of executor) (Date)

Michelle K. Murphy — 120 Ohio Avenue Washington, D.C., 20036 — 11-2-2004
(Signature of preparer (other than executor)) (Address) (Date)

For Paperwork Reduction Act Notice, see the separate instructions. Form 706-NA (Rev. 1-2003)

Form 706-NA (Rev. 1-2003) Page 2

Part III General Information

		Yes	No
1a	Did the decedent die testate?	X	
b	Were letters testamentary or of administration granted for the estate?	X	
	If granted to persons other than those filing the return, include names and addresses on page 1.		
2	Did the decedent, at the time of death, own any:		
a	Real property located in the United States?	X	
b	U.S. corporate stock?	X	
c	Debt obligations of (1) a U.S. person, or (2) the United States, a state or any political subdivision, or the District of Columbia?		X
d	Other property located in the United States?		X
3	Was the decedent engaged in business in the United States at the date of death?		X
4	At the date of death, did the decedent have access, personally or through an agent, to a safe deposit box located in the United States?		X
5	At the date of death, did the decedent own any property located in the United States as a joint tenant with right of survivorship; as a tenant by the entirety; or, with surviving spouse, as community property?		X
	If "Yes," attach Schedule E, Form 706.		
6a	Had the decedent ever been a citizen or resident of the United States (see page 2 of instructions)?		X
b	If "Yes," did the decedent lose U.S. citizenship or residency within 10 years of death?		X
7	Did the decedent make any transfer (of property that was located in the United States at either the time of the transfer or the time of death) described in sections 2035, 2036, 2037, or 2038 (see the instructions for Form 706, Schedule G)?		X
	If "Yes," attach Schedule G, Form 706.		
8	At the date of death, were there any trusts in existence that were created by the decedent and that included property located in the United States either when the trust was created or when the decedent died?		X
	If "Yes," attach Schedule G, Form 706.		
9	At the date of death, did the decedent:		
a	Have a general power of appointment over any property located in the United States?		X
b	Or, at any time, exercise or release the power?		X
	If "Yes" to either a or b, attach Schedule H, Form 706.		
10a	Have Federal gift tax returns ever been filed?		X
b	Periods covered ▶		
c	IRS offices where filed ▶		
11	Does the gross estate in the United States include any interests in property transferred to a "skip person" as defined in the instructions to Schedule R of Form 706?		X
	If "Yes," attach Schedules R and/or R-1, Form 706.		

Schedule A — Gross Estate in the United States (see page 2 of instructions)

	Yes	No
Do you elect to value the decedent's gross estate at a date or dates after the decedent's death (as authorized by section 2032)?		X

To make the election, you must check this box "Yes." If you check "Yes," complete all columns. If you check "No," complete columns (a), (b), and (e). You may leave columns (c) and (d) blank or you may use them to expand your column (b) description.

(a) Item no.	(b) Description of property and securities For securities, give CUSIP number.	(c) Alternate valuation date	(d) Alternate value in U.S. dollars	(e) Value at date of death in U.S. dollars
1	Condominium, 82 8th St., Washington, D.C.			447,774
2	2800 shares Power Co., Richmond, VA, common stock, $75.00 per share on date of death. Traded on NYSE.			210,000
	(If you need more space, attach additional sheets of same size.)			
Total				657,774

Schedule B — Taxable Estate

You must document lines 2 and 4 for the deduction on line 5 to be allowed.

1	Gross estate in the United States (Schedule A total)	1	657,774
2	Gross estate outside the United States (see page 3 of instructions)	2	1,738,870
3	Entire gross estate wherever located (add amounts on lines 1 and 2)	3	2,396,644
4	Amount of funeral expenses, administration expenses, decedent's debts, mortgages and liens, and losses during administration (attach itemized schedule) (see page 3 of instructions)	4	26,539
5	Deduction for expenses, claims, etc. (divide line 1 by line 3 and multiply the result by line 4)	5	7,284
6	Charitable deduction (attach Schedule O, Form 706) and marital deduction (attach Schedule M, Form 706, and computation)	6	8,500
7	Total deductions (add lines 5 and 6)	7	15,784
8	Taxable estate (subtract line 7 from line 1) (enter here and on line 1 of the Tax Computation)	8	641,990

Form 706-NA (Rev. 1-2003)

¶ 3270 Filled-in Form 706-QDT

The filled-in Form 706-QDT, U.S. Estate Tax Return for Qualified Domestic Trusts (Rev. Jan. 2003), illustrates a taxable distribution made from a qualified domestic trust. (See ¶ 1004 for a discussion of qualified domestic trusts.)

Corazon M. Costa, a nonresident alien, is the widow of Jose D. Costa, who died on July 18, 2000. The decedent left all of his estate to his surviving spouse, payable from a qualified domestic trust. In September 2004, pursuant to her general power over the trust, Costa appointed to herself 500 shares of X Corporation stock. This withdrawal was not made as a result of a hardship situation.

Form 706-QDT requires that the amounts entered on lines 10 and 11 be supported by attached computations. These computations are reproduced below:

Computation for Line 10:

Tentative tax on $804,418	$269,523
Less: Unified credit	220,550
Less: State death tax credit	23,012
Recomputed estate tax on amount on line 9	$ 25,961

Computation for Line 11:

Tentative tax on $781,168	$260,456
Less: Unified credit	220,550
Less: State death tax credit	21,896
Recomputed estate tax on amount on line 8	$ 18,010

Form **706-QDT** (Rev. January 2003) Department of the Treasury Internal Revenue Service

U.S. Estate Tax Return for Qualified Domestic Trusts

Calendar Year 2004

▶ See separate instructions.

OMB No. 1545-1212

Part I General Information

1a Name of surviving spouse (see Definitions on page 1 of the instructions) Corazon M. Costa	1b TIN of surviving spouse 491-23-8463
2a Name of trustee/designated filer (see page 1 of the instructions) Toni L. Costa (Trustee)	2b SSN or EIN of trustee/designated filer 484-26-1943
2c Address of trustee/designated filer 1428 Forest Avenue, Northbrook, IL 60062	
3a Surviving spouse's date of death (if applicable)	3b Surviving spouse's current marital status Widow
4a Name of decedent Jose D. Costa	4b SSN of decedent 480-29-1830
4c Service center where Form 706 (or 706-NA) for decedent's estate was filed Philadelpia, PA 19255	4d Decedent's date of death 7-18-2000

Part II Elections by the Trustee/Designated Filer (see page 3 of the instructions)

Please check the "Yes" or "No" box for each question.	Yes	No
1 Do you elect alternate valuation?		X
2 Do you elect special use valuation? If "Yes," you must complete and attach Schedule A-1 of Form 706.		X
3 Do you elect to pay the taxes in installments as described in section 6166? If "Yes," you must attach the additional information described in the instructions.		X
4 If the surviving spouse has become a U.S. citizen, does he or she elect under Code section 2056A(b)(12)(C) to treat all prior taxable distributions as taxable gifts and to treat any of the decedent's unified credit applied to the QDOT tax on those distributions as the surviving spouse's unified credit used under section 2505? (If not a U.S. citizen, enter "N/A")	N/A	

Part III Tax Computation

1	Current taxable trust distributions (total from Part II of Schedule A)	1	23,250
2	Value of taxable trust property at date of death (if applicable) (total from Part III of Schedule A)	2	0
3	Add lines 1 and 2	3	23,250
4	Charitable and marital deductions (see Schedule B instructions) (total from col. d, Part IV of Sch. A)	4	0
5	Net tentative taxable amount (subtract line 4 from line 3)	5	23,250
6	Prior taxable events (total from Part I of Schedule A)	6	0
7	Taxable estate of the decedent (see page 6 of the instructions)	7	781,168
8	Add lines 6 and 7	8	781,168
9	Add lines 5 and 8	9	804,418
10	Recomputation of decedent's estate tax based on the amount on line 9 (see page 6 of the instructions) (attach computation)	10	25,961
11	Recomputation of decedent's estate tax based on the amount on line 8 (see page 6 of the instructions) (attach computation)	11	18,010
12	Net estate tax (subtract line 11 from line 10)	12	7,951
13	Payment made with request for extension, if any, and credit under section 2056A(b)(2)(B)(ii)	13	0
14	**Tax due** — (If the amount on line 12 exceeds the amount on line 13, enter the difference here.) ▶	14	7,951
15	**Overpayment** — (If the amount on line 13 exceeds the amount on line 12, enter the difference here.)	15	0

Under penalties of perjury, I declare that I have examined this return, along with accompanying schedules and statements, and to the best of my knowledge and belief it is true, correct, and complete. Declaration of preparer (other than trustee or designated filer) is based on all information of which preparer has any knowledge.

Trustee's or designated filer's signature ▶ Toni L. Costa Date ▶ 4-15-2005

Preparer's signature (other than trustee or designated filer) ▶ Date ▶

Preparer's address (other than trustee or designated filer) ▶

For Paperwork Reduction Act Notice, see page 6 of the separate instructions for this form. Form **706-QDT** (Rev. 1-2003)

Form 706-QDT (Rev. 1-2003) Page 2

SCHEDULE A — Complete Schedule A only if you are a designated filer filing this return for multiple trusts.

Part I Summary of Prior Taxable Distributions

(a) Year	(b) Amount	(c) Year	(d) Amount
	$		$
	$		$
	$		$
	$		$
	$		$
	$		$
	$		$
	$		$
Total — Combine columns (b) and (d) ▶			

Part II Summary of Current Taxable Distributions

(a) EIN of QDOT	(b) Total Taxable Distributions for the Year	(c) EIN of QDOT	(d) Total Taxable Distributions for the Year
	$ 23,250		$
	$		$
	$		$
	$		$
	$		$
	$		$
	$		$
	$		$
Total — Combine columns (b) and (d) ▶			23,250

Part III Summary of Property Remaining in QDOTs at Death of Surviving Spouse

(a) EIN of QDOT	(b) Alternate Valuation Date (if applicable)	(c) Value	(d) EIN of QDOT	(e) Alternate Valuation Date (if applicable)	(f) Value
		$			$
		$			$
		$			$
		$			$
		$			$
		$			$
		$			$
		$			$
Total — Combine columns (c) and (f) ▶					

Part IV Summary of Marital and Charitable Deductions

(a) EIN of QDOT	(b) Total Marital Deduction	(c) Total Charitable Deduction	(d) Total Deductions (add cols. (b) and (c))
	$	$	$
	$	$	$
	$	$	$
	$	$	$
	$	$	$
	$	$	$
	$	$	$
	$	$	$
Total ▶			

Form 706-QDT (Rev. 1-2003)

Form 706-QDT (Rev. 1-2003) Page 3

SCHEDULE B

Part I **General Information** (see page 4 of the instructions)

1a Name of trust	1b EIN of trust
Jose D. Costa Trust	21-3683414
2a Name of trustee	2b SSN or EIN of trustee
2c Address of trustee	
3 Name of designated filer, if applicable	
4a Name of surviving spouse	4b TIN of surviving spouse
4c Surviving spouse's date of death (if applicable)	4d Surviving spouse's current marital status (or at death, if applicable)
5a Name of decedent	5b SSN of decedent
5c Service center where Form 706 (or 706-NA) for decedent's estate was filed	5d Decedent's date of death

Part II **Taxable Distributions From Prior Years**

(a) Year	(b) Amount	(c) Year	(d) Amount
	$		$
	$		$
	$		$
	$		$
	$		$
	$		$
	$		$
	$		$
	$		$
Total — Combine columns **(b)** and **(d)** ▶			

Part III **Current Taxable Distributions**

(a) Date of Distribution	(b) Description	(c) Value	(d) Amount of Hardship Exemption Claimed (see instructions)	(e) Net Transfer (col. (c) minus col. (d))
9-19-2004	500 shares of X Corp., common (traded on NYSE), $46.50 per share. CUSIP No. 109438765	23,250	0	23,250
Total ▶				23,250

Form **706-QDT** (Rev. 1-2003)

Form 706-QDT (Rev. 1-2003) Page 4

Schedule B (cont.)

Part IV Taxable Property in Trust at Death of Surviving Spouse

(a) Item No.	(b) Description	(c) Alternate Valuation Date	(d) Value
1			
Total ▶			

Part V Marital Deductions

(a) Item No.	(b) Description of property interests passing to spouse	(c) Value
1		
Total ▶		

Part VI Charitable Deductions

(a) Item No.	(b) Description	(c) Name and address of beneficiary	(d) Character of institution	(e) Amount
1				
Total ▶				

Form 706-QDT (Rev. 1-2003)

¶ 3280 Filled-In Form 709

The filled-in Form 709, United States Gift (and Generation-Skipping Transfer) Tax Return (2004), that follows illustrates the gift and generation-skipping transfer tax computations with respect to several transfers made by Robert A. Simon. Simon filed a Form 709 with respect to a taxable gift of $500,000 made to his sister in 1986. He made no further taxable gifts until 2004, when he gave $511,000 in cash to his daughter, Deborah Miller, and $1,011,000 to each of his two grandchildren, Matthew Miller and Mary Miller. Prior to the reporting of these two generation-skipping transfers on the 2004 Form 709, Simon had not allocated any part of his generation-skipping transfer tax exemption.

Form **709** Department of the Treasury Internal Revenue Service

United States Gift (and Generation-Skipping Transfer) Tax Return

(For gifts made during calendar year 2004)

▶ See separate instructions.

OMB No. 1545-0020

2004

Part 1—General Information

1 Donor's first name and middle initial	2 Donor's last name	3 Donor's social security number
Robert A.	Simon	362 54 7878
4 Address (number, street, and apartment number)		5 Legal residence (domicile) (county and state)
4700 N. Michigan Avenue		Cook County, IL
6 City, state, and ZIP code		7 Citizenship
Chicago, IL 60606		U.S.A.

		Yes	No
8	If the donor died during the year, check here ▶ ☐ and enter date of death .... , ...		
9	If you received an extension of time to file this Form 709, check here ▶ ☐ and attach the Form 4868, 2688, 2350, or 8892		
10	Enter the total number of donees listed on Schedule A—count each person only once. ▶ 3		
11a	Have you (the donor) previously filed a Form 709 (or 709-A) for any other year? If "No," skip line 11b	✓	
11b	If the answer to line 11a is "Yes," has your address changed since you last filed Form 709 (or 709-A)?		✓
12	Gifts by husband or wife to third parties.—Do you consent to have the gifts (including generation-skipping transfers) made by you and by your spouse to third parties during the calendar year considered as made one-half by each of you? (See instructions.) (If the answer is "Yes," the following information must be furnished and your spouse must sign the consent shown below. **If the answer is "No," skip lines 13–18 and go to Schedule A.**)		✓
13	Name of consenting spouse — 14 SSN		
15	Were you married to one another during the entire calendar year? (see instructions)		
16	If 15 is "No," check whether ☐ married ☐ divorced or ☐ widowed/deceased, and give date (see instructions) ▶		
17	Will a gift tax return for this year be filed by your spouse? (If "Yes," mail both returns in the same envelope.)		
18	**Consent of Spouse**—I consent to have the gifts (and generation-skipping transfers) made by me and by my spouse to third parties during the calendar year considered as made one-half by each of us. We are both aware of the joint and several liability for tax created by the execution of this consent.		

Consenting spouse's signature ▶ **Date ▶**

Part 2—Tax Computation

1	Enter the amount from Schedule A, Part 4, line 11	1	2,740,000
2	Enter the amount from Schedule B, line 3	2	500,000
3	Total taxable gifts (add lines 1 and 2)	3	3,240,000
4	Tax computed on amount on line 3 (see Table for Computing Tax in separate instructions)	4	1,376,000
5	Tax computed on amount on line 2 (see Table for Computing Tax in separate instructions)	5	155,800
6	Balance (subtract line 5 from line 4)	6	1,220,200
7	Maximum unified credit (nonresident aliens, see instructions)	7	345,800 00
8	Enter the unified credit against tax allowable for all prior periods (from Sch. B, line 1, col. C)	8	155,800
9	Balance (subtract line 8 from line 7)	9	190,000
10	Enter 20% (.20) of the amount allowed as a specific exemption for gifts made after September 8, 1976, and before January 1, 1977 (see instructions)	10	0
11	Balance (subtract line 10 from line 9)	11	190,000
12	Unified credit (enter the smaller of line 6 or line 11)	12	190,000
13	Credit for foreign gift taxes (see instructions)	13	0
14	Total credits (add lines 12 and 13)	14	190,000
15	Balance (subtract line 14 from line 6) (do not enter less than zero)	15	1,030,200
16	Generation-skipping transfer taxes (from Schedule C, Part 3, col. H, Total)	16	240,000
17	Total tax (add lines 15 and 16)	17	1,270,200
18	Gift and generation-skipping transfer taxes prepaid with extension of time to file	18	0
19	If line 18 is less than line 17, enter **balance due** (see instructions)	19	1,270,200
20	If line 18 is greater than line 17, enter **amount to be refunded**	20	

Attach check or money order here.

Sign Here Under penalties of perjury, I declare that I have examined this return, including any accompanying schedules and statements, and to the best of my knowledge and belief, it is true, correct, and complete. Declaration of preparer (other than donor) is based on all information of which preparer has any knowledge.

Robert A. Simon — Signature of donor — Date 4-15-2005

Paid Preparer's Use Only Preparer's signature ▶ Date Check if self-employed ▶ ☐

Firm's name (or yours if self-employed), address, and ZIP code ▶ Phone no. ▶ ( )

For Disclosure, Privacy Act, and Paperwork Reduction Act Notice, see page 12 of the separate instructions for this form. Cat. No. 16783M Form **709** (2004)

Form 709 (2004) Page 2

SCHEDULE A **Computation of Taxable Gifts** (Including transfers in trust) (see instructions)

A Does the value of any item listed on Schedule A reflect any valuation discount? If "Yes," see instructions . . . . Yes ☐ No ☑

B ☐ ◄ Check here if you elect under section 529(c)(2)(B) to treat any transfers made this year to a qualified tuition program as made ratably over a 5-year period beginning this year. See instructions. Attach explanation.

Part 1—Gifts Subject Only to Gift Tax. *Gifts less political organization, medical, and educational exclusions—see instructions*

A Item number	B • Donee's name and address • Relationship to donor (if any) • Description of gift • If the gift was of securities, give CUSIP no. • If closely held entity, give EIN	C	D Donor's adjusted basis of gift	E Date of gift	F Value at date of gift	G For split gifts, enter ½ of column F	H Net transfer (subtract col. G from col. F)
1	Cash to daughter, Deborah Miller 500 Manda Lane Wheeling,IL 60090		511,000	3-15-04	511,000		511,000
Gifts made by spouse—*complete* ***only*** *if you are splitting gifts with your spouse and he/she also made gifts.*							
Total of Part 1 (add amounts from Part 1, column H) . . . ▶							511,000

Part 2—Direct skips— gifts that are direct skips and are subject to both gift tax and generation-skipping transfer tax. You must list the gifts in chronological order.

A Item number	B • Donee's name and address • Relationship to donor (if any) • Description of gift • If the gift was of securities, give CUSIP no. • If closely held entity, give EIN	C 2632(b) election out	D Donor's adjusted basis of gift	E Date of gift	F Value at date of gift	G For split gifts, enter ½ of column F	H Net transfer (subtract col. G from col. F)
1	Cash to grandson, Matthew Miller 3907 Cleveland, Skokie, IL 60097		1,011,000	3-15-04	1,011,000		1,011,000
2	Cash to granddaughter, Mary Miller 4701 Oxnam, Norridge, IL 60656		1,011,000	3-15-04	1,011,000		1,011,000
Gifts made by spouse—*complete* ***only*** *if you are splitting gifts with your spouse and he/she also made gifts.*							
Total of Part 2 (add amounts from Part 2, column H) . . . ▶							2,022,000

Part 3—Indirect skips— gifts to trusts that are currently subject to gift tax and may later be subject to generation-skipping transfer tax. You must list these gifts in chronological order.

A Item number	B • Donee's name and address • Relationship to donor (if any) • Description of gift • If the gift was of securities, give CUSIP no. • If closely held entity, give EIN	C 2632(c) election	D Donor's adjusted basis of gift	E Date of gift	F Value at date of gift	G For split gifts, enter ½ of column F	H Net transfer (subtract col. G from col. F)
1							
Gifts made by spouse—*complete* ***only*** *if you are splitting gifts with your spouse and he/she also made gifts.*							
Total of Part 3 (add amounts from Part 3, column H) . . . ▶							

(If more space is needed, attach additional sheets of same size.) Form 709 (2004)

Form 709 (2004) Page 3

Part 4—Taxable Gift Reconciliation

1	Total value of gifts of donor (add totals from column H of Parts 1, 2, and 3)			1	2,533,000
2	Total annual exclusions for gifts listed on line 1 (see instructions)			2	33,000
3	Total included amount of gifts (subtract line 2 from line 1)			3	2,500,000
Deductions (see instructions)					
4	Gifts of interests to spouse for which a marital deduction will be claimed, based on items .... of Schedule A	4	0		
5	Exclusions attributable to gifts on line 4	5	0		
6	Marital deduction—subtract line 5 from line 4	6	0		
7	Charitable deduction, based on items .... less exclusions	7	0		
8	Total deductions—add lines 6 and 7			8	0
9	Subtract line 8 from line 3			9	2,500,000
10	Generation-skipping transfer taxes payable with this Form 709 (from Schedule C, Part 3, col. H, Total)			10	240,000
11	Taxable gifts (add lines 9 and 10). Enter here and on line 1 of the Tax Computation on page 1			11	2,740,000

12 Terminable Interest (QTIP) Marital Deduction. (See instructions for line 4 of Schedule A.)

If a trust (or other property) meets the requirements of qualified terminable interest property under section 2523(f), and

a. The trust (or other property) is listed on Schedule A, and

b. The value of the trust (or other property) is entered in whole or in part as a deduction on line 4, Part 4 of Schedule A,

then the donor shall be deemed to have made an election to have such trust (or other property) treated as qualified terminable interest property under section 2523(f).

If less than the entire value of the trust (or other property) that the donor has included in Parts 1 and 3 of Schedule A is entered as a deduction on line 4, the donor shall be considered to have made an election only as to a fraction of the trust (or other property). The numerator of this fraction is equal to the amount of the trust (or other property) deducted on line 6 of Part 4, Schedule A. The denominator is equal to the total value of the trust (or other property) listed in Parts 1 and 3 of Schedule A.

If you make the QTIP election (see instructions for line 4 of Schedule A), the terminable interest property involved will be included in your spouse's gross estate upon his or her death (section 2044). If your spouse disposes (by gift or otherwise) of all or part of the qualifying life income interest, he or she will be considered to have made a transfer of the entire property that is subject to the gift tax (see Transfer of Certain Life Estates on page 4 of the instructions).

13 Election Out of QTIP Treatment of Annuities

☐◀ Check here if you elect under section 2523(f)(6) **NOT** to treat as qualified terminable interest property any joint and survivor annuities that re reported on Schedule A and would otherwise be treated as qualified terminable interest property under section 2523(f). (See instructions.) Enter the item numbers (from Schedule A) for the annuities for which you are making this election ▶

SCHEDULE B Gifts From Prior Periods

If you answered "Yes" on line 11a of page 1, Part 1, see the instructions for completing Schedule B. If you answered "No," skip to the Tax Computation on page 1 (or Schedule C, if applicable).

A Calendar year or calendar quarter (see instructions)	B Internal Revenue office where prior return was filed	C Amount of unified credit against gift tax for periods after December 31, 1976	D Amount of specific exemption for prior periods ending before January 1, 1977	E Amount of taxable gifts
1986	IRS Service Center Kansas City, MO 64999	155,800		500,000
1 Totals for prior periods	1	155,800		500,000

2	Amount, if any, by which total specific exemption, line 1, column D, is more than $30,000	2	
3	Total amount of taxable gifts for prior periods (add amount, column E, line 1, and amount, if any, on line 2). (Enter here and on line 2 of the Tax Computation on page 1.)	3	500,000

(If more space is needed, attach additional sheets of same size.) Form 709 (2004)

Form 709 (2004) Page **4**

SCHEDULE C **Computation of Generation-Skipping Transfer Tax**

Note: *Inter vivos direct skips that are completely excluded by the GST exemption must still be fully reported (including value and exemptions claimed) on Schedule C.*

Part 1—Generation-Skipping Transfers

A Item No. (from Schedule A, Part 2, col. A)	B Value (from Schedule A, Part 2, col. H)	C Nontaxable portion of transfer	D Net Transfer (subtract col. C from col. B)
1	1,011,000	11,000	1,000,000
2	1,011,000	11,000	1,000,000
Gifts made by spouse (for gift splitting only)			

Part 2—GST Exemption Reconciliation (Section 2631) and Section 2652(a)(3) Election

Check box ▶ ☐ if you are making a section 2652(a)(3) (special QTIP) election (see instructions)

Enter the item numbers (from Schedule A) of the gifts for which you are making this election ▶ ....

		Line	Amount
1	Maximum allowable exemption (see instructions)	1	1,500,000
2	Total exemption used for periods before filing this return	2	0
3	Exemption available for this return (subtract line 2 from line 1)	3	1,500,000
4	Exemption claimed on this return (from Part 3, col. C total, below)	4	1,500,000
5	Automatic allocation of exemption to transfers reported on Schedule A, Part 3	5	0
6	Exemption allocated to transfers not shown on line 4 or 5, above. **You must attach a Notice of Allocation.** (See instructions.)	6	0
7	Add lines 4, 5, and 6	7	1,500,000
8	Exemption available for future transfers (subtract line 7 from line 3)	8	0

Part 3—Tax Computation

A Item No. (from Schedule C, Part 1)	B Net transfer (from Schedule C, Part 1, col. D)	C GST Exemption Allocated	D Divide col. C by col. B	E Inclusion Ratio (subtract col. D from 1.000)	F Maximum Estate Tax Rate	G Applicable Rate (multiply col. E by col. F)	H Generation-Skipping Transfer Tax (multiply col. B by col. G)
1	1,000,000	750,000	0.750	0.250	48% (.48)	0.120	120,000
2	1,000,000	750,000	0.750	0.250	48% (.48)	0.120	120,000
3					48% (.48)		
4					48% (.48)		
5					48% (.48)		
6					48% (.48)		
					48% (.48)		
					48% (.48)		
					48% (.48)		
					48% (.48)		
					48% (.48)		
					48% (.48)		
Total exemption claimed. Enter here and on line 4, Part 2, above. May not exceed line 3, Part 2, above		1,500,000	**Total generation-skipping transfer tax.** Enter here, on line 10 of Schedule A, Part 4, and on line 16 of the Tax Computation on page 1				240,000

(If more space is needed, attach additional sheets of same size.) Form **709** (2004)

¶ 4000
CODE FINDING LIST

This table lists the Internal Revenue Code Sections that are cited as authority in the *2005 U.S. Master ™ Estate and Gift Tax Guide*.

The citations appear at the paragraphs indicated.

Index

References are to (¶) numbers.

D

G

H

I

J

K

L

M

N

P

Q

R

T

U